EATCS
Monographs on Theoretical Computer Science
Volume 9

Editors: W. Brauer G. Rozenberg A. Salomaa

EATCS Monographs on Theoretical Computer Science

Vol. 1: K. Mehlhorn: Data Structures and Algorithms 1: Sorting and Searching. XIV, 336 pages, 87 figs. 1984.

Vol. 2: K. Mehlhorn: Data Structures and Algorithms 2: Graph Algorithms and NP-Completeness. XII, 260 pages, 54 figs. 1984.

Vol. 3: K. Mehlhorn: Data Structures and Algorithms 3: Multidimensional Searching and Computational Geometry. XII, 284 pages, 134 figs. 1984.

Vol. 4: W. Reisig: Petri Nets. An Introduction. X, 161 pages, 111 figs. 1985.

Vol. 5: W. Kuich, A. Salomaa: Semirings, Automata, Languages. IX, 374 pages. 23 figs. 1986.

Vol. 6: H. Ehrig, B. Mahr: Fundamentals of Algebraic Specification 1. Equations and Initial Semantics. XI, 321 pages. 1985.

Vol. 7: F. Gécseg: Products of Automata. VIII, 107 pages. 18 figs. 1986.

Vol. 8: Kröger: Temporal Logic of Programs. VIII, 148 pages. 1987.

Vol. 9: K. Weihrauch: Computability. X, 517 pages. 1987.

Klaus Weihrauch

Computability

Springer-Verlag
Berlin Heidelberg New York
London Paris Tokyo

Author

Prof. Dr. Klaus Weihrauch
FB Mathematik und Informatik, FernUniversität Hagen
Feithstr. 140, 5800 Hagen, Germany

Editors

Prof. Dr. Wilfried Brauer
Institut für Informatik, Technische Universität München
Arcisstrasse 21, 8000 München 2, Germany

Prof. Dr. Grzegorz Rozenberg
Institute of Applied Mathematics and Computer Science
University of Leiden, Wassenaarseweg 80, P.O. Box 9512
2300 RA Leiden, The Netherlands

Prof. Dr. Arto Salomaa
Department of Mathematics, University of Turku
20500 Turku 50, Finland

ISBN 3-540-13721-1 Springer-Verlag Berlin Heidelberg New York
ISBN 0-387-13721-1 Springer-Verlag New York Berlin Heidelberg

Library of Congress Cataloging-in-Publication Data
Weihrauch, K. (Klaus) Computability. (EATCS monographs on theoretical computer science; v. 9) Bibliography: p. Includes index. 1. Computable functions. 2. Recursive functions. I. Title. II. Series.
QA9.59.W45 1987 515'.25 87-4933

Offsetprinting: Druckhaus Beltz, Hemsbach
Binding: J. Schäffer GmbH & Co. KG, Grünstadt
2145/3140-543210

To Susanne, Stefan, and Katrin

Foreword

The theory of computability or recursion theory has grown rapidly from its beginning 50 years ago until today. While initially mainly logicians were interested in the theory of computability, today recursion theory supplies an important theoretical background to computer science and logic and its questions and methods are penetrating many other mathematical disciplines. It is impossible to present the whole theory of computability in a single book, since already branches of it (e.g. degree theory, α-recursion theory, general axiomatic recursion theory, recursion theory and logic, abstract complexity theory, domain theory and λ-calculus, recursive analysis, subrecursive functions, Turing machine complexity) would require extra volumes. This book deals with the pure theory of computability, which is the common basis for all these branches. It follows the line defined by Church's thesis, which separates computability from non-computability. Therefore, it presents rather a frame of recursion theory than a comprehensive view.

The book is divided into three consecutive parts which lead in a straightforward way from the very basic theory to modern concepts of computability. Part 1 is devoted to the introduction and discussion of the basic properties of computability on natural numbers and on words. Different computability models are introduced and proved to be equivalent, recursive and recursively enumerable sets are defined and their basic properties are investigated. Finally a standard numbering φ of the partial recursive number functions is defined and abstractly characterized. This part is written in a style appropriate for undergraduate students.

Part 2 contains the standard recursion theory on the natural numbers. The recursive and the recursively enumerable sets are studied in more detail. Numberings, the recursion theorem, and creativity and productivity are further focal points. Effectivity of numberings is discussed in detail. Excursions to computable ordinal numbers, to logic, to relativized computability and the Kleene hierarchy, and to axiomatic computational complexity complete Part 2. Readers with some knowledge in basic computability theory may skip Part 1 of the book since Part 2 is essentially self-contained.

In Part 3 computability on sets with the cardinality of the continuum, called Type 2 computability, is investigated. Since Type 2 computability has turned out to be a special case of a more general theory, Type 2 constructivity, which is expressed by means of topology, some knowledge of the basic concepts of topology will be helpful for the reader. Part 3 presents a unified systematic Type 2 theory of constructivity and computability which has no model in the previous literature. The basic Type 2 theory of constructivity and computability is developed and representations are discussed in detail. Domains which are used in semantics of programming languages are investigated systematically and the relation of Type 1 and Type 2 theory is studied. Finally applications to constructive and computable analysis are outlined. Readers familiar with ordinary recursion theory may skip Part 1 and Part 2 and read Part 3 directly.

This book developed from several courses I have given during the last years and from research which was partly supported by the Deutsche Forschungsgemeinschaft. It is largely influenced by the books of Hermes, Rogers, Mal'cev and Brainerd and Landweber on the same topics and by papers of Scott on cpo's and by Ershov on numberings. I am especially indebted to these authors. It should be remarked that the above list as well as the other bibliographical references in the book are far from being complete.

Valuable conversations, suggestions, or contributions have been offered by T. Deil, H.J. Dettki, N. Müller, C. Kreitz, D. Pumplün, G. Schäfer-Richter, U. Schreiber, D. Spreen, W. Tholen and several others. I am especially grateful to B. Heinemann for his very careful proof reading. Remaining errors are my sole responsibility. Finally thanks are due to B. Gramkow and U. Grunendahl who very carefully and reliably typed the text.

Hagen, February 1987 Klaus Weihrauch

Contents

Prerequisites and Notation

Throughout this book we use the language of naive set theory as our metalanguage. In most parts no particular knowledge from mathematics or computer science is assumed. Special concepts from mathematics are introduced shortly when they are needed.

The word "iff" abbreviates "if and only if" and means metalinguistically logical equivalence; "w.l.g." abbreviates "without loss of generality". If $X_1 \times X_2$ is the cartesian product of the sets X_1 and X_2 then $pr_1 : X_1 \times X_2 \longrightarrow X_1$ and $pr_2 : X_1 \times X_2 \longrightarrow X_2$ are the *projections* with $pr_1(x_2,x_2) = x_1$, $pr_2(x_1,x_2) = x_2$. Similarly pr_i is the projection to the i-th component in a cartesian product of k (with $i \leq k$) factors. The symbol $\mathbb{N}$ denotes the set of *natural numbers* $\{0,1,2,...\}$. Notice that 0 is a natural number. A *binary relation* (or simply *relation*) is a subset $\rho \subseteq X \times Y$ of a cartesian product of two sets. Often we shall write $x\rho y$ instead of $(x,y) \in \rho$.

It is customary in recursion theory to consider *partial functions*. A *partial function* or simply a *function* or *mapping* from X to Y is a triple

$$f = (X,Y,\rho)$$

where X and Y are sets and $\rho \subseteq X \times Y$ is a relation such that $(x\rho y \wedge x\rho y') \Rightarrow y = y'$ for all $x \in X$, $y,y' \in Y$. We define

$$\mathrm{dom}(f) := \{x \in X \mid (\exists y)(x,y) \in \rho\} \qquad (\textit{domain} \text{ of } f),$$
$$\mathrm{range}(f) := \{y \in Y \mid (\exists x)(x,y) \in \rho\} \qquad (\textit{range} \text{ of } f).$$

The relation ρ is called the *graph* of f. Of course, a partial function $f' = (X',Y',\rho')$ is equal to f, iff $X = X'$, $Y = Y'$, and $\rho = \rho'$. The notation

$$f : X \dashrightarrow Y$$

with dotted arrow indicates that f is a partial function from X to Y. For $x \in \mathrm{dom}(f)$, $f(x)$ or fx denotes the unique $y \in Y$ with $(x,y) \in \rho$. If $x \notin \mathrm{dom}(f)$, a value $f(x)$ does not exist. We say "$f(x)$ does not exist", or "$f(x)$ diverges", or we write "$f(x) = \mathrm{div}$", instead of $x \notin \mathrm{dom}(f)$. Notice that div is not a "value" of f. We shall write $f(x) = g(x)$ if $x \in \mathrm{dom}(f)$, $x \in \mathrm{dom}(g)$ and the values $f(x)$ and $g(x)$ are equal, or if $x \notin \mathrm{dom}(f)$ and $x \notin \mathrm{dom}(g)$. The function $f = (X,Y,\rho)$ is

- *injective* , iff $(f(x) = f(x') \Rightarrow x = x')$ for all $x, x' \in \mathrm{dom}(f)$,
- *surjective*, iff range $(f) = Y$,
- *total* , iff $\mathrm{dom}(f) = X$,
- *bijective* , iff it is injective, surjective and total.

If f is injective then its inverse $f^{-1}: Y \dashrightarrow X$ is the function defined by $f^{-1} = (Y, X, \rho^{-1})$ where $\rho^{-1} := \{(y,x) \mid (x,y) \in \rho\}$. For $A \subseteq X$ and $B \subseteq Y$ let

$$f(A) := fA := \{y \mid (\exists x \in A \cap \mathrm{dom}(f)) f(x) = y\},$$
$$f^{-1}(B) := f^{-1}B := \{x \mid (\exists y \in B \cap \mathrm{range}(f)) f(x) = y\}.$$

If $f: X \dashrightarrow Y$ is a total function we indicate this by writing $f: X \longrightarrow Y$ (as usual). We define $Y^X := \{f: X \longrightarrow Y\}$, $2^X := \{Z \mid Z \subseteq X\}$. If $f: X \dashrightarrow Y$ and $g: Y \dashrightarrow Z$ are partial functions, then the partial function $h := gf$ is defined as follows:

$$h : X \dashrightarrow Z$$

and

$$h(x) = z :\Leftrightarrow (\exists y \in Y)(f(x) = y \wedge g(y) = z).$$

Especially, $\mathrm{dom}(h) = \{x \in \mathrm{dom}(f) \mid f(x) \in \mathrm{dom}(g)\}$. Let $f: X \dashrightarrow X$ be a partial function. Then $f^i: X \dashrightarrow X$ for $i \in \mathbb{N}$ is defined as follows:

$$f^0 := \text{the identity on } X, \text{ i.e. } (\forall x \in X) f^0(x) = x,$$
$$f^1 := f,$$
$$f^{n+1} := ff^n = f^n f = \underbrace{ff \ldots f}_{(n+1)\text{ times}} .$$

An *alphabet* is a finite non-empty set. If we define an alphabet by explicitly listing the elements,

$$\Sigma := \{a_1, \ldots, a_n\},$$

we implicitly assume that $a_i \neq a_j$ for $1 \leq i < j \leq n$. A finite sequence of elements of some set X is called a *word over* X. Formally the words over X may be defined as follows. For any $n \in \mathbb{N}$ let

$$W_n(X) := \{(n,\rho) \mid (\exists x_1, \ldots, x_n \in X)\ \rho = \{(1,x_1), \ldots, (n,x_n)\}\}$$

be the set of words of length n over X, and let

$$W(X) := \cup \{W_n(X) \mid n \in \mathbb{N}\}$$

be the set of all words over X. If $w = (n, \{(1,x_1), \ldots, (n,x_n)\})$ then $\lg(x) := n$ is called the *length* and x_k is called the k'th symbol of w. The (only) word $(0,\emptyset) \in W_o(\Sigma)$ of length 0 is called the *the empty word* and is denoted by the symbol ε. Notice that $X \subseteq Y$ implies $W(X) \subseteq W(Y)$. Usually words are specified informally. Any informal specification of a word w must contain the following information:

- the length $n := \lg(w)$ of the word w,
- the k'th symbol of w for each $k \in \mathbb{N}$ with $1 \leq k \leq n$.

A word $w = (n, \{(1,a_1), \ldots, (n,a_n)\})$ is informally denoted by $a_1 a_2 \ldots a_n$. If $x = a_1 \ldots a_n$ and $y = b_1 \ldots b_m$ are words then xy denotes the word $a_1 \ldots a_n b_1 \ldots b_m$.

For emphasizing that a string from our metalanguage denotes a word over some (already defined) set X, it is put into quotation marks. Example: Let $X = \{a_o, a_1, \ldots\}$, let $y := a_3 a_1 a_1 \in W_3(X)$, $p(\lambda) := a_o a_4 a_o a_1 \in W_4(X)$. Then "$a_o y a_3 a_3 P(\lambda)$" denotes the word $a_o a_3 a_1 a_1 a_3 a_3 a_o a_4 a_o a_1 \in W_{1o}(X)$. Since ε denotes the empty word we have $\varepsilon x = x\varepsilon = x$ for all $x \in W(X)$. For $a \in X$ define $a^o := \varepsilon \in W_o(X)$, $a^1 =$ "a" $= (1,\{(1,a)\}) \in W_1(X)$, $a^2 := aa \in W_2(X)$, etc. For $w \in W(X)$ define $w^o := \varepsilon$, $w^1 := w$, $w^2 := ww$, etc. If $w,x,y,z \in W(X)$ and $w = xyz$, then x is called a *prefix*, z a *suffix*, and y a *subword* of w. If $w = b_1 \ldots b_n \in W_n(X)$, where $b_i \in X$ for $1 \leq i \leq n$, then $w^R := b_n b_{n-1} \ldots b_1$ is called the *reverse* of w.

Part 1: Basic Concepts of Computability

The aim of Part 1 of this book is to introduce the computable functions on numbers and on words and the decidable and the recursively enumerable sets and to study their basic properties. In the first chapter as a very general concept flowcharts and machines are defined and two transformations, refinement and simulation, are introduced which will be repeatedly used later. In the subsequent three chapters the computable function on numbers are defined in different ways, by register machines, as μ-recursive functions, and by WHILE-programs. It is proved in detail that these three definitions coincide. The computable word functions are defined by tape machines in Chapter 1.5 and by stack machines in Chapter 1.6. These two definitions also coincide. In Chapter 7 it is shown that by a standard numbering of words the computable word functions can be transformed into the computable number functions and vice versa. After this, Church's Thesis is formulated and discussed. The recursive and the recursively enumerable sets are defined in Chapter 8. In Chapter 9 the unary computable number functions are considered as a whole. An "effective" standard numbering is defined and two very important basic properties, the universal Turing machine theorem and the smn-theorem, are proved. As a first application it is shown that the halting problem and the self applicability problem for the standard numbering of the unary computable number functions are both recursively enumerable but not recursive. Finally in Chapter 10 some examples of unsolvable problems are studied, especially Post's Correspondence Problem and the word problem for Semi-Thue systems. After studying this Part 1 thoroughly the reader should have gained a precise intuition of computability, decidability and recursive enumerability which is independent of specific computational models.

BIBLIOGRAPHICAL NOTES

There are many good books which introduce the elementary theory of computability. They differ w.r.t. the computational models, the number of details, and the degree of formalization. The following list is far from being complete: Boolos (1974), Brainerd and Landweber (1974), Cutland (1980), Davis (1958), Hennie (1977), Heidler, Hermes, and Mahn (1977), Hermes (1978), Hopcroft and Ullman (1979), Jones (1977), Loeckx (1976), Machtey and Young (1978), Malcev (1974), Schnorr (1974), Börger (1985).

1.1 Flowcharts and Machines

Flowcharts are a common tool for describing everyday algorithms. Most computer programming languages admit flowchart programming. Also several definitions of computability use models based on the concept of flowchart. In this chapter general definitions of *flowcharts* and *machines* (machine := flowchart + input encoding + output encoding) and their semantics are given. Two very useful basic transformations for flowcharts, *simulation* and *refinement*, which we shall use repeatedly in later proofs, will be introduced and proved to be correct. Finally the change of input and output encoding is considered. The aim of this chapter is to give a framework for formulating several later proofs more rigorously and transparently and in addition to supply a precise method for developing programs together with correctness proofs. Roughly speaking, a flowchart is a list of operations and tests (called statements) on a dataset D, where the order of execution is determined by a finite table. Before defining a certain class of flowcharts formally we explain the idea by an example.

1 EXAMPLE

Let $D := \mathbb{N}^2$, let tests $s,t : D \to \{+,-\}$ and functions $f,g : D \to D$ be defined by

$s(a,b) := (+ \text{ if } a > b, - \text{ otherwise}),$
$t(a,b) := (+ \text{ if } a = b, - \text{ otherwise}),$
$f(a,b) := (a \dot{-} b, b) \ (\text{where } a \dot{-} b = (a - b \text{ if } a \geq b, 0 \text{ otherwise})),$
$g(a,b) := (b,a).$

We shall use the suggestive descriptions "$x > y$" := s, "$x = y$" := t, "$x := x \dot{-} y$" := f and "$x \leftrightarrow y$" := g. Then the following figure represents a flowchart F.

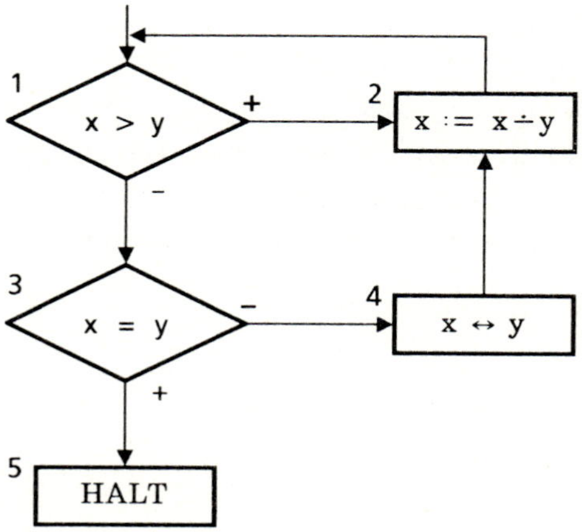

For a formal treatment it is useful to assign a name to each node in a flowchart. These names are called *states* (or *labels* in programming languages). In our case the states are the numbers 1,2,3,4, and 5. The incoming arrow indicates that 1 is the initial state of F. F has a single final state, namely 5. A flowchart can also be represented by a "program". The following text describes the flowchart F.

1 : $x > y$, 2 , 3 ;
2 : $x := x \dot{-} y$, 1 ;
3 : $x = y$, 5 , 4 ;
4 : $x \leftrightarrow y$, 2 ;
5 : HALT .

For better legibility we have divided the text into lines: one line for every state. Each line contains the statement (function or test) for the corresponding state and the next state (or states). The first line gives the initial state. It is obvious how this text corresponds to the above figure.

We shall now define flowcharts formally. The definition generalizes Example 1 in 4 ways.

(1) A test may have not only two but i alternatives ($i \geq 1$), which will be numbered consecutively 1,2,...,i .
(2) A test may also change the data.
(3) A test or function may be partial.
(4) A flowchart may have i HALT-statements HALT 1,...,HALT i ($i \geq 1$).

This means that every statement in a flowchart, which is not a HALT-statement, has the form

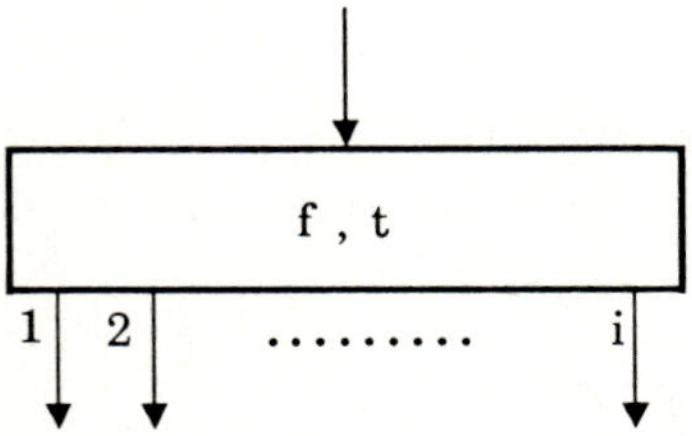

where f is a function and t is a test with i alternatives on D. Formally, a flowchart is a certain kind of tuple which yields all the information necessary for drawing a diagram or for writing the corresponding "program".

2 DEFINITION (*flowchart*)

A *flowchart* is a 6-tuple $F = (Q, D, \sigma, q_o, s, (q_1, \ldots, q_s))$ such that (1),...,(6) hold.

(1) Q is a finite set (*states*).

(2) D is a set (*dataset*).

(3) $q_o \in Q$ (*initial state*).

(4) $s \in \mathbb{N}$, $s \geq 1$ (number of *exists* of F).

(5) $q_1,\ldots,q_s \in Q$ with $q_o,q_1,\ldots,q_s$ pairwise different (*final states*).

(6) σ is a function which assigns to any $q \in Q \setminus \{q_1,\ldots,q_s\}$ a tuple

$$\sigma(q) = (f,t,(p_1,\ldots,p_k))$$

for some $k \geq 1$, $f : D \dashrightarrow D$, $t : D \dashrightarrow \{1,\ldots,k\}$, and $p_1,\ldots,p_k \in Q$ such that $\mathrm{dom}(f) = \mathrm{dom}(t)$.

$Q_e := \{q_1,\ldots,q_s\}$ is called the set of *final states*.

A flowchart, therefore, is an abstract 6-tuple. For specifying such 6-tuples informally, henceforth we shall normally use figures (diagrams) or program like notations (see Example 1). As we did in Example 1, we shall not explicitly mention the identity function on D, if a statement is a pure test, and we shall not explicitly mention the trivial test if a statement has only one exit. If a statement has two exits it is customary to sign them by + and - instead of 1 and 2.

3 EXAMPLE

Our flowchart from Example 1 formally is the following tuple:

$$F = (\{1,2,3,4,5\},\mathbb{N}^2,\sigma,1,1,(5))$$

with

$$\sigma(1) = (h\,,\,x > y\,,\,(2,3)),$$
$$\sigma(2) = (x := x \dot{-} y\,,\,t_o\,,\,(1)),$$
$$\sigma(3) = (h\,,\,x = y\,,\,(5,4)),$$
$$\sigma(4) = (x \leftrightarrow y\,,\,t_o\,,\,(2)),$$

where $h : D \to D$, $h(d) := d$, and $t_o : D \to \{1\}$, $t_o(d) := 1$ for all $d \in D$. Here and in future we shall identify "+" with alternative 1. Notice that the function table for σ is essentially the "program" from Example 1 describing F.

The following example gives a more general flowchart.

4 EXAMPLE

Let D be some set, $f,f' : D \dashrightarrow D$, $t : D \dashrightarrow \{1,2\}$, $t' : D \dashrightarrow \{1,2,3\}$ with $\mathrm{dom}(f) = \mathrm{dom}(t)$ and $\mathrm{dom}(f') = \mathrm{dom}(t')$. Define $F := (\{a,b,c,d,e\},D,\sigma,b,3,(d,c,e))$ with

$\sigma(a) := (f,t,(e,d))$,

$\sigma(b) := (f',t',(b,c,a))$.

Then F is a flowchart. The following figure shows F as a diagram.

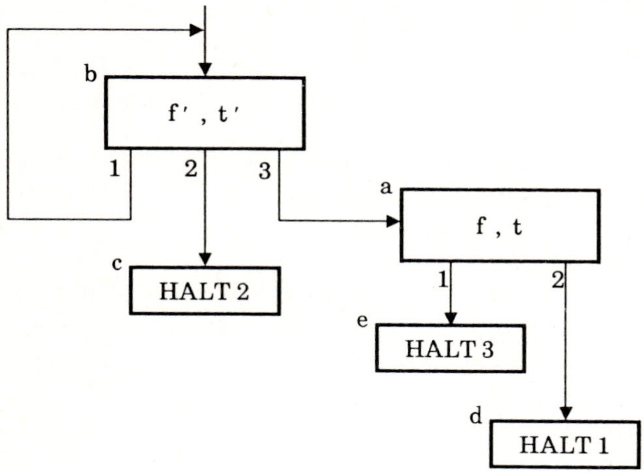

Our next aim is to define the meaning, the semantics, of a flowchart. The semantics of a flowchart F with dataset D and s final states will be a pair (f_F,t_F), where $f_F : D \dashrightarrow D$ is the function computed by F and $t_F : D \dashrightarrow \{1,\ldots,s\}$ is the test performed by F. We shall explain the definition of f_F and t_F by extending Example 1.

5 EXAMPLE

Let F be the flowchart from Example 1. For any state q which is not a final state and any data element $d \in D$ a (possibly new) data element d' and a (possibly new) state q' are determined. Thus, by F a "single step" function $SF : Q\times D \dashrightarrow Q\times D$ on the set $Q\times D$ of configurations is determined. A sequence $(\kappa, SF(\kappa), SF^2(\kappa),\ldots)$ of configurations is called a computation. Note that $SF(q,d) = \text{div}$, iff q is a final state. The above computation halts, iff for some number n of steps $SF^n(\kappa)$ is a final configuration, i.e. $SF^n(\kappa) = (q_e,d)$ for some final state $q_e \in Q$. The following table gives the values $(q_n,(a_n,b_n)) := SF^n(1,(4,14))$, $n = 0,1,\ldots,14$, for our flowchart F.

n	0	1	2	3	4	5	6	7	8	9	10	11	12	13	14
q_n	1	3	4	2	1	2	1	2	1	3	4	2	1	3	5
a_n	4	4	4	14	10	10	6	6	2	2	2	4	2	2	2
b_n	14	14	14	4	4	4	4	4	4	4	4	2	2	2	2

Obviously this computation is finite, where $SF^{14}(1,(4,14)) = (5,(2,2))$ is the last configuration. However the computation beginning with the configuration $\kappa := (1,(0,3))$ does not halt:

n	0	1	2	3	4	5	6	...
q_n	1	3	4	2	1	2	1	
a_n	0	0	0	3	3	3	3	etc.
b_n	3	3	3	0	0	0	0	

Since $SF^3(\kappa) = SF^5(\kappa)$, the computation obviously loops. The flowchart F defines a function $f : D \dashrightarrow D$ on its dataset D as follows. Let $d \in D$ be given. Perform the computation beginning with the configuration (q_o, d), where q_o is the initial state of F. If the computation is infinite, then f(d) does not exist. If the computation halts with some final configuration (q,d'), then $f(d) := d'$. In our example we have $f(4,14) = (2,2)$ and $f(0,3) = \text{div}$.

Now we shall define the semantics of a flowchart precisely.

6 <u>DEFINITION</u> (*semantics of a flowchart*)

Let $F = (Q,D,\sigma,q_o,s,(q_1,\ldots,q_s))$ be a flowchart.

(1) $CON := Q \times D$ is called the set of *configurations*, $\{q_1,\ldots,q_s\} \times D = Q_e \times D$ is called the set of *final configurations*.

(2) The *single step function* $SF : CON \dashrightarrow CON$ is defined as follows. Suppose $(q,d) \in Q \times D$.

<u>Case 1</u>: $q \in Q_e$. Then $SF(q,d) := \text{div}$.

<u>Case 2</u>: $q \in Q \setminus Q_e$. Suppose $\sigma(q) = (f,t,(p_1,\ldots,p_k))$.

<u>Case 2.1</u>: $d \notin \text{dom}(f)$. Then $SF(q,d) := \text{div}$.

<u>Case 2.2</u>: $d \in \text{dom}(f)$. Then $SF(q,d) := (p_{t(d)}, f(d))$.

(3) The *computation time function* $CT : CON \dashrightarrow \mathbb{N}$ is defined by

$$CT(q,d) := \begin{cases} \text{div if for no } n \in \mathbb{N}\ SF^n(q,d) \text{ is a final configuration} \\ \text{the unique n such that } SF^n(q,d) \text{ is a final configuration,} \\ \quad \text{otherwise.} \end{cases}$$

(4) The *total step function* $TF : CON \dashrightarrow CON$ is defined by

$$TF(q,d) := \begin{cases} SF^{CT(q,d)}(q,d) & \text{if } (q,d) \in \text{dom}(CT) \\ \text{div} & \text{otherwise.} \end{cases}$$

(5) The function $f_F : D \dashrightarrow D$ and the test $t_F : D \dashrightarrow \{1,\ldots,s\}$ are defined as follows:

$f_F(d)$ exists $\iff$ $t_F(d)$ exists $\iff$ $TF(q_o,d)$ exists,

and

$f_F(d) = d'$ and $t_F(d) = k$ if $TF(q_o,d) = (q_k,d')$.

Application of the single step function SF transforms a configuration into the next one. In order to determine TF(q,d), SF must be applied iteratively until a final configuration is reached. CT(q,d) is the number of steps after which a final configuration is reached. If TF(q,d) does not exist, two reasons are possible (see Def. 6(2)):

(1) $SF^n(q,d)$ exists for all $n \in \mathbb{N}$ (infinite computation),

(2) there is some n such that $\kappa := SF^n(q,d)$ exists, where $\kappa \notin dom(SF)$ and κ is not a final configuration (non executable statement).

Globally, a flowchart can be represented by a pair f_F, t_F where f_F is a function and t_F is a test on the dataset.

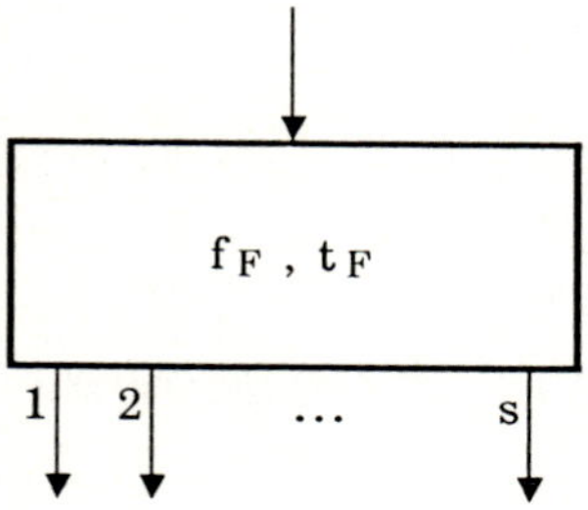

Therefore, the meaning of flowcharts and of statements within flowcharts are objects of the same type. Below we shall use this fact in the definition of refinement of flowcharts.

There are several partly very sophisticated transformations of flowcharts which preserve the semantics. For our purpose we shall introduce only two very basic ones: *renaming of states* and *refinement*. The definition of the semantics of a flowchart F (Def. 6) shows that the states of F play a secondary role. We show (the almost trivial) property that renaming of states does not change the semantics.

7 DEFINITION (*isomorphic flowcharts*)

Let $F = (Q,D,\sigma,q_o,s,(q_1,\dots,q_s))$
and $F' = (Q',D',\sigma',q'_o,s',(q'_1,\dots,q'_{s'}))$

be flowcharts. F and F' are called *isomorphic* iff: $D = D'$, $s = s'$, and there is a bijection $\tau : Q \to Q'$ with (1) and (2).

(1) $\tau(q_i) = q'_i$ for $i = 0,1,\dots,s$,

(2) $\sigma(q) = (f,t,(p_1,\dots,p_k)) \Rightarrow \sigma'\tau(q) = (f,t,(\tau(p_1),\dots,\tau(p_k)))$
for all $q \in Q, f, t, p_1,\dots,p_k$.

F' is obtained from F by renaming the states. Isomorphic flowcharts have the same semantics.

8 LEMMA

Let F and F' be isomorphic flowcharts. Then

$$f_F = f_{F'} \quad \text{and} \quad t_F = t_{F'} .$$

Proof

Let SF (SF') be the single step function and TF (TF') be the total step function of F (F'). Define $\hat{\tau}(q,d) := (\tau(q),d)$. Distinguishing the cases in Def. 6(2) one easily obtains

$$SF'\hat{\tau}(q,d) = \hat{\tau}SF(q,d) \quad (\text{for all } (q,d) \in CON) .$$

By induction we obtain for all $n \in \mathbb{N}$

$$(SF')^n\hat{\tau}(q,d) = \hat{\tau}SF^n(q,d) \quad (\text{for all } (q,d) \in CON) .$$

By Def. 7, (q,d) is a final configuration of F iff $\hat{\tau}(q,d)$ is a final configuration of F'. Therefore, $SF^n(q,d)$ is a final configuration of F iff $\hat{\tau}SF^n(q,d) = (SF')^n\hat{\tau}(q,d)$ is a final configuration of F'. This implies $TF'\hat{\tau} = \hat{\tau}TF$ and finally $f_F = f_{F'}$ and $t_F = t_{F'}$.
Q.E.D.

Obviously, for any flowchart there is an isomorphic one the states of which are elements of a given denumerable universal set M, e.g. $M = \mathbb{N}$. If necessary we may restrict our attention to such flowcharts. For convenience, if we specify flowcharts by figures, we shall usually omit names of states. They can be added if necessary.The most important transformation of flowcharts is *refinement*. Stepwise refinement is a very useful method for constructing correct programs. Here we define a special kind of refinement. It obtains its full power in connection with simulation which will be introduced afterwards. First we explain the idea by an example.

9 EXAMPLE

Consider flowchart F from Example 1. We want to replace the statement "$x = y$" at label 3 by a flowchart F' which only uses the statements "$x > y$" and "$x \leftrightarrow y$". Let F' be the following flowchart:

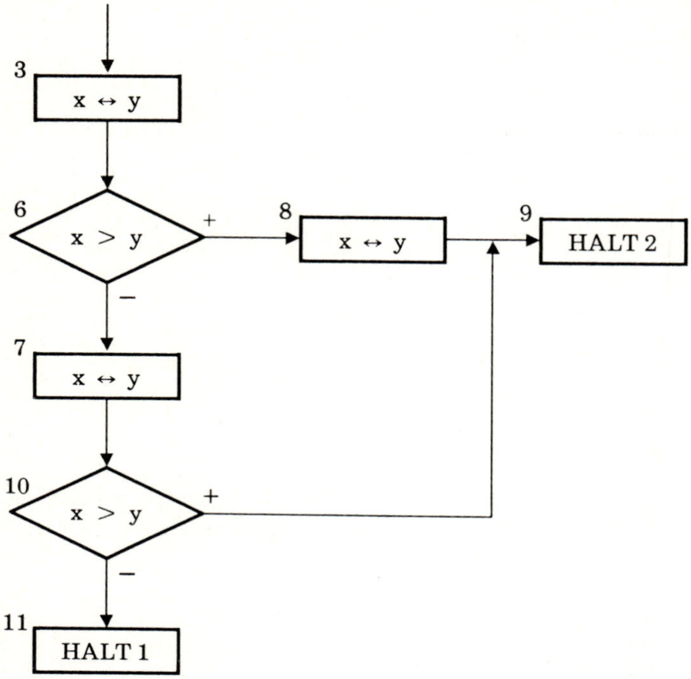

Distinguishing the cases $a > b$, $a = b$, and $a < b$ one easily obtains $f_{F'}(a,b) = (a,b)$, $t_{F'}(a,b) = (1 \text{ if } a=b,\ 2 \text{ otherwise})$. Therefore the operation and the test of F' coincide with those of state 3 in F. We replace the statement with label 3 in F by the flowchart F' and obtain a new flowchart $\overline{F}$ with the same semantics.

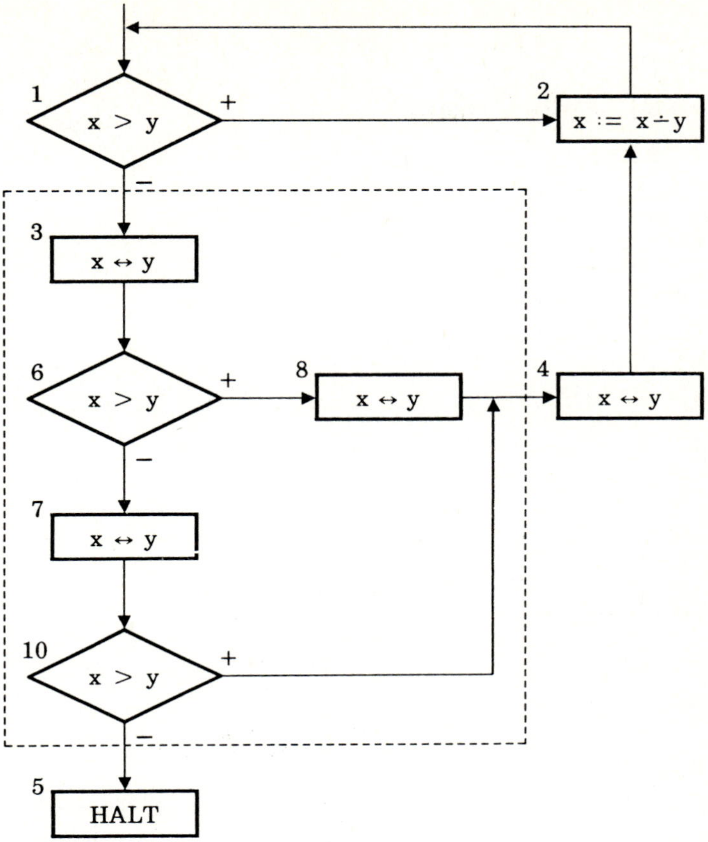

Notice that "3" is the only common state of F and F'. It is the state at which substitution in F is made and it is the initial state of F'.

This substitution can easily be understood using diagrams. Its formal definition is somewhat intricate.

10 DEFINITION (*substitution*)

Let F and F' be flowcharts,

$$F = (Q, D, \sigma, q_o, s, (q_1, \ldots, q_s)),$$
$$F' = (Q', D, \sigma', q_o', v, (q_1', \ldots, q_v'))$$

with $Q \cap Q' = \{q_o'\}$ and $\sigma(q_o') = (f, t, (p_1, \ldots, p_v))$ for some $f : D \dashrightarrow D$ and $t : D \dashrightarrow \{1, \ldots, v\}$.

Then define a flowchart

$$\overline{F} := (\overline{Q}, D, \overline{\sigma}, q_o, s, (q_1, \ldots, q_s))$$

as follows.

$\overline{Q} := (Q \cup Q') \setminus \{q'_1,\ldots,q'_v\}$,

$\overline{\sigma}(q) := \sigma(q)$ if $q \in Q \setminus \{q'_o\}$,

$\overline{\sigma}(q) := (g,u,(c(r_1),\ldots,c(r_i)))$

if $q \in Q' \setminus \{q'_1,\ldots,q'_v\}$ and $\sigma'(q) = (g,u,(r_1,\ldots,r_i))$,

where

$c(q'_1) := p_1,\ldots,c(q'_v) = p_v$ and $c(r) = r$, otherwise.

We say: $\overline{F}$ is defined by the *substitution* of F' into F at q'_o.

The next figure shows schematically the node of F which is replaced and the flowchart F' which is substituted for it.

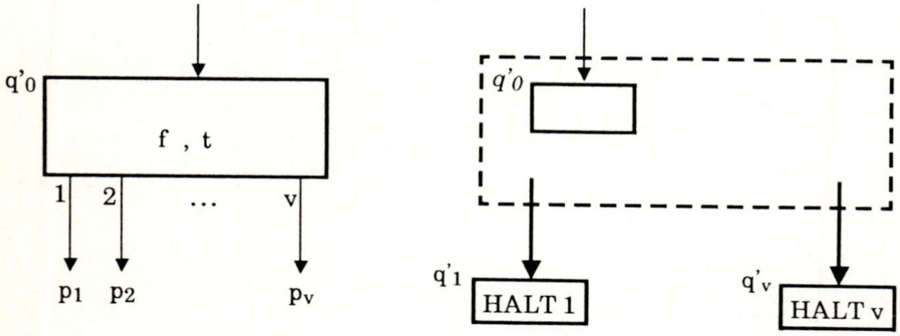

The following theorem on refinement is obvious. Its proof is tedious because all the formal definitions have to be used and several cases have to be distinguished.

11 THEOREM (*refinement*)

Let $\overline{F}$ be defined by the substitution of F' into F at q'_o (according to Def. 10). If $f = f_{F'}$ and $t = t_{F'}$ then $f_F = f_{\overline{F}}$ and $t_F = t_{\overline{F}}$. ("$\overline{F}$ is a *refinement* of F")

Proof

We use the notations from Def. 10. Let SF (SF',$\overline{SF}$) denote the single step function of F (F',$\overline{F}$), let TF (TF',$\overline{TF}$) denote the total step function of F (F',$\overline{F}$). Define $\hat{c} : Q' \times D \to \overline{Q} \times D$ by $\hat{c}(q,d) := (c(q),d)$. The following assertion relates computations in F' and $\overline{F}$.

Ass. 1: Let $d \in D$. For all $n \in \mathbb{N}$:

$$(SF')^n(q_o',d) \text{ exists} \Longrightarrow (\overline{SF})^n(q_o',d) = \hat{c}(SF')^n(q_o',d) .$$

Proof 1: $\overline{SF}(p,d) = \hat{c}SF'(p,d)$ for all $p \in Q' \setminus \{q_1',\dots,q_v'\}$ and all $d \in D$ follows immediately from the definitions. Ass. 1 is obtained from this by induction.

q.e.d. (1)

By the next assertion for any computation from the initial state of F there is a corresponding computation from the initial state of $\overline{F}$.

Ass. 2: Let $d \in D$. Then

$$(\forall n)\ (\exists \overline{n} \geq n)\ (SF^n(q_o,d) \text{ ex.} \Longrightarrow \overline{SF}^{\overline{n}}(q_o,d) = SF^n(q_o,d)) .$$

Proof 2: (By induction over n)

"n = 0": Choose $\overline{n} = 0$.

"n = n+1": Suppose $SF^{n+1}(q_o,d)$ exists. Then, by induction, there is some $(p,e) \in \text{dom}(SF)$ and some $\overline{n} \in \mathbb{N}$, $\overline{n} \geq n$, with

$$(p,e) = SF^n(q_o,d) = \overline{SF}^{\overline{n}}(q_o,d) .$$

(a) Case $p \neq q_o'$. Then $SF(p,e) = \overline{SF}(p,e)$, therefore $SF^{n+1}(q_o,d) = \overline{SF}^{\overline{n}+1}(q_o,d)$.

(b) Case $p = q_o'$. Since $(p,e) \in \text{dom}(SF)$, there exist $\tilde{e} \in D$ and $i \geq 1$ with $f(e) = \tilde{e}$ and $t(e) = i$. This implies $f_{F'}(e) = \tilde{e}$ and $t_{F'}(e) = i$. Hence there is some $k \geq 1$ with $(SF')^k(q_o',e) = TF'(q_o',e) = (q_i',\tilde{e})$. By Ass. 1, $\overline{SF}^k(q_o',e) = \hat{c}(q_i',\tilde{e}) = (p_i,\tilde{e}) = SF(q_o',e)$, and therefore $\overline{SF}^{\overline{n}+k}(q_o',e) = SF^{n+1}(q_o',e)$. Finally, $\overline{n} \geq n$ and $k \geq 1$ imply $\overline{n}+k \geq n+1$.

q.e.d. (2)

Since F and $\overline{F}$ have the same final configurations, Assertion 3 is an immediate consequence of Assertion 2.

Ass. 3: If $(q_o,d) \in \text{dom}(TF)$, then $TF(q_o,d) = \overline{TF}(q_o,d)$.

Now the case $(q_o,d) \notin \text{dom}(TF)$ is studied.

Ass. 4: If $(q_o,d) \notin \text{dom}(TF)$, then $(q_o,d) \notin \text{dom}(\overline{TF})$.

Proof 4: Suppose $(q_o,d) \notin \text{dom}(TF)$. If $SF^n(q_o,d)$ exists for all n, then $\overline{SF}^n(q_o,d)$ exists for all n by Ass. 2, i.e. $(q_o,d) \notin \text{dom}(\overline{TF})$. Therefore assume that $SF^n(q_o,d)$ does not exist for all n. Then there are some $p \in Q \setminus Q_e$, some $e \in D$, and some $n \in \mathbb{N}$ with $SF^n(q_o,d) = (p,e)$ such that $(p,e) \notin \text{dom}(SF)$. By Ass. 2 there is some $\overline{n}$ with $\overline{SF}^{\overline{n}}(q_o,d) = (p,e)$. Now three cases must be considered.

(1) $p \neq q_o'$. Then $(p,e) \notin \text{dom}(\overline{SF})$ and therefore $(q_o,d) \notin \text{dom}(\overline{TF})$.

(2) $p = q_o'$. $(p,e) \notin \text{dom}(SF)$ implies $e \notin \text{dom}(f) = \text{dom}(f_{F'})$ and $(q_o',e) \notin \text{dom}(TF')$. There may be two reasons for this.

(2.1) $(SF')^m(q_o',e)$ exists for all m. Then by Ass. 1 also $\overline{SF}^m(q_o',e)$ exists for all m, and therefore $\overline{TF}(q_o,d)$ does not exist.

(2.2) There are n',p',e' with $(SF')^{n'}(q_o',e) = (p',e')$, $(p',e') \notin \text{dom}(SF')$ and $p' \notin Q_e'$. Then $(p',e') \notin \text{dom}(\overline{SF})$ and by Ass. 1 $(p',e') = \overline{SF}^{n'}(q_o',e) = \overline{SF}^{\overline{n}+n'}(q_o,d)$. This implies $(q_o,d) \notin \text{dom}(\overline{TF})$, since p' is not a final state of $\overline{F}$.

q.e.d. (4).

We have proved $TF(q_o,d) = \overline{TF}(q_o,d)$ for all $d \in D$.

This implies $f_F = f_{\overline{F}}$ and $t_F = t_{\overline{F}}$.

Q.E.D.

In order to substitute a flowchart F' for a statement $p : f,t,p_1,\dots,p_v;$ in a flowchart F with the same dataset the essential condition is that the test $t_{F'}$ also has v alternatives. The condition $Q \cap Q' = \{q_o'\}$ is easily obtained by renaming states (Lemma 8). In order to apply Theorem 11 on refinement, the conditions $f = f_{F'}$ and $t = t_{F'}$ must be satisfied. In order to prove some property P (e.g. correctness) of $f_{\overline{F}}$ (or of $t_{\overline{F}}$) it is sufficient to prove this property for f_F (or t_F) and to prove $f = f_{F'}$ and $t = t_{F'}$. Thus not only the flowchart $\overline{F}$ but also the proof of property P is divided into simpler parts.

If a flowchart F uses the dataset D we assume a processor with a store for the elements of D. In Example 1 we have $D = \mathbb{N}^2$, hence the processor must have two counters. If, however, our processor doesn't have counters but e.g. two registers for words $w_1, w_2 \in W(\{0,1\})$, then the computations defined by F on pairs of numbers can be simulated on pairs of words which are used as binary notations for numbers by a simulating flowchart F'. F' is obtained from F by replacing each function and each test by a simulating one. We define this more precisely.

12 <u>DEFINITION</u> (*similarity*)

Let D,D' be sets, let $Sim \subseteq D \times D'$.

(1) Let $f : D \dashrightarrow D$, $f' : D' \dashrightarrow D'$. Then f and f' are *similar* w.r.t. Sim, $f =_{Sim} f'$, iff

$$f(d) \text{ exists} \iff f'(d') \text{ exists}$$

and

$$f(d) \text{ exists} \implies (f(d), f'(d')) \in Sim$$

for all $(d,d') \in Sim$.

(2) Let $t : D \dashrightarrow \{1,\dots,k\}$, $t' : D' \dashrightarrow \{1,\dots,k\}$. Then t and t' are *similar* w.r.t. Sim, $t =_{Sim} t'$, iff

$$t(d) \text{ exists} \iff t'(d') \text{ exists}$$

and

$$t(d) \text{ exists} \implies t(d) = t'(d')$$

for all $(d,d') \in Sim$.

By the following theorem the functions f_F and $f_{F'}$ and the tests t_F and $t_{F'}$ of flowcharts F and F' are similar, if F' is obtained from F by replacing each function and each test by a similar one.

13 THEOREM (*similar flowcharts*)

Let

$$F = (Q, D, \sigma, q_o, s, (q_1, \dots, q_s)) ,$$
$$F' = (Q, D', \sigma', q_o, s, (q_1, \dots, q_s))$$

be two flowcharts such that for each $q \in Q \setminus \{q_1, \dots, q_s\}$ there are functions f_q, f'_q, tests t_q, t'_q, and states $p_1, \dots, p_k$ such that

$$\sigma(q) = (f_q, t_q, p_1, \dots, p_k) ,$$
$$\sigma'(q) = (f'_q, t'_q, p_1, \dots, p_k) .$$

Let $Sim \subseteq D \times D'$ be a relation such that

$$f_q =_{Sim} f'_q \quad \text{and} \quad t_q =_{Sim} t'_q$$

for all $q \in Q \setminus \{q_1, \dots, q_s\}$. Then

$$f_F =_{Sim} f_{F'} \quad \text{and} \quad t_F =_{Sim} t_{F'} .$$

(Flowcharts satisfying the above conditions are called *similar w.r.t. the relation Sim*, one says: F' *simulates* F w.r.t. Sim.)

Proof

We extend the relation Sim to pairs of configurations by $(p,d)\, Sim\, (p',d') :\Longleftrightarrow (p = p' \text{ and } d\, Sim\, d')$. By the definitions $(p,d)\, Sim\, (p,d')$ implies $SF(p,d)\, Sim\, SF'(p,d')$ (or neither value exists). By induction, $(p,d)\, Sim\, (p,d')$ implies $SF^n(p,d)\, Sim\, (SF')^n(p,d')$ (or neither value exists) for all n. Therefore, $f_F(d)\, Sim\, f_{F'}(d')$ and $t_F(d) = t_{F'}(d')$ or none of these values exist, whenever $d\, Sim\, d'$.
Q.E.D.

Therefore, similar flowcharts compute similar functions and tests by computations which correspond to each other step by step. Refinement and simulation will be our main tools for transforming flowcharts into normal forms. The following example illustrates the relation between similar flowcharts.

14 EXAMPLE

Define flowcharts F and F' by the following diagrams:

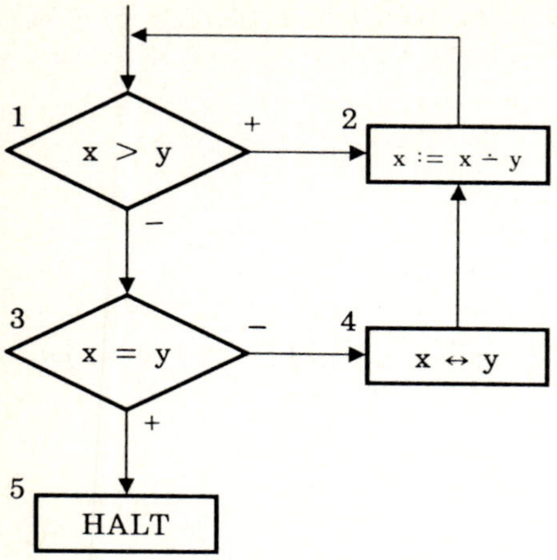

Flowchart F

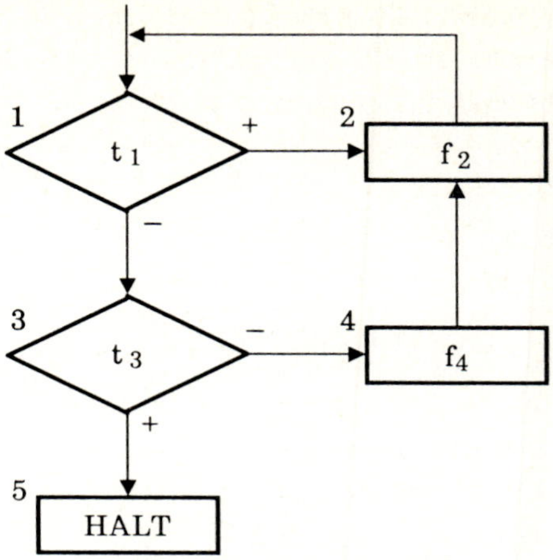

Flowchart F'

F is the flowchart from Example 1 with dataset $\mathbb{N}^2$. The functions $f_2, f_4 : D' \longrightarrow D'$ and the tests $t_1, t_3 : D' \longrightarrow \{1,2\}$ from F' are defined as follows.
Let $\beta : W(\{0,1\}) \longrightarrow \mathbb{N}$ be the function which decodes binary numbers (i.e. $\beta(\text{"}a_n a_{n-1} \ldots a_o\text{"}) = a_n 2^n + \ldots + a_o$). Let $D' := W(\{0,1\}) \times W(\{0,1\})$ and

$t_1(v,w) := 1$ if $\beta(v) > \beta(w)$, 2 otherwise,

$t_3(v,w) := 1$ if $\beta(v) = \beta(w)$, 2 otherwise,

$f_2(v,w) := (v',w)$ such that $\beta(v') = \beta(v) \dot{-} \beta(w)$ and v' has no leading zeros,

$f_4(v,w) := (w,v)$.

Define $Sim \subseteq D \times D'$ by $(a,b)\, Sim\, (u,v) :\Longleftrightarrow \beta(u) = a$ and $\beta(v) = b$. Then "x>y" $=_{Sim} t_1$, "x=y" $=_{Sim} t_3$, "x:=x∸y" $=_{Sim} f_2$, and "x↔y" $=_{Sim} f_4$. Therefore F and F' are similar w.r.t. Sim. Let $d = (5,3) \in D$ and $d' = (101,11) \in D'$. Then $d\, Sim\, d'$. The following tables show the values $(p_n,(a_n,b_n)) := SF^n(1,(5,3))$ and $(p_n',(v_n,w_n)) := (SF')^n(1,(101,11))$ for $n = 0,1,\ldots,12$.

n	0	1	2	3	4	5	6	7	8	9	10	11	12
p_n	1	2	1	3	4	2	1	3	4	2	1	3	5
a_n	5	5	2	2	2	3	1	1	1	2	1	1	1
b_n	3	3	3	3	3	2	2	2	2	1	1	1	1
p_n'	1	2	1	3	4	2	1	3	4	2	1	3	5
v_n	101	101	10	10	10	11	1	1	1	10	1	1	1
w_n	11	11	11	11	11	10	10	10	10	1	1	1	1

Notice that $p_n' = p_n$, $\beta(v_n) = a_n$ and $\beta(w_n) = b_n$ for all n.

In the above example the relation $Sim^{-1} \subseteq D \times D'$ is functional, i.e. for every d' there is exactly one d with $(d,d') \in Sim$. There are important other cases, consider for example, the simulation of binary numbers by decimal numbers. In this case neither Sim nor Sim^{-1} are functional. Notice that F simulates F' w.r.t Sim^{-1} if F' simulates F w.r.t. Sim.

If we want to define a function $f : X \dashrightarrow Y$ by a flowchart F, generally neither X nor Y coincide with the dataset of F. For adaption an input encoding $IC : X \longrightarrow D$ and an output encoding $OC : D \longrightarrow Y$ are needed. A flowchart together with an input and an output encoding will be called a *machine*.

15 EXAMPLE

Consider the flowchart F from Example 1. $D = \mathbb{N}^2$ is the dataset of F. Let $X := Y := \mathbb{N}$, define $IC : \mathbb{N} \longrightarrow \mathbb{N}^2$ and $OC : \mathbb{N}^2 \longrightarrow \mathbb{N}$ by $IC(a) = (2,a)$, $OC(a,b) := a$ for all $a,b \in \mathbb{N}$. By these data a machine M is defined which computes the function $f_M : X \dashrightarrow Y$, $f_M = OC \circ f_F \circ IC$. In our case

$$f_M(a) = \begin{cases} \text{div} & \text{if } a = 0 \\ 2 & \text{if } a > 0 \text{ and 2 divides a} \\ 1 & \text{otherwise} \end{cases}$$

(without proof).

16 DEFINITION (*machine, semantics of a machine*)

A machine is a quintuple $M = (F,X,Y,IC,OC)$ such that for some dataset D (1),...,(4) hold.

(1) F is a flowchart with dataset D,

(2) X (*input set*) and Y (*output set*) are sets,

(3) $IC : X \longrightarrow D$ (*input encoding*),

(4) $OC : D \longrightarrow Y$ (*output encoding*).

Suppose F has s exits. Then a function $f_M : X \dashrightarrow Y$ (*the function computed by* M) and a test $t_M : X \dashrightarrow \{1,\dots,s\}$ (*the test performed by* M) are defined by

$$f_M := OC \circ f_F \circ IC\,, \quad t_M := t_F \circ IC\,.$$

Thus, in order to determine $f_M(x)$, first encode x, execute the computation defined by the flowchart and decode the result. The value $f_M(x)$ is defined, iff the flowchart gives a result, i.e. iff $IC(x) \in dom(f_F)$. Clearly the choice of the input and the output encodings is essential. Usually classes of machines are defined by fixing the dataset D, the functions and tests which may be used for constructing flowcharts, and the input and the output encodings. We shall introduce several such classes in the following chapters.

Often it is desirable to change the dataset of a machine without changing the structure of the flowchart (the algorithm) such that the semantics remains unchanged. If in a machine the flowchart is substituted by a similar one, the encodings must be changed simultaneously. This is described by the following theorem.

17 THEOREM

Let $M=(F,X,Y,IC,OC)$ and $M'=(F',X,Y,IC',OC')$ be machines such that F' simulates F w.r.t. $Sim \subseteq D \times D'$. Let $IC(x)\, Sim\, IC'(x)$ for all $x \in X$ and $OC(d)=OC'(d')$ if $(d,d') \in Sim$. Then

$$f_M = f_{M'} \quad \text{and} \quad t_M = t_{M'} \, .$$

Proof (immediate from Theorem 13 and Definition 16)

Therefore in the case of simple simulation the encodings of a machine cannot be chosen arbitrarily. For changing encodings another transformation step is necessary. Applying Theorem 17 restricts the number of possible encodings too much. Therefore, a method for changing the encodings is needed. The problem is solved by adding an input adjustment and an output adjustment.

18 THEOREM (*change of encodings*)

Let $M=(F,X,Y,IC,OC)$ be a machine with dataset D. Let $M'=(F',X,Y,IC',OC')$ be a machine with dataset D such that F' is derived from F as follows

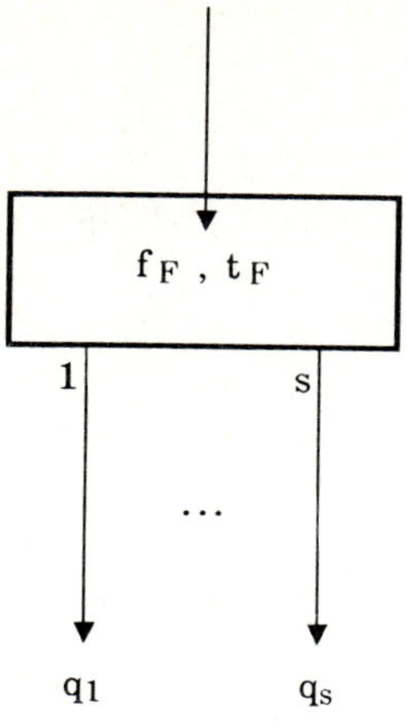

Flowchart F

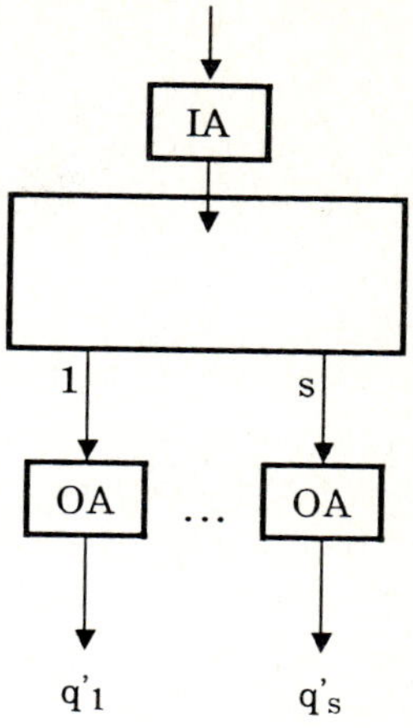

Flowchart F'

where the functions $IA: D \longrightarrow D$ (*input adjustment*) and $OA: D \longrightarrow D$ (*output adjustment*) satisfy the following equations:

$$(\forall x \in X) \quad IC(x) = IA \circ IC'(x) ,$$
$$(\forall d \in D) \quad OC(d) = OC' \circ OA(d) .$$

Then $f_M = f_{M'}$ and $t_M = t_{M'}$.

(We have defined F' from F informally by drawing figures, a formal definition can be derived unambiguously.)

Proof

By Definition 6, $f_{F'} = OA \circ f_F \circ IA$ and $t_{F'} = t_F \circ IA$. Therefore, by Definition 16, $f_{M'} = OC' \circ f_{F'} \circ IC' = OC \circ f_F \circ IC = f_M$ and $t_{M'} = t_{F'} \circ IC' = t_F \circ IC = t_M$.
Q.E.D.

The transformations refinement, simulation, and change of encodings provide a tool for a mathematically rigorous and clear stepwise development of (flowchart like) programs together with correctness proofs. So far we have assumed that at any stage of the development the functions and tests used in a machine are completely specified. In practice this restriction makes programming unnecessarily difficult. Usually it is not necessary to specify a function completely. If, e.g., we want to construct a machine for computing the greatest common divisor it suffices to find a machine $M = (F, \mathbb{N}^2, \mathbb{N}, IC, OC)$ such that $f_M : \mathbb{N}^2 \dashrightarrow \mathbb{N}$ satisfies the following property:

$(\forall a,b \in \mathbb{N})\quad [(a>0 \wedge b>0) \implies f\ (a,b) = \text{g.c.d.}(a,b)]$

For the case $a=0$ or $b=0$ the value $f_M(a,b)$ may be arbitrary. Suppose in a refinement step a flowchart F has to be found such that f_F satisfies a property Q (i.e. $Q(f_F)$). Let g be the function in F at some state q. In the proof of $Q(f_F)$ possibly only some property $Q'(g)$ of the function g is needed. Therefore g at state q may be substituted by any g' such that $Q'(g')$. Finally suppose a function f and a simulation Sim are given and a function f' has to be found such that $f =_{Sim} f'$. Then usually f' is not uniquely determined by the property $Q(f')$ where $Q(f') :\Longleftrightarrow f =_{Sim} f'$. In each of the cases it is not necessary to define the functions completely (in advance) but they may be specified incompletely by properties. Any function satisfying the given (sufficient) property may be used. In future we shall often use incompletely specified flowcharts and machines. This means that we assign a property of a function to a node rather than a specific function. The property is interpreted as follows: any function satisfying this property may be used for obtaining a completely specified correct flowchart or machine. The method of developing (flowchart) machines by stepwise construction of possibly incomplete machines using refinement, simulation, and change of encodings may be considered as a formalization of the informal method usually called "stepwise refinement".

EXERCISES

1) Let $M = (F, \mathbb{N}^2, \mathbb{N}, IC, OC)$ be the machine defined in Example 14.

   (a) Determine $SF^{10}(1,(3,8))$, $CT(1,(3,8))$, $TF(1,(3,8))$, $TF(1,(0,5))$ (cf. Definition 6).

   (b) Prove in detail:
   $(\forall a,b > 0)\ f_M(a,b) = \text{g.c.d.}(a,b)$.

   (c) Characterize $\text{dom}(f_M)$.

   (d) Prove: $(\forall a,b > 0)\ CT(1,(a,b)) \le 4\max(a,b) - 2$.

2) Let $F = (Q, D, \sigma, q_0, s, (q_1, \dots, q_s))$ be a flowchart. Show that there is a flowchart G with $f_F = f_G$ and $t_F = t_G$ which uses only pure function statements and pure test statements (i.e. if $\sigma_G(q) = (f,t,(p_1,\dots,p_k))$ is a statement, then either $k=1$ or $f(d) = (d$ if $d \in \text{dom}(t)$, div. otherwise$)$).

3) Let M be the machine defined in Example 14. Construct a machine $\overline{M} := (\overline{F}, \mathbb{N}^2, \mathbb{N}, \overline{IC}, \overline{OC})$ with $f_M = f_{\overline{M}}$ such that $\overline{IC}(a,b) := (b,a)$, $\overline{OC}(a,b) := b$

   (a) by simulation,

   (b) by input and output adjustments.

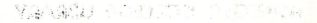

4) Let M be the machine defined in Example 14.

(a) Define a machine $M'=(F', \mathbb{N}^2, \mathbb{N}, IC' OC')$ which uses the dataset $D' = \mathbb{N}^3$ such that M' is similar to M via the relation $(a,b) \, Sim \, (a', b', c')$ $:\Longleftrightarrow (a = a' \wedge b = b')$.

(b) Change the functions of F', if necessary, such that each statement in F' can be computed by a flowchart which only uses the functions and tests given below and specify these corresponding flowcharts. The admitted functions and tests are f_i^+, f_i^- and s_i for $i = 1,2,3$, where

f_i^+ adds 1 in the i'th component,
f_i^- subtracts 1 in the i'th component,
s_i tests whether the i'th component is 0.

(c) Prove the correctness of the flowchart from (b) which corresponds to the statement simulating "$x > y$".

5) Let Z be a set of machines such that $f_M : X \dashrightarrow Y$ for any $M \in Z$. Define a machine $\overline{M}$ which computes the "universal function" $\overline{f} : Z \times X \dashrightarrow Y$ defined by $\overline{f}(M,x) := f_M(x)$.

BIBLIOGRAPHICAL NOTES

Flowcharts are investigated at different levels of abstraction. The theory of program schemes deals with properties of flowcharts which are independent of the appearing functions and tests. A pioneering paper is Luckham, Park, and Paterson (1970). Flowcharts which correspond to those ones defined in this book have e.g. been used by Manna (1974). The concept of machine used in this book is slightly different from that of Scott (1967) and Bird (1976).

1.2 Register Machines and Register Computability

In this chapter we introduce *register machines* and stüdy the functions computed by them, the *register computable* functions. As we shall discuss later, the register computable functions very likely represent those functions on the natural numbers which are "absolutely" computable in the intuitive sense.

Roughly speaking, register machines are flowchart programs of a very simple type for an idealized computer. This computer has a storage consisting of registers $R_o, R_1, R_2, \ldots$ each of which can store a natural number. The only operations and tests which may be used in the flowcharts are (for any $i \in \mathbb{N}$)

$R_i := R_i + 1$ (add 1 in register R_i),

$R_i := R_i - 1$ (substract 1 in register R_i),

$R_i = 0$? (test whether register R_i is empty).

The following figure shows the physical configuration of a register machine.

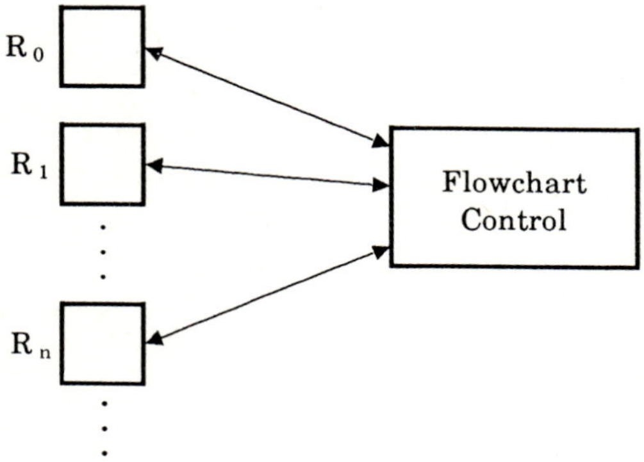

The model is appropriate for describing a real computer with registers for numbers as long as no overflow occurs during the considered computation. For our purpose the input encoding and the output encoding must be fixed: the input $(a_1, \ldots, a_k)$ is to be stored in registers R_1 to R_k, and the result will be found in register R_o (if a result exists).

1 <u>EXAMPLE</u>

By the following flowchart a register machine $M = (F, \mathbb{N}^2, \mathbb{N}, IC^{(2)}, OC)$ is defined.

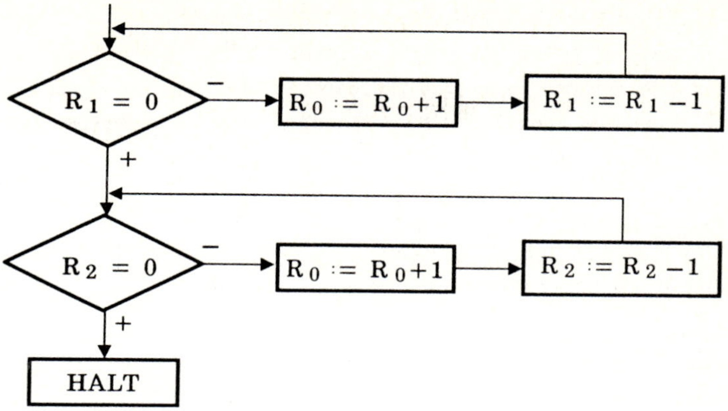

It computes the addition: $f_M(a,b) = a + b$.

Now we define register machines precisely. The dataset will be $D := \mathbb{N}^{\mathbb{N}} = \{d : \mathbb{N} \to \mathbb{N}\}$. Any $d \in D$ is a register assignment, where $d(i)$ is the content of register R_i. We shall write $d = (a_o, a_1, a_2, \ldots)$ in order to express $d(0) = a_o$, $d(1) = a_1, \ldots$.

2 DEFINITION (*register machine*)

Let k be a natural number. A (k-*ary*) *register machine* is a machine $M = (F, \mathbb{N}^k, \mathbb{N}, IC^{(k)}, OC)$ with flowchart $F = (Q, D, \sigma, q_o, s, (q_1, \ldots, q_s))$ such that (1),...,(4) hold.

(1) $D = \mathbb{N}^{\mathbb{N}}$.

(2) $IC^{(k)}(x_1, \ldots, x_k) = (0, x_1, \ldots, x_k, 0, \ldots)$ for all $(x_1, \ldots, x_k) \in \mathbb{N}^k$.

(3) $OC(a_o, a_1, \ldots) := a_o$ for all $a_o, a_1, \ldots \in \mathbb{N}$.

(4) Suppose $\sigma(q) = (f, t, (p_1, \ldots, p_j))$. Then either (a) or (b) holds.

(a) $j = 1$, $(\forall d \in D)$ $t(d) = 1$, and for some i $f =$ "$R_i := R_i + 1$" or $f =$ "$R_i := R_i - 1$" ,

(b) $j = 2$, $(\forall d \in D)$ $f(d) = d$, and for some i $t =$ "$R_i = 0$" ,

where

"$R_i := R_i + 1$"$(a_o, a_1, \ldots) := (a_o, a_1, \ldots, a_{i-1}, a_i + 1, a_{i+1}, \ldots)$,

"$R_i := R_i - 1$"$(a_o, a_1, \ldots) := (a_o, a_1, \ldots, a_{i-1}, a_i \dot{-} 1, a_{i+1}, \ldots)$,

$$\text{"}R_i{=}0\text{"}(d) := \begin{cases} 1 & \text{if } d(i) = 0 \\ 2 & \text{otherwise} \end{cases}$$

for all $a_o, a_1, \ldots \in \mathbb{N}$ and $d \in D$.

By (4) a statement in a register machine is either a pure function statement ("$R_i:=R_i+1$" , "$R_i:=R_i-1$") or a pure test statement ("$R_i=0$"). The set of k-ary register machines is determined by fixing the dataset, the input coding $IC^{(k)}$, the output coding OC, and the functions and tests which may be used. The functions and tests are the most simple ones: addition of 1, subtraction of 1, and test for 0 on any register R_i. Thus, operating on a register machine requires nothing else except the ability to count.

In Chapter 1, Definition 16 we have already defined the function f_M and the test t_M computed by a machine M. The functions and tests computed by register machines are called (absolutely) computable.

3 DEFINITION (*computability*)

A function $f:\mathbb{N}^k \dashrightarrow \mathbb{N}$ is *computable*, iff $f=f_M$ for some register machine M. A test $t:\mathbb{N}^k \dashrightarrow \{1,\dots,s\}$ is *computable*, iff $t=t_M$ for some register machine M. (Sometimes we shall say *register computable* instead of *computable*.)

In order to prove that a (somehow specified) function $f:\mathbb{N}^k \dashrightarrow \mathbb{N}$ is computable, it is sufficient to define an appropriate register machine M and to prove $f=f_M$. Example 1 shows that addition is computable (see Exercise 1). Many other functions can easily be proved to be computable. Lemma 4 gives some examples.

4 LEMMA

The functions

(a) $x \mapsto x+1$,

(b) $x \mapsto x$,

(c) $x \mapsto x \dot{-} 1$

from $\mathbb{N}$ to $\mathbb{N}$ are computable. The tests

(d) $x \mapsto$ (1 if $x=0$, 2 otherwise),

(e) $(x,y) \mapsto$ (1 if $x=y$, 2 otherwise)

on $\mathbb{N}$, $\mathbb{N}^2$ respectively, are computable.

We only prove the last statement. The other cases are left to the exercises.

Proof (e)

Let a 2-ary register machine M be defined by the following flowchart.

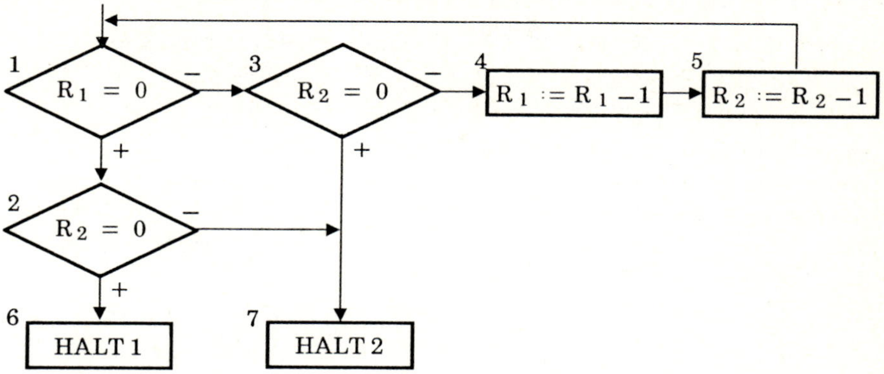

Let $(x,y) \in \mathbb{N}^2$. Then $IC^{(2)}(x,y) = (0,x,y,0,0,\dots) \in D$ by Definition 2(1). By simple inspection of the flowchart

$$SF^4(1,(0,a,b,0,\dots)) = (1,(0,a-1,b-1,0,\dots))$$

whenever $a > 0$ and $b > 0$. Complete induction on i yields:

$$SF^{4i}(1,(0,x,y,0,\dots)) = (1,(0,x-i,y-i,0,\dots)) \quad \text{if} \quad i \le x \quad \text{and} \quad i \le y.$$

Then

$$SF^{4x+2}(1,(0,x,y,0,\dots)) = (7,(0,0,y-x,0,\dots)) \quad \text{if} \quad x < y,$$

$$SF^{4x+2}(1,(0,x,y,0,\dots)) = (6,(0,0,0,0,\dots)) \quad \text{if} \quad x = y,$$

$$SF^{4y+2}(1,(0,x,y,0,\dots)) = (7,(0,x-y,0,0,\dots)) \quad \text{if} \quad x > y.$$

This implies $t(x,y) = (1$ if $x = y$, 2 otherwise$)$ by Definitions 1.1.6 and 1.1.16.
Q.E.D.

Any register machine M only uses a finite number of registers. Therefore, we could choose $D := \mathbb{N}^m$ for some $m \in \mathbb{N}$ as the dataset for M. The choice $D = \mathbb{N}^{\mathbb{N}}$ is made for technical reasons only. It is easy to write down for any given input $(x_1,\dots x_k)$ for M the corresponding computation (see Example 1.5), to notice when it halts, and to write down the result if it halts. (In practice the computation might be too long.) Altogether this is a mechanical task and could be also done by a machine. Therefore one can say: the register computable functions are "effectively" or "mechanically" computable.

Before showing that several other well known functions and tests are computable we prove a very useful theorem, which states that the computable functions and tests are closed w.r.t. flowchart programming. For a formal definition we generalize Definition 2. Instead of the three types of statements in (4), we now allow pure function statements $R_k := f(R_{i_1},\dots,R_{i_m})$ and pure test statements $t(R_{i_1},\dots,R_{i_m})$ with 2 exists, where $f : \mathbb{N}^m \dashrightarrow \mathbb{N}$ and $t : \mathbb{N}^m \dashrightarrow \{1,2\}$ are not restricted.

5 <u>DEFINITION</u> (*generalized register machine*)

The definition of a *generalized register machine* is obtained from Definition 2 by substituting (4) by (4').

(4') Suppose $\sigma(q) = (g,u,(p_1,\dots,p_k))$. Then either a) or b) holds:

a) $k = 1$, $g = "R_j := f(R_{i_1},\dots,R_{i_m})"$ for some $m,j,i_1,\dots,i_m \in \mathbb{N}$, and $f : \mathbb{N}^m \dashrightarrow \mathbb{N}$, $u(d) = (1$ if $d \in \mathrm{dom}(g)$, div otherwise), where

$$"R_j := f(R_{i_1},\dots,R_{i_m})"(a_o,a_1,\dots) := \begin{cases} (a_o,a_1,\dots,a_{j-1},x,a_{j+1},\dots) & \text{if } x := f(a_{i_1},\dots,a_{i_m}) \text{ exists} \\ \text{div otherwise} \end{cases}$$

b) $k = 2$, $u = "t(R_{i_1},\dots,R_{i_m})"$ for some $m,i_1,\dots,i_m \in \mathbb{N}$, and $t : \mathbb{N}^m \dashrightarrow \{1,2\}$, $g(d) = (d$ if $d \in \mathrm{dom}(u)$, div otherwise), where

$$"t(R_{i_1},\dots,R_{i_m})"(a_o,a_1,\dots) := t(a_{i_1},\dots,a_{i_m}) .$$

The following example gives a machine which multiplies numbers using additions as internal function.

6 <u>EXAMPLE</u>

Define a 2-ary generalized register machine by the following flowchart.

1 : $R_2 = 0$, 4 , 2 ;

2 : $R_o := R_o + R_1$, 3 ;

3 : $R_2 := R_2 - 1$, 1 ;

4 : HALT .

Then for any $x,y,z \in \mathbb{N}$, $z > 0$:

$$SF^3(1,(x,y,z,0,\dots,)) = (1,(x+y,y,z-1,0,\dots)) ,$$

and by induction for any y,z,i with $i \le z$:

$SF^{3i}(1,(0,y,z,0,\dots)) = (1,(y\cdot i,y,z-i,0,\dots))$.

The case $i = z$ implies

$SF^{3z+1}(1,(0,y,z,0,\dots)) = (4,(y\cdot z,y,0,\dots)) = TF(1,(0,y,z,0,\dots))$.

And therefore $f_M(y,z) = y \cdot z$.

From Example 1 we already know that addition is computable. The above example indicates that multiplication is also computable. The following theorem proves this.

7 THEOREM

Let M be a generalized register machine which uses only computable functions and tests (f and t in Definition 5(4')). Then f_M and t_M are computable.

This means a function $f : \mathbb{N}^k \dashrightarrow \mathbb{N}$ (or a test $t : \mathbb{N}^k \dashrightarrow \{1,\dots,m\}$) is computable if f (or t) is computed by a generalized register machine which uses only computable functions and tests. By Lemma 4, any register machine is a generalized register machine of this kind. The following lemma is used in the proof of Theorem 7.

8 LEMMA

Let $i,j,k \in \mathbb{N}$ be natural numbers where $k \neq i$, $k \neq j$, let $D := \mathbb{N}^{\mathbb{N}}$. Define "$R_i \leftarrow R_j$" : $D \to D$ and "$R_i :\underset{k}{=} R_j$" : $D \to D$ by

$$\text{"}R_i \leftarrow R_j\text{"}(d)(n) := \begin{cases} d(j) & \text{if } n = i \\ 0 & \text{if } n = j \text{ and } n \neq i \\ d(n) & \text{otherwise ,} \end{cases}$$

$$\text{"}R_i :\underset{k}{=} R_j\text{"}(d)(n) := \begin{cases} d(j) & \text{if } n = i \\ 0 & \text{if } n = k \\ d(n) & \text{otherwise} \end{cases}$$

for all $d \in D$, $n \in \mathbb{N}$. Then there are register flowcharts E and F with $f_E =$ "$R_i \leftarrow R_j$" and $f_F =$ "$R_i :\underset{k}{=} R_j$" .

Both functions transport the content of Register R_j into register R_i. In the first case R_j is empty afterwards, in the second case R_j keeps its value, however the auxiliary register R_k is empty afterwards.

Proof

We only specify an appropriate flowchart E, the rest of the proof is left as an exercise. Let E be the following flowchart.

1 : $R_i = 0$, 3 , 2 ;

2 : $R_i := R_i - 1$, 1 ;

3 : $R_j = 0$, 6 , 4 ;

4 : $R_j := R_j - 1$, 5 ;

5 : $R_i := R_i + 1$, 3 ;

6 : HALT .

Then $f_E = "R_i \leftarrow R_j"$ if $i \neq j$ (see Exercise 3).
In the case $i = j$ define E by

1 : $R_o = 0$, 2 , 2 ;

2 : HALT .

Q.E.D.

Proof (Theorem 7)

The main idea of the proof is to refine the nontrivial statements of the machine M by appropriate register machine flowcharts. The refining flowcharts will need auxiliary registers which are not used by M. Since the contents of all the auxiliary registers cannot be saved (proof?), a direct application of Theorem 1.1.11 is not possible. Note that any statement of M leaves these registers unchanged. The problem is solved by considering a machine M' which is similar to M via a similarity relation expressing that only the first (say) q registers are relevant. We shall only show how a general function statement, Case a) in Definition 5(4'), can be replaced by a register machine flowchart. The proof for test statements, Case b), is similar. Iterated application finally leads to the desired proper register machine.

Suppose $f : \mathbb{N}^m \dashrightarrow \mathbb{N}$ is computable and $g = "R_j := f(R_{i_1}, \dots, R_{i_m})"$ appears at some state s of M. Then there is a register machine with flowchart G which computes f. Let q be a number such that $q > k$ for any register R_k used in M or in G. Then for any $a_1, \dots, a_m, a_q, a_{q+1}, \dots$

$$f_G(0, a_1, \dots, a_m, \underbrace{0, \dots, 0}_{q-(m+1)\text{ times}}, a_q, a_{q+1}, \dots)$$

$$= \begin{cases} (f(a_1,\dots,a_m), b_1, \dots, b_{q-1}, a_q, a_{q+1}, \dots) & \text{for certain numbers } b_1, \dots, b_{q-1} \text{ if } f(a_1,\dots,a_m) \text{ exists} \\ \text{div} & \text{otherwise .} \end{cases}$$

Below, we shall define a register flowchart F with

$$f_F(a_o,a_1,\ldots) = (a_o,a_1,\ldots,a_{j-1},b_o,a_{j+1},\ldots,a_{q-1},c_q,c_{q+1},\ldots)$$

for certain values $c_q,c_{q+1},\ldots,$ if $b_o := f(a_{i_1},\ldots,a_{i_m})$ exists, and $f_F(a_o,a_1,\ldots) = \mathrm{div}$ otherwise. Now let $D' := D$ and $Sim \subseteq D \times D'$ be defined by

$$(a_o,a_1,\ldots)\,Sim\,(b_o,b_1,\ldots) :\Longleftrightarrow (a_o,\ldots,a_{q-1}) = (b_o,\ldots,b_{q-1}) .$$

Let M' be the machine which is obtained from machine M by substituting the function f_F for the function g in statement s. Then, obviously, M and M' are similar (Theorem 1.1.13). Substitution of flowchart F at state s into the flowchart of M' yields a machine M in which the nontrivial function g at s is eliminated and which computes the same function and test (Theorem 1.1.11).

It remains to define the flowchart F. First we define a flowchart H which

- shifts the contents of R_o to R_{q-1} q places to the right,
- initializes the operation for f_G,
- applies f_G and puts the result into R_{q+j}, and
- shifts the contents of R_q to R_{2q-1} q places to the left.

Let H be defined by the following flowchart.

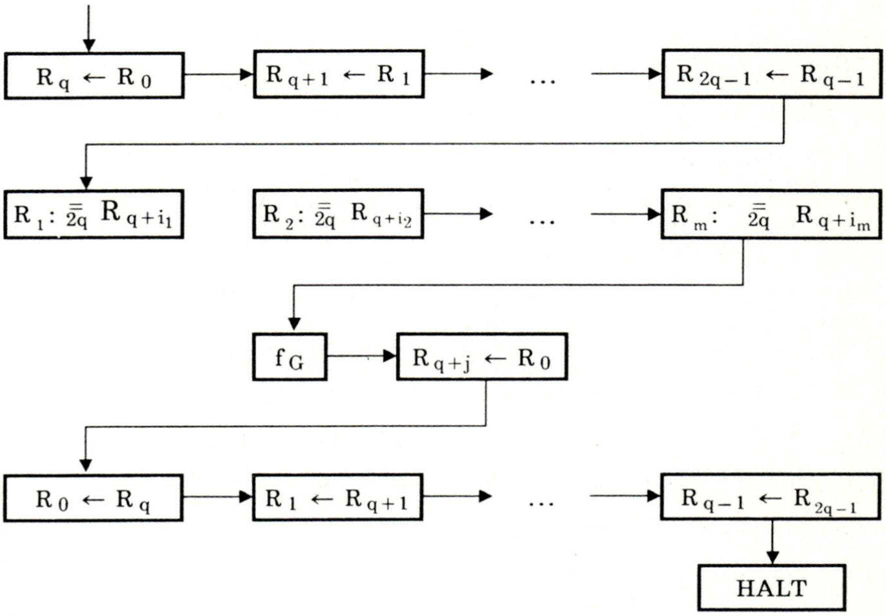

Suppose $d' = (a_o, a_1, a_2, \dots)$ is the initial assignment for H. Then the assignments at the end of the first, second, third, and fourth line of the above diagram are as follows. (Register R_q is marked by $\bar{\ }$). We assume that $b_o := f(a_{i_1}, \dots, a_{i_m})$ exists.

$(0,0,\dots,0,\bar{a}_o,a_1,\dots,a_{q-1},a_{2q},a_{2q+1},\dots)$,

$(0,a_{i_1},\dots,a_{i_m},0,\dots,0,\bar{a}_o,a_1,\dots,a_{q-1},0,a_{2q+1},\dots)$,

$(0,b_1,\dots,b_{q-1},\bar{a}_o,\dots,a_{j-1},b_o,a_{j+1},\dots,a_{q-1},0,a_{2q+1},\dots)$,

$(a_o,a_1,\dots,a_{j-1},b_o,a_{j+1},\dots,a_{q-1},\bar{0},0,\dots,0,0,a_{2q+1},\dots)$,

where $b_1,\dots,b_{q-1}$ are values without meaning for us.
If b_o does not exist then $f(\dots)$ and $f_H(\dots)$ do not exist either. For f_G and for the other functions appearing in H we have register machine flowcharts (Lemma 8). Therefore H can be refined into a register machine flowchart F with the desired property.
Q.E.D.

Now we can easily prove computability of a great number of well known functions. The next lemma summarizes some examples.

9 LEMMA (*some register computable functions*)

The following functions are computable.

(1) $\tilde{0} : \mathbb{N}^o \longrightarrow \mathbb{N}$, $\tilde{0}(\ ) := 0$,

(2) $Z : \mathbb{N} \longrightarrow \mathbb{N}$, $Z(x) := 0$,

(3) $pr_i^{(k)} : \mathbb{N}^k \longrightarrow \mathbb{N}$, $pr_i^{(k)}(x_1,\dots x_k) := x_i$ $(1 \le i \le k)$,

(4) $f_4 : \mathbb{N}^2 \longrightarrow \mathbb{N}$, $f_4(x,y) := x + y$,

(5) $f_5 : \mathbb{N}^2 \longrightarrow \mathbb{N}$, $f_5(x,y) := x \cdot y$,

(6) $f_6 : \mathbb{N}^2 \longrightarrow \mathbb{N}$, $f_6(x,y) := x \dot{-} y$,

(7) $f_7 : \mathbb{N}^2 \longrightarrow \mathbb{N}$, $f_7(x,y) := x^y$,

(8) $f_8 : \mathbb{N}^2 \longrightarrow \mathbb{N}$, $f_8(x,y) := (\lfloor \frac{x}{y} \rfloor$ if $y \neq 0$, div otherwise) ,

(9) $f_9 : \mathbb{N}^2 \longrightarrow \mathbb{N}$, $f_9(x,y) := x \dot{-} y \cdot f_8(x,y)$ (= rest under division) .

The following test $t : \mathbb{N}^2 \longrightarrow \{1,2\}$ is computable:

(10) $t_{10}(x,y) = (1$ if $x < y$, 2 otherwise) .

(Where $\lfloor z \rfloor$:= "the greatest integer n with $n \le z$" for any real number z.)

Proof

1. The machine $M = (F, \mathbb{N}^o, \mathbb{N}, IC^{(o)}, OC)$ where F is defined by:

   1 : $R_o = 0$, 2 , 2 ;

   2 : HALT .

   computes $\tilde{0}$.

2. The 1-ary register machine with the flowchart from 1 computes Z.

3. The k-ary register machine defined by the flowchart

   1 : $R_i = 0$, 4 , 2 ;

   2 : $R_i := R_i - 1$, 3 ;

   3 : $R_o := R_o + 1$, 1 ;

   4 : HALT

   computes $pr_i^{(k)}$. For the proof show by induction on m: $(\forall m \leq a_i)$
   $SF^{3m}(1,(a_o,a_1,\ldots,a_k,0,\ldots)) = (1,(a_o+m,a_1,\ldots,a_{i-1},a_i-m,a_{i+1},\ldots,a_k,0,\ldots))$.
   Then $SF^{3a_i+1}(1,(0,a_1,\ldots,a_k,0,\ldots)) = (4,(a_i,\ldots))$, therefore $f_M(a_1,\ldots,a_k) = a_i$.

4. (see Example 1)

5. (see Example 6)

6. (see Exercise 5)

7. (see Exercise 5)

10. Define a generalized register machine M by the following flowchart.

   1 : $R_o := R_2 \dot{-} R_1$, 2 ;

   2 : $R_o = 0$, 3 , 4 ;

   3 : HALT 2 ;

   4 : HALT 1 .

   Obviously, $t_{10} = t_M$. Since $\dot{-} = f_6$ is computable, t_{10} is computable by Theorem 7.

8., 9. (see Exercise 5)

Q.E.D.

Theorem 7 expresses a very general closure property of the computable functions: "the computable functions are closed under register programming". It is useful to formulate some more special consequences explicitly.

10 DEFINITION (*substitution, primitive and μ-recursion*)

(1) For any $k \in \mathbb{N}$ define

$$\mathbb{F}^{(k)} := \{f : \mathbb{N}^k \longrightarrow \mathbb{N}\}\,, \quad \mathbb{P}^{(k)} := \{f : \mathbb{N}^k \dashrightarrow \mathbb{N}\}\,,$$

$$\mathbb{F}^{(\infty)} := \bigcup\{\mathbb{F}^{(k)} \mid k \in \mathbb{N}\}\,, \quad \mathbb{P}^{(\infty)} := \bigcup\{\mathbb{P}^{(k)} \mid k \in \mathbb{N}\}\,.$$

(2) For any $k,m \in \mathbb{N}$ $(m \geq 1)$ and any $f \in \mathbb{P}^{(m)}$ and $g_1,\dots,g_m \in \mathbb{P}^{(k)}$ define $\mathrm{Sub}_m(f,g_1,\dots,g_m) \in \mathbb{P}^{(k)}$ by

$$\mathrm{Sub}_m(f,g_1,\dots,g_m)(\bar{x}) := f(g_1(\bar{x}),\dots,g_m(\bar{x}))$$

for all $\bar{x} \in \mathbb{N}^k$.

(3) For any $k \in \mathbb{N}$, and any $g \in \mathbb{P}^{(k)}$ and $h \in \mathbb{P}^{(k+2)}$ define $\mathrm{Prk}(g,h) \in \mathbb{P}^{(k+1)}$ by the unique function f which satisfies the two recursion equations

$$f(x_1,\dots,x_k,0) = g(x_1,\dots,x_k)$$

$$f(x_1,\dots,x_k,n+1) = h(x_1,\dots,x_k,n,f(x_1,\dots,x_k,n))$$

for all $x_1,\dots,x_k,n \in \mathbb{N}$.

(4) For any $k \in \mathbb{N}$ and any $h \in \mathbb{P}^{(k+1)}$ define $\tilde{\mu}(h) \in \mathbb{P}^{(k)}$ by

$$\tilde{\mu}(h)(x_1,\dots,x_k) := \begin{cases} \min(M) & \text{if } M := \{n \mid h(x_1,\dots,x_k,n) = 0 \\ & \quad \text{and } (\forall i < n)\ (x_1,\dots,x_k,i) \in \mathrm{dom}(h)\} \neq \emptyset \\ \mathrm{div} & \text{otherwise} \end{cases}$$

The operators $\mathrm{Sub}_m : (\mathbb{P}^{(\infty)})^{m+1} \dashrightarrow \mathbb{P}^{(\infty)}$ are called *substitution operators*, $\mathrm{Prk} : (\mathbb{P}^{(\infty)})^2 \dashrightarrow \mathbb{P}^{(\infty)}$ is the operator of *primitive recursion*, and $\tilde{\mu} : \mathbb{P}^{(\infty)} \dashrightarrow \mathbb{P}^{(\infty)}$ is the operator of *μ-recursion* or *minimization*.

In 10(2) and 10(3) we consider strict substitution of functions: $\mathrm{Sub}_m(f,g_1,\dots,g_m)(\bar{x}) = z$ iff there are values $y_1,\dots,y_m$ with $y_1 = g_1(\bar{x}),\dots$ $\dots, y_m = g_m(\bar{x})$ and $z = f(y_1,\dots,y_m)$. In 10(3) $f(x_1,\dots,x_k,n+1) = z$ iff there is some $y \in \mathbb{N}$ with $f(x_1,\dots,x_k,n) = y$ and $f(x_1,\dots,x_k,n+1) = h(x_1,\dots,x_k,n,y)$. Especially, if $f(x_1,\dots,x_k,n)$ is undefined then $f(x_1,\dots,x_k,n+1)$ is undefined. The value $f(x\ ,\dots,x\ ,n)$ can be determined by computing the values $f(x_1,\dots,x_k,0)$, $f(x_1,\dots,x_k,1)$, ... in this order using the two recursion equations (see the proof of Theorem 12).

The existence of a unique function f satisfying the recursion equations can be proved by complete induction. The substitution operators and the operator of primitive recursion transform functions from $\mathbb{F}$ (total functions) into functions from $\mathbb{F}$ (total functions), while for many functions $f \in \mathbb{F}$, $\tilde{\mu}(f)$ is not total.

11 EXAMPLES

(1) Let $pr_1^{(2)}$, f_6, and f_8 be the functions from Lemma 9. Then

$$Sub_2(f_8, pr_1^{(2)}, f_6)(x,y) = \begin{cases} \left\lfloor \frac{x}{x-y} \right\rfloor & \text{if } y < x \\ \text{div} & \text{otherwise} . \end{cases}$$

(2) Define $h : \mathbb{N}^3 \longrightarrow \mathbb{N}$ by $h(x,y,z) := z \dot{-} 1$. Then let $f := Prk(pr_1^{(1)}, h)$. This means f satisfies the recursion equations

$$f(x,0) = x ,$$

$$f(x,n+1) = f(x,n) \dot{-} 1 .$$

The function $(x,y) \longrightarrow x \dot{-} y$ also satisfies these equations. Since there is a unique solution of the recursion equations, $f(x,y) = x \dot{-} y$.

(3) Define $f : \mathbb{N}^3 \longrightarrow \mathbb{N}$ by $f(x,y,z) := (x+1) \dot{-} y \cdot z$. Then

$$\tilde{\mu}(f)(x,y) = 1 + f_8(x,y) \qquad (f_8 \text{ from Lemma 9}).$$

Define $f : \mathbb{N}^2 \dashrightarrow \mathbb{N}$ by $f(x,y) := x + f_8(y \dot{-} 1, y)$. Then $f(0,0) = \text{div}$, $f(0,1) = 0$. By Definition 10(4), $\tilde{\mu}(f)(0) = \text{div}$ although $f(0,n) = 0$ for some n.

12 THEOREM

The set of computable functions is closed under the operators of substitution, primitive recursion and μ-recursion.

Proof

(1) Suppose $f \in \mathbb{P}^{(m)}$ and $g_1, \ldots, g_m \in \mathbb{P}^{(k)}$ are computable. Define a k-ary generalized register machine M by the following flowchart.

1 : $R_{k+1} := g_1(R_1, \ldots, R_k)$, 2 ;

2 : $R_{k+2} := g_2(R_1, \ldots, R_k)$, 3 ;

⋮

m : $R_{k+m} := g_m(R_1, \ldots, R_k)$, m+1 ;

m+1 : $R_o := f(R_{k+1}, \ldots, R_{k+m})$, m+2 ;

m+2 : HALT .

Obviously $f_M = Sub_m(f, g_1, \ldots, g_m)$. By Theorem 7 f_M is computable.

(2) Suppose $g \in \mathbb{P}^{(k)}$ and $h \in \mathbb{P}^{(k+2)}$ are computable. Define a (k+1)-ary generalized register machine M by the following flowchart.

1 : $R_o := g(R_1,\ldots,R_k)$, 2 ;

2 : $R_{k+1} = R_{k+2}$, 5 , 3 ;

3 : $R_o := h(R_1,\ldots,R_k,R_{k+2},R_o)$, 4 ;

4 : $R_{k+2} := R_{k+2} + 1$, 2 ;

5 : HALT .

By Theorem 7 f_M is computable. We have to prove $f_M = f := Prk(g,h)$. Let $x_1,\ldots,x_k,y \in \mathbb{N}$. Then for all $i \le y$ the following equation holds:

$$SF^{3i+1}(1,(0,x_1,\ldots,x_k,y,0,\ldots)) = \begin{cases} (2,(z,x_1,\ldots,x_k,y,i,0,\ldots)) & \\ \qquad \text{if } z := f(x_1,\ldots,x_k,i) \text{ exists} \\ \text{div} \qquad \text{otherwise.} \end{cases}$$

This can easily be proved by induction on i using the recursion equations for f from Definition 10(3). From the special case $i = y$ we obtain

$$SF^{3y+2}(1,(0,x_1,\ldots,x_k,y,0,\ldots)) = \begin{cases} (5,(z,x_1,\ldots,x_k,y,y,0,\ldots)) & \\ \qquad \text{if } z := f(x_1,\ldots,x_k,y) \text{ exists} \\ \text{div} \qquad \text{otherwise} \end{cases}$$

This implies $f_M(x_1,\ldots,x_k,y) = f(x_1,\ldots,x_k,y)$. Therefore, $f = f_M$, and f is computable.

(3) Suppose $f \in \mathbb{P}^{(k+1)}$ is computable. Define a k-ary generalized register machine by the following flowchart.

1 : $R_{k+1} := f(R_1,\ldots,R_k,R_o)$, 2 ;

2 : $R_{k+1} = 0$, 4 , 3 ;

3 : $R_o := R_o + 1$, 1 ;

4 : HALT .

By Theorem 7 f_M is computable. The verification of $\tilde{\mu}(f) = f_M$ is left as an exercise. Q.E.D.

Of course, any kind of (strict) substitution transforms register computable functions into register computable functions. In future we shall use this fact without mentioning it explicitly.

In Definition 3 we have distinguished between computable functions $f : \mathbb{N}^k \dashrightarrow \mathbb{N}$ and computable tests $t : \mathbb{N}^k \dashrightarrow \{1,\ldots,s\}$. By the following lemma it is sufficient to study only functions.

13 LEMMA

Let $m,k \in \mathbb{N}$, $m \geq 1$, $t : \mathbb{N}^k \dashrightarrow \{1,\dots,m\}$. Then the following statements are equivalent:

(1) t is computable,

(2) The function $f : \mathbb{N}^k \dashrightarrow \mathbb{N}$, defined by $(\forall \bar{x} \in \mathbb{N}^k)\ f(\bar{x}) = t(\bar{x})$, is computable.

The easy proof is left as an exercise.

A function which is used very often in recursion theory is Cantor's pairing function $\pi : \mathbb{N}^2 \longrightarrow \mathbb{N}$, which encodes pairs of numbers by numbers. It is defined by a systematic diagonal counting of all pairs of natural numbers in the following way:

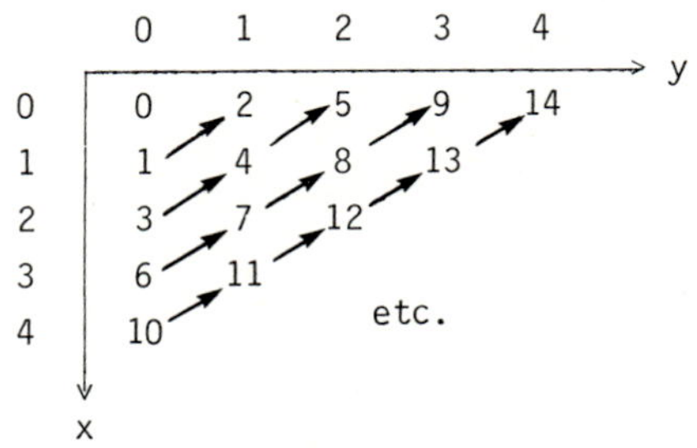

From the diagram we conclude $\pi(x,0) = \Sigma\{i \mid i \leq x\}$ and $\pi(x,y) = \pi(x+y,0) + y$, therefore, $\pi(x,y) = \Sigma\{i \mid i \leq x+y\} + y = \frac{1}{2}(x+y)(x+y+1) + y$.

14 DEFINITION (*Cantor's pairing function, k-tupling function*)

(1) Define $\pi : \mathbb{N}^2 \longrightarrow \mathbb{N}$ by $\pi(x,y) := \Sigma\{i \mid i \leq x+y\} + y$ for all $x,y \in \mathbb{N}$.

(2) For $k = 1,2,3,\dots$ define $\pi^{(k)} : \mathbb{N}^k \longrightarrow \mathbb{N}$ inductively by

$$\pi^{(1)}(x) := x$$

$$\pi^{(k+1)}(x_1,\dots,x_{k+1}) := \pi(\pi^{(k)}(x_1,\dots,x_k),x_{k+1})$$

for all $k,x,x_1,\dots,x_{k+1} \in \mathbb{N}$.

Notation: $\langle x_1,\dots,x_k\rangle := \pi^{(k)}(x_1,\dots,x_k)$. π is called *Cantor's pairing function*, $\pi^{(k)}$ is called the *standard k-tupling function*.

Notice that $\pi^{(2)} = \pi$. The following lemma summarizes the important properties of the functions $\pi^{(k)}$.

15 LEMMA

For any $k \geq 1$ the following properties hold.

(1) $\pi^{(k)}$ is bijective,

(2) $\pi^{(k)}$ is computable,

(3) $\pi_i^{(k)} := pr_i^{(k)}(\pi^{(k)})^{-1}$ is computable for any i, $1 \leq i \leq k$. ($\pi_1 := \pi_1^{(2)}$, $\pi_2 := \pi_2^{(2)}$)

Proof

First we consider the case $k = 2$. Define $f : \mathbb{N} \to \mathbb{N}$ and $q : \mathbb{N} \to \mathbb{N}$ by $f(w) := \Sigma\{i \mid i \leq w\} = \frac{1}{2}w(w+1)$ and $q(z) := \max\{v \mid f(v) \leq z\}$. Since $f(0) = 0$ and $f(w) < f(w+1)$, $q(z)$ exists for all z. From the definition of q, $fq(z) \leq z < f(q(z)+1) = fq(z) + q(z) + 1$ and therefore, $0 \leq z - fq(z) \leq q(z)$. Define $\pi_1, \pi_2 : \mathbb{N} \to \mathbb{N}$ by $\pi_2(z) := z - fq(z)$, $\pi_1(z) := q(z) - \pi_2(z)$. By the above inequality $\pi_2(z) \geq 0$ and $\pi_1(z) \geq 0$. Define $h : \mathbb{N} \to \mathbb{N}^2$ by $h(z) := (\pi_1(z), \pi_2(z))$. Then:

$$\pi h(z) = \pi(\pi_1(z), \pi_2(z)) = f(\pi_1(z) + \pi_2(z)) + \pi_2(z) = fq(z) + \pi_2(z) = z,$$

$$\pi_2\pi(x,y) = \pi(x,y) - fq\pi(x,y) = f(x+y) + y - f(x+y) = y,$$

$$\pi_1\pi(x,y) = q\pi(x,y) - \pi_2\pi(x,y) = x + y - y = x, \text{ therefore}$$

$$h\pi(x,y) = (\pi_1\pi(x,y), \pi_2\pi(x,y)) = (x,y).$$

Therefore, $h = \pi^{-1}$ and π is bijective. From Lemma 9 one easily concludes that f is computable. Define $g \in \mathbb{F}^{(2)}$ by $g(z,v) := (z+1) \dot{-} f(v)$. Then $q(z) = \tilde{\mu}(g)(z) \dot{-} 1$, and q is computable by Lemma 9 and Theorem 12. Also π_1 and π_2 are computable. Thus, we have proved (1), (2), and (3) for the case $k = 2$. A simple induction yields a proof for all $k \geq 1$.

Q.E.D.

The function $\pi^{(k)}$ relates k-ary functions and unary functions in such a way that computable functions correspond to computable functions:

16 LEMMA

Let $f : \mathbb{N} \dashrightarrow \mathbb{N}$ be a partial function, let $k \geq 1$. Then f is computable, iff $f\pi^{(k)}$ is computable.

Proof

Suppose f is computable. Then $f\pi^{(k)} = Sub_1(f, \pi^{(k)})$ is computable by Lemma 15(2) and Theorem 12. Suppose $g := f\pi^{(k)}$ is computable. Since $f(x) = g(\pi^{(k)})^{-1}(x) =$

$= g(\pi_1^{(k)}(x),\dots,\pi_k^{(k)}(x)) = \mathrm{Sub}_k(g,\pi_1^{(k)},\dots,\pi_k^{(k)})(x)$ and the $\pi_i^{(k)} := pr_i^{(k)}(\pi^{(k)})^{-1}$ are computable (Lemma 15), f is also computable by Lemma 12.
Q.E.D.

Since $\pi^{(k)}$ is bijective, any function $g : \mathbb{N}^k \dashrightarrow \mathbb{N}$ can be uniquely represented by its unary transform $f := g(\pi^{(k)})^{-1}$. Since $f\pi^{(k)} = g$, f is uniquely determined by the equation

$$f\langle x_1,\dots,x_k\rangle := g(x_1,\dots,x_k) .$$

By Lemma 16, f is computable iff g is computable. In future we shall repeatedly define a computable function by defining the computable function $f\pi^{(k)}$. Example: the equation $f\langle x,y,z\rangle := x^2 + yz$ defines a computable function $f : \mathbb{N} \to \mathbb{N}$.

Remark

The operator $\tilde{\mu}$ must be distinguished from the μ-notation which is defined as follows. Let A(i) be a predicate on $\mathbb{N}$. Then

$$\mu n[A(n)] := \begin{cases} \min(M) & \text{if } M := \{i \in \mathbb{N} \mid A(i)\} \neq \emptyset \\ \mathrm{div} & \text{otherwise .} \end{cases}$$

For example, define $f : \mathbb{N} \dashrightarrow \mathbb{N}$ by

$$f(x) := \mu n[n^2 = x] ,$$

then f(x) is the square root of x if x is a square number and f(x) is undefined otherwise. If $f : \mathbb{N}^{k+1} \longrightarrow \mathbb{N}$ is a total function, then

$$\tilde{\mu}(f)(x_1,\dots,x_k) = \mu i[f(x_1,\dots,x_k,i) = 0] .$$

Hence, in the case of total functions the operation $\tilde{\mu}$ can be expressed by the μ-notation.

EXERCISES

1) Let M be the machine defined in Example 1. Prove formally: $(\forall a,b \in \mathbb{N})f_M(a,b) = a+b$.

2) Prove Lemma 4(a) - (d).

3) (a) Let E be the flowchart defined in the proof of Lemma 8. Prove: $f_E = "R_i \longleftarrow R_j"$.
   (b) Define a register machine flowchart F with $f_F = "R_i :\underset{k}{=} R_j"$ (and prove this). Assume that $i \neq j$, $i \neq k$, $j \neq k$.

4) Consider Case b) in the proof of Theorem 7, replacement of a general test statement by a register machine flowchart. How must Case a) be modified?

5) Prove Lemma 9(6) - 9(9).

6) Verify $\tilde{\mu}(f) = f_M$ in (3) of the proof of Theorem 12.

7) Let $f : \mathbb{N} \dashrightarrow \mathbb{N}$ be an injective computable function. Show that $f^{-1} : \mathbb{N} \dashrightarrow \mathbb{N}$ is computable.

8) Prove that the function $f : \mathbb{N} \dashrightarrow \mathbb{N}$ with $f(n) :=$ "the n'th prime" is computable.

9) Define $f : \mathbb{N}^2 \dashrightarrow \mathbb{N}$ by $f(x,y) := 2^x(2y+1) \dot{-} 1$.

   (a) Show that f is bijective.

   (b) Show that f is computable.

   (c) Show that $pr_1^{(2)} f^{-1}$ and $pr_2^{(2)} f^{-1}$ are computable (f is another pairing function).

10) Let $f : \mathbb{N}^k \dashrightarrow \mathbb{N}$ be a bijective computable function. Prove that $pr_i^{(k)} f^{-1}$ is computable for any i with $1 \leq i \leq k$.

11) Prove Lemma 13.

12) A function $A : \mathbb{N}^2 \dashrightarrow \mathbb{N}$ is (uniquely) defined by the following recursion equations:

$$A(0,0) := 1,\ A(0,1) := 2,\ A(0,x) := x+2,$$
$$A(n+1,0) := 1,\ A(n+1,\ x+1) := A(n, A(n+1,x))$$

for all $n,x \in \mathbb{N}$. Show that A is computable. Hint: define a register machine M and prove that f_M satisfies the above equations. (A is essentially Ackermann's function which is computable but not primitive recursive.)

13) Let $g : \mathbb{N}^k \dashrightarrow \mathbb{N}$, $h : \mathbb{N}^{k+2} \dashrightarrow \mathbb{N}$. Show that there exists a unique function $f : \mathbb{N}^{k+1} \dashrightarrow \mathbb{N}$ which satisfies the recursion equations

$$f(x_1,\ldots,x_k,0) = g(x_1,\ldots,x_k),$$
$$f(x_1,\ldots,x_k,n+1) = h(x_1,\ldots,x_k,n,f(x_1,\ldots,x_k,n)).$$

14) An *indirect addressing register machine* (I-*register machine*) is a register machine in which the following statements which use indirect addressing are also admitted: "$IR_i := R_i + 1$", "$IR_i := R_i - 1$", "$IR_i = 0$" for any $i \in \mathbb{N}$, where

$$\text{"}IR_i := R_i + 1\text{"}(a_0,a_1,\ldots) := \text{"}R_{a_i} := R_{a_i} + 1\text{"}(a_0,a_1,\ldots),$$

$$\text{"}IR_i := R_i - 1\text{"}(a_0,a_1,\ldots) := \text{"}R_{a_i} := R_{a_i} - 1\text{"}(a_0,a_1,\ldots),$$

$$\text{"}IR_i = 0\text{"}(a_0,a_1,\ldots) := \text{"}R_{a_i} := 0\text{"}(a_0,a_1,\ldots).$$

Prove that f_M is computable for any indirect addressing register machine M.

15) An n-*counter flowchart* is a flowchart $F=(Q,D,\sigma,\ldots)$ with $D=\mathbb{N}^n$ such that any statement is either a pure function statement "$R_i := R_i + 1$" or "$R_i := R_i - 1$", where $1 \le i \le n$, defined by

$$"R_i := R_i + 1"(a_1,\ldots,a_n) = (a_1,\ldots,a_{i-1},a_i+1,a_{i+1},\ldots,a_n),$$
$$"R_i := R_i - 1"(a_1,\ldots,a_n) = (a_1,\ldots,a_{i-1},a_i \dot{-} 1,a_{i+1},\ldots,a_n)$$

or a pure test statement "$R_i=0$", where $1 \le i \le n$, defined by

$$"R_i = 0"(a_1,\ldots,a_n) = (1 \text{ if } a_i = 0, 2 \text{ otherwise}).$$

Prove that for any $k \in \mathbb{N}$ there are encodings $I^{(k)}$ and 0 such that

$$\{f_M \mid M=(F,\mathbb{N}^k,\mathbb{N},I^{(k)},0) \text{ for some 2-counter flowchart } F\}$$

is the class of the k-ary computable functions on $\mathbb{N}$.

16) Consider functions $f,g : \mathbb{N} \dashrightarrow \mathbb{N}$ defined by

$$f(x) := \begin{cases} 1 & \text{if a consecutive run of exactly } x \text{ 7's occurs} \\ & \text{in the decimal expansion of } \pi \\ 0 & \text{otherwise;} \end{cases}$$

and

$$g(x) := \begin{cases} 1 & \text{if a consecutive run of at least } x \text{ 7's occurs} \\ & \text{in the decimal expansion of } \pi \\ 0 & \text{otherwise.} \end{cases}$$

Discuss computability of f and g.

BIBLIOGRAPHICAL NOTES

Register Machines have been introduced by Shepherdson and Sturgis (1963) for defining computability.

1.3 Primitive Recursive and μ-Recursive Functions

In Chapter 1.2 we have defined the computable functions on $\mathbb{N}$ using register machines. This definition enables good understanding of the concept of computability. In this chapter we define the computable functions in a quite different way. We first define the *primitive recursive functions* and then the *μ-recursive functions* and finally prove that the μ-recursive functions coincide with the (register) computable functions. The primitive recursive functions form a class of total computable functions which contains all (total) functions of practical interest. However this class is too large to be of real importance outside of mathematical logic and theoretical computer science.

1 DEFINITION (*primitive recursive functions*)

A primitive recursive function is a function $f : \mathbb{N}^k \longrightarrow \mathbb{N}$ for some $k \in \mathbb{N}$, which can be constructed from functions from the set

$$Gr := \{\tilde{0}, Z, S\} \cup \{pr_i^{(k)} \mid 1 \le i \le k\}$$

by finitely many applications of operators from the set

$$\{Sub_m \mid m \in \mathbb{N}\} \cup \{Prk\},$$

where $S(x) := x+1$, $\tilde{0}(\ ) := 0$, $Z(x) := 0$, $pr_i^{(k)}(x_1,\dots,x_k) = x_i$ (see Lemma 1.2.9), the Sub_m are the substitution operators, and Prk is the operator of primitive recursion (see Definition 1.2.10).

Let PRK be the set of all primitive recursive functions.

The following definition is equivalent: The set of primitive recursive functions is the smallest subset $X \subseteq \mathbb{F}^{(\infty)}$ with $Gr \subseteq X$ which is closed under substitution (by Sub_m) and primitive recursion. (We state this without proof.) Many "effectively defined" sets are defined as "closures". Later we shall derive natural numberings from such definitions.

For the proof that the register computable functions are μ-recursive we need some practice in "programming" primitive recursive definitions. First we prove that the class of primitive recursive functions is closed under any kind of substitution. For this purpose we define certain terms.

2 DEFINITION

Let $Var = \{x_o, x_1, \ldots\}$ be the set of variables. A p-expression is a word which can be generated from the set $Var \cup \mathbb{N}$ by a finite number of applications of the following rule: if $f : \mathbb{N}^k \longrightarrow \mathbb{N}$ is primitive recursive and if $t_1, \ldots, t_k$ are p-expressions then "$f(t_1, \ldots, t_k)$" is a p-expression.

For example $t = f(3, h(x_1, x_3, 2, g()), x_1)$, where f, g, and h are primitive recursive, is a p-expression. It is clear what occurrence of a variable in a p-expression means, e.g. x_1 and x_3 are the variables which occur in the above p-expression. If $y_1, \ldots y_n$ are pairwise different variables and t is a p-expression such that $x \in \{y_1, \ldots, y_n\}$ for any variable x which occurs in t, then it is intuitively clear how a function $h : \mathbb{N}^n \longrightarrow \mathbb{N}$ is defined by $h(y_1, \ldots, y_n) := t$. (Of course all of this can be expressed and defined more formally.) Then the following holds.

3 LEMMA

Let t be a p-expression, let $y_1, \ldots, y_n$ be pairwise different variables such that $x \in \{y_1, \ldots, y_n\}$ for any variable which occurs in t. Then the function h defined by $h(y_1, \ldots, y_n) := t$ is primitive recursive.

Proof

We prove the statement by induction on the construction of p-expressions.

"$t \in Var$": Then the definition is $h(y_1, \ldots, y_n) = y_i$ for some i with $1 \le i \le n$, and $h = pr_i^{(n)} \in Gr \subseteq PRK$.

"$t \in \mathbb{N}$": We prove by complete induction on k that h, defined by $h(y_1, \ldots, y_n) := k$, is primitive recursive.

"$k = 0$": Then $h(a_1, \ldots, a_n) = 0 = Zpr_1^{(n)}(a_1, \ldots, a_n)$ for all $a_1, \ldots, a_n \in \mathbb{N}$. This implies $h = Sub_1(Z, pr_1^{(n)}) \in PRK$.

"$k \Longrightarrow k+1$": Suppose h defined by $h(y_1, \ldots, y_n) := k$ is primitive recursive. Define h' by $h'(y_1, \ldots, y_n) = k+1$. Then $h'(a_1, \ldots, a_n) = Sh(a_1, \ldots, a_n)$ for all $a_1, \ldots, a_n \in \mathbb{N}$. This implies $h' = Sub_1(S, h) \in PRK$ since $h \in PRK$.

"$t = f(t_1, \ldots, t_k)$": Let $h : \mathbb{N}^n \longrightarrow \mathbb{N}$ be defined by $h(y_1, \ldots, y_n) := f(t_1, \ldots, t_k)$, and assume that $h_i : \mathbb{N}^n \longrightarrow \mathbb{N}$ defined by $h_i(y_1, \ldots, y_n) := t_i$ is primitive recursive $(i = 1, \ldots, k)$. Then $h = Sub_k(f, h_1, \ldots, h_k) \in PRK$ since $f \in PRK$.

Q.E.D.

Let t be the p-expression of the above example. Then e.g. the function $d : \mathbb{N}^3 \longrightarrow \mathbb{N}$ defined by $d(x_2, x_1, x_4, x_3) := t = f(3, h(x_1, x_3, g()), x_1)$ is primitive recursive. From now on we shall apply Lemma 3 tacitly. In the case of the functions f_+ (addition), $f_\cdot$ (multiplication), etc. we use the more customary notations $t_1 + t_2$, $t_1 \cdot t_2$, etc. Also unnecessary parentheses are omitted. The following lemma lists some primitive recursive functions.

4 LEMMA

The following functions are primitive recursive:

(1) $V : \mathbb{N} \longrightarrow \mathbb{N}$, $V(x) := x \dot{-} 1$,

(2) $f_2 : \mathbb{N}^2 \longrightarrow \mathbb{N}$, $f_2(x,y) := x \dot{-} y$,

(3) $f_3 : \mathbb{N}^2 \longrightarrow \mathbb{N}$, $f_3(x,y) := x + y$,

(4) $f_4 : \mathbb{N}^2 \longrightarrow \mathbb{N}$, $f_4(x,y) := x \cdot \mathrm{sg}(y) = (0$ if $y = 0$, x otherwise$)$,

(5) $f_5 : \mathbb{N}^2 \longrightarrow \mathbb{N}$, $f_5(x,y) := x \cdot \overline{\mathrm{sg}}(y) = (x$ if $y = 0$, 0 otherwise$)$,

(6) $f_6 : \mathbb{N}^2 \longrightarrow \mathbb{N}$, $f_6(x,y) := |x - y|$,

(7) $f_7 : \mathbb{N} \longrightarrow \mathbb{N}$, $f_7(x) = \Sigma\{i \mid i \le x\}$,

(8) $\pi^{(k)}$, $\pi_i^{(k)} := pr_i^{(k)}(\pi^{(k)})^{-1}$ for any $1 \le i \le k$.

Proof

(1) V satisfies the recursion equations $V(0) = 0$, $V(x+1) = x$. Therefore, $V = \mathrm{Prk}(\tilde{0}, pr_1^{(2)})$. Since $\tilde{0}, pr_1^{(2)} \in \mathrm{PRK}$, also $V \in \mathrm{PRK}$ by Definition 1.

(2) f_2 satisfies the following equations. $f_2(x,0) = x$, $f_2(x,y+1) = V f_2(x,y)$. Define $h : \mathbb{N}^3 \longrightarrow \mathbb{N}$ by $h(x,y,z) := V(z)$. Then $h \in \mathrm{PRK}$ by (1) and Lemma 3, $f_2 = \mathrm{PRK}(pr_1^{(1)}, h)$, and therefore $f_2 \in \mathrm{PRK}$.

(3) $x + 0 = x$, $x + (y + 1) = (x + y) + 1$, therefore $f_3 = \mathrm{Prk}(pr_1^{(1)}, h)$ where $h(x,y,z) = S(z)$.

From now we only write down appropriate recursion equations.

(4) $x \cdot \mathrm{sg}(0) = 0$, $x \cdot \mathrm{sg}(y+1) = x$.

(5) $x \cdot \overline{\mathrm{sg}}(0) = x$, $x \cdot \overline{\mathrm{sg}}(y+1) = 0$.

(6) $|x - y| = (x \dot{-} y) + (y \dot{-} x)$ (see (2), (3)).

(7) $f_7(0) = 0$, $f_7(x+1) = f_7(x) + x + 1$.

(8) First we show that π and its inverses π_1 and π_2 are primitive recursive. Since $\pi(x,y) = f_7(x+y) + y$, π is primitive recursive. Define q, π_1, and π_2 as in the proof of Lemma 1.2.15. We have to show that π_1 and π_2 are primitive recursive. We have defined $q(z) = \max\{v \mid f_7(v) \le z\}$. Hence q satisfies the recursion equations:

$$q(0) = 0$$
$$q(z+1) = q(z) + 1 \cdot \overline{sg}\,((f_7 q(z) + q(z)) \mathbin{\dot{-}} z).$$

Since h where $h(z,y) = y + 1 \cdot \overline{sg}(z \mathbin{\dot{-}} (f_7(y) + y))$ is primitive recursive, q is also primitive recursive. Since $\pi_2(z) = z \mathbin{\dot{-}} f_7 q(z)$ and $\pi_1(z) = q(z) \mathbin{\dot{-}} \pi_2(z)$, also π_1 and π_2 are primitive recursive.

Now, we prove by induction on k that $\pi^{(k)}$ and $\pi_i^{(k)}$ $(1 \le i \le k)$ are primitive recursive (for $k \ge 1$).

"k = 1": $\pi^{(1)} = pr_1^{(1)}$, $\pi_1^{(1)} = pr_1^{(1)}$.

"k ⟹ k+1": $\pi^{(k+1)}(x_1,\ldots,x_{k+1}) = \pi(\pi^{(k)}(x_1,\ldots,x_k),x_{k+1})$. It follows from the induction assumption that $\pi^{(k+1)}$ is primitive recursive. By the definition $\pi_{k+1}^{(k+1)}(z) = \pi_2(z)$, $\pi_i^{(k+1)}(z) = \pi_i^{(k)}\pi_1(z)$ for $1 \le i \le k$. By induction assumption, $\pi_i^{(k)}$ is primitive recursive for all i with $1 \le i \le k$. Therefore $\pi_i^{(k+1)}$ is primitive recursive for all i with $1 \le i \le k$.

Q.E.D.

Lemma 4 already indicates that many interesting functions are primitive recursive. Some more examples are given in the exercises. Later we shall obtain a characterization of PRK as a register machine complexity class which provides a very good understanding of the richness of PRK. Every primitive recursive function is intuitively computable. In the past there has been the question of whether the primitive recursive functions are already the class of all the intuitively computable (total) functions. In 1928 Ackermann defined a total function which is not primitive recursive but intuitively computable. We shall define a similar but simpler function B which also has this property. Define a sequence $A_o, A_1, \ldots$ of functions from $\mathbb{N}$ to $\mathbb{N}$ inductively as follows.

$$A_o(x) := \begin{cases} 1 & \text{if } x = 0 \\ 2 & \text{if } x = 1 \\ x+2 & \text{otherwise} \end{cases}$$

$$A_{n+1}(x) := A_n^x(1)$$

i.e. A_{n+1} is defined by primitive recursion from A_n via the recursion equations $A_{n+1}(0) = 1$, $A_{n+1}(x+1) = A_n A_{n+1}(x)$. Define $B : \mathbb{N} \longrightarrow \mathbb{N}$ by $B(x) := A_x(x)$. The function B is register computable (see Chapter 1.2, Exercise 12). But B is not primitive recursive. In the proof, it is shown by several inductions that for any primitive recursive function $f : \mathbb{N} \longrightarrow \mathbb{N}$ there is some n such that A_n is more increasing than f, and that B is more increasing than any A_n. Therefore, B is more increasing than any (unary) primitive recursive function and cannot itself be primitive recursive.

There is another interesting way to construct an intuitively computable function which is not primitive recursive. By Definition 1, any primitive recursive function can be constructed from (finitely many) initial functions ($\in$ Gr) by applying substitution and primitive recursion finitely often. The construction can be finitely described. The strings (see the proof of Lemma 3) $\mathrm{Prk}(\tilde{0},\mathrm{pr}_1^{(2)})$ or $\mathrm{Sub}_1(S,\mathrm{Prk}(\mathrm{pr}_1^{(1)},\mathrm{Sub}_1(S,\mathrm{pr}_3^{(3)})))$ are examples of such descriptions. Given a description of some function f, for any input x the value f(x) can be determined. The descriptions of the unary functions can be ordered (first by length, then lexicographically) into a sequence. Let $f_i : \mathbb{N} \longrightarrow \mathbb{N}$ be the primitive recursive function determined by the i-th item of this sequence. Then there is an intuitively effective procedure, by which for any $i \in \mathbb{N}$ and $n \in \mathbb{N}$ the value $f_i(n)$ can be determined. The argument can be formulated precisely: A numbering $\nu : \mathbb{N} \longrightarrow \mathrm{PRK}^{(1)}$ of all the unary primitive recursive functions can be defined such that the universal function u of ν, defined by $u(i,n) := \nu(i)(n)$, is register computable. It is now easy to define a function which is computable but not primitive recursive. For this purpose we define a function $d : \mathbb{N} \longrightarrow \mathbb{N}$ which differs from any $\nu(i)$ $(i \in \mathbb{N})$. This is obtained by defining d such that $d(0) \neq \nu(0)(0)$, $d(1) \neq \nu(1)(1)$, ... The values $\nu(i)(i)$ are the values on the diagonal of the function table for the universal function u of ν.

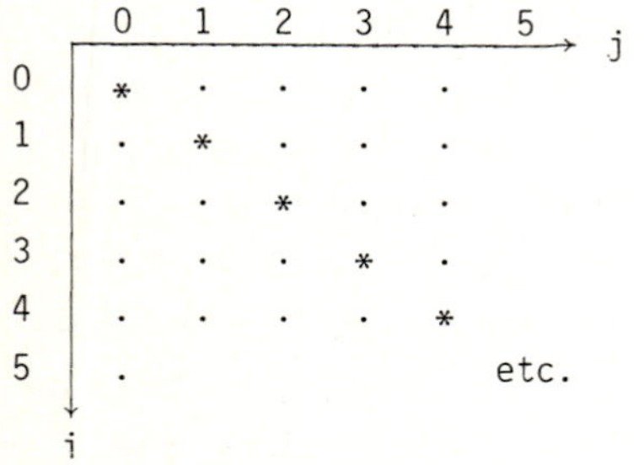

An appropriate definition of d is $(\forall i)\ d(i) := 1 + \nu(i)(i)$. Obviously, $d \neq \nu(k)$ for any k, since $d(k) \neq \nu(k)(k)$. Because $\nu(\mathbb{N}) = \mathrm{PRK}$, d cannot be primitive recursive. Since $d(i) = u(i,i) + 1$, d is computable and (u primitive recursive $\Longrightarrow$ d primitive recursive). Therefore, u also is not primitive recursive.

Above the existence of a computable not primitive recursive function is proved by *diagonalization*. Many important theorems in recursion theory are proved by diagonalization. A famous diagonal proof from set theory is given as an exercise.

Our arguments show that the primitive recursive functions are a proper subset of the total computable functions. We already know that the computable functions are closed under μ-recursion. We now define a class of functions by admitting μ-recursion also for generating new functions.

5 DEFINITION (*μ-recursive functions*)

A *μ-recursive function* is a function $f : \mathbb{N}^k \dashrightarrow \mathbb{N}$ for some $k \in \mathbb{N}$, which can be constructed from functions from the set Gr by finitely many applications of operators from the set

$$\{\mathrm{Sub}_m \mid m \in \mathbb{N}\} \cup \{\mathrm{Prk}, \tilde{\mu}\}$$

(see Definition 1).

Obviously, every primitive recursive function is also μ-recursive. Example 1.2.11(3) shows that μ-recursion applied to a primitive recursive function may lead to a partial (not total) function. Without further preparation we can now prove our main result, namely that the μ-recursive functions are exactly the register computable functions.

6 THEOREM (*register computable = μ-recursive*)

A function $f : \mathbb{N}^k \dashrightarrow \mathbb{N}$ is register computable, iff it is μ-recursive.

Proof

"⟹": By Lemma 1.2.4 and Lemma 1.2.9 any function from Gr is computable. By Theorem 1.2.12 the operators of substitution, primitive recursion, and μ-recursion transform computable functions into computable functions. Therefore, any μ-recursive function is computable.

"⟸": Let $M = (F, \mathbb{N}^k, \mathbb{N}, IC^{(k)}, OC)$ be a register machine with flowchart $F = (Q, D, \sigma, q_o, s, (q_1, \ldots, q_s))$. It is easy to show that for any flowchart G there is a flowchart G' with exactly one final state such that $f_G = f_{G'}$. Since we do not consider the test t_M, we may assume $s = 1$. By Lemma 1.1.8 we may assume $Q = \{0, 1, .., N\}$ for some $N \in \mathbb{N}$, $q_o = 0$, $q_1 = N \geq 1$. The flowchart F uses only finitely many registers. Let n be a number such that $n \geq k$ and $n \geq j$ for any register R_j which appears in the flowchart F.

Our next aim is to encode configurations of F by numbers such that a primitive recursive function on the code numbers describes the single step function SF of F. Define an injective function $\iota : \mathbb{N} \longrightarrow CON \subseteq \mathbb{N} \times \mathbb{N}^{\mathbb{N}}$ by

$$\iota\langle a_o, a_1, \ldots, a_n, q\rangle := (q, (a_o, a_1, \ldots, a_n, 0, \ldots))$$

for all $a_o, a_1, \ldots a_n, q \in \mathbb{N}$. We shall define a primitive recursive function sf such that

$$(*) \begin{cases} z \xrightarrow{\iota} \kappa \implies sf(z) \xrightarrow{\iota} SF(\kappa), & \text{if } \iota(z) = \kappa \in \mathrm{dom}(SF), \\ sf(z) = z & \text{if } \iota(z) \notin \mathrm{dom}(SF). \end{cases}$$

For any $p \in Q \setminus \{N\}$ define a function f_p as follows (see Definition 1.2.2).
If $\sigma(p) = (\text{"}R_i := R_i + 1\text{"}, t, j)$, then

$$f_p\langle a_o, a_1, \ldots, a_n, q\rangle := \langle a_o, a_1, \ldots, a_{i-1}, a_i + 1, a_{i+1}, \ldots, a_n, j\rangle \,;$$

if $\sigma(p) = (\text{"}R_i := R_i - 1\text{"}, t, j)$, then

$$f_p\langle a_o, a_1, \ldots, a_n, q\rangle := \langle a_o, a_1, \ldots, a_{i-1}, a_i \dot{-} 1, a_{i+1}, \ldots, a_n, j\rangle \,;$$

if $\sigma(p) = (h, \text{"}R_i = 0\text{"}, j, k)$, then

$$f_p\langle a_o, a_1, \ldots, a_n, q\rangle := \langle a_o, \ldots, a_n, j\rangle \cdot \overline{sg}(a_i) + \langle a_o, \ldots, a_n, k\rangle \cdot sg(a_i) \,.$$

Define $sf : \mathbb{N} \longrightarrow \mathbb{N}$ as follows. If $z = \langle a_o, a_1, \ldots, a_n, p\rangle$ then

$$\begin{aligned} sf(z) := {} & f_o(z) \cdot \overline{sg}(|p-0|) + f_1(z) \cdot \overline{sg}(|p-1|) + \ldots \\ & + f_{N-1}(z) \cdot \overline{sg}(|p-(N-1)|) + z \cdot \overline{sg}(N \dot{-} p) \,. \end{aligned}$$

Therefore $sf(z) = f_o(z)$ if $p = 0$, $sf(z) = f_1(z)$ if $p = 1$, ..., $sf(z) = f_{N-1}(z)$ if $p = N-1$, and $sf(z) = z$ if $p \geq N$.
By Definition 1.2.2 and Definition 1.1.6, the function sf satisfies Property (*).
By Lemma 1.3.4 and a lemma corresponding to Lemma 1.2.16 where "computable" is substituted by "primitive recursive", sf is primitive recursive. By complete induction on $t \in \mathbb{N}$, from (*) the following property can be derived easily:

$$\iota sf^t(z) = \begin{cases} SF^t(\iota(z)) & \text{if } \iota(z) \in \mathrm{dom}(SF^t) \\ TF(\iota(z)) & \text{otherwise}. \end{cases}$$

Define $g : \mathbb{N}^2 \longrightarrow \mathbb{N}$ by the recursion equations: $g(z,0) = z$, $g(z,t+1) = sf(g(z,t))$.
Then g is primitive recursive and $g(z,t) = sf^t(z)$. Define $h : \mathbb{N}^2 \longrightarrow \mathbb{N}$ by $h(z,t) := |\pi_{n+2}^{(n+2)} g(z,t) - N|$. Therefore, $h(z,t) = 0$, iff the "state component" of $sf^t(z)$ is the final state N, i.e. $\tilde{\mu}(h)(z) = CT(\iota(z))$ (if $\iota(z) \in CON$).
If $\iota(z) \in CON$ and $CT(\iota(z))$ exists then $TF(\iota(z)) = SF^{CT(\iota(z))}(\iota(z)) = \iota sf^{\tilde{\mu}(h)(z)}(z) = \iota g(z, \tilde{\mu}(h)(z))$. If $\iota(z) \in CON$ and $CT(\iota(z))$ does not exist, then neither $TF(\iota(z))$ nor $\iota g(z, \tilde{\mu}(h)(z))$ exist. Therefore $TF(\iota(z)) = \iota g(z, \tilde{\mu}(h)(z))$ whenever $\iota(z) \in CON$.
Define $ic : \mathbb{N}^k \longrightarrow \mathbb{N}$ by

$$ic(x_1, \ldots, x_k) = \langle 0, x_1, \ldots, x_k, 0, \ldots, 0, \underset{\substack{\uparrow \\ \text{place } (n+2)}}{0}\rangle \,.$$

Then $\iota(ic(\overline{x})) = (q_o, IC^{(k)}(\overline{x}))$ for any $\overline{x} \in \mathbb{N}^k$.
Define $oc : \mathbb{N} \longrightarrow \mathbb{N}$ by

$$oc(z) := \pi_1^{(n+2)}(z) \,.$$

Then $oc(z) = OC \circ pr_2 \circ \iota(z)$ (where $pr_2(p,d) := d$).
The functions ic and oc are primitive recursive. Combining our results we obtain:

$$\begin{aligned} f_M(\overline{x}) &= OC \circ f_F \circ IC^{(k)}(\overline{x}) = OC \circ pr_2 \circ TF(q_o, IC^{(k)}(\overline{x})) = OC \circ pr_2 \circ TF \circ \iota \circ ic(\overline{x}) = \\ &= OC \circ pr_2 \circ \iota \circ g(ic(\overline{x}), \tilde{\mu}(h) \circ ic(\overline{x})) = oc \circ g(ic(\overline{x}), \tilde{\mu}(h) \circ ic(\overline{x})) \,. \end{aligned}$$

Since the functions oc, ic, g, and h are primitive recursive, $\tilde{\mu}(h)$ is μ-recursive and f_M is μ-recursive.
Q.E.D.

The proof shows that in generating the function f_M the operator $\tilde{\mu}$ is only used once, namely in determining the computation time. It is also remarkable that $\tilde{\mu}$ has only to be applied to a primitive recursive function (h in the above proof). In this case the definition of $\tilde{\mu}$ is simpler (cf. Definition 1.2.10):

$$\tilde{\mu}(f)(\overline{x}) := \begin{cases} \min(M) & \text{if } M := \{n \mid f(\overline{x},n) = 0\} \neq \emptyset \\ \text{div} & \text{otherwise}. \end{cases}$$

Since the function sf leaves (codenumbers of) final configurations unchanged, any upper bound of the computation time would serve the same purpose. If an upper bound is primitive recursive, then also f_M is primitive recursive.

In Definition 1.1.6 we have defined the computation time function $CT_F : CON \dashrightarrow \mathbb{N}$ for a flowchart F. For a machine M we define the computation time function as follows (see Definition 1.1.16).

7 DEFINITION

Let $M = (F,X,Y,IC,OC)$ be a machine with flowchart $F = (Q,D,\sigma,q_o,s,(q_1,\ldots,q_s))$. Then define $Time_M : X \dashrightarrow \mathbb{N}$ by $Time_M(x) := CT_F(q_o,IC(x))$.

This means $Time_M(x)$ is the number of steps machine M needs for computing $f_M(x)$. We can now formulate the computation time characterization of the primitive recursive functions.

8 THEOREM

A function $f : \mathbb{N}^k \longrightarrow \mathbb{N}$ is primitive recursive, iff $f_M = f$ and $(\forall \overline{x} \in \mathbb{N}^k)$ $Time_M(\overline{x}) \le b(\overline{x})$ for some register machine M and some primitive recursive function $b : \mathbb{N}^k \longrightarrow \mathbb{N}$.

We only prove the "if"-part of the theorem. The only if direction is a lengthy estimation of upper bounds of computation times along the lines of the proofs of Lemma 1.2.8, Theorem 1.2.7, and Theorem 1.2.12, which we shall omit here.

Proof ("if")

Suppose $f_M = f$ for some register machine M and $(\forall \bar{x})$ $\text{Time}_M(\bar{x}) \leq b(\bar{x})$ for some primitive recursive function b. Consider the proof of Theorem 6. Then $\tilde{\mu}(h) \circ ic(\bar{x}) = CT(\iota \circ ic(\bar{x})) = CT(q_o, IC^{(k)}(\bar{x})) = \text{Time}_M(\bar{x}) \leq b(\bar{x})$. Since sf is defined such that $sf^t(z) = sf^{t_o}(z)$ if $t \geq t_o := CT(\iota(z))$, we obtain $g(ic(\bar{x}), \tilde{\mu}(h) \circ ic(\bar{x})) = g(ic(\bar{x}), b(\bar{x}))$ and $f_M(\bar{x}) = oc \circ g(ic(\bar{x}), b(\bar{x}))$. Therefore, f_M is primitive recursive.

Q.E.D.

The theorem is important since usually it is rather simple to bound the computation time of a register machine from above by a primitive recursive function. Appropriate bounds are the Ackermann functions A_n defined in the discussion after Lemma 4. Any function A_n is primitive recursive, and for any primitive recursive function $f : \mathbb{N}^k \longrightarrow \mathbb{N}$ there is some n such that $f(x_1,\dots,x_k) \leq A_n \circ \max_k(x_1,\dots,x_k) + n$ for all $x_1,\dots,x_k \in \mathbb{N}$ (without proof). Notice that $\max_k : \mathbb{N}^k \longrightarrow \mathbb{N}$ is primitive recursive. The first three functions of the sequence can hardly give any idea of how fast primitive recursive functions may grow:

$$A_o(x) = x+2 \ \text{ for } \ x \geq 2\,, \quad A_1(x) = 2x\,, \quad A_2(x) = 2^x\,, \quad A_3(x) = \left.2^{2^{\cdot^{\cdot^{\cdot^{2^1}}}}}\right\}\text{x-times} .$$

It is very unlikely that a register machine, the computation time of which is not bounded already by a function $A_3\max(x_1,\dots,x_k) + m$ has any practical interest. Since computation times for real world computers do not differ too much from computation times of register machines, any (total) function on $\mathbb{N}$ which can be computed in a reasonable time on a computer is a (very simple) primitive recursive function. Therefore the class of primitive recursive functions is too large to be of practical interest. The so called complexity classes of functions which can be computed on register machines e.g. in quadratic, cubic, polynomial, or exponential time are much more important.

Theorem 6 confirms that the computable functions defined by register machines are a natural class of functions. In the next chapter a further characterization is given.

EXERCISES

1. Prove that the following functions on $\mathbb{N}$ are primitive recursive.

   (a) $(x,y) \longmapsto x \cdot y$,

   (b) $(x,y) \longmapsto x^y$,

   (c) $x \longmapsto x! = 1 \cdot 2 \cdot 3 \cdot \ldots \cdot x$,

   (d) $(x,y) \longmapsto \mathrm{rest}(x,y) :=$ (0 if $y = 0$, the unique r with $(\exists m)(x = my + r \wedge r < y)$ otherwise),

   (e) $(x,y) \longmapsto \lfloor \frac{x}{y} \rfloor :=$ (0 if $y = 0$, the unique m with $(\exists r)(x = my + r \wedge r < y)$ otherwise),

   (f) $(x_1,\ldots,x_k) \longmapsto \max\{x_1,\ldots,x_k\}$ for any $k \geq 1$.

2. The Fibonacci function $F : \mathbb{N} \longrightarrow \mathbb{N}$ is defined by the following recursion equations:

   $F(0) = F(1) = 1$, $F(n+1) = F(n-1) + F(n)$ for all $n \geq 1$.

   Prove that F is primitive recursive.

3. Let $f : \mathbb{N}^k \longrightarrow \mathbb{N}$ be a function such that $f(\overline{x}) \neq 0$ for only finitely many $\overline{x} \in \mathbb{N}^k$. Prove that f is primitive recursive.

4. Let $g_i : \mathbb{N}^k \longrightarrow \mathbb{N}$ and $h_i : \mathbb{N}^{n+k+1} \longrightarrow \mathbb{N}$ where $k \in \mathbb{N}$, $n \geq 1$, $i = 1,\ldots,n$ be functions. Then there are functions $f_i : \mathbb{N}^{k+1} \longrightarrow \mathbb{N}$ $(1 \leq i \leq n)$ such that

   $$f_i(x_1,\ldots,x_k,0) = g_i(x_1,\ldots,x_k)$$

   $$f_i(x_1,\ldots,x_k, m+1) = h_i(x_1,\ldots,x_k,m,f_1(x_1,\ldots,x_k,m),\ldots,f_n(x_1,\ldots,x_k,m)).$$

   Prove that the functions f_i are primitive recursive, if the functions g_i and h_i are primitive recursive. (The class of primitive recursive functions is closed under *simultaneous recursion* or *vector recursion*.)

5. Let $f : \mathbb{N}^{k+1} \longrightarrow \mathbb{N}$ $(k \in \mathbb{N})$. Define $h : \mathbb{N}^{k+1} \longrightarrow \mathbb{N}$ by

   $$h(x_1,\ldots,x_k,n) := \mu(i \leq n)(f(x_1,\ldots,x_k,i) = 0)$$
   $$:= \min(\{i \leq y \mid f(x_1,\ldots,x_k,i) = 0\} \cup \{n+1\}).$$

   Prove that h is primitive recursive, if f is primitive recursive. (The class of primitive recursive functions is closed under *bounded minimization*.)

6. Assume that there is a numbering $\nu : \mathbb{N} \longrightarrow PRK^{(1)}$ of the unary primitive recursive functions such that the universal function of ν is computable.

   (a) Deduce that there is a 0-1 valued computable function which is not primitive recursive.

(b) Deduce that there is a computable non-primitive recursive function which increases faster than any $f \in PRK^{(1)}$.

7. Let $R^{(1)}$ be the set of all total computable unary functions, let $P^{(1)}$ be the set of all computable unary functions. Prove: There is no surjective function $\nu : \mathbb{N} \to R^{(1)}$, the universal function u of which is computable. The proof becomes incorrect if $R^{(1)}$ is replaced by $P^{(1)}$. Why? (In fact the corresponding statement for $P^{(1)}$ is false.)

8. Let M be any set, let 2^M be the set of subsets of M. Prove that there is no surjective (= onto) function $f : M \to 2^M$. (Hint: diagonalization).

9. Prove that for any computable function $f : \mathbb{N}^k \dashrightarrow \mathbb{N}$ there are primitive recursive functions $f_1 : \mathbb{N} \longrightarrow \mathbb{N}$ and $f_2 : \mathbb{N}^{k+1} \longrightarrow \mathbb{N}$ such that $f = f_1 \circ \tilde{\mu}(f_2)$. (Hint: Instead of h in the proof of Theorem 1.3.6 consider $f_2 : \mathbb{N}^{k+1} \longrightarrow \mathbb{N}$ defined by $f_2(x_1,\ldots,x_k,\langle y,t\rangle) :=$

$$|\pi^{(k+2)}_{k+2}\, g(ec(x_1,\ldots x_k),t) - N| + |\,\pi^{(k+2)}_{1}\, g(ec(x_1,\ldots,x_k),t) - y|.$$

BIBLIOGRAPHICAL NOTES

In earlier papers, e.g. in Hermes (1978), minimalization is only applied to total functions. Our proof shows that this suffices to generate all partial recursive functions. If some basis functions are added primitive recursion can be simulated by means of substitution and minimalization. Even minimalization may be substituted by other operations (see e.g. Machtey and Young (1978), Malcev (1974), Robinson (1950)). An extensive discussion of primitive recursive functions is in Peter (1951). The original Ackermann function can be found in Ackermann (1928). The functions A_n used in this chapter are from Brainerd and Landweber (1974).

1.4 WHILE-Programs and WHILE-Computability

The computable functions on numbers can also be defined by WHILE-programs. Here the idea of computing on registers is combined with the idea of inductive definition. While-programs allow constructing very transparent algorithms and support correctness proofs.

First we introduce the WHILE-programs syntactically, then for any WHILE-program P a function $\tau(P) : D \dashrightarrow D$, where $D = \mathbb{N}^{\mathbb{N}}$, is defined. Finally the k-ary function computed by P is defined by $\tau_k(P) := OC \circ f_P \circ IC^{(k)}$, where $IC^{(k)}$ and OC are the input and output encodings for register machines.

1 <u>DEFINITION</u> (*WHILE-programs*)

Let $\Sigma_o := \{+,-,(,),;,:,|\}$ be a set with 7 elements such that $\mathbb{N} \cap \Sigma_o = \emptyset$, let $\Sigma := \mathbb{N} \cup \Sigma_o$. Define $WHP \subseteq W(\Sigma)$, the set of WHILE-programs, as follows. A word $x \in W(\Sigma)$ is a WHILE-program, iff it can be generated from the set

$$\{"i+" \mid i \in \mathbb{N}\} \cup \{"i-" \mid i \in \mathbb{N}\} \subseteq W(\Sigma)$$

by finitely many applications of the following operations:

(1) $(P,Q) \longrightarrow$ "(P;Q)" ,

(2) $(P,Q) \longrightarrow$ "(i|P|Q)" for any $i \in \mathbb{N}$,

(3) $P \longrightarrow$ "(i:P)" for any $i \in \mathbb{N}$.

By Definition 1, WHILE-programs are words over the infinite set $\Sigma = \mathbb{N} \cup \Sigma_o$. If we specify a WHILE-program in our mathematical language, we usually use decimal notation for natural numbers. For example, by

w := "(13:54-)"

a WHILE-program $w \in W(\Sigma)$ is specified, where $(\in \Sigma_o$ is the first symbol, $13 \in \mathbb{N}$ is the second symbol,...,and $) \in \Sigma_o$ is the 6th symbol of w. One could also directly define WHILE-programs as words over the (finite) alphabet $\{0,1,\ldots,9\} \cup \Sigma_o$. The difference between the two ways is not essential, but the first one is slightly more suitable for our purpose.

The following strings over Σ are WHILE-programs: "3+" , "0-" , "(5+;(2-;4-))" , "(3|2-|(3+;3+))" , "(21:21-)" . A customary notation is "IF R_i=0 THEN P ELSE Q" instead of "(i|P|Q)", "WHILE $R_i \neq 0$ DO P" instead of "(i:P)".

Any WHILE-program can be uniquely decomposed into its constituents. We shall use this almost obvious fact without further proof in the next definition.

2 DEFINITION

For any WHILE-program P define a function $\tau(P) : D \dashrightarrow D$, where $D = \mathbb{N}^{\mathbb{N}}$, inductively as follows:

$$\tau(i+)(a_o,a_1,\ldots) := (a_o,a_1,\ldots,a_{i-1},a_i+1,a_{i+1},\ldots)$$

$$\tau(i-)(a_o,a_1,\ldots) := (a_o,a_1,\ldots,a_{i-1},a_i \dot{-} 1,a_{i+1},\ldots)$$

for any $i \in \mathbb{N}$,

$$\tau(\text{"(P;Q)"}) := \tau(Q) \circ \tau(P),$$

$$\tau(\text{"(i|P|Q)"})(d) := \begin{cases} \tau(P)(d) & \text{if } d(i) = 0 \\ \tau(Q)(d) & \text{if } d(i) \neq 0, \end{cases}$$

$$\tau(\text{"(i:P)"})(d) := \begin{cases} (\tau(P))^t(d) & \text{if } t := \min\{s \mid (\tau(P))^s(d)(i) = 0\} \text{ exists} \\ \text{div} & \text{otherwise}. \end{cases}$$

The following examples explain the definition of τ.

3 EXAMPLES

(1) Let $P_1 :=$ "(1-;0+)". Then $\tau(P_1)(a_o,a_1,\ldots) = (a_o+1,a_1 \dot{-} 1,\ldots)$.

(2) Let $P_2 :=$ "(1:P_1)". Since $(\tau(P_1))^i(a_o,a_1,\ldots) = (a_o+i,a_1 \dot{-} i,\ldots)$, $\tau(P_2)(a_o,a_1,\ldots) = ((P_1))^{a_1}(a_o,a_1,\ldots) = (a_o+a_1,0,a_2,\ldots)$.

(3) Similarly, if $P_3 =$ "(2 : (2-;0+))" then $\tau(P_2)(a_o,a_1,a_2,\ldots) = (a_o+a_2,a_1,0,a_3,\ldots)$.

(4) Let $P_4 =$ "(P_2;P_3)". Then $\tau(P_4)(0,a,b,0,\ldots) = (a+b,0,0,0,\ldots)$ (c f. Example 1.2.1).

(5) Let $P_5 =$ "(3|P_2|P_3)". Then $\tau(P_5)(0,a,b,0,0,\ldots) = (a,0,b,0,0,\ldots)$ and $\tau(P_5)(0,a,b,1,0,\ldots) = (b,a,0,1,0,\ldots)$.

For any $k \in \mathbb{N}$ and any WHILE-program P a function $\tau_k(P) : \mathbb{N}^k \dashrightarrow \mathbb{N}$ will now be defined.

4 DEFINITION

For any $k \in \mathbb{N}$ define $IC^{(k)} : \mathbb{N}^k \longrightarrow D$ and $OC : D \longrightarrow \mathbb{N}$ by

$$IC^{(k)}(a_1,\dots,a_k) := (0,a_1,\dots,a_k,0,0,\dots)\ ,$$
$$OC(a_o,a_1,\dots) := a_o\ .$$

Then for any $k \in \mathbb{N}$ and $P \in WHP$ define

$$\tau_k(P) := OC \circ \tau(P) \circ IC^{(k)}\ .$$

A function $f : \mathbb{N}^k \dashrightarrow \mathbb{N}$ is WHILE-computable, iff $f = \tau_k(P)$ for some WHILE-program P.

Let P_4 be the WHILE-program from Example 3. Then obviously, $\tau_2(P_4)(a,b) = a+b$ for all $a,b \in \mathbb{N}$.

We shall now prove that the WHILE-computable functions are exactly the register computable functions. The proof will show that WHILE-programs can be considered as very special register machine flowcharts.

5 THEOREM

A function $f : \mathbb{N}^k \dashrightarrow \mathbb{N}$ is WHILE-computable iff it is register computable.

Proof

"only if":

Since the input and the output encodings are the same for register machines and WHILE-computability, it is sufficient to prove that for any WHILE-program P there is some register machine flowchart F such that $f_F = \tau(P)$.

We prove by induction on the definition of WHILE-programs that for any WHILE-program P there is a register machine F with $\tau(P) = f_F$.

Suppose $P = $ "i+" for some $i \in \mathbb{N}$. Define a flowchart F by

0: $R_i := R_{i+1}, 1$;

1: HALT .

$P = $ "i-" for some i (correspondingly).

Let Q_1, Q_2 be WHILE-programs and let F_1, F_2 be register machine flowcharts with $\tau(Q_1) = f_{F_1}$, $\tau(Q_2) = f_{F_2}$ which can be presented graphically as follows.

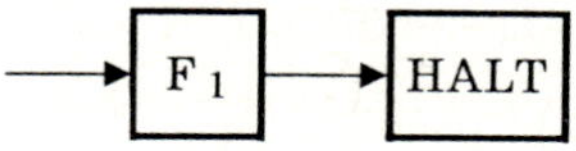

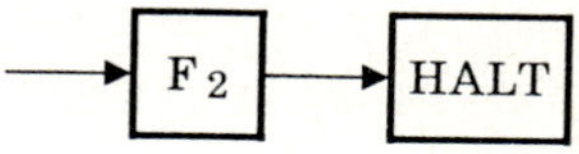

Suppose, $P = $ "$(Q_1;Q_2)$". Define a flowchart F by the following diagram

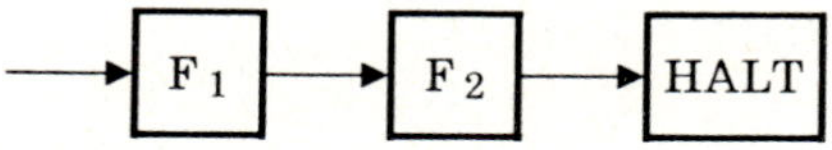

Then obviously $\tau(P)=f_F$.

Suppose $P=$"$(i|Q_1|Q_2)$". Define a flowchart F by the following diagram.

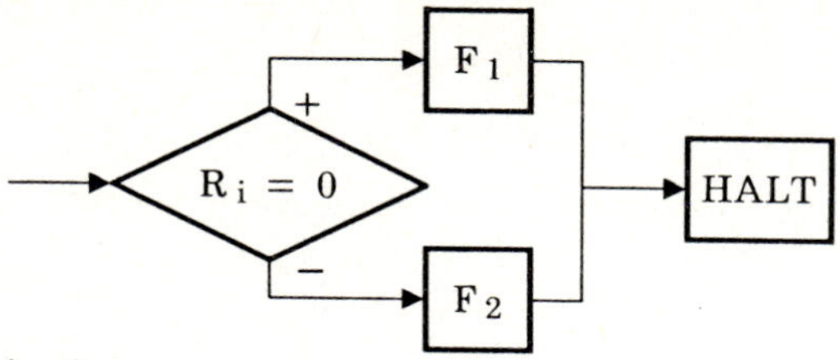

Then obviously $\tau(P)=f_F$.

Suppose $P=$"$(i:Q_1)$". Define a flowchart F by the following diagram.

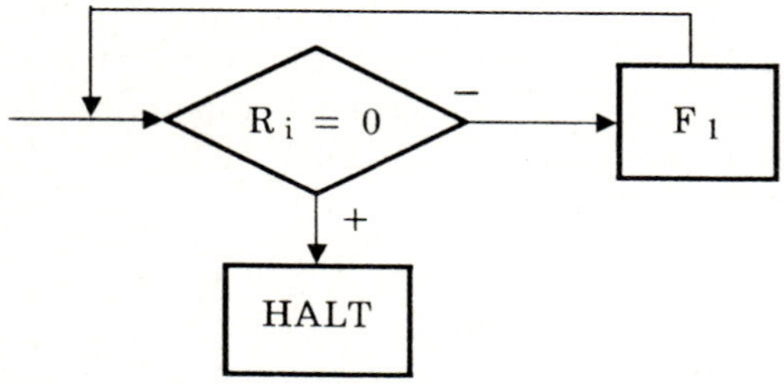

Then, by Definition 2, $\tau(P)=f_F$.

Therefore, for any WHILE-program P there is a register machine flowchart F with $\tau(P)=f_F$.

"if":

Let M be a k-ary register machine with flowchart $F=(Q,D,\sigma,q_o,s,(q_1,\ldots,q_s))$. As in the proof of Theorem 1.3.6 we may assume $Q=\{0,1,\ldots,N\}$; let $s=1$, $q_o=1$, $q_1=0$. In order to simulate the operations of a register machine, the configurations $(q,d)\in Q\times\mathbb{N}^{\mathbb{N}}$ of flowchart computations are encoded by data $d'\in\mathbb{N}^{\mathbb{N}}=D$ of WHILE-programs. Let $L>k$ be a number such that no register R_i with $i\geq L$ appears in F. Then define $\iota: Q\times D\longrightarrow D$ by

$$\iota(q,(a_o,a_1,\ldots)) := (a_o,a_1,\ldots,a_{L-1},q,0,\ldots)$$

for all $q\in Q$, $a_o,a_1,\ldots\in\mathbb{N}$. At first we define a WHILE-program P such that $\tau(P)\circ\iota(\kappa)=\iota\circ SF(\kappa)$ for any $\kappa\in\mathrm{dom}(SF)=\{1,\ldots,N\}\times D$. For $k\in\mathbb{N}$ define WHILE-programs $(L+)^k$ inductively by $(L+)^o :=$ "(L+;L-)", $(L+)^{k+1} :=$ "$((L+)^k;L+)$". Then

$$\tau((L+)^k)(a_o,\ldots,a_{L-1},0,\ldots) = (a_o,\ldots,a_{L-1},k,\ldots) .$$

For any state $m\in\{1,\ldots,N\}$ we define a WHILE-program P_m which performs the operation of this state on the configurations, where we assume that the state register R_L initially is 0.

If $\sigma(m) = (R_i := R_i+1 , k)$ then $P_m :=$ "$(i+;(L+)^k)$",

if $\sigma(m) = (R_i := R_i-1 , k)$ then $P_m :=$ "$(i-;(L+)^k)$",

if $\sigma(m) = (R_i = 0 , k , n)$ then $P_m :=$ "$(i|(L+)^k|(L+)^n)$".

We define WHILE-programs $S_1,\dots,S_N$ inductively by

$$S_N = P_N$$

$$S_m = \text{"}(L|P_m|(L-;S_{m+1}))\text{"} \quad \text{for} \quad 1 \le m < N .$$

An easy induction on i shows $(\forall i)\ (\forall n \ge 1,\ n+i \le N)$

$$\tau(S_n)(a_o,a_1,\dots,a_{L-1},i,\dots) = \tau(S_{n+i})(a_o,\dots,a_{L-1},0,\dots) .$$

This implies

$$\tau(S_1)(a_o,\dots,a_{L-1},i,\dots) = \tau(P_{1+i})(a_o,\dots,a_{L-1},0,\dots)$$

for all $i < N$.

As an immediate consequence we obtain:

$$\tau(\text{"}(L-;S_1)\text{"}) \circ \imath(q,d) = \imath \circ SF(q,d)$$

for all $d \in D$ and $q \in \{1,\dots,N\}$. Define $P_t := \text{"}(L:\ (L-;S_1))\text{"}$.

Then by Definition 2 and Definition 1.1.6,

$$\tau(P_t) \circ \imath(\kappa) = \imath \circ TF(\kappa)$$

for any configuration κ of F.

Now, $\imath \circ IC^{(k)}(\overline{x}) = \tau(\text{"}L+\text{"}) \circ IC^{(k)}(\overline{x})$, and $OC \circ \imath(d) = OC(d)$ for any $\overline{x} \in \mathbb{N}^k$ and $d \in D$. Define $P := \text{"}(L+;P_t)\text{"}$. Then

$$\begin{aligned} \tau_k(P)(\overline{x}) &= OC \circ \tau(P) \circ IC^{(k)}(\overline{x}) \\ &= OC \circ \tau(P_t) \circ \tau(\text{"}L+\text{"}) \circ IC^{(k)}(\overline{x}) \\ &= OC \circ \tau(P_t) \circ \imath \circ IC^{(k)}(\overline{x}) \\ &= OC \circ \imath \circ TF \circ IC^{(k)}(\overline{x}) \\ &= OC \circ TF \circ IC^{(k)}(\overline{x}) \\ &= f_M(\overline{x}) \end{aligned}$$

for all $\overline{x} \in \mathbb{N}^k$. Therefore the WHILE-program P computes f_M.

Q.E.D.

The proof that any register computable function is WHILE-computable resembles our previous proof that any register computable function is μ-recursive. In both cases the single step function is simulated and then iterated. In the case of WHILE-programs this iteration is obtained by a WHILE-statement, in the case of μ-recursive function, by using the operator $\tilde{\mu}$. As we shall prove later, generally there is no way to compute in advance whether a computation on a register machine will halt and yield a result or will diverge. Equivalently, in general there is no computable method to predict whether the loop of a WHILE-statement will ever be finished or not, or whether $\tilde{\mu}(f)$, f primitive recursive, exists or not for a given argument $\overline{x}$.

Every mechanism for defining the set of computable functions admits infinite non halting computations, which are essential for the theory of computability. We shall discuss this later in connection with the *halting problem*.

EXERCISES

1) Prove explicitly that the functions defined in Lemma 1.2.9 (1) to (7) are WHILE-computable.

2) Prove explicitly (without applying Theorem 1.3.6 or Theorem 1.4.5) that any WHILE-computable function is μ-recursive.

1.5 Tape Machines

In 1937, A.M. Turing proposed a machine model for defining computability. We shall use Turing's model for defining the computable word functions $f : (W(\Sigma))^k \dashrightarrow W(\Sigma)$, where Σ is an alphabet. The physical model of a Turing machine is a tape on which a read/write head operates controlled by a finite device (or a flowchart) like a computer operates on a potentially infinite magnetic tape.

The usual definition of a Turing machine does not immediately fit into our framework of flowcharts and machines. Therefore we introduce a machine model which is adapted to our previous definitions and which is essentially equivalent to Turing machines: the tape machines.

The physical mode we shall consider is a two way infinite tape which is divided into cells. Each cell of the tape holds exactly one symbol of the tape alphabet Γ. There is a tape head which scans one cell of the tape at a time. The following figure shows a tape, where the symbol $\downarrow$ indicates the position of the head.

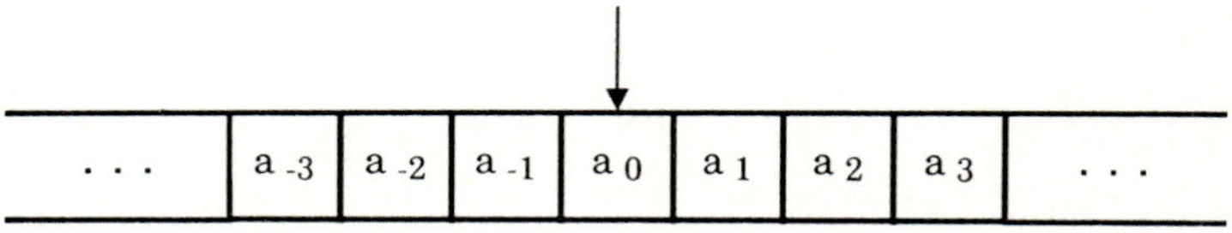

The symbols $a_o, a_1, a_{-1}, \ldots$ are elements of the tape alphabet Γ. Formally this physical situation can be described by a mapping $d : \mathbb{Z} \longrightarrow \Gamma$, where $d(0)$ is the symbol under the head, $d(-i)$ is the i-th symbol left of the head, and $d(i)$ is the i-th symbol right of the head ($i \in \mathbb{N}, i \neq 0$). Only the following operations may be performed on the tape

- move the head left one cell,
- move the head right one cell,
- replace the symbol under the head by another symbol,
- test which symbol is under the head.

We shall only consider tapes $d : \mathbb{Z} \longrightarrow \Gamma$ such that almost all tape cells contain a special symbol $B \in \Gamma$, the blank. The input encoding and the output encoding are standardized. The formal definition is as follows.

1 <u>DEFINITION</u> (*tape machine*)

Let Γ (the *tape alphabet*) and Σ (the *input/output alphabet*) be alphabets and let B (the *blank*) be an element such that $\Sigma \cup \{B\} \subseteq \Gamma$ and $B \notin \Sigma$. A k-*ary tape machine* over (Γ, Σ, B) is a machine

$$M = (F,(W(\Sigma))^k,W(\Sigma),IC^{(k)},OC)$$

such that (1),...,(4) hold.

(1) The dataset D is defined by

$$D = \{d : \mathbb{Z} \to \Gamma \mid d(z) \neq B \text{ only for finitely many } z \in \mathbb{Z}\}.$$

We shall use

$$[d(-i)d(-i+1)\ldots d(-1),\ d(0),\ d(1)\ldots d(j)]$$

as an informal (metalinguistic) notation for d, whenever $d(z) = B$ for $z < -i$ or $z > j$.

(2) The input encoding $IC^{(k)} : (W(\Sigma))^k \longrightarrow D$ is defined by

$$IC^{(k)}(w_1,\ldots,w_k) := [\varepsilon,B,w_1\ Bw_2\ldots Bw_k].$$

(3) The output encoding $OC : D \longrightarrow W(\Sigma)$ is defined by

$$OC([v,a,w]) := \text{the longest prefix } x \text{ of } w \text{ with } x \in W(\Sigma).$$

(4) Any statement in the flowchart F is either a pure function statement $f : D \longrightarrow D$ where $f \in \{L,R\} \cup \{f^a \mid a \in \Gamma\}$ or a pure test statement $t^a : D \longrightarrow \{+,-\}$ with $a \in \Gamma$, where:

$$L([vb,c,w]) := [v,b,cw] \quad \text{(left move)}$$

$$R([v,b,cw]) := [vb,c,w] \quad \text{(right move)}$$

$$f^a([v,b,w]) := [v,a,w]$$

$$t^a([v,b,w]) := \begin{cases} + & \text{if } a = b \\ - & \text{if } a \neq b \end{cases}$$

for all $a,b,c \in \Gamma$ and $v,w \in W(\Gamma)$.

Notice that any tape $d \in D$ has infinitely many informal notations since $[B^i v,a,wB^j] = [v,a,w]$ for all $i,j \in \mathbb{N}$. The statement L moves the head one position to the left, the statement R moves the head one position to the right, the function f^a prints the symbol a on the tape cell scanned by the head, and the test t^a checks whether a is the symbol under the head. In the diagram presentation of the tape flowcharts we use the symbol a for f^a and t^a $(a \in \Gamma)$. Notice that the definitions of L and R imply

$$L([\varepsilon,a,v]) = L([B,a,v]) = [\varepsilon,B,av],$$

$$R([v,a,\varepsilon]) = R([v,a,B]) = [va,B,\varepsilon].$$

2 EXAMPLE

Let $\Gamma := \{0,1,B\}$, $\Sigma := \{0,1\}$. Then the following flowchart F specifies a unary tape machine M.

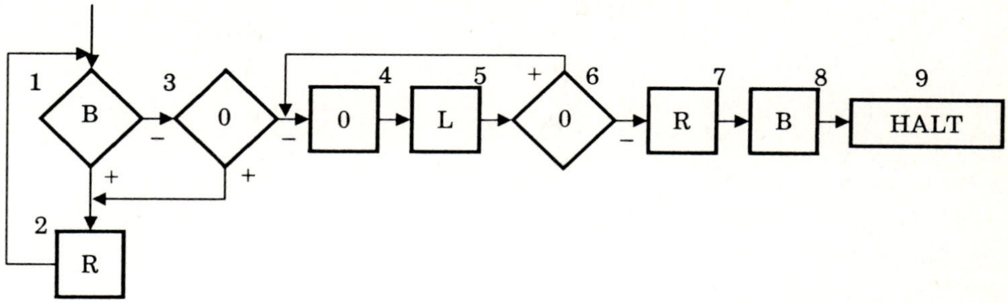

Beginning with the initial configuration $\alpha = (1,[\varepsilon,B,01])$ we obtain the following computation (see Def. 1.1.6, 1.1.16)

t	$SF^t(\alpha)$
0	$(1,[\varepsilon,B,01])$
1	$(2,[\varepsilon,B,01])$
2	$(1,[B,0,1])$
3	$(3,[B,0,1])$
4	$(2,[B,0,1])$
...	.....
7	$(4,[B0,1,\varepsilon])$
...	.....
15	$(9,[B,B,0])$

With $IC^{(1)}(01) = (\varepsilon,B,01)$ and $OC(B,B,0) = 0 \in W(\Sigma)$, we obtain $f_M(01) = 0$.

This example cannot show how powerful tape machines may be. Programming tape machines without further tools is rather cumbersome since the elementary operations and the dataset are so simple. In the next chapter we shall introduce stack machines which are equivalent to tape machines and for which it is easier to supply tools for programming.

The symbols from $\Gamma \setminus (\Sigma \cup \{B\})$ are called *auxiliary symbols*. Auxiliary symbols facilitate the construction of tape machines for given functions but they are not necessary. We shall use this result in Chapter 1.9 for defining an appropriate numbering $\varphi : \mathbb{N} \longrightarrow P^{(1)}$ of the set $P^{(1)}$ of computable functions $f : \mathbb{N} \dashrightarrow \mathbb{N}$. The proof is an extensive exercise in programming tape machines.

3 LEMMA (*auxiliary symbols*)

Let M be a k-ary tape machine over (Γ,Σ,B). Then there is a k-ary tape machine over (Γ',Σ,B), where $\Gamma' = \Sigma \cup \{B\}$, such that

$$f_M = f_{M'} \quad \text{and} \quad t_M = t_{M'} .$$

Proof

The main tools for the proof are refinement (Theorem 1.1.11), simulation (Theorems 1.1.13, 1.1.17) and change of encodings (Theorem 1.1.18). We shall use the method of incompletely specified flowcharts (see Chapter 1.1). Let

$$M = (F, (W(\Sigma))^k, W(\Sigma), IC^{(k)}, OC)$$

be a tape machine over (Γ,Σ,B). Our aim is to find an equivalent tape machine M' over (Γ',Σ,B) where $\Gamma' = \Sigma \cup \{B\}$. The datasets of M and M' are

$$D = \{d : \mathbb{Z} \longrightarrow \Gamma \mid d(z) = B \text{ almost everywhere}\},$$

$$D' = \{d' : \mathbb{Z} \longrightarrow \Gamma' \mid d'(z) = B \text{ almost everywhere}\},$$

respectively. The main idea is a simulation by which every symbol $c \in \Gamma$ is encoded by a word $\iota(c) \in W_m(\Gamma')$, the words over Γ' with length m, where m is appropriately chosen. The mapping ι can easily be extended to words and implies a simulation relation $Sim \subseteq D \times D'$ in a straightforward way.

Let $A \in \Sigma$ be a fixed symbol (we have assumed $\Sigma \neq \emptyset$), and let $m \in \mathbb{N}$ be such that $card(\Gamma) \leq 2^m = card\, W_m(\{A,B\})$. Let $\iota : \Gamma \longrightarrow W_m(\{A,B\})$ be an injective mapping such that $\iota(B) = B^m \in W_m(\{A,B\})$. For $c_1,\dots,c_n \in \Gamma$ we define

$$\iota(c_1c_2\dots c_n) := \iota(c_1)\iota(c_2)\dots\iota(c_n) \in W(\{A,B\}) .$$

The relation $Sim \subseteq D \times D'$ is defined by

$$[u,a,v]\, Sim\, [u',a',v'] :\Longleftrightarrow (\exists\, i,j,r,s \in \mathbb{N})\ (B^i u' = B^j \iota(u) \wedge a'v'B^r = \iota(av)B^s)$$

for all $a \in \Gamma$; $u,v \in W(\Gamma)$; $a' \in \Gamma'$; $u',v' \in W(\Gamma')$. Notice that this definition is independent of the representatives u,v,u',v' for informally denoting the tapes since $\iota(B) = B^m$. In our physical interpretation this means that the tape

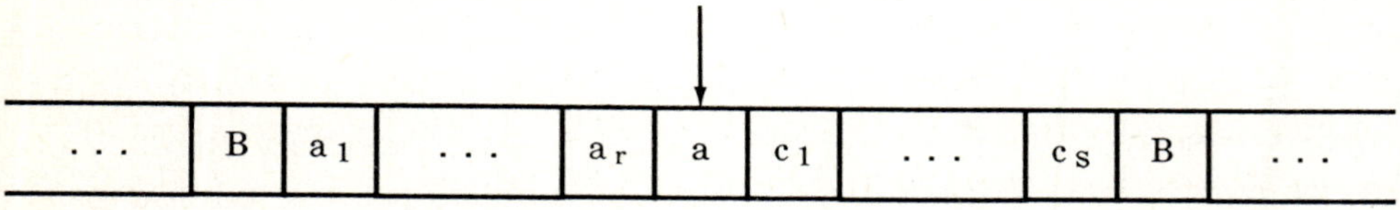

is simulated by the following tape.

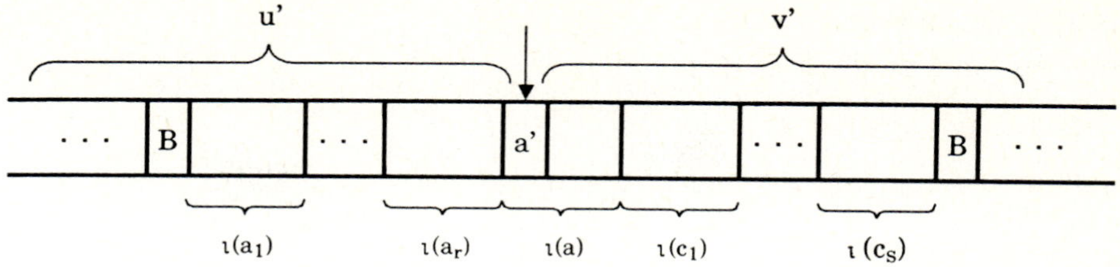

As the first step we specify (incompletely) a machine $M_1 = (F_1,(W(\Sigma))^k,W(\Sigma),I_1,O_1)$ which simulates the machine M w.r.t. Sim according to Theorem 1.1.17.

(a) Define $I_1 : (W(\Sigma))^k \longrightarrow D'$ by

$$I_1(w_1,\ldots,w_k) := [\varepsilon,B,B^{m-1}\iota(w_1B\ldots Bw_k)] .$$

(b) Define $O_1 : D' \longrightarrow W(\Sigma)$ as follows. For all $u',v' \in W(\Gamma')$, $a' \in \Gamma'$, and $y' \in W_{m-1}(\Gamma')$

$O_1[u',a',y'v']$:= the longest $x \in W(\Sigma)$ such that $\iota(x)$ is a prefix of v'.

(Any $d' \in D'$ can be written this way; the definition is independent of the choices of u' and v'.)

(c) Flowchart F_1 is obtained from F by replacing every function $f : D \longrightarrow D$ by a function $f_1 : D' \longrightarrow D'$ and every test $t : D \longrightarrow \{+,-\}$ by a test $t_1 : D' \longrightarrow \{+,-\}$ as follows:

- L_1 shifts the head m places to the left,
- R_1 shifts the head m places to the right,
- f_1^a substitutes the symbol under the head and the first (m-1) symbols to the right of the head by $\iota(a)$,
- t_1^a tests whether $\iota(a)$ is the word consisting of the symbol under the head and the first (m-1) symbols to the right of the head,

for any $a \in \Gamma$.

Then obviously $d \,\mathrm{Sim}\, d'$ implies $L =_{\mathrm{Sim}} L_1$, $R =_{\mathrm{Sim}} R_1$, $f_1^a =_{\mathrm{Sim}} f^a$, and $t_1^a =_{\mathrm{Sim}} t^a$. By Theorem 1.1.13 F_1 simulates F w.r.t. Sim. Since $IC^{(k)}(w_1,\ldots,w_k) \,\mathrm{Sim}\, I_1(w_1,\ldots,w_k)$ and since $d \,\mathrm{Sim}\, d'$ implies $OC(d) = O_1(d')$, $f_M = f_{M_1}$ and $t_M = t_{M_1}$ by Theorem 1.1.17.

As the second step we change the input and the output encodings of M_1 into the standard encodings of the tape machines by Theorem 1.1.18 using (incompletely specified) adjustments IA and OA. Let $M_2 = (F_2,(W(\Sigma))^n,W(\Sigma),IC^{(k)},OC)$ be the machine obtained from M_1 by adding adjustments IA and OA according to Theorem 1.1.18 where IA and OA satisfy the following conditions.

(d) For all $w_1,\ldots,w_k \in W(\Sigma)$

$$IA[\varepsilon,B,w_1B\ldots Bw_k] = [\varepsilon,B,B^{m-1}\iota(w_1B\ldots Bw_k)] .$$

(e) For all $u,w \in W(\Gamma')$, $a \in \Gamma'$, $y \in W_{m-1}(\Gamma')$, $x \in W(\Sigma)$, and $v \in W_m(\Gamma') \setminus \{\iota(b) \mid b \in \Sigma\}$ there are $u',v' \in W(\Gamma')$ with

$$OA\,[u,a,y\iota(x)vw] = [u',B,xBv'].$$

Then by Theorem 1.1.18, $f_{M_2} = f_{M_1}$ and $t_{M_2} = t_{M_1}$.

It remains to refine the (incompletely specified) flowchart F_2 into a tape machine flowchart. The refinements of the functions L_1, R_1, N_1, f_1^a and the tests t_1^a are very easy. As an example we give a tape machine flowchart F with $t_1^a = t_F$. Suppose $\iota(a) = b_1 \ldots b_m$ $(b_i \in \{A,B\})$. Then the following flowchart F has the desired property.

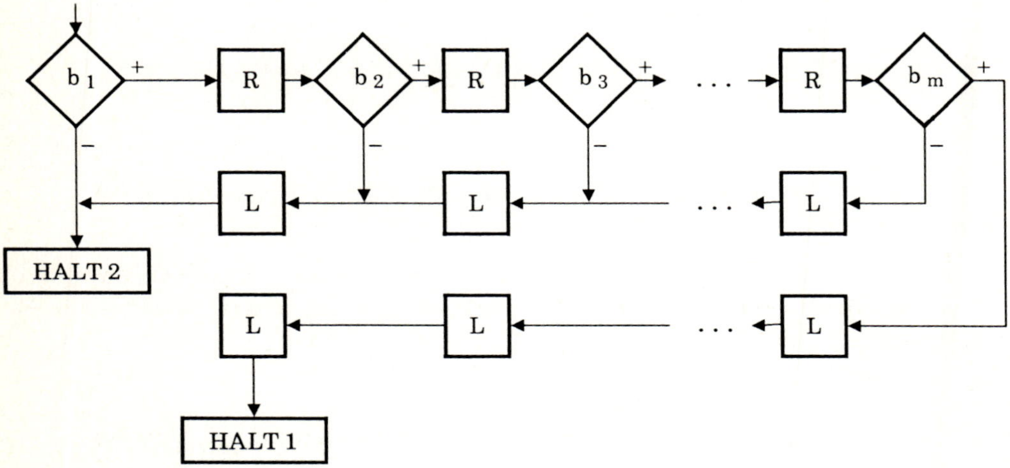

Finding appropriate flowcharts for IA and OA is more difficult. We only consider the case of IA here. Using the method of stepwise refinement of (incompletely specified) flowcharts we show how to construct a tape machine flowchart which computes a function IA satisfying

(d) $IA[\varepsilon,B,w_1B\ldots Bw_k] = [\varepsilon,B,B^{m-1}\iota(w_1B\ldots Bw_k)]$

for all $w_1,\ldots,w_k \in W(\Sigma)$.

Let RB satisfy (f) and let CB satisfy (g):

(f) $RB[x,B,uBy] = [xBu,B,y]$

for all $x,y \in W(\Gamma')$, $u \in W(\Sigma)$,

(g) $CB[u_1B\ldots u_jB,B,w] = [u_1B\ldots u_{j-1}B,B,\iota(u_jB)w]$ $(1 \le j \le k)$.

for all $u_1,\ldots,u_k \in W(\Sigma)$, $w \in W(\Gamma')$.

Define a flowchart G_1 by:

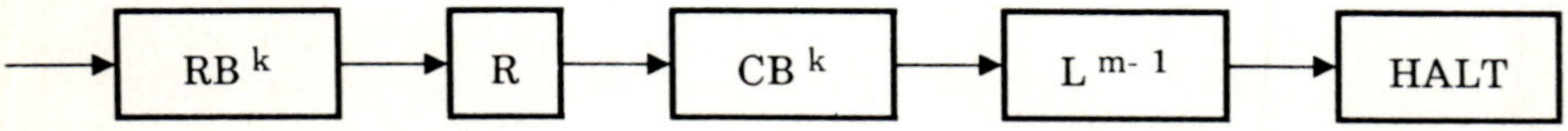

Then f_{G_1} satisfies Property (d). Now RB and CB must be refined. The refinement of RB is left as an exercise. Let SHIFT satisfy (h) and let CO satisfy (i):

(h) $SHIFT[u_1Bu_2B\ldots u_j,B,w] = [u_1B\ldots u_j,B,B^{m-1}w]$ for all j with $1 \leq j \leq k$

where $u_1,\ldots,u_k \in W(\Sigma)$, $w \in W(\Gamma')$.

(i) $CO[xa,B,B^{m-1}w] = [x,B,\iota(a)w]$

for all $x,w \in W(\Gamma')$, $a \in \Sigma$.

Define a flowchart G_2 by

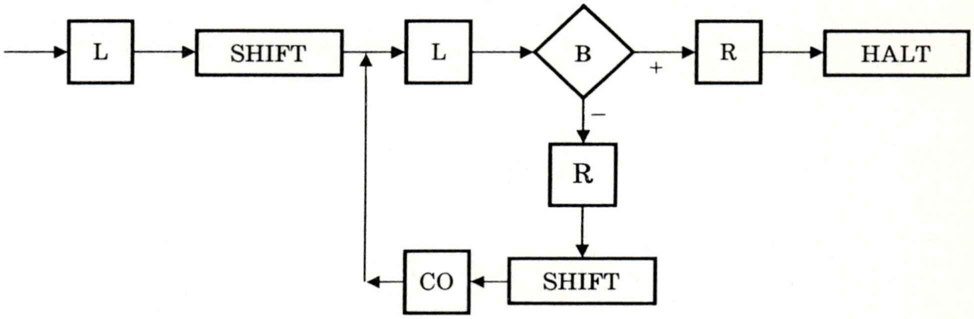

Then f_{G_2} satisfies Condition (g). Remember $\iota(B) = B^m$. The refinement of CO is left to the exercises. Let SB satisfy (j) and LB satisfy (k):

(j) $SB[x,B,B^{m-2}uBw] = [xuB,B,B^{m-2}w]$

for all $u \in W(\Sigma)$, $x,w \in W(\Gamma')$. (Notice that Lemma 3 is trivial if $m < 2$.)

(k) $LB[xBu,B,w] = [x,B,uBw]$

for all $u \in W(\Sigma)$, $x,w \in W(\Gamma')$.

Define a flowchart G_3 by

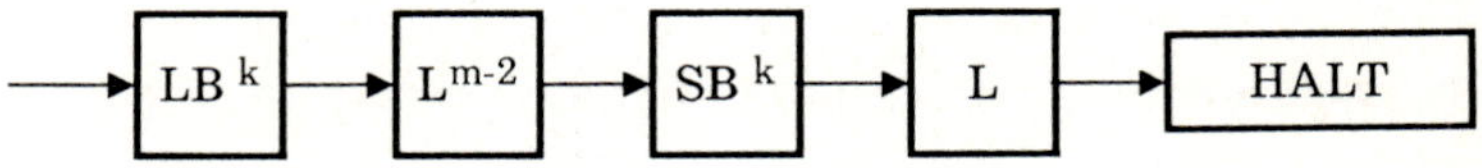

Then f_{G_3} satisfies Condition (h). The refinements of LB and of SB are easy and are left to the exercises. Altogether we have constructed a tape machine flowchart which computes a function satisfying Condition (d).

Q.E.D

As we have already mentioned our tape machines are essentially equivalent to Turing machines. A commonly used definition of a Turing machine is as follows. A Turing machine is a tuple

$T = (Q,\Gamma,\Sigma,\delta,q_o,F)$

where Γ and Σ are alphabets ($\Sigma \subseteq \Gamma$, $B \in \Gamma$, $B \notin \Sigma$), Q is a finite set of states, $q_o \in Q$ is the initial state, $F \subseteq Q$ is the set of final states (usually not ordered), and δ is a function

$$\delta : (Q \backslash F) \times \Gamma \longrightarrow Q \times \Gamma \times \{L,N,R\} .$$

The transition function δ is interpreted as follows: If $\delta(q,a) = (q',b,V)$ then in state q with a under the head the machine changes to state q', prints b and makes the move V (where $V = N$ means "no move"). In our framework, δ (essentially) defines a flowchart with dataset D (from Definition 1) and for each state q there is an operation $\sigma(q) = (f,t,(q_1,\ldots,q_n))$ which can be refined by a tape flowchart as follows (assume $\Gamma = \{b_1,\ldots,b_n\}$ and $\delta(q,b_i) = (q_i,c_i,V_i)$):

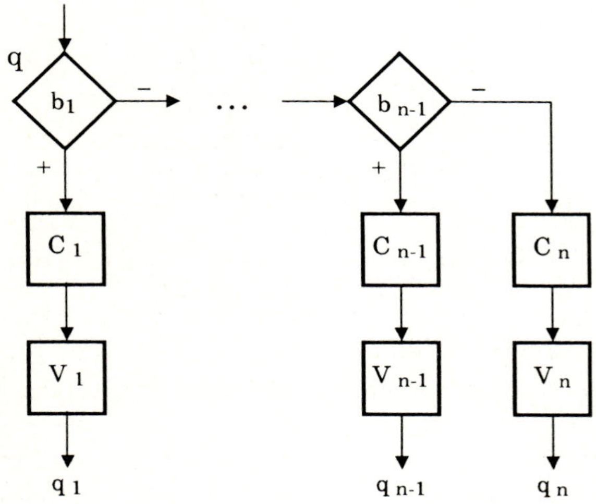

On the other hand, for each tape machine there is a Turing machine computing the same function. It is a matter of taste whether to use tape machines or Turing machines. We have defined tape machines in order to be able to directly apply refinement and simulation of our more general formalism. The functions computable by tape machines (or Turing machines) are (very likely) the intuitively computable word functions. This justifies the following definition.

4 DEFINITION (*computability of word functions*)

A word function $f : (W(\Sigma))^k \dashrightarrow W(\Sigma)$ is *computable* iff there is some tape machine M with $f = f_M$.

In order to prove that a function $f : (W(\Sigma))^k \dashrightarrow W(\Sigma)$ is computable, the existence of a tape machine M with $f = f_M$ has to be shown. Programming tape machines is not very convenient because it is difficult to handle different words on one tape independently. A theorem like Theorem 1.2.7 on generalized register machines could be proved in order to facilitate this task. Another way is to introduce tape machines (or Turing machines) with several tapes. In the next chapter we shall define the stack machines, which are essentially equivalent to the multitape Turing machines and which generalize the register machines from numbers to words.

In the literature there are almost as many definitions of Turing machines as there are authors studying them. Common to all these models is (the idea) that one or several heads which are controlled by a finite memory operate on one or several tapes. But even the idea of tape is generalized to n-dimensional "tapes" or tree like "tapes". There are Turing machines with one tape and with several tapes some of which may be reserved for input or output. There are Turing machines with several heads on the tape. Turing machines are also used for recognizing sets (i.e. computing tests). Here the nondeterministic Turing machines which have a transition relation instead of a transition function play an important role. Also many different input and output encodings are used. Almost all of these models compute the same class of word functions, the computable word functions, or recognize the same class of sets, the decidable and the recursively enumerable sets, which will be studied later. However, the different types of Turing machines may behave quite differently w.r.t. computation times and the space needed for computations. The resources needed by Turing machines in recognizing sets or computing functions is investigated in *Turing machine complexity theory*. One of the most challenging unsolved problems in this theory is the P-NP-*problem*, i.e. the question whether, in polynomial time, nondeterministic Turing machines are more powerful recognizers than deterministic ones.

EXERCISES

1) Consider the tape machine from Example 2.
   (a) Find some $u \in W(\Sigma)$ with $f_M(u) = 11$.
   (b) Find some $u \in W(\Sigma)$ with $f_M(u) = \text{div}$.
   (c) Characterize f_M explicitly (with proof).
2) Consider the proof of Lemma 3.
   (a) Construct simple tape machine flowcharts which compute the following functions: L_1, R_1, $f_1^a (a \in \Gamma)$.
   (b) Construct a simple tape machine flowchart for a function OA satisfying Condition (e).

(c) Construct a simple tape machine flowchart for a function RB satisfying Condition (f).

(d) Construct a simple tape machine flowchart for a function CO satisfying Condition (i).

3) Consider the proof of Lemma 3. Is there a tape machine flowchart which computes a function $f: D' \dashrightarrow D'$ satisfying

$$f[\varepsilon,B,w_1 B\ldots B\, w_k] = [\varepsilon,B,B^{m-1}\iota(w_1 B\ldots B\, w_k)]$$

for all $k\in\mathbb{N}$ and $w_1,\ldots,w_k \in W(\Sigma)$?

4) Consider the proof of Lemma 3. Let $\hat{M}$ be the class of all tape machines M such that f_M satisfies condition (d):

$$f_M[\varepsilon,B,w_1 B\ldots B\, w_k] = [\varepsilon,B,B^{m-1}\iota(w_1 B\ldots B\, w_k)]$$

for all $w_1,\ldots, w_k\in W(\Sigma)$. For $M\in\hat{M}$ let $T_M(w_1,\ldots,w_k)$ be the number of steps M performs with input $[\varepsilon,B,w_1 B\ldots B\, w_k]$.

(a) Show that there is a machine $M\in\hat{M}$ and constants $a,b\in\mathbb{N}$ such that

$$T_M(w_1,\ldots,w_k) \le an^2 + b \quad \text{where} \quad n = lg(w_1w_2\ldots w_k).$$

(b) Show that for no machine $M\in\hat{M}$ are there constants $a,b\in\mathbb{N}$ such that

$$T_M(w_1,\ldots,w_k) \le an + b \quad \text{where} \quad n = lg(w_1w_2\ldots w_k).$$

5) A machine with a queue as a storage (fifo = first in first out) is called a *queue machine*. More precisely queue machines are defined as follows (c f. Definition 1). Let Γ and Σ be alphabets with $\Sigma\subseteq\Gamma$, let $B\in\Gamma\setminus\Sigma$, let $k\in\mathbb{N}$. A k-*ary queue machine* over (Γ,Σ,B) is a machine

$$M = (F,(W(\Sigma))^k, W(\Sigma), I^{(k)},O)$$

satisfying the following properties (1),...,(4).

(1) $D = W(\Gamma)$

(2) $I^{(k)}(w_1,\ldots,w_k) = w_1B\ldots B\, w_k$

(3) $O(w)$:= the longest prefix x of w with $x\in W(\Sigma)$

(4) Any statement in the flowchart F is either a pure function statement cut or $app^a: D\longrightarrow D$ $(a\in\Gamma)$ where $cut(\varepsilon) := \varepsilon$, $cut(bw) := w$, $app^a(w) := wa$ or a pure test statement $head^a: D\longrightarrow\{+,-\}$ $(a\in\Gamma)$ defined by $head^a(w) = +$ if $w = ax$ for some $x\in W(\Gamma)$, $-$ otherwise.

(a) Show that every tape computable function is queue computable.

(b) Show that every queue computable function is tape computable.

BIBLIOGRAPHICAL NOTES

The idea to perform symbol manipulation on a tape is from Turing (1937). The Turing machine is the most commonly used model for defining computability, e.g. Davis (1958), Hermes (1978), Hopcroft and Ullman (1979), Loeckx (1976). The definition by means of μ-recursion is prefered by logicians.

1.6 Stack Machines

Since tape machines or one tape Turing machines are not very appropriate for practical programming of word functions, in this chapter we introduce a generalization of the register machines from numbers to words, the *stack machines*. Stack machines, especially the generalized stack machines, are a very useful and natural tool for formulating algorithms which operate on words. We shall prove that the stack machine computable word functions are exactly the (tape) computable word functions.

A stack machine has registers $R_o, R_1, \ldots$ each of which can store a word $w \in W(\Gamma)$. The following operations and tests may be used in the flowchart:

- "$R_i := R_i a$" (adds the symbol a to the right of the word in Register R_i),
- "$R_i := \text{pop } R_i$" (deletes the rightmost symbol of the word in Register R_i),
- "R top a" (tests whether a is the rightmost symbol of the word in Register R_i)

for any $a \in \Gamma$ and $i \in \mathbb{N}$.

The following figure shows the physical configuration of a stack machine .

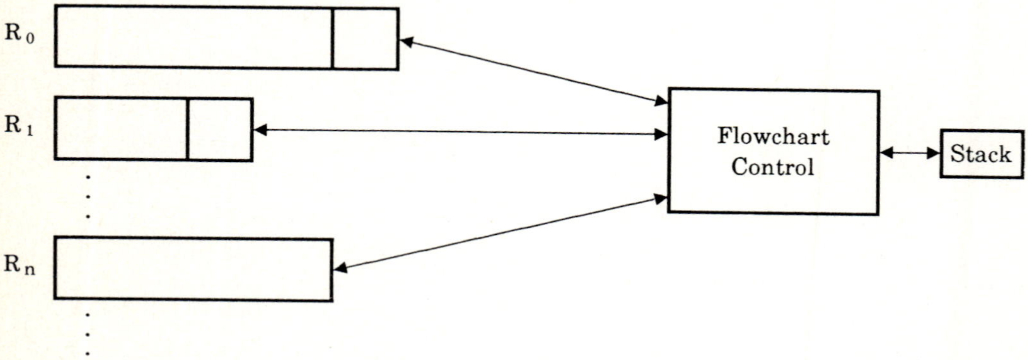

If the alphabet Γ has exactly one element, then the word of length n can be indentified with the number n ($n \in \mathbb{N}$), and the above operations on word registers become the operations of register machines. In this sense stack machines generalize register machines. A store for a word on which only the above operations on the right side are admitted is called a *stack* or *pushdown store*. Stack machines with stacks $R_o, R_1, \ldots$ which we introduce here must not be confused with *pushdown automata* (or stack automata) which have one oneway read only input tape and one stack and are used for recognizing the contextfree languages. The definition of stack machines is an obvious generalization of Definition 1.2.2 of register machines.

1 DEFINITION (*stack machine*)

Let Σ and Γ be alphabets with $\Sigma \subseteq \Gamma$, let $k \in \mathbb{N}$. A k-*ary stack machine over* (Γ,Σ) is a machine $M = (F,(W(\Sigma))^k,W(\Sigma),IC^{(k)},OC)$ with flowchart $F = (Q,D,\sigma,q_o,s,(q_1,\dots,q_s))$ such that (1),...,(4) hold.

(1) $D = (W(\Gamma))^{\mathbb{N}}$

Notation: Instead of $d(0) = w_o$, $d(1) = w_1$, ... we write $d = (w_o,w_1,\dots)$.

(2) $IC^{(k)}(w_1,\dots,w_k) := (\varepsilon,w_1,\dots,w_k,\varepsilon,\dots)$.

(3) $OC(w_o,w_1,\dots) := \begin{cases} w_o & \text{if } w_o \in W(\Sigma) \\ \varepsilon & \text{otherwise.} \end{cases}$

(4) Suppose $\sigma(q) = (f,t,(p_1,\dots,p_j))$. Then either (a) or (b) holds.

(a) $j = 1$, $(\forall d \in D)\ t(d) = 1$, and for some $i \in \mathbb{N}$, $a \in \Gamma$
$f = "R_i := R_i a"$ or $f = "R_i := \text{pop}\, R_i"$,

(b) $j = 2$, $(\forall d \in D)\ f(d) = d$, and for some $i \in \mathbb{N}$, $a \in \Gamma$
$t = "R_i \text{ top } a"$,

where

$"R_i := R_i a"(w_o,w_1,\dots) := (w_o,\dots,w_{i-1},w_i a,w_{i+1},\dots)$

$"R_i := \text{pop}\, R_i"(w_o,w_1,\dots) := (w_o,\dots,w_{i-1},\text{pop}(w_i),w_{i+1},\dots)$
(with $\text{pop}(\varepsilon) := \varepsilon$, $\text{pop}(wa) := w$ for $w \in W(\Gamma)$, $a \in \Gamma$),

$"R_i \text{ top } a"(w_o,w_1,\dots) := \begin{cases} + & \text{if } (\exists y \in W(\Gamma))\ w_i = ya \\ - & \text{otherwise,} \end{cases}$

for any $i \in \mathbb{N}$, $a \in \Gamma$, $(w_o,w_1,\dots) \in D$.

In Chapter 1 we have already defined the function f_M and the test t_M computed by a machine M. The definition of the stack computable functions and tests follows immediately.

2 DEFINITION (*stack computability*)

Let Σ be an alphabet.
A function $f : (W(\Sigma))^k \dashrightarrow W(\Sigma)$ is *stack computable* iff $f = f_M$ for some stack machine M.
A test $t : (W(\Sigma))^k \dashrightarrow \{1,\dots,s\}$ is *stack computable* iff $t = t_M$ for some stack machine M.

3 EXAMPLE

Let $\Sigma := \{a,b\}$ and $f : W(\Sigma) \longrightarrow W(\Sigma)$ with $f(w) := w^R :=$ reversal of word w. Define a unary stack machine over (Σ,Σ) by the following flowchart.

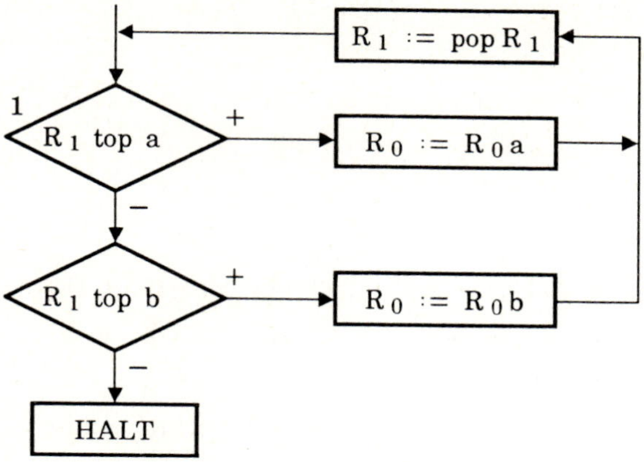

Then for any $u,w \in W(\Sigma)$, $c \in \Sigma$ there is some k with

$$SF^k(1,(u,wc,\varepsilon,\ldots)) = (1,(uc,w,\varepsilon,\ldots))$$

(namely $k = 2$ if $c = a$, $k = 3$ if $c = b$). By complete induction on the length of x the following property can be derived.

$(\forall x \in W(\Sigma))\ (\forall w \in W(\Sigma))\ (\exists n \in \mathbb{N})$

$$SF^n(1,(\varepsilon,wx,\varepsilon,\ldots)) = (1,(x^R,w,\varepsilon,\ldots))$$

(From Case x derive Case cx, $c \in \Sigma$.) Therefore for any $x \in W(\Sigma)$ there is some n with

$$SF^n(1,(\varepsilon,x,\varepsilon,\ldots)) = (1,(x^R,\varepsilon,\ldots)).$$

This implies $f_M = f$.

Let M be a stack machine over (Γ,Σ). The symbols from $\Gamma \setminus \Sigma$ are called auxiliary symbols. The set of auxiliary symbols may be increased without changing the function and test computed by M.

4 LEMMA

Let M be a stack machine over (Γ,Σ), let $\Gamma \subseteq \Gamma'$.
Then there is a stack machine M' over (Γ',Σ) such that $f_M = f_{M'}$ and $t_M = t_{M'}$.

The proof, a simple simulation, is left as an exercise. The theory of register machines can be easily transferred to stack machines. Especially a theorem corresponding to that on generalized register machines (Theorem 1.2.7) can be proved.

5 DEFINITION (*generalized stack machines*)

Replace "register machine" by "stack machine over (Γ,Σ)" and $\mathbb{N}$ by $W(\Sigma)$ in Definition 1.2.5 of generalized register machines.

6 THEOREM

Let M be a generalized stack machine over (Γ,Σ) which uses only stack computable functions and tests. Then there is some alphabet Γ' such that f_M and t_M can be computed by a stack machine over (Γ',Σ).

Proof (sketch)

For every function f_i (or test t_i) on $W(\Sigma)$ used in M there is an alphabet Γ_i such that f_i (or t_i) can be computed by a register machine over (Γ_i,Σ). Choose $\Gamma' := \Gamma \cup \bigcup \Gamma_i$. By Lemma 4 we may assume Γ' as the common alphabet for the new machine. The rest of the proof is almost identical to the proof of Theorem 1.2.7. The only change concerns the statements "$R_i \longleftarrow R_j$" (see Lemma 1.2.8). The stack flowchart corresponding to flowchart E in the proof of Lemma 1.2.8 would bring the reverse of Register R_j to Register R_i. In place of "$R_i \longleftarrow R_j$" the register function "$R_i \underset{k}{\longleftarrow} R_j$" $(k \neq i,\ k \neq j)$ with

$$"R_i \underset{k}{\longleftarrow} R_j"(d)(n) = \begin{cases} d(j) & \text{if } n = i \\ \varepsilon & \text{if } n = j \text{ or } n = k \\ d(n) & \text{otherwise} \end{cases}$$

can be used. In the main proof choose $k := 2q$ (see proof of Theorem 1.2.7).

The main result of this chapter is that the stack computable word functions are exactly the (Turing) computable word functions. For proving that a given word function is computable it is therefore sufficient to show that $f = f_M$ for some stack machine M.

7 THEOREM (*stack computable = computable*)

Let Σ be an alphabet, let $k \in \mathbb{N}$. A function $f : (W(\Sigma))^k \dashrightarrow W(\Sigma)$ is computable iff it is stack computable.

Proof

"$\Longrightarrow$": Let f be computable. Then $f = f_M$ for some tape machine

$M = (F,(W(\Sigma))^k,W(\Sigma),IC^{(k)},OC)$ over (Γ,Σ,B) with dataset D. By simulation (Theorem 1.1.13, 1.1.17), change of encodings (Theorem 1.1.18), and refinement (Theorem 1.1.11) we shall construct a stack machine $M' = (F',(W(\Sigma))^k,W(\Sigma),I^{(k)},0)$ over (Γ,Σ) which computes f.

M' has the dataset $(W(\Gamma))^{\mathbb{N}} =: D'$. The main idea of the proof is the simulation of the Turing tape by three stacks: one stack for the inscription left of the head, one stack for the symbol under the head, and one stack for the reverse of the inscription right of the head. More precisely, define $Sim \subseteq D \times D'$ by

$$Sim := \{([u,a,v],(\varepsilon,u,a,v^R,\varepsilon,\ldots)) \mid a \in \Gamma,\ u,v \in W(\Gamma)\}\ .$$

The word v has to be reversed since the stack operations act on the right side of a word. By the definition of Sim the tape

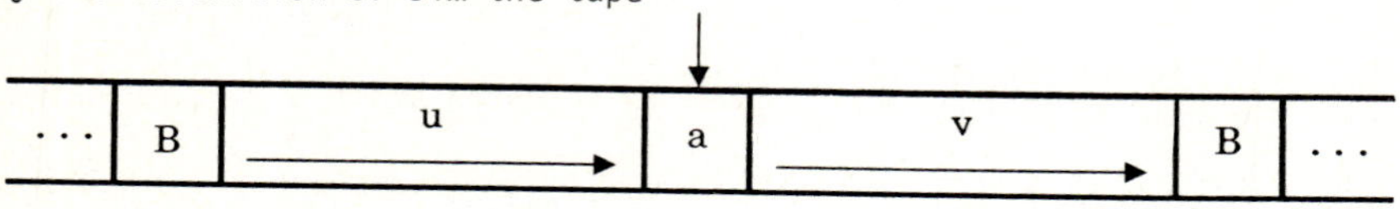

is simulated by the stack assignment

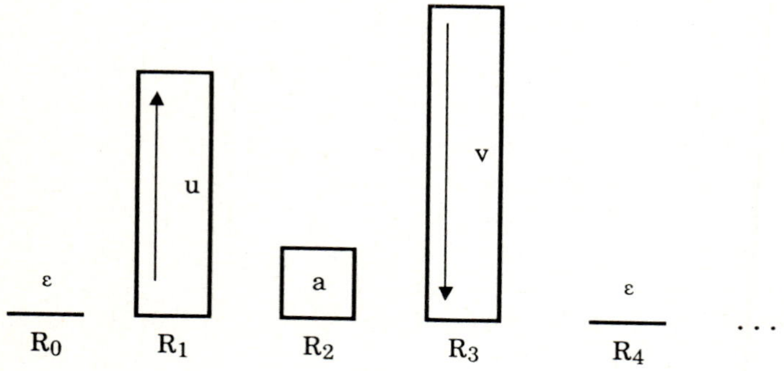

(the arrow points from the first to the last symbol of the word). Notice that by the tape [u,a,v] the word u is only determined up to blanks at the beginning. The corresponding remark holds for v. Thus, for any d there are infinitely many d' with $(d,d') \in Sim$. Let $M_1 = (F_1,(W(\Sigma))^k,W(\Sigma),I_1,0_1)$ be any machine with dataset D' which satisfies the following conditions (c f. Theorem 1.1.17)

(a) For all $w_1,\ldots,w_k \in W(\Sigma)$

$$I_1(w_1,\ldots,w_k) = (\varepsilon,\varepsilon,B,(w_1B\ldots Bw_k)^R,\varepsilon,\ldots)$$

(b) For all $y_o,y_1,\ldots \in W(\Gamma)$

$$0_1(y_o,y_1,\ldots) = x^R \quad \text{where x is the longest suffix y of } y_3 \text{ with } y \in W(\Sigma)$$

(c) Flowchart F_1 results from flowchart F by replacement of every function g (test t) by a function g_1 (test t_1) where g_1 (t_1) satisfies the following property in the respective case:

$$L_1(\varepsilon,ub,a,x,\varepsilon,\ldots) = (\varepsilon,u,b,xa,\varepsilon,\ldots)$$

$$L_1(\varepsilon,\varepsilon,a,x,\varepsilon,\dots) = (\varepsilon,\varepsilon,B,xa,\varepsilon,\dots)$$

$$R_1(\varepsilon,u,a,xb,\varepsilon,\dots) = (\varepsilon,ua,b,x,\varepsilon,\dots)$$

$$R_1(\varepsilon,u,a,\varepsilon,\varepsilon,\dots) = (\varepsilon,ua,B,\varepsilon,\varepsilon,\dots)$$

$$f_1^b(\varepsilon,u,a,x,\varepsilon,\dots) = (\varepsilon,u,b,x,\varepsilon,\dots)$$

$$t_1^b(\varepsilon,u,a,x,\varepsilon,\dots) = \begin{cases} + & \text{if } a=b \\ - & \text{else} \end{cases}$$

for any $a,b \in \Gamma$ and $u,x \in W(\Gamma)$.

Then $f = f_{M_1}$ by Theorem 1.1.17.
The next step is the change of the encoding I_1 and O_1 into the encodings $I^{(k)}$ and O of stack machines. By Theorem 1.1.18 the semantics remains unchanged, if appropriate adjustments are added to F_1. Let IA and OA be functions on D' which satisfy the following conditions:

(d) For all $w_1,\dots,w_k \in W(\Sigma)$

$$IA(\varepsilon,w_1,w_2,\dots,w_k,\varepsilon,\dots) = (\varepsilon,\varepsilon,B,(w_1B\dots Bw_k)^R,\varepsilon,\dots)$$

(e) For all $a \in \Gamma$, $u,v \in W(\Gamma)$

$$OA(\varepsilon,u,a,v,\dots) = (x^R,y_1,y_2,\dots)$$

for certain $y_1,y_2,\dots \in W(\Gamma)$ where x is the longest suffix y of v with $y \in W(\Sigma)$.

Let $M_2 = (F_2,(W(\Sigma))^k,W(\Sigma),I^{(k)},O)$, where F_2 is obtained from F_1 satisfying (c) by adding adjustments IA and OA which satisfy (d) and (e) according to Theorem 1.1.18. Then $f = f_{M_2}$.
The third step is the refinement of M_2 into a stack machine. This is an easy programming exercise with stack machines. We only consider the refinement of OA and leave the other cases to the exercises.
Define a stack machine flowchart G as follows (consider $\Sigma = \{a_1,\dots,a_i\}$):

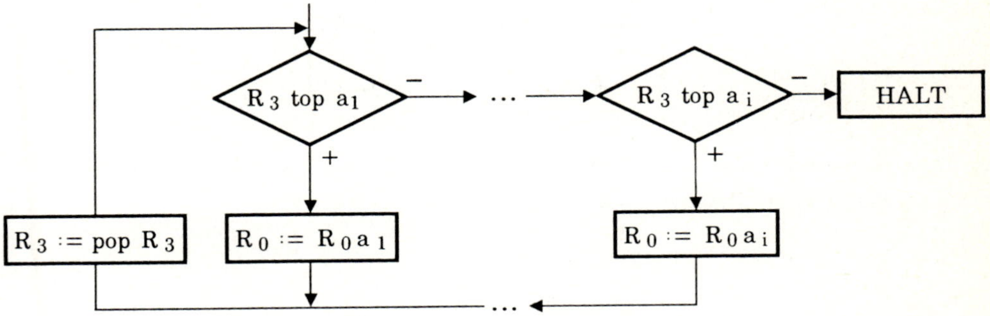

Then f_G satisfies Condition (e), i.e. G refines OA. Therefore we are able to construct a stack machine M' which computes f.

"$\Leftarrow$": Suppose f is stack computable. Then there are some Γ and some stack machine $M = (F,(W(\Sigma))^k, I^{(k)}, 0)$ over (Γ,Σ) which computes f. By simulation, change of encodings and refinement we construct a tape machine $M' = (F,(W(\Sigma))^k, W(\Sigma), IC^k, OC)$ over (Γ',Σ,B) which computes f.
Let $D = (W(\Gamma))^{\mathbb{N}}$, the dataset of M. Let \$ and B be two different symbols which are not elements of Γ, define $\Gamma' := \Gamma \cup \{\$,B\}$. Then the dataset of M' is $\{[v,a,w] \mid a \in \Gamma', v,w \in W(\Gamma')\}$. Again the main idea of the proof is the simulation of the stacks used by M by a Turing tape. Let m be a number such that no register R_i with $i \geq m$ is used by the stack machine M. Let $z = z_o z_1 z_2 \ldots z_s$ be a word over Γ', where $z_o, z_1, \ldots, z_s \in \Gamma'$. For any $i < m$ define $z^{(i)}$, the i-th "comb" of z, by

$$z^{(i)} = z_i z_{i+m} z_{i+2m} \ldots z_{i+rm}$$

where r is defined by $i + rm \leq s < i + (r+1)m$.
Example: $m = 3$,

z = a b a a B a b b B a B B a

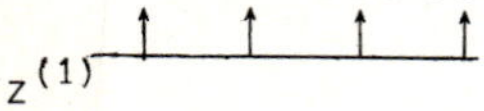

By the following simulation relation $Sim \subseteq D \times D'$ the i-th stack is encoded by the i-th comb of the inscription of the tape.

$$Sim := \{(d,[\varepsilon,\$,z]) \mid d \in D \wedge z \in W(\Gamma \cup \{B\}) \wedge (\forall i < m)(\exists n)\ z^{(i)} = d(i)B^n\}$$

It is clear, now, which properties the simulating functions and the adjustments IA and OA must have. We only specify a tape machine flowchart G such that the pair "$R_i := R_i a$" and f_G are similar w.r.t. Sim.

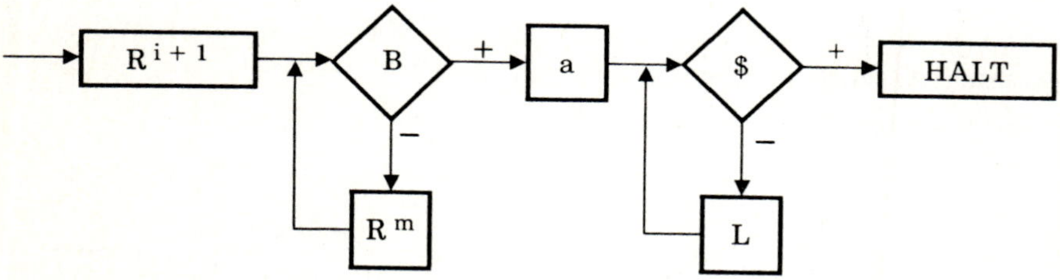

The other refinements are left to the exercises. Altogether we are able to construct a tape machine M' which computes f.
Q.E.D.

Finally we formulate a simple but useful lemma which studies the increase and the decrease of the alphabet.

8 LEMMA

Let Σ,Δ be alphabets with $\Sigma \subseteq \Delta$, let $k \in \mathbb{N}$.

(1) Let $f:(W(\Sigma))^k \dashrightarrow W(\Sigma)$ be computable. Then the function $g:(W(\Delta))^k \dashrightarrow W(\Delta)$ defined by

$$g(\overline{z}) := \begin{cases} f(\overline{z}) & \text{if } \overline{z} \in (W(\Sigma))^k \\ \varepsilon & \text{otherwise} \end{cases}$$

is computable.

(2) Let $g:(W(\Delta))^k \dashrightarrow W(\Delta)$ be computable. Then the function $f:(W(\Sigma))^k \dashrightarrow W(\Sigma)$ defined by

$$f(\overline{z}) = \begin{cases} \varepsilon & \text{if } g(\overline{z}) \in W(\Delta) \setminus W(\Sigma) \\ g(\overline{z}) & \text{otherwise} \end{cases}$$

is computable.

Proof (as an exercise)

As we have seen in the proof of Theorem 7 a Turing tape can easily be simulated by three stacks. Therefore, the n tapes of an n-tape Turing machine can be simulated by 3n stacks. On the other hand every stack can be considered as a special Turing tape. Therefore, there is no essential difference between multitape Turing machines and stack machines.

EXERCISES

1) Let $\Sigma := \{a,b,c\}$.

(a) Show that $f: W(\Sigma) \longrightarrow W(\Sigma)$ defined by $f(w) = www$ is stack computable.

(b) Show that the test $t: W(\Sigma) \longrightarrow \{1,2\}$ defined by $t(w) = (1$ if $w = w^R$, 2 otherwise) is stack computable.

2) Let $\Sigma = \{a_1,\dots,a_n\}$. A function $s: W(\Sigma) \longrightarrow W(\Sigma)$ is defined by the recursion equations

$$s(\varepsilon) = a_1$$

$$s(w\,a_i) = \begin{cases} w\,a_{i+1} & \text{if } i < n \\ s(w)a_1 & \text{otherwise} \end{cases}$$

for all $1 \le i \le n$, $w \in W(\Sigma)$. Show that s is stack computable.

3) Let $\Sigma = \{a_1, \dots, a_n\}$. A function $p: W(\Sigma) \longrightarrow W(\Sigma)$ is defined by the recursion equations

$$p(\varepsilon) = \varepsilon,$$

$$p(w\,a_i) = \begin{cases} w\,a_{i-1} & \text{if } i \neq 1 \\ p(w)a_n & \text{if } i = 1 \text{ and } w \neq \varepsilon \\ \varepsilon & \text{if } i = 1 \text{ and } w = \varepsilon. \end{cases}$$

Let s be the function defined in Exercise 2.

(a) Show $(\forall x \in W(\Sigma))\ ps(x) = x$.

(b) Show $(\forall x \in W(\Sigma),\ x \neq \varepsilon)\ sp(x) = x$.

(c) Show that p is stack computable.

4) Show that there is a stack machine flowchart F with $f_F =$ "$R_i \xleftarrow{k} R_j$" (c f. the comments to Theorem 5).

5) Consider the proof of Theorem 6.

(a) Construct stack machine flowcharts for refining the following functions: R_1, L_1, f_1^b, t_1^b, EA.

(b) Construct simple tape machines for the output adjustment OA, for the function which simulates "$R_i := \mathrm{pop}(R_i)$", and for the test which simulates "R_i top a" in the second part of the proof.

6) Prove Lemma 3.

7) Prove Lemma 7.

1.7 Comparison of Number and Word Functions, Church's Thesis

In Chapter 1.2 we introduced the computable functions on numbers using register machines, and in Chapter 1.5 we defined the computable word functions by means of Turing machines. Since numbers are not words and words are not numbers the two classes are incomparable. We shall prove, however, that by means of a *standard numbering* $\nu_\Sigma : \mathbb{N} \longrightarrow W(\Sigma)$ the computable number functions can be transformed into the computable word functions (over Σ) and vice versa. This shows that the two definitions of computability are not totally independent. *Church's thesis* which states that the computable number functions are exactly the intuitively computable number functions will be discussed. Finally, we prove that there are functions which are not computable.

For comparing number and word functions we define standard numberings of $W(\Sigma)$. The following example leads to the general definition.

1 EXAMPLE

Let $\Sigma := \{1,2\}$. It is easy to list the set $W(\Sigma)$ of words over Σ systematically:

ε ,
1 , 2 ,
11 , 12 , 21 , 22 ,
111 , 112 , 121 , 122 , 211 , 212 , 221 , 222 ,
1111 , ... , 2222 ,
etc.

Then the function $\nu_\Sigma : \mathbb{N} \longrightarrow W(\Sigma)$ with $\nu_\Sigma(i) :=$ "the i-th word in the list" is a bijective numbering of $W(\Sigma)$. For example, $\nu_\Sigma(0) = \varepsilon$, $\nu_\Sigma(8) = 112$.

2 DEFINITION (*standard numbering of* $W(\Sigma)$)

Let Σ be an alphabet, $n := \mathrm{card}(\Sigma)$. let $a : \{1,\dots,n\} \longrightarrow \Sigma$ be a bijection (*order function*). Notation: $a_i := a(i)$. Define $\sigma : W(\Sigma) \longrightarrow \mathbb{N}$ by

$$\sigma(\varepsilon) := 0 ,$$

$$\sigma(a(i_k)a(i_{k-1})\dots a(i_1)a(i_o)) := i_k n^k + i_{k-1} n^{k-1} + \dots + i_1 n + i_o$$

for all $k \in \mathbb{N}$, $i_o,\dots,i_k \in \{1,\dots,n\}$, and $\nu : \mathbb{N} \longrightarrow W(\Sigma)$ by $\nu = \sigma^{-1}$. Then ν is a *standard numbering* of $W(\Sigma)$.

The numbering ν_Σ from Example 1 is a standard numbering of $W(\{1,2\})$. The idea is to represent the natural numbers by n-adic numbers where the digits are $1,2,\dots,n$ and not $0,1,\dots,n-1$ as usual, based on the following modified division with remainder.

(*) For any $c,n \in \mathbb{N}$, $c > 0$, $n > 0$, there are two uniquely determined numbers $q,r \in \mathbb{N}$ such that

$$c = q\cdot n + r \quad \text{and} \quad 1 \le r \le n .$$

The values q and r can easily be computed from c and n using register machines. This means there are computable functions g_1 and g_2 with $c = n\cdot g_i(c,n) + g_2(c,n)$ and $1 \le g_2(c,n) \le n$ for all $c,n \ge 1$. An immediate consequence of Definition 2 is $\sigma(wa_i) = n\cdot\sigma(w) + i$ for all $w \in W(\Sigma)$, $1 \le i \le n$. Below we shall use these facts repeatedly. The definition of ν is correct only if σ is bijective.

3 LEMMA

σ and ν are bijective.

Proof

We show first that σ is injective. By complete induction on $lg(x)$ we prove $(\forall x)\ (\forall y)\ \ (\sigma(x) = \sigma(y) \Longrightarrow x = y)$.
$lg(x) = 0$: Then $x = \varepsilon$. Suppose $\sigma(x) = \sigma(y)$. Then $\sigma(y) = 0$ and $y = \varepsilon$, i.e. $x = y$.
$lg(x) = k+1$: Then $x = x_1 a_i$ for some x_1 and i. Suppose $\sigma(x) = \sigma(y)$. Then $y \neq \varepsilon$, i.e. $y = y_1 a_j$ for some y_1 and j. This implies $n\cdot\sigma(x_1) + i = \sigma(x) = \sigma(y) = n\cdot\sigma(y_1) + j$. By Property (*) we have $i = j$ and $\sigma(x_1) = \sigma(y_1)$, by the induction assumption, $x_1 = y_1$, therefore $x = y$.
We prove that σ is surjective: $\sigma(\varepsilon) = 0$, i.e. $0 \in \text{range}(\sigma)$. Let $m \in \mathbb{N}$, $m \ge 1$ and suppose $(\forall p < m)\ \ p \in \text{range}(\sigma)$. By Property (*) there are numbers q and r with $m = q\cdot n + r$ and $1 \le r \le n$. Since $q < m$, by the assumption we have $\sigma(x) = q$ for some $x \in W(\Sigma)$. Then $\sigma(xa_r) = n\sigma(x) + r = m$, hence $m \in \text{range}(\sigma)$. By complete induction, $\mathbb{N} = \text{range}(\sigma)$. Therefore σ and ν are bijective.
Q.E.D.

A numbering $\nu : \mathbb{N} \longrightarrow W(\Sigma)$ is neither a word function nor a number function, hence neither of our two definitions of computability is applicable to ν. Nevertheless standard numberings $\nu : \mathbb{N} \longrightarrow W(\Sigma)$ are intuitively effective. The following lemma expresses several effectivity properties of standard numberings of word sets.

4 LEMMA *(effectivity of standard numberings of word sets)*

Let Σ, Γ, and Δ be alphabets with $\Delta = \Sigma \cup \Gamma$. Let ν_Σ (ν_Γ) be a standard numbering of $W(\Sigma)$ ($W(\Gamma)$).

(1) Define $S, V : \mathbb{N} \longrightarrow \mathbb{N}$ by $S(x) := x+1$, $V(x) := x \dot{-} 1$.
Define $S_\Sigma, V_\Sigma : W(\Sigma) \longrightarrow W(\Sigma)$ by

$$S_\Sigma := \nu_\Sigma S \nu_\Sigma^{-1}, \quad V_\Sigma := \nu_\Sigma V \nu_\Sigma^{-1}.$$

Then S_Σ and V_Σ are computable.

(2) Let $b \in \Sigma$. Define $h^b : W(\Sigma) \longrightarrow W(\Sigma)$, $s^b : W(\Sigma) \longrightarrow \{1,2\}$ and $pop : W(\Sigma) \longrightarrow W(\Sigma)$ by $h^b(w) = wb$, $s^b(w) := (1$ if $w = xb$ for some $x \in W(\Sigma)$, 2 otherwise$)$, and $pop(\varepsilon) := \varepsilon$, $pop(wc) := w$. Define $h^b_\Sigma : \mathbb{N} \longrightarrow \mathbb{N}$, $s^b_\Sigma : \mathbb{N} \longrightarrow \{1,2\}$ and $pop_\Sigma : \mathbb{N} \longrightarrow \mathbb{N}$ by

$$h^b_\Sigma := \nu_\Sigma^{-1} h^b \nu_\Sigma, \quad pop_\Sigma := \nu_\Sigma^{-1} pop \nu_\Sigma, \quad s^b_\Sigma := s^b \nu_\Sigma.$$

Then h^b_Σ, pop_Σ, and s^b_Σ are computable.

(3) The following functions $p : W(\Delta) \longrightarrow W(\Delta)$ and $q : \mathbb{N} \longrightarrow \mathbb{N}$ are computable:

$$p(w) := (\nu_\Sigma \nu_\Gamma^{-1}(w) \text{ if } w \in W(\Gamma), \ \varepsilon \text{ otherwise}),$$
$$q(j) := (\nu_\Gamma^{-1} \nu_\Sigma(j) \text{ if } \nu_\Sigma(j) \in W(\Gamma), \ 0 \text{ otherwise}).$$

The transformation $T : f \longrightarrow \nu_\Sigma f \nu_\Sigma^{-1}$ for $f : \mathbb{N} \dashrightarrow \mathbb{N}$ is a bijection between the unary number functions and the unary word functions over $W(\Sigma)$. By Lemma 4(1) the transforms of the basic functions used in register machines are computable, by Lemma 4(2) the transforms of the basic functions used in stack machines are computable. Also the transform s^b_Σ of s^b is register computable. We shall use Lemma 4 to prove that T maps all the computable number functions bijectively onto the computable word functions. The function S_Σ (V_Σ) transforms any word into the word with the next number (predecessor number). In Example 1 we have $S_\Sigma(\varepsilon) = 1$, $S_\Sigma(1) = 2$, $S_\Sigma(2) = 11$, ... $V_\Sigma(1) = \varepsilon$, $V_\Sigma(2) = 1$, $V_\Sigma(11) = 2$, ...

Proof

Suppose ν_Σ is defined using the order function $a : \{1,\dots,n\} \longrightarrow \Sigma$.

(1) Define $g : W(\Sigma) \longrightarrow W(\Sigma)$ inductively by

$$g(\varepsilon) = a_1, \quad g(wa_i) = (wa_{i+1} \text{ if } i < n, \ g(w)a_1 \text{ if } i = n).$$

We show that g is computable by a tape machine over $(\Sigma \cup \{B\}, \Sigma, B)$. Define a unary tape machine M by the following flowchart.

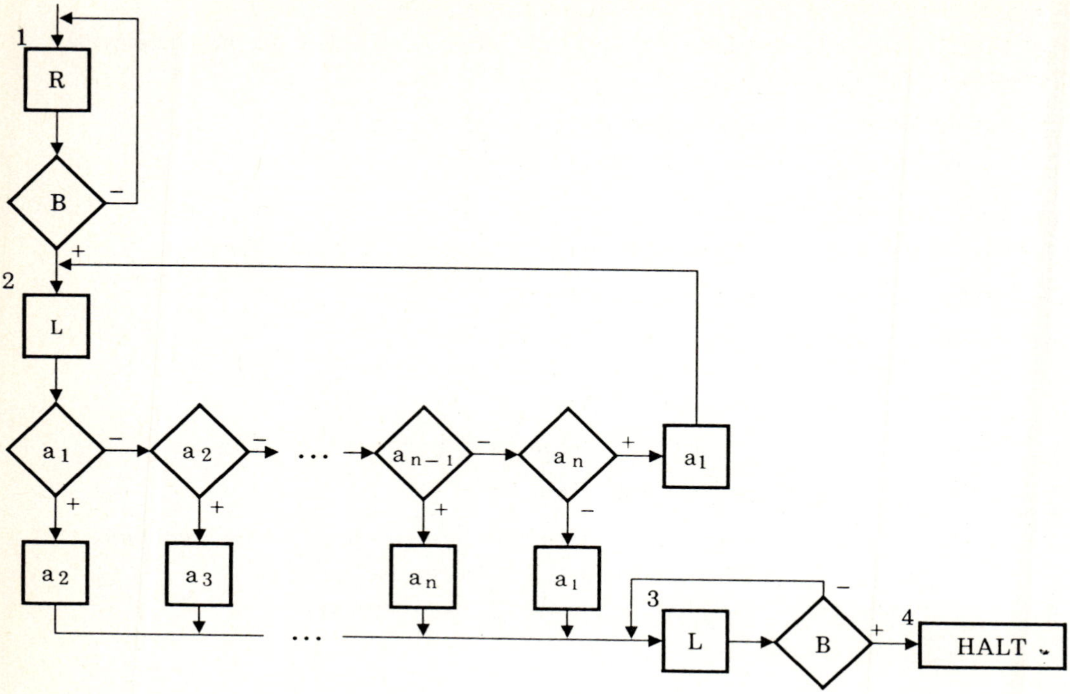

We shall prove $g = f_M$ and $g = S_\Sigma$. Let $\Gamma := \Sigma \cup \{B\}$.

Assertion: For all $w \in W(\Sigma)$:

$$(\forall a \in \Gamma)(\forall v \in W(\Gamma))\, TF\,(2,[w,a,v]) = (4,[\varepsilon,B,g(w)av])$$

Proof: (by induction on the length of w) If $w = \varepsilon$ the assertion is verified immediately. Consider the Case wa_i. If $1 \leq i < n$ the assertion is verified directly. Consider the case $i = n$. We obtain $SF^{n+2}(2,[wa_n,a,v]) = (2,[w,a_1,av])$ and by induction

$$\begin{aligned} TF(2,[wa_n,a,v]) &= TF(2,[w,a_1,av]) \\ &= (4,[\varepsilon,B,g(w)a_1\,av]) \\ &= (4,[\varepsilon,B,g(wa_n)\,av]). \end{aligned}$$

This proves the assertion.

We conclude $TF(1,[\varepsilon,B,w]) = TF(2,[w,B,\varepsilon]) = (4,[\varepsilon,B,g(w)])$, and $f_M(w) = OC \circ f_F \circ IC^{(1)}(w) = OC \circ f_F[\varepsilon,B,w] = OC \circ [\varepsilon,B,g(w)] = g(w)$ for all $w \in W(\Sigma)$, hence $g = f_M$. Finally we prove $(\forall w)\; g(w) = S_\Sigma(w)$ by induction on $lg(w)$. We have $S_\Sigma(\varepsilon) = \nu_\Sigma S \nu_\Sigma^{-1}(\varepsilon) = a_1$. Suppose $w = a_{i_k} \ldots a_{i_1} \in W(\Sigma)$ and $m := \nu_\Sigma^{-1}(w)$. For $1 \leq i < n$ we obtain $\nu_\Sigma S \nu_\Sigma^{-1}(wa_i) = \nu_\Sigma S(n \cdot m + i) = \nu_\Sigma(n \cdot m + (i+1)) = \nu_\Sigma(m)a_{i+1} = wa_{i+1} = g(wa_i)$. In the case $i = n$ we obtain $\nu_\Sigma S \nu_\Sigma^{-1}(wa_n) = \nu_\Sigma S(n\cdot m+n) = \nu_\Sigma(n\cdot(m+1)+1) = \nu_\Sigma(n\cdot S\nu_\Sigma^{-1}(w)+1) = \nu_\Sigma(n\cdot\nu_\Sigma^{-1}S_\Sigma(w)+1) = S_\Sigma(w)a_1 = g(w)a_1 = g(wa_n)$. Therefore, $S_\Sigma = g$, i.e. S_Σ is computable. Computability of V_Σ can be proved similarly (see the exercises).

(2) The functions $f_1, f_2 : \mathbb{N} \longrightarrow \mathbb{N}$ with $f_1(0) = f_2(0) = 0$ and

$$c = n \cdot f_1(c) + f_2(c) \quad \text{and} \quad 1 \le f_2(c) \le n \quad \text{for any} \quad c > 0$$

are computable. Then $h_\Sigma^{a_i}(m) = n\cdot m+i$, $pop_\Sigma = f_1$, and $s_\Sigma^{a_i}(m) = (1$ if $f_2(m) = i$, 2 otherwise) for all m, $1 \le i \le n$. Thus the h_Σ^b, pop, and s_Σ^b are computable.

(3) Define $S_\Sigma := \nu_\Sigma S \nu_\Sigma^{-1}$, $S_\Gamma := \nu_\Gamma S \nu_\Gamma^{-1}$ (see (1)).

Define a unary generalized stack machine over (Δ,Δ) by the following flowchart F.

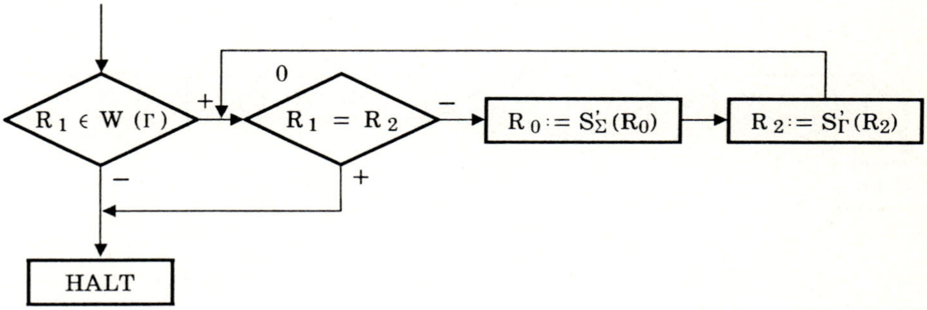

$S'_\Sigma, S'_\Gamma : W(\Delta) \longrightarrow W(\Delta)$ obtained from S_Σ and S_Γ according to Lemma 1.6.8(1) are computable by Lemma 4(1). By Theorem 1.6.6, f_M is computable. We shall prove $p = f_M$. The definition of S_Σ implies $S_\Sigma\nu_\Sigma(i) = \nu_\Sigma(i+1)$ and $S_\Gamma\nu_\Gamma(i) = \nu_\Gamma(i+1)$. Suppose $w \in W(\Gamma)$. Then the single step function SF of F satisfies

$$SF^{3i}(0,(\varepsilon,w,\varepsilon,\dots)) = (0,(\nu_\Sigma(i),w,\nu_\Gamma(i),\varepsilon,\dots))$$

for all $i \le \nu_\Gamma^{-1}(w)$ (proof by induction on i). The case $i = \nu_\Gamma^{-1}(w)$ yields $f_M(w) = \nu_\Sigma\nu_\Gamma^{-1}(w)$. If $w \notin W(\Gamma)$, then $f_M(w) = \varepsilon$. Thus we have proved $p = f_M$.

We shall prove now that q is computable. Let f_1, f_2 be defined as in the proof of (2). Suppose ν_Γ is defined via the order function $b : \{1,\dots,m\} \longrightarrow \Gamma$. The function $h : \mathbb{N} \longrightarrow \mathbb{N}$ defined by $h(j) := (b^{-1}a(j)$ if $a(j) \in \Gamma$, 0 otherwise) is computable. Define a unary register machine M by the following flowchart F.

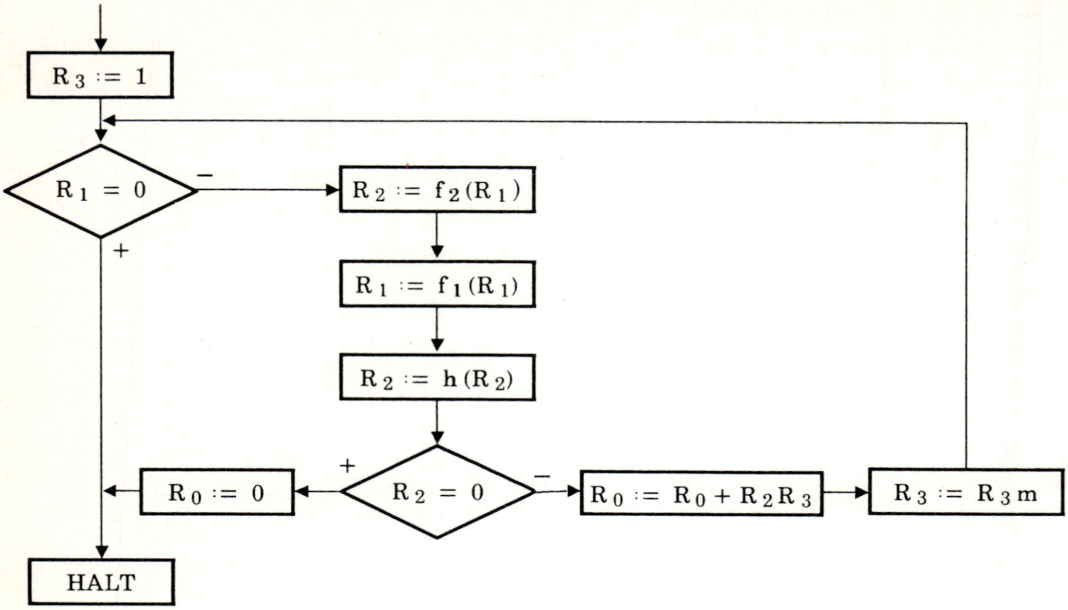

Then $q = f_M$ (proof as an exercise). Since all the functions used in F are computable, f_M is computable by Theorem 1.2.7.
Q.E.D.

After this preparation we can prove the main result of this chapter, namely that the computable word functions and the computable number functions coincide up to a transformation using a standard numbering of words.

5 THEOREM (*number computability* $\Longleftrightarrow$ *word computability*)

Let Σ be an alphabet, let ν be a standard numbering of $W(\Sigma)$. Let $k \in \mathbb{N}$, define $\vec{\nu} : \mathbb{N}^k \longrightarrow (W(\Sigma))^k$ by $\vec{\nu}(i_1,\dots,i_k) := (\nu(i_1),\dots,\nu(i_k))$

(1) Let $g : \mathbb{N}^k \dashrightarrow \mathbb{N}$ be computable. Then

$$\nu g \vec{\nu}^{-1} : (W(\Sigma))^k \dashrightarrow W(\Sigma)$$

is computed by a stack machine over (Σ,Σ).

(2) Let $f : (W(\Sigma))^k \dashrightarrow W(\Sigma)$ be computable. Then

$$\nu^{-1} f \vec{\nu} : \mathbb{N}^k \dashrightarrow \mathbb{N}$$

is computable.

Therefore, the mapping $g \longrightarrow \nu g \vec{\nu}^{-1}$ is a bijection from the k-ary computable number functions to the k-ary computable word functions.

Proof

(1) Let $M = (F, \mathbb{N}^k, \mathbb{N}, IC^{(k)}, OC)$ be a register machine with $g = f_M$. We define a machine $M' = (F', \mathbb{N}^k, \mathbb{N}, I'^{(k)}, O')$ similar to M (see Theorems 1.1.13, 1.1.17) which has a generalized stack machine flowchart F' over (Σ,Σ), where Register R_i of F is simulated by $\nu(R_i)$ in F'.
Let $D' := (W(\Sigma))^{\mathbb{N}}$, define $Sim \subseteq D \times D'$ by

$$d\,Sim\,d' \iff (\forall i \in \mathbb{N})\ d'(i) = \nu d(i).$$

This means $(i_o, i_1, \ldots)$ is simulated by $(\nu(i_o), \nu(i_1), \ldots)$.
Define $I'^{(k)}(i_1, \ldots, i_k) := (\varepsilon, \nu(i_1), \ldots, \nu(i_k), \ldots)$ and $O'(d') := \nu^{-1}d'(0)$. Then the input/output conditions of Theorem 1.1.17 are satisfied. Let F' be obtained from F by the following substitutions for any $i \in \mathbb{N}$:

"$R_i := R_i+1$" by "$R_i := S_\Sigma(R_i)$",

"$R_i := R_i-1$" by "$R_i := V_\Sigma(R_i)$",

"$R_i = 0$" by "$R_i = \varepsilon$",

where S_Σ and V_Σ are from Lemma 4(1). Then the conditions from Theorem 1.1.13 hold. This implies $f_M = f_{M'}$ by Theorem 1.1.17.
Define a stack machine $M_1 := (F', (W(\Sigma))^k, W(\Sigma), I^{(k)}, O)$. Then $I'^{(k)} = I^{(k)}\vec{\nu}$ and $O' = \nu^{-1}O$. This implies $\nu g \vec{\nu}^{-1} = \nu f_{M'} \vec{\nu}^{-1} = \nu \circ O' \circ f_{F'} \circ I'^{(k)} \vec{\nu}^{-1} = O \circ f_{F'} \circ I^{(k)} = f_{M_1}$.
By the proofs of Theorem 1.6.6 and Lemma 4, f_{M_1} is computable by a stack machine over (Σ,Σ). Therefore $\nu g \vec{\nu}^{-1}$ is computable.

(2) Let $M = (F, (W(\Sigma))^k, W(\Sigma), IC^{(k)}, OC)$ be a stack machine over (Γ,Σ) with $f_M = f$. Let ν_Γ be a standard numbering of $W(\Gamma)$. Using ν_Γ we shall now encode stacks by numbers. Let $D = (W(\Gamma))^{\mathbb{N}}$ be the dataset of M, let $D' = \mathbb{N}^{\mathbb{N}}$ be the dataset of the register machines. Define $Sim \subseteq D \times D'$ by

$$d\,Sim\,d' :\iff (\forall i \in \mathbb{N})\ d(i) = \nu_\Gamma d'(i).$$

Let $M' := (F', (W(\Sigma))^k, W(\Sigma), I'^{(k)}, O')$ be a machine with the flowchart of a generalized register machine defined as follows: $I'^{(k)}(w_1, \ldots, w_k) := (0, \nu_\Gamma^{-1} w_1, \ldots, \nu_\Gamma^{-1} w_k, 0, \ldots)$ $O'(d') = (\nu_\Gamma d'(0)$ if $\nu_\Gamma d'(0) \in W(\Sigma)$, ε otherwise$)$. Let F' be obtained from F by the substitutions for any $i \in \mathbb{N}$ and $c \in \Gamma$:

"$R_i := R_i c$" by "$R_i := h_\Gamma^c(R_i)$"

"$R_i := pop(R_i)$" by "$R_i := pop_\Gamma(R_i)$"

"R_i top c" by "$s_\Gamma^c(R_i)$"

where the number functions and tests h_Γ^c, pop_Γ, and s_Γ^c are from Lemma 4(2). Then F and F' are similar w.r.t. Sim and $f_M = f_{M'}$ by Theorem 1.1.17. Define a generalized register machine $M_1 := (F', \mathbb{N}^k, \mathbb{N}, I^{(k)}, 0)$. Then by Lemma 4(b) and Theorem 1.2.7, f_{M_1} is computable.

Let $q_1(j) := (\nu^{-1}\nu_\Gamma(j)$ if $\nu_\Gamma(j) \in W(\Sigma)$, 0 otherwise$)$, $q_2 := \nu_\Gamma^{-1}\nu$ (notice $\Sigma \subseteq \Gamma$). By Lemma 4(c), q_1 and q_2 are computable. From the definition we obtain $\nu^{-1}O'(d') = q_1O(d')$ and $I'^{(k)}\vec{\nu}(i_1,\dots,i_k) = I^{(k)}(q_2(i_1),\dots,q_2(i_k))$. Therefore,

$\nu^{-1}f\vec{\nu}(i_1,\dots,i_k) = \nu^{-1}O'f_{F'}I'^{(k)}\vec{\nu}(i_1,\dots,i_k) = q_1 O f_{F'} I^{(k)}(q_2(i_1),\dots,q_2(i_k)) =$
$= q_1 f_{M_1}(q_2(i_1),\dots,q_2(i_k))$. Since q_1, q_2, and f_{M_1} are computable, also $\nu^{-1}f\vec{\nu}$ is computable.

Q.E.D.

We discuss Theorem 5 for the case k=1. To prove that a word function $f : W(\Sigma) \dashrightarrow W(\Sigma)$ is computable it is sufficient to show that the transform $g : \mathbb{N} \dashrightarrow \mathbb{N}$ of f defined by $g = \nu^{-1}f\nu$ is computable. The equation $g = \nu^{-1}f\nu$ can be transformed to $\nu g = f\nu$. This means, if i is the number of a word w (i.e. $w = \nu(i)$) then g(i) is the number of f(w) (i.e. $\nu g(i) = f(w)$), thus g maps the number of a word w into the number of its image f(w).

The following diagram illustrates this.

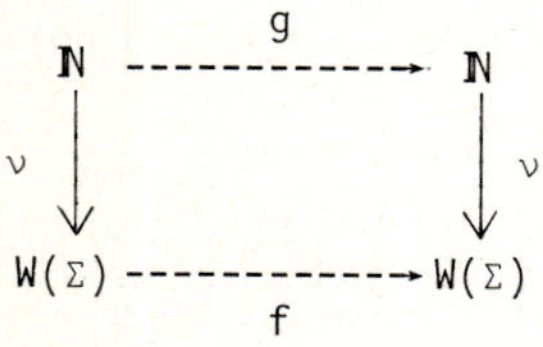

On the other hand, ν also defines a notation $\sigma := \nu^{-1} : W(\Sigma) \longrightarrow \mathbb{N}$ of the natural numbers by words ("modified" n-ary notation). For proving that a number function $g : \mathbb{N} \dashrightarrow \mathbb{N}$ is computable it suffices to show that its transform $f : W(\Sigma) \dashrightarrow W(\Sigma)$ defined by $f = \nu g \nu^{-1}$ is computable. The equation $f = \nu g \nu^{-1}$ can be transformed into $\sigma f = g\sigma$. This means if w is the name of a number i (i.e. $\sigma(w) = i$), then f(w) is the name of g(i) (i.e. $\sigma f(w) = g(i)$), thus f maps the name of a number i on to the name of its image g(i).

The following diagram illustrates this.

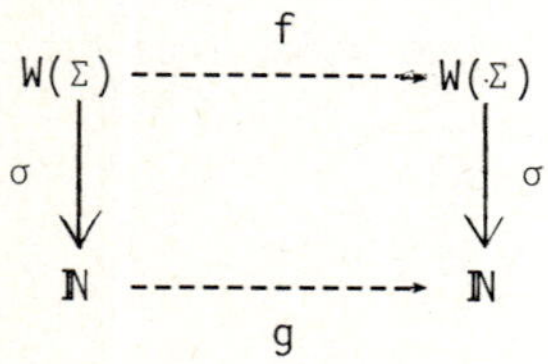

Later we shall study computability w.r.t. a numbering $\nu : \mathbb{N} \dashrightarrow S$ and computability w.r.t. a notation $\sigma : W(\Sigma) \dashrightarrow S$ in more detail.

Theorem 5 can be interpreted as a further definition of the computable word functions. There are several other definitions of the computable number functions and of the computable word functions all of which are equivalent to the definitions given here. Each of the definitions yields functions which are intuitively computable. On the other hand no function $f : \mathbb{N}^k \dashrightarrow \mathbb{N}$ has ever been found which is intuitively computable but not (register) computable. In 1935 A. Church formulated the thesis that the computable number functions are exactly those number functions which are intuitively computable.

CHURCH'S THESIS

The register computable functions are exactly the number functions which are intuitively computable.

Church's Thesis marks the border line between computability and noncomputability. It is not a theorem since the concept "intuitively computable" is not precisely defined. There is no doubt that every (register) computable function is intuitively computable. But although no number function which is intuitively computable but not register computable has been found, it is still possible that Church's Thesis does not hold. Church's Thesis does not influence the theory of computability developed in this book, it is only used for interpreting the results. Suppose some function $f : \mathbb{N} \dashrightarrow \mathbb{N}$ is not (register) computable. Then by Church's Thesis we may say that there is no algorithmic method, no algorithm, for computing f.

A corresponding thesis can be formulated for word functions: the (stack) computable functions are exactly the intuitively computable word functions. It cannot be derived from Church's Thesis, but by Theorem 5 the two theses are not independent.

6 DEFINITION

(1) For any k $\mathbb{N}$ define:

$$P^{(k)} := \{f : \mathbb{N}^k \dashrightarrow \mathbb{N} \mid f \text{ computable}\} ,$$

$$R^{(k)} := \{f : \mathbb{N}^k \longrightarrow \mathbb{N} \mid f \text{ computable}\} .$$

(2) $P^{(\infty)} := \bigcup_{k \in \mathbb{N}} P^{(k)}$ is called the class of *computable number functions* or *partial recursive functions*.

$R^{(\infty)} := \bigcup_{k \in \mathbb{N}} R^{(k)}$ is called the class of *total computable number functions* or *total recursive functions*.

Remark

Any total recursive function is partial recursive since $R^{(\infty)} \subseteq P^{(\infty)}$. Some authors say *general recursive* instead of *total recursive*, some say *recursive* instead of *total recursive*, and others say *recursive* instead of *partial recursive*. We shall use the terms with meanings as in Definition 6.

As we have shown Cantor's tupling function $\pi^{(k)}$ maps the unary partial recursive functions on to the k-ary partial recursive functions (Lemma 1.2.16), more precisely we have $P^{(k)} = P^{(1)}\pi^{(k)}$ and $R^{(k)} = R^{(1)}\pi^{(k)}$. As already mentioned we shall usually consider unary functions. Instead of defining $g : \mathbb{N}^k \dashrightarrow \mathbb{N}$ by $g(x_1,\dots,x_k) := \dots$ we define $f : \mathbb{N} \dashrightarrow \mathbb{N}$ by $f\pi^{(k)}(x_1,\dots,x_k) := \dots$ or $f\langle x_1,\dots,x_k\rangle := \dots$ where $f = g(\pi^{(k)})^{-1}$.

It is useful to generalize the concept of computability for word functions slightly.

7 DEFINITION (*computable word functions*)

Let $k \in \mathbb{N}$, let $\Sigma_o,\Sigma_1,\dots,\Sigma_k$ be alphabets, let $f : W(\Sigma_1) \times \dots \times W(\Sigma_k) \dashrightarrow W(\Sigma_o)$, let $\Delta := \Sigma_o \cup \Sigma_1 \cup \dots \cup \Sigma_k$.

(1) The function f is called *computable* iff there is some computable $g : (W(\Delta))^k \dashrightarrow W(\Delta)$ with $g(x) = f(x)$ for all $x \in W(\Sigma_1) \times \dots \times W(\Sigma_k)$.

(2) The function f is *total computable* iff it is computable and $\mathrm{dom}(f) = W(\Sigma_1) \times \dots \times W(\Sigma_k)$.

It is easy to show that the function g in Definition 7(1) can be normed such that $g(x) = \mathrm{div}$ if $x \notin W(\Sigma_1) \times \dots \times W(\Sigma_k)$ or such that $g(x) = \varepsilon$ if $x \notin W(\Sigma_1) \times \dots \times W(\Sigma_k)$.

So far we have only considered computable functions. The question arises whether there are noncomputable functions at all.

8 THEOREM

There is a function $f : \mathbb{N} \dashrightarrow \mathbb{N}$ which is not computable.

Proof

First we show that there is a surjective function $\psi : \mathbb{N} \longrightarrow P^{(1)}$. (This means the set $P^{(1)}$ of (unary) partial recursive functions is denumerable.) For any $n \in \mathbb{N}$ let

G_n be the set of those unary register machines the flowcharts of which satisfy:

(1) $q \in \mathbb{N}$ and $q \leq n$ for any state q of F,

(2) $i \leq n$ for any register R_i used in F.

Then G_n is finite for any n. Listing the elements of $G_o, G_1, G_2, \ldots$ we obtain a surjective function $\eta : \mathbb{N} \longrightarrow G_\infty$, where $G_\infty = \bigcup_{n \in \mathbb{N}} G_n$. Define ψ by $\psi(i) := f_{\eta(i)}$ (= the function computed by the i-th register machine). Then for any $g \in P^{(1)}$ there are some n and some $M \in G_n$ with $g = f_M$, and since $M = \eta(i)$ for some i, $g \in \text{range}(\psi)$. Therefore ψ is surjective, since also $\psi(i) \in P^{(1)}$ for any i.

Now, we use the numbering ψ of $P^{(1)}$ to define a function $f : \mathbb{N} \dashrightarrow \mathbb{N}$ which is not an element of $P^{(1)}$ i.e. not computable. The following diagram shows the function table for the values $\psi(i)(k)$ for $i \in \mathbb{N}$ and $k \in \mathbb{N}$. (Since we have not fully specified ψ we do not know any value actually; any dot indicates a natural number or "div".)

	0	1	2	3	4	5	→ k
$\psi(0)$	•	•	∘	∘	∘	•	
$\psi(1)$	•	•	•	∘	∘	∘	
$\psi(2)$	∘	∘	•	•	•	∘	
$\psi(3)$	•	•	∘	•	•	∘	
$\psi(4)$	•	•	•	•	•	•	
$\psi(5)$	∘	∘	∘	∘	∘	•	
⋮						etc.	

Line 0 contains the values $\psi(0)(0)$, $\psi(0)(1), \ldots$, Line 1 contains the values $\psi(1)(0)$, $\psi(1)(1), \ldots$ etc. Now, let $f : \mathbb{N} \dashrightarrow \mathbb{N}$ be a function which differs from $\psi(0)$ at argument 0, from $\psi(1)$ at argument 1, etc. Such a function exists. Then $f \neq \psi(0)$ since $f(0) \neq \psi(0)(0)$, $f \neq \psi(1)$ since $f(1) \neq \psi(1)(1)$, etc. This means, f differs from any function $\psi(i)$, $i \in \mathbb{N}$, and since $\psi : \mathbb{N} \longrightarrow P^{(1)}$ numbers all the computable functions, f cannot be computable.

More formally, define $f : \mathbb{N} \dashrightarrow \mathbb{N}$ by

$$f(x) := \begin{cases} \text{div} & \text{if } \psi(x)(x) \text{ exists} \\ 0 & \text{otherwise}. \end{cases}$$

Suppose f is computable. Then $f = \psi(i)$ for some i. But each of the assumptions "f(i) exists" and "f(i) does not exist" yields a contradiction:

$$f(i) \text{ exists} \implies \psi(i)(i) \text{ exists} \implies f(i) = \text{div},$$
$$f(i) = \text{div} \implies \psi(i)(i) = \text{div} \implies f(i) = 0.$$

Therefore, the assumption that f is computable is false.

Q.E.D.

From the view of set theory we have proved in detail that the set $P^{(1)}$ is denumerable and that there is some $f : \mathbb{N} \dashrightarrow \mathbb{N}$ which is not an element of $P^{(1)}$. Later we shall define an "effective" numbering φ of $P^{(1)}$ and repeat the proof in various versions. The method used in the second part of the proof is called *diagonal method* or *diagonalization*. The function f is defined in such a way that for any argument i it differs from the diagonal value $\psi(i)(i)$ of the sequence $\psi(0), \psi(1), \ldots$ of functions. Notice that any other path $\psi(i)(k_i)$ where $i \neq j \Longrightarrow k_i \neq k_j$ would serve the same purpose as the diagonal where $k_i = i$. Diagonal proofs have been used by G. Cantor in set theory. Diagonalization is one of the important proof methods in recursion theory.

It is easy to define a non computable function $f : \mathbb{N}^k \dashrightarrow \mathbb{N}$, a non computable function $f : \mathbb{N}^k \longrightarrow \mathbb{N}$ (i.e. f total), and a non computable function $f : (W(\Sigma))^k \longrightarrow W(\Sigma)$ for any Σ, where $k \geq 1$ (see the exercises). Theorem 8 can easily be proved by a set theoretic cardinality argument: The set $\mathbb{P}^{(1)} = \{f : \mathbb{N} \dashrightarrow \mathbb{N}\}$ is not denumerable, the set $P^{(1)}$ is denumerable, therefore, most of the functions in $\mathbb{P}^{(1)}$ are not computable. The proof that $\mathbb{P}^{(1)}$ is not denumerable, however, uses a diagonal argument (see the exercises).

EXERCISES

1) Let Σ be an alphabet, $\Sigma = \{a_1, \ldots, a_n\}$.

   For numberings ν of $W(\Sigma)$ define the following effectivity property $P(\nu)$:

   The functions $f : \mathbb{N} \longrightarrow \mathbb{N}$ and $g : \mathbb{N}^2 \longrightarrow \mathbb{N}$ defined by $f(i) := lg(\nu(i))$, $g(i,m) :=$ (0 if $\nu(i)$ has no m-th symbol, k where a_k is the m-th symbol of $\nu(i)$ otherwise) are computable.

   Let ν be any numbering and let ν_Σ be the standard numbering w.r.t. (a_i) of $W(\Sigma)$. Then:

   $$P(\nu) \iff \nu \equiv \nu_\Sigma$$

   ($\nu \equiv \nu_\Sigma$ if $\nu = \nu_\Sigma h_1$ and $\nu_\Sigma = \nu h_2$ for some computable functions $h_1, h_2 : \mathbb{N} \longrightarrow \mathbb{N}$)

2) Let ν_Σ be a standard numbering of $W(\Sigma)$. Show that $V_\Sigma = \nu_\Sigma V \nu_\Sigma^{-1}$ (c f. Lemma 4(1)) is computable

   (a) by a proof similar to that for S_Σ,

   (b) by using computability of S_Σ.

3) Consider the register machine M which is defined by the third flowchart in the proof of Lemma 4. Prove $q = f_M$.

4) Consider the proof of Lemma 4(2). Verify the equations $h_\Sigma^{a_i}(m) = n \cdot m + i$, $pop_\Sigma = f_1$, and $s_\Sigma^{a_i}(m) = (1 \text{ if } f_2(m) = i, 2 \text{ otherwise})$.

5) Let Σ, Γ, and Δ be alphabets with $\Sigma \cup \Gamma \subseteq \Delta$, let ν_Σ (ν_Γ) be a standard numbering of $W(\Sigma)$ ($W(\Gamma)$).

   (a) Let $f: W(\Delta) \dashrightarrow W(\Delta)$ be computable. Show that $\nu_\Sigma^{-1} f \nu_\Gamma$ is computable.

   (b) Let $g: \mathbb{N} \dashrightarrow \mathbb{N}$ be computable. Show that $h: W(\Delta) \dashrightarrow W(\Delta)$ defined by

$$h(w) = \begin{cases} \nu_\Gamma g \nu_\Sigma^{-1}(w) & \text{if } w \in W(\Sigma) \\ \varepsilon & \text{otherwise} \end{cases}$$

   is computable.

6) Let $f: W(\Sigma_1) \times \ldots \times W(\Sigma_n) \dashrightarrow W(\Sigma_o)$ be computable. Show that the function $g: (W(\Delta))^k \dashrightarrow W(\Delta)$, where $\Delta = \Sigma_o \cup \Sigma_1 \cup \ldots \cup \Sigma_n$, defined by

$$g(\tilde{x}) = \begin{cases} f(\tilde{x}) & \text{if } \tilde{x} \in W(\Sigma_1) \times \ldots \times W(\Sigma_n) \\ \varepsilon & \text{otherwise,} \end{cases}$$

   is computable.

7) Show that for any stack machine M over (Γ, Σ) there is some stack machine M' over (Σ, Σ) such that $f_M = f_{M'}$.

8) Let Σ be an alphabet, let $k \geq 1$. Define a noncomputable function g where

   (a) $g : \mathbb{N} \longrightarrow \mathbb{N}$

   (b) $g : \mathbb{N}^k \longrightarrow \mathbb{N}$

   (c) $g : W(\Sigma) \longrightarrow W(\Sigma)$

   (d) $g : (W(\Sigma))^k \longrightarrow W(\Sigma)$

   (e) $g : \mathbb{N} \longrightarrow \mathbb{N}$ and $\text{range}(g) \subseteq \{0,1\}$

9) Let $2^{\mathbb{N}} = \{A \subseteq \mathbb{N}\}$, $\mathbb{F} := \{f : \mathbb{N} \longrightarrow \mathbb{N}\}$, $\mathbb{P} := \{f : \mathbb{N} \dashrightarrow \mathbb{N}\}$, $Z = \{f : \mathbb{N} \dashrightarrow \mathbb{N} \mid \text{range}(f) \subseteq \{0\}\}$, $\mathbb{R} :=$ the set of real numbers. Prove that these sets have the same cardinality. Show that none of these sets can be numbered.

BIBLIOGRAPHICAL NOTES

Alonzo Church was the first one who proposed that the λ-definable functions (which are equivalent to our total register computable functions) are all the effectively calculable (total) functions. Kleene (1952) called this proposition "Church's thesis". Rogers (1967) usually refers to Church's thesis, when he states that a function defined by an informal algorithm is computable. But although Church's thesis cannot be proved, an informal algorithm usually can be refined into a Turing machine together with a correctness proof. Therefore, reference to Church's thesis is not adequate in this case. During the 1930's and since then several formal characterizations of the computable functions have been proposed all of which were shown to be equivalent (e.g. Church (1936), Post (1936), Kleene (1936), Turing (1936), Markov (1951), Shepherdson and Sturgis (1963)).

1.8 Recursive and Recursively Enumerable Sets

In the previous chapters we have studied computable functions $f: \mathbb{N}^k \dashrightarrow \mathbb{N}$ and $f: (W(\Sigma))^k \dashrightarrow W(\Sigma)$. The concept of computability is now used to define *recursiveness* and *recursive enumerability* of subsets $A \subseteq \mathbb{N}^k$ and $B \subseteq (W(\Sigma))^k$.

1 DEFINITION

Let $k \in \mathbb{N}$, $A \subseteq \mathbb{N}^k$.

(1) A is *recursive* iff $A = f^{-1}\{0\}$ for some total recursive function $f: \mathbb{N}^k \longrightarrow \mathbb{N}$ (i.e. $f \in R^{(k)}$).

(2) A is *recursively enumerable* iff $A = \mathrm{dom}(f)$ for some partial recursive function $f: \mathbb{N}^k \dashrightarrow \mathbb{N}$ (i.e. $f \in P^{(k)}$).

Notations: *decidable* instead of *recursive*, *partially decidable* or *provable* or *r.e.* instead of *recursively enumerable*.

The set A is recursive iff there is a register machine M which halts for any input $\bar{x} \in \mathbb{N}^k$ yielding $f_M(\bar{x}) = 0$ if $\bar{x} \in A$ and $f_M(\bar{x}) \neq 0$ if $\bar{x} \notin A$. This means that the machine M (or the function f_M) is an effective procedure for deciding for any $\bar{x} \in \mathbb{N}^k$ the question "$\bar{x} \in A$?" definitely. With input $\bar{x}$ after a finite number of steps the machine M halts and gives the answer.

The set A is r.e. (recursively enumerable) iff there is a register machine M which halts on input $\bar{x} \in \mathbb{N}^k$ iff $\bar{x} \in A$. With input $\bar{x}$ the machine M gives a positive answer (by halting after a finite number of steps) if $\bar{x} \in A$, but it gives no answer if $\bar{x} \notin A$ since it computes forever without halting. If A is decidable then there is an effective procedure which answers any question "$\bar{x} \in A$?" correctly, if A is r.e. then there is an effective procedure which gives the answer yes if $\bar{x} \in A$ and gives no answer otherwise.

2 EXAMPLES

(1) The set $\emptyset$ is recursive: define $f \in R^{(1)}$ by $(\forall x)\ f(x) = 1$. Then $\emptyset = f^{-1}\{0\}$.

(2) The set $\emptyset$ is r.e.: define $f \in P^{(1)}$ by $(\forall x)\ f(x) = \mathrm{div}$ (remember $f(x) = \mathrm{div} :\Longleftrightarrow x \notin \mathrm{dom}(f)$). Then $\emptyset = \mathrm{dom}(f)$.

(3) $\{x \in \mathbb{N} \mid x \text{ even}\}$ is recursive: it is easy to define a register machine M with $f_M \in R^{(1)}$ and $f_M(x) = 0 \Longleftrightarrow x$ is even.

(4) The equality relation $\{(x,y) \mid x = y\} \subseteq \mathbb{N}^2$ is recursive: it is easy to define a register machine M with $f_M(x,y) = 0$ if $x = y$, $f_M(x,y) = 1$ otherwise.

(5) $\{x \in \mathbb{N} \mid x \text{ is prime}\}$ is recursive and r.e.: Using the rest function which is computable by Lemma 1.2.9 we can easily define a generalized register machine M which only uses computable functions such that $f_M \in R^{(1)}$ and $f_M(x) = 0 \iff x$ is prime. If in M the statement q : HALT is substituted by

q : $R_o = 0, r, q$;
r : HALT .

we obtain a machine M' with $x \in \text{dom } f_{M'} \iff x$ is prime.

We shall prove later that any recursive set is recursively enumerable (see Example 2(5)) but that there are recursively enumerable sets which are not recursive. First we show that there are sets $A \subseteq \mathbb{N}$ which are not recursive and sets which are not r.e.

3 THEOREM

(1) There is a set $A \subseteq \mathbb{N}$ which is not recursive.

(2) There is a set $A_1 \subseteq \mathbb{N}$ which is not r.e.

The theorem can be proved by a simple cardinality argument. Since $P^{(1)}$ and $R^{(1)}$ are denumerable, also the set of recursive sets and the set of r.e. sets are denumerable. The set $2^{\mathbb{N}}$ of subsets of $\mathbb{N}$, however, is nondenumerable. Therefore, most of the subsets of $\mathbb{N}$ are not recursive and not r.e. We shall prove the theorem directly by diagonalizations.

Proof

As we have shown in the proof of Theorem 1.7.8 there is a surjective function $\psi : \mathbb{N} \longrightarrow P^{(1)}$.

(1) By diagonalization we define a set which differs from any recursive set. Let $A := \{x \mid \psi(x)(x) \neq 0\}$. Let $B \subseteq \mathbb{N}$ be any recursive set. Then $B = (\psi(i))^{-1}\{0\}$ for some $i \in \mathbb{N}$ with $\psi(i) \in R^{(1)}$. We show $A \neq B$: $i \in A \Rightarrow \psi(i)(i) \neq 0 \Rightarrow i \notin B$, $i \notin A \Rightarrow \psi(i)(i) = 0 \Rightarrow i \in B$, this means A and B differ at place i. Therefore A is not recursive.

(2) Let $A_1 := \{x \mid \psi(x)(x) = \text{div}\}$. Then A_1 diagonalizes over all r.e. sets: Suppose B is r.e. Then $B = \text{dom}\,\psi(i)$ for some $i \in \mathbb{N}$. We show that A_1 and B differ at place i.

$i \in A_1 \Rightarrow \psi(i)(i) = \text{div} \Rightarrow i \notin B$, $i \notin A_1 \Rightarrow \psi(i)(i)$ exists $\Rightarrow i \in B$. Therefore $A_1 \neq B$, and A_1 differs from any r.e. B, i.e. A_1 is not r.e.
Q.E.D.

A set A is r.e. iff $A = \text{dom}(f_M)$ for some register machine M. By the definition of f_M, x is in the domain of f_M, iff for some time t the machine M with input x operates t steps and halts. While it is not possible in general (as we shall prove) to decide whether $x \in \text{dom}(f_M)$, we can (intuitively) decide whether a given machine M with input x halts in at most t steps. To decide this, at most t steps of the computation have to be performed which can be done with pencil and paper in a finite amount of time. The proof of the following fundamental theorem is based on this simple idea.

4 THEOREM (*projection theorem*)

Let $k \in \mathbb{N}$, let $A \subseteq \mathbb{N}^k$. Then A is r.e. iff there is some recursive set $B \subseteq \mathbb{N}^{k+1}$ with

$$A = \{(x_1,\dots,x_k) \mid (\exists t)\ (x_1,\dots,x_k,t) \in B\}$$

(i.e. A is the projection of B to the first k components).

Proof

"$\Rightarrow$" : Let $M = (F, \mathbb{N}^k, \mathbb{N}, IC^{(k)}, OC)$ be a register machine with $A = \text{dom}\, f_M$. We construct a generalized register machine M' which with input $(x_1,\dots,x_k,t)$ performs the operations which M performs with input $(x_1,\dots,x_k)$ and for any step of M subtracts 1 of an additional counter with initial value t. The computation halts if the simulation of M reaches a HALT statement or if the counter is empty.

From the flowchart F we define the flowchart F' of M' as follows. Let $m \in \mathbb{N}$ be a number such that no register R_n with $m \leq n$ is used in F.

(1) If q_o is the initial state of F, let q_o' (a new state) be the initial state of F' and add the statements

$$q_o' : \ R_m := R_{k+1} , r_1 ;$$

$$r_1 : \ R_{k+1} := 0 , q_o ;$$

where r_1 is a new state.

(2) If q_e is the final state of F (we may assume that F has exactly one final state) then let q_e' (a new state) be the final state of F' and add the statements

q_e : $R_o := 0$, q'_e ;

q'_e : HALT .

(3) Replace any function statement in F

q : h , r ;

by the statements

q : $R_m = 0$, r_1 , r_2 ;

r_1 : $R_o := 1$, q'_e ;

r_2 : $R_m := R_m - 1$, r_3 ;

r_3 : h , r ;

where r_1, r_2, r_3 are new states.

(4) Replace any test statement in F

q : $R_j = 0$, r , s ;

by the statements

q : $R_m = 0$, r_1 , r_2 ;

r_1 : $R_o := 1$, q'_e ;

r_2 : $R_m := R_m - 1$, r_3 ;

r_3 : $R_j = 0$, r , s ;

where r_1, r_2, r_3 again are new states.

We prove now that $B := f_{M'}^{-1}\{0\}$ has the desired properties. $f_{M'}$ is computable since F' uses only computable functions.

<u>Assertion:</u> For any $x_1,\dots,x_k,t,i,b_o,\dots,b_{m-1} \in \mathbb{N}$ with $i \le t$ the following holds: if

$$SF^i(q_o,(0,x_1,\dots,x_k,0,\dots)) = (q,(b_o,b_1,\dots,b_{m-1},0,\dots))$$

then

$$(SF')^{3i+2}(q'_o,(0,x_1,\dots,x_k,t,0,\dots)) = (q,(b_o,\dots,b_{m-1},t-i,0,\dots)) .$$

<u>Proof:</u> (by easy induction on i, not executed here)

Suppose $x_1,\dots,x_k \in \mathbb{N}$. Then

$(x_1,\dots,x_k) \in \mathrm{dom}(f_M) = A$

$\Longrightarrow (\exists t)\ SF^t(q_o,(0,x_1,\dots,x_k,0,\dots)) = (q_e,(\dots))$

$\Longrightarrow (\exists t)\ (SF')^{3t+3}(q'_o,(0,x_1,\dots,x_k,t,0,\dots)) = (q'_e,(0,\dots))$
(by the above assertion)

$\Longrightarrow (\exists t)\ f_{M'}(x_1,\dots,x_k,t) = 0$

and

$(x_1,\ldots,x_k) \notin \mathrm{dom}(f_M) = A$

$\Longrightarrow (\forall t)\ SF^t(q_o,(0,x_1,\ldots,x_k,0,\ldots)) = (q,(\ldots))$ with $q \neq q_e$

$\Longrightarrow (\forall t)\ (SF')^{3t+4}(q_o',(0,x_1,\ldots,x_k,t,0,\ldots)) = (q_e',(1,\ldots))$
(by the above assertion)

$\Longrightarrow (\forall t)\ f_{M'}(x_1,\ldots,x_k,t) = 1$.

Therefore, the set $B := f_{M'}^{-1}\{0\}$ has the desired property.

"$\Longleftarrow$": Suppose $B \subseteq \mathbb{N}^{k+1}$ is recursive. Then $B = f^{-1}\{0\}$ for some $f \in R^{(k+1)}$. Define $g := \tilde{\mu}(f)$. Then $g \in P^{(k)}$ by Theorem 1.2.12. Since f is a total function,

$$\mathrm{dom}(g) = \{(x_1,\ldots,x_k) \subseteq \mathbb{N}^k \mid (\exists t)\ f(x_1,\ldots,x_k,t) = 0\} = A ,$$

hence A is recursively enumerable.
Q.E.D.

By the projection theorem any r.e. set is the projection of a recursive set. The next theorem gives another fundamental relation between r.e. and recursive sets.

5 <u>THEOREM</u> (*relation recursive $\leftrightarrow$ r.e.*)

Let $k \in \mathbb{N}$, $A \subseteq \mathbb{N}^k$. Then

A recursive $\Longleftrightarrow$ (A r.e. and $\mathbb{N}^k \setminus A$ r.e.)

<u>Proof</u>

"$\Longrightarrow$": Suppose A is recursive. Then $A = f^{-1}\{0\}$ for some $f \in R^{(k)}$. Define $g_1, g_2 : \mathbb{N}^k \dashrightarrow \mathbb{N}$ by

$g_1(\overline{x}) = (0$ if $f(\overline{x}) = 0$, div otherwise) ,

$g_2(\overline{x}) = (0$ if $f(\overline{x}) \neq 0$, div otherwise)

for all $\overline{x} \in \mathbb{N}^k$. Then g_1 and g_2 are computable and $A = \mathrm{dom}(g_1)$, $\mathbb{N} \setminus A = \mathrm{dom}(g_2)$, hence A and $\mathbb{N}^k \setminus A$ are r.e.

"$\Longleftarrow$": Let us write $(\overline{x})$ for $(x_1,\ldots,x_k)$ and $(\overline{x},t)$ for $(x_1,\ldots,x_k,t)$. Suppose A and $\mathbb{N}^k \setminus A$ are r.e. One way to prove the statement is to take two register machines M_1 and M_2 with $\mathrm{dom}(f_{M_1}) = A$ and $\mathrm{dom}(f_{M_2}) = \mathbb{N}^k \setminus A$ and run these two machines in parallel by a "product machine" M. For any input $\overline{x}$ either the computation of M_1 or the computation of M_2 halts, and $\overline{x} \in A$ iff the first case occurs. We shall use the projection theorem for the proof. By Theorem 4 there are $f_1, f_2 \in R^{(k+1)}$ with

$A = \{(\bar{x}) \mid (\exists t)\ f_1(\bar{x},t) = 0\}$,

$\mathbb{N}^k \setminus A = \{(\bar{x}) \mid (\exists t)\ f_2(\bar{x},t) = 0\}$.

Define $f \in R^{(k+1)}$ by $f(\bar{x},t) := f_1(\bar{x},t) \cdot f_2(\bar{x},t)$ and $h := \tilde{\mu}(f)$. Let $(\bar{x}) \in \mathbb{N}^k$. Since $(\bar{x}) \in A$ or $(\bar{x}) \in \mathbb{N}^k \setminus A$, $i := h(\bar{x})$ exists and $f(\bar{x},i) = 0$. If $(\bar{x}) \in A$ then $(\forall t)\ f_2(\bar{x},t) \neq 0$, hence $f_1(\bar{x},i) = 0$. If $(\bar{x}) \notin A$ then $(\forall t)\ f_1(\bar{x},t) \neq 0$, hence $f_2(\bar{x},i) = 0$. Therefore, $(\bar{x}) \in A \Longleftrightarrow f_1(\bar{x},\tilde{\mu}(f)(\bar{x})) = 0$. Define $g \in R^{(1)}$ by $g(\bar{x}) := f_1(\bar{x},\tilde{\mu}(f)(\bar{x}))$. Then $g^{-1}\{0\} = A$, i.e. A is recursive.
Q.E.D.

As a simple corollary we obtain that $\mathbb{N}^k \setminus A$ is recursive if A is recursive. By Lemma 1.2.16 it is sufficient to consider only unary computable functions. By the following lemma it is sufficient in computability theory to consider only recursive and r.e. subsets of $\mathbb{N}$.

6 LEMMA

Let $k > 1$ and $A \subseteq \mathbb{N}^k$. Then

A is recursive $\Longleftrightarrow$ $\pi^{(k)}(A)$ is recursive,

A is r.e. $\Longleftrightarrow$ $\pi^{(k)}(A)$ is r.e.

Proof

Let A be recursive. Then $A = f^{-1}\{0\}$ for some $f \in R^{(k)}$. Since f is recursive, $f(\pi^{(k)})^{-1} : \mathbb{N} \longrightarrow \mathbb{N}$ is recursive by Lemma 1.2.16 and $(f(\pi^{(k)})^{-1})^{-1}\{0\} = \pi^{(k)} f^{-1}\{0\} = \pi^{(k)}(A)$. Therefore, $\pi^{(k)}(A)$ is recursive.
The other cases are proved similarly.
Q.E.D.

Recursive and recursively enumerable subsets of $\mathbb{N}$ will be studied in more detail in Part 2 of this book. Using the computable word functions we define the recursive and the recursively enumerable languages (= sets of words).

7 DEFINITION

Let Δ be an alphabet, let $k \in \mathbb{N}$, $A \subseteq (W(\Delta))$.

A is *recursive* iff $A = f^{-1}\{\varepsilon\}$ for some total computable function $f : (W(\Delta))^k \longrightarrow W(\Delta)$.

A is *recursively enumerable* iff $A = \mathrm{dom}(f)$ for some computable function $f : (W(\Delta))^k \dashrightarrow W(\Delta)$.

Notations: *decidable* instead of *recursive*, *partially decidable*, *provable*, or *r.e.* instead of *recursively enumerable*.

Obviously Definition 7 generalizes Definition 1. It remains to prove that the definition of a recursive or r.e. set A is independent of the alphabet Δ.

8 LEMMA

Let Γ, Δ be alphabets, $\Gamma \subseteq \Delta$, let $k \in \mathbb{N}$, $A \subseteq (W(\Gamma))^k$, then:

(1) $(\exists f : (W(\Gamma))^k \longrightarrow W(\Gamma))$ (f computable and $A = f^{-1}\{\varepsilon\}$)

$\Longleftrightarrow$

$(\exists g : (W(\Delta))^k \longrightarrow W(\Delta))$ (g computable and $A = g^{-1}\{\varepsilon\}$)

(2) $(\exists f : (W(\Gamma))^k \dashrightarrow W(\Gamma))$ (f computable and $A = \mathrm{dom}(f)$)

$\Longleftrightarrow$

$(\exists g : (W(\Delta))^k \dashrightarrow W(\Delta))$ (g computable and $A = \mathrm{dom}(g)$).

Proof

(1) "$\Longrightarrow$": Let $f : (W(\Gamma))^k \longrightarrow W(\Gamma)$ be computable and $A = f^{-1}\{\varepsilon\}$. By Lemma 1.6.8(1) there is some computable function $g' : (W(\Delta))^k \dashrightarrow W(\Delta)$ with $f(\bar{z}) = g'(\bar{z})$ for all $\bar{z} \in (W(\Gamma))^k$. Define a k-ary generalized stack machine M over (Π, Δ), where Π is appropriately chosen, by the flowchart

1 : $(R_1 \in W(\Gamma) \wedge \ldots \wedge R_k \in W(\Gamma))$, 2, 3;

2 : $R_o := f'(R_1, \ldots, R_k)$, 4;

3 : $R_o := R_o a$, 4;

4 : HALT

where $a \in \Delta$ is fixed. Then $A = f_M^{-1}\{\varepsilon\}$ and f_M is computable by Theorem 1.6.6. Define $g := f_M$.

"$\Longleftarrow$": (accordingly by use of Lemma 1.6.8(2))

(2) (accordingly)

Q.E.D.

The standard numberings relate the recursive (r.e.) sets of numbers and the recursive (r.e.) sets of words.

9 THEOREM

Let Δ be an alphabet, let ν be a standard numbering of $W(\Delta)$. Let $k \in \mathbb{N}$. For any $A \subseteq \mathbb{N}^k$ define $\vec{\nu}(A) := \{(\nu(i_1),\ldots,\nu(i_k)) \mid (i_1,\ldots,i_k) \in A\}$. Then the following holds:

A recursive $\iff$ $\vec{\nu}(A)$ recursive ,

A r.e. $\iff$ $\vec{\nu}(A)$ r.e.

Proof

Suppose A is recursive. Then $A = g^{-1}\{0\}$ for some total recursive $g : \mathbb{N}^k \longrightarrow \mathbb{N}$. By Theorem 1.7.5(1), $f := \nu g(\vec{\nu})^{-1}$ is computable and total, and $f^{-1}\{\varepsilon\} = \vec{\nu} g^{-1} \nu^{-1}\{\varepsilon\} = \vec{\nu} g^{-1}\{0\} = \vec{\nu} A$, therefore $\vec{\nu} A$ is recursive. The other implication and the case "A r.e." is proved accordingly by use of Theorem 1.7.5.
Q.E.D.

Recursive and recursively enumerable sets of word tuples have similar properties to recursive and recursively enumerable sets of number tuples. A set $A \subseteq (W(\Sigma))^k$ is r.e. iff it is the projection of some recursive set $B \subseteq (W(\Sigma))^{k+1}$ (projection theorem), and a set $A \subseteq (W(\Sigma))^k$ is recursive iff A and $(W(\Sigma))^k \setminus A$ are recursively enumerable. This can be derived from Theorem 4 and Theorem 5 by Theorem 9 or proved directly. Non recursive (r.e.) sets of words can be defined directly by diagonalization or from non recursive (r.e.) sets of numbers using Theorem 9.

There is a one-one correspondence between the predicates P on M and the subsets $A \subseteq M$, where $M = \mathbb{N}^k$ or $M = (W(\Sigma))^k$:

$P(x)$ iff $x \in A$ (for all $x \in M$) .

A predicate P is called recursive or decidable iff the corresponding set A is recursive, a predicate P is called recursively enumerable, semirecursive, or partially decidable iff the corresponding set A is r.e.

EXERCISES

1) Let $A \subseteq \mathbb{N}$ be finite. Prove that A is recursive.

2) For $A \subseteq \mathbb{N}$ define $c_A : \mathbb{N} \longrightarrow \mathbb{N}$, the characteristic function of A, by $c_A(x) = (1$ if $x \in A$, 0 otherwise). Show: A is decidable <=> c_A is computable.

3) Let $A \subseteq \mathbb{N}^k$. Then A is r.e. iff $A = f^{-1}\{0\}$ for some partial recursive function $f : \mathbb{N}^k \dashrightarrow \mathbb{N}$.

4) Let $A, B \subseteq \mathbb{N}$ be decidable, let $f : \mathbb{N} \longrightarrow \mathbb{N}$ be computable. Show that the following sets are decidable: $A \cup B$, $A \cap B$, $\mathbb{N} \setminus A$, $f^{-1}A$.

5) For $A, B \subseteq \mathbb{N}$ define $A \oplus B := \{2a \mid a \in A\} \cup \{2b+1 \mid b \in B\}$.
Prove:
(a) A recursive $\wedge$ B recursive <=> $A \oplus B$ recursive
(b) A r.e. $\wedge$ B r.e. <=> $A \oplus B$ r.e.

6) Let $A, B \subseteq \mathbb{N}$, $A \neq \emptyset$ and $B \neq \emptyset$. Prove:
(a) A recursive $\wedge$ B recursive <=> $A \times B$ recursive
(b) A r.e. $\wedge$ B r.e. <=> $A \times B$ r.e.
(Is the condition $A \neq \emptyset \wedge B \neq \emptyset$ necessary?)

7) In the proof of the projection theorem it has been shown that for any register machine M the set

$$B = \{(x_1,\dots,x_k,t) \mid M \text{ with input } (x_1,\dots,x_k) \text{ halts within at most } t \text{ steps}\}$$

is recursive. Prove that the set

$$C := \{(x_1,\dots,x_k,t) \mid M \text{ with input } (x_1,\dots,x_k) \text{ halts in exactly } t \text{ steps}\}$$

is recursive.

8) Let M_1, M_2 be k-ary register machines. Construct register machines M and N such that
(a) $\mathrm{dom}(f_M) = \mathrm{dom}(f_{M_1}) \cap \mathrm{dom}(f_{M_2})$,
(b) $\mathrm{dom}(f_N) = \mathrm{dom}(f_{M_1}) \cup \mathrm{dom}(f_{M_2})$.

9) For $p \in \mathbb{F} := \{f : \mathbb{N} \longrightarrow \mathbb{N}\}$ define

$$\mathbb{M}_p := \{n \mid n+1 \in \mathrm{range}\,(p)\}.$$

(a) Prove for any $A \subseteq \mathbb{N}$:
A is r.e. <=> $(\exists p \in R^{(1)})\ A = \mathbb{M}_p$.

(b) Prove for any $A \subseteq \mathbb{N}$, $A \neq \emptyset$:
A is r.e. <=> $(\exists p \in R^{(1)})\ A = \mathrm{range}\,(p)$.

10) Consider Fermat's conjecture: $(\forall n>2)(\forall x,y,z\geq 1)x^n+y^n\neq z^n$.

(a) Show that $A:=\{n\geq 1 \mid (\exists x,y,z\geq 1)x^n+y^n=z^n\}$ is r.e.

(b) Define a 0-ary register machine M such that

$$f_M() = \begin{cases} 0 & \text{if Fermat's conjecture is false} \\ \text{div} & \text{otherwise.} \end{cases}$$

(The solution of the halting problem for M solves Fermat's problem.)

1.9 The Standard Numbering φ of $P^{(1)}$

In the previous chapters we have studied different kinds of machines, the computable functions and recursive and r.e. sets. The theorems we have proved are generally of a constructive nature themselves. We have shown e.g.: "for any $f \in P^{(2)}$, $\tilde{\mu}(f) \in P^{(1)}$" (Theorem 1.2.12), "for any stack machine *there is* a Turing machine computing the same function" (Theorem 1.6.7), "for any r.e. $A \subseteq \mathbb{N}$ *there is* some recursive $B \subseteq \mathbb{N}^2$ such that A is the projection of B" (Theorem 1.8.4). The proofs of these and many other theorems, however, yield more information. We have for example shown: "there is an *effective procedure* which for *any* register machine M produces a register machine M' such that $f_{M'} = \tilde{\mu}(f_M)$", or "there is an *effective procedure* which for *any* register machine M produces a register machine M' such that $f_{M'}$ is a total function and $\mathrm{dom}(f_M)$ is the projection of $f_{M'}^{-1}\{0\}$". In order to formulate these observations precisely one can introduce standard names for register machines (or the corresponding computable functions) which are appropriate words. Then the *effective procedures* can be represented by computable functions on the names. Since computability on words can be reduced to computability on numbers (Theorem 1.7.5), we shall use numbers as names which yields a formally simpler theory.

In this chapter we shall define a standard numbering $\varphi : \mathbb{N} \longrightarrow P^{(1)}$ of the unary partial recursive functions. We shall prove that this numbering φ satisfies two fundamental effectivity properies, the *utm-theorem* and the *smn-theorem*, by which it is characterized already up to equivalence. The numbering φ will be defined in three steps:

- A notation $\mathrm{tm} : W(\Omega) \dashrightarrow \mathrm{TM}$ of a suitable class of tape machines TM for the computable functions $W(\{1\}) \dashrightarrow W(\{1\})$ is introduced.
- A notation $\varphi' : W(\Omega) \dashrightarrow P^{(1)}$ of $P^{(1)}$ is derived by: $\varphi'(w) :=$ the function from $P^{(1)}$ computed by the tape machine $\mathrm{tm}(w)$.
- By a standard numbering ν_{TP} of $\mathrm{dom}(\mathrm{tm}) = \mathrm{dom}(\varphi')$ the numbering φ is obtained: $\varphi := \varphi'\nu_{TP}$.

The definition of the notation tm is the crucial one. By Theorem 1.7.5, the mapping $f \longrightarrow \iota^{-1}f\iota$ where $\iota : \mathbb{N} \longrightarrow W(\{1\})$ is a standard numbering maps the computable functions $f : W(\{1\}) \dashrightarrow W(\{1\})$ onto $P^{(1)}$. By Lemma 1.5.3 for any computable function $f : W(\{1\}) \dashrightarrow W(\{1\})$ there is a tape machine M over $(\{B,1\},\{1\},B)$ with $f = f_M$. By Lemma 1.1.7 we may assume that the states of the flowchart of M are natural numbers. Furthermore we may assume that M has only one exit. We shall define a simple notation for all tape machines with one exit over $(\{B,1\},\{1\},B)$ the states of which are natural numbers.

1 EXAMPLE

Consider a flowchart for a tape machine.

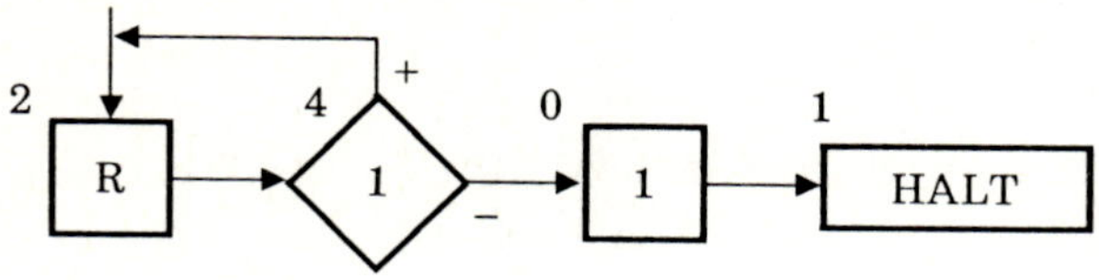

Then the following word denotes this flowchart:

$((\varepsilon:1,1)(1^2:R,1^4)(1^4:1,1^2,\varepsilon)\ ,\ 1^2\ ,\ 1)$

Thus, a state $i \in \mathbb{N}$ is denoted by the word 1^i of length i, a statement $i : R,j$ is denoted by the word "$(1^i:R,1^j)$" of length $i+j+5$, etc. The above program is a list of such statement words followed by the name of the initial state and by the name of the final state.

For formal convenience we shall admit that there are two or more statement words for each state in the list. In this case only the leftmost one is considered. Furthermore we admit that the list is incomplete. If necessary we implicitly add statement-words $(1^p:B,1^{q_e},1^{q_e})$ where q_e is the final state. (Thus we shift some complications from the syntax to the semantics.) The precise definition of the notation is lengthly but not difficult.

2 DEFINITION (*notation of tape machines*)

(1) Let $\Omega := \{1|B|(|)|:|,|R|L\}$ be an alphabet with 8 elements. (The symbol | is used for metalinguistic separation since the comma is an element of Ω, i.e. , $\in \Omega$.)

(2) Let TM be the set of the unary tape machines with one exit over $(\{B,1\},\{1\},B)$ such that the states are natural numbers.

(3) Define $TS \subseteq W(\Omega)$ (the *tape statements*) and $TP \subseteq W(\Omega)$ (the *tape programs*) as follows.

$$TS := \{"(1^m:\beta,1^n)" \mid \beta \in \{B,1,R,L\};\ m,n \in \mathbb{N}\} \cup \{"(1^m:\beta,1^k,1^n)" \mid \beta \in \{B,1\};\ k,m,n \in \mathbb{N}\}$$

$$TP := \{"(z_1z_2\ldots z_k,1^i,1^j)" \mid i,j,k \in \mathbb{N}\ ;\ i \neq j;\ z_1,\ldots,z_k \in TS\}$$

(4) A mapping $tm : W(\Omega) \dashrightarrow TM$ is defined as follows.

$$dom(tm) := TP\ ,$$

$$tm("(w,1^i,1^j)") := M \in TM$$

such that the flowchart $F = (Q,D,\sigma,q_o,1,q_1)$ of M has the following properties:

$q_o = i$,

$q_1 = j$,

$Q = \{n \in \mathbb{N} \mid$ "$(1^n$:" or ",1^n," or ",1^n)" is a subword of "$(w,1^i,1^j)$"$\}$,

and for all $n \in Q \setminus \{j\}$, $\sigma(n)$ is defined as follows:

$\sigma(n) =$

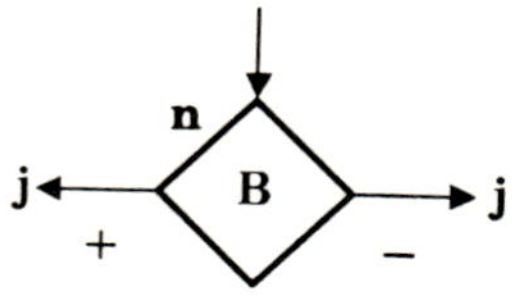

if "$(1^n$:" is not a subword of w

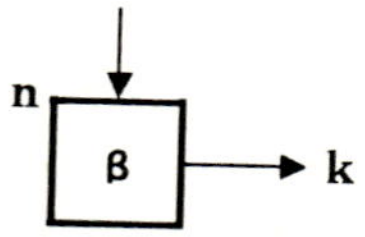

if "$(1^n:\beta,1^k)$" with $\beta \in \{1,B,R,L\}$ is the leftmost statement in w with prefix "$(1^n$:"

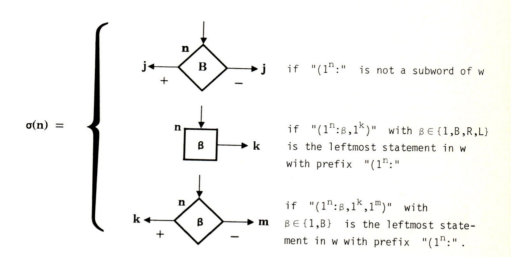

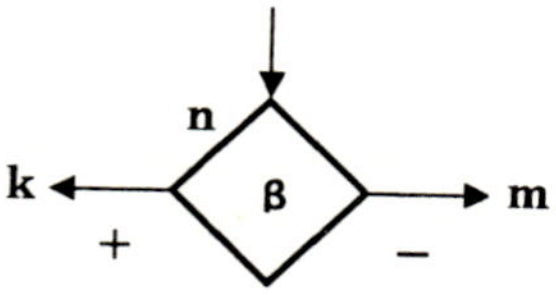

if "$(1^n:\beta,1^k,1^m)$" with $\beta \in \{1,B\}$ is the leftmost statement in w with prefix "$(1^n$:" .

Each tape machine from TM receives a name w.r.t. tm. Furthermore, $TP = dom(tm)$ is a recursive set of words.

LEMMA

(1) TP is a recursive set.

(2) The mapping $tm : W(\Omega) \dashrightarrow TM$ is surjective.

Proof

(1) It is easy to construct a stack machine M over (Ω,Ω) such that $f_M : W(\Omega) \longrightarrow W(\Omega)$ is a total function and $TP = f_M^{-1}\{\varepsilon\}$. Details are left to the reader.

(2) Obviously, for any $M \in TM$ there is some $w \in TP$ with $tm(w) = M$.

Q.E.D.

Proof

The essential part is to show that there is a computable function $q_u : W(\Omega) \times W(\Omega) \dashrightarrow W(\Omega)$ with $q_u(x,w) = f_{tm(x)}(w)$ for all $x \in TP = dom(tm)$ and all $w \in W(\Sigma)$, where $\Sigma = \{1\}$. There is a pencil and paper method for performing the computation for any tape program x with input w step by step. Our aim is to construct a stack machine for q_u.

For any tape program $x \in TP$ let

$$M_x := tm(x) = (F_x, W(\{1\}), W(\{1\}), I', O')$$

be the unary tape machine defined by x, and let

$$F_x = (Q_x, D, \sigma_x, q_{ox}, 1, q_{ex})$$

be the flowchart of M_x. Let SF_x (TF_x) be the single step function (total step function) of F_x. Notice that the dataset $D = \{[u,a,v] \mid a \in \{B,1\},\ u,v \in W(\{B,1\})\}$ is independent of x and that $Q_x \subseteq \mathbb{N}$.

Define a universal machine $\overline{M} := (\overline{F}, (W(\Omega))^2, W(\Omega), \overline{I}, \overline{O})$ as follows. The flowchart $\overline{F}$ is given by the diagram

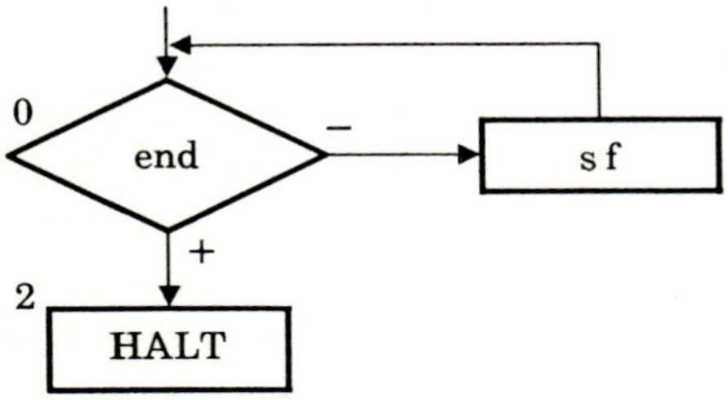

together with the following specification.

$$\overline{D} := W(\Omega) \times (\mathbb{N} \times D)$$

If $\overline{d} = (x,(i,d))$ then x is the program under consideration and (i,d) is a tape machine configuration.

$$end(x,(i,d)) := \begin{cases} + & \text{if } i = q_{ex} \text{ and } x \in TP \\ - & \text{otherwise,} \end{cases}$$

$$sf(x,(i,d)) := \begin{cases} (x, SF_x(i,d)) & \text{if } x \in TP \text{ and } i \in Q_x \setminus \{q_{ex}\} \\ (x,(i,d)) & \text{otherwise,} \end{cases}$$

$$\overline{I}(x,w) := \begin{cases} (x,(q_{ox}, I'(w))) & \text{if } x \in TP \text{ and } w \in W(\Sigma) \\ \overline{d} & \text{otherwise,} \end{cases}$$

where $\overline{d} \in \overline{D}$ is arbitrary,

$\overline{O}(x,(i,d)) := O'(d)$

for all $x,w \in W(\Omega)$, $i \in \mathbb{N}$, $d \in D$. It is now almost obvious that $q_u := f_{\overline{M}}$ has the desired property. We prove this formally. By a simple induction on t we obtain

$\overline{SF}^{2t}(0,(x,(q_{ox},d))) = (0,(x,SF_x^t(q_{ox},d)))$

for all $x \in TP$, $d \in D$ if $SF_x^t(q_{ox},d)$ exists. From this

$\overline{TF}(0,(x,(q_{ox},d))) = (2,(x,TF_x(q_{ox},d)))$

follows for all $x \in TP$ and $d \in D$. Therefore, for any $x \in TP$ and $w \in W(\Sigma)$ we obtain by Definition 1.1.6 and 1.1.16:

$$
\begin{aligned}
f_{\overline{M}}(x,w) &= \overline{O} \circ f_{\overline{F}} \circ \overline{I}(x,w) && \text{(Def. of } f_{\overline{M}}) \\
&= \overline{O} \circ f_{\overline{F}}(x,(q_{ox},I'(w))) && \text{(Def. of } \overline{I}) \\
&= \overline{O} \circ pr_2 \circ \overline{TF}(0,(x,(q_{ox},I'(w)))) && \text{(Def. of } f_{\overline{F}}) \\
&= \overline{O}(x,TF_x(q_{ox},I'(w))) && \text{(proved above)} \\
&= O' \circ pr_2 \circ TF_x(q_{ox},I'(w)) && \text{(Def. of } \overline{O}) \\
&= O' \circ f_{F_x} \circ I'(w) && \text{(Def. of } f_{F_x}) \\
&= f_{M_x}(w) && \text{(Def. of } f_{M_x}) \\
&= f_{tm(x)}(w) && \text{(Def. of } M_x) .
\end{aligned}
$$

To prove that $f_{\overline{M}}$ is computable, we show that $\overline{M}$ can be transformed into a stack machine M over (Ω,Ω). We use a simulation relation $Sim \subseteq \overline{D} \times \hat{D}$, $\hat{D} = (W(\Omega))^{\mathbb{N}}$, which is defined as follows.

$$Sim := \{((x,(i,[u,a,v])),(x,1^i,u,a,v^R,\varepsilon,\dots)) \mid x \in W(\Omega),\ i \in \mathbb{N},\ a \in \{B,1\},\ u,v \in W(\{B,1\})\}$$

This is a generalization of the simulation relation in the proof of Theorem 1.6.7 where a fixed tape machine is simulated by a stack machine. We define a machine $\hat{M} = (\hat{F},(W(\Omega))^2,W(\Omega),\hat{I},\hat{O})$ which is similar to $\overline{M}$ via Sim as follows (see Theorem 1.1.17). $\hat{F}$ results from $\overline{F}$ by replacing "end" by any $\widehat{end}$ and "sf" by any $\widehat{sf}$ which have the properties:

$$\widehat{end}(x,1^i,u,a,v,\varepsilon,\dots) = \begin{cases} + & \text{if i is the final state of tm(x)} \\ - & \text{otherwise} \end{cases}$$

and

$$\widehat{sf}(x,1^i,u,a,v,\varepsilon,\dots) = (x,1^j,u',a',v',\varepsilon,\dots)$$

where j,u',a',v' are such that $SF_x(i,[u,a,v^R]) = (j,[u',a',v'^R])$. Define
$\hat{I}(x,w) := (x,1^i, ,B,w^R,\varepsilon,\dots)$ with $i :=$ initial state of tm(x)
$\hat{O}(x,1^i,u,y,v,\dots) := z^R$ where z is the longest suffix z' of v with $z' \in W(\{1\})$

(cf. Conditions (a) and (b) in the proof of Theorem 1.6.7). Adjustments IA and OA to the standard encodings of stack machines can also be defined easily (see Conditions (d) and (e) in the proof of Theorem 1.6.7). Routine programming shows that $\widehat{end}$, $\widehat{sf}$, IA and OA can be refined by stack machine flowcharts. Therefore, $q_u := f_{\overline{M}}$ is computable.

For any $i,j \in \mathbb{N}$ we have

$$\varphi_i(j) = u_\varphi(i,j) = \iota^{-1} f_{tm(\nu_{TP}(i))}\iota(j) = \iota^{-1} q_u(\nu_{TP}(i),\iota(j))$$
$$= \iota^{-1}\nu_\Omega\nu_\Omega^{-1} q_u(\nu_\Omega\nu_\Omega^{-1}\nu_{TP}(i),\nu_\Omega\nu_\Omega^{-1}\iota(j))$$

where ν_Ω is a standard numbering of $W(\Omega)$.

We show that this expression can be decomposed into computable functions. Define $q_1 := \nu_\Omega^{-1}\iota$ and $q_2(i) := (\iota^{-1}\nu_\Omega(i)$ if $\nu_\Omega(i) \in W(\Sigma)$, 0 otherwise). Then q_1 and q_2 are computable by Lemma 1.7.4. Define $q'(m,n) := \nu_\Omega^{-1} q_u(\nu_\Omega(m),\nu_\Omega(n))$. q' is computable by Theorem 1.7.5. Let $i_o := \nu_\Omega^{-1}("(,,1)")$. Then

$$q_3(i) := \nu_\Omega^{-1}\nu_{TP}(i) = \begin{cases} i_o & \text{if } \nu_\Omega(i) \notin TP \\ i & \text{otherwise.} \end{cases}$$

Since TP is decidable, also $\nu_\Omega^{-1}(TP)$ is decidable, therefore q_3 is computable. We obtain $u_\varphi(i,j) = q_2 q'(q_3(i),q_1(j))$, hence u_φ is computable.

Q.E.D.

The effectivity property of φ which guarantees the possibility of effective programming can be formulated as follows.

7 THEOREM (*smn-theorem, translation lemma*)

For any partial recursive function $f \in P^{(2)}$ there is a total recursive function $r \in R^{(1)}$ with

$$(\forall i,j)\ f(i,j) = \varphi_{r(i)}(j).$$

The function r computes (the number of) a program. It is important that r is total recursive. The names *smn-theorem* and *translation lemma* will be explained later. The relevance of the smn-theorem will become clear by its applications.

Proof

Suppose $f : \mathbb{N}^2 \dashrightarrow \mathbb{N}$ is computable. Then there is a 2-ary tape machine M such that $f(i,j) = \iota^{-1} f_M(\iota(i),\iota(j))$ for all $i,j \in \mathbb{N}$ (Theorem 1.7.5). By Lemma 1.5.3 we may assume that the states of M are natural numbers and that M is a machine over $(\{1,B\},\{1\},B)$. Let

$$M = (F,(W(\{1\}))^2,W(\{1\}),I^{(2)},0).$$

For any $i \in \mathbb{N}$ let $M_i \in TM$ be a unary tape machine which on input 1^j first transforms the initial tape

$$[\varepsilon,B,1^j]$$

into the tape

$$[\varepsilon,B,1^iB1^j]$$

and then operates with flowchart F like machine M. Then obviously $f_{M_i}(1^j) = f_M(1^i,1^j)$. We shall show in detail that there is a computable function r which transforms any number i into a number k of machine M_i (i.e. $M_i = tm\nu_{TP}r(i)$).

Let $x = "(w,1^m,1^n)"$ be a tape program such that

$$tm(x) = (F,W(\{1\}),W(\{1\}),I,0) \in TM$$

(where F is the flowchart from M). Let $k := 1 + \max(Q)$, where Q is the set of states of F. For any $i \in \mathbb{N}$ define $x_i \in TP$ as follows

$$x_i := "(w_i,1^k,1^n)"$$

where w_i is the following word over the alphabet Ω:

$$"(1^k{:}L,1^{k+1})(1^{k+1}{:}1,1^{k+2})$$
$$(1^{k+2}{:}L,1^{k+3})(1^{k+3}{:}1,1^{k+4})$$
$$\vdots$$
$$(1^{k+2i-2}{:}L,1^{k+2i-1})(1^{k+2i-1}{:}1,1^{k+2i})$$
$$(1^{k+2i}{:}L,1^m)\,w\,".$$

(This includes the special case $w_o = "(1^k{:}L,1^m)w"$.)
Let SF_i be the single step function of the tape machine $tm(x_i)$. Then

$$SF_i^{2i+1}(k,[\varepsilon,B,1^j]) = (m,[\varepsilon,B,1^iB1^j])$$

and hence $f_{tm(x_i)}(1^j) = f_M(1^i,1^j)$. Let $r : \mathbb{N} \longrightarrow \mathbb{N}$ be a function such that $x_i = \nu_{TP}r(i)$. Then

$$\begin{aligned}
f(i,j) &= \iota^{-1}f_M(\iota(i),\iota(j)) \\
&= \iota^{-1}f_{tm(x_i)}(\iota(j)) && \text{(see above)} \\
&= \varphi'(x_i)(j) && \text{(see Def. 4)} \\
&= \varphi'\nu_{TP}r(i)(j) \\
&= \varphi_{r(i)}(j) && \text{(see Def. 4)}.
\end{aligned}$$

It remains to show that a computable function $r : \mathbb{N} \longrightarrow \mathbb{N}$ with $x_i = \nu_{TP} r(i)$ exists. There is a computable function $r' : W(\Omega) \dashrightarrow W(\Omega)$ with $r'(1^i) = x_i$ (proof by a stack machine). Define $r := \nu_\Omega^{-1} r' \iota$. Then

$$\begin{aligned} \nu_{TP} r(i) &= \nu_{TP} \nu_\Omega^{-1} r' \iota(i) \\ &= r'\iota(i) \qquad (\text{since } r'\iota(i) \in TP) \\ &= x_i \end{aligned}$$

and using Lemma 1.7.4(3) and Theorem 1.7.5 one easily shows that r is computable.
Q.E.D.

Theorem 7 has a non effective formulation: for any $f \in P^{(2)}$ there exists ...
To formulate an effective version we need a numbering of $P^{(2)}$. Remember that $P^{(2)} = \{f\pi^{(2)} \mid f \in P^{(1)}\}$ (Lemma 1.2.16). Therefore, $\varphi_i^{(2)}$ defined by $\varphi_i^{(2)}(j,k) := \varphi_i \pi^{(2)}(j,k) = \varphi_i\langle j,k\rangle$ is a numbering of $P^{(2)}$. The effective version of Theorem 7 can be formulated as follows:

8 COROLLARY (*effective smn-theorem*)

There is a total recursive function $s : \mathbb{N}^2 \longrightarrow \mathbb{N}$ with

$$(\forall i,j,k)\ \varphi_i\langle j,k\rangle = \varphi_{s(i,j)}(k) .$$

The translation lemma can easily be derived from this effective version. The proof of Corollary 8 is a typical application of the utm-theorem and the (non effective version of) the smn-theorem.

Proof

By the utm-theorem the universal function u_φ of φ is computable. Define a function $f : \mathbb{N}^2 \dashrightarrow \mathbb{N}$ by

$$f(\langle i,j\rangle,k) := u_\varphi(i,\langle j,k\rangle) .$$

Since u_φ, π, and the projections of π^{-1} are computable (Lemma 1.2.15), the function f is computable. By Theorem 7 there is a function $r \in R^{(1)}$ such that $\varphi_{r\langle i,j\rangle}(k) = f(\langle i,j\rangle,k)$. Define $s \in R^{(2)}$ by $s := r\pi^{(2)}$. Then

$$\varphi_{s(i,j)}(k) = \varphi_{r\langle i,j\rangle}(k) = f(\langle i,j\rangle,k) = u_\varphi(i,\langle j,k\rangle) = \varphi_i\langle j,k\rangle .$$

Q.E.D.

Let ψ be any numbering of a subset $S \subseteq P^{(1)}$ such that the universal function $u_\psi : \mathbb{N}^2 \dashrightarrow \mathbb{N}$ is computable. Then, by Theorem 7, there is some recursive function $r \in R^{(1)}$ with $\psi_i(n) = u_\psi(i,n) = \varphi_{r(i)}(n)$ for all $i,n \in \mathbb{N}$. This means that the function r *translates* the numbering ψ into the standard numbering φ of $P^{(1)}$. This "universal" property of φ explains the name *translation lemma*. The name smn-theorem comes from a more general effective version: for any $n,m \in \mathbb{N}$ there exists a total recursive function $s_n^m : \mathbb{N}^{m+1} \longrightarrow \mathbb{N}$ with

$$\varphi_{s_n^m(i,x_1,\ldots,x_m)}\langle y_1,\ldots,y_n\rangle = \varphi_i\langle x_1,\ldots,x_m,y_1,\ldots,y_n\rangle$$

(see the exercises). The utm-theorem and the translation lemma are independent. There is a numbering ψ of $P^{(1)}$ which satisfies the utm-theorem and not the translation lemma, and there is a numbering ψ' of $P^{(1)}$ which satisfies the translation lemma and not the utm-theorem (see the exercises). The utm-theorem and the translation lemma determine the numbering φ up to equivalence.

9 DEFINITION (*reducibility, equivalence of numbering*)

(1) A numbering ν of a set S is a surjective function $\nu : \mathbb{N} \dashrightarrow S$.

Let ν_i be a numbering of S_i $(i = 1,2)$.

(2) $\nu_1 \leq \nu_2 :\Longleftrightarrow (\exists r \in P^{(1)})(\forall i \in \mathrm{dom}(\nu_1))\ \nu_1(i) = \nu_2 r(i)$
(ν_1 is *reducible to* ν_2, ν_1 is *translatable into* ν_2)

(3) $\nu_1 \equiv \nu_2 :\Longleftrightarrow (\nu_1 \leq \nu_2 \wedge \nu_2 \leq \nu_1)$
(ν_1 is *equivalent to* ν_2)

With these preparations we can formulate the characterization of our standard numbering φ by the utm-theorem and the translation lemma. Roughly speaking, it says that there is essentially only one single effective numbering of $P^{(1)}$.

10 THEOREM (*characterization of* φ)

Let ψ,ψ' be total numberings of $P^{(1)}$.

(1) If ψ satisfies the utm-theorem and ψ' satisfies the translation lemma, then $\psi \leq \psi'$.

(2) $\psi \equiv \varphi$ iff ψ satisfies the utm-theorem and the translation lemma.

Proof

(1) If ψ satisfies the utm-theorem, then the universal function u_ψ of ψ defined by

$u_\psi(i,x) = \psi_i(x)$ is computable. If ψ' satisfies the translation lemma, $u_\psi(i,x) = \psi'_{r(i)}(x)$ for some $r \in R^{(1)}$, therefore $\psi_i = \psi'_{r(i)}$ for all i, i.e. $\psi \le \psi'$.
(2) "$\Rightarrow$": Suppose $\psi \equiv \varphi$. Then there are functions $r,s \in R^{(1)}$ with $\psi_i = \varphi_{r(i)}$ and $\varphi_i = \psi_{s(i)}$ for all $i \in \mathbb{N}$. We obtain $u_\psi(i,x) = \psi_i(x) = \varphi_{r(i)}(x) = u_\varphi(r(i),x)$, hence u_ψ is computable, i.e. ψ satisfies the utm-theorem. Let $h \in P^{(2)}$. Then $h(i,x) = \varphi_{t(i)}(x) = \psi_{st(i)}(x)$ for some $t \in R^{(1)}$. Since $s \circ t \in R^{(1)}$, ψ satisfies the translation lemma.
"$\Leftarrow$": Suppose ψ satisfies the utm-theorem and the translation lemma. Then $\psi \le \varphi$ and $\varphi \le \psi$ by (1), hence $\varphi \equiv \psi$.
Q.E.D.

The following diagram of the ordering $\le$ on the set of total numberings of $P^{(1)}$ illustrates the theorem.

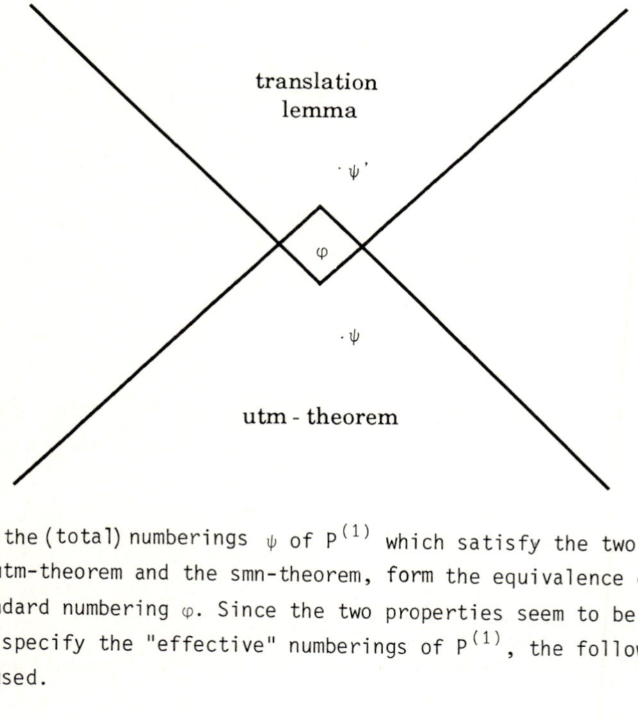

By Theorem 10 the (total) numberings ψ of $P^{(1)}$ which satisfy the two effectivity properties, the utm-theorem and the smn-theorem, form the equivalence class which contains our standard numbering φ. Since the two properties seem to be necessary and sufficient to specify the "effective" numberings of $P^{(1)}$, the following notations are commonly used.

11 DEFINITION

A numbering ψ of $P^{(1)}$ is called "*effective*" or "*admissible*" or an "*effective* (or *admissible*) *Gödel numbering* (or *indexing*)" of $P^{(1)}$, iff $\psi \equiv \varphi$.

For almost all purposes in recursion theory any admissible numbering is as suitable as the standard numbering φ. Only in some applications do the details of the definition of φ (or some other admissible numbering) have to be considered.

The belief that the numbering φ is (up to equivalence) the only intuitively effective numbering of $P^{(1)}$ can be expressed by a thesis like Church's thesis, which also cannot be proved.

THESIS

A numbering ψ of $P^{(1)}$ is *intuitively effective*, iff $\psi \equiv \varphi$.

The question how to define "effective numberings" will be discussed later in a more general context.

As we have mentioned earlier, the translation lemma guarantees the possibility of effective programming. The following lemma is one of the consequences.

12 LEMMA

There is a total recursive function $h \in R^{(2)}$ such that

$$\varphi_{h(i,j)} = \varphi_i \circ \varphi_j$$

for all $i,j \in \mathbb{N}$.

This means that the composition operation on $P^{(1)}$ is "effective w.r.t. φ". The proof is easy.

Proof

Define $f : \mathbb{N}^2 \dashrightarrow \mathbb{N}$ by $f(\langle i,j\rangle,n) := \varphi_i \circ \varphi_j(n)$. Since $f(\langle i,j\rangle,n) = u_\varphi(i,u_\varphi(j,n))$, f is computable by the utm-theorem. The translation lemma yields some $g \in R^{(1)}$ with $\varphi_{g\langle i,j\rangle}(n) = f(\langle i,j\rangle,n) = \varphi_i \circ \varphi_j(n)$. The function h with $h(i,j) = g\langle i,j\rangle$ has the desired property.

Q.E.D.

Instead of $\varphi_i \circ \varphi_j(n)$ in Lemma 12 any other similar expression can be used, e.g. there are total recursive functions h with $\varphi_{h(i)} = \tilde{\mu}(\varphi\circ\pi)$, $\varphi_{h(i)}(n) = (i+n)^2$,

$\varphi_{h(i,j,k)}(n) = (\varphi_i(n))^2 + \varphi_j(n) \cdot \varphi_k(n)$, etc. It is remarkable that a total numbering of $P^{(1)}$ with computable universal function satisfies the translation lemma iff it satisfies Lemma 12, i.e. iff composition is effective (see the exercises).

The use of non total computable functions gives rise to many difficulties in computability theory. One could try to consider only the tape programs of the total computable functions. But there is no reasonable total numbering of $R^{(1)}$.

13 THEOREM

Let ψ be any total numbering of the total recursive (unary) functions i.e. $\psi : \mathbb{N} \longrightarrow R^{(1)}$. Then the universal function $u_\psi : \mathbb{N}^2 \longrightarrow \mathbb{N}$ of ψ is not computable.

We have proved in Chapter 1.3 that the universal function of a total numbering of the unary primitive recursive functions cannot be primitive recursive itself. By the same diagonalization argument we prove Theorem 13.

Proof

Define $h : \mathbb{N} \longrightarrow \mathbb{N}$ by $h(i) := u_\psi(i,i) + 1$. Then h diagonalizes over the sequence $(\psi_i)_{i\in\mathbb{N}}$ of total recursive functions: for all i, $h \neq \psi_i$ since $h(i) \neq \psi_i(i)$. Therefore $h \notin R^{(1)}$. But $u_\psi \in R^{(2)}$ would imply $h \in R^{(1)}$.
Q.E.D.

The non total computable functions would lose their importance if for any $f \in P^{(1)}$ there were a total computable function $g \in R^{(1)}$ which extends f, i.e. $(\forall x \in dom(f))$ $f(x) = g(x)$. By the following theorem this is impossible.

14 THEOREM

The function f with $(\forall i)\ f(i) = \varphi_i(i) + 1$ is computable, but it has no total recursive extension.

Proof

Let $g : \mathbb{N} \longrightarrow \mathbb{N}$ be any total extension of f. Then g diagonalizes over all computable functions $h : \mathbb{N} \dashrightarrow \mathbb{N}$ which are total: Let $h \in R^{(1)}$; then $h = \varphi_i$ for some $i \in \mathbb{N}$. Since $\varphi_i(i)$ exists, $g(i) = f(i) = \varphi_i(i) + 1 \neq \varphi_i(i) = h(i)$, hence $g \neq h$. Therefore, g cannot be computable. By the utm-theorem, f is computable.
Q.E.D.

The domain A of the function f in Theorem 14 cannot be recursive. Otherwise the function $g : \mathbb{N} \longrightarrow \mathbb{N}$ with $g(x) = (f(x)$ if $x \in A$, 0 otherwise) would be a total recursive extension of f. We prove this directly.

15 DEFINITION

$K_\varphi := \{i \mid i \in \mathrm{dom}(\varphi_i)\}$,

$K^\circ_\varphi := \{\langle i,x\rangle \mid x \in \mathrm{dom}(\varphi_i)\}$.

We have already mentioned that it is not generally possible to know in advance whether a given (register, stack, tape) machine with input x will eventually halt or not. The set K°_φ formalizes this problem for the numbering φ. The set K_φ formalizes the problem of whether a tape machine is applicable to its own number ("to itself"). We shall prove now that both problems are recursively enumerable and not recursive, i.e. recursively unsolvable.

16 THEOREM

(1) K_φ and K°_φ are recursively enumerable.

(2) K_φ and K°_φ are not recursive.

(3) $\mathbb{N} \setminus K_\varphi$ and $\mathbb{N} \setminus K^\circ_\varphi$ are not recursively enumerable.

Instead of "K_φ is not recursive" one usually says "the *self applicability problem* is unsolvable", and instead of "K°_φ is not recursive" one usually says "the *halting problem* is unsolvable".

Proof

(1) Define $f : \mathbb{N} \dashrightarrow \mathbb{N}$ by $f(i) := u_\varphi(i,i)$. By the utm-theorem f is computable. Since $K_\varphi = \mathrm{dom}(f)$, f is r.e. Define $g : \mathbb{N} \dashrightarrow \mathbb{N}$ by $g\langle i,x\rangle := u_\varphi(i,x)$. Then $g \in P^{(1)}$ and $K^\circ_\varphi = \mathrm{dom}(g)$, hence K°_φ is r.e.

(2) Define a function $g : \mathbb{N} \dashrightarrow \mathbb{N}$ by

$$g(x) := \begin{cases} \mathrm{div} & \text{if } x \in K_\varphi \\ 0 & \text{otherwise}. \end{cases}$$

For any $i \in \mathbb{N}$ we have $i \in \mathrm{dom}(\varphi_i) \iff i \in K_\varphi \iff i \notin \mathrm{dom}(g)$. This means g and φ_i differ at argument i, hence $g \neq \varphi_i$. (The function g diagonalizes over the sequence $(\varphi_i)_{i\in\mathbb{N}}$.) Therefore g cannot be computable. But if K_φ is recursive then there is a register machine which computes g. Therefore K_φ cannot be recursive. Since K_φ is not decidable, the more complicated problem K^o_φ cannot be decidable. We formalize this *proof by reduction*. Define $f : \mathbb{N} \longrightarrow \mathbb{N}$ by $f(i) := \langle i,i \rangle$. Then $f \in R^{(1)}$ and $i \in K_\varphi \iff f(i) \in K^o_\varphi$ for all $i \in \mathbb{N}$, i.e. $K_\varphi = f^{-1}K^o_\varphi$. Suppose K^o_φ is recursive. Then $K^o_\varphi = g^{-1}\{0\}$ for some $g \in R^{(1)}$, hence $K_\varphi = f^{-1}g^{-1}\{0\} = (gf)^{-1}\{0\}$. Since $gf \in R^{(1)}$, K_φ must be recursive, a contradiction.

(3) This follows from (1) and (2) together with Theorem 1.8.5 which relates r.e. and recursive sets. There is annother interesting way to prove that $\mathbb{N} \setminus K_\varphi$ is not r.e. For any $i \in \mathbb{N}$ the following holds:

$$i \in \mathbb{N} \setminus K_\varphi \iff i \notin \mathrm{dom}(\varphi_i)\ .$$

Since $\{\mathrm{dom}(\varphi_i) \mid i \in \mathbb{N}\}$ is the set of all r.e. subsets of $\mathbb{N}$, $\mathbb{N} \setminus K_\varphi$ differs from any r.e. set $A \subseteq \mathbb{N}$. ($\mathbb{N} \setminus K_\varphi$ diagonalizes over the sequence $(\mathrm{dom}\ \varphi_i)_{i \in \mathbb{N}}$.) Therefore $\mathbb{N} \setminus K_\varphi$ is not r.e.

Q.E.D.

We have considered the halting problem for our model programming language $(\mathbb{N},\varphi)$ of $P^{(1)}$. But also for any other reasonable sufficiently rich programming language the halting problem is unsolvable.

17 THEOREM (*unsolvability of the general halting problem*)

Let Σ,Δ be alphabets, let $\psi : W(\Delta) \dashrightarrow P_\Sigma$ be a notation (= surjective mapping) of a class of functions $W(\Sigma) \dashrightarrow W(\Sigma)$. Define

$$K^o_\psi := \{(w,x) \in \mathrm{dom}(\psi) \times W(\Sigma) \mid x \in \mathrm{dom}(\psi_w)\}\ .$$

Suppose there is a function $g \in R^{(1)}$ such that

(*) $\varphi_i(k) = \nu_\Sigma^{-1}\psi_{\nu_\Delta g(i)}\nu_\Sigma(k)$ for all $i,k \in \mathbb{N}$.

Then there is no computable function $f : W(\Gamma) \times W(\Gamma) \dashrightarrow W(\Gamma)$, where $\Gamma = \Sigma \cup \Delta$, such that $\mathrm{dom}(\psi) \times W(\Sigma) \subseteq \mathrm{dom}(f)$ and $f(w,x) = \varepsilon \iff x \in \mathrm{dom}(\psi_w)$ for all $(w,x) \in \mathrm{dom}(\psi) \times W(\Sigma)$.

The theorem states that for a programming language L with "syntax" $\mathrm{dom}(\psi)$ and "semantics" ψ by which the partial recursive functions can be appropriately expressed (Condition (*)), the halting problem is unsolvable. Clearly, if the halting problem for ψ is unsolvable then this is true also for any extension ψ' of ψ. Condition (*) is satisfied for the usual programming languages like PASCAL, etc. Therefore the halting problem for these languages is unsolvable.

Proof

Suppose a function f with the specified properties exists. Define $h : \mathbb{N} \dashrightarrow \mathbb{N}$ by

$$h\langle i,j\rangle = \nu_\Gamma^{-1} f(\nu_\Delta g(i), \nu_\Sigma(j)) \ .$$

Then h is a total function and $K_\varphi^\circ = h^{-1}\{0\}$. From Lemma 1.7.4 and Theorem 1.7.5 one easily concludes that h is computable. Therefore, K_φ° is decidable which contradicts Theorem 16.

Q.E.D.

Many other properties of our model programming language $(\mathbb{N},\varphi)$ can be transferred to more general programming languages in a similar way. Because of its formal simplicity we shall henceforward consider only the programming language $(\mathbb{N},\varphi)$.

The halting problem seems to be a very special problem at the first glance. The following example shows, however, that many interesting particular problems are instances of the halting problem. Consider Fermat's conjecture $(\forall n > 2)\ (\forall x,y,z \geq 1)$ $x^n + y^n \neq z^n$. Today it has been proved that for all n with $2 < n \lessapprox 500\,000$ the statement is true. But no proof for the whole conjecture exists. There is a register machine M_1 which for input n,x,y,z checks whether $x^n + y^n \neq z^n$. From M_1 a register machine M_2 can be constructed such that for any input M_2 operates in stages $m = 0,1,2,\ldots$ as follows.

Stage m:

Let $m = \langle n,x,y,z\rangle$. If $(n > 2,\ x \geq 1,\ y \geq 1,\ z \geq 1,\ x^n + y^n = z^n)$ then HALT else continue with Stage (m+1).

Therefore the machine M_2 halts on input 0 if Fermat's conjecture is false and diverges otherwise. From the register machine M_2 a number i of a tape machine M can be constructed such that $f_{M_2} = \varphi_i$. But then $\langle i,0\rangle \in K_\varphi^\circ \iff$ Fermat's conjecture is false. Therefore this instance of the halting problem solves Fermat's conjecture. Many other unsolved problems are instances of the halting problem in a similar way.

Let i be a natural number and consider the question "$i \in K_\varphi$?". In order to answer it either a proof of "$i \in \mathrm{dom}(\varphi_i)$" or a proof of "$i \notin \mathrm{dom}\ \varphi_i$" has to be found. For a rigorous proof we need a proof system (like Peano arithmetic or ZF-set theory) with axioms and rules from which either the theorem "$i \in \mathrm{dom}\ \varphi_i$" or the theorem "$i \notin \mathrm{dom}\ \varphi_i$" must be derived. For any reasonable proof system the set of derivable sentences is a recursively enumerable set (of words). Suppose A is the set of derivable sentences in our proof system, where A is recursively enumerable. (Of course, we assume that only true sentences of the form "$i \in \mathrm{dom}\ \varphi_i$" or "$i \notin \mathrm{dom}\ \varphi_i$" are in A.) Unfortunately, A is incomplete, i.e. there are numbers j such that neither

"$j \in \text{dom } \varphi_j$" nor "$j \notin \text{dom } \varphi_j$" are in A. This can be seen as follows: Suppose all the true statements "$j \notin \text{dom } \varphi_j$" are in A. Then since A is recursively enumerable also $\{j \mid j \notin \text{dom } \varphi_j\}$ becomes recursively enumerable which contradicts Theorem 16. Let $k \in \mathbb{N}$ be a number such that $k \notin \text{dom } \varphi_k$ but "$k \notin \text{dom } \varphi_k$" is not a sentence of A. How can we be sure that $k \notin \text{dom } \varphi_k$ holds? Our proof system, which is incomplete does not give any answer.

Surprisingly it is possible to determine a concrete number k such that $k \notin \text{dom } \varphi_k$ and "$k \notin \text{dom } \varphi_k$" is no sentence of A. Let

$$B := \{i \mid \text{"} i \notin \text{dom } \varphi_i \text{" is a sentence of A}\} .$$

Since A is r.e., also B is r.e., thus $B = \text{dom } \varphi_k$ for some k. Later it will become clear that k can be determined from A. We show that k already has the desired properties. Suppose $k \in \text{dom } \varphi_k = B$. Then $k \notin \text{dom } \varphi_k$ by the definition of B (contradiction). Therefore we have $k \notin \text{dom } \varphi_k$. Suppose "$k \notin \text{dom } \varphi_k$" is a sentence of A. Then we obtain $k \in B = \text{dom } \varphi_k$ (contradiction). Of course we have proved "$k \notin \text{dom } \varphi_k$" not by means of our formal proof system but in a more general system. We can express our result by saying that our formal proof system is *effectively incomplete*. This is a very remarkable result. The recursion theoretical reason for this result is that $\mathbb{N} \setminus K_\varphi$ is a *productive* set. Productive sets will be studied in detail in Part 2 of this book.

EXERCISES

1) Define an order function $a : \{1,\dots,9\} \longrightarrow \Omega$ (cf. Definition 1) by $a(1) := 1$, $a(2) = B, \dots, a(9) := L$.
   (a) Determine $\nu_{TP}(i)$ for all $i \le 20$.
   (b) Determine the smallest number i such that

   $\nu_{TP}(i) \neq$ "(,,q)"

2) Consider Definition 4. Show that $h := \nu_\Omega^{-1} \nu_{TP}$ is computable.
3) Prove Lemma 3(1) by defining a tape machine M such that $f_M : W(\Omega) \longrightarrow W(\Omega)$ and $TP = f_M^{-1}\{\varepsilon\}$.
4) Consider the proof of Theorem 6.
   (a) Construct a stack machine flowchart F over (Ω,Ω) such that f_F is some function $\widehat{sf}$.
   (b) Construct a stack machine flowchart F over (Ω,Ω) such that t_F is some test $\widehat{end}$.

5) Which of the following functions are computable?

(a) $f(i,j) := \varphi_i(j) + \varphi_i(i)$,

(b) $f(i,j,k) := \varphi_{\varphi_i(j)}(k)$,

(c) $f(i) := \max\{\varphi_n(i) \mid n \le i \wedge i \in \mathrm{dom}(\varphi_n)\}$,

(d) $f(i) := i^2 + 0 \cdot \varphi_i(i)$.

6) (a) Show that there is a numbering $\eta : \mathbb{N} \longrightarrow P^{(1)}$ of $P^{(1)}$ which does not satisfy the utm-theorem.

(b) From η construct a numbering ψ of $P^{(1)}$ which satisfies the smn-theorem but not the utm-theorem. (Hint: $\psi_{<i,0>} := \eta_i$, $\psi_{<i,x,n+1>}(y) := \psi_{<i,n>}<x,y>$.)

7) Define $\psi : \mathbb{N} \longrightarrow P^{(1)}$ by

$$\psi_{<x,y>}(z) := \begin{cases} \mathrm{div} & \text{if } z = 0 \text{ and } x = 0 \\ x - 1 & \text{if } z = 0 \text{ and } x > 0 \\ \psi_y(z) & \text{if } z > 0. \end{cases}$$

Show that ψ is a numbering of $P^{(1)}$ which satisfies the utm-theorem but not the smn-theorem. (Hint: Use Exercise 8.)

8) Prove that $M = \{i \mid 0 \in \mathrm{dom}(\varphi_i)\}$ is r.e. and not recursive.
(Hint: Apply the translation lemma to h with $h(i,x) = \varphi_i(i)$.)

9) Prove that there is some $h \in R^{(1)}$ such that $K^o_\varphi = h^{-1}K$.
(Hint: Consider the function f with $f<<i,x>,n> = \varphi_i(x)$.)

10) Let ψ be a numbering of $P^{(1)}$ which satisfies the utm-theorem. Then the following properties are equivalent

(1) ψ satisfies the smn-theorem.

(2) There is some $h \in R^{(2)}$ with $(\forall i,j)\psi_{h(i,j)} = \psi_i \circ \psi_j$.

11) For any $m \ge 1$ define $\varphi^{(m)} : \mathbb{N} \longrightarrow P^{(m)}$ by

$$\varphi_i^{(m)} := \varphi_i \circ \pi^{(m)}$$

(a) Show that $\varphi_i^{(m)}$ is surjective.

(b) Show that the universal function of $\varphi_i^{(m)}$ is computable (utm-theorem).

(c) Show that for any $m, n \ge 1$ there is a total recursive function $s^n_m : \mathbb{N}^{m+1} \longrightarrow \mathbb{N}$

$$\varphi^{(n)}_{s^n_m(i,x_1,\dots,x_m)}(y_1,\dots,y_n) = \varphi_i^{(m+n)}(x_1,\dots,x_m,y_1,\dots,y_n).$$

(This is the original smn-theorem.)

12) Let $\psi : \mathbb{N} \longrightarrow P^{(1)}$ be any numbering of $P^{(1)}$ which satisfies the smn- and the utm-theorem. Show that the self applicability problem K_ψ and the halting problem K^o_ψ of ψ are recursively enumerable and not recursive.

13) Let ψ be a total numbering of $P^{(1)}$. Show that ψ is admissible iff ψ satisfies the utm-theorem and $\psi' \leq \psi$ for any total numbering ψ' of $P^{(1)}$ which satisfies the utm-theorem.

BIBLIOGRAPHICAL NOTES

The unsolvability of the halting problem is due to Turing (1936) who also constructed a universal Turing machine. The formulation of the smn-theorem is due to Kleene (1952). The characterization theorem of ψ (Theorem 1.9.10) is from Rogers (1967, p.41 and 1958).

1.10 Some Unsolvable Problems

In Chapter 1.9 we have proved that the halting problem and the self applicability problem for φ are (recursively) unsolvable (Theorem 1.9.16(2)). In Part 2 of this book several other problems which can be derived from φ will be shown to be unsolvable, and we shall study "degrees of unsolvability". The discussion at the end of Chapter 1.9 indicates that there are fundamental applications of recursion theory in logic. A special chapter in Part 2 will be devoted to some of these questions. In this chapter some decision problems from other parts of mathematics will be considered. A decision problem is defined by a set M and a subset $M_o \subseteq M$. The problem is to decide for any $m \in M$ whether m belongs to M_o or not. In the case of the halting problem $M = \mathbb{N}$ and $M_o = K_\varphi^o$. If M is not a set of the numbers or of the words over some alphabet then it is not clear what "decide" means. In this case more information has to be supplied to specify the decision problem. Usually a notation ν of M, i.e. a surjective function $\nu : W(\Sigma) \dashrightarrow M$, is given. Also a numbering $\nu : \mathbb{N} \dashrightarrow M$ could be used. W.l.g. we consider the case of a notation here. By Theorem 1.8.9 both approaches yield the same decidability results.

1 DEFINITION (*decision problem*)

A decision problem is a triple $P = (M, M_o, \nu)$ where M is some set, $M_o \subseteq M$, and $\nu : W(\Sigma) \dashrightarrow M$ is a notation of M (for some alphabet Σ). A solution of the problem P is a computable function $f : W(\Sigma) \dashrightarrow W(\Sigma)$ such that $\mathrm{dom}(\nu) \subseteq \mathrm{dom}(f)$ and

$$\nu(w) \in M_o \iff f(w) = \varepsilon$$

for any $w \in \mathrm{dom}(\nu)$. The decision problem P is *decidable* or *solvable* iff it has a solution.

The function f (or a program for f) decides the membership in M_o, given any name w of an element $\nu(w) \in M$. We shall formulate some famous decision problems which are undecidable. The undecidability proofs usually are rather long, therefore we present only two of them here.

2 DEFINITION (*Post correspondence problem*)

Let Σ be an alphabet.

(1) Let $PL := \{((x_1,y_1),\dots,(x_n,y_n)) \mid n \geq 1;\ x_i, y_i \in W(\Sigma)\}$ be the set of *pair lists* over Σ.

(2) Let $\Delta := \{(\,|\,)\,|\,,\}$ be a three element alphabet (w.l.g. $\Delta \cap \Sigma = \emptyset$). A standard notation $\nu : W(\Sigma\cup\Delta) \dashrightarrow PL$ is defined by

$$\mathrm{dom}(\nu) = \{"((x_1,y_1),\ldots,(x_n,y_n))" \mid n \geq 1,\ x_i,y_i \in W(\Sigma)\}\,,$$

$$\nu("((x_1,y_1),\ldots,(x_n,y_n))") := ((x_1,y_1),\ldots,(x_n,y_n))\,.$$

(3) Let $\bar{p} = ((x_1,y_1),\ldots,(x_n,y_n)) \in PL$ be a pair list. A *correspondence* of $\bar{p}$ is a sequence $(i_1,\ldots,i_k)$ with $1 \leq i_j \leq n$ such that

$$x_{i_1}x_{i_2}\ldots x_{i_k} = y_{i_1}y_{i_2}\ldots y_{i_k}$$

where the word $x_{i_1}\ldots x_{i_k}$ is called a *solution* of $\bar{p}$.

(4) The triple (PL, PL_o, ν) where

$$PL_o = \{\bar{p} \in PL \mid \bar{p} \text{ has a correspondence}\}$$

is the *Post Correspondence Problem* (over Σ), the PCP.

The function ν is a simple "effective" notation of PL. Notice that the domain of ν is a set of words over $\Sigma \cup \Delta$ and that the range of ν is the set PL of pairlists.

3 EXAMPLES

Let $\bar{p} = ((a,ba),(b^2a,a^3),(a^2b,ba))$. If $(i_1,\ldots,i_k)$ is a correspondence of $\bar{p}$ then x_{i_1} must be a prefix of y_{i_1} or vice versa. This condition cannot be satisfied. Let $\bar{p} = ((b^3,b^2),(ab^2,bab^3))$. Then $(1,2,1)$ is a correspondence since $b^3ab^2b^3 = b^2bab^3b^2$.

For technical reasons we introduce the *Special Post Correspondence Problem* (SPCP, for short).

4 DEFINITION

Let Σ, ν, and PL be as in Definition 2.

(1) A correspondence $(i_1,\ldots,i_k)$ of a pair list $\bar{p} \in PL$ is a *special correspondence*, iff $i_1 = 1$.

(2) The triple (PL, PL_1, ν) where

$$PL_1 = \{\bar{p} \in PL \mid \bar{p} \text{ has a special correspondence}\}$$

is the *Special Post Correspondence Problem* (over Σ).

In the second example from above, (1,2,1) is a special correspondence of $\hat{p}$. We shall prove 3 statements in turn: 1. the SPCP is unsolvable for some special alphabet, 2. the PCP is unsolvable for some special alphabet, 3. the PCP is unsolvable for any alphabet Σ with $\mathrm{card}(\Sigma) \geq 2$.

5 LEMMA

There is an alphabet Δ such that the SPCP over Δ is unsolvable.

Proof

The lemma is proved by reduction to the halting problem. We show that for any tape program $v \in TP$ (c f. Definition 1.9.2) and input $x \in W(\{1\})$ a pair list $\hat{p}$ can be constructed such that the tape machine tm(v) halts on input x, if and only if the pair list $\hat{p}$ has a special correspondence $(1,i_2,i_3,\dots,i_k)$. The word $x_1 x_{i_2} \dots x_{i_k}$ is (or encodes) the protocol of the computation. Now, if the SPCP were solvable, also the halting problem for Turing machines would be solvable: for given $v \in TP$ and input x construct the corresponding pair list $\hat{p}$ and decide whether $\hat{p}$ has a special correspondence. But we already know that the halting problem is unsolvable. We go into the details now.

Consider the definitions 1.9.2 and 1.9.4. Define a surjective mapping $\psi : W(\Omega) \dashrightarrow P_\Sigma$ $(\Sigma := \{1\})$ by $\mathrm{dom}(\psi) := TP \subseteq W(\Omega)$ and $\psi_v(x) := f_{tm(v)}(x)$ for all $v \in TP$ and $x \in W(\{1\})$. We show by Theorem 1.9.17 that the halting problem for ψ is unsolvable. By Definition 1.9.4 there is a function $g \in R^{(1)}$ such that $\nu_{TP}(i) = \nu_\Omega g(i)$. This function satisfies Condition (*) from Theorem 1.9.17:

$$\varphi_i(k) = \iota^{-1} f_{tm\nu_{TP}(i)} \iota(k) = \iota^{-1} \psi_{\nu_\Omega g(i)} \iota(k) .$$

Therefore there is no computable function $f : W(\Omega) \times W(\Omega) \dashrightarrow W(\Omega)$ with $TP \times W(\{1\}) \subseteq \mathrm{dom}(f)$ and $f(v,x) = \varepsilon \Longleftrightarrow x \in \mathrm{dom}(\psi_v)$ for all $v \in TP$ and $x \in W(\{1\})$.

We shall now, for given $v \in TP$ and $x \in W(\{1\})$, construct (the name w.r.t. a standard notation of) a pair list $\hat{p}$ such that $\hat{p}$ has a special correspondence, iff $x \in \mathrm{dom}\,\psi_v$. Let $\Delta := \{B,0,1,¢,\$,\#\}$. Let $D = \{[y,a,z] \mid a \in \{B,1\},\ y,z \in W(\{B,1\})\}$ be the data set of the tape machines from TM (c f. Def. 1.9.2, Def. 1.5.1). The configurations of these machines are in the set $\mathbb{N} \times D$ (c f. Def. 1.1.6, Def. 1.9.2). We define a notation $\gamma : W(\{B,0,1\}) \longrightarrow \mathbb{N} \times D$ as follows:

$$\mathrm{dom}(\gamma) := \{ya0^{i+1}az \mid i \in \mathbb{N},\ y,z \in W(\{B,1\}),\ a \in \{B,1\}\} ,$$

$$\gamma(ya0^{i+1}az) := (i,[y,a,z]) .$$

(Notice that γ is not injective.) Let SF be the single step function of the machine $tm(v) \in TM$. It is our aim to construct a pair list $\hat{p}$ such that every solution begins with

$\$¢u_o\#¢u_1\#\ldots¢u_k\#\ldots$

where $\gamma(u_o) = (q_o,[\varepsilon,B,x])$ (= the initial configuration) and $SF\gamma(u_i) = \gamma(u_{i+1})$. Let $F = (Q,D,\sigma,q_o,1,q_e)$ be the flowchart of the tape machine tm(v). Then let $\hat{p}$ consist of the following pairs (x_i,y_i).

i	x_i	y_i
1	\$	$\$¢B0^{q_o+1}Bx\#$
2	¢	¢
3	#	#
4	1	1
5	B	B

For all $p \in Q \setminus \{q_e\}$, $q,q' \in Q$ and $a,b \in \{B,1\}$ add the following pairs (in lexicographic order)

$$\left.\begin{array}{l}(1\,0^{p+1}\,1\,,\,1\,0^{q+1}\,1)\\(B\,0^{p+1}\,B\,,\,B\,0^{q'+1}\,B)\end{array}\right\}\quad \text{if}\quad \sigma(p) = q$$

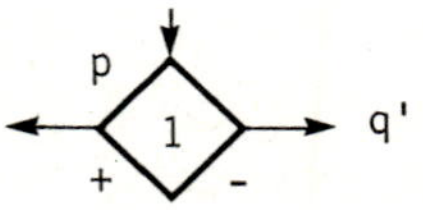

$$\left.\begin{array}{l}(1\,0^{p+1}\,1\,,\,1\,0^{q'+1}\,1)\\(B\,0^{p+1}\,B\,,\,B\,0^{q+1}\,B)\end{array}\right\}\quad \text{if}\quad \sigma(p) = q$$

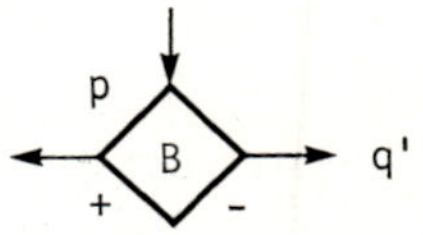

$$(a\,0^{p+1}\,a\,,\,b\,0^{q+1}\,b)\quad \text{if}\quad \sigma(p) =$$

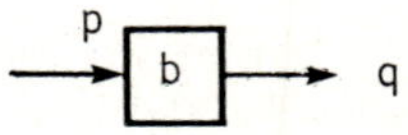

$$\left.\begin{array}{l}(a\,0^{p+1}\,a\,b\,,\,a\,b\,0^{q+1}\,b)\\(a\,0^{p+1}\,a\#\,,\,a\,B\,0^{q+1}\,B\#)\end{array}\right\}\quad \text{if}\quad \sigma(p) =$$

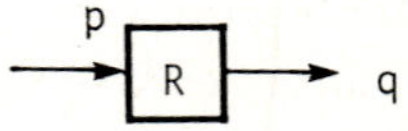

$$\left.\begin{array}{l}(b\,a\,0^{p+1}\,a\,,\,b\,0^{q+1}\,b\,a)\\(¢\,a\,0^{p+1}\,a\,,\,¢\,B\,0^{q+1}\,B\,a)\end{array}\right\}\quad \text{if}\quad \sigma(p) =$$

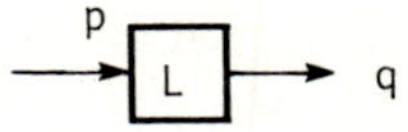

$$(b\,a\,0^{q_e+1}\,a\,,\,a\,0^{q_e+1}\,a)$$

$$(¢\,a\,0^{q_e+1}\,a\,b\,,\,¢\,a\,0^{q_e+1}\,a)$$

$$(¢\,a\,0^{q_e+1}\,a\#\,,\,\varepsilon)\;.$$

Let us call a sequence $(1,i_2,\ldots,i_m)$ a partial correspondence if $u := x_1x_{i_2}\ldots x_{i_m}$ is a prefix of $v := y_1y_{i_2}\ldots y_{i_m}$ or v is a prefix of u. In this case (u,v) is called a partial solution of $\hat{p}$.

<u>Assertion:</u>

Let $(1,i_2,\ldots,i_m)$ be a partial correspondence of $\hat{p}$ determining the partial solution $(z,z¢u\#)$ where $u \in \mathrm{dom}(\gamma)$ and $\gamma(u)$ is not a final configuration of the tape machine tm(v). Then:

1. There is a partial correspondence $(1,i_2,\dots,i_m,i_{m+1},\dots,i_n)$ with a partial solution $(z¢u\#, z¢u\#¢u'\#)$ such that $SF\gamma(u)=\gamma(u')$. (Existence)

2. Let $(1,i_2,\dots,i_m,i'_{m+1},\dots,i'_k)$ be a partial correspondence with partial solution (w_1,w_2) such that $z¢u\#$ is a prefix of w_1. Then $k\geq n$ and $i_j=i'_j$ for $m<j\leq k$. (Uniqueness)

Proof:
Suppose $u=y_1a0^{p+1}ay_2$: For extending the partial solution $(z,z¢u\#)$ a sequence $(i_{m+1},\dots,i_n)$ of indices must be determined such that $¢u\#$ is a prefix of $x_{i_{m+1}}\dots x_{i_n}$. Since p is not the final state, there is only one pair (x_i,y_i) in the list such that 0^{p+1} is a subword of x_i, and (x_i,y_i) can be correctly appended. Therefore, using also pairs with numbers 2,3,4, and 5 the word $¢u\#$ can be produced in a unique way. The y-components yield a word $¢u'\#$ such that $SF\gamma(u)=\gamma(u')$. This proves the assertion.

Now, suppose that the tape machine tm(v) on input x halts after k steps. Obviously, $(\$,\$¢\ B0^{q_0+1}Bx\#)$ is a partial solution. Using the above assertion, by an induction we obtain $u_0:=B0^{q_0+1}Bx, u_1,\dots,u_k$ such that $SF(\gamma(u_i))=\gamma(u_{i+1})$ for $i<k$, u_k is a final configuration of tm(v), and

$$(z,z') := (\$¢u_0\#¢u_1\#\dots¢u_{k-1}\#\ ,\ \$¢u_0\#\dots\ ¢u_{k-1}\#¢u_k\#)$$

is a partial solution of $\hat{p}$. There are $y_1,y_2\in W(\{B,1\})$ and $a\in\{B,1\}$ with $u_k=y_1a0^{p_e+1}ay_2$. By appending pairs from $\hat{p}$ given in the last 3 lines of the table and pairs 2 - 5 the first component of (z,z') can gradually catch up with the second component until by appending a pair from the last line a correspondence is obtained. This shows that $\hat{p}$ has a special correspondence.

On the other hand, suppose $\hat{p}$ has a correspondence $(1,i_1,\dots,i_n)$. By induction using the above assertion the solution must extend partial solutions

$$(\$¢u_0\#¢u_1\#\dots¢u_{k-1}\#\ ,\ \$¢u_0\#\dots¢u_k\#)$$

where $u_0=B0^{q_0+1}Bx$ and $SF(\gamma(u_i))=\gamma(u_{i+1})$ for $i<k$. Suppose k is maximal with this property. Then u_k must be a final configuration of tm(v). Hence the Turing machine tm(v) halts on input x.

Therefore, we have proved that tm(v) halts on input x iff $\hat{p}$ has a special correspondence. It is easy to specify the numbers of the pairs (x_i,y_i) given in our list for $\hat{p}$ such that the function h with $h(v,x)=\nu^{-1}(\hat{p})$ (ν from Definition 2) becomes computable (use lexicographic order) (see Def. 1.7.7).

Now suppose that the SPCP for the alphabet $\Delta=\{B,0,1,¢,\$,\#\}$ is solvable. Then there is some computable function g with $dom(\nu)\subseteq dom(g)$, $range(g)\subseteq\{\varepsilon,1\}$, and $g(w)=\varepsilon\Leftrightarrow\nu(w)$ has a special solution. There is a computable word function with $f(v,x)=gh(v,x)$ for all $v\in TP$ and $x\in W(\{1\})$. Then $TP\times W(\{1\})\subseteq dom(f)$ and $f(v,x)=\varepsilon\Leftrightarrow$

tm(v) halts on input $x \Longleftrightarrow x \in \mathrm{dom}\,\psi_v$. But we have shown above that such a function f cannot exist. Therefore the SPCP over $\Delta = \{B,0,1,¢,\$,\#\}$ is unsolvable.

Q.E.D.

Of course, the SPCP is also unsolvable for any alphabet Δ with more than six symbols.

6 LEMMA

8 There is some alphabet Σ with 8 elements such that the PCP over Σ is unsolvable.

Proof

Let Δ be the alphabet from Lemma 5 with 6 elements, let $\Sigma := \Delta \cup \{A,B\}$ where $A,B \notin \Delta$. Let ν_1 (ν_2) be the notation of the pair lists PL(Δ) over Δ (PL(Σ) over Σ) (c f. Definition 2). We shall define a function $h : PL(\Delta) \longrightarrow PL(\Sigma)$ such that for any pair list $\bar{p} \in PL(\Delta)$ $\bar{p}$ has a special correspondence iff $h(\bar{p})$ has a correspondence. Moreover, h will be computable w.r.t. (ν_1,ν_2) , i.e. there is a computable function f which transforms a name of $\bar{p}$ into a name of $h(\bar{p})$; more precisely there is a computable word function f such that $h\nu_1(v) = \nu_2 f(v)$ for any $v \in \mathrm{dom}(\nu_1)$. Then, if the PCP over Σ were solvable then also the SPCP over Δ would be solvable. We go into details now. Define $\varphi_L(a) := Aa$ and $\varphi_R(a) = aA$ for any $a \in \Delta$ and extend φ_L and φ_R to W(Δ) by $\varphi_L(\varepsilon) = \varphi_R(\varepsilon) = \varepsilon$, $\varphi_L(wa) = \varphi_L(w)\varphi_L(a)$, $\varphi_R(wa) = \varphi_R(w)\varphi_R(a)$ for any $w \in W(\Delta)$ and $a \in \Delta$. For any pair list $\bar{p} = ((x_1,y_1),\dots,(x_n,y_n))$ over Δ define the pair list $h(\bar{p}) := ((x'_1,y'_1),\dots,(x'_{n+2},y'_{n+2}))$ over Σ as follows.

$$x'_1 := A\varphi_R(x_1) \ , \quad y'_1 := \varphi_L(y_1) \ ,$$

$$x'_{i+1} := \varphi_R(x_i) \ , \quad y'_{i+1} := \varphi_L(y_i)$$

for $i = 1,\dots,n$ and

$$x'_{n+2} := B \ , \quad y'_{n+2} := AB \ .$$

Suppose $(1,i_1,\dots,i_k)$ is a correspondence of $\bar{p}$. Then

$$\begin{aligned} & x'_1 x'_{i_1+1} \dots x'_{i_k+1}\, x'_{n+2} \\ &= A\varphi_R(x_1 x_{i_1} \dots x_{i_k})B \\ &= A\varphi_R(y_1 y_{i_1} \dots y_{i_k})B \\ &= \varphi_L(y_1 y_{i_1} \dots y_{i_k})AB \\ &= y'_1 y'_{i_1+1} \dots y'_{i_k+1} y'_{n+2} \ , \end{aligned}$$

therefore $(1,i_1+1,\dots,i_k+1,n+2)$ is a correspondence of $h(\bar{p})$. Suppose $(j_1,\dots,j_k)$

is a correspondence of $h(\bar{p})$. Since (x'_{n+2},y'_{n+2}) is the only pair which ends with the same symbol, $j_k = n+2$. Let m be the least integer such that $j_m = n+2$. Let $u := x'_{j_1}\dots x'_{j_m}$, $v := y'_{j_1}\dots y'_{j_m}$. Then either u is a prefix of v or v is a prefix of u. By assumption on m there is only one appearance of B in u and in v respectively (namely the last symbol). Hence $u = v$, and $(j_1,\dots,j_m)$ is a correspondence with $j_m = n+2$ and $j_i < n+2$ for $i = 1,\dots,m-1$. Since (x'_1,y'_1) is the only pair which starts with the same symbol (namely A), $j_1 = 1$. If $j_i = 1$ for some other i, $1 < i < m$, then u would have more A's than v. Hence, $2 \le j_i \le n+1$ for all i with $1 < i < m$ and

$$\begin{aligned}
&A\varphi_R(x_1 x_{j_2-1}\dots x_{j_{m-1}-1})B \\
&= x'_1 x'_{j_2}\dots x'_{j_{m-1}} x'_{j_m} \\
&= y'_1 y'_{j_2}\dots y'_{j_{m-1}} y'_{j_m} \\
&= \varphi_L(y_1 y_{j_2-1}\dots y_{j_{m-1}-1})AB \\
&= A\varphi_R(y_1 y_{j_2-1}\dots y_{j_{m-1}-1})B\ .
\end{aligned}$$

Since φ_R is injective, $(1,j_2-1,\dots,j_{m-1}-1)$ is a correspondence for $\bar{p}$. Therefore, $\bar{p}$ has a special correspondence iff $h(\bar{p})$ has a correspondence. It is easy to define a stack machine M which for any ν_1-name v of some $\bar{p}$ yields a ν_2-name of $h(\bar{p})$. Now suppose that the PCP over Σ is solvable. Then there is a computable word function f such that $\mathrm{dom}(\nu_2) \subseteq \mathrm{dom}(f)$ and $\nu_2(w)$ has a correspondence iff $f(w) = \varepsilon$. Consider the function $\bar{f} := ff_M$. Then for any $v \in \mathrm{dom}(\nu_1)$, $\bar{f}(v)$ is defined, $\bar{f}$ is computable and $\nu_1(v)$ has a special correspondence, iff $\nu_2 f_M(v)$ has a correspondence, iff $ff_M(v) = \bar{f}(v) = \varepsilon$. Therefore the SPCP over Δ would be solvable. This contradicts Lemma 5.

Q.E.D.

By a further very simple reduction we derive now that the PCP over Γ is unsolvable if Γ has at least two elements.

7 THEOREM (*Unsolvability of the PCP*)

Let Γ be an alphabet with at least two elements. Then the Post Correspondence Problem over Γ is unsolvable.

Proof

Let $A,B \in \Gamma$, $A \neq B$ arbitrary symbols from Γ. Let Σ be the alphabet from Lemma 6 with 8 elements. Let $\sigma : \Sigma \longrightarrow W(\{A,B\})$ be an injective mapping such that $\sigma(a)$ has length 3 for any $a \in \Sigma$. Define a function $\gamma : W(\Sigma) \longrightarrow W(\Gamma)$ by $\gamma(\varepsilon) = \varepsilon$ and

$\gamma(wa) = \gamma(w)\sigma(a)$ for any $w \in W(\Sigma)$, $a \in \Sigma$. Then γ is injective. Let γ_1 (γ_2) be the standard notation of the pair lists over Σ (over Γ). Then there is a computable word function h such that $\mathrm{dom}(\nu_1) \subseteq \mathrm{dom}(h)$ and

$$h(\hat{p}) = \text{"}((\gamma(x_1),\gamma(y_1)),\ldots,(\gamma(x_n),\gamma(y_n)))\text{"} \quad \text{for any pair list}$$
$$\hat{p} = \text{"}((x_1,y_1),\ldots,(x_n,y_n))\text{"}$$

over Σ. Obviously, $\hat{p}$ has a correspondence iff $h(\hat{p})$ has a correspondence. As in the proof of Lemma 6 it can easily be shown that the PCP over Σ is solvable if the PCP over Γ is solvable. By Lemma 6, the PCP over Γ is unsolvable.
Q.E.D.

It can be shown that the Post Correspondence Problem is solvable if the alphabet has only one element. For any alphabet Σ the set of pair lists over Σ which have a correspondence (more precisely, the set of all $\nu^{-1}(\hat{p})$ for which $\hat{p}$ has a correspondence) is recursively enumerable (c f. the exercises).

Another famous problem is the word problem for *Semi-Thue systems*. Informally, a Semi-Thue system is a finite set $R \subseteq W(\Sigma) \times W(\Sigma)$ of pairs of words called *rewrite* or *production rules* or *productions*. The rules are used for transforming words. If $(x,y) \in R$ is a rule and $w = uxv$ then w may be transformed into $w' = uyv$, i.e. any subword x of w may be replaced by the subword y. The word problem for the Semi-Thue system defined by R is to decide for any $z,z' \in W(\Sigma)$ whether z can be transformed into z' by finitely many replacements with rules from R. The general word problem for Semi-Thue problems is to decide for any (finite) set of rules R and any $z,z' \in W(\Sigma)$ whether z can be transformed into z' by finitely many replacements with rules from R. We shall now define the concepts more precisely.

8 <u>DEFINITION</u> (*Semi-Thue system, derivability*)

(1) A *Semi-Thue system* is a pair $T = (\Sigma, R)$ where Σ is an alphabet and $R \subseteq W(\Sigma) \times W(\Sigma)$ is finite.

(2) A relation $\xrightarrow[T]{} \subseteq W(\Sigma) \times W(\Sigma)$ is defined by

$$\xrightarrow[T]{} := \{(uxv,uyv) \mid u,v \in W(\Sigma),\ (x,y) \in R\}.$$

(3) Let $\xrightarrow[T]{*}$ $W(\Sigma) \times W(\Sigma)$ be the reflexive (w.r.t. $W(\Sigma) \times W(\Sigma)$) and transitive closure of $\xrightarrow[T]{}$ ($u \xrightarrow[T]{*} v$ means "v is derivable from u by means of T").

9 <u>EXAMPLE</u>

Let $\Sigma = \{a,b,c,S,B\}$, $R = \{(S,\varepsilon),(S,aSBc),(cB,Bc),(aB,ab),(bB,bb)\}$. Then e.g.

$S \xrightarrow[T]{} aSBC \xrightarrow[T]{} aaSBcBc \xrightarrow[T]{} aaBcBc \xrightarrow[T]{} aabcBc \xrightarrow[T]{} aabBcc \xrightarrow[T]{} aabbcc$, i.e. $S \xrightarrow[T]{} a^2b^2c^2$.

By the next theorem the general word problem for Semi-Thue systems is unsolvable.

10 THEOREM (*unsolvability of the word problem for STS's*)

Let Σ be an alphabet with at least two elements. Let

$$M := \{(T,v,w) \mid T \text{ is a Semi-Thue system over } \Sigma,\ v,w \in W(\Sigma)\},$$

let ν be a "canonical" notation of M. Let

$$M_o = \{(T,v,w) \in M \mid v \xrightarrow[T]{*} w\}.$$

Then the word problem for Semi-Thue systems over Σ, (M, M_o, ν) is unsolvable.

It should be clear what is meant by "canonical" notation. For example the notation ν with

$$\nu(\text{"}(\{(x_1,y_1),\ldots,(x_n,x_n)\},u,v)\text{"}) := (\{(x_1,y_1),\ldots,(x_n,y_n)\},u,v)$$

for all $n \in \mathbb{N}$, $x_i, y_i, u, v \in W(\Sigma)$ is canonical, c f. Definition 2(2). Theorem 10 is a corollary of the following lemma.

11 LEMMA

Let $L \subseteq W(\Sigma)$ be recursively enumerable. Then there is a Semi-Thue system $T = (\Delta, R)$ with $\Sigma \subseteq \Delta$ and $S \in \Delta \setminus \Sigma$ such that

$$L = \{w \in W(\Sigma) \mid S \xrightarrow[T]{*} w\}.$$

Proof

Let $L \subseteq W(\Sigma)$ be a recursively enumerable set of words. By Definition 1.8.7 there is a tape machine $M = (F, W(\Sigma), W(\Sigma), I, O)$ over (Γ, Σ, B) such that $L = \mathrm{dom}(f_M)$. Let $F = (Q, D, \sigma, q_o, 1, q_e)$ be the flowchart of the tape machine M. We may assume $Q \cap \Gamma = \emptyset$. Let $\{¢,\$,S,C,D\}$ be a set with five elements such that $\{¢,\$,S,C,D\} \cap (Q \cup \Gamma) = \emptyset$, let $\Delta := Q \cup \Gamma \cup \{¢,\$,S,C,D\}$. The Semi-Thue system will operate on names of tape machine configurations. Define a notation $\gamma : W(\Delta) \dashrightarrow \mathrm{CON}$ as follows:

$$\mathrm{dom}(\gamma) := \{¢uqav\$ \mid q \in Q;\ a \in \Gamma;\ u,v \in W(\Gamma)\}$$

$$\gamma(¢uqav\$) := (q, [u,a,v])$$

for all $q \in Q$; $a \in \Gamma$; $u,v \in W(\Gamma)$. By Definition 1.5.4

$$w \in \mathrm{dom}(f_M) \iff (\exists t \in \mathbb{N})(\exists a,u,v)\ SF^t(q_o,[\varepsilon,B,w]) = (q_e,[u,a,v])$$

for all $w \in W(\Sigma)$. We shall define finite sets of productions $R_1,\ldots,R_4$ with the following properties:

- The productions from R_1 generate from S all words z such that $\gamma(z)$ is a final configuration.
- The productions from R_2 allow any name of a configuration to be transformed into the equivalent names. (Notice that $\gamma(¢B^m uqavB^n\$) = \gamma(¢uqav\$)$ for all $m,n \in \mathbb{N}$.)
- The productions from R_3 reverse (on the encodings) the single step function of the flowchart F.
- The productions from R_4 generate the input value from the encoding of any initial configuration.

The set of rules are defined as follows

$$R_1 := \{(S,¢C)\} \cup \{(C,aC),(C,q_e a\$),(q_e,q_e a) \mid a \in \Gamma\}$$

$$R_2 := \{(¢B,¢),(¢,¢B),(aB\$,a\$),(\$,B\$) \mid a \in \Gamma\}$$

$$\begin{aligned} R_3 := &\{(aqb,pab) \mid a,b \in \Gamma;\ p,q \in Q;\ \sigma(p) = \text{"R,q"}\} \\ &\cup \{(qab,apb) \mid a,b \in \Gamma;\ p,q \in Q;\ \sigma(p) = \text{"L,q"}\} \\ &\cup \{(qa,pa),(q'b,pb) \mid a,b \in \Gamma;\ p,q,q' \in Q;\ a \neq b;\ \sigma(p) = \text{"a,q,q'"}\} \end{aligned}$$

$$R_4 := \{(¢q_o B,D),(Da,aD),(D\$,\varepsilon) \mid a \in \Sigma\}.$$

We shall prove some basic properties of the sets $R_1,\ldots,R_4$ of rules. For short we write $\xrightarrow[i]{}$ instead of $\xrightarrow[R_i]{}$, $\xrightarrow[i,j]{}$ instead of $\xrightarrow[R_i \cup R_j]{}$, etc. Define $R := R_1 \cup R_2 \cup R_3 \cup R_4$.

<u>Proposition 1:</u>

$$\{z \in W(\Delta) \mid S \xrightarrow[1,2]{*} z\} = \{S\} \cup \{¢xC, ¢xq_e y\$ \mid x,y \in W(\Gamma),\ y \neq \varepsilon\}$$

<u>Proof:</u> (as an exercise)

<u>Proposition 2:</u>

$$u' \xrightarrow[2,3]{*} u \iff (\exists n)\ SF^n\gamma(u) = \gamma(u')$$

for all $u,u' \in \mathrm{dom}(\gamma)$

<u>Proof:</u>

"$\Longrightarrow$": Show $(\forall m)\ u' \xrightarrow[2,3]{m} u \Longrightarrow (\exists n) \ldots$ by induction.

"$\Longleftarrow$": Show $(\forall n)\ SF^n\gamma(u) = \gamma(u') \Longrightarrow u' \xrightarrow[2,3]{*} u$ by induction on n (as exercises).

<u>Proposition 3:</u>

$$Dv\$ \xrightarrow[R]{*} w \iff (\exists i)\ v = wB^i$$

for all $v \in W(\Gamma)$, $w \in W(\Sigma)$.

<u>Proof:</u>

"$\Longrightarrow$": Show by induction on m: $Dv\$ \xrightarrow[R]{m} w \Longrightarrow (\exists i)\ v = wB^i$.

"$\Longleftarrow$": Show by induction on $lg(v)$: $(\exists i)\ v = wB^i \Longrightarrow \ldots$ (as exercises).

Now, suppose $w \in L = \mathrm{dom}(f_M)$. Then for some $n \in \mathbb{N}$, $SF^n(q_o,[\varepsilon,B,w]) =: \kappa'$ is a final configuration. Let $u := ¢q_oBw\$$, then $\gamma(u) = (q_o,[\varepsilon,B,w])$. Let $u' \in \mathrm{dom}(\gamma)$ such that $\gamma(u') = \kappa'$. Then

$$S \xrightarrow[1,2]{*} u' \quad \text{(by Prop. 1)}$$

$$\xrightarrow[2,3]{*} u \quad \text{(by Prop. 2)}$$

$$\xrightarrow[R]{} Dw\$$$

$$\xrightarrow[R]{*} w \quad \text{(by Prop. 3)}$$

On the other hand suppose $S \xrightarrow[R]{*} w$ with $w \in W(\Sigma)$. By Proposition 1, $S \xrightarrow[1,2]{*} w$ is false. Therefore there are words w_1, w_2 with $S \xrightarrow[1,2]{*} w_1 \xrightarrow[3,4]{} w_2 \xrightarrow[R]{*} w$. Hence $w_1 = ¢xq_eay\$$ for certain $a \in \Gamma$, $x,y \in W(\Gamma)$ by Proposition 1.

Case $w_1 \xrightarrow[3]{} w_2$: Then $w_2 = ¢x'q'a'y'\$$ for certain x', y', a', and q' where $q' \neq q_e$ by Definition of R_3. There are words w_3, w_4 with $w_2 \xrightarrow[2,3]{*} w_3 \xrightarrow[1,4]{} w_4 \xrightarrow[R]{*} w$. By Proposition 2, $\gamma(w_3)$ is not a final configuration, hence $w_3 \xrightarrow[4]{} w_4$ by Definition of R_1. Therefore $w_3 = ¢q_oBv'\$$ and $w_4 = Dv'\$$ for some $v' \in W(\Gamma)$.

Case $w_1 \xrightarrow[4]{} w_2$: Then $(¢q_oB,D)$ is the only applicable production from R_4 but since $q_e \neq q_o$ this is impossible.

Therefore there is a word v' with

$$S \xrightarrow[1,2]{*} ¢xq_eay\$ \xrightarrow[2,3]{*} ¢q_oBv'\$ \xrightarrow[4]{} Dv'\$ \xrightarrow[R]{*} w .$$

By Proposition 3, $v' = wB^i$ for some $i \in \mathbb{N}$. By Proposition 2 there is some n such that

$$SF^n(q_o,[\varepsilon,B,w]) = SF^n\gamma(¢q_oBv'\$) = \gamma(¢xq_eay\$) = (q_e,[x,a,y]) ,$$

hence $w \in \mathrm{dom}(f_M) = L$.

Q.E.D.

The proof of Theorem 10 is left as an exercise. Remember that there is a nonrecursive set $L \subseteq W(\Sigma)$. The word problem for Semi-Thue systems is recursively enumerable.

12 THEOREM

Let Σ be an alphabet, let ν be a canonical notation of the Semi-Thue systems over Σ. Then the set

$$\{(w,x,y) \mid x \xrightarrow[\nu(w)]{*} y\}$$

is recursively enumerable.

Proof

As the main tool we use the projection theorem for sets of word tuples (Theorem 1.8.4, see also the comment after Theorem 1.8.9). It is easy to see that the set

$$\{(w,x,y,x_o\$x_1\$\ldots\$x_k) \mid k \geq 1,\ x_o = x,\ x_k = y,\ x_i \xrightarrow[\nu(w)]{} x_{i+1} \text{ for } i < k\}$$

is recursive (assume $\$ \notin \Sigma$). The projection theorem immediately yields that $\{(w,x,y) \mid x \xrightarrow[\nu(w)]{} y\}$ is r.e.

Q.E.D.

A *Thue system* is a Semi-Thue system $T = (\Sigma,R)$ such that $(u,v) \in R \Longrightarrow (v,u) \in R$. The *word problem* for *Thue systems* is unsolvable. This problem is also called the *word problem for semigroups*. This will now be explained. Let $T = (\Sigma,R)$ be a Thue system. The elements of Σ generate the free semigroup with unit ε $S_\Sigma := (W(\Sigma),\circ,\varepsilon)$ where $\circ$ is the concatenation on $W(\Sigma)$. The relation $\xrightarrow[R]{*}$ on $W(\Sigma)$ is an equivalence relation since R is symmetric. It is compatible with the concatenation: $x \xrightarrow[R]{*} y \Longrightarrow uxv \xrightarrow[R]{*} uyv$, i.e. $\xrightarrow[R]{*}$ is a congruence relation on S_Σ which we denote by "$\equiv$". For any $x \in W(\Sigma)$ let $[x] := \{y \mid x \equiv y\}$, $W(\Sigma)/\equiv\ := \{[x] \mid x \in W(\Sigma)\}$. Since $\equiv$ is a congruence relation, by $[x]\circ[y] := [xy]$ an associative product with unit $[\varepsilon]$ is defined. Therefore, $S_\Sigma/\equiv\ := (W(\Sigma)/\equiv,\circ,[\varepsilon])$ is a semigroup with unit $[\varepsilon]$. The mapping $h : x \longmapsto [x]$ is a semigroup homomorphism from S_Σ to $S_\Sigma/\equiv$ which can be considered as a notation of $W(\Sigma)/\equiv$. Since $x \xrightarrow[R]{*} y \Longleftrightarrow x \equiv y \Longleftrightarrow [x] = [y] \Longleftrightarrow h(x) = h(y)$, the word problem for the Thue system T is the equivalence problem for the notation h of the semigroup $W(\Sigma)/\equiv$.

By a further specialization we obtain the *word problem for group systems* which is also unsolvable. Let $T = (\Sigma,R)$ be a Thue system with the following additional property: There is a mapping $\sigma : \Sigma \longrightarrow \Sigma$ with

$$(\forall a \in \Sigma)\quad (a\sigma(a),\varepsilon) \in R\,.$$

Then T is called a group system. Notice that for a group system T the Semigroup $S_\Sigma/\equiv$ defined above is a group.

A further unsolvable problem is *Hilbert's 10th problem* on *diophantine equations*. Let

$$\tilde{P} := \{p : \mathbb{Z}^n \longrightarrow \mathbb{Z} \mid p \text{ a polynomial function with coefficients from } \mathbb{Z}, n \in \mathbb{N}\}.$$

A function $p : \mathbb{Z}^n \longrightarrow \mathbb{Z}$ has a zero if $p(a_1,\ldots,a_n) = 0$ for some tuple $(a_1,\ldots,a_n) \in \mathbb{Z}^n$. Let

$$\tilde{P}_o := \{p \in \tilde{P} \mid p \text{ has a zero}\}\,.$$

Let ν be a canonical notation of $\tilde{P}$. Then Hilbert's 10th problem is the decision problem $(\tilde{P},\nu,\tilde{P}_o)$. It is unsolvable, i.e. there is no computable function f with $dom(\nu) \subseteq dom(f)$ and $f(v) = \varepsilon \Longleftrightarrow v \in \tilde{P}_o$. Therefore, by Church's Thesis there is no effective method for deciding for any integer polynomial function p whether p has a zero or not. Notice, however, that $\nu^{-1}\tilde{P}_o$ is recursively enumerable.

In our examples we have proved unsolvability by reduction to the unsolvability of the halting problem. Reduction of this kind and more general ones will be discussed in detail in the second part of this book.

EXERCISES

1) Let ν be the notation of pair lists over Σ introduced in Definition 2.
   (a) Show that $\mathrm{dom}(\nu)$ is decidable.
   (b) Show that $\nu^{-1}(PL_o)$ is recursively enumerable.
   (c) Show that $\nu^{-1}(PL_1)$ is recursively enumerable (cf. Def. 3).
2) Which of the following pair lists has a correspondence?
   (a) ((111,1), (10,10111), (0,10)),
   (b) ((10,101), (011,11), (101,011)).
3) Show that the Post Correspondence Problem over Σ is solvable if Σ has only one element.
4) Consider the Semi-Thue system T from Example 9. Prove:

$$\{w \in W(\{a,b,c\}) \mid S \xrightarrow[T]{*} w\} = \{a^n b^n c^n \mid n \in \mathbb{N}\}$$

5) Prove the propositions in the proof of Lemma 11.
6) Prove Theorem 10. (Hint: If $\Delta = \{a_1,\ldots,a_k\}$ in Lemma 11 and $A,B \in \Sigma$, encode a_i by AB^iA.)
7) Prove that there is a Semi-Thue system $T = (\Sigma,R)$, $\Sigma = \{A,B\}$, such that $\{(x,y) \mid x \xrightarrow[T]{*} y\}$ is not recursive.
8) Let M be defined as in Theorem 10. Define a surjective mapping $\nu : W(\Delta) \dashrightarrow M$ (Δ appropriately chosen) such that the following sets are decidable:
   $\mathrm{dom}(\nu)$,
   $\{(x,y,w) \mid (x,y) \in pr_1\nu(w)\}$,
   $\{(x,w) \mid x = pr_2\nu(w)\}$,
   $\{(x,w) \mid x = pr_3\nu(w)\}$.
9) Define a surjective mapping ν from $W(\Delta)$ (Δ appropriately chosen) onto the Semi-Thue systems over Σ such that $\mathrm{dom}(\nu)$ and $\{(x,y,w) \mid (x,y) \in \nu(w)\}$ are decidable.

BIBLIOGRAPHICAL NOTES

The Post correspondence problem is from Post (1946); our proof follows Hopcroft and Ullman (1979). The problem from Theorem 1.10.9 was posed by Thue (1914) and it was solved by Post (1947). Hilbert's 10th problem was solved finally by Matijasevic (1970).

Part 2: Type 1 Recursion Theory

This part contains the standard recursion theory on the natural numbers. It is assumed that the reader is familiar with some definition of the partial recursive (or computable) functions $f: \mathbb{N}^k \dashrightarrow \mathbb{N}$. The formalism which will be developed is based on a pair (φ, Φ) (a Blum complexity measure) which satisfies certain axioms. The details are explained in Chapter 2.1. Numberings are a tool for transferring computability from numbers to other denumerable sets. In Chapter 2.2 numberings and relativized computability, decidability and enumerability are studied from a general point of view. Chapter 2.3 continues the investigation of the recursive and the recursively enumerable sets. Standard numberings are introduced and different characterizations are shown to be equivalent. Finally, theorems are proved which show that no non-trivial property on $P^{(1)}$ is φ-decidable (Rice's theorem) and that most interesting properties on $P^{(1)}$ are not even φ-recursively enumerable. Many-one and one-one reducibility are investigated in Chapter 2.4. Many interesting numberings are precomplete. They satisfy the recursion theorem which is a useful tool for answering difficult questions in recursion theory. In Chapter 2.5 precomplete numberings are introduced and some applications of the recursion theorem, especially the isomorphism theorem for precomplete numberings, are proved. The theory of creativity is developed in Chapter 2.6. Chapter 2.7 deals with the question of effectivity of numberings. A general principle for defining effective numberings is proposed. It can be regarded as an extension of Church's thesis. Chapter 2.8 is an excursion to ordinal trees and ordinal numbers. The computable ordinal numbers are introduced and investigated and a standard numbering of this set is defined. In Chapter 2.9 recursion theory is applied to some questions in logic, where the abstract concepts of creativity, productivity and recursive inseparability obtain very interesting interpretations. Relativized recursion theory is introduced in Chapter 2.10. Chapter 2.11 is devoted to Turing reducibility and a classification of the arithmetical sets by means of recursion theory and finally, Chapter 2.12 is an outline of recursion theoretical complexity theory. The presentation is far from being comprehensive. For more details the reader should consult other books or recent publications in journals.

BIBLIOGRAPHICAL NOTES

The standard reference for Type 1 recursion theory is the excellent book by Rogers (1967). There are several other good books covering this topic, e.g. Brainerd and Landweber (1974), Davis (1958), Schnorr (1974), Malcev (1974), and Machtey and Young (1978). The main sources for the theory of numberings are Ershov (1973), and Malcev (1974).

2.1 The Basic Concepts of Computability Theory

The fundamental notion of computability theory is that of the computable functions $f : \mathbb{N}^k \dashrightarrow \mathbb{N}$, where $\mathbb{N} = \{0,1,2,...\}$ is the set of natural numbers and the dotted arrow indicates a partial function. By definition, a function $f : \mathbb{N}^k \dashrightarrow \mathbb{N}$ $(k \in \mathbb{N})$ is computable iff there is a register machine which computes it (c f. Chapter 1.2, Def. 3). The domain of f consists of those inputs for which the register machine halts. There are several other equivalent definitions (see Part 1 of this book).
By Church's Thesis the computable functions are exactly those number functions which are intuitively computable. This thesis is not a theorem since the concept "intuitively computable" is not precisely defined. The theory of computability does not depend on the validity of Church's Thesis which is only used for interpreting the results. By $P^{(k)}$ we denote the set of k-ary partial recursive functions $f : \mathbb{N}^k \dashrightarrow \mathbb{N}$, by $R^{(k)}$ we denote the set of k-ary total recursive functions (c f. Def. 1.7.6). For proving that a function $f : \mathbb{N}^k \dashrightarrow \mathbb{N}$ is computable, usually it is shown that a register machine exists which computes f. In practice such a proof is not elaborated in all details. The first essential step consists of the definition of an abstract machine M (= input encoding + output encoding + flowchart, c f. Chapter 1.1) and a proof of $f = f_M$ (correctness). The flowchart of the machine should be sufficiently detailed such that transformation of the machine M into a register machine by refinement and simulation is a routine exercise which generally is not executed. Usually it suffices to specify the flowchart only informally and incompletely using e.g. ALGOL like notation such that a precise specification can be derived easily. In future we shall proceed in this manner.

A function $f : (W(\Sigma))^k \dashrightarrow W(\Sigma)$, where $W(\Sigma)$ is the set of words over the alphabet Σ, is computable iff there is a stack machine or a tape machine which computes it (c f. Chapters 1.5 and 1.6). By means of a standard numbering $\nu : \mathbb{N} \longrightarrow W(\Sigma)$ the computable number functions can be transformed bijectively onto the computable word functions: $f \in P^{(k)}$ is transformed into $g : (W(\Sigma))^k \dashrightarrow W(\Sigma)$, where $g(w_1,...,w_k) = \nu f(\nu^{-1}w_1,...,\nu^{-1}w_k)$ (c f. Chapter 1.7). To obtain formal simplicity in recursion theory mainly number functions are considered. The results can be transferred to word functions by means of a standard numbering ν of words.

The properties "recursive" (or "decidable") and "recursively enumerable" (for short "r.e.") are derived from the concept of computability. A subset $A \subseteq \mathbb{N}^k$ is recursive iff $A = f^{-1}\{0\}$ for some $f \in R^{(k)}$; A is r.e. iff $A = dom(f)$ for some $f \in P^{(k)}$ (Definition 1.8.1). A subset $B \subseteq (W(\Sigma))^k$ is recursive (r.e.) iff

$$\vec{\nu}^{-1}B := \{(\nu^{-1}a_1,...,\nu^{-1}a_k) \mid (a_1,...,a_k) \in B\}$$

is recursive (r.e.) (c f. Def. 1.8.7 and Theorem 1.8.9).

Computability of functions $f : \mathbb{N}^k \dashrightarrow \mathbb{N}$ $(k \geq 2)$ can be reduced to computability of functions $g : \mathbb{N} \dashrightarrow \mathbb{N}$ by means of the tupling function $\pi^{(k)} : \mathbb{N}^k \longrightarrow \mathbb{N}$:

$$g : \mathbb{N} \dashrightarrow \mathbb{N} \text{ is computable } \iff g\pi^{(k)} : \mathbb{N}^k \dashrightarrow \mathbb{N} \text{ is computable}$$

(c f. Lemma 1.2.16). By Lemma 1.8.6, $B \in \mathbb{N}^k$ is recursive (r.e.) iff $\pi^{(k)}(B) \subseteq \mathbb{N}$ is recursive (r.e.). In order to obtain further simplicity in recursion theory usually only functions $f : \mathbb{N} \dashrightarrow \mathbb{N}$ and subsets $A \subseteq \mathbb{N}$ are considered. The results can be transferred to the k-ary case by means of the bijection $\pi^{(k)}$.

The set $P^{(1)}$ of partial recursive unary number functions can be numbered in a very particular way. There is a numbering $\varphi : \mathbb{N} \longrightarrow P^{(1)}$ of $P^{(1)}$ which satisfies the utm-theorem ("universal Turing machine") (Theorem 1.9.6) and the smn-theorem (Theorem 1.9.7) :

$$\text{utm}(\varphi) : \; u_\varphi \in P^{(2)} , \text{ where } (\forall i,x) \; u_\varphi(i,x) := \varphi_i(x) ,$$

$$\text{smn}(\varphi) : \; (\forall f \in P^{(2)}) \, (\exists r \in R^{(1)}) \, (\forall i,j) \; f(i,x) = \varphi_{r(i)}(x) .$$

In Chapter 1.9 such a numbering φ is defined where $\varphi_i := \varphi(i)$ is that function from $P^{(1)}$ which is computed by the i'th tape machine. The utm-theorem and the smn-theorem are effectivity properties of φ. Remarkably, by these two properties the numbering φ is already uniquely determined (up to equivalence) (Theorem 1.9.10). A numbering ψ of $P^{(1)}$ is called "admissible" or "effective" iff it is total and satisfies the utm-theorem and the smn-theorem or iff it is equivalent to φ.

So far we have not explicitly considered the fact that any value $\varphi_i(x)$ is the result of a computation. For any $i,j \in \mathbb{N}$ let $T_i(j)$ be the number of steps and $L_i(j)$ the number of tape squares which the i'th tape machine with input j needs for the computation if $\varphi_i(j)$ exists. If $j \notin \text{dom}(\varphi_i)$ then define $T_i(j) = \text{div}$ and $L_i(j) = \text{div}$. The family $(T_i)_{i \in \mathbb{N}}$ is called the *time complexity measure* and the family $(L_i)_{i \in \mathbb{N}}$ is called the *tape complexity measure* associated with our numbering $\text{tm}\nu_{TP}$ of tape machines (c f. Def. 1.9.1). It can be shown that $\text{dom}(\varphi_i) = \text{dom}(T_i) = \text{dom}(L_i)$ for all $i \in \mathbb{N}$ and that the sets $\{(i,j,t) \mid T_i(j) = t\}$ and $\{(i,j,t) \mid L_i(j) = t\}$ are recursive; in words: it can be decided whether the i'th Turing machine with input j needs exactly t steps of computation (t tape squares, respectively) for halting. We do not prove these properties here but formulate axioms for a complexity measure.

1 DEFINITION (*complexity measure*)

8 A *complexity measure* is a pair (ψ,Ψ) with the following properties.

(1) $\psi : \mathbb{N} \longrightarrow Q$ is a numbering of some subset $Q \subseteq P^{(1)}$ such that ψ satisfies the utm-theorem.

(2) Ψ is a total numbering of a subset of $P^{(1)}$ such that the following axioms are satisfied:

(B 1) $(\forall i)\ \mathrm{dom}(\psi_i) = \mathrm{dom}(\Psi_i)$,

(B 2) $\{(i,x,t) \mid \Psi_i(x) = t\}$ is recursive.

(Notation $\psi_i := \psi(i)$, $\Psi_i := \Psi(i)$)

A complexity measure (ψ,Ψ) such that ψ is an admissible numbering of $P^{(1)}$ is called a *Blum (computational) complexity measure*. The axioms (B 1) and (B 2) are called *Blum's axioms*. The pairs (φ,T) and (φ,L) (see above) are Blum complexity measures. Generally, if (ψ,Ψ) is a complexity measure, then $\Psi_i(j) = t$ is interpreted as follows: t is the "resource" needed by the "machine" with number i for computing the value $\psi_i(j)$. For any reasonable machine model (for $P^{(1)}$) the time (or space) requirement of the computations yields a complexity measure.

The set $\{(i,x,t) \mid \Psi_i(x) = t\}$ is recursive iff the set $\{(i,x,t) \mid \Psi_i(x) \le t\}$ is recursive. We shall use this fact without explicitly mentioning it.

Now we shall show that for any ψ which satisfies the utm-theorem there is a complexity measure (ψ,Ψ). For the proof we apply the projection theorem. Remember that a computation time argument is already used in the proof of the projection theorem.

2 LEMMA (*existence of complexity measures*)

Let ψ be a total numbering of a subset of $P^{(1)}$ which satisfies the utm-theorem. Then there is a complexity measure (ψ,Ψ).

Proof

By assumption the universal function u of ψ is computable. The set dom(u) is r.e. By the projection theorem (Thm. 1.8.4) there is a recursive set $B \subseteq \mathbb{N}^3$ with

$$\mathrm{dom}(u) = \{(i,j) \mid (\exists t)\ (i,j,t) \in B\} .$$

There is some $f \in R^{(3)}$ with $B = f^{-1}\{0\}$. Define $\Psi_i(j) := \tilde{\mu}(f)(i,j)$. Thus, $\Psi_i(j)$ is the smallest number t such that $(i,j,t) \in B$ if it exists, see Def. 1.2.10(4). Since f is a total function we have for any $i,j \in \mathbb{N}$: $j \in \mathrm{dom}(\psi_i) \Longleftrightarrow (i,j) \in \mathrm{dom}(u)$ $\Longleftrightarrow (\exists t)\ (i,j,t) \in B \Longleftrightarrow (i,j) \in \mathrm{dom}\tilde{\mu}(f) \Longleftrightarrow j \in \mathrm{dom}(\Psi_i)$, therefore (B 1) is satisfied. Axiom (B 2) is easily verified: $\Psi_i(j) = t \Longleftrightarrow ((i,j,t) \in B$ and $(\forall s < t)$

$(i,j,s) \notin B)$. To decide this property, for all $s \le t$ the property $(i,j,s) \in B$ has to be decided. Hence, $\{(i,j,t) \mid \psi_i(j) = t\}$ is decidable.
Q.E.D.

From the proof of the projection theorem it follows that $(i,j,t) \in B$ iff t is the computation time of an arbitrarily chosen register machine which computes the universal function u of ψ. Hence, in the proof of Lemma 2 Ψ is defined by the computation time of a universal register machine for the numbering ψ. The projection theorem, on the other hand, is a corollary of Lemma 2 (see the exercises). Two simple but useful properties are formulated in the next lemma.

3 LEMMA

Let (ψ,Ψ) be a complexity measure. Then the following properties hold.

(1) $A := \{(i,x,y,z) \mid \psi_i(x) = y$ and $\Psi_i(x) = z\}$ is decidable.

(2) Ψ is a numbering of a subset of $P^{(1)}$ which satisfies the utm-theorem.

Proof

(1) Define a generalized register machine M by the following flowchart (c f. Chapter 1.2):

1 : $\Psi(R_1)(R_2) = R_4$, 2 , 4 ;

2 : $R_5 := \psi(R_1)(R_2)$, 3 ;

3 : $R_3 = R_5$, 5 , 4 ;

4 : $R_o := 1$, 5 ;

5 : HALT .

Let (i,x,y,z) be the input to the registers R_1,R_2,R_3,R_4. If $\Psi_i(x) \neq z$ the output is 1. Suppose $\Psi_i(x) = z$. Then $\psi_i(x)$ exists by Axiom (B 1). If $\psi_i(x) = y$ the output is 0, otherwise 1. Hence f_M is a total function such that $f_M^{-1}\{0\}$ is the desired set A. By the utm-theorem and Axiom (B 2) the functions and tests used in M are computable. By Theorem 1.2.7 f_M is computable.

(2) Let $B = \{(i,x,t) \mid \Psi_i(x) = t\}$. Since B is recursive, the function $h : \mathbb{N}^2 \dashrightarrow \mathbb{N}$ defined by $h(i,x) = \mu t[(i,x,t) \in B]$ is computable. Since h is the universal function of Ψ, Ψ satisfies the utm-theorem. Obviously $\Psi_i \in P^{(1)}$ for all $i \in \mathbb{N}$.
Q.E.D.

Another theorem which is closely related to the projection theorem and to Lemma 2 with Axioms (B 1) and (B 2) is Kleene's Normal Form Theorem.

4 <u>THEOREM</u> (*Kleene's Normal Form Theorem*)

Let ψ be a total numbering of a subset of $P^{(1)}$ which satisfies the utm-theorem. Then there are functions $g \in R^{(3)}$ and $h \in R^{(1)}$ such that

$$\psi_i(x) = h\tilde{\mu}(g)(i,x)$$

for all $i,x \in \mathbb{N}$. Furthermore (ψ,Ψ) is a complexity measure, where

$$\Psi_i(x) := \tilde{\mu}(g)(i,x)\ .$$

Since $g \in R^{(3)}$, $\tilde{\mu}(g)(i,x) = \mu t[g(i,x,t) = 0]$ (c f. Chapter 1.2). If ψ is an admissible total numbering of $P^{(1)}$ then the corresponding predicate T defined by $T(i,x,t) :\Longleftrightarrow g(i,x,t) = 0$ is called *Kleene's T-predicate*. Kleene's T-predicate, a complexity measure for φ, or the projection theorem can be used equally well in proofs. In this book we shall generally use formulations with complexity measures which seem to be the most intuitive ones.

<u>Proof</u>

By Lemma 2 there is a complexity measure (ψ,Ψ). Define $g : \mathbb{N}^3 \longrightarrow \mathbb{N}$ by

$$g(i,x,\langle y,z\rangle) := \begin{cases} 0 & \text{if } \psi_i(x) = y \text{ and } \Psi_i(x) = z \\ 1 & \text{otherwise} \end{cases}$$

for all $i,x,y,z \in \mathbb{N}$. By Lemma 3, g is computable. Let $h := \pi_1^{(2)}$ (c f. Def. 1.2.14, Lemma 1.2.15). Then g and h have the desired properties.
Q.E.D.

We have seen that essential properties of the numbering φ of $P^{(1)}$ defined in Chapter 1.9 can be derived from the utm-theorem and the smn-theorem for φ, and that essential properties of computational complexity can be derived from Blum's Axioms (B 1) and (B 2). Henceforth the symbol φ will no longer denote the particular numbering of $P^{(1)}$ defined in Chapter 1.9 but any admissible total numbering of $P^{(1)}$, and Φ will be any numbering such that (φ,Φ) is a complexity measure.

5 DEFINITION (*axioms for recursion theory*)

Let $\varphi : \mathbb{N} \longrightarrow P^{(1)}$ be a total numbering of $P^{(1)}$ and let Φ be a numbering of a subset of $P^{(1)}$ such that the following axioms hold.

(utm) : $u_\varphi \in P^{(2)}$, where $u_\varphi(i,x) := \varphi_i(x)$,

(smn) : $(\forall f \in P^{(2)})\ (\exists r \in R^{(1)})\ (\forall i,x)\ \ \varphi_{r(i)}(x) = f(i,x)$,

(B 1) : $(\forall i)\ \ \mathrm{dom}(\varphi_i) = \mathrm{dom}(\Phi_i)$,

(B 2) : $\{(i,x,t) \mid \Phi_i(x) = t\}$ is recursive.

Then {utm,smn, B1,B2} is said to be an *axiom system for recursion theory w.r.t.* (φ,Φ).

For the rest of this book we shall assume that (φ,Φ) is some arbitrarily fixed pair which satisfies Definition 5. The recursion theory which will be developed does not depend on particular properties of φ and Φ but only on the axioms given in Definition 5. From time to time we shall show this explicitly.

EXERCISES

1) Show that the projection theorem can be easily derived from Lemma 2.
2) Let ψ be a total numbering of a subset $Q \subseteq P^{(1)}$. Suppose there are $g \in R^{(1)}$ and $h \in R^{(1)}$ such that $(\forall i,x)\psi_i(x) = h\tilde{\mu}(g)(i,x)$. Show that there is a numbering Ψ such that (ψ,Ψ) is a complexity measure.
3) Let ψ be an admissible numbering of $P^{(1)}$ and let (ψ,Ψ) be a complexity measure. In which of the following cases is $(\psi,\widehat{\Psi})$ a complexity measure?
   (a) $\widehat{\Psi}_i(j) := \psi_i(j)$
   (b) $\widehat{\Psi}_i(j) := 0$
   (c) $\widehat{\Psi}_i(j) := i^2 + j^2 + (\psi_i(j))^2$
   (d) $\widehat{\Psi}_i(j) := \psi_i(j) + \Psi_i(j)$
   (e) $\widehat{\psi}_i(j) := \langle\psi_i(j), \Psi_i(j)\rangle$
   (f) $\widehat{\Psi}_i(j) := (i \text{ if } i \in A, \psi_i(j) \text{ otherwise})$ where $A \subseteq \mathbb{N}$ such that $(\forall i \in A)\psi_i \in R^{(1)}$.
4) Prove that Axiom (B2) can be replaced by:

   $\{(i,x,t) \mid \Phi_i(x) \leq t\}$ is recursive.

BIBLIOGRAPHICAL NOTES

The characterization of the numbering φ by the smn-theorem and the utm-theorem is by H. Rogers (1958). The axioms (B1) and (B2) have been introduced by M. Blum (1967).

2.2 Numberings

In Part 1 of this book we have defined the computable functions $f : \mathbb{N}^k \dashrightarrow \mathbb{N}$ and the computable functions $f : (W(\Sigma))^k \dashrightarrow W(\Sigma)$. These definitions, however, are not applicable to functions on the rational numbers, on finite graphs, on the real numbers, etc. It is not even defined whether a "standard numbering" $\nu : \mathbb{N} \longrightarrow W(\Sigma)$ is computable or not. Obviously, new definitions are needed. One method for defining the computable functions $f : M_1 \dashrightarrow M_2$ is to develop a new computability model for the sets M_1 and M_2. As we have seen in Part 1, any new computability model requires the development of an extended theory and the justification of a thesis like Church's Thesis. We already know that a computability theory may be reducible to another one, e.g. computability on words may be reduced to computability on numbers by a standard numbering $\nu : \mathbb{N} \longrightarrow W(\Sigma)$ (Theorem 1.7.5), or computability of functions $\mathbb{N}^k \dashrightarrow \mathbb{N}$ can be reduced to computability of functions $\mathbb{N} \dashrightarrow \mathbb{N}$ by the tupling function $\pi^{(k)}$ (Lemma 1.2.16). This indicates a second method for introducing computability of functions $M_1 \dashrightarrow M_2$. The elements of M_1 and M_2 are named (or encoded) by numbers, and a function $f : M_1 \dashrightarrow M_2$ is called computable iff it results from a computable function which transforms names (i.e. numbers) into names. In this case no new theory of computability has to be developed, but still theses corresponding to Church's Thesis have to be discussed, namely whether the "namings" of M_1 and M_2 are "intuitively effective". Of course, this method is only applicable to denumerable sets since the set of available names, namely $\mathbb{N}$, is only denumerable. A naming by natural numbers will be called a *numbering*. In this chapter we shall study effectivity w.r.t. given numberings. The question of effectivity of numberings will be discussed later in a separate chapter.

Consider a numbering of a set M. Then any $m \in M$ must have a number and any number is the name of at most one element of M. Hence, formally a numbering of M is a partial surjective function $\nu : \mathbb{N} \dashrightarrow M$.

1 DEFINITION (*numbering*)

Let M be a set. A *numbering* of M is a partial surjective function $\nu : \mathbb{N} \dashrightarrow M$. Let

$$N(M) := \{\nu \mid \nu \text{ is a numbering of } M\} ,$$

$$TN(M) := \{\nu \in N(M) \mid \nu \text{ is total}\} .$$

Furthermore, let $\widehat{N}$ be the class of all numberings and $\widehat{TN}$ be the class of all total numberings.

The following definition gives a list of some standard numberings.

2 <u>DEFINITION</u> (*some standard numberings*)

$1\!\!1_A \in N(A)$ for $A \subseteq \mathbb{N}$,

$\mathrm{dom}(1\!\!1_A) := A$, $1\!\!1_A(a) := a$ for all $a \in A$.

$\nu_a \in N(\Sigma)$ for bijective $a : \{1,\ldots,n\} \longrightarrow \Sigma$,

$\mathrm{dom}(\nu_a) := \{1,\ldots,n\}$, $\nu_a(i) := a(i)$ for $1 \le i \le n$.

$\nu_{Ck} \in TN(\mathbb{N}^k)$ for $k \ge 2$ (*Cantor numbering*),

$\nu_{Ck} := (\pi^{(k)})^{-1}$ (cf. Def. 1.2.14).

$\nu_\Sigma \in TN(W(\Sigma))$,

ν_Σ is the standard numbering of $W(\Sigma)$ w.r.t. some fixed order function $a : \{1,\ldots,n\} \longrightarrow \Sigma$ (cf. Def. 1.7.2).

$\nu^* \in TN(W(\mathbb{N}))$,

$\nu^*(0) := \varepsilon$ (empty word),

$\nu^*(\langle\langle x_o,\ldots,x_k\rangle,k\rangle+1) := x_o x_1 \ldots x_k$ for all $k \in \mathbb{N}$, $x_o,x_1,\ldots,x_k \in \mathbb{N}$ (cf. Def. 1.2.14).

$\nu_G \in N(W(\Sigma))$ (*Gödel numbering*).

Let $a : \{1,\ldots,n\} \longrightarrow \Sigma$ be bijective, $a_i := a(i)$, let p_i be the i'th prime $(i = 1,2,\ldots)$.

$\mathrm{dom}(\nu_G) := \{p_1^{i_1} \cdot p_2^{i_2} \cdot \ldots \cdot p_k^{i_k} \mid k \in \mathbb{N},\ i_1,\ldots,i_k \in \{1,\ldots,n\}\}$,

$\nu_G(p_1^{i_1} \cdot p_2^{i_2} \cdot \ldots \cdot p_k^{i_k}) := a_{i_1} a_{i_2} \ldots a_{i_k}$.

$e \in TN(E(\mathbb{N}))$, $E(\mathbb{N}) := \{A \subseteq \mathbb{N} \mid A \text{ finite}\}$.

Define $\eta : E(\mathbb{N}) \longrightarrow \mathbb{N}$ by $\eta(A) := \Sigma\{2^i \mid i \in A\}$. Then η is bijective. Define $e := \eta^{-1}$, $e_i := e(i)$.

$\nu_Z \in TN(\mathbb{Z})$, ($\mathbb{Z} := \{\ldots,-2,-1,0,1,2,\ldots\}$ = set of integers),

$\nu_Z\langle i,j\rangle := i - j$.

$\nu_Q \in TN(\mathbb{Q})$, ($\mathbb{Q}$:= set of rational numbers),

$\nu_Q\langle i,j,k\rangle := (i-j)/(1+k)$.

For example $\mathbb{I}_{\emptyset}(2) = \text{div}$, $\nu_{C2}(11) = (3,1)$, $\nu_{\Sigma}(8) = a_1 a_1 a_2$, $\nu_G(630) = a_1 a_2 a_1 a_1$ if $\Sigma = \{a_1, a_2\}$, $\nu^*(355) = (1)(0)(1)(2)$, $e(77) = \{0,2,3,6\}$, $\nu_Z(13) = -2$, $\nu_Q(122) = -2/3$. Further numberings will be introduced in the course of the text. All the numberings from the above definition are "effective" in a certain sense. This will be discussed later. It remains to show that the numbering e of the finite subsets of $\mathbb{N}$ is well-defined.

3 LEMMA

The function η from the definition of e is bijective.

Proof

From the definiton of η we conclude $(\eta(X)$ is odd $\iff 0 \in X)$ and $\eta(X+1) = 2 \cdot \eta(X)$. By induction on n one easily proves: $(\forall n \in \mathbb{N})\ (\forall\ i \leq n)\ (\exists X)\ \ \eta(X) = i$. Therefore, η is surjective. Also by induction on n the following property can be proved: $(\forall n \in \mathbb{N})\ \ (\forall X \subseteq \{0,\ldots,n-1\})\ (\forall Y)\ \ (\eta(X) = \eta(Y) \Longrightarrow X = Y)$. Therefore, η is injective. Q.E.D.

From the binary notation u of a number $n \in \mathbb{N}$ one can easily obtain the elements of the set e_n: the i'th position of u is 1 iff $i \in e_n$. Example: $e(834_{10}) = e(1101000010_2) = \{1,6,8,9\}$. The numbering ν_G is injective. Its inverse is sometimes called the standard *gödelization* of $W(\Sigma)$.

Now we shall introduce effectivity w.r.t. given numberings. Not only functions may be effective but also predicates of the form

$$(\forall x \in X)\ (\exists y \in Y)\ \ P(x,y)\ .$$

This predicate is "effective" iff for any $x \in X$ some $y \in Y$ can be "determined" with P(x,y). Notice that there may be several elements y with P(x,y). Many theorems in mathematics are of this form. Consider e.g. the predicate (theorem)

$$(\forall x \in \mathbb{Z})\ (\exists y \in \mathbb{Q})\ \ x < y\ .$$

It is effective w.r.t. the numberings ν_Z and ν_Q: For any ν_Z-number m of some $x \in \mathbb{Z}$ a ν_Q-number n of some $y \in \mathbb{Q}$ can be determined such that $x < y$. Define a function $f : \mathbb{N} \longrightarrow \mathbb{N}$ by

$$f\langle i,j\rangle := \langle i+1,0,0\rangle\ .$$

Then $f \in R^{(1)}$ and for any $i,j \in \mathbb{N}$, $\nu_Z\langle i,j\rangle = i-j \in \mathbb{Z}$ and $\nu_Q f\langle i,j\rangle = \nu_Q\langle i+1,0,0\rangle = i+1 \in \mathbb{Q}$, hence $\nu_Z(m) < \nu_Q f(m)$ for all $m \in \mathbb{N}$.

The concept of *correspondence* seems to be adequate for a formal definition. A *correspondence* is a triple $f = (X,Y,\rho)$ where X and Y are sets and $\rho \subseteq X \times Y$. By definition, $dom(f) = \{x \mid (\exists y)\ (x,y) \in \rho\}$, $range(f) = \{y \mid (\exists x)\ (x,y) \in \rho\}$, $f^{-1} = (Y,X,\rho^{-1})$ where $\rho^{-1} = \{(y,x) \mid (x,y) \in \rho\}$. A *partial function* $f : X \dashrightarrow Y$ is a correspondence $f = (X,Y,\rho)$ such that $((x,y) \in \rho \wedge (x,y') \in \rho) \Longrightarrow y = y'$ for all $x \in X$, $y,y' \in Y$. The partial function $f = (X,Y,\rho)$ is total iff $X = dom(f)$. Effectivity of a correspondence w.r.t. given numberings is defined as follows.

4 DEFINITION (*relative computability*)

Let $\nu_X \in N(X)$ and $\nu_Y \in N(Y)$ be numberings, let $f = (X,Y,\rho)$ be a correspondence.

(1) f is (ν_X,ν_Y)-*computable* iff there is some $g \in P^{(1)}$ with

$$(\forall i \in \nu_X^{-1} dom(f))\quad (\nu_X(i), \nu_Y g(i)) \in \rho .$$

(2) f is *strongly* (ν_X,ν_Y)-*computable* iff there is some $g \in P^{(1)}$ with

$$(\forall i \in \nu_X^{-1} dom(f))\quad (\nu_X(i), \nu_Y g(i)) \in \rho$$

and

$$(\forall i \in \nu_X^{-1}(X \setminus dom(f)))\quad i \notin dom(g) .$$

The correspondence f is (ν_X,ν_Y)-computable iff for any ν_X-number i of some $x \in dom(f)$ a ν_Y-number j of some y with $(x,y) \in \rho$ can be computed.. The correspondence is strongly (ν_X,ν_Y)-computable iff the function g also respects the domain of f: g diverges for all $i \in dom(\nu_X)$ for which $\nu_X(i) \notin dom(f)$. The function g may behave arbitrarily for all $i \notin dom(\nu_X)$. For any function $g : \mathbb{N} \dashrightarrow \mathbb{N}$ we shall say: "the correspondence f is (ν_X,ν_Y)-*effective via* g" iff $(\nu_X(i),\nu_Y g(i)) \in \rho$ for all $i \in \nu_X^{-1} dom(f)$ and "f is *strongly* (ν_X,ν_Y)-*effective via* g" iff $(\nu_X(i),\nu_Y g(i)) \in \rho$ for all $i \in \nu_X^{-1} dom(f)$ and $i \notin dom(g)$ for all $i \in \nu_X^{-1}(X \setminus dom(f))$. Notice that the correspondence f is strongly effective if it is effective and if $X = dom(f)$. Let $f = (X,Y,\rho)$ be a correspondence. Define $f' := (dom(f),Y,\rho)$, and $\nu' \in N(dom(f))$ by restriction of ν_X as follows: $dom(\nu') = \nu_X^{-1} dom(f)$, $\nu'(i) = \nu_X(i)$ for all $i \in dom(\nu')$. Then obviously, f is (ν_X,ν_Y)-computable $\Longleftrightarrow$ f' is strongly (ν',ν_Y)-computable. As we have shown above, the correspondence $(\mathbb{Z},\mathbb{Q},\{(x,y) \in \mathbb{Z} \times \mathbb{Q} \mid x < y\})$ is strongly (ν_Z,ν_Q)-computable. Notice that in Definition 4(1) the condition $(\nu_X(i) = \nu_X(i') \Longrightarrow \nu_Y g(i) = \nu_Y g(i'))$ is not required. In our example we have $\nu_Z(\langle 0,0\rangle) = \nu_Z(\langle 1,1\rangle)$ but $\nu_Q f\langle 0,0\rangle \neq \nu_Q f\langle 1,1\rangle$.

The following picture illustrates Definition 4.

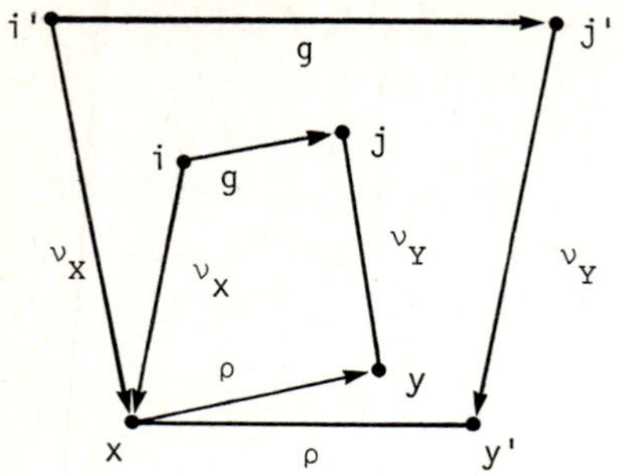

Here we have

$(\nu_X(i), \nu_Y g(i)) \in \rho$,

$(\nu_X(i'), \nu_Y g(i')) \in \rho$.

If the correspondence f is a partial function $f : X \dashrightarrow Y$ then Definition 4 can be expressed as follows.

5 COROLLARY (*(ν_X,ν_Y)-computability of a function*)

Let $f : X \dashrightarrow Y$ be a function, let ν_X (ν_Y) be a numbering of X (Y).

(1) f is *(ν_X,ν_Y)-computable* iff there is some $g \in P^{(1)}$ with $f\nu_X(i) = \nu_Y g(i)$ for all $i \in \text{dom}(f\nu_X)$.

(2) f is *strongly* *(ν_X,ν_Y)-computable* iff in addition to (1) $i \notin \text{dom}(g)$ for all $i \in \text{dom}(\nu_X) \setminus \text{dom}(f\nu_X)$.

The following diagram illustrates Corollary 5.

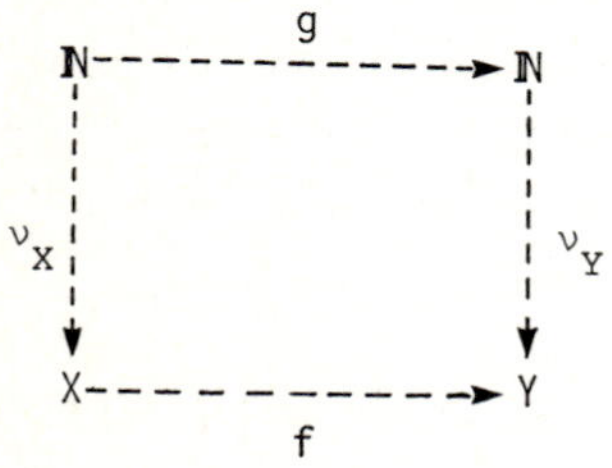

The function g operates on names and the functions ν_X and ν_Y are the semantic mappings which assign meanings to the names. If f is (ν_X,ν_Y)-computable the diagram must commute for all $i \in \text{dom}(f\nu_X)$. If f is strongly (ν_X,ν_Y)-computable the function g must diverge for all $i \in \text{dom}(\nu_X)$ which are not in $\text{dom}(f\nu_X)$. If $X = \text{dom}(f)$ then Condition (2) in Def. 4 (Corollary 5 respectively) is trivial. In this case any (ν_X,ν_Y)-computable correspondence (function) is strongly (ν_X,ν_Y)-computable. In Chapter 1.7 we have defined standard numberings $\nu : \mathbb{N} \longrightarrow W(\Sigma)$. The case $k = 1$ of Theorem 1.7.5 can be expressed as follows: $g : W(\Sigma) \dashrightarrow W(\Sigma)$ is computable iff g is strongly (ν,ν)-computable, where ν is a standard numbering of $W(\Sigma)$. Lemma 1.2.16

can be expressed as follows: $f : \mathbb{N}^k \dashrightarrow \mathbb{N}$ is computable iff f is strongly $(\nu_{Ck}, \mathrm{I\!I}_{\mathbb{N}})$-computable (see Def. 2). If ν_X and ν_Y are bijective, then $f : X \dashrightarrow Y$ is strongly (ν_X,ν_Y)-computable iff $\nu_Y^{-1} f \nu_X \in P^{(1)}$.

As an example we show that inversion $f : q \dashrightarrow 1/q$ on $\mathbb{Q}$ is strongly (ν_Q,ν_Q)-computable. Define a function $g : \mathbb{N} \dashrightarrow \mathbb{N}$ by

$$g(\langle i,j,k\rangle) := \begin{cases} \langle 1+k\,,\,0\,,\,i \dot{-} (j+1)\rangle & \text{if } i > j \\ \text{div} & \text{if } i = j \\ \langle 0\,,\,1+k\,,\,j \dot{-} (i+1)\rangle & \text{if } j > i\,. \end{cases}$$

Clearly, g is computable. Suppose $\langle i,j,k\rangle \in \mathrm{dom}(f\nu_Q)$. Then $\nu_Q\langle i,j,k\rangle \neq 0$, i.e. $i \neq j$. If $i > j$, then $f\nu_Q\langle i,j,k\rangle = f((i-j)/(1+k)) = (1+k)/(i-j) = (1+k)/(1+(i \dot{-} (j+1))) = \nu_Q\langle 1+k,0,i\dot{-}(j+1)\rangle = \nu_Q g\langle i,j,k\rangle$. If $i < j$ one similarly obtains $f\nu_Q\langle i,j,k\rangle = \nu_Q g\langle i,j,k\rangle$. Therefore, Condition (1) of Corollary 5 is satisfied. Suppose $\langle i,j,k\rangle \notin \mathrm{dom}(f\nu_Q)$. Then $\nu_Q\langle i,j,k\rangle = 0$, i.e. $i = j$, and $\langle i,j,k\rangle \notin \mathrm{dom}(g)$. Therefore Condition 2 of Corollary 5 holds.

The concept of (ν_X,ν_Y)-computability behaves well w.r.t. composition of functions.

6 LEMMA (*closure under composition*)

Let $f : X \dashrightarrow Y$ and $g : Y \dashrightarrow Z$ be partial functions, let ν_X (ν_Y,ν_Z) be a numbering of X (Y,Z).

(1) gf is (ν_X,ν_Z)-computable if f is (ν_X,ν_Y)-computable and g is (ν_Y,ν_Z)-computable.

(2) gf is strongly (ν_X,ν_Z)-computable if f is strongly (ν_X,ν_Y)-computable and g is strongly (ν_Y,ν_Z)-computable.

Proof

(1) By assumption there are $f',g' \in P^{(1)}$ with $f\nu_X(i) = \nu_Y f'(i)$ for all $i \in \mathrm{dom}(f\nu_X)$ and $g\nu_Y(j) = \nu_Z g'(j)$ for all $j \in \mathrm{dom}(g\nu_Y)$. Suppose $i \in \mathrm{dom}(gf\nu_X)$. Then $i \in \mathrm{dom}(f\nu_X)$, $gf\nu_X(i) = g\nu_Y f'(i)$, $f'(i) \in \mathrm{dom}(g\nu_Y)$, $g\nu_Y f'(i) = \nu_Z g'f'(i)$, hence $gf\nu_X(i) = \nu_Z g'f'(i)$. Since $g'f' \in P^{(1)}$, gf is (ν_X,ν_Z)-computable.

(2) By assumption $i \notin \mathrm{dom}(f')$ if $i \in \mathrm{dom}(\nu_X) \setminus \mathrm{dom}(f\nu_X)$ and $j \notin \mathrm{dom}(g')$ if $j \in \mathrm{dom}(\nu_Y) \setminus \mathrm{dom}(g\nu_Y)$. Suppose $i \in \mathrm{dom}(\nu_X) \setminus \mathrm{dom}(gf\nu_X)$. Case 1: $i \notin \mathrm{dom}(f\nu_X)$. Then $i \notin \mathrm{dom}(f')$ and $i \notin \mathrm{dom}(g'f')$. Case 2: $i \in \mathrm{dom}(f\nu_X)$. Then $f\nu_X(i) \notin \mathrm{dom}(g)$. By (1) $f\nu_X(i) = \nu_Y f'(i) \notin \mathrm{dom}(g)$, i.e. $f'(i) \notin \mathrm{dom}(g\nu_Y)$, hence $f'(i) \notin \mathrm{dom}(g')$ and $i \notin \mathrm{dom}(g'f')$.

Q.E.D.

In Definition 1.9.9 we have introduced reducibility and equivalence of numberings: $\nu \le \nu' \iff (\exists g \in P^{(1)})(\forall i \in \mathrm{dom}(\nu))\ \nu(i) = \nu' g(i)$, $\nu \equiv \nu' \iff (\nu \le \nu' \wedge \nu' \le \nu)$. Reducibility can be also expressed in terms of relative computability of the identical embedding $1\!\!1_{X,Y}$ of X into Y.

7 LEMMA

Let ν be a numbering of X, let ν' be a numbering of Y. Then:

$$\nu \le \nu' \iff (X \subseteq Y \text{ and } 1\!\!1_{X,Y} \text{ is } (\nu,\nu')\text{-computable}).$$

Proof

"$\Longrightarrow$": Since $1\!\!1_{X,Y}$ is a total function, $\mathrm{dom}\, 1\!\!1_{X,Y}\nu = \mathrm{dom}(\nu)$, hence $\forall i \in \mathrm{dom}(\nu)$ $\nu(i) = 1\!\!1_{X,Y}\nu(i) = \nu' g(i)$.

"$\Longleftarrow$": By assumption $\mathrm{range}(\nu) \subseteq \mathrm{range}(\nu')$. Since $1\!\!1_{X,Y}$ is a total function $\mathrm{dom}(\nu) = \mathrm{dom}(1\!\!1_{X,Y}\nu)$, hence $(\forall i \in \mathrm{dom}(1\!\!1_{X,Y}\nu))\ 1\!\!1_{X,Y}\nu(i) = \nu(i) = \nu' g(i)$. Furthermore $\mathrm{dom}(\nu) \setminus \mathrm{dom}(1\!\!1_{X,Y}\nu) = \emptyset$, hence $\nu \le \nu'$.
Q.E.D.

By Lemma 7, $\nu \le \nu'$ iff there is a computable function which for any ν-number i of some $x \in X$ determines a ν'-number $j = g(i)$ of x. A numbering ν can be interpreted to be a "language", where $\mathrm{dom}(\nu)$ (the *syntax*) is the set of possible names and ν (the *semantics*) associates a meaning $\nu(i) \in X$ with any name i. Under this interpretation, $\nu \le \nu'$ means that the language ν can be translated into the language ν'.

As an example, we have already proved (Theorem 1.9.10) that two numberings of $P^{(1)}$ which satisfy the smn-theorem and the utm-theorem are equivalent. We have also proved that any two standard numberings of $W(\Sigma)$ (c f. Chapter 1.7) are equivalent (see the exercises). The concept of equivalence is important since two numberings of a set M define the same kind of computability theory for M if and only if they are equivalent. The following lemma expresses the essential properties.

8 LEMMA

Let $\nu, \nu' \in N(M)$. Then the following properties are equivalent.

(1) $\nu \le \nu'$.

(2) (f is (ν_1,ν)-computable $\Longrightarrow$ f is (ν_1,ν')-computable) for any numbering $\nu_1 \in N(M_1)$ and any $f : M_1 \dashrightarrow M$.

(3) (f is (ν',ν_2)-computable $\Longrightarrow$ f is (ν,ν_2)-computable) for any numbering $\nu_2 \in N(M_2)$ and any $f: M \dashrightarrow M_2$.

In (2) and (3) the property "strongly" may be added.

Proof

The essential tool is Lemma 6.

"(1) $\Longrightarrow$ (2)": By assumption $1\!\!1_{M,M}$ is (ν,ν')-computable. If f is (ν_1,ν)-computable, then $f = 1\!\!1_{M,M} f$ is (ν_1,ν')-computable.

"(2) $\Longrightarrow$ (1)": Choose $\nu_1 = \nu$, $f = 1\!\!1_{M,M}$. Then $1\!\!1_{M,M}$ is (ν,ν')-computable, i.e. $\nu \leq \nu'$.

"(1) $\Longrightarrow$ (3)" and "(3) $\Longrightarrow$ (1)" are proved similarly. The case of strong computability is proved accordingly.

Q.E.D.

9 CONCLUSION

Two numberings ν and ν' of a set M define the same kind of computability for M, if and only if they are equivalent.

Equivalent numberings yield the same kind of computability also for correspondences. The proof follows immediately from the definitions.

10 LEMMA

Let $\nu_i, \nu_i' \in N(M_i)$ $(i = 1,2)$ be numberings, let $f = (M_1, M_2, \rho)$ be a (ν_1,ν_2)-computable correspondence. If $\nu_1' \leq \nu_1$ and $\nu_2 \leq \nu_2'$, then f is (ν_1',ν_2')-computable. The same property holds in the case of strong computability.

The definition of recursive and of recursively enumerable subsets of $\mathbb{N}$ (Def. 1.8.1) can be generalized to an arbitrary numbered set M.

11 DEFINITION (*ν-recursive sets, ν-r.e. sets*)

Let M be a set, let ν be a numbering of M, and let $A \subseteq M$ be a subset of M.

(1) A is *ν-recursive* or *ν-decidable* iff $A = f^{-1}\{0\}$ for some total function $f: M \longrightarrow \{0,1\}$ which is $(\nu, 1\!\!1_{\{0,1\}})$-computable.

(2) A is *ν-recursively enumerable* (*ν-r.e.*) iff $A = \mathrm{dom}(f)$ for some $f: M \dashrightarrow \{0\}$ which is strongly $(\nu, 1\!\!1_{\{0\}})$-computable.

From Corollary 5 we obtain a more direct characterization of the ν-recursive and the ν-r.e. subsets of M.

12 COROLLARY

Let $\nu \in N(M)$ and $A \subseteq M$.

(1) A is ν-recursive iff there is some $g \in P^{(1)}$ with: $g(i) = 0$ if $\nu(i) \in A$ and $g(i) = 1$ if $\nu(i) \notin A$ for all $i \in dom(\nu)$.

(2) A is ν-r.e. iff there is some $h \in P^{(1)}$ with: $h(i) = 0$ if $\nu(i) \in A$ and $h(i) = div$ if $\nu(i) \notin A$ for all $i \in dom(\nu)$.

Roughly speaking, g decides the membership of A on the names in the first case, and $\nu^{-1}A = dom(h) \cap dom(\nu)$ in the second case. Our standard numberings induce the correct recursive and r.e. subsets on $\mathbb{N}^k$, $W(\Sigma)$ resp.:

$A \subseteq \mathbb{N}^k$ is recursive (r.e.) $\Longleftrightarrow$ A is ν_{Ck}-recursive (ν_{Ck}-r.e.),

$A \subseteq W(\Sigma)$ is recursive (r.e.) $\Longleftrightarrow$ A is ν_Σ-recursive (ν_Σ-r.e.)

for any standard numbering ν_Σ of $W(\Sigma)$. As another example, the set $\mathbb{Z}$ of integers is a $\nu_\mathbb{Q}$-recursive subset of the set $\mathbb{Q}$ of rational numbers. Define $g : \mathbb{N} \longrightarrow \mathbb{N}$.

$$g\langle i,j,k\rangle := \begin{cases} 0 & \text{if } (k+1) \text{ divides } (i-j) \\ 1 & \text{otherwise}. \end{cases}$$

Then $g \in R^{(1)}$, $g(n) = 0$ if $\nu_\mathbb{Q}(n) \in \mathbb{Z}$, $g(n) = 1$ if $\nu_\mathbb{Q}(n) \notin \mathbb{Z}$. If $dom(\nu)$ is recursive then A is ν-recursive iff $\nu^{-1}(A)$ is recursive; if $dom(\nu)$ is r.e., then A is ν-r.e. iff $\nu^{-1}(A)$ is r.e.. The well-known relation between "recursive" and "r.e." for subsets of $\mathbb{N}$ (Theorem 1.8.5) can be transferred to the relativized case.

13 THEOREM

Let ν be a numbering of M, let $A \subseteq M$. Then

$$A \ \nu\text{-recursive} \Longleftrightarrow (A \ \nu\text{-r.e. and } M \setminus A \ \nu\text{-r.e.}).$$

Proof

"$\Longrightarrow$": Let $g \in P^{(1)}$ be a function which satisfies the property of Corollary 12(1). Define a function $h : \mathbb{N} \dashrightarrow \mathbb{N}$ by $h(i) := (0$ if $g(i) = 0$, div otherwise). Then $h \in P^{(1)}$, and h satisfies the property of Corollary 12(2). Therefore A is ν-r.e. The case of $M \setminus A$ is proved correspondingly.

"$\Longleftarrow$": Let $h_1 \in P^{(1)}$ and $h_2 \in P^{(1)}$ be the functions for A, $M \setminus A$ respectively, according to Corollary 12(2). There are numbers $i,j \in \mathbb{N}$ with $h_1 = \varphi_i$ and $h_2 = \varphi_j$.

Define $g_1 : \mathbb{N} \dashrightarrow \mathbb{N}$ by $g_1(x) := \mu t[\Phi_i(x) = t \vee \Phi_j(x) = t]$. By Definition 2.1.5, g_1 is computable. Define $g : \mathbb{N} \dashrightarrow \mathbb{N}$ by

$$g(x) := \begin{cases} 0 & \text{if } x \in \mathrm{dom}(g_1) \text{ and } \Phi_i(x) = g_1(x) \\ 1 & \text{if } x \in \mathrm{dom}(g_1) \text{ and } \Phi_i(x) \neq g_1(x) \\ \mathrm{div} & \text{if } x \notin \mathrm{dom}(g_1) . \end{cases}$$

Then g is computable. Let $x \in \mathrm{dom}(\nu)$ and $\nu(x) \in A$. Then $x \in \mathrm{dom}(\varphi_i)$ and $x \notin \mathrm{dom}(\varphi_j)$, hence $\Phi_i(x)$ exists and $g_1(x) = \Phi_i(x)$ and $g(x) = 0$. Let $x \in \mathrm{dom}(\nu)$ and $\nu(x) \notin A$. Then $x \notin \mathrm{dom}(\varphi_i)$ and $x \in \mathrm{dom}(\varphi_j)$, hence $\Phi_i(x)$ diverges, $\Phi_j(x)$ exists and $g_1(x) = \Phi_j(x)$. This implies $g(x) = 1$. Therefore g satisfies the conditions of Corollary 12(1), and A is ν-recursive.

Q.E.D.

There are several natural operations by which new numberings can be constructed from given ones.

14 <u>DEFINITION</u>

In the following definitions let $\nu_i \in N(M_i)$ for $i \in \mathbb{N}$.

(1) $[\nu_1,\ldots,\nu_n] \in N(M_1 \times \ldots \times M_n)$ $(n \geq 1)$,

$$\mathrm{dom}[\nu_1,\ldots,\nu_n] := \{<i_1,\ldots,i_n> \mid i_1 \in \mathrm{dom}(\nu_1),\ldots,i_n \in \mathrm{dom}(\nu_n)\},$$

$$[\nu_1,\ldots,\nu_n]<i_1,\ldots,i_n> := (\nu_1(i_1),\ldots,\nu_n(i_n)) .$$

(2) $\nu_1 \sqcup \nu_2 \in N(M_1 \cup M_2)$,

$$\mathrm{dom}(\nu_1 \sqcup \nu_2) := \{2i \mid i \in \mathrm{dom}(\nu_1)\} \cup \{2i+1 \mid i \in \mathrm{dom}(\nu_2)\},$$

$$(\nu_1 \sqcup \nu_2)(2i) := \nu_1(i) , \quad (\nu_1 \sqcup \nu_2)(2i+1) := \nu_2(i) .$$

(3) $\nu_1 \sqcap \nu_2 \in N(M_1 \cap M_2)$,

$$\mathrm{dom}(\nu_1 \sqcap \nu_2) := \{<i_1,i_2> \mid i_1 \in \mathrm{dom}(\nu_1) \wedge i_2 \in \mathrm{dom}(\nu_2) \wedge \nu_1(i_1) = \nu_2(i_2)\},$$

$$(\nu_1 \sqcap \nu_2)<i_1,i_2> := \nu_1(i_1) .$$

(4) $WD(\nu_o) \in N(W(M_o))$,

$$\mathrm{dom}(WD(\nu_o)) := \{0\} \cup \{<<x_o,\ldots,x_k>,k> + 1 \mid k \in \mathbb{N} , x_o,\ldots,x_k \in \mathrm{dom}(\nu_o)\},$$

$$WD(\nu_o)(0) := \varepsilon,$$

$$WD(\nu_o)(<<x_o,\ldots,x_k>,k> + 1) := \nu_o(x_o)\nu_o(x_1)\ldots\nu_o(x_k) .$$

(5) $FS(\nu_o) \in N(E(M_o))$ where $E(M_o) = \{X \subseteq M_o \mid X \text{ finite}\}$,

$dom(FS(\nu_o)) := \{k \mid e_k \subseteq dom(\nu_o)\}$,

$FS(\nu_o)(k) := \{\nu_o(i) \mid i \in e_k\}$.

If $\nu := \nu_1 = \nu_2 = \ldots = \nu_n$ we define $\nu^n := [\nu_1,\ldots,\nu_n]$.

If $\nu_o, \nu_1, \ldots$ are "effective" then certainly the above defined numberings are "effective". The numbering $[\nu_1,\ldots,\nu_k]$ is derived from ν_{Ck}, the numbering $WD(\nu_o)$ is derived from ν^*, and the numbering $FS(\nu_o)$ is derived from the numbering e. Obviously, $\nu_{Ck} = 1\!\!1^k_{\mathbb{N}}$ (for $k \geq 1$) , $\nu^* = WD(1\!\!1_{\mathbb{N}})$, and $e = FS(1\!\!1_{\mathbb{N}})$. The numbering $\nu_1 \sqcup \nu_2$ is "the least upper bound" and the numbering $\nu_1 \sqcap \nu_2$ is "the greatest lower bound" of ν_1 and ν_2. The standard numbering ν of $W(\Sigma)$ derived from the order function $a : \{1,\ldots,n\} \longrightarrow \Sigma$ is equivalent to $WD(\nu_a)$ (c f. Def. 2). The operations introduced in Definition 14 are isotone w.r.t. the reducibility order $\leq$.

15 LEMMA

Suppose $\nu_i \leq \nu_i'$ $(i \in \mathbb{N})$. Then

$$[\nu_1,\ldots,\nu_n] \leq [\nu_1',\ldots,\nu_n'] \quad (n \geq 1) ,$$

$$\nu_1 \sqcup \nu_2 \leq \nu_1' \sqcup \nu_2' ,$$

$$\nu_1 \sqcap \nu_2 \leq \nu_1' \sqcap \nu_2' ,$$

$$WD(\nu_o) \leq WD(\nu_o') ,$$

$$FS(\nu_o) \leq FS(\nu_o') .$$

Proof (as an exercise)

By using standard numberings (e.g. from Definition 2) and standard operations we can formulate even more computability properties.

16 EXAMPLES

(1) Multiplication $f : \mathbb{Q} \times \mathbb{Q} \longrightarrow \mathbb{Q}$ is $([\nu_{\mathbb{Q}},\nu_{\mathbb{Q}}],\nu_{\mathbb{Q}})$-computable:
Consider the function $g : \mathbb{N} \longrightarrow \mathbb{N}$ with
$g(\langle\langle i,j,k\rangle,\langle i',j',k'\rangle\rangle) := \langle ii'+jj', ij'+ji', k+k'+kk'\rangle$. Then $f[\nu_{\mathbb{Q}},\nu_{\mathbb{Q}}](n) = \nu_{\mathbb{Q}}g(n)$ for all $n \in \mathbb{N}$.

(2) Composition $f : P^{(1)} \times P^{(1)} \longrightarrow P^{(1)}$ is $([\varphi,\varphi],\varphi)$-computable:
By Lemma 1.9.12 there is some $h \in R^{(2)}$ such that $\varphi_{h(i,j)} = f(\varphi_i,\varphi_j) = \varphi_i \circ \varphi_j$.
Define $g \in R^{(1)}$ by $g\langle i,j\rangle := h(i,j)$. Then $f[\varphi,\varphi]\langle i,j\rangle = f(\varphi_i,\varphi_j) = \varphi g\langle i,j\rangle$ for all $\langle i,j\rangle \in \mathbb{N}$.

(3) Union on $E(\mathbb{N})$ is $([e,e],e)$-computable (as an exercise).

The following lemma shows that the new definitions are consistent with older ones.

17 LEMMA

(1) Let $f : \mathbb{N}^k \dashrightarrow \mathbb{N}$ $(k \geq 1)$. Then f is computable iff f is strongly $(\mathbb{1}^k_{\mathbb{N}}, \mathbb{1}_{\mathbb{N}})$-computable.

(2) Let $f : (W(\Sigma))^k \dashrightarrow W(\Sigma)$ $(k \geq 1)$, let ν be a standard numbering of $W(\Sigma)$. Then f is computable iff f is strongly (ν^k,ν)-computable.

Proof

(1) follows immediately from $(\pi^{(k)})^{-1} = \nu_{Ck} = \mathbb{1}^k_{\mathbb{N}}$ and Lemma 1.2.16.

(2) Let f be computable. By Theorem 1.7.5 $g_1 := \nu^{-1} f \vec{\nu}$ is computable. By Lemma 1.2.16 $g := g_1 \nu_{Ck}$ is computable. We have $f\nu^k\langle i_1,\dots,i_k\rangle = f\vec{\nu}(i_1,\dots,i_k) = \nu g_1(i_1,\dots,i_k) = \nu g\langle i_1,\dots,i_k\rangle$, hence f is strongly (ν^k,ν)-computable. Now suppose that f is strongly (ν^k,ν)-computable. Then $f\nu^k(m) = \nu g(m)$ for some $g \in P^{(1)}$ (notice that ν is a total numbering). We conclude $f = f\vec{\nu}\vec{\nu}^{-1} = f\nu^k\pi^{(k)}\vec{\nu}^{-1} = \nu g\pi^{(k)}\vec{\nu}^{-1}$. By Lemma 1.2.16, $g\pi^{(k)}$ is computable, hence by Theorem 1.7.5, f is computable.
Q.E.D.

We have introduced numberings in order to reduce computability on the numbered sets to computability on $\mathbb{N}$. For practical reasons it is sometimes more useful to consider computability on words as the basic computability concept. In this case notations $\nu : W(\Sigma) \dashrightarrow M$ are used instead of numberings. Apart from some (inessential) additional formal complications because of the many different possible alphabets the theory of notations corresponds to that of numberings. The standard numberings ν_Σ of $W(\Sigma)$ connect the results of the two approaches.

18 DEFINITION (*notation*)

A *notation* of a set M is a surjective mapping $\nu : W(\Sigma) \dashrightarrow M$ where Σ is some alphabet.

The binary notation $\nu_B : W(\{0,1\}) \longrightarrow \mathbb{N}$ with $\nu_B(\text{"}a_n a_{n-1} \ldots a_1 a_o\text{"}) := \Sigma\{a_i \cdot 2^i \mid i \le n\}$ is a well-known example. An obvious modification of Definition 4 yields the definition of (ν,ν')-computability for notations ν and ν'. The two computability concepts are related via the standard numberings of word sets.

19 LEMMA

Let $\nu_i : W(\Sigma_i) \dashrightarrow M_i$ be notations, let λ_i be standard numberings of $W(\Sigma_i)$ $(i = 1,2)$, let $f : M_1 \dashrightarrow M_2$ be a function. Then f is (strongly) (ν_1,ν_2)-computable if and only if f is (strongly) $(\nu_1\lambda_1,\nu_2\lambda_2)$-computable.

The lemma is easily proved by Theorem 1.7.5. Since a notation $\nu : W(\Sigma) \dashrightarrow M$ and the corresponding numbering $\nu\lambda : \mathbb{N} \dashrightarrow M$, where λ is a standard numbering of $W(\Sigma)$, yield the same computability theory on M we shall say informally that ν and $\nu\lambda$ are *equivalent*. In Chapter 1.10 we introduced decision problems $P = (M,M_o,\nu)$ where ν is a notation of M and $M_o \subseteq M$. Then a decision problem (M,M_o,ν) is decidable (Def. 1.10.1) iff the set M_o is ν-recursive (cf. Def. 2.2.11).

EXERCISES

1) Let $a : \{1,2,3\} \longrightarrow \Sigma$, $\Sigma := \{A,B,C\}$ be defined by $a(1) = A$, $a(2) = B$, $a(3) = C$. Define ν_Σ and ν_G w.r.t. the order function a.
   (a) Determine $\nu(1000)$ for $\nu = 1\!\!1_{\{2,5\}}, \nu_a, \nu_\Sigma, \nu^*, \nu_G, e, \nu_Z, \nu_Q$.
   (b) Determine $x \in \mathbb{N}$ with: $\nu_{C4}(x) = (4,3,2,1)$, $\nu_\Sigma(x) = CAA$, $\nu^*(x) = 0 \mid 0 \mid 0 \mid 0 \mid 1 \mid 0$, $\nu_G(x) = BBA$, $e(x) = \{0,1,3,8\}$, $\nu_Z(x) = -13$, $\nu_Q(x) = 3/4$.
2) Execute the two inductions from the proof of Lemma 3.
3) Define a correspondence $f := (\mathbb{Q},\mathbb{Z},\rho)$ by $(x,y) \in \rho :\Leftrightarrow (x \ge 2 \Rightarrow x < y < x^2)$. Prove that f is strongly (ν_Q,ν_Z)-computable.
4) Show that the function $f : E(\mathbb{N}) \longrightarrow E(\mathbb{N})$ defined by $f(A) := \{0,\ldots,10\} \setminus A$ is (e,e)-computable.
5) Define a function $f : \mathbb{N} \dashrightarrow \mathbb{N}$ which is $(1\!\!1_{\mathbb{N}}, 1\!\!1_{\mathbb{N}})$-computable but not strongly $(1\!\!1_{\mathbb{N}}, 1\!\!1_{\mathbb{N}})$-computable. Define a function $g : \mathbb{N} \longrightarrow \mathbb{N}$ which is not $(1\!\!1_{\mathbb{N}}, 1\!\!1_{\mathbb{N}})$-computable.

6) Let $\nu_X \in N(X)$, $\nu_Y \in N(Y)$ be numberings. Characterize those $g : \mathbb{N} \dashrightarrow \mathbb{N}$ such that there is some
   (a) correspondence f which is (ν_X, ν_Y)-effective via g,
   (b) correspondence f which is strongly (ν_X, ν_Y)-effective via g,
   (c) partial function f which is (ν_X, ν_Y)-effective via g,
   (d) partial function f which is strongly (ν_X, ν_Y)-effective via g.
7) Prove that any two standard numberings of $W(\Sigma)$ (where Σ is an alphabet) are equivalent.
8) Prove Lemma 10.
9) Let ν_1 and ν_2 be numberings.
   (a) Prove: $\nu_1 \le \nu_1 \sqcup \nu_2, \nu_2 \le \nu_1 \sqcup \nu_2$.
   (b) Prove: $(\nu_1 \le \nu \wedge \nu_2 \le \nu) \Rightarrow \nu_1 \sqcup \nu_2 \le \nu$ for any numbering ν.
10) Let ν_1 and ν_2 be numberings.
   (a) Prove: $\nu_1 \sqcap \nu_2 \le \nu_1$, $\nu_1 \sqcap \nu_2 \le \nu_2$.
   (b) Prove: $(\nu \le \nu_1 \wedge \nu \le \nu_2) \Rightarrow \nu \le \nu_1 \sqcap \nu_2$ for any numbering ν.
11) Prove that addition on $\mathbb{Q}$ is $(\nu_{\mathbb{Q}}^2, \nu_{\mathbb{Q}})$-computable.
12) Prove Lemma 15.
13) Prove that union on $E(\mathbb{N})$ is (e,e)-computable.
14) Let $\nu, \nu' \in N(M), \nu \le \nu'$, let $A \subseteq M$. Prove:

    A ν'-r.e. $\Rightarrow A$ ν-r.e.,
    A ν'-recursive $\Rightarrow A$ ν-recursive.

15) Show $\nu_G \equiv \nu_\Sigma$ (see Definition 2).
16) Let $A \subseteq \mathbb{N}$ be finite, let $\nu : \mathbb{N} \longrightarrow A$ be a total numbering of A. Show that $\nu \equiv 1\!\!1_A$ iff $(\forall a \in A)\ \nu^{-1}\{a\}$ is recursive.
17) Let ν be a total numbering of $E(\mathbb{N})$. Show that $\nu \equiv e$ (c f. Def. 2) iff ν satisfies the following properties:

    $card : E(\mathbb{N}) \longrightarrow \mathbb{N}$ is $(\nu, 1\!\!1_{\mathbb{N}})$-computable, $\{(i,j) \mid i \in \nu(j)\}$ is decidable.

18) Let $\mathbb{P}_o = \{f : \mathbb{N} \dashrightarrow \mathbb{N} \mid dom(f) \text{ is finite}\}$. For total numberings ν of $\mathbb{P}_o$ define the following properties:
    $Q_1(\nu) :\Longleftrightarrow$ the function $\alpha : \mathbb{P}_o \longrightarrow E(\mathbb{N})$, $\alpha(f) := dom(f)$, is (ν,e)-computable,
    $Q_2(\nu) :\Longleftrightarrow \{(i,j,k) \mid \nu(i)(j) = k\}$ is recursive.
   (a) Show that there is a numbering $\nu_o \in TN(\mathbb{P}_o)$ such that $Q_1(\nu_o)$ and $Q_2(\nu_o)$.
   (b) Show that for any numbering $\nu \in TN(\mathbb{P}_o)$ the following holds:
   $\nu_o \equiv \nu \Longleftrightarrow (Q_1(\nu) \wedge Q_2(\nu))$.
19) Let a and b be order functions of the alphabet Σ. Show: $\nu_a \equiv \nu_b$ (see Def. 2).

20) A *finite graph* with nodes from $\mathbb{N}$ is a pair $G = (A,B)$ where $A \in E(\mathbb{N})$ and $B \subseteq A \times A$. Define an "effective" numbering of the set of all finite graphs with nodes form $\mathbb{N}$.

21) Let $\nu \in N(M)$, $A \subseteq M$.
    (a) Assume that $\mathrm{dom}(\nu)$ is recursive. Prove:
    A ν-recursive $\iff \nu^{-1}(A)$ is recursive.
    (b) Assume that $\mathrm{dom}(\nu)$ is r.e. Prove:
    A is ν-r.e. $\iff \nu^{-1}(A)$ is r.e.

BIBLIOGRAPHICAL NOTES

The theory of numberings has been developed by Russians. Malcev (1974) and Ershov (1973, 1975) are good sources for further studies.

2.3 Recursive and Recursively Enumerable Sets (Continued)

In this chapter we continue the study of the recursive and the recursively enumerable subsets of $\mathbb{N}$. First more examples for recursively enumerable sets which are not recursive are given. The non-recursiveness is proved by reduction to the self applicability problem or in one case by a new kind of diagonalization. Several characterizations of the recursive and the recursively enumerable sets are introduced and the corresponding numberings are compared w.r.t. reducibility. In most cases the non-existence of a computable function can be reduced to the unsolvability of the halting problem. Finally the φ-recursive and the φ-recursively enumerable subsets of $P^{(1)}$ are studied. Rice's theorem states that no non-trivial property $P^{(1)}$ is φ-recursive. A more general lemma gives two necessary conditions for φ-r.e. sets, by which many subsets of $P^{(1)}$ can be proved to be not φ-r.e.

By Definition 1.8.1 a subset $A \subseteq \mathbb{N}$ is recursive iff $A = f^{-1}\{0\}$ for some total recursive function $f : \mathbb{N} \longrightarrow \mathbb{N}$ (i.e. $f \in R^{(1)}$), and A is recursively enumerable iff $A = \mathrm{dom}(f)$ for some partial recursive function $f : \mathbb{N} \dashrightarrow \mathbb{N}$ (i.e. $f \in P^{(1)}$). By Theorem 1.8.5 a set A is recursive iff A and $\mathbb{N} \setminus A$ are recursively enumerable. Sets which are recursively enumerable but not recursive are of particular interest. In Definition 1.9.15 we introduced two sets of this type, K_φ and K^o_φ (see Theorem 1.9.16). Because of the independent definition of φ in Part 2 of this book (c f. Definition 2.1.5), we give a new definition.

1 <u>DEFINITION</u>

$K := \{i \in \mathbb{N} \mid i \in \mathrm{dom}(\varphi_i)\}$,

$K^o := \{\langle i,j\rangle \in \mathbb{N} \mid j \in \mathrm{dom}(\varphi_i)\}$.

The sets K and K^o have the following properties.

2 <u>THEOREM</u>

(1) K and K^o are recursively enumerable,

(2) K and K^o are not recursive,

(3) $\mathbb{N} \setminus K$ and $\mathbb{N} \setminus K^o$ are not recursively enumerable.

The proof is essentially that of Theorem 1.9.16. Property (1) is a consequence of the utm-theorem for φ, Property (2) for K already follows from the fact that φ is a total numbering of $P^{(1)}$. The proof is a typical proof by *diagonalization*. The non recursiveness of K^o is proved by *reduction* to K. A function $f \in R^{(1)}$ (i.e. f is total recursive) is defined such that $i \in K \iff f(i) \in K^o$ for all $i \in \mathbb{N}$, or expressed differently $K = f^{-1}(K^o)$. Suppose K^o is recursive. Then $K^o = g^{-1}\{0\}$ for some $g \in R^{(1)}$. Then $K = f^{-1}g^{-1}\{0\} = (gf)^{-1}\{0\}$. Since $gf \in R^{(1)}$, K is recursive, a contraction. We shall use *proofs by reduction* repeatedly. This concept is formalized by Definition 3 and Lemma 4.

3 DEFINITION (*reducibility for subsets of* $\mathbb{N}$)

Let $A, B \subseteq \mathbb{N}$.

$$A \leq B :\iff (\exists f \in R^{(1)})\ A = f^{-1}(B) \quad (\text{"A is } \textit{reducible} \text{ to B"}),$$

$$A \equiv B :\iff (A \leq B \wedge B \leq A) \quad (\text{"A is } \textit{equivalent} \text{ to B"}).$$

Reduction proofs are based on the following simple lemma.

4 LEMMA

Suppose $A \leq B$. Then:

(1) B recursive $\Longrightarrow$ A recursive,

(2) B r.e. $\Longrightarrow$ A r.e.,

(3) $\mathbb{N} \setminus A \leq \mathbb{N} \setminus B$.

Proof

$A = f^{-1}(B)$ for some $f \in R^{(1)}$. If B is recursive, then $B = g^{-1}\{0\}$ for some $g \in R^{(1)}$. Since $gf \in R^{(1)}$ and $A = (gf)^{-1}\{0\}$, A is recursive. If B is r.e., then $B = \text{dom}(g)$ for some $g \in P^{(1)}$. Since $gf \in P^{(1)}$ and $A = f^{-1}(B) = f^{-1}(\text{dom}(g)) = \text{dom}(gf)$, A is r.e. Property (3) is obvious.

Q.E.D.

In proofs usually the contrapositive formulations A not recursive (r.e.) $\Longrightarrow$ B not recursive (r.e.) are used. Lemma 4 (1) has an intuitive proof. $A = f^{-1}(B)$ means $(\forall i \in \mathbb{N})\ (i \in A \iff f(i) \in B)$. Suppose B is decidable. For deciding whether $i \in A$ or whether not, compute f(i) and decide whether $f(i) \in B$ or whether not. There are many other sets which are recursively enumerable but not recursive.

We give some examples.

5 LEMMA (*r.e. but not recursive sets*)

The following sets are recursively enumerable but not recursive.

$$M_1 := \{i \mid \mathrm{dom}(\varphi_i) \neq \emptyset\},$$

$$M_2 := \{\langle i,j\rangle \mid j \in \mathrm{range}(\varphi_i)\},$$

$$M_3 := \{\langle i,j,k\rangle \mid \varphi_i(j) = k\},$$

$$M_{4,k} := \{i \mid k \in \mathrm{dom}(\varphi_i)\} \quad (k \in \mathbb{N}),$$

$$M_{5,k} := \{i \mid k \in \mathrm{range}(\varphi_i)\} \quad (k \in \mathbb{N}).$$

Proof

(a) The sets A and B where

$$A = \{(i,x,t) \mid \Phi_i(x) = t\},$$

$$B = \{(i,x,y,t) \mid \Phi_i(x) = t \wedge \varphi_i(x) = y\}$$

are recursive (Definition 2.1.5, Lemma 2.1.3). We obtain

$$M_1 = \{i \mid (\exists \langle x,t\rangle)\ (i,x,t) \in A\}$$

$$M_2 = \{\langle i,j\rangle \mid (\exists \langle x,t\rangle)\ (i,x,j,t) \in B\}$$

$$M_3 = \{\langle i,j,k\rangle \mid (\exists t)\ (i,j,k,t) \in B\}$$

$$M_{4,k} = \{i \mid (\exists t)\ (i,k,t) \in A\}$$

$$M_{5,k} = \{i \mid (\exists \langle x,t\rangle)\ (i,x,k,t) \in B\}$$

The sets $\{(i,\langle x,t\rangle) \mid (i,x,t) \in A\}$, $\{(\langle i,j\rangle,\langle x,t\rangle \mid (i,x,j,t) \in B\}$, etc. are recursive. By the projection theorem (Theorem 1.8.4) the sets M_1, M_2, M_3, $M_{4,k}$, and $M_{5,k}$ are r.e. for any $k \in \mathbb{N}$.

(b) The non recursiveness of the five sets is proved by reduction to K (Lemma 4(1)). Define a function $g : \mathbb{N}^2 \dashrightarrow \mathbb{N}$ by

$$g(i,x) := \begin{cases} x & \text{if } i \in \mathrm{dom}(\varphi_i) \\ \mathrm{div} & \text{otherwise.} \end{cases}$$

Then $g \in P^{(2)}$, and by the smn-theorem (Def. 2.1.5) there is some $r \in R^{(1)}$ with $\varphi_{r(i)}(x) = g(i,x)$. Therefore, $\varphi_{r(i)}$ is the identity on $\mathbb{N}$ if $i \in K$ and the nowhere defined function if $i \notin K$. We obtain $i \in K \iff r(i) \in M_1 \iff r(i) \in M_{4,k} \iff r(i) \in M_{5,k}$ for all $i \in \mathbb{N}$, hence M_1, $M_{4,k}$ and $M_{5,k}$ are not recursive by Theorem 2 and Lemma 4. Define $r_2(i) := \langle r(i),0\rangle$, $r_3(i) := \langle r(i),0,0\rangle$. Then $r_2, r_3 \in R^{(1)}$ and $i \in K \iff r_2(i) \in M_2$ and $i \in K \iff r_3(i) \in M_3$ for all $i \in \mathbb{N}$. By Theorem 2 and

Lemma 4, M_2 and M_3 are not recursive.
Q.E.D.

The non recursiveness of K is proved by diagonalization (Theorem 1.9.16, Theorem 2), the non recursiveness of each set from Lemma 2 has been proved by reduction to K. There are, however, sets $B \subseteq \mathbb{N}$ which are recursively enumerable and not recursive for which $K \leq B$ does not hold. We shall introduce a certain class of such sets now, the simple sets.

6 DEFINITION (*simple sets*)

A set $B \subseteq \mathbb{N}$ is *simple* iff it is recursively enumerable and satisfies (1) and (2).

(1) $\mathbb{N} \setminus B$ is infinite ,

(2) $B \cap A \neq \emptyset$ for any infinite r.e. set $A \subseteq \mathbb{N}$.

We show that simple sets exist and that a simple set is not recursive.

7 THEOREM

(1) $B \subseteq \mathbb{N}$ is not recursive if B is simple.

(2) Define $S := \text{range}(f)$ where

$$f(x) := \pi_1 \mu\langle y,t\rangle[y > 2x \wedge \Phi_x(y) = t]$$

for all x. Then S is simple.

Proof

(1) Let $B \subseteq \mathbb{N}$ be simple. Suppose that B is recursive. By Definition 6(1) and Theorem 1.8.5, $\mathbb{N} \setminus B$ is an infinite r.e. set. By Definition 6(2), B must intersect $\mathbb{N} \setminus B$ which is impossible. Therefore, B is not recursive.

(2) Let $A \subseteq \mathbb{N}$ be r.e. and infinite. Then there are $x,y,t \in \mathbb{N}$ with $A = \text{dom}(\varphi_x)$, $y > 2x$ and $\Phi_x(y) = t$. Let $\langle y',t'\rangle$ be the smallest number $\langle y,t\rangle$ with $y > 2x$ and $\Phi_x(y) = t$. Then $f(x) = y' \in A$, hence $S \cap A \neq \emptyset$. By Axiom (B 2) (Def. 2.1.5) the function f is computable, hence $f = \varphi_i$ for some $i \in \mathbb{N}$. Let $A := \{(y,\langle x,t\rangle) \mid \varphi_i(x) = y \wedge \Phi_i(x) = t\}$. By Lemma 2.1.3 (see Def. 2.1.5) A is recursive. We obtain $S = \text{range}(f) = \{y \mid (\exists \langle x,t\rangle)\ (y,\langle x,t\rangle) \in A\}$, hence S is recursively enumerable. It remains to show that $\mathbb{N} \setminus S$ is infinite. Since $f(x) = \text{div}$ or $f(x) > 2x$

for any $x \in \mathbb{N}$ we obtain

$$\begin{aligned} &\mathrm{card}(\{0,1,\dots,2x\} \setminus \mathrm{range}(f)) \\ &= \mathrm{card}(\{0,1,\dots,2x\} \setminus f\{0,1,\dots,x-1\}) \\ &\geq 2x+1-x = x+1 . \end{aligned}$$

Therefore $\mathbb{N} \setminus S = \mathbb{N} \setminus \mathrm{range}(f)$ is infinite.
Q.E.D.

Let $X \subseteq \mathbb{N}$ be such that $\mathbb{N} \setminus X$ is r.e. and infinite. By Def. 6(2) of a simple set A, $A \setminus X = A \cap (\mathbb{N} \setminus X) \neq \emptyset$, hence $A \neq X$. This means that A diagonalizes over all $X \subseteq \mathbb{N}$ for which $\mathbb{N} \setminus X$ is r.e. and infinite. Since $\mathbb{N} \setminus A$ is infinite, $\mathbb{N} \setminus A$ must not be recursively enumerable, hence A must not be recursive. This is a new kind of diagonalization argument. In Chapter 2.6 we shall see that $K \leq A$ does not hold if A is simple.

By Definition 1.8.1, a subset $A \subseteq \mathbb{N}$ is recursive iff $A = f^{-1}\, 0$ for some $f \in R^{(1)}$, and A is recursively enumerable iff $A = \mathrm{dom}(f)$ for some $f \in R^{(1)}$. These definitions induce standard numberings of the recursive and the r.e. sets which are derived from the admissible numbering φ of $P^{(1)}$.

8 DEFINITION (*standard numberings of the recursive and the r.e. sets*)

(1) Let $RE := \{A \subseteq \mathbb{N} \mid A \text{ r.e.}\}$ be the set of all recursively enumerable subsets of $\mathbb{N}$. Define a total numbering W of RE by

$$W_i := W(i) := \mathrm{dom}(\varphi_i) .$$

(2) Let $REC := \{A \subseteq \mathbb{N} \mid A \text{ recursive}\}$ be the set of all recursive subsets of $\mathbb{N}$. Define a partial numbering Z of REC by

$$\mathrm{dom}(Z) = \{i \mid \varphi_i \in R^{(1)}\}$$

$$Z_i := Z(i) := \varphi_i^{-1}\{0\} \quad \text{for all } i \in \mathrm{dom}(Z) .$$

The definition of the numbering W depends on the numbering φ. Suppose φ' is another admissible numbering of $P^{(1)}$ and let $W'_i := \mathrm{dom}(\varphi'_i)$. As we already know, $\varphi \equiv \varphi'$. As a direct consequence we obtain $W_i \equiv W'_i$. Therefore the computability theory on RE induced by the numbering W does not depend on particular properties of φ but only on the axioms formulated in Definition 2.1.5. The corresponding remark holds for the numbering Z.

We are now able to formulate "effective" versions of theorems concerning recursive and recursively enumerable sets. As an example we consider Theorem 1.8.5: $A \subseteq \mathbb{N}$ is recursive iff A and $\mathbb{N} \setminus A$ are r.e. Let f be the correspondence

$$(\mathrm{REC}, \mathrm{RE} \times \mathrm{RE}, \{(A,(B,C)) \mid A = B \wedge \mathbb{N} \setminus A = C\}) .$$

We shall prove that f is strongly (Z,W^2)-computable and that f^{-1} is (W^2,Z)-computable. We shall express this more directly in Lemma 9. Define a numbering W^c of the complements of the r.e.sets by $W_i^c := \mathbb{N} \setminus W_i$. Then Lemma 9(1)(2) can be formulated very shortly as follows: $Z \equiv W \sqcap W^c$ (see Definition 2.2.14). Especially $Z \le W$, or in other words the correspondence $f = (\mathrm{REC},\mathrm{RE},\{(A,B) \mid A = B\})$ is strongly (Z,W)-computable. The question arises whether f^{-1} is (W,Z)-computable. Lemma 9(3) answers this question negatively.

9 LEMMA

(1) There are $g,h \in R^{(1)}$ such that for all $i \in \mathrm{dom}(Z)$:

$$Z_i = W_{g(i)} \quad \text{and} \quad \mathbb{N} \setminus Z_i = W_{h(i)} .$$

(2) There is a function $g \in P^{(1)}$ such that

$$W_i = Z_{g<i,j>}$$

for all i,j with $W_j = \mathbb{N} \setminus W_i$.

(3) There is no $g \in P^{(1)}$ with

$$Z_{g(i)} = W_i$$

for all $i \in \mathbb{N}$ such that W_i is recursive.

Proof

(1) By the smn-theorem there is some $g \in R^{(1)}$ with $\varphi_{g(i)}(n) = (0$ if $\varphi_i(n) = 0$, div otherwise$)$. Then for all $i \in \mathrm{dom}(Z)$: $Z_i = \varphi_i^{-1}\{0\} = \mathrm{dom}(\varphi_{g(i)}) = W_{g(i)}$. Similarly there is some $h \in R^{(1)}$ with $\varphi_{h(i)}(n) = (0$ if $\varphi_i(n)$ exists and $\varphi_i(n) \neq 0$, div otherwise$)$. Then $\mathbb{N} \setminus Z_i = \{n \mid \varphi_i(n) \neq 0\} = \mathrm{dom}(\varphi_{h(i)}) = W_{h(i)}$ for all $i \in \mathrm{dom}(Z)$.

(2) Define functions $h \in P^{(3)}$ and $p \in P^{(2)}$ by

$$h(i,j,n) := \mu t[\Phi_i(n) = t \vee \Phi_j(n) = t] ,$$

$$p(<i,j>,n) := \begin{cases} 0 & \text{if } h(i,j,n) \text{ exists and } \Phi_i(n) = h(i,j,n) \\ 1 & \text{if } h(i,j,n) \text{ exists and } \Phi_i(n) \neq h(i,j,n) \\ \text{div} & \text{otherwise.} \end{cases}$$

There is some $g \in R^{(1)}$ with $\varphi_{g<i,j>}(n) = p(<i,j>,n)$. Let $i,j \in \mathbb{N}$ with $W_j = \mathbb{N} \setminus W_i$, let $n \in \mathbb{N}$. If $n \in W_i$, then $n \notin W_j$, $h(i,j,n) = \Phi_i(n)$, and $\varphi_{g<i,j>}(n) = 0$. If $n \notin W_i$, then $n \in W_j$, $h(i,j,n)$ exists, $\Phi_i(n) \neq h(i,j,n)$, and $\varphi_{g<i,j>}(n) = 1$. Therefore $Z_{g<i,j>} = W_i$ if $W_j = \mathbb{N} \setminus W_i$.

(3) As we have shown in the proof of Lemma 5 there is some $r \in R^{(1)}$ such that $\varphi_{r(i)} = 1\!\!1_{\mathbb{N}}$ if $i \in K$ and $\varphi_{r(i)}$ is the nowhere defined function if $i \notin K$. Suppose some function g with the above property exists. Then $r(i) \in \mathrm{dom}(g)$ for all i since $W_{r(i)} = \emptyset$ or $W_{r(i)} = \mathbb{N}$, and $i \in K \iff 0 \in W_{r(i)} \iff 0 \in Z_{gr(i)} \iff \varphi_{gr(i)}(0) = 0$ for all $i \in \mathbb{N}$. The function h with $h(i) := \varphi_{gr(i)}(0)$ is total recursive (utm-theorem). We conclude $K = h^{-1}\{0\}$ which means that K is recursive (contradiction).
Q.E.D.

The recursively enumerable subsets of $\mathbb{N}$ can be characterized in different ways. Several characterizations induce natural numberings of the set RE (c f. Definition 8(1)). The following theorem summarizes some important characterizations the derived numberings of which are equivalent to W.

10 <u>THEOREM</u> (*characterizations of the r.e. sets*)

The following functions are equivalent numberings of the set RE of recursively enumerable subsets of $\mathbb{N}$.

(1) W with $W_i := \mathrm{dom}(\varphi_i)$,

(2) V_1 with $V_{1,i} := \mathrm{range}(\varphi_i)$,

(3) V_2 with $\mathrm{dom}(V_2) = \{i \mid \varphi_i \in R^{(1)}\}$ and $V_{2,i} := \{n \mid n+1 \in \mathrm{range}(\varphi_i)\}$,

(4) V_3 with $\mathrm{dom}(V_3) = \{i \mid \varphi_i \in R^{(1)}\}$ and $V_{3,i} := \{n \mid (\exists t)\ \langle n,t\rangle \in Z_i\}$,

(5) V_4 with $V_{4,i} := \{n \mid (\exists t)\ \langle n,t\rangle \in W_i\}$.

Especially for any $M \subseteq \mathbb{N}$ the following properties are equivalent.

(1') M is recursively enumerable.

(2') $M = \mathrm{range}(f)$ for some $f \in P^{(1)}$.

(3') $M = \{i \mid i+1 \in \mathrm{range}(g)\}$ for some $g \in R^{(1)}$.

(4') $M = \{n \mid (\exists t)\ \langle n,t\rangle \in A\}$ for some recursive set $A \subseteq \mathbb{N}$.

(5') $M = \{n \mid (\exists t)\ \langle n,t\rangle \in B\}$ for some recursively enumerable set $B \subseteq \mathbb{N}$.

<u>Proof</u>

We shall prove $W \le V_3 \le V_4 \le V_2 \le V_1 \le W$. Then by Lemma 2.2.6(2) and Lemma 2.2.7, the five numberings are equivalent numberings of RE.

"$W \le V_3$": We shall prove that a function $r \in R^{(1)}$ exists with $Z_{r(i)} = \{\langle n,t\rangle \mid \Phi_i(n) = t\}$. Then $W_i = \{n \mid n \in \mathrm{dom}(\varphi_i)\} = \{n \mid (\exists t)\ \Phi_i(n) = t\} = \{n \mid (\exists t)\ \langle n,t\rangle \in Z_{r(i)}\} = V_{3,r(i)}$, for all i, hence $W \le V_3$. By Axiom (B 2) there is some $f \in R^{(2)}$ with $f(i,\langle n,t\rangle) = 0 \iff \Phi_i(n) = t$ for all i,n,t. By the smn-theorem there is some $r \in R^{(1)}$ with $\varphi_{r(i)}\langle n,t\rangle = f(i,\langle n,t\rangle)$ for all i,n,t. Therefore, $Z_{r(i)} = \{\langle n,t\rangle \mid \Phi_i(n) = t\}$, as desired.

"$V_3 \leq V_4$": By Lemma 9, there is some $g \in R^{(1)}$ with $Z_i = W_{g(i)}$ for all $i \in \mathrm{dom}(Z) = \mathrm{dom}(V_3)$. Then $V_{3,i} = V_{4,g(i)}$ for all $i \in \mathrm{dom}(V_3)$, i.e. $V_3 \leq V_4$.

"$V_4 \leq V_2$": We shall show that there is a function $r \in R^{(1)}$ with the following property: if x "proves" $n \in V_{4,i}$ then $\varphi_{r(i)}(x) = n+1$, otherwise $\varphi_{r(i)}(x) = 0$. Define $h \in R^{(2)}$ by

$$h(i,\langle n,t,v\rangle) := \begin{cases} n+1 & \text{if } \Phi_i\langle n,t\rangle = v \\ 0 & \text{otherwise.} \end{cases}$$

By the smn-theorem there is some $r \in R^{(1)}$ with $\varphi_{r(i)}\langle n,t,v\rangle = h(i,\langle n,t,v\rangle)$ and $\varphi_{r(i)} \in R^{(1)}$. We obtain for any $i,n \in \mathbb{N}$: $n \in V_{4,i} \iff (\exists t,v)\ \Phi_i\langle n,t\rangle = v \iff n+1 \in \mathrm{range}(\varphi_{r(i)}) \iff n \in V_{2,r(i)}$, hence $V_4 \leq V_2$.

"$V_2 \leq V_1$": By the smn-theorem there is a function $r \in R^{(1)}$ with

$$\varphi_{r(i)}(k) = \begin{cases} \varphi_i(k) \dot{-} 1 & \text{if } \varphi_i(k) \text{ exists and } \varphi_i(k) \geq 1 \\ \mathrm{div} & \text{otherwise.} \end{cases}$$

Obviously, $V_{2,i} = V_{1,r(i)}$ for all $i \in \mathrm{dom}(V_2)$.

"$V_1 \leq W$": By the smn-theorem and Lemma 2.1.3 there is a function $r \in R^{(1)}$ with $\varphi_{r(i)}(n) = \mu\langle x,t\rangle[\varphi_i(x) = n \text{ and } \Phi_i(x) = t]$. Then we have $n \in V_{1,i} \iff (\exists x,t)$ $[\varphi_i(x) = n$ and $\Phi_i(x) = t] \iff n \in \mathrm{dom}(\varphi_{r(i)}) \iff n \in W_{r(i)}$. Therefore, $V_1 \leq W$.
Q.E.D.

The following corollary of the property $W \equiv V_2$ is often used as the original definition of the recursively enumerable sets.

11 COROLLARY

Let $A \subseteq \mathbb{N}$. Then A is recursively enumerable iff $A = \emptyset$ or $A = \mathrm{range}(f)$ for some total recursive function $f: \mathbb{N} \longrightarrow \mathbb{N}$ (i.e. $f \in R^{(1)}$).

A set $A \neq \emptyset$ is recursively enumerable iff there is some total function $f: \mathbb{N} \longrightarrow \mathbb{N}$ which "*enumerates*" A "*recursively*": $A = \{f(0),f(1),f(2),\ldots\}$. Notice that the list may have repetitions, i.e. f is not injective in general. Suppose we have determined some initial segment $f(0),f(1),\ldots,f(i)$ of the enumeration. Let $n \in \mathbb{N}$. If n is one of the $f(j)$ $(j \leq i)$ then surely $n \in A$. But if n has not yet been found, we cannot be sure that $n \notin A$. If $n \notin A$ we cannot be sure of this fact at any stage of the enumeration procedure. The characterization from Corollary 11 has the disadvantage that it needs the non-effective distinction between the empty set and the non-empty sets. The modified enumeration, $A = \{n \mid n+1 \in \text{range}(g)\}$ does not have this disadvantage. The enumeration functions can be normed in different ways, e.g. every infinite r.e. set A can be enumerated without repetition, i.e. $A = \text{range}(f)$ where f is injective. By the following lemma which states two additional useful properties the restrictions must not be too strong.

12 LEMMA

(1) Let $M \subseteq \mathbb{N}$, $M \neq \emptyset$. Then M is recursive iff $M = \text{range}(g)$ for some isotone $g \in R^{(1)}$.

(2) Let $M \subseteq \mathbb{N}$ be infinite and r.e. Then there is some infinite recursive set $A \subseteq M$.

Proof

(1) "$\Longrightarrow$": Let $M \neq \emptyset$ be recursive. Then $M = f^{-1}\{0\}$ for some $f \in R^{(1)}$. Define a function $h : \mathbb{N} \dashrightarrow \mathbb{N}$ inductively as follows.

$$h(0) := \mu n[f(n) = 0],$$

$$h(x+1) := \begin{cases} h(x) & \text{if } f(x+1) \neq 0 \\ x+1 & \text{if } f(x+1) = 0. \end{cases}$$

It is easy to design a generalized register machine which computes h, hence $h \in R^{(1)}$. Let $m := \text{Min}\, M$. The following property can be easily proved by induction on y:

$$h\{0,\dots,y\} = \{m\} \cup (M \cap \{0,\dots,y\}) \quad \text{for all } y \in \mathbb{N}.$$

Therefore, $z \in \text{range}(h) \iff (\exists y)\ z \in h\{0,\dots,y\} \iff (\exists y)\ (z = m \text{ or } z \in M \cap \{0,\dots,y\}) \iff z \in M$. Finally, an easy induction shows that h is isotone.

(1) "$\Longleftarrow$": If M is finite then M is recursive. Let M be infinite. Define $h : \mathbb{N} \dashrightarrow \mathbb{N}$ by $h(y) := \mu x[g(x) > y]$. Since M is infinite, $h \in R^{(1)}$. For any $x \geq h(y)$ we have $g(x) \geq gh(y) > y$ by definition of h and isotonicity of g. Therefore

$$y \in M = \text{range}(g) \iff (\exists x < h(y))\ g(x) = y,$$

hence for searching y in M only a list of known length has to be tested. Define $f \in R^{(1)}$ by

$$f(y) := \begin{cases} 0 & \text{if } (\exists x < h(y))\ g(x) = y \\ 1 & \text{otherwise}. \end{cases}$$

Then $M = f^{-1}\{0\}$, i.e. M is recursive.

(2) Since M is infinite, $M = \text{range}(f)$ for some $f \in R^{(1)}$. Define $h : \mathbb{N} \dashrightarrow \mathbb{N}$ inductively by

$h(0) := f(0)$,

$h(x+1) := f(\mu z[f(z) > h(x)])$.

Then h is computable. By induction we show that h is a total function: h(0) exists, if h(x) exists, then h(x+1) exists since f is unbounded. By the definition of h, $h(x+1) = f(z)$ for some z with $f(z) > h(x)$, hence $h(x+1) > h(x)$. Therefore h is isotone and range(h) is infinite, i.e. range(h) is recursive by (1). Finally we prove $\mathrm{range}(h) \subseteq M$: $h(0) = f(0) \in M$, for all x, $h(x+1) = f(z)$ for some z, hence $h(x+1) \in \mathrm{range}(f) = M$. Therefore, $A := \mathrm{range}(h)$ is an infinite recursive subset of M. Q.E.D.

In the proof of (1) "$\Longleftarrow$" the cases "M finite" and "M infinite" have to be distinguished. In fact, there is no $f \in P^{(1)}$ such that for all $i \in \mathbb{N}$, $Z_{f(i)} = \mathrm{range}(\varphi_i)$ whenever $\varphi_i \in R^{(1)}$ and φ_i is isotone (see the exercises).

The sets RE and REC are closed under several standard operations. We immediately prove effective versions. Remember that <,> is Cantor's pairing function.

13 THEOREM (*closure properties of* REC *and* RE)

(1) Let $A, B \subseteq$ REC, let $f \in R^{(1)}$. Then the following sets are recursive:

$$A \cup B,\ A \cap B,\ \mathbb{N} \setminus A,\ \langle A,B \rangle,\ f^{-1}(A).$$

The corresponding operations are computable w.r.t. the numberings Z and φ.

(2) Let $A, B \subseteq$ RE, let $f \in P^{(1)}$. Then the following sets are recursively enumerable:

$$A \cup B,\ A \cap B,\ \langle A,B \rangle,\ f^{-1}(A),\ f(A),\ \bigcup\{W_x \mid x \in A\}.$$

The corresponding operations are computable w.r.t. the numberings W and φ.

Proof

(1) Define a function $g \in P^{(2)}$ by

$g(\langle i,j \rangle, n) := \varphi_i(n) \cdot \varphi_j(n)$.

By the smn-theorem there is some $r \in R^{(1)}$ such that $\varphi_{r\langle i,j \rangle}(n) = g(\langle i,j \rangle, n)$. We obtain $r\langle i,j \rangle \in \mathrm{dom}(Z)$ if $\langle i,j \rangle \in \mathrm{dom}([Z,Z])$ (see Def. 2.2.14), and $Z_{r\langle i,j \rangle} = Z_i \cup Z_j$ for all $i,j \in \mathrm{dom}(Z)$. Therefore, $A \cup B$ is recursive if A and B are recursive, and the function $H : \mathrm{REC} \times \mathrm{REC} \longrightarrow \mathrm{REC}$ with $H(A,B) = A \cup B$ is ([Z,Z],Z)-computable. Similarly, for the other operations there are recursive functions r with:

$$\varphi_{r<i,j>}(n) = \varphi_i(n) + \varphi_j(n) \qquad \text{(for the case } Z_i \cap Z_j),$$

$$\varphi_{r(i)}(n) = 1 \dot{-} \varphi_i(n) \qquad \text{(for the case } \mathbb{N} \setminus Z_i),$$

$$\varphi_{r<i,j>}<m,n> = <\varphi_i(m), \varphi_j(n)> \qquad \text{(for the case } <Z_i, Z_j>,$$

$$\varphi_{r<i,j>}(n) = \varphi_i\varphi_j(n) \qquad \text{(for the case } \varphi_j^{-1}Z_i).$$

(2) By the smn-theorem and Axiom (B 2) there is a function $r \in R^{(1)}$ such that

$$\varphi_{r<i,j>}(n) = \mu t[\Phi_i(n) = t \vee \Phi_j(n) = t].$$

We obtain $n \in W_{r<i,j>}$ iff $n \in W_i$ or $n \in W_j$, i.e. $W_{r<i,j>} = W_i \cup W_j$. Therefore the union is (W^2, W)-computable on RE. Similarly for the other operations there are recursive functions r with:

$$\varphi_{r<i,j>}(n) = \varphi_i(n) + \varphi_j(n) \qquad \text{(for the case } W_i \cap W_j),$$

$$\varphi_{r<i,j>}<m,n> = <\varphi_i(m), \varphi_j(n)> \qquad \text{(for the case } <W_i, W_j>),$$

$$\varphi_{r<i,j>}(n) = \varphi_i\varphi_j(n) \qquad \text{(for the case } \varphi_j^{-1}W_i),$$

$$\varphi_{r<i,j>}(n) = \mu<x,s,t>[\Phi_i(x) = t \wedge \varphi_i(x) = n \wedge \Phi_j(x) = t] \qquad \text{(for the case } \varphi_i(W_j)).$$

In the last case apply Lemma 2.1.3.
Q.E.D.

Notice that f(A) may be non-recursive if $f \in R^{(1)}$ and A is recursive, e.g. $K = f(\mathbb{N})$ for some $f \in R^{(1)}$ (Corollary 11, Theorem 2), and that for $A \in RE$ the complement $\mathbb{N} \setminus A$ is recursive only if A is recursive.

In our approach we have reduced the definition of the recursively enumerable subsets of $\mathbb{N}$ to the definition of computable functions on $\mathbb{N}$. The converse procedure is possible: A function $f : \mathbb{N} \dashrightarrow \mathbb{N}$ is computable iff its graph is recursively enumerable. Similarly the total recursive functions can be characterized by recursive graphs.

14 <u>THEOREM</u> (*graph-theorem*)

(1) Let $f : \mathbb{N} \dashrightarrow \mathbb{N}$. Then

$$f \in P^{(1)} \iff \{<i, f(i)> \mid i \in \mathrm{dom}(f)\} \text{ is r.e.}$$

(2) Let $f : \mathbb{N} \longrightarrow \mathbb{N}$. Then

$$f \in R^{(1)} \iff \{<i, f(i)> \mid i \in \mathrm{dom}(f)\} \text{ is recursive.}$$

By the smn-theorem there is some $r \in R^{(1)}$ with $\varphi_{r(i)}(x) = h(i,x)$. If $i \notin K$ and $x \notin \mathrm{dom}(\varphi_m)$ then $x \notin \mathrm{dom}(\varphi_{r(i)})$. If $i \notin K$ and $x \in \mathrm{dom}(\varphi_m)$ then $g(i,x)$ exists, $g(i,x) = \Phi_m(x)$, and $\varphi_{r(i)}(x) = \varphi_m(x)$. Therefore, $i \notin K$ implies $\varphi_{r(i)} = \varphi_m \in M$. Let $i \in K$. Then $g(i,x)$ exists. If $g(i,x) = \Phi_m(x)$ then $\varphi_{r(i)}(x) = \varphi_m(x) = \varphi_n(x)$ since $\mathrm{graph}(\varphi_m) \subseteq \mathrm{graph}(\varphi_n)$. If $g(i,x) \neq \Phi_m(x)$ then $\varphi_{r(i)}(x) = \varphi_n(x)$. Therefore $i \in K$ implies $\varphi_{r(i)} = \varphi_n \notin M$. Altogether we obtain $i \notin K \iff r(i) \in \varphi^{-1}(M)$. By assumption on M and by Lemma 4, $\mathbb{N} \setminus K$ is r.e. in contradiction to Theorem 2. This proves our lemma.
Q.E.D.

A complete characterization of the φ-r.e. subsets of M can be easily derived from Lemma 16 (as an exercise). We shall prove the complete theorem in a more general framework in Part 3 of this book. As a simple corollary we obtain Rice's theorem which characterizes the φ-recursive subsets of $P^{(1)}$.

17 <u>COROLLARY</u> (*Rice's theorem*)

8 Let $M \subseteq P^{(1)}$. If $\varphi^{-1}(M)$ is recursive then either $M = \emptyset$ or $M = P^{(1)}$.

<u>Proof</u>

Let $\varphi^{-1}M$ be recursive. Then $\varphi^{-1}M$ and $\varphi^{-1}(P^{(1)} \setminus M)$ are recursively enumerable. Let $f_o \in P^{(1)}$ be the function with $\mathrm{dom}(f_o) = \emptyset$. If $f_o \in M$, then $f \in M$ for any $f \in P^{(1)}$ by Lemma 16, hence $M = P^{(1)}$. If $f_o \in P^{(1)} \setminus M$ then $f \in P^{(1)} \setminus M$ for any $f \in P^{(1)}$ by Lemma 16, hence $M = \emptyset$.
Q.E.D.

In other words, Rice's theorem states that no non-trivial subset (= "property") of $P^{(1)}$ is φ-recursive (see Def. 2.2.11). Rice's theorem and Lemma 16 are used to show that certain sets are not recursive or not recursively enumerable. For example, the following sets are not recursive by Rice's theorem.

$\{i \mid \mathrm{dom}(\varphi_i) = \emptyset\}$

$\{i \mid \mathrm{dom}(\varphi_i) \neq \emptyset\}$

$\{i \mid \varphi_i \in R^{(1)}\}$

$\{i \mid n \in \mathrm{dom}(\varphi_i)\}$ $(n \in \mathbb{N})$

$\{i \mid \mathrm{range}(\varphi_i) \subseteq A\}$ $(A \subseteq \mathbb{N},\ A \neq \mathbb{N})$

$\{i \mid f = \varphi_i\}$ $(f \in P^{(1)})$

Each of the following sets is not recursively enumerable since it violates either Condition (1) or Condition (2) of Lemma 16.

$\{i \mid \mathrm{dom}(\varphi_i)$ is finite$\}$

$\{i \mid \varphi_i \in R^{(1)}\}$

$\{i \mid \mathrm{range}(\varphi_i)$ is infinite$\}$

$\{i \mid \varphi_i = f\} \quad (f \in P^{(1)})$

$\{i \mid \varphi_i \neq f\} \quad (f \in P^{(1)},\ \mathrm{dom}(f) \neq \emptyset)$

$\{i \mid \varphi_i \notin R^{(1)}\}$

By an easy reduction we obtain the unsolvability of the equivalence problem of φ.

18 LEMMA

(1) For any $f \in P^{(1)}$ the set

$$M_f := \{i \mid \varphi_i = f\}$$

is not r.e.

(2) Neither the set

$$M_e := \{\langle i,j\rangle \mid \varphi_i = \varphi_j\}$$

nor its complement is r.e.

Proof

If $\mathrm{dom}(f) \neq \emptyset$, neither $M_f = \{i \mid \varphi_i = f\}$ nor $\mathbb{N} \setminus M_f$ is r.e. by Lemma 16. Let $m \in \mathbb{N}$ be such that $\mathrm{dom}(\varphi_m) \neq \emptyset$. Define $f := \varphi_m$. Define $h \in R^{(1)}$ by $h(x) := \langle x,m\rangle$. Then $k \in M_f \iff h(k) \in M_e$, hence $M_f \leq M_e$. By Lemma 4, M_e and $\mathbb{N} \setminus M_e$ are not r.e. since M_f and $\mathbb{N} \setminus M_f$ are not r.e.
Q.E.D.

With the interpretation that φ_i is the function which is computed by the i-th tape machine, Lemma 18(1) says that the correctness problem for tape machines is unsolvable (even not r.e.) and Lemma 18(2) says that the equivalence problem for tape machines is unsolvable (even not r.e.). It can be easily shown that these two problems are unsolvable for any reasonable programming language.

The definitions of the numbering W of the r.e. sets and of Z of the recursive sets depend on φ. Let ψ be another numbering of $P^{(1)}$ which satisfies the smn-theorem and the utm-theorem. Define $W'_i = \mathrm{dom}(\psi_i)$, $Z'_i := \psi_i^{-1}\{0\}$ if $\psi_i \in R^{(1)}$. Then $W \equiv W'$

and $Z \equiv Z'$ since $\varphi \equiv \psi$. By Conclusion 2.2.9, W and W' as well as Z and Z' define the same computability theories.

EXERCISES

1) Prove that the set $\{i \mid \varphi_i(0) = 0\}$ is recursively enumerable and not recursive.
2) Let e be the standard numbering of $E(\mathbb{N})$.
   (a) Prove: $e \le Z$.
   (b) Prove that there is no $g \in P^{(1)}$ such that $e_{g(i)} = Z_i$ for all $i \in \mathrm{dom}(Z)$ such that Z_i is finite.
   (c) Prove that there is no $h \in P^{(1)}$ such that $e_{h(i)} = W_i$ for all $i \in \mathbb{N}$ such that W_i is finite.
3) (a) Prove that the correspondence
   $$(RE, \mathbb{N}, \{(A,i) \mid i \in A\})$$
   is strongly $(W, 1_{\mathbb{N}})$-computable.
   (b) Prove that there is no function $f: RE \dashrightarrow \mathbb{N}$ with $f(A) \in A$ if $A \neq \emptyset$, which is $(W, 1_{\mathbb{N}})$-computable.
4) Prove that the set $\{\langle i,k\rangle \mid (\exists j)(i \in W_j \wedge j \in W_k)\}$ is recursively enumerable and not recursive.
5) (a) Let $A, B \subseteq \mathbb{N}$ be recursively enumerable. Prove that by
   $U(A,B) := \bigcup \{e_m \mid (\exists n)(\langle m,n\rangle \in A \wedge e_n \subseteq B)\}$
   a function $U: RE^2 \longrightarrow RE$ is defined.
   (b) Prove that the above defined function U is strongly (W^2, W)-computable.
6) A set $A \subseteq \mathbb{N}$ is a *segment* of $\mathbb{N}$ iff ($i < j$ and $j \in A$) implies $i \in A$ for all $i, j \in \mathbb{N}$.
   (a) Define a numbering V_s of r.e. subsets of $\mathbb{N}$ by
   $$\mathrm{dom}(V_s) := \{i \mid \mathrm{dom}(\varphi_i) \text{ is a segment, } \varphi_i \text{ is injective}\},$$
   $$V_s(i) := \mathrm{range}\,(\varphi_i) \quad \text{for all } i \in \mathrm{dom}(V_s).$$
   Prove: $V_s \equiv W$.
   (b) Define a numbering Z_s of subsets of $\mathbb{N}$ by
   $$\mathrm{dom}(Z_s) := \{i \mid \varphi_i \text{ is injective and isotone and } \mathrm{dom}(\varphi_i) \text{ is a segment}\}$$
   $$Z_s(i) := \mathrm{range}\,(\varphi_i) \quad \text{for all } i \ \mathrm{dom}(Z_s).$$
   Prove that Z_s is a numbering of the recursive subsets of $\mathbb{N}$.
   Prove: $Z \le Z_s$, $Z_s \not\le Z$.
7) Complete the proof of Theorem 13.
8) Prove Corollary 11.
9) Formulate and prove the effective versions (w.r.t. φ, W, and Z) of Lemma 12.

10) Let $f \in R^{(1)}$, $K = \text{range}(f)$, f injective.

(a) Prove that there is some isotone unbounded $g : \mathbb{N} \longrightarrow \mathbb{N}$ with $(\forall n) g(n) \leq f(n)$.

(b) Prove that the function g from (a) is not recursive.

11) Define $h : \mathbb{N}^2 \dashrightarrow \mathbb{N}$ by

$$h(i,x) := \mu y[\langle x,y\rangle \in W_i].$$

Show that h is not computable.

12) Consider the single-valuedness theorem. Prove that the additional condition $W_i = W_j \Rightarrow W_{g(i)} = W_{g(j)}$ cannot be satisfied.

13) Call a subset $A \subseteq \mathbb{N}$ "e-isotone" iff $(\langle i,j\rangle \in A$ and $\langle m,n\rangle \in A$ and $e_i \subseteq e_m) \Rightarrow e_j \subseteq e_n$. Prove that there is a function $g \in R^{(1)}$ such that

(1) $W_{g(i)} \subseteq W_i$,

(2) $W_{g(i)}$ is e-isotone,

(3) $W_{g(i)} = W_i$ if W_i is e-isotone,

(4) $\pi_1 W_i = \pi_1 W_{g(i)}$

for all $i \in \mathbb{N}$.

14) Define a numbering ν_F of the set $F_o := \{f : \mathbb{N} \dashrightarrow \mathbb{N} \mid \text{dom}(f) \text{ finite}\}$ by $\nu_F(i)(j) := \mu k[\langle j,k\rangle \in e_i]$ for all $i,j \in \mathbb{N}$. For any $i \in \mathbb{N}$ define $[\nu_F(i)] := \{f \in P^{(1)} \mid \text{graph}(\nu_F(i)) \subseteq \text{graph}(f)\}$. Prove the following characterization of the φ-r.e. sets. Let $M \subseteq P^{(1)}$. M is φ-r.e. iff there is some r.e. set $A \subseteq \mathbb{N}$ such that $M = \bigcup\{[\nu_F(i)] \mid i \in A\}$.

15) Let $H \subseteq RE$ be a W-r.e. set. Prove the following properties for any $A \in M$.

(1) There is some $B \in H$, B finite, such that $B \subseteq A$.

(2) $C \in H$ for all $C \in RE$ with $A \subseteq C$.

(Hint: Use Lemma 16.)

16) Characterize the pairs (A, B) of recursive sets for which $A \leq B$.

17) Prove by a diagonalization (not by reduction) that $\{x \mid \varphi_x \text{ is total}\}$ is not r.e.

18) Let $M_1 := \{x \mid \varphi_x \text{ is total}\}$.

(a) Let $M_2 := \{x \mid W_x \text{ is infinite}\}$. Prove that $M_1 \equiv M_2$.

(b) Prove that there are recursive sets $A_i \, (i = 1,2)$ such that $M_i = \{x \mid (\forall y)(\exists z)\langle x,y,z\rangle \in A_i\}$.

(c) Let A be recursive and $M := \{x \mid (\forall y)(\exists z)\langle x,y,z\rangle \in A\}$. Prove: $M \leq M_1$.

19) Prove $A \leq K^o$ for any recursively enumerable set A.

20) Prove $K^o \leq K$.

21) Let $A_1, \ldots, A_n$ be r.e. sets such that $A_i \cap A_j = \emptyset$ if $1 \leq i < j \leq n$ and $\mathbb{N} = \cup \{A_i \mid 1 \leq i \leq n\}$. Prove that A_i is recursive for all i.

22) Let A be simple, let B be recursively enumerable and infinite. Show that $A \cap B$ is infinite.

23) Show that $A \cap B$ is simple if A and B are simple.

BIBLIOGRAPHICAL NOTES

The theory of recursive and recursively enumerable sets is part of standard recursion theory, see e.g. Rogers (1967). The concept of numbering admits a concise formulation of many properties. Lemma 16 is a special case of a theorem by Rice et al., see Rice (1956). A general version of this theorem will be proved in Part 3 of this book (Chapter 3.6). Usually only the special case corollary 17 is called Rice's theorem. The term simple set is due to Post (1944).

2.4 Many-one and One-one Reducibility

In Chapter 1.9 we have introduced the reducibility relation $\le$ for numberings, and in Chapter 2.2 we have proved that two numberings of a set M define the same computability theory for M iff they are equivalent. We shall now introduce a stronger reducibility, the *one-one reducibility*, together with the induced *one-one equivalence* and *isomorphism* of numberings. We shall prove *Myhill's theorem* which states that (for total numberings) isomorphism and one-one equivalence coincide. We introduce *cylinders* and study the relation between reducibility and one-one reducibility. We conclude with some further useful properties.

In the course of the book we shall study several kinds of reducibilities all of which define pre-orders. From any pre-order an equivalence relation and a partial order on the corresponding equivalence classes can be derived.

1 DEFINITION (*pre-order*, *partial order*)

(1) A *pre-order* is a pair $(A,\le)$ where A is a class and $\le$ is a subclass of $A\times A$ satisfying $a\le a$ and $(a\le b \wedge b\le c) \Longrightarrow a\le c$ for all $a,b,c\in A$.

(2) A *partial order* is a pre-order $(A,\le)$ which in addition satisfies $(a\le b\wedge b\le a)\Longrightarrow a=b$ for all $a,b\in A$.

Therefore, in a pre-order ($a\le b$ and $b\le a$) is possible for different elements a and b. It is convenient to generalize some concepts which are originally defined for partial orders to pre-orders.

2 DEFINITION

Let $(A,\le)$ be a pre-order.

(1) Define $a\equiv b :\Longleftrightarrow (a\le b\wedge b\le a)$. (Obviously, $(A,\equiv)$ is an equivalence relation.)

(2) $a\in A$ is *minimal* if $(b\le a \Longrightarrow b\equiv a)$ for all $b\in A$. *Maximality* is defined accordingly.

(3) Let $B\subseteq A$.

$$\mathrm{Sup}(B) := \{a \mid (\forall b\in B)\ b\le a \text{ and } (\forall c\in A)\ [(\forall b\in B)\ b\le c \Longrightarrow a\le c]\}$$

The set Inf(B) is defined accordingly.

If $a \in \mathrm{Sup}(B)$ and $b \in \mathrm{Sup}(B)$, then $a \equiv b$. Hence $\mathrm{Sup}(B)$ is either empty or consists of a single equivalence class. If $(A,\leq)$ is a partial order then $\mathrm{Sup}(B) = \{b\}$ if the least upper bound $b = \mathrm{l.u.b.}(B)$ exists, and $\mathrm{Sup}(B) = \emptyset$ otherwise. We shall say "a *is a least upper bound of* B" if $a \in \mathrm{Sup}(B)$. The corresponding remarks hold for "Inf" instead of "Sup".

Let $(A,\leq)$ be a pre-order. For $a,b \in A$ define $[a] := \{b \in A \mid b \equiv a\}$, $A/\equiv\, := \{[a] \mid a \in A\}$, $[a] \leq' [b] :\Longleftrightarrow a \leq b$. Then $(A/\equiv, \leq')$ is a partial order of the equivalence classes of the pre-order $(A,\leq)$. Let $B \subseteq A$, $\leq_B := B \times B \cap \leq$. For simplicity we shall denote $(B,\leq_B)$ by $(B,\leq)$, which also is a pre-order.

In Chapter 1.9 we have defined the reducibility relation $\leq$ on the class $\hat{N}$ of numberings. Now we shall define a more special relation $\leq_1$ on $\hat{N}$ and isomorphism of total numberings.

3 DEFINITION (*one-one reducibility, isomorphism*)

Let ν,ν' be numberings. Define:

(1) $\nu \leq_1 \nu' \;:\Longleftrightarrow\; (\exists f \in P^{(1)})\,[(\forall i,j \in \mathrm{dom}(\nu))(\nu(i) = \nu' f(i) \wedge (f(i) = f(j) \Longrightarrow i = j))]$

(ν is 1-*reducible* or *one-one reducible* to ν')

(2) $\nu \equiv_1 \nu' \;:\Longleftrightarrow\; (\nu \leq_1 \nu' \wedge \nu' \leq_1 \nu)$

(ν is 1-*equivalent* or *one-one equivalent* to ν')

Let ν,ν' be total numberings, Define:

(3) $\nu \simeq \nu' \;:\Longleftrightarrow\; (\exists f \in R^{(1)})\,(f \text{ bijective} \wedge (\forall i)\; \nu(i) = \nu' f(i))$

(ν is *isomorphic* to ν')

In contrast to one-one reducibility the ordinary reducibility $\leq$ is sometimes called *Many-one reducibility* or *m-reducibility* and is denoted by $\leq_m$. The next lemma summarizes some properties which immediately follow from the definitions. Notice that $f^{-1} \in R^{(1)}$ if $f \in R^{(1)}$ is bijective.

4 LEMMA

Consider Definition 2.2.1. Then:

(1) $(\hat{N},\leq)$ and $(\hat{N},\leq_1)$ are pre-orders.

(2) $\nu \leq_1 \nu' \Longrightarrow \nu \leq \nu'$ (for any $\nu,\nu' \in \hat{N}$).

(3) $\nu \equiv_1 \nu' \Longrightarrow \nu \equiv \nu'$ (for any $\nu, \nu' \in \hat{N}$).

(4) $\nu \approx \nu' \Longrightarrow \nu \equiv_1 \nu'$ (for any $\nu, \nu' \in \hat{TN}$).

While equivalent numberings define the same computability theory, isomorphic numberings can be called indistinguishable within recursion theory. Obviously $(A, \leq)$ and $(A, \leq_1)$ are pre-orders and $(A, \equiv)$ and $(A, \equiv_1)$ are equivalence relations for any subclass $A \subseteq \hat{N}$. Total numberings of $\{0,1\}$ can be considered as characteristic functions of the non-trivial subsets of $\mathbb{N}$. The reducibilities on the numberings induce reducibilities on the sets.

5 DEFINITION

(1) For any $A \subseteq \mathbb{N}$, $A \neq \emptyset$, $A \neq \mathbb{N}$, define $cf_A \in TN(\{0,1\})$, the characteristic function of A, by

$$cf_A(i) := \begin{cases} 1 & \text{if } i \in A \\ 0 & \text{otherwise.} \end{cases}$$

(2) Let $A, B \subseteq \mathbb{N}$, $A, B \neq \emptyset$, $A, B \neq \mathbb{N}$. Then define:

$$A \leq B :\Longleftrightarrow cf_A \leq cf_B,$$

$$A \equiv B :\Longleftrightarrow cf_A \equiv cf_B,$$

$$A \leq_1 B :\Longleftrightarrow cf_A \leq_1 cf_B,$$

$$A \equiv_1 B :\Longleftrightarrow cf_A \equiv_1 cf_B,$$

$$A \approx B :\Longleftrightarrow cf_A \approx cf_B.$$

Notice that this definition of $A \leq B$ is consistent with that from Def. 2.3.3. Hence for the non-trivial subsets of $\mathbb{N}$, reducibility theory can be embedded into the more general reducibility theory for numberings. Of course, $(\hat{P}, \leq)$ and $(\hat{P}, \leq_1)$ are pre-orders and $(\hat{P}, \equiv)$, $(\hat{P}, \equiv_1)$, and $(\hat{P}, \approx)$ are equivalence relations, where $\hat{P} := \{A \mid A \subseteq \mathbb{N}, A \neq \emptyset, A \neq \mathbb{N}\}$.

As a fundamental result we prove that for total numberings 1-equivalence and isomorphism coincide.

6 THEOREM (*Myhill*)

Let ν, ν' be total numberings, then:

$$\nu \equiv_1 \nu' \Longleftrightarrow \nu \approx \nu'.$$

Proof

"$\Longleftarrow$": Let $\nu \approx \nu'$. Then $\nu = \nu' f$ for some bijective $f \in R^{(1)}$. Since f is bijective, $\nu' = \nu f^{-1}$. Therefore $\nu \leq_1 \nu'$ and (since $f^{-1} \in R^{(1)}$) $\nu' \leq_1 \nu$, i.e. $\nu \equiv_1 \nu'$.

"$\Longrightarrow$": Let $\nu \equiv_1 \nu'$. Then there are injective functions $f, g \in R^{(1)}$ with $\nu = \nu' f$ and $\nu' = \nu g$. It is our aim to construct a bijection $h \in R^{(1)}$ with $\nu = \nu' h$. In this proof any finite subset of the graph of such a function will be called a *correspondence*. More formally, a correspondence is a sequence $((x_o, y_o), (x_1, y_1), \ldots$ $\ldots, (x_k, y_k))$ of pairs of numbers such that (1) and (2) hold.

(1) $x_i \neq x_j$ and $y_i \neq y_j$ for all $0 \leq i < j \leq k$,

(2) $\nu(x_i) = \nu'(y_i)$ for all $0 \leq i \leq k$.

We shall prove now (a) and (b).

(a) For every correspondence $((x_o, y_o), \ldots, (x_k, y_k))$ and every $x \notin \{x_o, \ldots, x_k\}$ a number y can be determined such that $((x_o, y_o), \ldots, (x_k, y_k), (x, y))$ is a correspondence.

(b) With the procedure from (a) a bijection $h \in R^{(1)}$ with $\nu = \nu' h$ can be determined.

Proof of (a): Let $((x_o, y_o), \ldots, (x_k, y_k))$ be a correspondence, let $x \notin \{x_o, \ldots, x_k\}$. We define a sequence $(a_o, b_o), (a_1, b_1), \ldots$ inductively as follows:

Step 0:

$$a_o := x \ , \quad b_o := f(a_o) \ .$$

Step n+1:

If (a_n, b_n) is not defined then (a_{n+1}, b_{n+1}) is not defined. Suppose (a_n, b_n) is defined. Let

$$m(n) := \mu j[j \leq k \wedge b_n = y_j] \ .$$

If m(n) does not exist then (a_{n+1}, b_{n+1}) does not exist.

Otherwise:

$$a_{n+1} := x_{m(n)} \ , \quad b_{n+1} := f(a_{n+1}) \ .$$

We prove three propositions about the sequence $(a_i, b_i)_i$.

Prop. 1: $\nu(x) = \nu(a_n) = \nu'(b_n)$ if (a_n, b_n) exists.

Proof 1: From $\nu(i) = \nu' f(i)$ and $\nu(x_i) = \nu'(y_i)$ by induction.

Prop. 2: If (a_n, b_n) exists then $a_n \notin \{a_o, \ldots, a_{n-1}\}$ and $b_n \notin \{b_o, \ldots, b_{n-1}\}$.

Proof 2: (by induction on n). This is true for $n = 0$. Consider the case $n+1$. Since $a_o \notin \{x_o, \ldots, x_k\}$ and $a_{n+1} \in \{x_o, \ldots, x_k\}$, we have $a_{n+1} \neq a_o$. Let $1 \leq r \leq n$. By the construction $(a_{n+1}, b_n) = (x_i, y_i)$ and $(a_r, b_{r-1}) = (x_j, y_j)$ for some $i, j \leq k$. By induction we have $b_n \neq b_{r-1}$, hence $y_i \neq y_j$, $i \neq j$, and by Condition (1) $x_i \neq x_j$, i.e. $a_{n+1} \neq a_r$. Therefore, we have proved $a_{n+1} \notin \{a_o, \ldots, a_n\}$.

Since $(\forall i \le n+1)\ b_i = f(a_i)$ by the definition and since f is injective we conclude $b_{n+1} \notin \{b_o,\dots,b_n\}$.

Prop. 3: There is a greatest number N such that (a_N,b_N) exists, and for this N $((x_o,y_o),\dots,(x_k,y_k),(x,b_N))$ is a correspondence.

Proof 3: Since $b_n \in \{y_o,\dots,y_k\}$ if b_n exists and the b_i are pairwise different by Prop. 2, there is a greatest number N such that (a_N,b_N) exists. From the construction we have $b_N \notin \{y_o,\dots,y_k\}$ and from Prop. 1 we know $\nu(x) = \nu'(b_N)$. This proves Prop. 3.

The construction of $y = b_N$ from a correspondence $\alpha = ((x_o,y_o),\dots,(x_k,y_k))$ and a value x is effective. More precisely, there is a stack machine M which on input (α,x) (appropriately encoded) yields output y. Correspondingly, for any correspondence $((x_o,y_o),\dots,(x_k,y_k))$ and any $y \notin \{y_o,\dots,y_k\}$ a number x can be determined such that $((x_o,y_o),\dots,(x_k,y_k),(x,y))$ is a correspondence.

Proof of (b): We define two functions $x : \mathbb{N} \longrightarrow \mathbb{N}$ and $y : \mathbb{N} \longrightarrow \mathbb{N}$ by the following procedure:

Step 0:

$$x_o := 0\ ,\quad y_o := f(x_o)\ .$$

Step 2n+1:

$y_{2n+1} := \mu t[t \notin \{y_o,\dots,y_{2n}\}]$

$x_{2n+1} :=$ that number x' determined from the list $((x_o,y_o),\dots,(x_{2n},y_{2n}))$ and y_{2n+1} by the function defined in (a).

Step 2n+2:

$x_{2n+2} := \mu t[t \notin \{x_o,\dots,x_{2n+1}\}]$

$y_{2n+2} :=$ that number y' determined from the list $((x_o,y_o),\dots,(x_{2n+1},y_{2n+1}))$ and x_{2n+2} by the function defined in (a).

By induction on i one easily shows that for all i the sequence $((x_o,y_o),\dots,(x_i,y_i))$ exists and is a correspondence. The procedure for determining x(i) and y(i) can be programmed, hence x and y are total recursive functions. The functions x and y are injective since $((x_o,y_o),\dots,(x_i,y_i))$ is a correspondence (for any i). An easy induction yields:

$$(\forall i)\ \ \{0,\dots,i\} \subseteq \{x_o,x_1,\dots,x_{2i}\}\ ,$$

$$(\forall i)\ \ \{0,\dots,i\} \subseteq \{y_o,y_1,\dots,y_{2i+1}\}\ .$$

Therefore, the functions x and y are surjective. Altogether we have shown that x and y are bijective and computable and $\nu(x_i) = \nu'(y_i)$ for all i. Define $h := yx^{-1}$. Then h is a computable bijection with $\nu(n) = \nu x x^{-1}(n) = \nu' y x^{-1}(n) = \nu' h(n)$ for all $n \in \mathbb{N}$. Therefore, $\nu \approx \nu'$.

Q.E.D.

We have only defined isomorphism for total numberings. Any partial numbering $\nu \in N(S)$ can be extended into a total numbering $\nu_\perp$ defined by $\nu_\perp(i) := (\nu(i)$ if $i \in \mathrm{dom}(\nu)$, $\perp$ otherwise) for all $i \in \mathbb{N}$, where $\perp \notin S$. But this extension is not always appropriate. By Definition 5, Myhill's theorem can be formulated for non-trivial subsets of $\mathbb{N}$ as follows: $A \equiv_1 B \iff A \approx B$. The next question we shall study is the relation between 1-reducibility and m-reducibility. If $\nu \le \nu'$ then there is a computable function f with $(\forall i \in \mathrm{dom}(\nu))\ \nu(i) = \nu' f(i)$. The function f may map many numbers i into a single number j. This is forbidden in the case of 1-reducibility. If, however, ν' has the property that for any $j \in \mathrm{dom}(\nu')$ arbitrarily many equivalent numbers can be determined effectively, from the many-one translation f a one-one translation g can be derived. Numberings ν' with this property are called cylinders.

7 DEFINITION (*cylinder*)

(1) For any numbering $\nu \in N(M)$ define a numbering $c(\nu) \in N(M)$, the *cylindrification* of ν, by

$$\mathrm{dom}(c(\nu)) := \{\langle i,j\rangle \mid i \in \mathrm{dom}(\nu)\},$$

$$c(\nu)\langle i,j\rangle := \nu(i) \quad \text{for all } \langle i,j\rangle \in \mathrm{dom}(c(\nu)).$$

(2) A numbering $\nu \in N(M)$ is called a *cylinder* iff $\nu \equiv_1 c(\nu')$ for some $\nu' \in N(M)$.

Obviously, $c(\nu)\langle i,j\rangle = c(\nu)\langle i,0\rangle = c(\nu)\langle i,1\rangle = \ldots$, therefore for any $n \in \mathrm{dom}(c(\nu))$ infinitely many equivalent numbers can be determined. If $\nu' \equiv_1 c(\nu)$ then the corresponding property holds for ν'. The following elementary theorem gives some insight into the relation between 1-reducibility and m-reducibility.

8 THEOREM (*cylinder theorem*)

Let ν and ν' be numberings.

(1) $\nu \le_1 c(\nu)$,

(2) $c(\nu) \le \nu$,

(3) ν is a cylinder $\iff (\forall \nu_1 \in \hat{N})\ (\nu_1 \le \nu \Rightarrow \nu_1 \le_1 \nu)$,

(4) $\nu \le \nu' \iff c(\nu) \le_1 c(\nu')$.

Proof

(1) Define $f \in R^{(1)}$ by $f(n) = \langle n,0\rangle$. Then f is injective and $\nu(n) = c(\nu)\langle n,0\rangle =$

$= c(\nu)f(n)$ for all $n \in \mathrm{dom}(\nu)$, hence $\nu \le_1 c(\nu)$.

(2) $c(\nu)\langle i,j\rangle = \nu(i) = \nu\pi_1\langle i,j\rangle$ for all $\langle i,j\rangle \in \mathrm{dom}(c(\nu))$, hence $c(\nu) \le \nu$.

(3) "$\Longrightarrow$": Assume $\nu \equiv_1 c(\nu')$ for some ν' and assume $\nu_1 \le \nu$. Then $\nu_1 \le \nu'$ by (2). Let $f \in P^{(1)}$ with $\nu_1(i) = \nu' f(i)$ for all $i \in \mathrm{dom}(\nu_1)$. Define $g \in P^{(1)}$ by $g(i) := \langle f(i), i\rangle$ for all $i \in \mathbb{N}$. Then g is injective and $\nu_1(i) = c(\nu')g(i)$ for all $i \in \mathrm{dom}(\nu')$, hence $\nu_1 \le_1 c(\nu')$. We conclude $\nu_1 \le_1 \nu$.

"$\Longleftarrow$": Assume $(\forall \nu_1 \in \hat{N})\ (\nu_1 \le \nu \Longrightarrow \nu_1 \le_1 \nu)$. Set $\nu_1 := c(\nu)$. By (2) we have $c(\nu) \le \nu$, therefore $c(\nu) \le_1 \nu$. With (1) we obtain $c(\nu) \equiv_1 \nu$, i.e. ν is a cylinder.

(4) $\nu \le \nu' \Longrightarrow c(\nu) \le c(\nu')$ (by (1) and (2)) $\Longrightarrow c(\nu) \le_1 c(\nu')$ (by(3)) $\Longrightarrow \nu \le \nu'$ (by (1) and (2)).

Q.E.D.

Property (3) characterizes cylinders: ν is a cylinder iff m-reducibility to ν implies 1-reducibility to ν. Let ν be a numbering, let $N_o := \{\nu' \mid \nu \equiv \nu'\}$ be the equivalence class of ν. Then the pre-order $(N_o, \le_1)$ has $c(\nu)$ as a maximum: $\nu' \le_1 c(\nu)$ for all $\nu' \in N_o$ by Property (3). By Property (4) the pre-orders $(\{c(\nu) \mid \nu \in \hat{N}\}, \le_1)$ and $(\hat{N}, \le)$ are isomorphic. There are two other characterizations of cylinders both of which express that for any number infinitely many other equivalent numbers can be determined.

9 <u>THEOREM</u> (*characterization of cylinders*)

Let $\nu \in N(S)$ be a numbering. The following properties are equivalent.

(1) ν is a cylinder.

(2) $c(\nu) \le_1 \nu$.

(3) There is some $f \in P^{(1)}$ which is injective on $\langle \mathrm{dom}(\nu), \mathbb{N}\rangle$ with

$$\nu(n) = \nu f\langle n,i\rangle$$

for all $n \in \mathrm{dom}(\nu)$ and $i \in \mathbb{N}$.

The function f in (3) is called a *padding function* for ν.

<u>Proof</u>

"(2) $\Longrightarrow$ (1)": Since $\nu \le_1 c(\nu)$, $c(\nu) \le_1 \nu$ implies $\nu \equiv_1 c(\psi)$, hence ν is a cylinder.

"(1) $\Longrightarrow$ (3)": Assume that ν is a cylinder. Then there are some numbering $\nu' \in N(S)$ and functions $p, p' \in P^{(1)}$ such that p is injective on $\mathrm{dom}(\nu')$, p' is injective on $dom(\nu)$, $(\forall i \in dom(\nu))\ \nu(i) = c(\nu')p'(i)$, $(\forall i \in dom(c(\nu')))\ c(\nu')(i) = \nu p(i)$. Define $f \in P^{(1)}$ by $f\langle n,i\rangle := p\langle \pi_1 p'(n), \langle i,n\rangle\rangle$. Assume $n \in dom(\nu)$, $i \in \mathbb{N}$. Then $\nu(n) = c(\nu')p'(n) = \nu'\pi_1 p'(n) = c(\nu')\langle \pi_1 p'(n), \langle i,n\rangle\rangle = \nu p\langle \pi_1 p'(n), \langle i,n\rangle\rangle = \nu f\langle n,i\rangle$. Assume $n' \in dom(\nu)$, $i' \in \mathbb{N}$ with $(n',i') \neq (n,i)$. Then correspondingly $\nu(n') = f\langle n',i'\rangle$ and $f\langle n,i\rangle \neq f\langle n',i'\rangle$.

"(3) $\Longrightarrow$ (2)": For all $n \in dom(\nu)$ and $i \in \mathbb{N}$ we have $c(\nu)\langle n,i\rangle = \nu(n) = \nu f\langle n,i\rangle$. Since f is injective on $dom(c(\nu)) = \langle dom(\nu), \mathbb{N}\rangle$, $c(\nu) \leq_1 \nu$.
Q.E.D.

We shall prove that the numberings $\varphi \in TN(P^{(1)})$, $W \in TN(RE)$, and $Z \in N(REC)$ are cylinders. For total numberings Condition 9(3) can be weakened.

10 LEMMA

Let $\nu \in TN(S)$ be a total numbering. Then ν is a cylinder iff there is some $h \in R^{(1)}$ with (1) and (2).

(1) $(\forall i,n)\ \ \nu(n) = \nu h\langle n,i\rangle$,

(2) $(\forall i,i',n)\ \ i \neq i' \Longrightarrow h\langle n,i\rangle \neq h\langle n,i'\rangle$.

Notice that injectivity of h is not required.

Proof

If ν is a cylinder then the property of Theorem 9(3) holds. Define $h := f$. Then h satisfies (1) and (2). On the other hand let $h \in R^{(1)}$ satisfy (1) and (2). Define a function $f \in R^{(1)}$ inductively by

$f(0) := h(0)$,

$f\langle n,i\rangle := h\langle n,j\rangle$

where

$j := \mu k[h\langle n,k\rangle \neq f(m)$ for all $m < \langle n,i\rangle]$.

The function f is total since $\{h\langle n,i\rangle \mid i \in \mathbb{N}\}$ is infinite for all n. Clearly f is injective by the construction, and for all n,i there is some j with

$\nu f\langle n,i\rangle = \nu h\langle n,j\rangle = \nu(n)$.

Q.E.D.

Let $\psi \in TN(P^{(1)})$ be the numbering which we called φ in Chapter 1.9: ψ_i is the function computed by the i-th Turing machine. It is easy to add an arbitrary number of dummy statements to any Turing machine such that the computed function remains unchanged. Therefore, there is a computable function $h \in R^{(1)}$ with $\psi_i = \psi_{h<i,j>}$ for all i,j and $h<i,j> \neq h<i,j'>$ if $j \neq j'$. By Lemma 10, ψ is a cylinder. We cannot conclude directly, however, that φ is a cylinder for all φ with $\varphi \equiv \psi$. For proving that any $\varphi \in N(P^{(1)})$ which satisfies the smn-theorem and the utm-theorem is a cylinder more sophisticated methods are required.

In Definition 5 a bijective function $cf : \hat{P} \longrightarrow TN(\{0,1\})$ is given by $cf(A)(i) = 1 :\Longleftrightarrow i \in A$, and reducibility concepts on $\hat{P}$ are defined by the corresponding concepts on $TN(\{0,1\})$. Also the theory of cylinders can be transferred to $\hat{P}$.

11 DEFINITION

Let $A \subseteq \mathbb{N}$, $A \notin \{\emptyset, \mathbb{N}\}$.

(1) A is a cylinder iff $cf(A) \in TN(\{0,1\})$ is a cylinder.

(2) The cylindrification of A is defined by

$$c(A) := cf^{-1}(c(cf(A))) .$$

12 THEOREM

(1) $c(A) = <A,\mathbb{N}> = \{<a,n> \mid a \in A,\ n \in \mathbb{N}\}$

(2) Theorems 8 and 9 and Lemma 10 can be transferred to subsets of $\mathbb{N}$.

Proof (obvious)

For example, $A \subseteq \mathbb{N}$ is a cylinder iff $<A,\mathbb{N}> \leq_1 A$. Later we shall prove that the set $K = \{i \mid i \in W_i\}$ is a cylinder. The question arises whether every r.e. set which is not recursive is a cylinder. The answer is negative:

13 THEOREM

If $S \subseteq \mathbb{N}$ is simple then S is not a cylinder.

Proof

Let S be simple. Suppose S is a cylinder. Then $<S,\mathbb{N}> \leq_1 S$ by Theorem 9(2), hence

$\langle \mathbb{N}\setminus S, \mathbb{N}\rangle = \mathbb{N}\setminus\langle S,\mathbb{N}\rangle \leq_1 \mathbb{N}\setminus S$ via some injective $f \in R^{(1)}$. Choose $i \in \mathbb{N}\setminus S$ arbitrarily. Then the set $A := f\{\langle i,k\rangle \mid k \in \mathbb{N}\}$ is r.e. and infinite and satisfies $A \subseteq \mathbb{N}\setminus S$. This is impossible. Therefore, S is not a cylinder.
Q.E.D.

The pre-order $(\hat{N},\leq)$ is very rich. For any two numberings ν_1 and ν_2, $\mathrm{Sup}\{\nu_1,\nu_2\}$ and $\mathrm{Inf}\{\nu_1,\nu_2\}$ are not empty.

14 LEMMA

Let $\nu_1,\nu_2 \in \hat{N}$. Then

(1) $\nu_1 \sqcup \nu_2 \in \mathrm{Sup}\{\nu_1,\nu_2\}$,

(2) $\nu_1 \sqcap \nu_2 \in \mathrm{Inf}\{\nu_1,\nu_2\}$.

Proof

(1) Define $f_1,f_2 \in R^{(1)}$ by $f_1(i) := 2i$, $f_2(i) = 2i+1$. Then $\nu_1(i) = (\nu_1 \sqcup \nu_2)f_1(i)$ for all $i \in \mathrm{dom}(\nu_1)$ and $\nu_2(i) = (\nu_1 \sqcup \nu_2)f_2(i)$ for all $i \in \mathrm{dom}(\nu_2)$. Therefore, $\nu_1 \leq \nu_1 \sqcup \nu_2$ and $\nu_2 \leq \nu_1 \sqcup \nu_2$. Assume $\nu_1 \leq \nu$ and $\nu_2 \leq \nu$. Then there are $g_1,g_2 \in P^{(1)}$ such that $\nu_1(i) = \nu g_1(i)$ for all $i \in \mathrm{dom}(\nu_1)$ and $\nu_2(i) = \nu g_2(i)$ for all $i \in \mathrm{dom}(\nu_2)$. Define $h \in P^{(1)}$ by

$$h(k) := \begin{cases} g_1(k/2) & \text{if } k \text{ is even} \\ g_2((k-1)/2) & \text{if } k \text{ is odd}. \end{cases}$$

Let $k \in \mathrm{dom}(\nu_1 \sqcup \nu_2)$. Then either $k = 2i$ and $i \in \mathrm{dom}(\nu_1)$ or $k = 2i+1$ and $i \in \mathrm{dom}(\nu_2)$. In the first case $(\nu_1 \sqcup \nu_2)(k) = \nu_1(i) = \nu g_1(i) = \nu h(k)$, and in the second case, $(\nu_1 \sqcup \nu_2)(k) = \nu_2(i) = \nu g_2(i) = \nu h(k)$, hence $(\nu_1 \sqcup \nu_2) \leq \nu$. Therefore, $\nu_1 \sqcup \nu_2 \in \mathrm{Sup}\{\nu_1,\nu_2\}$.

(2) $(\nu_1 \sqcap \nu_2)(i) = \nu_1\pi_1(i) = \nu_2\pi_2(i)$ for all $i \in \mathrm{dom}(\nu_1 \sqcap \nu_2)$. Therefore $(\nu_1 \sqcap \nu_2) \leq \nu_1$ and $(\nu_1 \sqcap \nu_2) \leq \nu_2$. Assume $\nu \leq \nu_1$ via $g_1 \in P^{(1)}$ and $\nu \leq \nu_2$ via $g_2 \in P^{(1)}$. Define $h \in P^{(1)}$ by $h(i) := \langle g_1(i), g_2(i)\rangle$. Then $\nu \leq \nu_1 \sqcap \nu_2$ via h. Therefore, $\nu_1 \sqcap \nu_2 \in \mathrm{Inf}\{\nu_1,\nu_2\}$.
Q.E.D.

Even for the set of numberings of a single (non-trivial) set the reducibility order is very complicated. The set TN(S) has the cardinality of the continuum. Since any equivalence class has only denumberably many elements (because the set $P^{(1)}$ is denumerable) the set of many-one equivalence classes also has the cardinality of the continuum.

Partial numberings which are not total are more difficult to handle than total ones. Under certain circumstances there is an equivalent total numbering, which by Conclusion 2.2.9 defines the same computability theory.

15 LEMMA

Let $S \neq \emptyset$, $\nu \in N(S)$, $dom(\nu)$ recursively enumerable. Then there is a total numbering $\nu' \in TN(S)$ with $\nu \equiv \nu'$.

Proof

By Corollary 2.3.11 there is some $f \in R^{(1)}$ with $range(f) = dom(\nu)$. Define ν' by $\nu'(i) := \nu f(i)$. Then $\nu' \in TN(S)$ and $\nu' \leq \nu$. Define $g \in P^{(1)}$ by $g(n) := \mu i[f(i) = n]$. Then $dom(g) = range(f) = dom(\nu)$ and $\nu' g(n) = \nu f g(n) = \nu(n)$ for all $n \in dom(\nu)$, hence $\nu \leq \nu'$.
Q.E.D.

Of particular interest are numberings the equivalence problem of which is recursive or recursively enumerable.

16 DEFINITION (*decidable, positive, negative numberings*)

(1) Let $\nu \in \hat{N}$ be a numbering. Define

$$\varepsilon_\nu := \{\langle x,y \rangle \mid x,y \in dom(\nu),\ \nu(x) = \nu(y)\}$$

("*the equivalence problem of* ν")

(2) Let $\nu \in \widehat{TN}$. Then ν is *decidable* (*positive*, *negative*) iff ε_ν is recursive (ε_ν is r.e., $\mathbb{N} \setminus \varepsilon_\nu$ is r.e.).

By Lemma 2.3.18(2) the numbering φ is neither positive nor negative. If $\nu \in TN(S)$ and S is finite, then ν is decidable if it is positive or negative. If S is infinite and $\nu \in TN(S)$, then ν is decidable $\iff \nu \equiv \nu_o$ for some injective $\nu_o \in TN(S)$. The properties decidable, positive, and negative are passed on downwards under reducibility. If $\nu, \nu' \in TN(S)$ and $\nu \leq \nu'$ then ν is decidable (positive, negative) if ν' is decidable (positive, negative). The proofs are easy and are left as exercises. The positive numberings $\nu \in TN(S)$ are minimal elements in the pre-order $(TN(S), \leq)$.

17 LEMMA

Let $\nu \in TN(S)$ be positive. Then $\nu \equiv \nu'$ for any $\nu' \in TN(S)$ with $\nu' \leq \nu$.

Especially injective total numberings are positive. Therefore injective total numberings are minimal in $(TN(S), \leq)$.

Proof

Assume $\nu' \leq \nu$ via $f \in R^{(1)}$. Since ε_ν is r.e., $\varepsilon_\nu = dom(\varphi_m)$ for some $m \in \mathbb{N}$. Define $g \in P^{(1)}$ by

$$g(k) := \pi_1^{(3)} \mu\langle i,j,t\rangle[f(i) = j \wedge \Phi_m\langle j,k\rangle = t] .$$

Let $s := \nu(k)$. Then there is some i with $\nu'(i) = s$, hence $\nu(j) = s$ where $j = f(i)$ and $\langle j,k\rangle \in dom(\Phi_m)$. Therefore, $g \in R^{(1)}$. The definition of g implies $\langle fg(k),k\rangle \in dom(\varphi_m) = \varepsilon_\nu$. Therefore $\nu' g(k) = \nu f g(k) = \nu(k)$ for all k, hence $\nu \leq \nu'$ and $\nu \equiv \nu'$.

Q.E.D.

As we have already mentioned, a numbering $\nu \in TN(S)$ for infinite S is decidable iff $\nu \equiv \nu_o$ for some injective numbering $\nu_o \in TN(S)$. The following theorem studies the case of negative numberings.

18 THEOREM

Let $\nu \in TN(S)$ be a total numbering of an infinite set S. Let ν be negative. Then (1) and (2) hold.

(1) $M := \{i \mid (\forall j < i) \ \ \nu(i) \neq \nu(j)\}$ is r.e.

(2) There is some injective numbering $\nu_o \in TN(S)$ with $\nu_o \leq_1 \nu$.

Proof

Since ν is negative, $\{\langle i,j\rangle \mid \nu(i) \neq \nu(j)\} = dom(\varphi_m)$ for some $m \in \mathbb{N}$. Define $g \in P^{(1)}$ by

$$g(i) = \begin{cases} 0 & \text{if } (\forall j < i) \ \langle i,j\rangle \in dom(\varphi_m) \\ div & \text{otherwise}. \end{cases}$$

Then $dom(g) = \{i \mid (\forall j < i) \ \ \nu(i) \neq \nu(j)\} = M$, hence M is r.e. The set M is infinite since S is infinite. There is some injective $f \in R^{(1)}$ with $range(f) = M$ (see Exer-

cise 2.3.6). Define $\nu_o \in TN(S)$ by $\nu_o := \nu f$. Then $\nu_o \leq_1 \nu$ via f. Assume $\nu_o(i_1) = \nu_o(i_2)$, let $j_1 := f(i_1)$ and $j_2 := f(i_2)$. Then $j_1 \neq j_2$ since f is injective. Finally $j_1 \in M$ and $j_2 \in M$ implies $\nu(j_1) \neq \nu(j_2)$, i.e. $\nu_o(i_1) \neq \nu_o(i_2)$. Therefore, ν_o is injective.
Q.E.D.

EXERCISES

1) Let $\hat{P} := \{A \subseteq \mathbb{N} \mid A \neq \emptyset, A \neq \mathbb{N}, A \text{ recursive}\}$.
   (a) Prove: $cf_A \leq cf_B$ iff $(\exists f \in R^{(1)})(\forall i)(i \in A \Longleftrightarrow f(i) \in B)$.
   (b) Characterize $(\hat{P},\leq)$ and $(\hat{P},\equiv)$.
   (c) Characterize $(\hat{P},\leq_1)$ and $(\hat{P},\equiv_1)$.

2) Let $\nu,\nu' \in TN(M)$. Let $\nu \leq \nu'$ via $f \in R^{(1)}$ and $\nu' \leq \nu$ via $g \in R^{(1)}$ such that $2i \leq f(i) < f(i+1)$ and $2i \leq g(i) < g(i+1)$ for all i. Give a simple proof of $\nu \approx \nu'$ without applying Theorem 6.

3) Let $\nu \in N(M)$. Define a property Q by
   $$(\exists g \in P^{(1)})(\forall a \in M)(\forall i \in \mathbb{N})(\emptyset \neq e_i \subseteq \nu^{-1}\{a\} \Rightarrow g(i) \in \nu^{-1}\{a\} \setminus e_i).$$
   Prove:
   (a) ν is a cylinder $\Rightarrow$ Q,
   (b) (Q and ν is total) $\Rightarrow$ ν is a cylinder.

4) Let $\nu,\nu' \in \hat{N}$ be cylinders. Which of following numberings are cylinders: $[\nu,\nu']$, $\nu \sqcup \nu'$, $\nu \sqcap \nu'$, WD(ν), FS(ν)? (see Definition 2.2.14) Give counterexamples if possible.

5) Let $\nu \in N(S)$ be a cylinder, let $H: S \dashrightarrow S'$ be surjective. Show that $H\nu \in N(S')$ is a cylinder.

6) Prove Theorem 12(1). Formulate Theorems 8 und 9 and Lemma 10 for subsets of $\mathbb{N}$.

7) Define numberings $\nu,\nu' \in N(S)$, such that $\nu \equiv \nu'$, ν is total, and dom(ν') is not r.e.

8) Let $\nu_o,\nu_1 \in TN(S)$ with $\nu_o \leq \nu_1$. Show:
   (a) ($\nu_o \leq \nu_1$ via some f with $f(\mathbb{N}) = \mathbb{N}$) $\Rightarrow \nu_o \equiv \nu_1$,
   (b) ν_1 injective $\Rightarrow \nu_o \equiv \nu_1$,
   (c) (ν_o injective and ν_1 injective) $\Rightarrow \nu_o \approx \nu_1$.

9) Let $Z \in N(REC)$ be the numbering from Definition 2.3.8. Show that there is no total numbering ν of REC with $\nu \leq Z$.

10) Let S be a finite set and $\nu \in TN(S)$. Prove:
   (a) ν positive $\Rightarrow$ ν decidable,
   (b) ν negative $\Rightarrow$ ν decidable.

11) Let S be infinite and $\nu \in TN(S)$. Prove:

ν is decidable $\Longleftrightarrow$ $\nu \equiv \nu_o$ for some bijective $\nu_o \in TN(S)$.

12) Give an example of a positive (total) numbering which is not decidable. Give an example of a negative (total) numbering which is not decidable.

13) Show that a numbering ν is a cylinder iff $\nu \sqcup \nu \leq_1 \nu$.

14) Show that there are numberings $\nu_1, \nu_2 \in TN(\mathbb{N})$ such that ν is not total for any $\nu \in Inf\{\nu_1, \nu_2\}$.

15) Prove $c(\nu_1 \sqcap \nu_2) \equiv c(\nu_1) \sqcup c(\nu_2)$.

16) Show that there is a total numbering $\nu : \mathbb{N} \longrightarrow S$ such that $(\forall s \in S)\nu^{-1}\{s\}$ is recursive and ν is not decidable.

BIBLIOGRAPHICAL NOTES

Theorem 6 is due to Myhill (1955) who proved the theorem for reducibility on the subsets of $\mathbb{N}$.

2.5 The Recursion Theorem

In this chapter we present a simple theorem, the *recursion theorem* or the *fixed-point theorem of recursion theory*, which provides a means for answering a number of seemingly difficult problems for *precomplete* numberings among which are the numberings φ, W, and cf_K, the characteristic function of the self applicability problem.

1 DEFINITION (*precomplete*, *complete*)

Let ν be a total numbering of a set S.

(1) ν is *precomplete* iff for all $g \in P^{(1)}$ there is some $f \in R^{(1)}$ such that

$$\nu f(i) = \nu g(i)$$

for all $i \in \mathrm{dom}(g)$.

(2) ν is *complete* iff there is some $a \in S$ (*a distinguished element* of ν) such that for all $g \in P^{(1)}$ there is some $f \in R^{(1)}$ with

$$\nu f(i) = \begin{cases} \nu g(i) & \text{if } i \in \mathrm{dom}(g) \\ a & \text{otherwise.} \end{cases}$$

Obviously, every complete numbering is precomplete. If S has only one element, every $\nu \in TN(S)$ is precomplete. The identity on $\mathbb{N}$, $1\!\!1_{\mathbb{N}}$ is not precomplete. Otherwise any partial recursive function $g \in P^{(1)}$ could be extended into a total recursive function $f \in R^{(1)}$. But this is impossible by Theorem 1.9.14 . On the other hand, the numbering φ of the partial recursive functions is complete where the function t with empty domain is a distinguished element of φ (see below). Finally, there are precomplete numberings which are not complete.

2 THEOREM

The following numberings are complete:

(1) $\varphi \in TN(P^{(1)})$ (distinguished element f with $\mathrm{dom}(f) = \emptyset$),

(2) $W \in TN(RE)$ (distinguished element $\emptyset$),

(3) $cf_K \in TN(\{0,1\})$ (distinguished element 0).

Proof

(1) Assume $g \in P^{(1)}$. By the smn-theorem there is some $f \in R^{(1)}$ such that $\varphi_{f(i)}(x) = u_\varphi(g(i),x)$ for all $i \in \mathbb{N}$ (where u_φ is the universal function of φ). Therefore, $\varphi_{f(i)} = \varphi_{g(i)}$ if $i \in \mathrm{dom}(g)$ and $\varphi_{f(i)}$ is the nowhere defined function f_o otherwise. Hence, φ is complete with f_o as a distinguished element.

(2) Assume $g \in P^{(1)}$. Let f be the function introduced in (1). Then $W_{f(i)} = \mathrm{dom}(\varphi_{f(i)}) = \mathrm{dom}(\varphi_{g(i)}) = W_{g(i)}$ if $i \in \mathrm{dom}(g)$ and $W_{f(i)} = \emptyset$ otherwise. Therefore W is complete with $\emptyset$ as a distinguished element.

(3) Assume $g \in P^{(1)}$. Let $v \in P^{(1)}$ with $K = \mathrm{dom}(v)$. By the smn-theorem there is some $f \in R^{(1)}$ with $\varphi_{f(i)}(x) = vg(i)$ for all $i,x \in \mathbb{N}$. If $i \in \mathrm{dom}(g)$ and $g(i) \in \mathrm{dom}(v) = K$ then $f(i) \in K$ and $cf_K g(i) = 1 = cf_K f(i)$. If $i \in \mathrm{dom}(g)$ and $g(i) \notin K$ then $f(i) \notin K$ and $cf_K g(i) = 0 = cf_K f(i)$. If $i \notin \mathrm{dom}(g)$ then $f(i) \notin K$ and $cf_K f(i) = 0$. Therefore, cf_K is complete with 0 as a distiguished element. Q.E.D.

In order to show that the two concepts "completeness" and "precompleteness" differ we construct a numbering which is precomplete but not complete.

3 LEMMA

8 There is a numbering ν which is precomplete and not complete.

Proof

Define $q \in P^{(1)}$ by $q(x) := \varphi_x(x)$. Define an equivalence relation $\sim$ on $\mathbb{N}$ by

$$x \sim y :\Longleftrightarrow (\exists m,n)\ [q^m(x) \text{ exists} \wedge q^n(y) \text{ exists} \wedge q^m(x) = q^n(y)] .$$

The set $M = \{\langle x,y\rangle \mid x \sim y\}$ is r.e. Define a numbering ν by $\nu(x) := A_x := \{y \mid x \sim y\}$. We shall prove that ν is precomplete and not complete.

(1) Suppose ν is complete and A_z is a distinguished element of ν. If $x,y \in \mathbb{N}\setminus K$ and $x \neq y$ then not $x \sim y$. Since $\mathbb{N}\setminus K$ is infinite, there is some y with $A_y \neq A_z$. Define $g \in P^{(1)}$ by $\mathrm{dom}(g) = K$ and $g(i) = y$ for all $i \in K$. Since ν is assumed to be complete there is some $f \in R^{(1)}$ with

$$\nu f(i) = \begin{cases} \nu g(i) = A_y & \text{if } i \in K \\ A_z & \text{otherwise} . \end{cases}$$

Therefore we obtain $i \in \mathbb{N}\setminus K \Longleftrightarrow \nu f(i) = A_z \Longleftrightarrow f(i) \in A_z$, hence $\mathbb{N}\setminus K \le A_z$. A_z is r.e. since M is r.e., but this is impossible by Theorem 2.3.2 and Lemma 2.3.4. Therefore ν is not complete.

(2) There is some $h \in R^{(1)}$ such that $W_i = \mathrm{range}(\varphi_{h(i)})$ and $\varphi_{h(i)} \in R^{(1)}$ if $W_i \neq \emptyset$.

Assume $g \in P^{(1)}$. There is some $s \in R^{(1)}$ such that $\nu g(x) = A_{g(x)} = W_{s(x)}$ if $x \in \mathrm{dom}(g)$ (and $W_{s(x)} = \emptyset$ otherwise). We prove that $f := hs$ has the desired property. Assume $x \in \mathrm{dom}(g)$. Then $\nu g(x) = W_{s(x)}$, $g(x) \in W_{s(x)}$, $W_{s(x)} \neq \emptyset$, range $\varphi_{hs(x)} = W_{s(x)}$ and $\varphi_{hs(x)} \in R^{(1)}$. Therefore, $qf(x) = \varphi_{hs(x)} hs(x) \in W_{s(x)} = \nu g(x)$, hence $f(x) \sim g(x)$. This implies $\nu f(x) = \nu g(x)$. Therefore, ν is precomplete. Q.E.D.

There are many complete and many precomplete numberings. The following theorem summarizes some properties which can be used for constructing new precomplete and complete numberings.

4 THEOREM

(1) Let $\nu, \nu' \in TN(S)$ with $\nu \equiv \nu'$. If ν is precomplete then ν' is precomplete. If ν is complete with distinguished element a then ν' is complete with distinguished element a.

(2) Let $\nu, \nu' \in TN(S)$. If ν and ν' are precomplete (complete) then $[\nu, \nu']$ is precomplete (complete).

(3) Let $\nu \in TN(S)$ and $H : S \twoheadrightarrow S'$ be a surjective function. If ν is precomplete (complete) then $H\nu$ is precomplete (complete).

(4) Let $\nu \in TN(S)$ be a total numbering. Then the numbering $\tilde{\nu}$ defined by

$$\tilde{\nu}(i) := \begin{cases} \{\nu u(i)\} & \text{if } i \in \mathrm{dom}(u) \\ \emptyset & \text{otherwise}, \end{cases}$$

is complete with $\emptyset$ as a distinguished element (u is the universal function of φ) defined by $u\langle i,x\rangle = \varphi_i(x)$).

Proof

The proofs of (1), (2), and (3) are straightforward (see the exercises).

(4) Assume $g \in P^{(1)}$. By the smn-theorem there is some $r \in R^{(1)}$ with $\varphi_{r(i)}(x) = ug(i)$ for all $i, x \in \mathbb{N}$. Define $f \in R^{(1)}$ by $f(i) := \langle r(i), 0\rangle$. Then $uf(i) = \varphi_{r(i)}(0) = ug(i)$ for all $i \in \mathbb{N}$. Assume $i \in \mathrm{dom}(g)$. If $g(i) \in \mathrm{dom}(u)$ then $f(i) \in \mathrm{dom}(u)$ and $\tilde{\nu}g(i) = \{\nu ug(i)\} = \{\nu uf(i)\} = \tilde{\nu}f(i)$. If $g(i) \notin \mathrm{dom}(u)$ then $f(i) \notin \mathrm{dom}(u)$ and $\tilde{\nu}g(i) = \emptyset = \tilde{\nu}f(i)$. If $i \notin \mathrm{dom}(g)$ then $f(i) \notin \mathrm{dom}(u)$ and $\tilde{\nu}f(i) = \emptyset$. Therefore $\emptyset$ is the distinguished element of the complete numbering $\tilde{\nu}$. Q.E.D.

Precomplete numberings are of interest because they satisfy the recursion theorem ("$\Longrightarrow$" in Theorem 5). On the other hand the recursion property is already a sufficient condition for precompleteness ("$\Longleftarrow$" in Theorem 5).

5 THEOREM (*recursion theorem*)

Let ν be a total numbering. Then ν is precomplete iff there is a function $h \in R^{(1)}$ such that

$$\nu\varphi_i h(i) = \nu h(i)$$

for all i with $\varphi_i \in R^{(1)}$.

Proof

"$\Longrightarrow$": Define $p \in P^{(1)}$ by $p(z) := \varphi_z(z)$. Since ν is precomplete there is some $g \in R^{(1)}$ such that $\nu g(z) = \nu p(z)$ for all $z \in \mathrm{dom}(p)$. There is some $q \in R^{(1)}$ with $\varphi_{q(i)} = \varphi_i g$. Define $h \in R^{(1)}$ by $h := gq$. Then $\nu\varphi_i h(i) = \nu\varphi_i gq(i) = \nu\varphi_{q(i)} q(i) = \nu pq(i) = \nu gq(i) = \nu h(i)$ whenever $\varphi_i \in R^{(1)}$.

"$\Longleftarrow$": Let $h \in R^{(1)}$ such that $\nu\varphi_i h(i) = \nu h(i)$ for all i with $\varphi_i \in R^{(1)}$. Assume $g \in P^{(1)}$. There is some $q \in R^{(1)}$ with $\varphi_{q(x)}(y) = g(x)$ for all x. Define $f := hq$. Then $f \in R^{(1)}$ and for all $x \in \mathrm{dom}(g)$ we have $\varphi_{q(x)} \in R^{(1)}$ and $\nu g(x) = \nu\varphi_{q(x)} hq(x) = \nu hq(x) = \nu f(x)$. Therefore, ν is precomplete.

Q.E.D.

Although the proof of the recursion theorem is short it is very difficult to grasp. If $\nu f(n) = \nu(n)$ then n could be called a fixed-point of f. But there is a better explanation of this name.

6 COROLLARY (*fixed point theorem*)

Let $\nu \in TN(S)$ be precomplete and let $F : S \longrightarrow S$ be (ν,ν)-computable. Then F has a fixed point, i.e. $F(s) = s$ for some $s \in S$.

Proof

If F is (ν,ν)-computable, then $F\nu(i) = \nu g(i)$ for some $g \in R^{(1)}$. By Theorem 5 there is some $n \in \mathbb{N}$ with $\nu g(n) = \nu(n)$. Define $s := \nu(n)$. Then

$$F(s) = F\nu(n) = \nu g(n) = \nu(n) = s .$$

Q.E.D.

For more convenient application we state some derived versions of the recursion theorem.

7 COROLLARY

(1) Let ν be a precomplete numbering. Then for all $f \in R^{(1)}$ there is some $t \in R^{(1)}$ such that

$$(\forall i) \quad \nu f\langle i,t(i)\rangle = \nu t(i) .$$

(2) Let ν be a precomplete numbering. Then for all $g \in R^{(1)}$ there is some n such that

$$\nu g(n) = \nu(n) .$$

(3) For all $f \in P^{(1)}$ there is some $t \in R^{(1)}$ with

$$\varphi_{t(i)}(x) = f\langle x,i,t(i)\rangle$$

for all $i,x \in \mathbb{N}$.

(4) For all $g \in P^{(1)}$ there is some $n \in \mathbb{N}$ with

$$\varphi_n(x) = g\langle x,n\rangle$$

for all $x \in \mathbb{N}$.

Proof

(1) By the smn-theorem there is some $r \in R^{(1)}$ such that $f\langle i,x\rangle = \varphi_{r(i)}(x)$. Define $t := hr$, where h is the recursion function from Theorem 5.

(2) For some i, $g = \varphi_i$. Define $n := h(i)$.

(3) Let h be the function from the standard recursion theorem for φ (Theorem 5). Define $f_1 \in P^{(1)}$ by $f_1\langle i,z,x\rangle := f\langle x,i,z\rangle$. Twofold application of the smn-theorem yields a function $g \in R^{(1)}$ such that $\varphi_{g(i)} \in R^{(1)}$ for all i and

$$\varphi_{\varphi_{g(i)}(z)}(x) = f_1\langle\langle i,z\rangle,x\rangle = f\langle x,i,z\rangle .$$

Define $t \in R^{(1)}$ by $t = hg$. Then for all $i \in \mathbb{N}$:

$$\varphi_{t(i)}(x) = \varphi_{hg(i)}(x) = \varphi_{\varphi_{g(i)}hg(i)}(x) = f\langle x,i,t(i)\rangle .$$

(4) Define $f' \in P^{(1)}$ by $f'\langle x,i,z\rangle := g\langle x,z\rangle$. Then apply (3) and define $n := t(0)$. Q.E.D.

Still more surprising than the proof of the recursion theorem for precomplete numberings are many of its applications. The recursion theorem for φ (which is complete) yields a number m such that $(\forall x)\ \varphi_m(x) = m$: Define $f \in P^{(2)}$ by $(\forall i,x)\ f(x,i) = i$. By Corollary 6(4) there is a number m with $\varphi_m(x) = f(x,m) = m$ for all x. The tape program with number m can be called *self-reproducing*: for all inputs x it halts and produces its own name. Similarly, there are numbers m with $\text{range}(\varphi_m) = \{m^2\}$, $W_m = \{m\}$, etc. (see the exercises). As a first application we prove a generalization of Rice's theorem for precomplete numberings.

8 THEOREM (*Rice's theorem generalized*)

Let $\nu \in TN(S)$ be a precomplete numbering, let $S_o \subseteq S$. Then (1) and (2) hold.

(1) $\nu^{-1}(S_o) \not\leq \nu^{-1}(S \setminus S_o)$

(2) If $\nu^{-1}(S_o)$ is recursive then $S_o = S$ or $S_o = \emptyset$.

Property 7(2) applied to φ is Rice's theorem (Corollary 2.3.17).

Proof

Suppose there is some $f \in R^{(1)}$ with $i \in \nu^{-1}(S_o) \iff f(i) \in \nu^{-1}(S \setminus S_o)$. By Corollary 6(2), there is a number n with $\nu f(n) = \nu(n)$, hence $n \in \nu^{-1}(S_o) \iff \nu(n) \in S_o \iff \nu f(n) \in S_o \iff f(n) \in \nu^{-1}(S_o)$; on the other hand $n \in \nu^{-1}(S_o) \iff f(n) \notin \nu^{-1}(S_o)$ (by the reduction). This is a contradiction, hence (1) is proved. If $A = \nu^{-1}(S_o)$ is recursive then $B := \mathbb{N} \setminus A = \nu^{-1}(S \setminus S_o)$ is recursive. If $S_o \neq S$ and $S_o \neq \emptyset$ then $A, B \neq \mathbb{N}$ and $A, B \neq \emptyset$. This implies $A \leq B$ which contradicts (1).
Q.E.D.

Theorem 8(2) can be expressed as follows: no non-trivial property on S is ν-recursive if ν is precomplete. Our next aim is to prove that any precomplete numbering is a cylinder. There is a very elegant proof for the important special case $\nu = \varphi$ which we present here before we prove the general result.

9 THEOREM (*injective smn-theorem*)

For all $f \in P^{(2)}$ there is some injective $t \in R^{(1)}$ with

$$(\forall i,x)\quad \varphi_{t(i)}(x) = f(i,x).$$

Therefore we may assume that the index function t is injective whenever we apply the smn-theorem (see e.g. the proof of Lemma 2.3.5).

Proof

By assumption, the numbering φ satisfies the smn-theorem and the utm-theorem. The (easy) proof of Corollary 1.9.8 shows that these properties imply an effective version of the smn-theorem: There is some $s \in R^{(2)}$ such that $(\forall i,j,k)$ $\varphi_{s(i,j)}(k) = \varphi_i\langle j,k\rangle$. Define a function $g \in P^{(1)}$ as follows:

$$g\langle\langle i,x\rangle,z\rangle := \begin{cases} 0 & \text{if } (\exists j < i)\ s(z,j) = s(z,i) \\ 1 & \text{if } (\forall j < i)\ s(z,j) \neq s(z,i) \text{ and } i < x \text{ and } s(z,i) = s(z,x) \\ f(i,x) & \text{otherwise}. \end{cases}$$

By Corollary 7(4) there is some $n \in \mathbb{N}$ with $\varphi_n\langle i,x\rangle = g\langle\langle i,x\rangle,n\rangle$. Define $t \in R^{(1)}$ by $t(i) := s(n,i)$. Then $g\langle\langle i,x\rangle,n\rangle = \varphi_n\langle i,x\rangle = \varphi_{s(n,i)}(x) = \varphi_{t(i)}(x)$ and

$$\varphi_{t(i)}(x) = \begin{cases} 0 & \text{if } (\exists j < i)\ t(j) = t(i) \\ 1 & \text{if } (\forall j < i)\ t(j) \neq t(i) \text{ and } i < x \text{ and } t(i) = t(x) \\ f(i,x) & \text{otherwise}. \end{cases}$$

Suppose t is not injective. Then there are $i_o, j_o \in \mathbb{N}$ with

$$j_o := \mu j[(\exists i > j)\ t(i) = t(j)], \quad i_o := \mu i[i > j_o \wedge t(i) = t(j_o)],$$

hence $j_o < i_o$ and $0 = \varphi_{t(i_o)}(i_o) = \varphi_{t(j_o)}(i_o) = 1$. Therefore, t is injective and in any case $\varphi_{t(i)}(x) = f(i,x)$.

Q.E.D.

Essentially we have proved that φ is a cylinder.

10 COROLLARY

8 φ is a cylinder.

Proof

By Theorem 2.4.9 it suffices to prove $c(\varphi) \leq_1 \varphi$. We already know $c(\varphi) \leq \varphi$, therefore $c(\varphi)$ satisfies the utm-theorem. Let $f \in P^{(2)}$ be the universal function of $c(\varphi)$, i.e. $f(i,x) = c(\varphi)(i)(x)$. By Theorem 9 there is an injective function $t \in R^{(1)}$ with $c(\varphi)(i)(x) = f(i,x) = \varphi_{t(i)}(x)$, hence $c(\varphi) \leq_1 \varphi$ via t.

Q.E.D.

As a further corollary we obtain that any two admissible numberings of $P^{(1)}$ are isomorphic. This improves Theorem 1.9.10.

11 COROLLARY (*isomorphism theorem (Rogers)*)

Let ψ be a total numbering of $P^{(1)}$. Then the following properties are equivalent.

(1) $\varphi \approx \psi$.

(2) ψ satisfies the utm-theorem and the smn-theorem.

Proof

By Theorem 1.9.10, (2) is equivalent to $\varphi \equiv \psi$. Assume ψ satisfies the utm-theorem and the smn-theorem. For proving Corollary 10 we only needed the utm-theorem and the smn-theorem for φ. Therefore ψ is also a cylinder. By Theorem 2.4.8 we obtain $\varphi \equiv_1 \psi$ and Myhill's theorem (2.4.6) implies $\varphi \approx \psi$.
Q.E.D.

Corollary 11 can be interpreted as follows. Up to recursive isomorphisms there is only one reasonable programming language for the set $P^{(1)}$ of partial recursive functions.

Now we shall study the more general case of arbitrary precomplete numberings. By Theorem 8, no set $\nu^{-1}\{a\}$ is recursive (if $a \in S$, $S \neq \{a\}$). We shall prove even more: whenever we know that $Z_j \subseteq \nu^{-1}\{a\}$ then we can determine a number k with $k \in \nu^{-1}\{a\} \setminus Z_j$. Thus the sets $\nu^{-1}\{a\}$ are "effectively nonrecursive". As a corollary we obtain that ν is a cylinder.

12 LEMMA (*precomplete numberings are effectively nonrecursive*)

Let $\nu \in TN(S)$ be precomplete, let $card(S) \geq 2$. Then there is some $g \in P^{(1)}$ such that

$$g(j) \text{ exists and } g(j) \in \nu^{-1}\{d\} \setminus Z_j$$

whenever $d \in S$, $j \in dom(Z)$, and $\emptyset \neq Z_j \subseteq \nu^{-1}\{d\}$.

Proof

Since $card(S) \geq 2$, there are $a,b \in \mathbb{N}$ with $\nu(a) \neq \nu(b)$. Define two functions $F,G : \mathbb{N} \dashrightarrow \mathbb{N}$ as follows.

$$F\langle j,y\rangle := \begin{cases} a & \text{if } \varphi_j(y) \text{ exists and } \varphi_j(y) = 0 \\ i & \text{if } \varphi_j(y) \text{ exists and } \varphi_j(y) \neq 0 \text{ and} \\ & i := \pi_1 \mu\langle k,t\rangle[\Phi_j(k) = t \wedge \varphi_j(k) = 0] \text{ exists} \\ \text{div} & \text{otherwise}, \end{cases}$$

$$G\langle j,y\rangle := \begin{cases} b & \text{if } \varphi_j(y) \text{ exists and } \varphi_j(y) = 0 \\ a & \text{if } \varphi_j(y) \text{ exists and } \varphi_j(y) \neq 0 \\ \text{div} & \text{otherwise.} \end{cases}$$

By Lemma 2.1.3 the functions F and G are computable. Since ν is precomplete, there are functions $F_1, G_1 \in R^{(1)}$ such that $\nu F_1(i) = \nu F(i)$ for all $i \in \mathrm{dom}(F)$ and $\nu G_1(i) = \nu G(i)$ for all $i \in \mathrm{dom}(G)$. By the recursion theorem (Corollary 7(1)) there are functions $m \in R^{(1)}$ and $n \in R^{(1)}$ (we write m_j instead of $m(j)$ and n_j instead of $n(j)$) such that

$$\nu F_1\langle j,m_j\rangle = \nu(m_j)\,,$$
$$\nu G_1\langle j,n_j\rangle = \nu(n_j)$$

for all $j \in \mathbb{N}$. Define $g \in P^{(1)}$ by

$$g(j) := \begin{cases} m_j & \text{if } \varphi_j(m_j) \text{ exists and } \varphi_j(m_j) \neq 0 \\ n_j & \text{if } \varphi_j(m_j) \text{ exists and } \varphi_j(m_j) = 0 \\ \text{div} & \text{otherwise.} \end{cases}$$

We prove that g has the desired property. Assume $j \in \mathrm{dom}(Z)$ and $\emptyset \neq Z_j \subseteq \nu^{-1}\{d\}$ for some $d \in S$. Then $\varphi_j \in R^{(1)}$ and $\varphi_j(m_j)$ and $g(j)$ exist.

<u>Case</u> $\varphi_j(m_j) \neq 0$:
Then $g(j) = m_j \notin \varphi_j^{-1}\{0\} = Z_j$. Since $Z_j \neq \emptyset$, a number $i := \pi_i \mu\langle k,t\rangle[\Phi_j(k) = t \wedge \varphi_j(k) = 0]$ exists, hence $F\langle j,m_j\rangle = i \in Z_j$. We conclude

$$\begin{aligned} \nu g(j) &= \nu(m_j) \\ &= \nu F_1\langle j,m_j\rangle && \text{(by Def. of } m_j) \\ &= \nu F\langle j,m_j\rangle && \text{(since } \langle j,m_j\rangle \in \mathrm{dom}(F)) \\ &= \nu(i) \\ &= d && \text{(since } i \in Z_j \subseteq \nu^{-1}\{d\}). \end{aligned}$$

This proves $g(j) \in \nu^{-1}\{d\} \setminus Z_j$.

<u>Case</u> $\varphi_j(m_j) = 0$:
Then $m_j \in Z_j \subseteq \nu^{-1}\{d\}$, hence $\nu(m_j) = d$. Furthermore we have

$$\begin{aligned} \nu(m_j) &= \nu F_1\langle j,m_j\rangle && \text{(by Def. of } m_j) \\ &= \nu F\langle j,m_j\rangle && \text{(since } \langle j,m_j\rangle \in \mathrm{dom}(F)) \\ &= \nu(a)\,. \end{aligned}$$

Suppose $\varphi_j(n_j) = 0$. Then $n_j \in Z_j \subseteq \nu^{-1}\{d\}$, hence $\nu(n_j) = d$. We conclude

$$\begin{aligned} \nu(a) &= \nu(m_j) \\ &= d \\ &= \nu(n_j) \\ &= \nu G_1\langle j,n_j\rangle && \text{(by Def. of } n_j) \\ &= \nu G\langle j,n_j\rangle && \text{(since } \langle j,n_j\rangle \in \mathrm{dom}(G)) \\ &= \nu(b)\,. \end{aligned}$$

But we had presumed $\nu(a) \neq \nu(b)$. Therefore $\varphi_j(n_j)$ exists (since $j \in dom(Z)$) and $\varphi_j(n_j) \neq 0$, hence $n_j \notin Z_j$. Finally

$$\begin{aligned}\nu g(j) &= \nu(n_j) \qquad (\text{since } \varphi_j(m_j) = 0)\\ &= \nu G_1\langle j, n_j\rangle\\ &= \nu G\langle j, n_j\rangle \qquad (\text{since } \langle j, n_j\rangle \in dom(G))\\ &= \nu(a)\\ &= d,\end{aligned}$$

hence $g(j) \in \nu^{-1}\{d\}$. Since $g(j) = n_j \notin Z_j$ we have $g(j) \in \nu^{-1}\{d\} \setminus Z_j$.
Q.E.D.

The above proof is another rather sophisticated application of the recursion theorem. The next theorem gives two basic properties of precomplete numberings. It can be derived in a straightforward way from Lemma 12.

13 THEOREM

Let $\nu \in TN(S)$ be a precomplete numbering, assume $card(S) \geq 2$. Then the following holds:

(1) $(\forall \nu' \in \hat{N})\ (\nu' \leq \nu \Longrightarrow \nu' \leq_1 \nu)$ (i.e. ν is a cylinder),

(2) $(\forall \nu' \in \hat{N})\ (\nu \leq \nu' \Longrightarrow \nu \leq_1 \nu')$.

This means that many-one reducibility from ν as well as to ν can be replaced by one-one reducibility.

Proof

(1) There is some $q \in R^{(1)}$ such that

$$\varphi_{q\langle i,k\rangle}(x) = \begin{cases} \varphi_i(x) & \text{if } x \neq k \\ 0 & \text{otherwise}. \end{cases}$$

Then $Z_{q\langle i,k\rangle} = Z_i \cup \{k\}$ if $i \in dom(Z)$. Let $a \in \mathbb{N}$ such that $Z_a = \emptyset$. Define a function $p \in P^{(2)}$ inductively by

$$\begin{aligned} p(m,0) &= q\langle a,m\rangle\\ p(m,n+1) &= q\langle p(m,n), gp(m,n)\rangle \end{aligned}$$

where g is the function from Lemma 12. By an easy induction on n we obtain:

$p(m,n)$ exists,

$Z_{p(m,n)} \subseteq \nu^{-1}\nu(m)$,

$gp(m,n) \in Z_{p(m,n+1)} \setminus Z_{p(m,n)}$

for all $m,n \in \mathbb{N}$. Therefore $\nu gp(m,n) = \nu(m)$ for all m,n, and $gp(m,n) \neq gp(m,n')$ if $n \neq n'$ for all m,n,n'. Define $h \in R^{(1)}$ by $h\langle m,n\rangle := gp(m,n)$. Then ν is a cylinder by Lemma 2.4.10 and it satisfies (1) by Theorem 2.4.8(3).

(2) Suppose $\nu(x) = \nu' f(x)$ with $f \in R^{(1)}$. Let g be the function from Lemma 12. There is some $p \in R^{(1)}$ with

$$\varphi_{p(z)}(x) = \begin{cases} 0 & \text{if } f(x) \in e_z \\ 1 & \text{otherwise .} \end{cases}$$

Then $Z_{p(z)} = f^{-1}(e_z)$ (cf. Def. 2.2.2). Define a function $q \in P^{(1)}$ inductively by

$q\langle i,0\rangle = f(i)$,

$q\langle i,n+1\rangle = fgpe^{-1}\{q\langle i,0\rangle,\dots,q\langle i,n\rangle\}$.

For any i the following properties can be proved by induction on n.

(1) $q\langle i,x\rangle$ exists for all $x \le n$,

(2) $q\langle i,x\rangle \neq q\langle i,x'\rangle$ whenever $0 \le x < x' \le n$,

(3) $\nu' q\langle i,x\rangle = \nu(i)$ for all $x \le n$.

The properties hold for the case $n = 0$. Suppose the case n is true. Define $z := e^{-1}\{q\langle i,0\rangle,\dots,q\langle i,n\rangle\}$. Then $\{\nu(i)\} = \nu' e_z = \nu' f f^{-1} e_z = \nu Z_{p(z)}$. By Lemma 12, $gp(z)$ exists and $gp(z) \in \nu^{-1}\{\nu(i)\} \setminus Z_{p(z)}$, hence $\nu gp(z) = \nu(i)$ and $gp(z) \notin Z_{p(z)} = f^{-1} e_z$. Therefore, $q\langle i,n+1\rangle$ exists, $\nu' q\langle i,n+1\rangle = \nu' fgp(z) = \nu gp(z) = \nu(i)$, and $q\langle i,n+1\rangle = fgp(z) \notin e_z = \{q\langle i,0\rangle,\dots,q\langle i,n\rangle\}$. Now we define an injective function $h \in R^{(1)}$ such that $(\forall x)\ \nu(x) = \nu' h(x)$:

$h(0) := q\langle 0,0\rangle$,

$h(x+1) := q\langle x+1,w\rangle$ where $w := \mu n[q\langle x+1,n\rangle \notin \{h(0),\dots,h(x)\}]$.

Since for any x the values $q\langle x+1,n\rangle$ for $n = 0,1,2,\dots$ are pairwise different, h is a total recursive function. The function h is injective by construction, and $\nu' h(x+1) = \nu' q\langle x+1,w\rangle = \nu(x+1)$ for all x (and $\nu' h(0) = \nu' q\langle 0,0\rangle = \nu(0)$). Therefore, $\nu \le_1 \nu'$ via h.
Q.E.D.

The isomorphism theorem for admissible numberings of $P^{(1)}$ can easily be generalized to precomplete numberings.

14 THEOREM (*isomorphism theorem for precomplete numberings*)

Let $\nu,\nu' \in TN(S)$, let ν be precomplete. Then

$$\nu \equiv \nu' \Longleftrightarrow \nu \approx \nu' .$$

Proof

The implication "$\Longleftarrow$" is trivial. Assume $\nu \equiv \nu'$. If $card(S) = 1$ then clearly $\nu \approx \nu'$. If $card(S) \geq 2$, then by Theorem 13, $\nu \leq_1 \nu'$ and $\nu' \leq_1 \nu$, hence $\nu \approx \nu'$ by Myhill's theorem.

Q.E.D.

It is easy to show that K and K^{o} (Def. 2.3.1) are m-equivalent. Since cf_K is complete, $cf_K \approx cf_{K^o}$, hence $K \approx K^{o}$. Instead of Theorem 14, Theorem 9 can be used.

15 THEOREM

$$K \approx K^{o}$$

Proof

Define $f \in R^{(1)}$ by $f(x) := \langle x,x \rangle$. Then f is injective and $K = f^{-1}K^{o}$, hence $K \leq_1 K^{o}$. Define $h \in P^{(2)}$ by $h(\langle i,x \rangle, y) := \varphi_i(x) = u\langle i,x \rangle$. By Theorem 9 there is an injective $t \in R^{(1)}$ with $\varphi_{t\langle i,x \rangle}(y) = \varphi_i(x)$ for all i,x,y. We obtain $\langle i,x \rangle \in K^{o} \Longleftrightarrow t\langle i,x \rangle \in K$, hence $K^{o} \leq_1 K$. $K \approx K^{o}$ follows from Myhill's theorem.

Q.E.D.

There are recursively enumerable,not recursive sets A such that cf_A is not precomplete.

16 THEOREM

cf_A is not precomplete if A is a simple set.

Proof

By Theorem 13(1) cf_A is a cylinder if cf_A is precomplete. Since a simple set A is not a cylinder (Theorem 2.4.13) cf_A cannot be precomplete.

Q.E.D.

Many numberings which will be used later are precomplete, and repeatedly we shall use the recursion theorem as a powerful tool.

So far we have defined precompleteness only for total numberings. We extend Definition 1 to partial numberings as follows.

17 DEFINITION *(precomplete partial numberings)*

Let $\nu: \mathbb{N} \dashrightarrow S$ be a partial numbering. Let $\bot$ be an element with $\bot \notin S$. Extend ν to a total numbering $\bar{\nu}: \mathbb{N} \longrightarrow S \cup \{\bot\}$ as follows:

$$\bar{\nu}(i) := \begin{cases} \nu(i) & \text{if } i \in \mathrm{dom}(\nu) \\ \bot & \text{otherwise.} \end{cases}$$

Then ν is called *precomplete* iff $\bar{\nu}$ is precomplete.

Theorem 4(1) cannot be generalized to partial numberings. Consider the numberings $1\!\!1_{\mathbb{N}}$ and ν of $\mathbb{N}$, where $\nu(i) := (\varphi_i(i)$ if $\varphi_i(i)$ exists, div otherwise). Then ν is precomplete (proof?), $1\!\!1_{\mathbb{N}}$ is not precomplete, and $1\!\!1_{\mathbb{N}} \equiv \nu$. Any restriction w.r.t. the range of a precomplete numbering is precomplete.

18 LEMMA

Let $\nu: \mathbb{N} \dashrightarrow S$ be a precomplete numbering. Let $S_1 \subseteq S$ and define $\nu_1: \mathbb{N} \dashrightarrow S_1$ by $\nu_1(i) := (\nu(i)$ if $\nu(i) \in S_1$, div otherwise). Then ν_1 is a precomplete numbering.

The easy proof is left as an exercise.

EXERCISES

1) In each of the following cases prove or disprove the existence of an $m \in \mathbb{N}$ with the asserted property.
   (a) $W_m = \{m^2\}$
   (b) $W_m = \mathbb{N} \setminus \{m\}$
   (c) $W_m = \{x \mid (\exists y)\, my^2 = x\}$
   (d) $W_m = \{x \mid \langle x,m\rangle \in A\}$ (A any r.e. set)
   (e) $W_m = \{x \mid x \in \mathrm{dom}(\varphi_m)\}$
   (f) $W_m = \{0\} \cup \{x \mid (\exists y)\, [x = 3y \wedge y \in W_m]\}$

2) Is there a function $f \in R^{(1)}$ with $\varphi_{t(i)}(x) = x \cdot t(i)$ for all $i, x \in \mathbb{N}$?

3) Show that there is some $f \in R^{(1)}$ such that $\{i \mid \varphi_i = \varphi_{f(i)}\}$ is not recursive.

4) Prove (1), (2) and (3) of Theorem 4.

5) Let ν be complete.
   (a) Is $WD(\nu)$ complete?
   (b) Is $FS(\nu)$ complete?

6) Which of the (total) numberings from Definition 2.2.2 are precomplete?

7) In which of the following cases is cf_L precomplete or even complete?
   (a) $L = \mathbb{N} \setminus K$,
   (b) $L = \{i \mid \varphi_i \in R^{(1)}\}$.

8) Let ν be a complete numbering, let a be a distinguished element of ν. Define a total numbering $\bar{\nu}$ by

$$\bar{\nu}(i) := \begin{cases} \nu u(i) & \text{if } i \in Def(u) \quad (\text{where } u\langle i,x\rangle := \varphi_i(x)) \\ a & \text{otherwise.} \end{cases}$$

   Prove $\nu \equiv \bar{\nu}$. (Hint: (3) and (4) from Theorem 4 may be used.)

9) Let $\nu \in TN(S)$ be complete, let a be a distinguished element of ν, let $S_o \subseteq S$. Prove: $S_o = S$ whenever $a \in S_o$ and $\nu^{-1}(S_o)$ is r.e. (cf. Lemma 2.3.14).

10) Show that there is some injective function $s \in R^{(1)}$ with $\varphi_{s\langle i,j\rangle}(x) = \varphi_i\langle j,x\rangle$ for all i, j, x.

11) Let ν be a precomplete numbering. Show that there is an injective function $p \in R^{(1)}$ with

$$\varphi_{p(i)} \in R^{(1)} \text{ and } (\forall x \in dom(\varphi_i))\nu\varphi_i(x) = \nu\varphi_{p(i)}(x)$$

   for all $i \in \mathbb{N}$.

12) Show that there is some $f \in P^{(1)}$ with $f(j) \in K \setminus Z_j$ whenever $j \in dom(Z)$ and $Z_j \subseteq K$.

13) (a) Is there some $m \in K$ with $W_m = K$?
   (b) Is there some $m \in \mathbb{N} \setminus K$ with $W_m = K$?

14) Define a numbering ν of $\mathbb{N}$ by $\nu(i) := (\varphi_i(0)$ if $\varphi_i(0)$ exists, div otherwise). Show that ν is precomplete.

15) Prove Lemma 18.

BIBLIOGRAPHICAL NOTES

The recursion theorem for φ is due to Kleene as are many of its applications, see e.g. Kleene (1952) and Rogers (1967). The general version presented here is from Ershov (1973). The isomorphism theorem for φ has originally been proved by Rogers (1958). The proof of the general isomorphism theorem (Theorem 14) is from Ershov (1973).

2.6 Creative, Productive, Complete Sets

As we already know the set $K = \{i \mid i \in \mathrm{dom}(\varphi_i)\}$ is recursively enumerable and not recursive. In the set RE of recursively enumerable subsets of $\mathbb{N}$ the set K has several characteristic remarkable properties: it is creative, it is m-complete, it is 1-complete, and its complement is the smallest productive set. As we shall see, creativity and productivity have interesting applications in logic. As a kind of generalization of creativity we finally introduce effective inseparability and prove a further generalization of Rice's theorem for precomplete numberings.

A set $A \subseteq \mathbb{N}$ is m-complete (1-complete) in a set T of subsets of $\mathbb{N}$ iff it is a maximum in the preorder $(T, \leq_m)$ $((T, \leq_1))$. If A is m-complete (1-complete), it is "the most difficult" set, w.r.t. $\leq$ $(\leq_1)$ in T.

1 DEFINITION (m-*complete*, 1-*complete*)

Let T be a set of subsets of $\mathbb{N}$, let A be a subset of $\mathbb{N}$.

(1) A is m-*complete* in T iff $A \in T$ and $B \leq A$ for all $B \in T$.

(2) A is 1-*complete* in T iff $A \in T$ and $B \leq_1 A$ for all $B \in T$.

(If $T = RE$, the set of r.e. subsets of $\mathbb{N}$, one usually omits the supplement "in RE".)

The basic observation is that K^o is 1-complete in RE: Let $B \in RE$. Then $B = W_i$ for some $i \in \mathbb{N}$. Define $f \in R^{(1)}$ by $f(x) := \langle i,x \rangle$. Then f is injective and $x \in B \Longleftrightarrow f(x) \in K^o$, hence $B \leq_1 K^o$. The other statements of the following theorem are easy consequences of what we have already proved.

2 THEOREM

Let A be a recursively enumerable subset of $\mathbb{N}$. Then the following properties are equivalent.

(1) A is m-complete (in RE),

(2) A is 1-complete (in RE),

(3) $K \leq A$,

(4) $K \leq_1 A$,

(5) $K \equiv A$,

(6) $K \approx A$,

(7) cf_A is complete with distinguished element 0, and $A \neq \emptyset$.

Proof

As we have shown above, K^o is 1-complete in RE. Since $K \approx K^o$ (Theorem 2.5.15), K is 1-complete. We have

$$\begin{aligned} A \text{ is m-complete} &\Longrightarrow K \leq A \quad (\text{since } K \in RE) \\ &\Longrightarrow K \equiv A \quad (\text{since K is 1-complete}) \\ &\Longrightarrow K \approx A \quad (\text{by Theorem 2.5.2, Theorem 2.5.14}) \\ &\Longrightarrow K \leq_1 A \\ &\Longrightarrow A \text{ is 1-complete} \quad (\text{since K is 1-complete}) \\ &\Longrightarrow A \text{ is m-complete}. \end{aligned}$$

Therefore (1),...,(6) are equivalent. Let $K \approx A$. Then $A \neq \emptyset$ and cf_A is complete with distinguished element 0 by Theorem 2.5.2 and Theorem 2.5.4. On the other hand assume (7). Let $i_o \in A$. Define $g \in P^{(1)}$ by $dom(g) = K$ and $g(x) = i_o$ for all $x \in K$. Since cf_A is complete there is some $f \in R^{(1)}$ with $cf_A f(x) = cf_A g(x) = 1$ if $x \in dom(g) = K$ and $cf_A f(x) = 0$ if $x \notin K$. Therefore, $x \in K \Longleftrightarrow f(x) \in A$, i.e. $K \leq A$.
Q.E.D.

In Lemma 2.3.5 we have introduced several recursively enumerable sets M for which $K \leq M$ holds. By Theorem 2 all of these sets are 1-complete in RE and isomorphic to K. However simple sets as well as their cylinders are not isomorphic to K.

3 COROLLARY

(1) If A is m-complete in RE then A is a cylinder.

(2) If A is simple, then $K \not\leq A$ and $K \not\leq c(A)$.

Proof

(1) If A is m-complete then A is 1-complete by Theorem 2. Since $c(A) \in RE$, $c(A) \leq_1 A$, hence A is a cylinder.

(2) If A is a simple set then A is not a cylinder (Theorem 2.4.13). By (1) and Theorem 2, $K \not\leq A$. $K \leq c(A)$ would imply $K \leq A$.
Q.E.D.

The set K has another remarkable property. As we already know $\mathbb{N} \setminus K$ is not recursively enumerable. Indeed it is effectively non r.e.: $i \in (\mathbb{N} \setminus K) \setminus W_i$ if $W_i \subseteq \mathbb{N} \setminus K$. Whenever the name i of an r.e. subset of $\mathbb{N} \setminus K$ is known, a new element of $\mathbb{N} \setminus K$ which is not in W_i, in this case the number i, can be found. Sets with this property are called *productive* (cf. Lemma 2.5.12).

4 DEFINITION (*productive*, *creative*)

(1) Let $A \subseteq \mathbb{N}$. A is *productive* iff there is a function $g \in P^{(1)}$ such that

$$g(i) \text{ exists and } g(i) \in A \setminus W_i$$

whenever $W_i \subseteq A$. Any function g with the above property is called a *productive function* of A.

(2) A set $A \subseteq \mathbb{N}$ is *creative* iff A is r.e. and $\mathbb{N} \setminus A$ is productive.

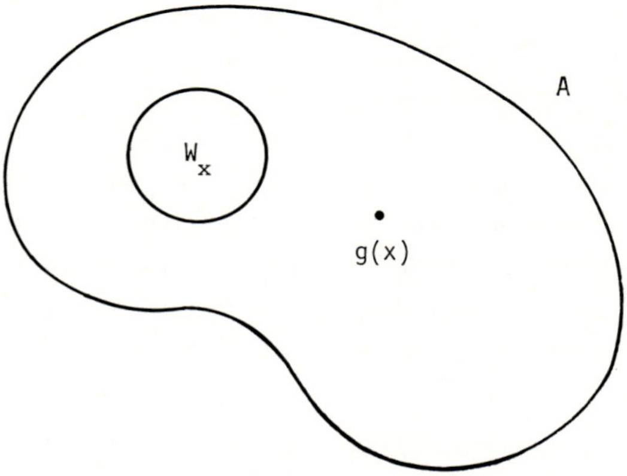

5 LEMMA

K is creative; $\mathbb{N} \setminus K$ is productive with $1\!\!1_{\mathbb{N}}$ as a productive function.

Proof

Since K is r.e. it suffices to show that $\mathbb{N} \setminus K$ is productive. We show that $1\!\!1_{\mathbb{N}}$ is a productive function. Suppose $W_i \subseteq \mathbb{N} \setminus K$. If $i \in W_i$ then $i \in K$ on the one hand and $i \in W_i \subseteq \mathbb{N} \setminus K$, i.e. $i \notin K$ on the other hand. This is a contradiction. Therefore $i \notin W_i$, i.e. $i \in \mathbb{N} \setminus K$. This proves $1\!\!1_{\mathbb{N}}(i) \in (\mathbb{N} \setminus K) \setminus W_i$.
Q.E.D.

The following theorem gives a simple characterization of the productive sets.

6 THEOREM (*characterization of productive sets*)

Let $A \subseteq \mathbb{N}$. Then the following properties are equivalent.

(1) A is productive ,

(2) $\mathbb{N} \setminus K \leq A$,

(3) $\mathbb{N} \setminus K \leq_1 A$.

Proof

"(1) $\Longrightarrow$ (2)": Let g be a productive function of A. Define $h \in P^{(1)}$ by

$$h\langle z,y,w\rangle := \begin{cases} 0 & \text{if } g(w) \text{ exists, } y \in K \text{, and } g(w) = z \\ \text{div} & \text{otherwise.} \end{cases}$$

By the recursion theorem for φ (Corollary 2.5.7(3)) there is some $t \in R^{(1)}$ with $\varphi_{t(y)}(z) = h\langle z,y,t(y)\rangle$. We obtain

$$\varphi_{t(y)}(z) = \begin{cases} 0 & \text{if } gt(y) \text{ exists, } y \in K \text{, and } gt(y) = z \\ \text{div} & \text{otherwise,} \end{cases}$$

hence

$$W_{t(y)} = \begin{cases} \{gt(y)\} & \text{if } gt(y) \text{ exists and } y \in K \\ \emptyset & \text{otherwise.} \end{cases}$$

We show that $\mathbb{N} \setminus K \leq A$ via gt. Suppose $t(y) \notin \mathrm{dom}(g)$ for some y. Then $W_{t(y)} = \emptyset \subseteq A$ and gt(y) exists since g is a productive function of A. Therefore gt(y) exists for all y. Assume $y \in K$. Then $W_{t(y)} = \{gt(y)\}$ by Def. of t. Since g is a productive function of A, $W_{t(y)} \subseteq A$ implies $gt(y) \notin W_{t(y)}$. Therefore $W_{t(y)} \not\subseteq A$, hence $gt(y) \notin A$. Assume $y \notin K$. Then $W_{t(y)} = \emptyset$ and $gt(y) \in A \setminus \emptyset = A$. This proves $K \leq \mathbb{N} \setminus A$, i.e. Property (2) holds.

"(2) $\Longrightarrow$ (3)": Since cf_K is complete, by Theorem 2.5.13(2) we obtain $K \leq_1 \mathbb{N} \setminus A$, i.e. Property (3) holds.

"(3) $\Longrightarrow$ (1)": Suppose $\mathbb{N} \setminus K \leq_1 A$ via $\varphi_i \in R^{(1)}$. By Theorem 2.3.13(2) there is some $r \in R^{(1)}$ with $W_{r\langle i,x\rangle} = \varphi_i^{-1} W_x$. Define $f \in R^{(1)}$ by $f(x) := \varphi_i r\langle i,x\rangle$. We show that f is a productive function of A. Assume $W_x \subseteq A$. Then $W_{r\langle i,x\rangle} = \varphi_i^{-1} W_x \subseteq \varphi_i^{-1} A = \mathbb{N} \setminus K$, hence $r\langle i,x\rangle \in (\mathbb{N} \setminus K) \setminus \varphi_i^{-1} W_x$ and $f(x) = \varphi_i r\langle i,x\rangle \in A \setminus W_x$.

Q.E.D.

7 COROLLARY

(A productive $\wedge$ $A \leq B$) $\Longrightarrow$ B productive

Proof

(A productive $\wedge$ $A \le B$) $\Longrightarrow$ ($\mathbb{N} \setminus K \le A \wedge A \le B$) $\Longrightarrow$ ($\mathbb{N} \setminus K \le B$) $\Longrightarrow$ B productive.
Q.E.D.

For any productive set there is a productive function with very special additional properties.

8 COROLLARY (*completely productive*)

Let A be productive. Then A is *completely productive*, i.e. there is a productive function $f \in P^{(1)}$ with:

(1) $f \in R^{(1)}$,

(2) f is injective,

(3) $(\forall x)\ \ f(x) \in A \setminus W_x \cup W_x \setminus A$.

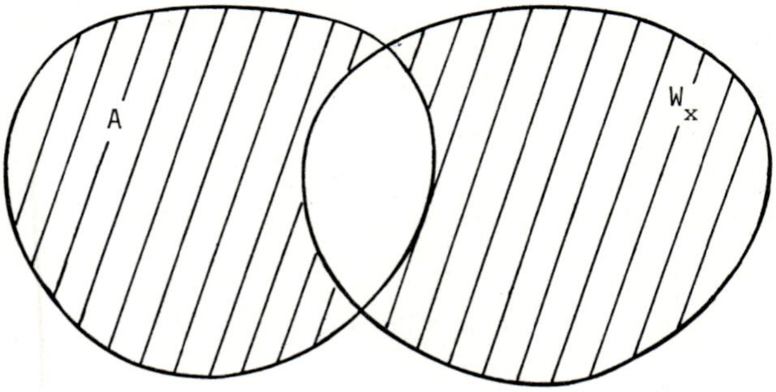

The value f(x) is in the hatched region, especially in the case $W_x \subseteq A$.

Proof

At first we show that $\mathbb{N} \setminus K$ is completely productive with productive function $1\!\!1_{\mathbb{N}}$. Only (3) must be shown. For any $x \in \mathbb{N}$ we have $x \in \mathbb{N} \setminus K \Longleftrightarrow x \notin W_x$, i.e. $1\!\!1_{\mathbb{N}}(x) \in (\mathbb{N} \setminus K) \setminus W_x \cup W_x \setminus (\mathbb{N} \setminus K)$. Assume that A is productive. By Theorem 6 there is some injective $h \in R^{(1)}$ such that $\mathbb{N} \setminus K = h^{-1}A$. By the injective smn-theorem (Theorem 2.5.9) there is some injective $q \in R^{(1)}$ with $\varphi_{q(x)}(y) = \varphi_x h(y)$, hence $W_{q(x)} = \{y \mid h(y) \in W_x\} = h^{-1}W_x$. We obtain

$$\begin{aligned} q(x) &\in (\mathbb{N} \setminus K) \setminus W_{q(x)} \cup W_{q(x)} \setminus (\mathbb{N} \setminus K) \\ &= h^{-1}A \setminus h^{-1}W_x \cup h^{-1}W_x \setminus h^{-1}A \\ &= h^{-1}(A \setminus W_x \cup W_x \setminus A) \end{aligned}$$

and therefore $hq(x) \in A \setminus W_x \cup W_x \setminus A$. The function $f := hq$ has the desired property.
Q.E.D.

The productive function g of A produces a new element $g(x) \in A$ if $W_x \subseteq A$. Since $W_x \cup \{g(x)\}$ is also r.e., say the set W_y, g produces a new element g(y) of A. Iteration of this process yields an infinite r.e. set $W_z \subseteq A \setminus W_x$. By the following theorem a number z can be computed from x.

9 <u>THEOREM</u>

Let $A \subseteq \mathbb{N}$ be productive. Then there is a function $g \in R^{(1)}$ such that $W_{g(x)} \subseteq A \setminus W_x$ and $W_{g(x)}$ is infinite if $W_x \subseteq A$.

<u>Proof</u>

There is some $q \in R^{(1)}$ with $W_{q(x)} = W_x \cup \{f(x)\}$ where f is a productive function of A. There is some $g \in R^{(1)}$ with $\varphi_{g(x)}(y) = \mu i[y = fq^i(x)]$. Then $W_{g(x)} = \{fq^i(x) \mid i \in \mathbb{N}\}$. Assume $W_x \subseteq A$. Then

$$W_x \subseteq W_{q(x)} \subseteq W_{q^2(x)} \subseteq \ldots \subseteq A$$

and $fq^i(x) \in A \setminus W_{q^i(x)}$ and $fq^i(x) \in W_{q^{i+1}(x)}$ for all i. Therefore $W_{g(x)} \subseteq A \setminus W_x$ and $W_{g(x)}$ is infinite.

Q.E.D.

Beginning from $W_{g(x)} \subseteq A$ the process of production can be continued. Essentially two operations are available for this procedure:

(1) G produces one new element using the productive function f,

(2) H is the effective countable union of r.e. subsets which are already produced.

Each possible stage of production can be characterized by a computable tree with leaves from $\mathbb{N}$ and inner nodes G and H where G has one successor and H has infinitely many successors. This set of *finite path trees* will be studied in more detail in Chapter 2.8. As a simple corollary of Theorem 9 we obtain that any productive set has an infinite recursive subset.

10 <u>COROLLARY</u>

If A is productive, then A has an infinite recursive subset.

<u>Proof</u>

Let $k \in \mathbb{N}$ such that $W_k = \emptyset$. Then $W_k \subseteq A$ and $W_{g(k)} \subseteq A$ where $W_{g(k)}$ is infinite, by Theorem 9. By Lemma 2.3.12, $W_{g(k)}$ has an infinite recursive subset.

Q.E.D.

From Theorem 6 and Theorem 2 we can easily characterize the creative sets.

11 THEOREM

A set $A \subseteq \mathbb{N}$ is creative iff $A \approx K$.

Proof

Assume that A is creative. Then by Theorem 6 $\mathbb{N} \setminus K \leq \mathbb{N} \setminus A$, hence $K \leq A$. Since A is r.e., $A \approx K$ by Theorem 2. Assume $A \approx K$. Then A is r.e. and $K \leq A$, hence $\mathbb{N} \setminus K \leq \mathbb{N} \setminus A$. By Theorem 6, $\mathbb{N} \setminus A$ is productive, therefore A is creative.
Q.E.D.

The definition of creativity and productivity depends formally on the numbering W, hence on φ. Similarly the definition of K depends on φ. By Theorem 2 and Theorem 11, a set A is creative iff it is m-complete (in RE). Therefore the concept of creativity does not really depend on φ. Although the definition of K depends on φ, the isomorphism class $\{A \mid A \approx K\}$ is the set of all creative sets and therefore does not depend on φ.

The concept of creativity can be generalized from one to two sets as follows.

12 DEFINITION (*effectively inseparable sets*)

Two sets $A, B \subseteq \mathbb{N}$ are effectively inseparable iff $A \cap B = \emptyset$ and there is some $g \in P^{(1)}$ (a *productive function* for A and B) with

$$g<i,j> \text{ exists and } g<i,j> \in \mathbb{N} \setminus (W_i \cup W_j)$$

whenever $A \subseteq W_i$, $B \subseteq W_j$ and $W_i \cap W_j = \emptyset$.

The following diagram illustrates the definition.

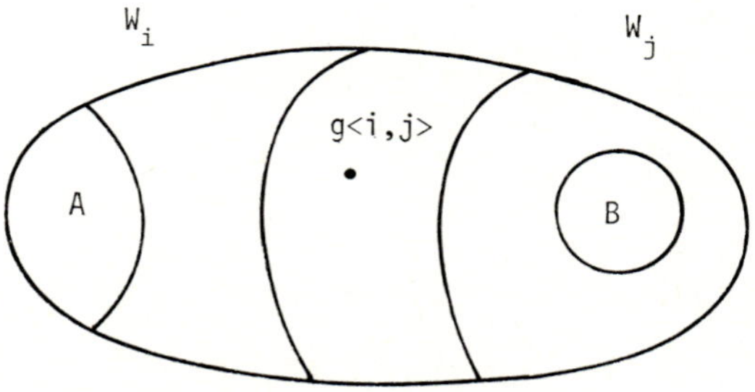

Lemma 13 summarizes some useful properties of effective inseparability.

13 LEMMA

Let A and B be effectively inseparable. Then:

(1) A and B are not recursive.

(2) If $A \subseteq A'$, $B \subseteq B'$ and $A' \cap B' = \emptyset$. Then A' and B' are effectively inseparable.

(3) If $h \in R^{(1)}$ and $h(A) \cap h(B) = \emptyset$ then h(A) and h(B) are effectively inseparable.

(4) If A and B are recursively enumerable then A and B are creative.

Proof

Let g be a productive function of A and B.

(1) Suppose that A is recursive. There are $i,j \in \mathbb{N}$ with $W_i = A$, $W_j = \mathbb{N} \setminus A$. Then $A \subseteq W_i$, $B \subseteq W_j$, but $g\langle i,j\rangle \in \mathbb{N} \setminus (W_i \cup W_j) = \emptyset$ for no $g \in P^{(1)}$.

(2) g is a productive function of A' and B'.

(3) There is a function $f \in R^{(1)}$ with $W_{f(i)} = h^{-1}W_i$ for all i. Define $g' \in P^{(1)}$ by $g'\langle i,j\rangle := hg\langle f(i),f(j)\rangle$. We show that g' is a productive function of h(A) and h(B). Let $h(A) \subseteq W_i$, $h(B) \subseteq W_j$, $W_i \cap W_j = \emptyset$. Then $A \subseteq W_{f(i)}$, $B \subseteq W_{f(j)}$ and $W_{f(i)} \cap W_{f(j)} = \emptyset$. Therefore, $g\langle f(i),f(j)\rangle \in \mathbb{N} \setminus (W_{f(i)} \cup W_{f(j)}) = h^{-1}(\mathbb{N} \setminus (W_i \cup W_j))$, hence $g'\langle i,j\rangle \in \mathbb{N} \setminus (W_i \cup W_j)$. Since $h(A) \cap h(B) = \emptyset$, h(A) and h(B) are effectively inseparable.

(4) We show that $\mathbb{N} \setminus A$ is productive. There is $a \in \mathbb{N}$ with $W_a = A$ and there is $p \in R^{(1)}$ with $W_{p(x)} = B \cup W_x$ for all $x \in \mathbb{N}$. Define $g' \in P^{(1)}$ by $g'(x) := g\langle a,p(x)\rangle$. We obtain:

$$\begin{aligned} W_x \subseteq \mathbb{N} \setminus A &\Longrightarrow B \subseteq W_x \cup B = W_{p(x)} \subseteq \mathbb{N} \setminus A \\ &\Longrightarrow A \subseteq W_a \wedge B \subseteq W_{p(x)} \wedge W_a \cap W_{p(x)} = \emptyset \\ &\Longrightarrow g'(x) \in \mathbb{N} \setminus (W_a \cup W_{p(x)}) \\ &\Longrightarrow g'(x) \in (\mathbb{N} \setminus A) \setminus W_x . \end{aligned}$$

Therefore A is creative. Similarly it is shown that B is creative.
Q.E.D.

Definition 12 and Lemma 13 would be useless, if we could not prove that effectively inseparable sets exist.

14 LEMMA

The sets

$A_o := \{i \mid \varphi_i(i) = 0\}$,

$A_1 := \{i \mid \varphi_i(i) = 1\}$

are effectively inseparable.

Proof

Define $p,q \in P^{(1)}$ as follows:

$$p\langle i,j,y\rangle := \mu t[\Phi_i(y) = t \vee \Phi_j(y) = t]$$

$$q\langle i,j,y,t\rangle := \begin{cases} 1 & \text{if } \Phi_i(y) = t \wedge \Phi_j(y) \neq t \\ 0 & \text{if } \Phi_j(y) = t \\ \text{div} & \text{otherwise} . \end{cases}$$

Then there is some $g \in R^{(1)}$ with $\varphi_{g\langle i,j\rangle}(y) = q\langle i,j,y,p\langle i,j,y\rangle\rangle$. Assume $A_o \subseteq W_i$, $A_1 \subseteq W_j$, $W_i \cap W_j = \emptyset$. Suppose $g\langle i,j\rangle \in W_i$. Then $g\langle i,j\rangle \notin W_j$, $g\langle i,j\rangle \in \mathrm{dom}\,\Phi_i$ and $g\langle i,j\rangle \notin \mathrm{dom}(\Phi_j)$. Therefore $p\langle i,j,g\langle i,j\rangle\rangle = \Phi_i g\langle i,j\rangle$, hence $\varphi_{g\langle i,j\rangle} g\langle i,j\rangle = 1$, i.e. $g\langle i,j\rangle \in A_1 \subseteq W_j$ (a contradiction). Similarly the assumption $g\langle i,j\rangle \in W_j$ yields a contradiction. Therefore $g\langle i,j\rangle \in \mathbb{N} \setminus (W_i \cup W_j)$. Since $A_o \cap A_1 = \emptyset$, the two sets are effectively inseparable with g as a productive function.

Q.E.D.

By Rice's theorem (Theorem 2.5.8(2)) no non-trivial property of S is ν-recursive, if ν is precomplete. We shall prove now a stronger theorem. Every disjoint pair of non-trivial properties is effectively inseparable (w.r.t. ν) if ν is precomplete.

15 THEOREM (*Rice's theorem generalized*)

Let $\nu \in TN(S)$ be precomplete, let $S_o, S_1 \subseteq S$ such that $S_o, S_1 \neq \emptyset$, $S_o, S_1 \neq S$, and $S_o \cap S_1 = \emptyset$. Then:

(1) There are effectively inseparable recursively enumerable sets B_o and B_1 with $B_o \subseteq \nu^{-1}(S_o)$ and $B_1 \subseteq \nu^{-1}(S_1)$.

(2) $\nu^{-1}(S_o)$ and $\nu^{-1}(S_1)$ are effectively inseparable.

(3) $\nu^{-1}(S_o)$ is creative if it is r.e.

(4) $\nu^{-1}(S_o)$ is not recursive.

Proof

(1) By Lemma 14 there are recursively enumerable sets A_o and A_1 which are effectively inseparable. Let $n_o \in \nu^{-1}(S_o)$ and $n_1 \in \nu^{-1}(S_1)$. Define $h \in P^{(1)}$ by

$$h(x) = \begin{cases} n_o & \text{if } x \in A_o \\ n_1 & \text{if } x \in A_1 \\ \text{div} & \text{otherwise.} \end{cases}$$

Since ν is precomplete there is a function $g \in R^{(1)}$ such that $\nu g(x) = \nu h(x)$ if $x \in \mathrm{dom}(h)$. We obtain $g(A_o) \subseteq \nu^{-1}(S_o)$ and $g(A_1) \subseteq \nu^{-1}(S_1)$. The sets $B_o := g(A_o)$ and $B_1 := g(A_1)$ are recursively enumerable and effectively inseparable by Lemma 13(3).

(2) This follows from (1) by Lemma 13(2).

(3) Suppose $\nu^{-1}(S_o)$ is r.e. Then $\nu^{-1}(S_o)$ and B_1 are r.e. and effectively inseparable (from (1) by Lemma 13(2)). By Lemma 13(4), $\nu^{-1}(S_o)$ is creative.

(4) This follows from (2) by Lemma 13(1).

Q.E.D.

EXERCISES

1) Let $A \subseteq \mathbb{N}$, $A \neq \emptyset$. Define $RE(A) := \{g^{-1}(A) \mid g \in P^{(1)}\}$. Define $L := u^{-1}(A)$ where u is the universal function of φ.
   (a) Prove that L is 1-complete in $RE(A)$.
   (b) Prove that $L \approx K$ if A is recursively enumerable.
   (c) Show that for any $B \subseteq \mathbb{N}$ the following properties are equivalent:
      (1) B is m-complete in $RE(A)$,
      (2) B is 1-complete in $RE(A)$,
      (3) $L \leq B$,
      (4) $L \leq_1 B$,
      (5) $L \equiv B$,
      (6) $L \equiv_1 B$,
      (7) cf_B is complete with 0 as a distinguished element.

2) Let $M = \{x \mid \varphi_x \in R^{(1)}\}$.
   (a) Show that M is productive. (Use a diagonalization argument and do not apply Theorem 6.)
   (b) Show $\mathbb{N} \setminus K \leq M$ (hence M is productive).
   (c) Show $M \approx u^{-1}(M)$. (Use Exercise 1.)

3) Let g be a productive function of $A \subseteq \mathbb{N}$. Show that there are $i, j \in \mathbb{N}$ such that $W_i = W_j = \emptyset$ but $g(i) \neq g(j)$.

4) Show that there are sets B, C such that B is creative, C is productive, $A = B \cup C$, $\emptyset = B \cap C$, if

(a) A is infinite and recursively enumerable

or

(b) A is productive.

5) Prove: (B r.e. $\wedge$ $A \cap B$ productive) $\Rightarrow$ A productive.

6) Let $Prd(A) := \{x \mid W_x \subseteq A\}$.

(a) Show: A productive $\Rightarrow$ $Prd(A)$ productive.

Let g be a productive function of A. Show:

(b) $g\,Prd(A) \subseteq A$,

(c) $g\,Prd(A) \subseteq B \subseteq A \Rightarrow B$ productive.

7) Show that there are two simple sets S_1 and S_2 with $S_1 \cup S_2 = \mathbb{N}$.

8) Let A be creative, B productive, and S simple.

(a) Show that $A \cap S$ is creative.

(b) Show that $B \cup S$ productive.

9) Show that A is creative if $\langle A, \mathbb{N} \rangle = c(A)$ is creative.

BIBLIOGRAPHICAL NOTES

The theory of creativity has been developed by Post, Dekker et al. A final general theory of creativity and m-completeness is presented in Ershov (1973).

2.7 Effective Numberings

In Chapter 2.2 we have defined how a numbering ν of a set S induces a computability theory on the set S. We have shown that the numbering ν of a set S is determined uniquely (up to equivalence) by the computability theory induced by it (Lemma 2.2.8, Conclusion 2.2.9). In this chapter we shall study for which effectivity conditions numberings satisfying these conditions exist. As a main result we shall show that for sets which are defined as closures numberings defined via generation trees are natural.

There are three main types of requirements for the computability theory induced by a numbering ν of S.

(a) A function $f : S' \dashrightarrow S$ shall become (ν',ν)-computable, where ν' is already defined.

(b) A function $g : S^n \dashrightarrow S'$ shall become (ν^n,ν')-computable, where ν' is already defined.

(c) An operation $h : S^n \dashrightarrow S$ shall become (ν^n,ν)-computable.

Often there are many non-equivalent numberings which satisfy a given set of effectivity conditions. Since $\nu \leq \nu'$ informally means that ν is simpler than ν', an effective numbering should be as small as possible w.r.t. many-one reducibility. Sometimes, precompleteness or completeness are required as further conditions.

First we consider finite sets. The set of numberings of a finite set has a minimum w.r.t. $\leq$ which is highly effective.

1 THEOREM (*effective numbering of a finite set*)

Let S be a finite set, $S \neq \emptyset$. Let ν_S be any numbering of S with $\mathrm{dom}(\nu_S) = \{0,1,\ldots,\mathrm{card}(S)-1\}$. Then:

(1) $\nu_S \leq \nu$ for any numbering ν of S.

(2) $\nu_S \equiv \nu \iff \nu$ is decidable, for any total numbering ν of S (see Definition 2.4.16).

(3) Any function $f : S^n \dashrightarrow S'$ is strongly (ν_S^n,ν')-computable where ν' is an arbitrary numbering of S'.

By (1) the numbering ν_S is as simple as possible, by (3) any function from S^n is computable w.r.t. ν_S. Especially characteristic functions on S^2 are computable, hence the equivalence problem of ν_S is decidable. By (2) this last property already characterizes the equivalence class of ν_S. The easy proof of Theorem 1 is left as an exercise. Of course the numbering ν_a from Definition 2.2.2, where $S = \Sigma$, is equivalent to ν_S.

The next theorem shows that conditions of type (a) can always be satisfied.

2 THEOREM

(1) Let $\nu_i \in N(S_i)$ and $f_i : S_i \dashrightarrow S$ $(i = 1,\dots,n)$. There is a numbering ν_o of $S_o := \bigcup \mathrm{range}(f_i)$ such that for any numbering ν of S:

$$\nu_o \le \nu \iff (\forall i)\ f_i \text{ is } (\nu_i,\nu)\text{-computable.}$$

(2) Let $\nu_i \in N(S_i)$ and $f_i : S_i \dashrightarrow S$ $(i \in \mathbb{N})$. Then there is a numbering ν_o of $S_o := \bigcup \mathrm{range}(f_i)$ such that ($\nu_o \le \nu$ iff there is some $g \in P^{(1)}$ with $(\forall i,n$ with $n \in \mathrm{dom}(f_i\nu_i))$ $f_i\nu_i(n) = \nu g\langle i,n\rangle$) for any numbering ν of S.

Proof

(1) Define $S_i' := \mathrm{range}(f_i)$ and $\nu_i' \in N(S_i')$ by $\nu_i'(k) := (f_i\nu_i(k)$ if $k \in \mathrm{dom}(f_i\nu_i)$, div otherwise). Let $\nu_o := \nu_1' \sqcup (\nu_2' \sqcup (\dots \sqcup \nu_n')\dots)$. Then $\nu_o \in \mathrm{Sup}\{\nu_i' \mid 1 \le i \le n\}$ (see Lemma 2.4.14), hence $\nu_o \le \nu \iff (\forall i)\ \nu_i' \le \nu$. Finally observe that $\nu_i' \le \nu$ holds iff f_i is (ν_i,ν)-computable.

(2) Define ν_o by $\langle i,n\rangle \in \mathrm{dom}(\nu_o) \iff n \in \mathrm{dom}(f_i\nu_i)$, and $\nu_o\langle i,n\rangle := f_i\nu_i(n)$ for $\langle i,n\rangle \in \mathrm{dom}(\nu_o)$. It can easily be verified that ν_o has the desired property.
Q.E.D.

Remember that for a total function $f_i : S_i \longrightarrow S$, f is strongly (ν_i,ν)-computable, iff f_i is (ν_i,ν)-computable. In (1) or (2) any numbering ν with $\nu_o \le \nu$ can be called effective w.r.t. the given computability requirement. If $S \setminus S_o$ is finite then $\{\nu \in N(S) \mid \nu_o \le \nu\}$ has a least element, e.g. $\nu' := \nu_o \sqcup \nu_T$ where $T = S \setminus S_o$ and ν_T is defined as in Theorem 1 (see the exercises). In this case there is a distinguished, up to equivalence unique effective numbering.

As we have shown infinitely many requirements of Type (a) can be satisfied. By the next theorem finitely many requirements of Type (b) can be satisfied.

3 THEOREM

Let $\nu_i \in N(S_i)$ and $f_i : S \dashrightarrow S_i$ $(i = 1,\dots,n)$. Then there is a numbering ν of S such that f_i is (ν,ν_i)-computable for all $i = 1,\dots,n$.

Proof

For $i = 1,\dots,n$ let $\nu_i' \in N(S)$ be a numbering such that $\nu_i'(n) \in f_i^{-1}\{\nu_i(n)\}$ for all n with $\nu_i(n) \in \mathrm{range}(f_i)$. Then f_i is (ν_i',ν_i)-computable (via $1_{\mathbb{N}}$). Let $\nu := \nu_1' \sqcap (\nu_2' \sqcap (\dots \sqcap \nu_n')\dots)$. Then $\nu \le \nu_i'$ and f_i is (ν,ν_i)-computable for all i.
Q.E.D.

Clearly, any numbering $\tilde{\nu} \in N(S)$ with $\tilde{\nu} \le \nu$ can be chosen in Theorem 3 instead of ν. Probably Theorem 3 cannot be generalized to the case of n-ary functions $(n \ge 2)$ or to the case of infinitely many functions. The requirements of Type (b) include predicates (the special case $S' = \{0,1\}$, ν' effective as in Theorem 1). Exercise 3 shows that ν cannot be a total numbering in general.

Computability conditions of Type(c) are of particular importance, since for many fundamental sets S the "effective" numberings can be defined by requiring computability of certain operators. We shall study the following case: There are some subset $B \subseteq S$ and a set of operations F on S such that each element of S can be generated from the elements of B by repeated applications of operations from F.

4 EXAMPLES

(1) $\mathbb{N}$: $B = \{0\}$, $F = \{\text{successor on } \mathbb{N}\}$.

(2) $W(\Sigma)$: $B = \{\varepsilon\}$, $F = \{\lambda_a \mid a \in \Sigma\}$ where $\lambda_a(x) = ax$.

(3) $E(\mathbb{N})$: $B = \emptyset$, $F = \{X \longmapsto X+1, X \longmapsto X \cup \{0\}\}$.

(4) P = set of partial recursive functions: $B = Gr$, $F = \{$substitutions, primitive recursion, μ-recursion$\}$ (see Definition 1.3.5).

The computation rules which specify in which order functions have to be applied can be represented by trees. We shall define these trees formally, we shall show how trees can be evaluated if a generating system $\hat{A}$ which interprets the nodes in the trees is given, and we shall define and study a standard notation and a standard numbering of the set of trees. If i is the number of a tree t which evaluated w.r.t. $\hat{A}$ yields the element x, then i is a number of x which is canonical w.r.t. $\hat{A}$. First we define the set of trees of a given signature.

5 <u>DEFINITION</u> (*trees over an f.b. signature* σ)

(1) A *finitely branched (f.b.) signature* is a mapping $\sigma : \mathbb{N} \dashrightarrow \mathbb{N}$ such that $0 \notin \mathrm{range}(\sigma)$.

(2) Define sets $T_n(\sigma)$ for $n \in \mathbb{N}$ inductively by

$$T_o(\sigma) = \mathbb{N},$$

$$T_n(\sigma) = T_{n-1}(\sigma) \cup \{(i,t_1,\ldots,t_k) \mid \sigma(i) = k,\ t_1,\ldots,t_k \in T_{n-1}(\sigma)\}$$

for all $n > 0$. Define $T(\sigma)$, the *set of trees over* σ, by

$$T(\sigma) := \bigcup_n T_n(\sigma).$$

(3) The *height* of a tree is defined by:

$$\mathrm{height}(t) = 0 \quad \text{if} \quad t \in T_o(\sigma),$$

$$\mathrm{height}(t) = n \quad \text{if} \quad t \in T_n(\sigma) \setminus T_{n-1}(\sigma).$$

$T(\sigma)$ is the set of (ordered, finitely branched) trees with leaves from $\mathbb{N}$ and nodes from $\mathrm{dom}(\sigma)$ the branching of which is given by the signature function σ. Trees can be represented graphically.

6 <u>EXAMPLE</u>

Let $\sigma(0) = 2$, $\sigma(2) = 1$, $\sigma(n) = \mathrm{div}$ otherwise. Then e.g. the tree $t = (0,(2,(0,1,1)),(2,1))$ with height 3 can be represented by the following figure:

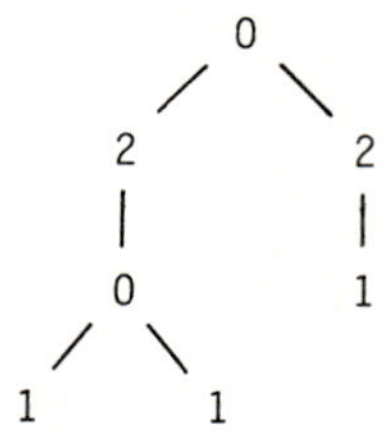

The existence of the unique set $T(\sigma)$ in Definition 5 is guaranteed by set theory. In the following, i will be the number of a k-ary operation if $\sigma(i) = k$. The value $\sigma(i) = 0$ is reserved for ω-ary operations (see Chapter 2.8).

7 DEFINITION (*algebra with signature* σ)

Let σ be an f.b. signature. An *algebra with signature* σ is a triple

$$\hat{A} = (A, \hat{f}, \nu_o)$$

where A is a set, ν_o is a numbering of a subset of A, and $\hat{f}$ is a numbering of operations on A with

$$\mathrm{dom}(\hat{f}) = \mathrm{dom}(\sigma),$$

$$\hat{f}(n) : A^{\sigma(n)} \dashrightarrow A$$

for all $n \in \mathrm{dom}(\sigma)$.

Thus, an algebra assigns values $\nu_o(i) \in A$ to the leaves $i \in \mathrm{dom}(\nu_o)$ and a $\sigma(n)$-ary operation $\hat{f}(n)$ on A to any $n \in \mathrm{dom}(\hat{f})$. Any tree $t \in T(\sigma)$ can be interpreted as a prescription for determining a value $a \in A$.

8 DEFINITION (*evaluation mapping*)

Let σ be a signature and let $\hat{A} = (A, \hat{f}, \nu_o)$ be an algebra with signature σ. Define the *evaluation mapping* $H : T(\sigma) \dashrightarrow A$ of $\hat{A}$ inductively as follows:

$$H(t) = \nu_o(i)$$

if $\mathrm{height}(t) = 0$ and $t = i$, and

$$H(t) = \hat{f}(i)(H(t_1), \ldots, H(t_{\sigma(i)}))$$

for all t with $\mathrm{height}(t) > 0$, where $t = (i, t_1, \ldots, t_{\sigma(i)})$.

Intuitively, any tree has height 0 or it can be uniquely decomposed into a root and subtrees of smaller height, hence the function H is welldefined. We prove the existence and uniqueness of H more rigorously.

9 LEMMA

The evaluation mapping H is welldefined.

Proof

(1) By an induction on $N \in \mathbb{N}$ one can easily show: for each $N \in \mathbb{N}$ there is a unique function $H_N : T_N(\sigma) \dashrightarrow A$ such that

$$H_N(t) = \nu_o(i) \quad \text{if} \quad t = i,$$

$$H_N(t) = \hat{f}(i)(H_N(t_1),\ldots,H_N(t_{\sigma(i)})) \quad \text{if} \quad t = (i,t_1,\ldots,t_{\sigma(i)})$$

for all $t \in T_N(\sigma)$. Define H by $H(t) := H_N(t)$ if $t \in T_N(\sigma)$ for some $N \in \mathbb{N}$. Then H has the desired properties.

(2) Uniqueness of H: Let $H' : T(\sigma) \dashrightarrow A$ be another function satisfying Definition 8. An easy induction on height(t) shows $(\forall t \in T(\sigma))\ H(t) = H'(t)$.
Q.E.D.

10 EXAMPLE (Example 6 continued)
Let σ be the signature from Example 6. Define an algebra $\hat{A} = (\mathbb{R},\hat{f},\nu_o)$ with signature σ by $\nu_o(1) = 2$, $\nu_o(i) = \text{div}$ otherwise, $\text{dom}(\hat{f}(0)) := \mathbb{Q} \times \mathbb{Q}$, $\hat{f}(0)(x,y) := x + y$, $\text{dom}(\hat{f}(2)) := \mathbb{Z}$, $\hat{f}(2)(z) := z^2$. Then

$$H(1) = \nu_o(1) = 2$$

$$H((2,1)) = \hat{f}(2)H(1) = 4$$

$$H((0,1,1)) = 4$$

$$H((2,(0,1,1))) = 16$$

$$H(t) = 16 + 4 = 20\,.$$

So far we have denoted trees informally in our metalanguage, e.g. the tree (0,(2,(0,1,1)),(2,1)) from Example 6. For a formal treatment of trees a notation or a numbering is needed (see Chapter 2.2). Usually trees are denoted by terms or expressions which are certain words over an appropriate alphabet. The above tree could be denoted by the word

"(0,(2,(0,1,1)),(2,1))"

or by the word

"0(2(0(1,1)),2(1))"

or by the word

"$f_o f_2 f_o 11 f_2 1$".

There are many other reasonable notations, but the above and some other similar ones have the advantage that the names of subtrees are subwords. A standard prefix notation $\nu : W(\Sigma) \dashrightarrow T(\sigma)$ where $\Sigma = \{1|(|)|,\}$ (we use the sign | for separation in our metalanguage since $, \in \Sigma$) can be defined as follows. Define $H : T(\sigma) \longrightarrow W(\Sigma)$ by

$$H(t) := 1^t \quad \text{if} \quad \text{height}(t) = 0\,, \quad \text{i.e.} \quad t \in \mathbb{N}$$

$$H(t) := \text{"}1^i(H(t_1),\ldots,H(t_k))\text{"}$$

where $t = (i,t_1,\ldots,t_k)$ for all t with height(t) > 0. It can be shown that H is welldefined and injective. Then let $\nu := H^{-1}$. The elements of dom(ν) are usually called *terms* in *prefix notation with parentheses*. An equivalent notation is obtained if instead of 1^t a word $w \in \beta_1^{-1}\{t\}$ and instead of 1^i a word $x \in \beta_2^{-1}\{i\}$ are used, where $\beta_1, \beta_2 : W(\Delta) \dashrightarrow \mathbb{N}$ are $(\nu_\Delta, 1\!\!1_{\mathbb{N}})$-computable notations of $\mathbb{N}$ with $\Delta \cap \{(,|,),|,\} = \emptyset$. Let e.g. $\sigma(0) = 1$, $\sigma(1) = \sigma(2) = 2$, let $\beta_1(\text{"x"}) := 0$, $\beta_1(\text{"y"}) = 1$, $\beta_2(\text{"S"}) = 0$, $\beta_2(\text{"add"}) = 1$, $\beta_2(\text{"mult"}) = 2$. Then for an appropriate alphabet Γ

"add(mult(x,y),S(y))" $\in W(\Gamma)$

is a name for the tree

$(1,(2,0,1),(0,1)) \in T(\sigma)$.

From the above notation ν a numbering $\nu' := \nu\nu_\Sigma$ of $T(\sigma)$ can be derived. We shall now explicitly define a numbering ν_σ which is equivalent to ν'.

11 DEFINITION (*standard numbering of* $T(\sigma)$)

Let σ be an f.b. signature. Define the *standard numbering* ν_σ of $T(\sigma)$ inductively as follows.

$$\nu_\sigma(n) = \begin{cases} i \in T_o(\sigma) & \text{if } n = \langle i,0\rangle \\ (i,\nu_\sigma(j_1),\ldots,\nu_\sigma(j_k)) & \text{if } n = \langle i,\langle j_1,\ldots,j_k\rangle+1\rangle \text{ and } \sigma(i) = k \\ & \text{and } j_1,\ldots,j_k \in \text{dom}(\nu_\sigma) \\ \text{div} & \text{otherwise.} \end{cases}$$

Since $j_m < n$ for $m = 1,\ldots,k$ if $n = \langle i,\langle j_1,\ldots,j_k\rangle+1\rangle$, $\nu_\sigma(n)$ is welldefined for all $n \in \mathbb{N}$. It remains to show that $T(\sigma) = \text{range}(\nu_\sigma)$.

12 LEMMA

$T(\sigma) = \text{range}(\nu_\sigma)$

Proof

An easy induction shows $(\forall n)\ T_n(\sigma) \subseteq \text{range}(\nu_\sigma)$, hence $T(\sigma) \subseteq \text{range}(\nu_\sigma)$. Also by induction $(\forall n \in \text{dom}(\nu_\sigma))(\exists m)\ \nu_\sigma(n) \in T_m(\sigma)$ can be proved, hence $\text{range}(\nu_\sigma) \subseteq T(\sigma)$.

Q.E.D.

Two interesting properties of ν_σ are given by the following lemma.

13 LEMMA

(1) ν_σ is injective.

(2) $\mathrm{dom}(\nu_\sigma)$ is recursively enumerable if σ is computable.

Proof

The following property can be shown by induction: $(\forall n)\ (\forall m,m' < n)$ $(\nu_\sigma(m) = \nu_\sigma(m') \Longrightarrow m = m')$. Therefore ν_σ is injective. By the recursion theorem (Corollary 2.5.7(4)) there is a function $h(=\varphi_s) \in P^{(1)}$ with

$$h(n) = \begin{cases} 0 & \text{if } n = \langle i,0\rangle \text{ or if} \\ & n = \langle i,\langle j_1,\ldots,j_k\rangle + 1\rangle \text{ and } \sigma(i) = k \text{ and } h(j_1) = \ldots = h(j_k) = 0 \\ \text{div} & \text{otherwise} \end{cases}$$

if σ is computable. By complete induction on n one obtains

$$(\forall m \le n)\quad (m \in \mathrm{dom}(\nu_\sigma) \Longleftrightarrow m \in \mathrm{dom}(h)),$$

hence $\mathrm{dom}(\nu_\sigma) = \mathrm{dom}(h)$ and $\mathrm{dom}(\nu_\sigma)$ is recursively enumerable.
Q.E.D.

Let σ be an f.b. signature and let $\hat{A} = (A, \hat{f}, \nu_o)$ be an algebra with signature σ. Let $H : T(\sigma) \dashrightarrow A$ be the evaluation mapping associated with $\hat{A}$. Then by $\nu(i) := (H\nu_\sigma(i)$ if $i \in \mathrm{dom}\, H\nu_\sigma$, div otherwise) a numbering ν of $\mathrm{range}(H) \subseteq A$ is defined. If $i \in \mathrm{dom}(\nu)$ then $\nu_\sigma(i)$ is a tree composed of functions $\hat{f}(n)$ which is a rule for determining the element $\nu(i) = H\nu_\sigma(i) \in A$. The numbering ν can be called effective w.r.t. the algebra $\hat{A}$. Often not all trees but only a subset $T' \subseteq T(\sigma)$ is considered for generating elements.

14 DEFINITION (*tree numberings*)

Let $\hat{A} = (A, \hat{f}, \nu_o)$ be an algebra with f.b. signature σ. Let $H : T(\sigma) \dashrightarrow A$ be the evaluation mapping of $\hat{A}$. Let $T' \subseteq T(\sigma)$. Then the numbering ν of $H(T')$ defined by

$$\nu(i) := \begin{cases} H\nu_\sigma(i) & \text{if } \nu_\sigma(i) \in T' \\ \text{div} & \text{otherwise} \end{cases}$$

is called the numbering *canonical* w.r.t. $\hat{A}$ and T'.

If $T' = T(\sigma)$, $\mathrm{range}(\nu)$ is the set of elements which can be determined from the elements of $\mathrm{range}(\nu_o)$ by finitely many applications of functions from $\mathrm{range}(\hat{f})$, i.e. the closure of $\mathrm{range}(\nu_o)$ by $\mathrm{range}(\hat{f})$. It is the smallest set which contains $\mathrm{range}(\nu_o)$

and which is closed under the operations from range($\hat{f}$). In this case the numbering ν is the smallest numbering of range(ν) for which the operations from range($\hat{f}$) become weakly computable w.r.t. ν in a uniform way:

15 THEOREM

Let $\tilde{A}$ be an algebra with the computable f.b. signature σ. Let ν be the numbering canonical w.r.t. $\tilde{A}$ and $T(\sigma)$. Let $\tilde{B} = (B, \hat{g}, \nu_o)$ where $B = \text{range}(\nu)$ and for all n, $\hat{g}(n) : B^{\sigma(n)} \dashrightarrow B$ is defined by restricting f. Let

$$N'(\tilde{B}) := \{\nu' \in N(B) \mid \nu_o \le \nu' \text{ and } (\exists g \in P^{(1)})\ (\forall n \in \text{dom}(\sigma))\ (\forall i \in \text{dom}(\nu'^{\sigma(n)})\ \hat{g}(n)\nu'^{\sigma(n)}(i) = \nu' g\langle n,i\rangle\} .$$

Then $\nu \in N'(\tilde{B})$ and $\nu \le \nu'$ for all $\nu' \in N'(\tilde{B})$.

Proof

We show $\nu \in N'(\tilde{B})$. Define $g\langle n,i\rangle := \langle n,i+1\rangle$. Let $n \in \text{dom}(\sigma)$, $i \in \text{dom}(\nu^{\sigma(n)})$. Then there are numbers $i_1,\dots,i_{\sigma(n)}$ with $i = \langle i_1,\dots,i_{\sigma(n)}\rangle$. We obtain

$$\begin{aligned}
\hat{g}(n)\nu^{\sigma(n)}(i) &= \hat{g}(n)(\nu(i_1),\dots,\nu(i_{\sigma(n)})) && \text{(Def. 2.2.14)}\\
&= \hat{f}(n)(H\nu_\sigma(i_1),\dots,H\nu_\sigma(i_{\sigma(n)}))\\
&= H(n,\nu_\sigma(i_1),\dots,\nu_\sigma(i_{\sigma(n)})) && \text{(Def. 8)}\\
&= H\nu_\sigma\langle n,\langle i_1,\dots,i_{\sigma(n)}\rangle+1\rangle && \text{(Def. 11)}\\
&= \nu g\langle n,i\rangle .
\end{aligned}$$

This proves the second condition. Furthermore we have for all $i \in \text{dom}(\nu_o)$:

$$\nu_o(i) = H(i) = H\nu_\sigma\langle i,0\rangle = \nu\langle i,0\rangle ,$$

hence $\nu_o \le \nu$. This proves $\nu \in N'(\tilde{B})$.
Now assume $\nu' \in N'(\tilde{B})$. Assume $\nu_o \le \nu'$ via $f \in P^{(1)}$. By the recursion theorem (Corollary 2.5.7(4)) there is a function $q \in P^{(1)}$ $(q = \varphi_s)$ such that

$$q(n) = \begin{cases} f(i) & \text{if } n = \langle i,0\rangle \\ g\langle i,\langle q(j_1),\dots,q(j_k)\rangle\rangle & \text{if } n = \langle i,\langle j_1,\dots,j_k\rangle+1\rangle \text{ and } \sigma(i) = k \\ \text{div} & \text{otherwise} . \end{cases}$$

By induction on n we prove:

$$(\forall n)\quad (\forall m \le n)\quad (m \in \text{dom}(\nu) \Longrightarrow \nu(m) = \nu' q(m))$$

"n = 0": Assume $0 \in \text{dom}(\nu)$. $\nu(0) = H\nu_\sigma\langle 0,0\rangle = H(0) = \nu_o(0) = \nu' f(0) = \nu' q(0)$.

"n-1 $\Longrightarrow$ n": Assume $n \in \text{dom}(\nu)$. If $n = \langle i,0\rangle$ then $\nu(n) = H\nu_\sigma\langle i,0\rangle = H(i) = \nu_o(i) = \nu' f(i) = \nu' q(n)$. Otherwise there are $i,j_1,\dots,j_k$ with $n = \langle i,\langle j_1,\dots,j_k\rangle+1\rangle$, $\sigma(i) = k$, and $j_1,\dots,j_k \in \text{dom}(\nu_\sigma)$. Then

$$\begin{aligned}
\nu(n) &= H\nu_\sigma(n) \\
&= H(i,\nu_\sigma(j_1),\dots,\nu_\sigma(j_k)) && \text{(Def. 11)} \\
&= \hat{f}(i)(H\nu_\sigma(j_1),\dots,H\nu_\sigma(j_k)) && \text{(Def. 8)} \\
&= \hat{g}(i)(\nu(j_1),\dots,\nu(j_k)) \\
&= \hat{g}(i)(\nu'q(j_1),\dots,\nu'q(j_k)) && \text{(by induction since } j_1 < n,\dots,j_k < n) \\
&= \hat{g}(i)\nu'^k\langle q(j_1),\dots,q(j_k)\rangle \\
&= \nu' g\langle i,\langle q(j_1),\dots,q(j_k)\rangle\rangle \\
&= \nu' q(n) .
\end{aligned}$$

Therefore in any case $\nu(n) = \nu'q(n)$. This proves $\nu \le \nu'$.
Q.E.D.

Roughly speaking, if a set B is defined as the closure of a set B_o (numbered by ν_o) by operations $\hat{f}(n)$, then there is a distinguished numbering ν of B which makes the closure operations computable and which satisfies $\nu_o \le \nu$. For ν the "tree numbering" of B can be chosen. The following examples show that many natural numberings are minimal effective numberings of this kind.

16 EXAMPLES

(1) $A = \mathbb{N}$, $\nu_o(0) = 0 \in \mathbb{N}$, $\nu_o(i) = \mathrm{div}$ otherwise, $\hat{f}(0)(n) := n+1$, $\hat{f}(i) = \mathrm{div}$ otherwise. Then $\mathrm{range}(\nu) = \mathbb{N}$, $\tilde{B} = \tilde{A}$ and $\nu \equiv 1\!\!1_{\mathbb{N}}$ can be shown easily.

(2) $A = E(\mathbb{N})$, $\nu_o(0) = \emptyset$, $\nu_o(i) = \mathrm{div}$ otherwise, $\hat{f}(0)(X) := X \cup \{0\}$, $\hat{f}(1)(X) := X + 1$, $\hat{f}(i) = \mathrm{div}$ otherwise. Then $\mathrm{range}(\nu) = E(\mathbb{N})$, $\tilde{B} = \tilde{A}$ and $\nu \equiv e$ (see Def. 2.2.2).

(3) $A = W(\mathbb{N})$, $\nu_o(0) = \varepsilon$, $\nu_o(i) = \mathrm{div}$ otherwise, $\hat{f}(n)(w) := nw$. Then $\mathrm{range}(\nu) = W(\mathbb{N})$, $\tilde{B} = \tilde{A}$ and $\nu \equiv \nu^*$ (see Def. 2.2.2).

(4) $A = \{f : \mathbb{N}^k \dashrightarrow \mathbb{N} \mid k \in \mathbb{N}\}$, $\nu_o\langle 0,0\rangle := \tilde{0} \in A$, $\nu_o\langle 0,1\rangle := Z \in A$, $\nu_o\langle 0,2\rangle := S \in A$, $\nu_o\langle 1,\langle i,k\rangle\rangle := pr_i^{(k)}$ for $1 \le i \le k$, $\nu(n) = \mathrm{div}$ otherwise. (Then $\mathrm{range}(\nu_o) = Gr$, see Def. 1.3.1.) $\hat{f}\langle 0,m\rangle := Sub_m$, $\hat{f}\langle 1,0\rangle := Prk$, $\hat{f}\langle 1,1\rangle := \tilde{\mu}$ (see Def. 1.3.5). Then $\mathrm{range}(\nu) = P =$ the set of partial recursive functions. Define $\nu^{(1)} \in N(P^{(1)})$ by $\nu^{(1)}(i) = (\nu(i)$ if $\nu(i) \in P^{(1)}$, div otherwise$)$. Then $\nu^{(1)} \equiv \varphi$.

There are many other examples. They confirm that numberings defined via generating trees according to Definition 14 (and the numberings which are equivalent to those ones) play a distinguished role. We formulate this observation as a heuristic rule: Whenever a set is defined from a subset by generating operations the canonical numbering according to Definition 14 is appropriate. Later we shall also consider trees which contain operations with infinitely many arguments.

EXERCISES

1) Prove Theorem 1.

2) Let $S := \{a_1,\ldots,a_n\}$, $S_i := \{a_i\}$, $\nu_i : \mathbb{N} \longrightarrow S_i$ defined by $\nu_i(k) = a_i$ (for $k \in \mathbb{N}$) for $i = 1,\ldots,n$. Show that the numbering ν_o from Theorem 2(1) is equivalent to ν_S from Theorem 1.

3) Show that there are sets S, S_1, S_2, numberings $\nu_1 \in TN(S_1)$, $\nu_2 \in TN(S_2)$ and functions $f_1 : S \longrightarrow S_1$ and $f_2 : S \longrightarrow S_2$ such that for no total numbering ν of S, f_i becomes (ν,ν_i)-computable for $i = 1,2$ (cf. Theorem 3).

4) (a) Show that $N(S)$ has a minimum if S is finite.

   (b) Show that $TN(S)$ has infinitely many incomparable minimal elements if S is infinite.

   (c) Show that $N(S)$ has no minimum if S is infinite.

   (d) Let S, S_o be sets, $S_o \subseteq S$, and $\nu_o \in N(S_o)$. Show that $\{\nu \in N(S) \mid \nu_o \leq \nu\}$ has a minimum iff $S \setminus S_o$ is finite.

5) Let $\sigma : \mathbb{N} \dashrightarrow \mathbb{N}$ be a computable f.b. signature, let $T(\sigma)$ be the set of trees over σ. For numberings $\nu \in N(T(\sigma))$ define a predicate P by: $P(\nu) :\Longleftrightarrow$

   There are functions $f, g \in P^{(1)}$ such that

   $(\forall n \in dom(\nu))\ [f(n) = \langle 0,i\rangle$ if $\nu(n) = i \in \mathbb{N}$, $f(n) = \langle 1,i\rangle$
   if $\nu(n) = (i,t_1,\ldots,t_k)$ for some k and $t_1,\ldots,t_k \in T(\sigma)]$,

   $(\forall n \in dom(\nu))\ [\nu(n) = (i, \nu g\langle n,1\rangle,\ldots, g\langle n,k\rangle)$
   if $f(n) = \langle 1,i\rangle$ and $\sigma(i) = k]$.

   Prove for any numbering ν of $T(\sigma)$:

   (a) $\nu \leq \nu_\sigma$ if $P(\nu)$,

   (b) $\nu \equiv \nu_\sigma \iff P(\nu)$, if $dom(\nu)$ is recursively enumerable.

6) Let σ be a computable f.b. signature, let ν_σ be the standard numbering of $T(\sigma)$. Show that height: $T(\sigma) \longrightarrow \mathbb{N}$ is $(\nu_\sigma, 1_{\mathbb{N}})$-computable.

BIBLIOGRAPHICAL NOTES

The concepts presented in this chapter are based on Reiser and Weihrauch (1980).

2.8 Ordinal Trees and Computable Ordinals

In chapter 2.6 we have indicated how appropriate finite path trees can be used for specifying infinite computable production processes. We shall generalize Definition 2.7.5 of trees by also admitting nodes with infinite branching. Such nodes will serve as names for functions with infinitely many arguments such as "$\lim_{n\to\infty}$". For measuring the height of such trees the denumerable ordinal numbers, i.e. the numbers of Cantor's second number class, are needed. We shall define the effective numberings of the computable trees over the (unrestricted) signature σ. As the main application we derive a standard numbering of the computable ordinals. We prove that the computable ordinals can be characterized by total numberings of well-orders for which $\nu(i) \le \nu(j)$ is decidable. Our approach differs slightly from Kleene's original one.

Before we define ordinal trees and the numberings of the computable ordinals we give a very short introduction to well-orders and ordinal numbers. A well-order is a total order such that every non-empty subset has a least element.

1 DEFINITION (*well-order*)

A *well-order* is a pair $(M,<)$, where M is a set and $< \subseteq M \times M$ satisfies the following properties for all $a,b,c \in M$:

(1) not $a < a$,

(2) $(a < b$ and $b < c) \implies a < c$,

(3) $a < b$ or $b < a$ or $a = b$,

(4) for all $A \subseteq M$, $A \neq \emptyset$, there is some $a \in A$ with $(\forall b \in A)\ a \le b$.

The least element of M is called 0 (if $M \neq \emptyset$). As usual, $a \le b$ means $a = b$ or $a < b$, $a > b$ means $b < a$, and $a \ge b$ means $b \le a$. We shall use the same symbols $<, \le, \ldots$ for all well-orders if no confusion is possible. A subset $A \subseteq M$ is $\le$-bounded if $(\forall a \in A)\ a \le b$ for some $b \in M$. For a non-empty $\le$-bounded subset A the least element of the set $\{b \in M \mid (\forall a \in A)\ a \le b\}$ of upper bounds of A is called $\sup(A)$. If A is empty or unbounded then $\sup(A)$ does not exist. A subset $A \subseteq M$ with $(b < a \implies b \in A)$ for all $a \in A$ and $b \in M$ is called a *segment* of $(M,<)$.

The natural numbers $\mathbb{N}$ with natural order $<$ yield a well-order $(\mathbb{N},<)$. The set $\mathbb{N}^2$ can be well-ordered as follows: $(a_1,a_2) < (b_1,b_2) :\iff (a_1 < b_1$ or $(a_1 = b_1 \wedge a_2 < b_2))$.

By the axiom of choice, every set M can be well-ordered. The method of complete induction on $\mathbb{N}$ can be generalized to arbitrary well-orders.

2 THEOREM (*transfinite induction*)

Let $(M,<)$ be a well-order, let Q be a property of M (i.e. for all $m \in M$, $Q(m)$ is either true or false). Assume that Q is *progressive*; this means $[(\forall n < m)\ Q(n) \Longrightarrow Q(m)]$ holds for all $m \in M$. Then $Q(m)$ holds for all $m \in M$.

Proof

Assume the set $A = \{m \in M \mid Q(m) \text{ is false}\}$ is not empty. Then by Def. 1(4), A has a least element $a \in A$, i.e. $Q(n)$ holds for all $n < a$. Since Q is progressive, $Q(a)$ is true, hence $a \notin A$, a contradiction. Therefore A is empty.
Q.E.D.

The definition by induction on $\mathbb{N}$ (see Def. 1.2.10(3), Exercise 1.2.13) can be generalized to arbitrary well-orders.

3 THEOREM (*definition by transfinite induction*)

Let $(M,<)$ be a well-order, let Y be a set. Let $M_a := \{b \in M \mid b < a\}$ and $F_a := \{q : M_a \longrightarrow Y\}$ for all $a \in M$. Let

$$h : \cup\{F_a \mid a \in M\} \dashrightarrow Y$$

be a partial function. Then there is a unique function $f : M \dashrightarrow Y$ such that

$$f(a) = h(f_a) \quad \text{for all } a \in M,$$

where $f_a : M_a \dashrightarrow Y$ is the restriction of f to M_a. The domain of f is a segment of $(M,<)$.

Any value $f(a)$ is determined by the values $f(b)$ with $b < a$. If $a = 0$ then $M_a = \emptyset$, hence $h(f_a)$ is any constant $y_o \in Y$ or undefined.

Proof (outline)

The following property $Q(a)$ on M is progressive: There is a unique function $g^a : M \dashrightarrow Y$ such that

$$\text{dom}(g^a) \subseteq \{b \in M \mid b \leq a\}, \quad g^a(b) = h(g^a_b) \quad \text{for all } b \leq a,$$

where g^a_b is the restriction of g^a to M_b. Define f by $f(a) := g^a(a)$.
Q.E.D.

On the class of well-orders a pre-order can be defined as follows.

4 DEFINITION

Let $(M,<)$ and $(N,<)$ be well-orders. Then $(M,<) \leq (N,<)$ iff there is some function $f: M \longrightarrow N$ such that

(1) f is <-isotone, i.e. $m < m' \implies f(m) < f(m')$,

(2) range(f) is a segment of $(N,<)$.

Define *isomorphism* by

$$(M,<) \equiv (N,<) \quad \text{iff} \quad (M,<) \leq (N,<) \quad \text{and} \quad (N,<) \leq (M,<).$$

Finally define

$$(M,<) < (N,<) \quad \text{iff} \quad (M,<) \leq (N,<) \quad \text{and} \quad (M,<) \not\equiv (N,<).$$

Therefore, $(M,<) \leq (N,<)$ iff $(M,<)$ is isomorphic to a segment of $(N,<)$. It can be shown by transfinite induction on $(M,<)$ that f is determined uniquely by (1) and (2) if it exists (see the exercises). By the following fundamental theorem, for any two well-orders one is isomorphic to a segment of the other one.

5 THEOREM

Let $(M,<)$ and $(N,<)$ be well-orders. Then $(M,<) < (N,<)$ or $(N,<) < (M,<)$ or $(M,<) \equiv (N,<)$.

Proof (outline)

By Theorem 3 there is a unique function $f: M \dashrightarrow N$ such that

$$f(m) = \min\{n \in N \mid (\forall m' < m)\ f(m') < n\}$$

for all $m \in M$. If $m = 0$, $f(m) = \min N = 0$. If there is no $n \in N$ such that $(\forall m' < m)\ f(m') < n$, then f(m) is undefined. By Theorem 3, dom(f) is a segment of $(M,<)$. The following property Q(m) is progressive:

$$m \in \mathrm{dom}(f) \Rightarrow (\forall m' < m)\ f(m') < f(m) \text{ and } \{f(m') \mid m' < m\} \text{ is a segment.}$$

Therefore, f is <-isotone and range(f) is a segment. Assume that $\mathrm{dom}(f) \neq M$ and

$\mathrm{range}(f) \neq N$. Let $a := \min(M \setminus \mathrm{dom}(f))$ and $b := \min(N \setminus \mathrm{range}(f))$. It is easy to show that then $f(a) = b$ which contradicts the assumption. One obtains $(M,<) < (N,<)$ if $\mathrm{range}(f) \neq N$, $(N,<) < (M,<)$ if $\mathrm{dom}(f) \neq M$, and $(M,<) \equiv (N,<)$ if $\mathrm{dom}(f) = M$ and $\mathrm{range}(f) = N$.
Q.E.D.

The function f defined in the proof of Theorem 5 can be illustrated by one of the following diagrams.

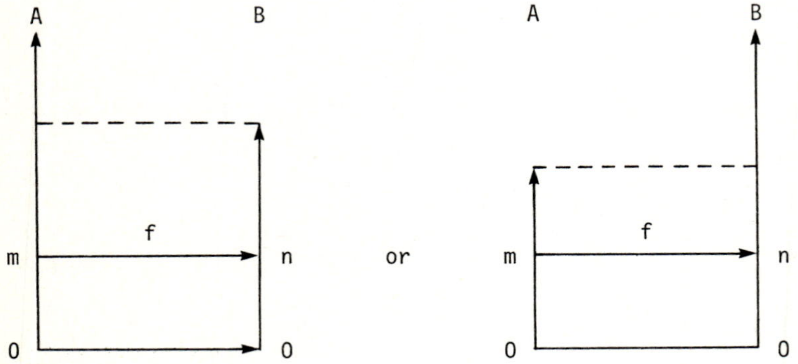

The class of isomorphic well-orders are called ordinal types. The class of ordinal types is well-ordered by: $T < T'$ iff $\alpha < \alpha'$ for some $\alpha \in T$ and $\alpha' \in T'$.

We are interested in well-orders $(M,<)$ with a denumerable carrier M. There is a well-order $(\mathbb{O},<)$ such that $(M,<) < (\mathbb{O},<)$ iff M is denumerable. It is determined uniquely up to isomorphism. As in the case of the natural numbers we shall choose one fixed representative $(\mathbb{O},<)$ and call the elements of $\mathbb{O}$ the *ordinals* (or *ordinal numbers*) of the *second number class*. The elements of $\mathbb{O}$ correspond to the denumerable order types as follows: $\alpha \in \mathbb{O}$ corresponds to the order type of $(\mathbb{O}(\alpha),<')$ where $\mathbb{O}(\alpha)$ is the segment $\{\beta \in \mathbb{O} \mid \beta < \alpha\}$ and $<' := < \cap (\mathbb{O}(\alpha) \times \mathbb{O}(\alpha))$.

6 DEFINITION (*second number class*)

Let $(\mathbb{O},<)$ be a fixed well-order which satisfies Axiom I and Axiom II :

Ax. I : $\mathbb{O}(\alpha)$ is denumerable for any $\alpha \in \mathbb{O}$.

Ax. II : For any denumerable $M \subseteq \mathbb{O}$ there is some $\alpha \in \mathbb{O}$ with $M \subseteq \mathbb{O}(\alpha)$

(where $\mathbb{O}(\alpha) := \{\beta \in \mathbb{O} \mid \beta < \alpha\}$). $\mathbb{O}$ is called the *second number class*.

Thus, the denumerable subsets $M \subseteq \mathbb{O}$ are exactly the <-bounded subsets. The existence of $(\mathbb{O},<)$ is guaranteed by set theory. $(\mathbb{O},<)$ is (up to isomorphism) the smallest well-order such that $(M,<) < (\mathbb{O},<)$ for all denumerable well-orders $(M,<)$ (see exercises), hence the well-orders $(\mathbb{O}(\alpha),<)$ with $\alpha \in \mathbb{O}$ represent exactly all the denumerable order types.

The least element of $\mathbb{O}$ is called 0. The function $S:\mathbb{O}\to\mathbb{O}$, defined by $S(\alpha)=\min\{\beta \mid \alpha<\beta\}$, is the *successor function* on $\mathbb{O}$. Notice that $\{\beta \mid \alpha<\beta\} \neq \emptyset$ by Axiom II hence $S(\alpha)$ exists for all $\alpha \in \mathbb{O}$. The elements of range(S) are called *successors*. The elements 0,S0,SS0,... can be identified with the natural numbers $\mathbb{N}=\{0,1,2,\ldots\}$. By Axiom II, $\mathbb{N}$ has a least upper bound which is called ω. The number ω is not a successor. A number which is not 0 and not a successor is called a *limit number*. ω is the smallest limit number of $\mathbb{O}$. We are now able to generalize Definition 2.7.5 to trees with ω-branching.

7 DEFINITION (*trees over a signature*)

(1) A *signature* is a function $\sigma:\mathbb{N} \dashrightarrow \mathbb{N}$.

(2) Define a mapping $\alpha \longmapsto T_\alpha(\sigma)$ for all $\alpha \in \mathbb{O}$ inductively as follows:

$$T_o(\sigma) = \mathbb{N},$$

$$T_\alpha(\sigma) = T_{<\alpha} \cup \{(i,t_1,\ldots,t_k) \mid \sigma(i)=k>0 \wedge \{t_1,\ldots,t_k\} \subset T_{<\alpha}\}$$
$$\cup \{(i,t_o,t_1,\ldots) \mid \sigma(i)=0 \wedge \{t_o,t_1,\ldots\} \subset T_{<\alpha}\}$$

where $T_{<\alpha} := \bigcup\{T_\beta(\sigma) \mid \beta<\alpha\}$ for all $\alpha>0$.

(3) Let $T(\sigma) := \bigcup\{T_\alpha(\sigma) \mid \alpha\in\mathbb{O}\}$ be the set of all σ-*trees*.

(4) The *height* of a tree $t \in T(\sigma)$ is defined by

$$\text{height}(t) := \min\{\alpha\in\mathbb{O} \mid t \in T_\alpha(\sigma)\}.$$

(5) Let $T'_\alpha(\sigma) := T_\alpha(\sigma) \setminus T_{<\alpha}$.

By Theorem 3 the mapping f with $f(\alpha)=T_\alpha(\sigma)$ exists uniquely. In this special case the function h maps ordinal sequences of sets of trees into sets of trees. The existence of the objects $(i,t_1,\ldots,t_k)$ and $(i,t_o,t_1,\ldots)$ is guaranteed by set theory. The generalized trees can also be presented graphically.

8 EXAMPLE

Let $\sigma(0)=1$, $\sigma(1)=0$, $\sigma(i)=\text{div}$ otherwise.

The finite trees of $T(\sigma)$ are $j,(0,j),(0,(0,j)),\ldots$ for $j\in\mathbb{N}$, which can be presented graphically by

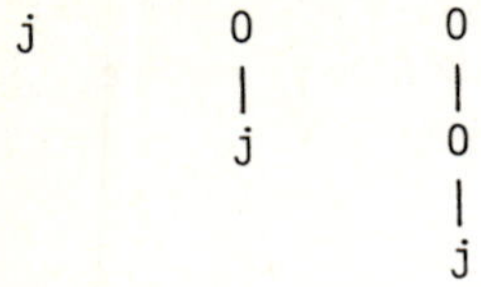

etc.

The tree $t_1 = (1,(0,4),(0,4),\ldots)$ is infinite, its height is 2.

t_1 :

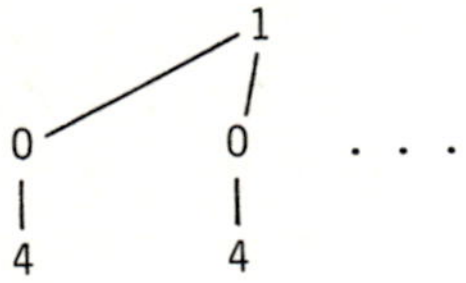

The tree $t_2 = (1,3,(0,3),(0,(0,3)),\ldots)$ is infinite, its height is ω, the least ordinal which is greater than the height of any subtree.

t_2 :

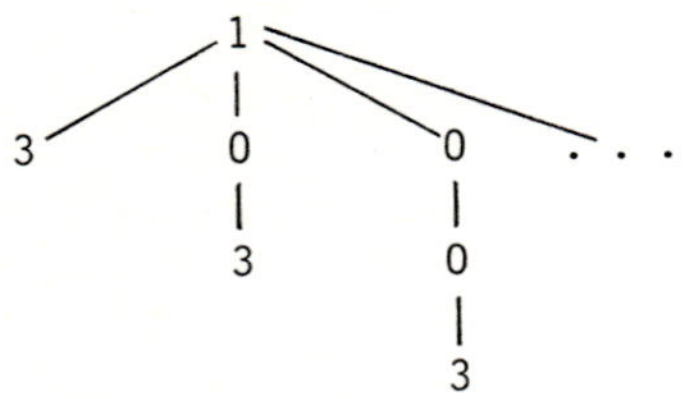

We can now generalize Definitions 2.7.7 and 2.7.8 and Lemma 2.7.9 to the case of arbitrary signatures.

9 <u>DEFINITION</u> (*algebra with signature* σ)

Let σ be a signature. An *algebra with signature* σ is a triple

$$\hat{A} = (A, \hat{f}, \nu_o)$$

where A is a set, ν_o is a numbering of a subset of A and $\hat{f}$ is a numbering of operations on A with

$$\mathrm{dom}(\hat{f}) = \mathrm{dom}(\sigma)\,,$$

$$\hat{f}(n) : A^{\sigma(n)} \dashrightarrow A \quad \text{if} \quad \sigma(n) > 0\,,$$

$$\hat{f}(n) : A^{\omega} \dashrightarrow A \quad \text{if} \quad \sigma(n) = 0\,,$$

for all $n \in \mathrm{dom}(\sigma)$.

10 DEFINITION (*evaluation mapping*)

Let σ be a signature, let $\hat{A} = (A, \hat{f}, \nu_o)$ be an algebra with signature σ. Define the *evaluation mapping* $H : T(\sigma) \dashrightarrow A$ of $\hat{A}$ inductively as follows:

$$H(t) = \begin{cases} \nu_o(t) & \text{if } t \in T_o(\sigma) \\ \hat{f}_i(H(t_1), \ldots, H(t_k)) & \text{if } t = (i, t_1, \ldots, t_k) \\ \hat{f}_i(H(t_o), H(t_1), \ldots) & \text{if } t = (i, t_o, t_1, \ldots) . \end{cases}$$

11 LEMMA

The evaluation mapping is welldefined.

Proof

Let $T'_\alpha := T_\alpha \setminus T_{<\alpha}$ be the set of σ-trees with height α. Then H is uniquely determined by the restrictions H_α of H to T'_α for all $\alpha \in \mathbb{O}$. The definition of H can be transformed into a definition of the functions H_α by transfinite induction:

$$H_\alpha = h((H_\beta)_{\beta<\alpha})$$

for some function h defined by the equation from Def. 10. Therefore H is welldefined by Theorem 3.

Q.E.D.

The range of the evaluation mapping H is the least subset $B \subseteq A$ such that $\text{range}(\nu_o) \subseteq B$ and B is closed under the operations $\hat{f}_i$ for $i \in \text{dom}(\sigma)$. Any tree $t \in T(\sigma)$ can serve as a program for generating the element $H(t) \in B$. For Definition 10 the fact is used that any tree can be uniquely decomposed into a root and subtrees of smaller height. Before we define the standard numbering of the computable trees in $T(\sigma)$ we give some non-trivial examples of algebras.

12 EXAMPLES

(1) Let $A := \mathbb{R}$ (= the set of real numbers), let ν_Q be a standard numbering of the rational numbers (see Def. 2.2.2), let $\text{dom}(\sigma) = \{0\}$, $\sigma(0) := 0$, let $\hat{f}(0) := h : \mathbb{R}^\omega \dashrightarrow \mathbb{R}$ be defined by

$$\text{dom}(h) = \{(x_i)_{i\in\mathbb{N}} \mid (x_i) \text{ Cauchy-sequence}\} ,$$

$$h((x_i)_i) := \lim_i x_i .$$

Then $(\mathbb{R}, \hat{f}, \nu_Q)$ is an algebra with signature σ. Since every real number is the limit of a Cauchy-sequence of rational numbers we have $\mathbb{R} = H(T_1(\sigma))$, hence $\mathbb{R} = \text{range}(H)$.

(2) The same as (1) but with the stronger condition

$$\mathrm{dom}(h) = \{(x_i)_{i\in\mathbb{N}} \mid (\forall i>j)\ |x_i - x_j| < 2^{-j}\}.$$

Again $\mathbb{R} = H(T_1(\sigma))$.

(3) Let $A := \mathbb{O}$, $\mathrm{dom}(\sigma) = \{0\}$, $\sigma(0) := 0$, $\hat{f}(0) := h_2 : \mathbb{O}^\omega \longrightarrow \mathbb{O}$ with $h_2(\alpha_o,\alpha_1,\ldots) := \sup\{S\alpha_o, S\alpha_1,\ldots\}$, let $\mathrm{dom}(\nu_o) = \{0\}$, $\nu_o(0) := 0 \in \mathbb{O}$.

(4) Let A,σ, and ν_o as in (3). Let $\hat{f}(0) := h_3 : \mathbb{O}^\omega \dashrightarrow \mathbb{O}$ with $\mathrm{dom}(h_3) = \{(\alpha_o,\alpha_1,\ldots) \mid \alpha_o \le \alpha_1 \le \alpha_2 \ldots\}$ and $h_3(\alpha_o,\alpha_1,\ldots) := \sup\{S\alpha_o, S\alpha_1,\ldots\}$.

(5) Let $A = \mathbb{O}$, $\mathrm{dom}(\sigma) := \{0,1\}$, $\sigma(0) := 0$, $\sigma(1) := 1$, $\hat{f}(0) := h_4 : \mathbb{O}^\omega \dashrightarrow \mathbb{O}$ with $\mathrm{dom}(h_4) := \{(\alpha_o,\alpha_1,\ldots) \mid \alpha_o < \alpha_1 < \ldots\}$, $h_4(\alpha_o,\alpha_1,\ldots) := \sup\{\alpha_o,\alpha_1,\ldots\}$, and let $\hat{f}(1) := S$. Let $\mathrm{dom}(\nu_o) = \{0\}$, $\nu_o(0) := 0 \in \mathbb{O}$.

In each of the cases (3), (4), and (5), $\mathrm{range}(H) = \mathbb{O}$ for the corresponding evaluation function H.

If the signature σ is not finitely branched (i.e. $\sigma(i) = 0$ for some i) then the set of trees $T(\sigma)$ is not denumerable. In this case $T(\sigma)$ cannot be numbered. The best one can do is to define a *numbering of the computable trees* of $T(\sigma)$.

13 DEFINITION (*standard numbering of computable trees*)

Let σ be a signature. Define a mapping $N : T(\sigma) \longrightarrow 2^{\mathbb{N}}$ by the following conditions:

$$N(t) = \begin{cases} \{\langle i,0\rangle\} & \text{if } t = i \in \mathbb{N}, \\ \{\langle i,\langle j_1,\ldots,j_k\rangle+1\rangle \mid j_1 \in N(t_1),\ldots,j_k \in N(t_k)\} & \text{if } t = (i,t_1,\ldots,t_k), \\ \{\langle i,n+1\rangle \mid \varphi_n \in R^{(1)} \text{ and } (\forall j)\ \varphi_n(j) \in N(t_j)\} & \text{if } t = (i,t_o,t_1,\ldots). \end{cases}$$

Define a numbering ν_σ by $\mathrm{range}(\nu_\sigma) = \mathrm{dom}(N)$, $\mathrm{dom}(\nu_\sigma) = \bigcup\{N(t) \mid t \in T(\sigma)\}$, $\nu_o(i) = t$ iff $i \in N(t)$. $\mathrm{range}(\nu_\sigma)$ is the set of *computable trees* over σ.

It has to be shown that ν_σ is welldefined. Notice that we obtain Definition 2.7.11 if σ is finitely branched.

14 LEMMA

ν_σ is welldefined.

Proof

By Theorem 3, N is welldefined. By an easy transfinite induction one shows

$$(\forall \alpha \in \mathbb{O})\ (\forall t,t' \in T_\alpha(\sigma))\ \ (N(t) \cap N(t') = \emptyset \ \text{ if } \ t \neq t')\,.$$

Therefore ν_σ is welldefined.

Q.E.D.

We formulate Definition 2.7.14 for the more general case.

15 DEFINITION

Let $\hat{A} = (A, \hat{f}, \nu_o)$ be an algebra with signature σ. Let $H : T(\sigma) \dashrightarrow A$ be the evaluation mapping of $\hat{A}$. Let $T' \subseteq T(\sigma)$. Then the numbering ν defined by

$$\nu(i) = \begin{cases} H\nu_\sigma(i) & \text{if } \ \nu_\sigma(i) \in T' \\ \text{div} & \text{otherwise} \end{cases}$$

is called *the numbering canonical w.r.t.* $\hat{A}$ *and* T'.

16 EXAMPLES

(1) Let $\hat{A}$ be the algebra from Example 12(2). The numbering canonical w.r.t. $\hat{A}$ and $T_1(\sigma)$ is called the (or a) *standard numbering* of the *computable real numbers*.

(2) Let $\hat{A}$ be the algebra from Example 12(5). The numbering canonical w.r.t. $\hat{A}$ and $T(\sigma)$ is called a numbering of the *computable ordinals which is effective in Kleene's sense*.

For justifying Definition 15 a generalization of Theorem 2.7.15 can be proved (see the exercises and Theorem 19). There doesn't seem to be an essential reason to make an explicit distinction between limit numbers and successor numbers as in Kleene's numbering. The numbering of ordinals canonical w.r.t. the algebra $\hat{A}$ of Example 12(3) seems to be (up to equivalence) the most natural one.

17 DEFINITION (*standard numbering of the computable ordinals*)

Define an algebra $\hat{A} = (\mathbb{O}, \hat{f}, \nu_o)$ with signature σ by

$$\text{dom}(\sigma) := \{0\}\,, \quad \sigma(0) := 0\,,$$

$$\hat{f}(0) : \mathbb{O}^\omega \longrightarrow \mathbb{O}\,,$$

$$\hat{f}(0)(\alpha_o, \alpha_1, \ldots) := \text{l.u.b.}\{\alpha_o, \alpha_1, \ldots\} := \sup\{S\alpha_o, S\alpha_1, \ldots\}\,,$$

$\mathrm{dom}(\nu_o) := \{0\}$, $\nu_o(0) := 0$.

Then the *standard numbering of the computable ordinals* is the numbering $\hat{\nu}$ which is canonical w.r.t. $\hat{A}$ and $T(\sigma)$.

The computable ordinals are a segment of $(\mathbb{O}, <)$. The following lemma also gives a more direct characterization of $\hat{\nu}$.

18 LEMMA

(1) $\hat{\nu}$ is defined uniquely by the recursion equations

$$\hat{\nu}^{-1}\{0\} = \{<0,0>\} = \{0\},$$

$$\hat{\nu}^{-1}\{\alpha\} = \{<0,n+1> \mid \varphi_n \in R^{(1)}, \ \alpha = \mathrm{l.u.b.}\{\hat{\nu}\varphi_n(i) \mid i \in \mathbb{N}\}\} \quad \text{if} \quad \alpha > 0 .$$

(2) The computable ordinals are a segment of $(\mathbb{O}, <)$.

Proof

(1) By Theorem 3, there is a unique function $f : \mathbb{O} \longrightarrow 2^{\mathbb{N}}$ satisfying the equations. Definitions 10, 13, and 17 imply that $\alpha \longmapsto \hat{\nu}^{-1}\{\alpha\}$ satisfies the equations.

(2) It suffices to show that the following property $Q(\alpha)$ is progressive:

$$\alpha \in \mathrm{range}(\hat{\nu}) \implies (\forall \beta < \alpha) \ \beta \in \mathrm{range}(\hat{\nu}) .$$

Suppose $Q(\alpha')$ holds for all $\alpha' < \alpha$. If $\alpha = 0$ then $Q(\alpha)$ holds trivially. Suppose $\alpha > 0$ and $\alpha \in \mathrm{range}(\hat{\nu})$. Then $\alpha = \hat{\nu}<0,n+1>$ for some $n \in \mathbb{N}$. By (1) we have

$$\alpha = \hat{\nu}<0,n+1> = \mathrm{l.u.b.}\{\hat{\nu}\varphi_n(0), \hat{\nu}\varphi_n(1), \ldots\} .$$

Suppose $\beta < \alpha$. Then $\beta = \hat{\nu}\varphi_n(k)$ for some k or $\beta < \hat{\nu}\varphi_n(k)$ for some k. In the first case $\beta \in \mathrm{range}(\hat{\nu})$, in the second case $\beta \in \mathrm{range}(\hat{\nu})$ since $\hat{\nu}\varphi_n(k) < \alpha$ and $Q(\hat{\nu}\varphi_n(k))$.
Q.E.D.

Of course, the computable ordinals are a proper segment of $(\mathbb{O}, <)$ by Axiom II. If γ is the least ordinal which is not computable then $\mathbb{O}(\gamma)$ is the set of computable ordinals. The standard numbering $\hat{\nu}$ is maximal in the class of "effective" numberings of ordinals. We prove a theorem which corresponds to Theorem 2.7.15.

19 **THEOREM** (*universality of the standard numbering*)

Let $\tilde{N}$ be the set of all numberings ν of subsets of $\mathbb{O}$ such that (1) and (2) hold:

(1) $\{0\}$ is ν-decidable.

(2) There is a function $q \in R^{(1)}$ such that for all $k \in \mathrm{dom}(\nu)$ with $\nu(k) \neq 0$ $\varphi_{q(k)}(i) \in \mathrm{dom}(\nu)$ for all i and $\nu(k) = \mathrm{l.u.b.}\{\nu\varphi_{q(k)}(0), \nu\varphi_{q(k)}(1), \ldots\}$.

Then $\hat{\nu} \in \tilde{N}$ and $(\forall \nu \in \tilde{N})\ \nu \leq \hat{\nu}$.

Proof

Since $\hat{\nu}^{-1}\{0\} = 0$, $\{0\}$ is $\hat{\nu}$-decidable. Define q such that $q\langle 0,n+1\rangle = n$. By Lemma 18, q satisfies (2). Therefore $\hat{\nu} \in \tilde{N}$. Assume $\nu \in \tilde{N}$. Then there is a function $s \in P^{(1)}$ with $(\forall k \in \mathrm{dom}(\nu))\ (k \in \mathrm{dom}(s) \wedge (s(k) = 0 \iff \nu(k) = 0))$, and there is a function q satisfying (2). There is a function $r \in R^{(1)}$ with $\varphi_{r\langle i,k\rangle} = \varphi_i \varphi_{q(k)}$. By the recursion theorem (Corollary 2.5.7(4)) there is a number $m \in \mathbb{N}$ with

$$\varphi_m(k) = \begin{cases} 0 & \text{if } s(k) = 0 \\ \langle 0, r\langle m,k\rangle + 1\rangle & \text{if } s(k) \text{ exists and } s(k) \neq 0 \\ \text{div} & \text{otherwise.} \end{cases}$$

We show that the following property Q is progressive, where $Q(\alpha)$ holds iff

$$(\forall k \in \mathbb{N})(\nu(k) = \alpha \implies \nu(k) = \hat{\nu}\varphi_m(k)) .$$

If $\alpha = 0$ then $s(k) = 0$ and $\hat{\nu}\varphi_m(k) = \hat{\nu}(0) = 0$. Suppose $\alpha > 0$ and $\nu(k) = \alpha$. Then

$$\begin{aligned} \nu(k) &= \mathrm{l.u.b.}\{\nu\varphi_{q(k)}(0), \ldots\} \\ &= \mathrm{l.u.b.}\{\hat{\nu}\varphi_m\varphi_{q(k)}(0), \ldots\} \qquad (\text{since } Q(\alpha') \text{ for } \alpha' < \alpha) \\ &= \mathrm{l.u.b.}\{\hat{\nu}\varphi_{r\langle m,k\rangle}(0), \ldots\} \\ &= \hat{\nu}\langle 0, r\langle m,k\rangle + 1\rangle \\ &= \hat{\nu}\varphi_m(k) . \end{aligned}$$

Therefore $\nu \leq \hat{\nu}$ via φ_m.
Q.E.D.

As in the proof of Theorem 19, the recursion theorem is the main tool for proving that certain functions on $\mathbb{O}$ are computable. We give some further examples.

20 **LEMMA**

The maximum function $\max : \mathbb{O} \times \mathbb{O} \longrightarrow \mathbb{O}$ is $(\hat{\nu}^2, \hat{\nu})$-computable.

Proof

Let $q \in R^{(1)}$ be such that $q<0,m+1> = m$. There is a function $s \in R^{(3)}$ with $\varphi_{s(a,j,k)}(i) = \varphi_a<\varphi_{q(j)}(i),\varphi_{q(k)}(i)>$. By the recursion theorem there is a number $b \in \mathbb{N}$ with

$$\varphi_b<j,k> = \begin{cases} j & \text{if } k=0 \\ k & \text{if } k \neq 0 \text{ and } j=0 \\ <0,s(b,j,k)+1> & \text{otherwise.} \end{cases}$$

The following property Q is progressive, where $Q(\alpha)$ is defined by

$$(\forall j,k)[(\hat{\nu}(j) \le \alpha \wedge \hat{\nu}(k) \le \alpha) \Rightarrow \hat{\nu}\varphi_b<j,k> = \max(\hat{\nu}(j),\hat{\nu}(k))].$$

Suppose $j,k \in \mathbb{N}$, $\hat{\nu}(j) \le \alpha$ and $\hat{\nu}(k) \le \alpha$. If $j=0$ or $k=0$ then the desired property holds. Suppose $j \neq 0$ and $k \neq 0$ and $Q(\alpha')$ for all $\alpha' < \alpha$. Then the definitions and assumptions yield $\hat{\nu}\varphi_b<j,k> = \max(\hat{\nu}(j),\hat{\nu}(k))$. Therefore Q is progressive and max is computed w.r.t. $\hat{\nu}$ via φ_b.

Q.E.D.

Addition is another $(\hat{\nu}^2,\hat{\nu})$-computable function.

21 DEFINITION

Addition on $\mathbb{O}$ is defined inductively by the following recursion equation

$$\alpha + 0 = \alpha$$

$$\alpha + \beta = \text{l.u.b.}\{\alpha + \gamma \mid \gamma < \beta\}$$

for all $\alpha,\beta \in \mathbb{O}$.

Since $\alpha + \beta$ is defined by means of $\alpha + \gamma$ for all $\gamma < \beta$, by Theorem 3 addition is welldefined. Addition is isotone in each argument and l.u.b.-continuous in the second argument.

22 LEMMA

(1) $\alpha \le \alpha' \Rightarrow \alpha + \beta \le \alpha' + \beta$.

(2) $\beta < \beta' \Rightarrow \alpha + \beta < \alpha + \beta'$.

(3) $\alpha + \text{l.u.b.}\{\beta_i \mid i \in I\} = \text{l.u.b.}\{\alpha + \beta_i \mid i \in I\}$ where $(\beta_i)_{i \in I}$ is a denumerable family of ordinals from $\mathbb{O}$.

Proof

(1) Let $\alpha \le \alpha'$. We apply transfinite induction. Define $Q(\beta) :\Longleftrightarrow \alpha + \beta \le \alpha' + \beta$. We have to show that Q is progressive. Q(0) is true. Assume $(\forall \gamma < \beta)\, Q(\gamma)$. Then $\alpha + \beta = \text{l.u.b.}\{\alpha + \gamma \mid \gamma < \beta\} \le \text{l.u.b.}\{\alpha' + \gamma \mid \gamma < \beta\} = \alpha' + \beta$, hence $Q(\beta)$ is true.

(2) Assume $\beta < \beta'$. Then $\alpha + \beta \in \{\alpha + \gamma \mid \gamma < \beta'\}$, hence $\alpha + \beta < \alpha + \beta'$.

(3) For any j, $\beta_j < \text{l.u.b.}\{\beta_i\}$, hence $\alpha + \beta_j < \alpha + \text{l.u.b.}\{\beta_i\}$ by (2). We obtain $\text{l.u.b.}\{\alpha + \beta_i\} \le \alpha + \text{l.u.b.}\{\beta_i\}$. We have $\alpha + \text{l.u.b.}\{\beta_i\} = \text{l.u.b.}\{\alpha + \gamma \mid \gamma < \text{l.u.b.}\{\beta_i\}\}$. Since $\gamma < \text{l.u.b.}\{\beta_i\} \Longleftrightarrow (\exists j)\ \gamma \le \beta_j$, we obtain
$\alpha + \text{l.u.b.}\{\beta_i\} = \text{l.u.b.}\{\alpha + \gamma \mid (\exists j)\ \gamma \le \beta_j\} \le \text{l.u.b.}\{\alpha + \beta_i\}$.

Q.E.D.

By the next theorem addition on the computable ordinals is computable w.r.t. $\hat{\nu}$.

23 THEOREM

8 Addition on the computable ordinals is $(\hat{\nu}^2,\hat{\nu})$-computable.

Proof

Let $q \in R^{(1)}$ such that $q\langle 0,m+1\rangle = m$. There is a function $s \in R^{(3)}$ with $\varphi_{s(a,j,k)}(i) = \varphi_a\langle j,\varphi_{q(k)}(i)\rangle$ for all $a,j,k \in \mathbb{N}$. By the recursion theorem there is a number $b \in \mathbb{N}$ with

$$\varphi_b\langle j,k\rangle = \begin{cases} j & \text{if } k = 0 \\ \langle 0,s(b,j,k)+1\rangle & \text{otherwise}. \end{cases}$$

Let $\alpha = \hat{\nu}(j)$. By transfinite induction on β we prove $\hat{\nu}\varphi_b\langle j,k\rangle = \hat{\nu}(j) + \hat{\nu}(k)$ for all k with $\hat{\nu}(k) = \beta$. If $\beta = 0$ and $\hat{\nu}(k) = \beta$ then $k = 0$ and $\hat{\nu}\varphi_b\langle j,0\rangle = \hat{\nu}(j) + \hat{\nu}(0)$. Assume that the above equation holds for all $\gamma < \beta$, assume $\hat{\nu}(k) = \beta$. Then

$$\begin{aligned} \hat{\nu}(j) + \hat{\nu}(k) &= \hat{\nu}(j) + \text{l.u.b.}\{\hat{\nu}\varphi_{q(k)}(i) \mid i \in \mathbb{N}\} \\ &= \text{l.u.b.}\{\hat{\nu}(j) + \hat{\nu}\varphi_{q(k)}(i) \mid i \in \mathbb{N}\} \qquad \text{(by Lemma 22(3))} \\ &= \text{l.u.b.}\{\hat{\nu}\varphi_b\langle j,\varphi_{q(k)}(i)\rangle \mid i \in \mathbb{N}\} \qquad \text{(by induction)} \\ &= \text{l.u.b.}\{\hat{\nu}\varphi_{s(b,j,k)}(i) \mid i \in \mathbb{N}\} \\ &= \hat{\nu}(\langle 0,s(b,j,k)+1\rangle) \\ &= \hat{\nu}\varphi_b\langle j,k\rangle . \end{aligned}$$

Therefore, addition is $(\hat{\nu}^2,\hat{\nu})$-computable via φ_b.
Q.E.D.

There is another way for defining computability on certain segments of $\mathbb{O}$.

24 DEFINITION *(recursive ordinals)*

An ordinal $\alpha \in \mathbb{O}$ is *recursive* iff $\alpha = 0$ or there is a total numbering ν of $\mathbb{O}(\alpha) = \{\beta \mid \beta < \alpha\}$ such that $\{\langle i,j\rangle \mid \nu(i) \le \nu(j)\}$ is decidable.

We shall prove now that an ordinal is computable (i.e. $\in \mathrm{range}(\hat{\nu})$) iff it is recursive.

25 THEOREM

Every recursive ordinal is computable.

Proof

Let $\alpha > 0$ and let ν be a numbering of $\mathbb{O}(\alpha)$ such that $\{\langle i,j\rangle \mid \nu(i) \le \nu(j)\}$ is decidable. Then $A := \nu^{-1}\{0\}$ is decidable and there is a function $r \in R^{(1)}$ such that $\varphi_{r(z)} \in R^{(1)}$ and $\{i \mid \nu(i) < \nu(z)\} = \mathrm{range}(\varphi_{r(z)})$ for all $z \notin A$. There is a function $s \in R^{(2)}$ with $\varphi_{s(m,z)}(i) = \varphi_m \varphi_{r(z)}(i)$. By the recursion theorem there is a number $a \in \mathbb{N}$ with

$$\varphi_a(z) = \begin{cases} 0 & \text{if } z \in A \\ \langle 0, s(a,z)+1\rangle & \text{otherwise.} \end{cases}$$

Since $s \in R^{(2)}$, $\varphi_a(z)$ exists for all z, hence φ_a is total recursive. We prove $\nu \le \hat{\nu}$ via φ_a by showing that the property Q defined by

$$(\forall z)[(\beta < \alpha \wedge \nu(z) = \beta) \Rightarrow \nu(z) = \hat{\nu}\varphi_a(z)]$$

is progressive. Obviously, Q(0) is true. Assume $0 < \beta < \alpha$ and $\nu(z) = \beta$, assume $Q(\beta')$ for all $\beta' < \beta$. Then

$$\begin{aligned} \hat{\nu}\varphi_a(z) &= \hat{\nu}\langle 0, s(a,z)+1\rangle \\ &= \mathrm{l.u.b.}\{\hat{\nu}\varphi_{s(a,z)}(i) \mid i \in \mathbb{N}\} \\ &= \mathrm{l.u.b.}\{\hat{\nu}\varphi_a\varphi_{r(z)}(i) \mid i \in \mathbb{N}\} \\ &= \mathrm{l.u.b.}\{\nu\varphi_{r(z)}(i) \mid i \in \mathbb{N}\} \qquad \text{(by induction)} \\ &= \nu(z)\,. \end{aligned}$$

This proves $\nu \le \hat{\nu}$ via φ_a. We obtain

$$\begin{aligned} \hat{\nu}\langle 0, a+1\rangle &= \mathrm{l.u.b.}\{\hat{\nu}\varphi_a(i) \mid i \in \mathbb{N}\} \\ &= \mathrm{l.u.b.}(\mathbb{O}(\alpha)) \\ &= \alpha\,, \end{aligned}$$

hence α is computable.
Q.E.D.

Notice that we have shown $\nu \le \hat{\nu}$.

The proof of the converse of Theorem 25 is divided into parts. The essential idea is to restrict the numbering $\hat{\nu}$ to those numbers which have the *subname property*.

26 DEFINITION (*subname property*)

(1) Let $SN : \mathrm{dom}(\hat{\nu}) \longrightarrow 2^{\mathrm{dom}(\hat{\nu})}$ be defined as follows:

$$SN(<0,0>) = \{<0,0>\}$$

$$SN(<0,n+1>) = \{<0,n+1>\} \cup \bigcup \{SN(\varphi_n(i)) \mid i \in \mathbb{N}\}$$

for all $<0,n+1> \in \mathrm{dom}(\hat{\nu})$.

$$i \le_s j :\Longleftrightarrow i \in SN(j) \Longleftrightarrow: (i \text{ is a } \textit{subname} \text{ of } j).$$

(2) Let $SP : \mathbb{O} \dashrightarrow 2^{\mathbb{N}}$ be defined as follows:

$$SP(0) = \{<0,0>\}$$

$$SP(\alpha) = \{<0,n+1> \mid \hat{\nu}<0,n+1> = \alpha \text{ and } (\forall i)\ [\varphi_n(i) \in \bigcup \{SP(\beta) \mid \beta < \alpha\} \text{ and } \varphi_n(i) \le_s \varphi_n(i+1)]\}$$

$$SP := \bigcup \{SP(\alpha) \mid \alpha \in \mathbb{O}\}.$$

$i \in SP :\Longleftrightarrow i$ has the *subname property*.

(3) Let $\tilde{\nu}$ be a numbering of ordinals such that

$$\mathrm{dom}(\tilde{\nu}) = SP,$$

$$\tilde{\nu}(k) = \hat{\nu}(k) \quad \text{for all } k \in SP.$$

By Theorem 3, SN and SP are welldefined. Notice that the relation $\le_s$ is a partial order on the set $\mathrm{dom}(\hat{\nu})$. Obviously, SP is a subset of $\mathrm{dom}(\hat{\nu})$, hence $\tilde{\nu}$ is a restriction of $\hat{\nu}$. We shall show that $\mathrm{range}(\tilde{\nu}) = \mathrm{range}(\hat{\nu})$, that A_k is r.e., $\tilde{\nu}$ is injective on A_k, and $\hat{\nu}(A_k)$ is a segment for all $k \in \mathrm{dom}(\tilde{\nu})$, where $A_k = \{i \in SP \mid i \le_s k\}$.

27 LEMMA

For $k \in \mathrm{dom}(\tilde{\nu})$ define $A_k := \{i \in SP \mid i \le_s k\}$. Then:

(1) $\tilde{\nu}(A_k)$ is a segment for all $k \in \mathrm{dom}(\tilde{\nu})$.

(2) $\tilde{\nu}$ is injective on A_k for all $k \in \mathrm{dom}(\tilde{\nu})$.

(3) There is some $p \in R^{(1)}$ such that

$$W_{p(k)} = B_k := \{\langle i,j\rangle \mid i \in A_k \wedge j \in A_k \wedge i \le_s j\}$$

for all $k \in \mathrm{dom}(\tilde{\nu})$.

Proof

From Definition 26(1) an easy induction yields $\hat{\nu}(i) < \hat{\nu}(j)$ if $i \le_s j$ and $i \neq j$.

(1) We show that the following property Q on $\mathbb{O}$ is progressive: $Q(\alpha)$ holds iff

$$(\forall k)[\tilde{\nu}(k) = \alpha \Rightarrow \tilde{\nu}(A_k) \text{ is a segment}].$$

If $\alpha = 0$ then $k = 0$, $A_k = \{0\}$, and $\tilde{\nu}(A_k) = \{0\}$ is a segment. Assume $\alpha > 0$ and $Q(\alpha')$ for all $\alpha' < \alpha$, assume $\tilde{\nu}\langle 0,n+1\rangle = \alpha$ and $\beta < \alpha$. Since $\tilde{\nu}\langle 0,n+1\rangle = \text{l.u.b.}\ \{\tilde{\nu}\varphi_n(i) \mid i \in \mathbb{N}\}$, $\beta \le \tilde{\nu}\varphi_n(j) =: \alpha'$ for some j. Since $Q(\alpha')$, $\tilde{\nu}A_{\varphi_n(j)}$ is a segment, hence $\beta = \tilde{\nu}(i)$ for some $i \in SP$ with $i \le_s \varphi_n(j)$. We obtain $i \le_s \varphi_n(j) <_s \langle 0,n+1\rangle$, hence $\beta \in \tilde{\nu}A_{\langle 0,n+1\rangle}$.

(2) The following property Q is progressive, where $Q(\alpha)$ holds iff for all i,j,k:

$$[\tilde{\nu}(k) = \alpha \wedge i \in A_k \wedge j \in A_k] \Rightarrow (i \le_s j \text{ or } j \le_s i)$$

(easy proof). Assume $k \in \mathrm{dom}(\tilde{\nu})$ and $i,j \in A_k$ with $\tilde{\nu}(i) = \tilde{\nu}(j)$. As we have shown $i \le_s j$ or $j \le_s i$. $i <_s j$ would imply $\tilde{\nu}(i) < \tilde{\nu}(j)$, similarly for $j <_s i$. Therefore we obtain $i = j$.

(3) By the recursion theorem there is a function $p \in R^{(1)}$ (where $p := \varphi_d t, \varphi_d = \mathbb{1}_{\mathbb{N}}$ and t from Corollary 2.5.7(3))

$$\varphi_{p(k)}(x) = \begin{cases} 0 & \text{if } \langle k,k\rangle = x \text{ or: } k = \langle 0,n+1\rangle \text{ and } [(\exists i)\ x \in W_{p\varphi_n(i)} \text{ or} \\ & \quad (\exists i,y)\ (x = \langle y,k\rangle \text{ and } \langle y,y\rangle \in W_{p\varphi_n(i)})] \\ \text{div} & \text{otherwise.} \end{cases}$$

An induction on $\alpha \in \mathbb{O}$ shows that p has the desired property. Notice that

$$B_k = \bigcup \{B_j \mid j <_s k\} \cup \{\langle j,k\rangle \mid j <_s k\} \cup \{\langle k,k\rangle\} \qquad \text{for } k \in \mathrm{dom}(\tilde{\nu}).$$

Q.E.D.

By Lemma 23, addition on range($\hat{\nu}$) is $\hat{\nu}$-computable.

28 LEMMA

There is a function $\varphi_b \in P^{(1)}$ such that for all $j,k \in \mathrm{dom}(\tilde{\nu})$:

(1) $\varphi_b\langle j,k\rangle \in \mathrm{dom}(\tilde{\nu})$

(2) $\tilde{\nu}\varphi_b\langle j,k\rangle = \tilde{\nu}(j) + \tilde{\nu}(k)$

(3) $j \le_s \varphi_b\langle j,k\rangle$.

Proof

For φ_b choose the function defined in the proof of Lemma 23. Since $\tilde{\nu}$ is a restriction of $\hat{\nu}$, (2) follows from (1) and Lemma 23. We show that the following property Q is progressive where $Q(\beta)$ holds iff for all $k,k' \in \mathbb{N}$:

$$(\tilde{\nu}(k) = \beta \wedge k' \leq_s k) \implies (\varphi_b\langle j,k'\rangle \leq_s \varphi_b\langle j,k\rangle \in \mathrm{dom}(\tilde{\nu}) \text{ for all } j \in \mathrm{dom}(\tilde{\nu})).$$

If $\beta = 0$, then $k = 0$, and $k' \leq_s k$ implies $k' = 0$. Hence $\varphi_b\langle j,k\rangle = j \in \mathrm{dom}(\tilde{\nu})$ and $\varphi_b(j,k') \leq_s \varphi_b\langle j,k\rangle$. Assume $\beta > 0$, $\tilde{\nu}(k) = \beta$, and $Q(\beta')$ for all $\beta' < \beta$. Since $k \in \mathrm{dom}(\tilde{\nu})$, $\varphi_{q(k)}(i) \leq_s \varphi_{q(k)}(i+1)$ and $\tilde{\nu}\varphi_{q(k)}(i) < \beta$ for all i. Since $Q(\beta')$ for all $\beta' < \beta$, we obtain $\varphi_b\langle j,\varphi_{q(k)}(i)\rangle \leq_s \varphi_b\langle j,\varphi_{q(k)}(i+1)\rangle$ and $\varphi_b\langle j,\varphi_{q(k)}(i)\rangle \in \mathrm{dom}(\tilde{\nu})$ for all i. From the definition of s (Proof of Theorem 23) and Definition 26 we obtain $\varphi_b\langle j,k\rangle = \langle 0,s(b,j,k)+1\rangle \in \mathrm{dom}(\tilde{\nu})$. If $k' =_s k$ nothing else is to show. Assume $k' <_s k$. Then $k' \leq_s \varphi_{q(k)}(i) <_s k$ for some i. By induction, $\varphi_b\langle j,k'\rangle \leq_s \varphi_b\langle j,\varphi_{q(k)}(i)\rangle = \varphi_{s(b,j,k)}(i) <_s \langle 0,s(b,j,k)+1\rangle = \varphi_b\langle j,k\rangle$. Therefore, $Q(\beta)$ is progressive. This proves (1) and (3).
Q.E.D.

Especially, addition on $\mathrm{range}(\tilde{\nu})$ is $\tilde{\nu}$-computable. We are now able to prove that for any $\alpha \in \mathrm{range}(\hat{\nu})$ there is some $\beta \in \mathrm{range}(\tilde{\nu})$ with $\alpha \leq \beta$.

29 LEMMA

8 There is a function $\varphi_a \in P^{(1)}$ such that $\hat{\nu}(m) \leq \tilde{\nu}\varphi_a(m)$ for all $m \in \mathrm{dom}(\hat{\nu})$.

Proof

Let $q \in R^{(1)}$ with $q\langle 0,n+1\rangle = n$, let φ_b be the function from Lemma 28. By the recursion theorem, Corollary 2.5.7(3), there is a function $t \in R^{(1)}$ with

$$\varphi_{t\langle k,n\rangle}(0) = \varphi_k\varphi_{q(n)}(0),$$

$$\varphi_{t\langle k,n\rangle}(i+1) = \varphi_b\langle \varphi_{t\langle k,n\rangle}(i), \varphi_k\varphi_{q(n)}(i+1)\rangle.$$

If $\varphi_k\varphi_{q(n)}(i) \in \mathrm{dom}(\tilde{\nu})$ for all i, then by Lemma 28 $\varphi_{t\langle k,n\rangle}(i) \leq_s \varphi_{t\langle k,n\rangle}(i+1)$, $\varphi_{t\langle k,n\rangle}(i) \in \mathrm{dom}(\tilde{\nu})$, and $\tilde{\nu}\varphi_{t\langle k,n\rangle}(i) \geq \varphi_k\varphi_{q(n)}(i)$ (since $\alpha + \beta \geq \beta$) for all i. By the recursion theorem there is a number $a \in \mathbb{N}$ with

$$\varphi_a(n) = \begin{cases} 0 & \text{if } n = 0 \\ \langle 0,t\langle a,n\rangle+1\rangle & \text{otherwise.} \end{cases}$$

An induction on α shows that φ_a has the desired property.
Q.E.D.

30 <u>COROLLARY</u>

$\tilde{\nu}$ is a numbering of the computable ordinals.

<u>Proof</u>

By Lemma 27, range($\tilde{\nu}$) is the union of segments of $(\mathbb{O}, <)$, hence a segment. By Lemma 29, range$(\hat{\nu}) \subseteq$ range$(\tilde{\nu})$, hence range$(\hat{\nu})$ = range$(\tilde{\nu})$.
Q.E.D.

31 <u>THEOREM</u>

Every computable ordinal is recursive.

<u>Proof</u>

Let α be a computable ordinal. If $\alpha = 0$ then α is recursive. Assume $\alpha > 0$. Then $\tilde{\nu}(k) = \alpha$ for some $k \in \mathbb{N}$ by Corollary 30. Define a numbering ν_1 by $\mathrm{dom}(\nu_1) = \{i \in \mathrm{dom}(\tilde{\nu}) \mid i <_s k\}$ and $\nu_1(i) = \tilde{\nu}(i)$. By Lemma 27(1) and (2), ν_1 is an injective numbering of $\mathbb{O}(\alpha)$. From Lemma 27(3) one derives easily that $\{<i,j> \mid i,j \in \mathrm{dom}(\nu_1),\ i \leq_s j\} =: B$ is r.e. Since $i <_s j \implies \tilde{\nu}(i) < \tilde{\nu}(j)$ for $i,j \in \mathrm{dom}(\tilde{\nu})$, $B = \{<i,j> \mid i,j \in \mathrm{dom}(\nu_1) \wedge \nu_1(i) \leq \nu_1(j)\}$. Since B is r.e. also $\mathrm{dom}(\nu_1) = \{i \mid <i,i> \in B\}$ is r.e. By Lemma 2.4.15 there is a total numbering ν of $\mathbb{O}(\alpha)$ with $\nu \equiv \nu_1$. Since ν_1 is injective, the set $C_1 := \{<i,j> \mid \nu(i) = \nu(j)\}$ is decidable. Since B is r.e. the sets

$$C := \{<i,j> \mid \nu(i) \leq \nu(j)\},$$

$$C_2 := \{<i,j> \mid \nu(i) \geq \nu(j)\} = \{<i,j> \mid <j,i> \in C\},$$

$$C_3 := \{<i,j> \mid \nu(i) > \nu(j)\} = C_2 \setminus C_1$$

are r.e. Since $\mathbb{N} = C \cup C_3$ and $C \cap C_3 = \emptyset$, C is recursive by Theorem 1.8.5. Therefore α is recursive by Definition 24.
Q.E.D.

Definition 24 induces a numbering ν_r of the recursive (= computable) ordinals as follows:

$$\mathrm{dom}(\nu_r) := \{<i,n> \mid \text{for some total numbering } \nu \text{ of a segment } \mathbb{O}(\alpha),\ \nu(i) = 0 \text{ and } \varphi_n \in R^{(1)} \text{ and } \varphi_n^{-1}\{0\} = \{<i,j> \mid \nu(i) \leq \nu(j)\}\}.$$

(Notice that α is determined uniquely by $<i,n> \in \mathrm{dom}(\nu_r)$.)

$\nu_r<i,n>$:= the unique α determined by $<i,n>$.

Our proofs have essentially shown:

$$\tilde{\nu} \le \nu_r \le \hat{\nu}$$

Very likely, $\hat{\nu}$ is not reducible to ν_r and ν_r is not reducible to $\tilde{\nu}$. For defining $\hat{\nu}$ (and $\tilde{\nu}$) we have generated $\mathbb{O}$ from $\{0\}$ by a single ω-ary function, $\hat{f}(0)$, with $\hat{f}(0)(\alpha_o,\alpha_1,\ldots) = \text{l.u.b.}\{\alpha_i\}$. In his original definition, Kleene used two functions, the successor and sup for strictly increasing ω-sequences (see Example 12(5)). This approach leads to a numbering ν' of the same set, namely the computable ordinals, but the numbers (i.e. names) contain more information. If $\nu'(k) = \alpha$, then from k numbers i and j can be determined such that $\nu'(k) = \nu'(i) + j$ where $\nu'(i)$ is a limit number and $j < \omega$. This is impossible for $\hat{\nu}$. However even more information can be made accessible. There is a numbering ν'' such that for any $k \in \text{dom}(\nu'')$ numbers j,m,n can be determined such that $\nu''(k) = \nu''(j) + \omega\cdot n + m$ where $\nu''(j)$ is the limit of a sequence (α_i) such that $\alpha_i + \omega \le \alpha_{i+1}$ for all i. This concept can be generalized to define a large number of other numberings of the computable ordinals. The numbering $\hat{\nu}$ is the simplest and therefore most natural one among these.

In Chapter 2.6 we have indicated how big r.e. subsets of a productive set can be generated from a number m with $W_m = \emptyset$ by applying iteratedly two functions to numbers of r.e. subsets already generated, a function G which adds one new element, and a function H which is the countable union of sets. Let $A \subseteq \mathbb{N}$ be productive, let $g \in P^{(1)}$ be a productive function of A. Then there is a function $p \in R^{(1)}$ such that

$$W_{p(x)} = W_x \cup \{g(x)\} \quad \text{if} \quad W_x \subseteq A,$$

and there is a function $q \in R^{(1)}$ such that

$$W_{q(n)} = \bigcup\{W_i \mid i \in \text{range}(\varphi_n)\}.$$

Define a signature $\sigma : \mathbb{N} \dashrightarrow \mathbb{N}$ by $\sigma(0) = 1$, $\sigma(1) = 0$, $\sigma(i) = \text{div}$ otherwise. Let ν_σ be the standard numbering of the computable trees over σ (Def. 13). Every $n \in \text{dom}(\nu_\sigma)$ corresponds to a rule for producing an r.e. subset $W_{h(n)} \subseteq A$ as follows.

$$h\langle j,0\rangle = m \qquad \text{for all } j,$$

$$h\langle 0,n+1\rangle = p(n) \qquad \text{for } \langle 0,n+1\rangle \in \text{dom}(\nu_\sigma),$$

$$h\langle 1,n+1\rangle = q(n) \qquad \text{for } \langle 1,n+1\rangle \in \text{dom}(\nu_\sigma)$$

(see Definition 13). Thus the number k of a "big" tree allows a "big" r.e. subset $W_{h(k)}$ of A to be determined.

EXERCISES

1) Let $\hat{M}_i = (M_i, R_i)$ $(i = 1,2)$ be well-orders.
   (a) Define $\hat{M} := (M_1 \times M_2, R)$ by
   $(a_1,a_2) R (b_1,b_2) :\iff a_1 R_1 b_1$ or $(a_1 = b_1$ and $a_2 R_2 b_2)$.
   Show that $\hat{M}$ is a well-order.
   (b) Assume $M_1 \cap M_2 = \emptyset$. Show that $\hat{M} := (M_1 \cup M_2, R)$ with aRb iff $(a,b \in M_1$ and $aR_1 b)$ or $(a \in M_1$ and $b \in M_2)$ or $(a,b \in M_2$ and $a R_2 b)$ is a well-order.

2) Let (M,R) be a well-order. Let $M' \subseteq M$ and $R' := R \cap (M' \times M')$.
   (a) Show that (M',R') is a well-order.
   (b) Show $(M',R') \leq (M,R)$.

3) Show that $\mathbb{O}$ is not denumerable.

4) (a) Let $(M,<)$ be a denumerable well-order.
   Show that $(M,<) < (\mathbb{O},<)$.
   (b) Let $(N,<)$ be a well-order such that $(M,<) \leq (N,<)$ for all denumerable well-orders $(M,<)$.
   Show: $(\mathbb{O},<) \leq (N,<)$.

5) Let σ be a signature such that $\sigma^{-1}\{0\} \neq \emptyset$.
   (a) Show that $(\forall \alpha \in \mathbb{O}) T'_\alpha(\sigma) \neq \emptyset$.
   (b) Show that $T(\sigma)$ has the cardinality of the continuum.

6) Consider Definition 10. Show that range(H) is the smallest subset $B \subseteq A$ such that range$(\nu_o) \subseteq B$ which is closed under the operations $\hat{f}(i)$, $i \in$ dom(σ).

7) Show that for each of the examples 12(3), (4), and (5), range(H) $= \mathbb{O}$.

8) Generalize Theorem 2.7.15 to the case of arbitrary signatures.

9) Complete the proof of Lemma 14.

10) Complete the proof of Lemma 18(1).

11) Prove $(\alpha+\beta)+\gamma = \alpha+(\beta+\gamma)$ for all $\alpha,\beta,\gamma \in \mathbb{O}$.
    Show directly: $(\alpha < \beta$ and β recursive$) \Rightarrow \alpha$ recursive.

12) Consider the proof of Lemma 27.
    (a) Verify in (2) that $Q(\alpha)$ is progressive.
    (b) Verify in (3) the property $W_{P(k)} = B_k$.

13) Define a relation $(W(\mathbb{N}),R)$ as follows:

$$R := \{(\varepsilon,x) \mid x \in W(\mathbb{N}) \setminus \{\varepsilon\}\} \cup \{(i_1 i_2 \dots i_m, j_1 j_2 \dots j_n) \mid m < n \text{ or } [m = n \text{ and } (\exists k \leq m)((\forall a < k) i_a = j_a \text{ and } i_k < j_k)]\}$$

(a) Show that $(W(\mathbb{N}),R)$ is a well-order. (The ordinal α such that $\mathbb{O}(\alpha)$ is order isomorphic to $(W(\mathbb{N}),R)$ is called ω^ω.)

(b) Let φ be the standard numbering of $P^{(1)}$ defined in Chapter 1.9, let $\hat{\nu}$ be the numbering of the computable ordinals defined via Lemma 18 using this standard numbering φ. Explain how a concrete number $n \in \mathbb{N}$ can be determined such that $\hat{\nu}(n) = \omega^\omega$.

14) Complete the proof of Theorem 3.

15) Complete the proof of Theorem 5.

BIBLIOGRAPHICAL NOTES

A short introduction to the second number class can e.g. be found in Schütte (1977) or Rogers (1967). Church (1938) and Kleene (1938) initiated the general theory of systems of notation (i.e. numberings) for ordinal numbers.

2.9 Some Applications to Logic

In mathematics statements about mathematical objects are formulated and proved. In logics the formulation of statements (the *syntax*), the meaning of statements (the *semantics*), *truth*, *proofs*, etc. are studied. In this chapter we shall exhibit some applications of recursion theory to logics. Decidability, productivity, and effective inseparability will play an important role.

The words which are used to formulate the statements of a mathematical theory constitute a formal language $L \subseteq W(\Sigma)$ over some alphabet Σ. Since it should be possible to decide whether a word $w \in W(\Sigma)$ formulates a statement of the mathematical theory or whether not, the set L should be decidable. The words which denote true statements are a subset $T \subseteq L$. For being sure that a word $w \in L$ denotes a true statement a *proof* w.r.t. a *proof system* (usually a set of *axioms* with *deduction rules*) is needed. Let $T_P \subseteq L$ be the set of words which can be deduced in the proof system P. Among others the following questions arise:

- Is T decidable?
- Is T recursively enumerable?
- Is T_P correct, i.e. $T_P \subseteq T$?
- Is T_P recursive?
- Is $T_P = T$ for some appropriate proof system?

As an example we introduce *first order arithmetic*. We shall prove that the recursively enumerable sets are *arithmetically representable* and derive that the set of true arithmetical expressions is productive (especially not recursive or recursively enumerable). We define (formal) theories with negation function and define formal *consistency* and formal *completeness*. As a main result we show that any axiomatic formally consistent theory, which is sufficiently rich in order to express certain properties of Turing machine computations, is creative and formally incomplete. The application of this theorem to Peano arithmetic is the *Gödel-Rosser incompleteness theorem* which strengthens *Gödel's first incompleteness theorem*.

The properties we have studied so far in recursion theory can be expressed in *first order arithmetic*, which we shall introduce now as an important example of a theory. In first order arithmetic properties on $\mathbb{N}$ are formulated using addition, multiplication, equality, the logical connectives "not" and "or", and "$(\forall x)$" i.e. quantification over individual variables. The theory is called "first order theory" since quantification over set variables (e.g. "for all subsets $A \subseteq \mathbb{N}$") is not allowed. First we define the language L of first order arithmetic.

1 DEFINITION (*language of first order arithmetic*)

(1) Let Σ_A be an alphabet defined by

$$\Sigma_A := \{0,S,V,(,),+,\cdot,=,\vee,\sim,\forall\} .$$

(2) Let Var_A be the set of variables defined by

$$Var_A = \{V0^n \mid n \in \mathbb{N}\} \subseteq W(\Sigma_A) .$$

(3) For $n = 0,1,2,\dots$ define $Tm_n \subseteq W(\Sigma_A)$ inductively by

$$Tm_o := \{"0"\} \cup Var_A ,$$

$$Tm_{n+1} := Tm_n \cup \{"St_1","(t_1+t_2)","(t_1\cdot t_2)" \mid t_1,t_2 \in Tm_n\} .$$

Let $Tm_A := \bigcup\{Tm_n \mid n \in \mathbb{N}\}$ be the set of *terms*.

(4) For $n = 0,1,2,\dots$ define $L_n \subseteq W(\Sigma_A)$ inductively by

$$L_o := \{"(t_1 = t_2)" \mid t_1,t_2 \in Tm_A\} ,$$

$$L_{n+1} := \{"\sim p","(p \vee q)","(\forall x)p" \mid p,q \in L_n , x \in Var_A\} .$$

Then $L_A := \bigcup\{L_n \mid n \in \mathbb{N}\}$ is the set of (arithmetical) *expressions* or *formulas*.

Thus the set of arithmetical terms, Tm_A, is the smallest subset $X \subseteq W(\Sigma_A)$ such that $0 \in X$, $Var \subseteq X$ and St_1, (t_1+t_2), and $(t_1 \cdot t_2)$ are elements of X if t_1 and t_2 are elements of X. The set L_A can be characterized similarly. The definition resembles that of trees (Def. 2.7.4). Any tree which is not a leaf can be uniquely decomposed into the root and the direct subtrees. Terms and expressions have a corresponding property.

2 LEMMA (*unique decomposition*)

(1) $Tm_A \cap L_A = \emptyset$

(2) For each term $t \in Tm_A$ exactly one of the following four cases occurs.
- $t \in Tm_o = \{"0"\} \cup Var_A$,
- there is a unique $t' \in Tm_A$ with $t = "St'"$,
- there are unique $t_1,t_2 \in Tm_A$ with $t = "(t_1+t_2)"$,
- there are unique $t_1,t_2 \in Tm_A$ with $t = "(t_1 \cdot t_2)"$.

(3) For each expression $p \in L_A$ exactly one of the following four cases occurs.
- there are unique $t_1,t_2 \in Tm_A$ with $p = "t_1=t_2"$,

- there is a unique $q \in L_A$ with $p = "\sim q"$,
- there are unique $q_1, q_2 \in L_A$ with $p = "(q_1 \vee q_2)"$,
- there are a unique $x \in Var_A$ and a unique $q \in L_A$ with $p = "(\forall x)q"$.

Proof (outline)

(1) Obviously, $Tm_A \subseteq W(\Sigma \setminus \{=\})$ and $L_A \cap W(\Sigma \setminus \{=\}) = \emptyset$, hence $Tm_A \cap L_A = \emptyset$.

(2) The following prefix property Q(n) can be proved by complete induction:

$$(t_1 \in Tm_n \wedge t_2 \in Tm_n \wedge t_1 \text{ is a prefix of } t_2) \implies (t_1, t_2 \in Var_A \vee t_1 = t_2) .$$

The unique decomposition property for terms follows immediately.

(3) The proof is similar to that of (2).

Q.E.D.

The following words are arithmetical terms: "0", "V000", "SV0", "(S0+V00)", "(SV0000·S(0+SS0))". In our metalanguage we shall use the abbreviations $\underline{n} := S^n0 = SS\ldots S0$ and $v_n := V0^n = V00\ldots0$ for $n \in \mathbb{N}$. For example, "$(v_4 \cdot S(0+\underline{2}))$" abbreviates the term "(V0000·S(0+SS0))". The following word is an expression:

$$((v_2 = v_1) \vee \sim(\forall v_1)\sim(\forall v_3)(v_4 = (\underline{3} + (\underline{1} \cdot v_1))))$$

Furthermore we shall use the following abbreviations in our metalanguage for specifying expressions from L_A:

$(\exists x)\, p$	abbreviates	$\sim(\forall x)\sim p$
$(p \wedge q)$	abbreviates	$\sim(\sim p \vee \sim q)$
$(p \Longrightarrow q)$	abbreviates	$(\sim p \vee q)$
$(p \Longleftrightarrow q)$	abbreviates	$((p \Longrightarrow q) \wedge (q \Longrightarrow p))$

Parentheses will be omitted in the metalanguage if no misunderstanding is possible. By Lemma 2, every term can be represented by a tree and every expression can be represented by a tree. A canonical approach corresponding to that indicated in Chapter 2.7 would be to introduce the set of trees which are (or represent) arithmetical statements and to define a canonical notation for these trees. The language L_A and the mapping $L_A \longrightarrow$ set of trees is such a canonical notation. Definition 2.7.8 and Lemma 2.7.9 are consequences of the unique decomposability of trees. The definition can be applied correspondingly to terms and expressions. We shall do this without further comments.

For operating on terms and expressions, free and bound occurrences of variables and substitution of free variables by terms have to be defined.

3 **DEFINITION** *(substitution)*

For $x \in Var_A$ and $t \in Tm_A$ define $[w: x/t]$ for all $w \in Tm_A \cup L_A$ inductively as follows.

$$
\begin{aligned}
[0 : x/t] &= \text{"0"},\\
[x : x/t] &= \text{"t"},\\
[y : x/t] &= \text{"y" for } y \in Var_A,\ y \neq x,\\
[St_1 : x/t] &= \text{"}S[t_1 : x/t]\text{"},\\
[(t_1+t_2) : x/t] &= \text{"}([t_1 : x/t] + [t_2 : x/t])\text{"},\\
[(t_1 \cdot t_2) : x/t] &= \text{"}([t_1 : x/t] \cdot [t_2 : x/t])\text{"},\\
[t_1=t_2 : x/t] &= \text{"}[t_1 : x/t] = [t_2 : x/t]\text{"},\\
[\sim p : x/t] &= \text{"}\sim[p : x/t]\text{"},\\
[(p \vee q) : x/t] &= \text{"}([p : x/t] \vee [q : x/t])\text{"},\\
[(\forall x)\, p : x/t] &= \text{"}(\forall x)p\text{"},\\
[(\forall y)\, p : x/t] &= \text{"}(\forall y)\ [p : x/t]\text{" if } y \neq x.
\end{aligned}
$$

If, e.g., t is the term $((v_1 + \underline{1}) \cdot v_1)$ and p is the expression $v_o = 0 \vee (\forall v_o)\ Sv_o = v_1$, then $[p: v_o/t]$ is the expression

$$((v_1 + \underline{1}) \cdot v_1) = 0 \vee (\forall v_o)\ Sv_o = v_1.$$

Notice that v_o is only replaced by the term t if it is not in the "scope" of a quantification $(\forall v_o)$. In our context we only need substitution of variables by terms of the type $\underline{n}$ (i.e. "S00...0"). A variable x occurs free in a term or expression w, iff substitution of any t (where $t \neq x$) for x changes w.

4 **DEFINITION** *(free variables)*

Let $x \in Var_A$ be a variable and let $w \in Tm_A \cup L_A$. Then x *occurs free* in w iff $w \neq [w: x/\underline{0}]$. Let $FV(w)$ be the set of variables which occur free in w. Expressions and terms without free variables are called *closed*.

The variable x does not occur free in $[w: x/\underline{n}]$ for any $w \in Tm_A \cup L_A$ and $n \in \mathbb{N}$. It is easy to show that $[[w: x/\underline{m}] : y/\underline{n}] = [[w: y/n] : x/\underline{m}]$ if $x \neq y$. We shall abbreviate $[\ldots[w: x_1/\underline{m_1}] : x_2/\underline{m_2}] : \ldots : x_j/\underline{m_j}]$ (where the variables $x_1,\ldots,x_j$ are pairwise different) by $[w: x_1/\underline{m_1},\ x_2/\underline{m_2},\ldots,x_j/\underline{m_j}]$.

Although terms and expressions have already an intended meaning, so far we have only defined formal languages Tm_A and L_A and studied formal properties without using the intended meaning.

We shall now *interpret* the closed terms and expressions arithmetically. The symbol "0" will be interpreted by $0 \in \mathbb{N}$, "S" by the successor function on $\mathbb{N}$, "+" by addition, "·" by multiplication, "=" by equality on $\mathbb{N}$, "~" by logical negation, "v" by logical or, and "$(\forall x)$" by "for all natural numbers x".

5 DEFINITION *(value of closed terms and expressions)*

(1) For all closed terms $t \in Tm_A$ define $val(t) \in \mathbb{N}$ inductively as follows.

$$val(\text{"0"}) = 0 \in \mathbb{N},$$

$$val(\text{"St"}) = 1 + val(t),$$

$$val(\text{"}(t_1+t_2)\text{"}) = val(t_1) + val(t_2),$$

$$val(\text{"}(t_1 \cdot t_2)\text{"}) = val(t_1) \cdot val(t_2).$$

(2) For all closed expressions $p \in L_A$ define $val(p) \in \{\text{true, false}\}$ inductively as follows:

$val(\text{"}t_1=t_2\text{"}) = \text{true}$, iff $val(t_1) = val(t_2)$,

$val(\text{"}\sim p\text{"}) = \text{true}$, iff $val(p) = \text{false}$,

$val(\text{"}(p \vee q)\text{"}) = \text{true}$, iff at least one of the values $val(p)$, $val(q)$ is true,

$val(\text{"}(\forall x)\ p\text{"}) = \text{true}$, iff $val[p : x/\underline{n}] = \text{true}$ for all $n \in \mathbb{N}$.

From the definition we obtain $val(\underline{n}) = val(S^n0) = n$ for all $n \in \mathbb{N}$ and e.g. $val(\text{"}(\underline{5} \cdot (\underline{3} + SSS\underline{1}))\text{"}) = 35$, $val(\text{"}\underline{5} = \underline{3}\text{"}) = \text{false}$, $val(\text{"}(\forall v_0)(\forall v_1)(\sim Sv_0 = Sv_1 \vee v_0 = v_1)\text{"}) = \text{true}$. Thus Definition 5 expresses exactly the intended meaning of arithmetical terms and expressions. The definition takes for granted that we know the natural numbers with addition and multiplication, and that we know the meaning of "equal", "not", "or", and "for all $x \in \mathbb{N}$". It is a *semantical* definition. Our abbreviations $(\exists x)\ p$, $p \wedge q$, $p \Rightarrow q$, and $p \Leftrightarrow q$ obtain the intended meaning by Definition 5. Arithmetical expressions allow formulation of very complicated properties of numbers.

6 EXAMPLES

(1) Let $p_1 := "(\exists z)\ x+z=y" = "\sim(\forall z)\sim(x+z)=y"$, where $x,y,z \in Var_A$. Then $val[p : x/\underline{m}, y/\underline{n}] = true$ iff $m \le n$. Thus p_1 can be abbreviated by $"x \le y"$.

(2) A number $x \in \mathbb{N}$ is prime iff (in metalinguistic formulation)

$$2 \le x \wedge (\forall y)\ ((2 \le y \wedge \sim x \le y) \Longrightarrow (\forall z)\ \sim(y \cdot z) = x)\ .$$

Using expressions similar to p_1 this metalinguistic expression can be transformed into an expression $p_2 \in L_A$ with the only free variable x such that $val[p : x/\underline{n}] = true$ iff n is a prime number.

The examples show how subsets of $\mathbb{N}^k$ can be defined by arithmetical expressions. The general definition of arithmetical sets and arithmetically representable functions is as follows.

7 DEFINITION (*arithmetical sets and functions*)

(1) Let $M \subseteq \mathbb{N}^k$, $k \ge 1$. M is *arithmetical* iff there are an expression $p \in L_A$ and pairwise different variables $\{x_1,\ldots,x_k\} \subseteq Var_A$ with $FV(p) \subseteq \{x_1,\ldots,x_k\}$ such that

$$M = \{(n_1,\ldots,n_k) \mid val[p : x_1/\underline{n}_1,\ldots,x_k/\underline{n}_k] = true\}\ .$$

(2) Let $f : \mathbb{N}^k \dashrightarrow \mathbb{N}$, $k \in \mathbb{N}$. Then f is *arithmetically representable* iff $graph(f) = \{(n_1,n_2,\ldots,n_k,m) \mid f(n_1,\ldots,n_k) = m\}$ is arithmetical.

From Example 6 we obtain that $\{(a,b) \mid a \le b\}$ and $\{n \mid n \text{ is prime}\}$ are arithmetical sets. Our next aim is to show that the recursively enumerable sets are arithmetical and that the computable functions are arithmetically representable. In the proof we have to encode finite sequences of numbers. For this purpose we introduce a certain arithmetical set G, called Gödel's set.

8 DEFINITION (*Gödel's set* G)

The set $G := \{(a,b,i,k) \in \mathbb{N}^4 \mid k \le ib$ and $(\exists v)\ a = v(1+ib) + k\}$ is called *Gödel's set*.

The condition in the definition of G can also be written as follows: $k = a \bmod (1+ib)$. The following lemma expresses the essential properties of G.

9 LEMMA

(1) G is arithmetical.

(2) For all a,b and all i there is exactly one k with $(a,b,i,k) \in G$.

(3) Let $r \geq 1$ and $m_1,\ldots,m_r \in \mathbb{N}$. Then there are $a,b \in \mathbb{N}$ such that $(a,b,i,m_i) \in G$ for $i = 1,\ldots,r$.

Let $a,b \in \mathbb{N}$, let k_i be the unique number (by(2)) with $(a,b,i,k_i) \in G$. Then the pair of numbers (a,b) can be used to encode the sequence $(k_1,k_2,\ldots,k_r)$, $r \geq 1$. By (3) any sequence $(m_1,\ldots,m_r)$ can be encoded this way.

Proof

(1) Define $p := "(\exists u)\ (z{+}u) = (y{\cdot}x) \wedge (\exists v)\ w = ((v \cdot (\underline{1} + (y{\cdot}x))) + z)"$ where $w,x,y,z \in Var_A$, then $(a,b,i,k) \in G$ iff $val[p : w/\underline{a}, x/\underline{b}, y/\underline{i}, z/\underline{k}] = true$. Therefore, G is arithmetical.

(2) k as a remainder under division is uniquely determined.

(3) Let $s := \max\{r,m_1,\ldots,m_r\}$, $b := s! = 1{\cdot}2{\cdot}\ldots{\cdot}s$. For $i = 1,\ldots,r$ define $b_i := 1 + ib$.

Proposition: b_i and b_j have no common divisor greater than 1 if $1 \leq i < j \leq r$.

Proof: Suppose $q \in \mathbb{N}$ such that $q \mid b_i$ and $q \mid b_j$. Then $q \mid (b_j - b_i)$, hence $q \mid (j-i)b$, and $q \mid (j-i)$ or $q \mid b$. If $q \mid (j-i)$, then $q < r \leq s$, hence $q \mid b$. In any case $q \mid b$, hence $q \mid ib$. Since $q \mid b_i$ we conclude $q \mid 1$. Therefore, b_i and b_j have no common divisor greater than 1 if $1 \leq i < j \leq r$.

q.e.d.

By the definitions we have $(a,b,i,k) \in G \iff k = a \bmod b_i$. We want to prove $m_i = a \bmod b_i$ for $i = 1,\ldots,r$, if a is appropriately chosen. Define a mapping

$$\rho : \{0,1,\ldots,b_1 b_2 \ldots b_r - 1\} \longrightarrow \{0,\ldots,b_1 - 1\} \times \ldots \times \{0,\ldots,b_r - 1\}$$

by $\rho(a) := (a \bmod b_1, a \bmod b_2, \ldots, a \bmod b_r)$.

Proposition: ρ is bijective.

Proof: Assume $\rho(a) = \rho(a')$. Then $b_i \mid (a - a')$ for $1 \leq i \leq r$, hence $b_1 \ldots b_r \mid (a - a')$ by the first proposition, and $a = a'$. Therefore ρ is injective and bijective by a cardinality argument.

q.e.d.

Since $m_i \leq s \leq b < b_i$ for $1 \leq i \leq r$, there is some $a < b_1 \ldots b_r$ with $(m_1,\ldots,m_r) = \rho(a) = (a \bmod b_1,\ldots,a \bmod b_r)$, therefore $m = a \bmod (1 + ib)$, i.e. (a,b,i,m_i) for $i = 1,\ldots,r$.

Q.E.D.

10 EXAMPLE

We show that the set $M = \{(b,c,a) \mid a = b^c\}$ is arithmetical. We have

$$a = b^c \iff (\exists m_1,\dots,m_{c+1})\ (m_1 = 1 \land m_{c+1} = a \land (\forall 1 \le i \le c)\ m_i \cdot b = m_{i+1})$$
$$\iff (\exists a',b')\ [G(a',b',1,1) \land G(a',b',c+1,a) \land (\forall 1 \le i \le c)(\exists m,m')\ (G(a',b',i,m) \land G(a',b',i+1,m') \land m \cdot b = m')] .$$

Since G is arithmetical, this last (informal) metalinguistic expression can be transformed into an expression p with the three free variables $x,y,z \in Var_A$ such that $a = b^c \iff val[p : x/\underline{b}, y/\underline{c}, z/\underline{a}] = true$. Therefore, the function f with $f(b,c) := b^c$ is arithmetically representable and $M = graph(f)$ is arithmetical.

11 THEOREM

Every computable function $f : \mathbb{N}^k \dashrightarrow \mathbb{N}$ is arithmetically representable.

The theorem can be proved in different ways depending on the definition of computability which is considered. Here we shall use the definition of the μ-recursive functions given in Chapter 1.3. Remember that a function $f : \mathbb{N}^k \dashrightarrow \mathbb{N}$ is μ-recursive iff it can be generated from functions belonging to

$$Gr = \{\tilde{0}, Z, S\} \cup \{pr_i^{(k)} \mid 1 \le i \le k\}$$

by finitely many applications of the operators of substitution, primitive recursion, and μ-recursion.

Proof

(1) The functions from Gr are arithmetical: $\tilde{0}$: $graph(\tilde{0}) = \{0\}$. Let x be any variable and p := "x=0". Then $\{n \mid val[p : x/\underline{n}] = true\} = \{0\} = graph(\tilde{0})$. The proof that Z,S, and the projections $pr_i^{(k)}$ are arithmetical is left as an exercise.

(2) Let $k,m \in \mathbb{N}$ $(m \ge 1)$, let $f : \mathbb{N}^m \dashrightarrow \mathbb{N}$ and $g_i : \mathbb{N}^k \dashrightarrow \mathbb{N}$ $(i = 1,\dots,m)$ be arithmetically representable (cf. Definition 1.2.10(2)). Then there are pairwise different variables $z,y_1,\dots,y_m,x_1,\dots,x_k$ and expressions p and $q_1,\dots,q_m$ such that

$$c = f(b_1,\dots,b_m) \iff val[p : y_1/\underline{b}_1, \dots, y_m/\underline{b}_m, z/\underline{c}] = true$$
$$b_i = g_i(a_1,\dots,a_k) \iff val[q_i : x_1/\underline{a}_1, \dots, x_k/\underline{a}_k, y_i/\underline{b}_i] = true .$$

Let $q' := "(\exists y_1)\dots(\exists y_m)(p \land q_1 \land \dots \land q_m)"$. Then the expression q' represents the function $h := Sub_m(f,g_1,\dots,g_m)$ according to Definition 7, hence h is arithmetically representable.

(3) Let $k \in \mathbb{N}$, let $g : \mathbb{N}^k \dashrightarrow \mathbb{N}$ and $h : \mathbb{N}^{k+2} \dashrightarrow \mathbb{N}$ be arithmetically representable. Let $f : \mathbb{N}^{k+1} \dashrightarrow \mathbb{N}$, $f := \mathrm{Prk}(g,h)$ (see Definition 1.2.10(3)). Then

$$f(a_1,\ldots,a_k,0) = g(a_1,\ldots,a_k)$$
$$f(a_1,\ldots,a_k,n+1) = h(a_1,\ldots,a_k,n,f(a_1,\ldots,a_k,n))$$

for all $a_1,\ldots,a_k,n \in \mathbb{N}$. Therefore, $f(a_1,\ldots,a_k,n) = c$ iff there is a sequence $b_1,\ldots,b_{n+1}$ such that

$$b_1 = g(a_1,\ldots,a_k)\,,$$
$$(\forall i \le n)\ \ b_{i+1} = h(a_1,\ldots,a_k,i,b_i)\,,$$
$$b_{n+1} = c\,.$$

Using Gödel's set G we can formulate this as follows.

$$f(a_1,\ldots,a_k,n) = b$$

iff

$$(\exists a,b)\ \ [(\exists b_1)\ (G(a,b,1,b_1) \wedge b_1 = g(a_1,\ldots,a_k)) \wedge G(a,b,n+1,c)$$
$$\wedge\ (\forall i\,,\ 1 \le i \le n)\ (\exists b',b'')\ \ (G(a,b,i,b') \wedge G(a,b,i+1,b'')$$
$$\wedge\ b'' = h(a_1,\ldots,a_k,i,b'))]\,.$$

Since G is arithmetical and g and h are arithmetically representable, this metalinguistic condition can be transformed into an expression which represents f according to Definition 7.

(4) Let $f : \mathbb{N}^{k+1} \dashrightarrow \mathbb{N}$ be arithmetically representable. Then $\tilde{\mu}(f) : \mathbb{N}^k \dashrightarrow \mathbb{N}$ (see Definition 1.2.10(4)) is arithmetically representable (as an exercise).

Thus we have shown that any function which can be constructed from the functions of the set Gr by finitely many applications of operators from $\{\mathrm{Sub}_m \mid m \in \mathbb{N}\} \cup \{\mathrm{Prk},\tilde{\mu}\}$ is arithmetically representable. By Definition 1.3.5 the μ-recursive (i.e. the computable) functions are arithmetically representable.
Q.E.D.

As a corollary we obtain that the recursively enumerable sets are arithmetical.

12 COROLLARY

8 The recursively enumerable subsets $M \subseteq \mathbb{N}^k$ are arithmetical.

Proof

Let $M \subseteq \mathbb{N}^k$ $(k \ge 1)$ be r.e. Then $M = \mathrm{dom}(f)$ for some computable $f : \mathbb{N}^k \dashrightarrow \mathbb{N}$.

By Theorem 11, f is arithmetically representable, hence there is some arithmetical expression p with

$$f(a_1,\dots,a_k) = b \iff \mathrm{val}[p : x_1/\underline{a}_1 , \dots , x_k/\underline{a}_k , y/\underline{b}] = \text{true} .$$

We obtain

$$(a_1,\dots,a_k) \in M \iff \mathrm{val}[(\exists y)\ p : x_1/\underline{a}_1 , \dots , x_k/\underline{a}_k] = \text{true} .$$

Therefore M is arithmetical.

Q.E.D.

This result is related to Hilbert's famous 10th problem which had been unsolved for 70 years (c f. Chapter 1.10). We formulate the problem in our context. A diophantine equation is an expression "$t_1=t_2$" $\in L_A$ where $t_1,t_2 \in Tm_A$. Let $\{x_1,\dots,x_k\}$ be the set of free variables of "$t_1=t_2$". A solution (in $\mathbb{N}^k$) of "$t_1=t_2$" is a tuple $(a_1,\dots,a_k) \in \mathbb{N}^k$ such that

$$\mathrm{val}[\text{"}t_1=t_2\text{"} : x_1/\underline{a}_1 , \dots , x_k/\underline{a}_k] = \text{true} .$$

Then Hilbert's 10th Problem can be stated as follows: "Is the set of diophantine equations which have a solution recursive?" A negative answer was given in 1970, by Matijasevic who proved that for any recursively enumerable set $M \subseteq \mathbb{N}^k$ there is an expression

$$p = \text{"}(\exists y_1)\dots(\exists y_n)\ t_1 = t_2\text{"}$$

with the only free variables $x_1,\dots,x_k$ such that

$$(a_1,\dots,a_k) \in M \iff \mathrm{val}[p : x_1/\underline{a}_1 , \dots , x_k/\underline{a}_k] = \text{true} .$$

This is a very strong version of Corollary 12. Our brute force proof does not yield this very special normal form of expressions. For deriving the negative answer to Hilbert's question consider the set K which is recursively enumerable but not recursive (Theorem 2.3.2). By the projection theorem there is a recursive set A such that $K = \{i \mid (\exists b)\ (i,b) \in A\}$. By Matijasevic's result

$$(i,b) \in A \iff \mathrm{val}[p : x/\underline{i} , y/\underline{b}] = \text{true}$$

where p has the form $(\exists y_1)\dots(\exists y_n)\ t_1 = t_2$. Then $i \in K$ iff $[\text{"}t_1=t_2\text{"} : x/\underline{i}]$ has a solution. Let ν be a standard numbering of $W(\Sigma_A)$. Let $DS := \{i \mid \nu(i) \text{ is a solvable diophantine equation}\}$. Define $f : \mathbb{N} \longrightarrow \mathbb{N}$ by $f(i) := \nu^{-1}[\text{"}t_1=t_2\text{"} : x/\underline{i}]$. Then $K \le DS$ via f, hence DS is not recursive, and the set of diophantine equations which have a solution is not recursive.

From Corollary 12 we derive that arithmetical truth is not decidable and not even recursively enumerable. A set $B \subseteq W(\Sigma_A)$ is called productive iff $\nu^{-1}B$ is productive for some standard numbering ν.

13 THEOREM

Each of the following sets is productive.

(1) $L_A^t = \{p \in L_A \mid p$ is closed $\wedge$ val(p) = true$\}$,

(2) $L_A^f = \{p \in L_A \mid p$ is closed $\wedge$ val(p) = false$\}$.

Therefore, none of these sets is recursive or recursively enumerable. There is no programmable procedure which lists exactly all the true closed arithmetical expressions.

Proof

Since $K = \{i \mid i \in \mathrm{dom}(\varphi_i)\}$ is r.e., by Corollary 12 there is an expression p with the only free variable x such that

$$n \in K \iff \mathrm{val}[p : x/\underline{n}] = \mathrm{true}$$

hence

$$n \in \mathbb{N} \setminus K \iff \mathrm{val}[p : x/\underline{n}] = \mathrm{false}$$
$$\iff \mathrm{val}[\sim p : x/\underline{n}] = \mathrm{true}$$

for all $n \in \mathbb{N}$. Let ν be a standard numbering of $W(\Sigma_A)$. Then the functions h_1 and h_2 defined by

$$h_1(n) := \nu^{-1}[p : x/\underline{n}] ,$$
$$h_2(n) := \nu^{-1}[\sim p : x/\underline{n}]$$

are computable. We obtain $\mathbb{N} \setminus K \leq \nu^{-1} L_A^t$ via h_2 and correspondingly $\mathbb{N} \setminus K \leq \nu^{-1} L_A^f$ via h_1. By Theorem 2.6.6 the two sets are productive.
Q.E.D.

The set of true closed arithmetical expressions is productive, i.e. from a name (number) i of a r.e. set B of true closed expressions a new true closed expression $p = f(i) \notin B$ can be computed by means of a productive function f.

For proving theorems mathematicians use calculi. A calculus determines how sentences can be derived from axioms by means of rules in a purely mechanical way. More formally, a *calculus* or a *proof system* is a triple $T := (\Sigma, A, R)$, where Σ is an alphabet, $A \subseteq W(\Sigma)$ is a recursive set of words (the *axioms*) and R is a finite set of recursive sets $\rho \subseteq (W(\Sigma))^n \times W(\Sigma)(n \geq 1)$ (the *inference rules*). A *proof* in PS is a sequence $(w_o, w_1, \ldots, w_k)$ of words such that for all $i \leq k$ one of the following conditions holds:

- $w_i \in A$ (i.e. w_i is an axiom)
- there is a rule $\rho \subseteq (W(\Sigma))^n \times W(\Sigma)$ and numbers $i_1, \ldots, i_n \in \{0, \ldots, k-1\}$ such that $((w_{i_1}, \ldots, w_{i_n}), w_k) \in \rho$.

A word w is *provable* in the proof system T, iff there is a proof $(w_o, \ldots, w_k)$ with $w_k = w$. It is easy to see that the set $T_P \subseteq W(\Sigma)$ of the words which are provable in the proof system P is recursively enumerable. On the other hand, for any recursively enumerable set $X \subseteq W(\Sigma)$ there is a proof system such that $X = T_P$. For this reason, recursively enumerable sets are sometimes called *provable*. A simple but important consequence of Theorem 13 is that there is no proof system P such that exactly the true closed arithmetical expressions can be proved. Whenever $T_P \subseteq L_A^t$, then $T_P \neq L_A^t$ since L_A^t is productive. This means that every sound proof system for arithmetic is incomplete.

The above considerations depend on the semantical definition of truth in arithmetic. We shall now study formal theories from a purely formal and recursion theoretical point of view. The main aim is to outline a proof of the non logical part of the *Gödel-Rosser incompleteness theorem*. The following definition is an abstraction of the examples already given.

14 **DEFINITION** (*formal language, formal theory, axiomatic theory*)

(1) A *formal language with negation* is a triple $\bar{L} = (\Sigma, L, neg)$ where Σ is an alphabet, $L \subseteq W(\Sigma)$ is a recursive set and $neg : W(\Sigma) \dashrightarrow W(\Sigma)$ is a computable function such that $neg(L) \subseteq L$ and $neg^{-1}(L) \subseteq L$.

(2) A *formal theory* is a pair $\bar{T} = (\bar{L}, T)$ where $\bar{L}$ is a formal language with negation and $T \subseteq L$. T is called the set of *theorems*.

(3) A formal theory $\bar{T} = (\bar{L}, T)$ is an *axiomatic theory*, iff T is recursively enumerable.

Therefore, $\bar{L}_A = (\Sigma_A, L_A, neg)$ where $neg(w) = "\sim w"$ is a formal language with negation, and $(\bar{L}_A, L_A^t)$ is a formal theory which is not axiomatic. Since L is recursive the function neg can always be chosen such that the condition $neg^{-1}(L) \subseteq L$ is satisfied. Notice that in Definition 14 no semantics is used and that "truth" is not defined.

Formal consistency and formal completeness of a formal theory are defined by the behaviour of its negation function.

15 DEFINITION (*consistency, completeness*)

Let $\overline{T} = (\overline{L}, T)$ be a formal theory with $\overline{L} = (\Sigma, L, neg)$.

(1) $\overline{T}$ is *formally consistent* iff $(\forall w \in L)$ $(w \notin T$ or $neg(w) \notin T)$.

(2) $\overline{T}$ is *formally complete* iff $(\forall w \in L)$ $(w \in T$ or $neg(w) \in T)$.

The following figure illustrates the definition. The arrows indicate typical instances of the negation function neg, while the dotted arrows are forbidden.

$\overline{T}$ is formally consistent:

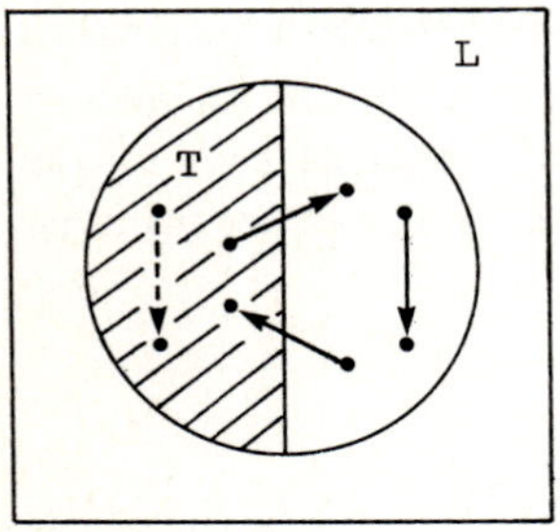

$\overline{T}$ is formally complete:

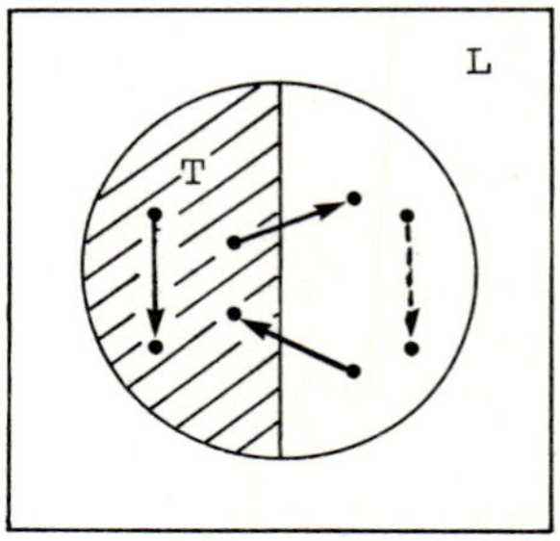

If $\overline{T}$ is formally consistent then $(w \in T$ and $neg(w) \in T)$ is forbidden; if $\overline{T}$ is formally complete then $(w \notin T$ and $neg(w) \notin T)$ is forbidden. The intended semantics of the definition is obvious. The above theory $(\overline{L}_A, L_A^t)$ is formally consistent and formally complete (proof as an exercise). If $\overline{T}$ is formally consistent then T and $neg^{-1}(T)$, the set of those expressions the negation of which is in T, are disjoint. An axiomatic theory which is formally consistent and formally complete must be recursive.

16 THEOREM

Let $\overline{T} = (\overline{L}, T)$ be a formally consistent and formally complete axiomatic theory. Then T is recursive.

Proof

The proof is essentially an application of Theorem 1.8.5 which states that a set A is recursive iff A and $\mathbb{N}\setminus A$ are recursively enumerable. By assumption, T is r.e. Formal consistency implies $T \cap neg^{-1}(T) = \emptyset$, formal completeness implies $T \cup neg^{-1}(T) = L$. Let $S := neg^{-1}(T) \cup (W(\Sigma)\setminus L)$. Then S and T are r.e. and S is the complement of T. By Theorem 1.8.5, T is recursive.
Q.E.D.

If T is formally consistent, then $T \cap neg^{-1}(T) = \emptyset$, thus the expressions $w \in L$ which are in T and those the negation of which are in T are separated by T. If T is sufficiently rich in order to express some special properties of Turing machine computations, then T and $neg^{-1}(T)$ become effectively inseparable (see Definition 2.6.12). If furthermore T is recursively enumerable, then T is creative and $\overline{T}$ is formally incomplete. Here we call a set of words $A \subseteq W(\Sigma)$ creative, productive, etc. if the corresponding set of numbers $\nu^{-1}(A)$, ν a standard numbering of $W(\Sigma)$, has this property.

17 THEOREM

Let $\overline{L} = (\Sigma, L, neg)$ be a formal language with negation, let ν ba a standard numbering of $W(\Sigma)$ and let $\overline{T} = (\overline{L}, T)$ be an axiomatic theory. Suppose that the following conditions hold.

(1) $\overline{T}$ is formally consistent.

(2) There is some $f \in R^{(1)}$ such that

$$\varphi_i(i) = 0 \implies \nu f(i) \in T,$$

$$\varphi_i(i) = 1 \implies neg\, \nu f(i) \in T$$

for all $i \in \mathbb{N}$.

Then:

(1) T and $neg^{-1}(T)$ are effectively inseparable.

(2) T is creative.

(3) $\overline{T}$ is not formally complete.

The following diagram illustrates the situation.

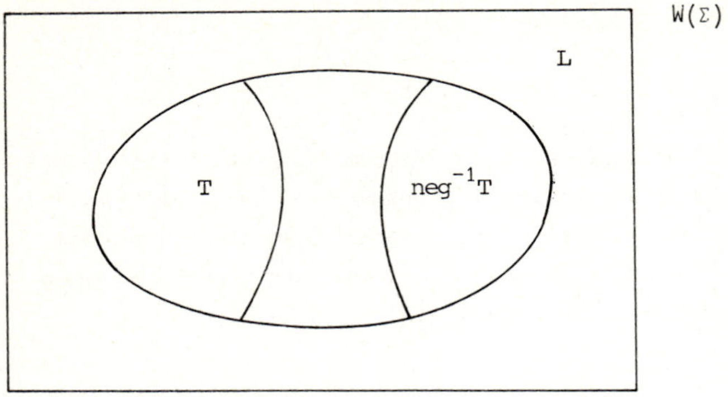

Proof

By Lemma 2.6.14 the sets $A_0 := \{i \mid \varphi_i(i) = 0\}$ and $A_1 = \{i \mid \varphi_i(i) = 1\}$ are effectively inseparable. By assumption $f(A_0) \subseteq \nu^{-1}T$ and $f(A_1) \subseteq \nu^{-1}neg^{-1}(T)$. By Lemma 2.6.13 $\nu^{-1}T$ and $\nu^{-1}neg^{-1}(T)$ are effectively inseparable, hence T and $neg^{-1}(T)$ are effectively inseparable by convention. Since T is r.e., also $neg^{-1}(T)$ is r.e., and T is creative by Lemma 2.6.13(4). Since T is creative, it is not recursive. By Theorem 16, $\overline{T}$ cannot be formally complete.

Q.E.D.

If an axiomatic theory $\overline{T}$ satisfies the conditions of Theorem 17, then every formally consistent extension satisfies these conditions. An extension of $\overline{T} = (\overline{L},T)$ is a theory $\overline{T}' = (\overline{L}',T')$ with $\overline{L}' = (\Sigma',L',neg')$ such that $\Sigma \subseteq \Sigma'$, $L \subseteq L'$, $T \subseteq T'$ and $neg(w) = neg'(w)$ for all $w \in L$. Therefore we obtain as a corollary:

18 COROLLARY

If $\overline{T}$ is an axiomatic theory which satisfies the conditions of Theorem 17, and if $\overline{T}'$ is a formally consistent extension of $\overline{T}$, then T' is creative and $\overline{T}'$ is formally incomplete.

A well known proof system for arithmetic is defined by the Peano axioms with first order induction. The derived axiomatic theory $\overline{T}_A = (\overline{L}_A,T_P)$ can be shown to satisfy Condition 2 of Theorem 17. If the theory $\overline{T}_A$ is consistent (we have not defined consistency of a first order theory here) then it is formally consistent. Therefore, the theory $\overline{T}_A$ is formally incomplete (hence an incomplete first order theory) if it is consistent. The same holds for any consistent extension of it. This is the Gödel-Rosser incompleteness theorem.

Notice that the Gödel-Rosser incompleteness theorem does not depend on the semantical concept of truth. The theorem holds even for those consistent extensions of the theory $\overline{T}_A$ which contain semantically false sentences. Consistency of $\overline{T}_A$ can be proved, but not by means of the Peano axioms. This is stated by *Gödel's second incompleteness theorem.*

If the theory $\overline{T}_A$ is consistent (as we believe) there is an arithmetical expression $p \in L_A$ such that neither $p \in T_A$ nor "$\sim p$"$\in T_A$. This means that p can be neither proved nor disproved by means of the Peano axioms.

As a concluding example we consider Fermat's famous problem. Fermat has conjectured:

$$(\forall x)(\forall y)(\forall z)(\forall n) \quad (x > 0 \wedge y > 0 \wedge z > 0 \wedge n > 2 \implies x^n + y^n \neq z^n)$$

This is an abbreviation of a closed arithmetical expression which we shall call F. Until today it is unknown whether Fermat's conjecture is true. One could try to solve the problem in different ways:

1. One could try to derive the expression F in a generally accepted proof system P (e.g. by the peano axioms).

2. One could try to derive "~F" in a generally accepted proof system P.

Since we believe that our proof system P is formally consistent, it is formally incomplete (provided it is sufficiently rich). Therefore, possibly neither "F" nor "~F" are derivable.

3. As we have shown, the set L_A^t of true arithmetical expressions, is productive. The set T_p of expressions derivable in our proof system is recursively enumerable and (we assume) $T_p \subseteq L_A^t$. Hence, using a productive function of L_A^t from a number of the r.e. set T_p many new true arithmetical expressions can be determined. At the end of Chapter 2.8 we have indicated how to perform many such production steps by a single "super step", which is defined by any number of a "big" computable ordinal tree. Therefore, the problem can be reduced to finding numbers of ordinal trees until a proof of F or a proof of "~F" is found. But even this method might fail.

4. The last method is to find more powerful proof systems by inventing new axioms or new derivation rules which are semantically correct. But how can we be sure that an axiom is semantically true if we don't have a proof for it?

EXERCISES

1) Prove Lemma 2 in detail.
2) Show for closed expressions $p, q \in L$:
   (a) val("$p \wedge q$") = true iff val(p) = true and val(q) = true,
   (b) val("$p \Rightarrow q$") = true iff val(p) = false or val(q) = true,
   (c) val("$p \Leftrightarrow q$") = true iff val(p) = val(q),
   (d) val("$(\exists x)p$") = true iff $\text{val}[p : x/\underline{n}]$ = true for some $n \in \mathbb{N}$.
3) Prove without applying Theorem 11 or Corollary 12:
   (a) Each finite set $A \subseteq \mathbb{N}$ is arithmetical.
   (b) For any $k \geq 1$ the set $B_k = \{n^k \mid n \in \mathbb{N}\}$ is arithmetical.
   (c) Define the Fibonacci function $f : \mathbb{N} \longrightarrow \mathbb{N}$ by
   $f(0) = f(1) = 1$, $f(n+1) = f(n-1) + f(n)$ for $n > 1$.
   Show that f is arithmetically representable.
4) Show that there is a set $X \subseteq \mathbb{N}$ which is not arithmetically representable.
5) Show directly that the functions $Z, S : \mathbb{N} \longrightarrow \mathbb{N}$ $(Z(n) = 0,\ S(n) = n+1)$ and the projections $pr_i^{(k)}$ are arithmetically representable.
6) Prove in detail that $\tilde{\mu}f$ is arithmetically representable if f is arithmetically representable (c f. the proof of Theorem 11).
7) Consider Theorem 18. Show that $L \setminus (T \cup neg^{-1}(T))$ is productive.
8) Determine a productive function for the set L_A^t of the true closed arithmetical expressions.

BIBLIOGRAPHICAL NOTES

There are several books which discuss the relation between recursion theory and logic more extendedly, e.g. Kleene (1952), Rogers (1967), Shoenfield (1967), and Machtey and Young (1978). Gödel's first incompleteness theorem is published in Gödel (1931). The idea of the proof presented in this chapter is from Rosser (1936).

2.10 Oracle Machines and Relativized Recursion Theory

For comparing the difficulty of sets of numbers, in Chapter 2.3 we have introduced (many-one) reducibility: $A \le B$ iff $(\forall x)\ (x \in A \Longleftrightarrow f(x) \in B)$ for some total recursive function $f \in R^{(1)}$. If $A \le B$ then by Lemma 2.3.4, B recursive $\Longrightarrow$ A recursive and B r.e. $\Longrightarrow$ A r.e. Let $A \le B$. Thus, for deciding $x \in A$ it is sufficient to answer the question "$f(x) \in B$?". The following examples show that there are more general possibilities to reduce questions "$x \in A$?" computably to questions "$y \in B$?".

1 EXAMPLE

(a) $x \in A$ iff $f(x) \in B$ (where $f \in R^{(1)}$)

(b) $x \in A$ iff $f(x) \in B$ (where $f \in P^{(1)}$)

(c) $x \in A$ iff $2x \in B \wedge (4x \in B \vee 5x \notin B)$

(d) $x \in A$ iff $e_{x^2} \subseteq B \vee e_{2x} \subseteq \mathbb{N} \setminus B$

(e) $x \in A$ iff $1 + \mu y[y > x \wedge y \in B] \notin B$

(f) $x \in A$ iff $(\exists u)\ (\langle x,u\rangle \in C \wedge e_u \subseteq B)$ (where C is r.e.)

(g) $x \in A$ iff $(\exists u,v)\ (\langle x,u,v\rangle \in C \wedge e_u \subseteq B \wedge e_v \subseteq \mathbb{N} \setminus B)$ (where C is r.e.)

where e is the standard numbering of the finite subsets of $\mathbb{N}$ (Def. 2.2.2).

In each of the above cases the characteristic function or an enumeration of the set A can be obtained by a computable procedure from the characteristic function or an enumeration of the set B. A very general theory of continuous and of computable operators $\Gamma : 2^{\mathbb{N}} \dashrightarrow 2^{\mathbb{N}}$ will be developed in Part 3 of this book.

In the next two chapters we shall consider a fixed set $A \subseteq \mathbb{N}$ as a parameter rather than an argument of a function. Essentially we shall study the A-computable functions, i.e. those functions which would become computable if the set A were decidable. The set of A-computable functions could be called the computable neighbourhood (not in the topological sense) of the characteristic function of A. This concept of relativized computability will be used for classifying nonrecursive sets in Chapter 2.11.

The new kind of computability will be defined by machines, so-called *oracle machines*, which generalize register machines, stack machines, or tape machines. These machines compute functions $2^{\mathbb{N}} \times \mathbb{N}^k \dashrightarrow \mathbb{N}$ or $2^{W(\Sigma)} \times (W(\Sigma))^k \dashrightarrow W(\Sigma)$, respectively. Oracle register machines are defined as follows (cf. Definition 1.2.2).

2 <u>DEFINITION</u> (*oracle register machines*)

An *oracle register machine* is a machine

$$M = (F, 2^{\mathbb{N}} \times \mathbb{N}^k, \mathbb{N}, I^{(k)}, O)$$

such that the following conditions hold.

(1) $D = 2^{\mathbb{N}} \times \mathbb{N}^{\mathbb{N}}$ is the data set of the flowchart F.

(2) $I^{(k)}(A, x_1, \ldots, x_k) := (A, (0, x_1, \ldots, x_k, 0, \ldots))$

(3) $O(A, (x_o, x_1, \ldots)) := x_o$

(4) The flowchart F may contain pure function statements of the form "$R_i := R_i+1$" or "$R_i := R_i-1$" and pure test statements of the form "$R_i = 0$" or "R_i" for $i \in \mathbb{N}$, where for any $d = (A, (a_o, a_1, \ldots)) \in D$:

$$\text{"}R_i := R_i+1\text{"}(d) := (A, (a_o, a_1, \ldots, a_{i-1}, a_i+1, a_{i+1}, \ldots))$$

$$\text{"}R_i := R_i-1\text{"}(d) := (A, (a_o, a_1, \ldots, a_{i-1}, a_i-1, a_{i+1}, \ldots))$$

$$\text{"}R_i = 0\text{"}(d) := \begin{cases} + & \text{if } a_i = 0 \\ - & \text{if } a_i \neq 0, \end{cases}$$

$$\text{"}R_i\text{"}(d) := \begin{cases} + & \text{if } a_i \in A \\ - & \text{if } a_i \notin A. \end{cases}$$

Notice that the set component A of $d \in D$ remains unchanged during any computation. (For simplicity we use the informal notation "$R_i := R_i+1$" etc. for register machines as well as for oracle register machines.) By the above definition, an oracle register machine works on the registers in the same way as a register machine, but in addition it may ask questions "$a_i \in A$?". If A is not recursive then by Church's Thesis only an "oracle" can answer all the questions of this kind. Therefore, machines with this ability are called *oracle machines*. The semantics of oracle register machines is given by the general definitions 1.1.6 and 1.1.16.

3 <u>EXAMPLE</u> (see Example 1)

(a) Define a (generalized) unary oracle register machine by the following flowchart:

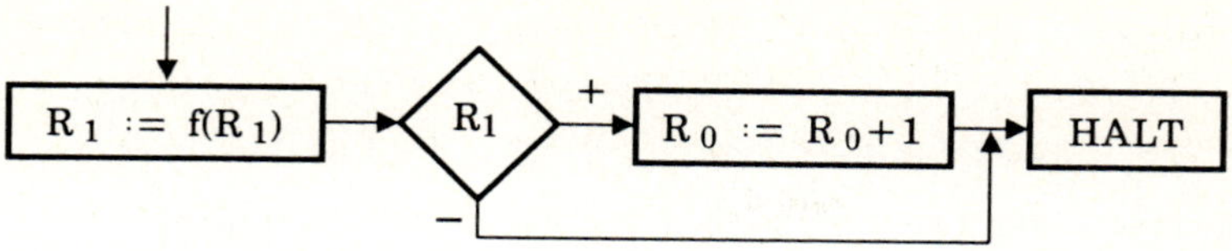

where $f \in R^{(1)}$. Then $f_M : 2^{\mathbb{N}} \times \mathbb{N} \longrightarrow \mathbb{N}$, the function computed by M, is total and satisfies

$$f_M(B,x) = 1 \iff f(x) \in B .$$

for all $x \in \mathbb{N}$. Machine M can be refined into an oracle register machine according to Definition 2. If we define $\Gamma : 2^{\mathbb{N}} \longrightarrow 2^{\mathbb{N}}$ by $x \in \Gamma(B) :\iff f_M(B,x) = 1$, then $\Gamma(B) \le B$ via f.

(b) Define a generalized unary oracle register machine M by the following flowchart:

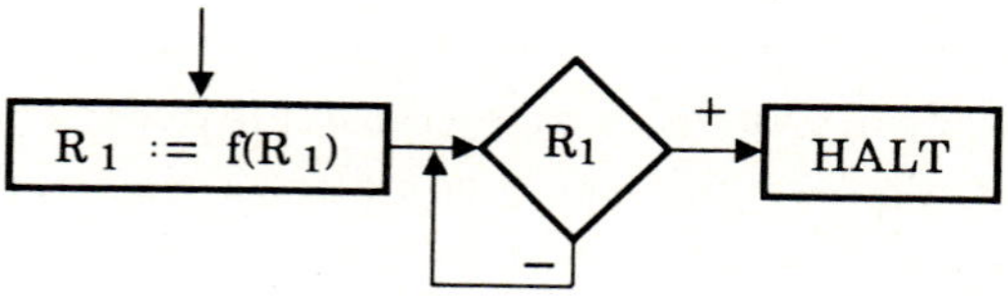

where $f \in P^{(1)}$. This flowchart can be refined into an oracle register machine flowchart. For the function f_M computed by M we obtain

$$(B,x) \in \mathrm{dom}(f_M) \iff g(x) \in B$$

for all $x \in \mathbb{N}$. Define $\Gamma(B)$ by $x \in \Gamma(B) :\iff (B,x) \in \mathrm{dom}(f_M)$, then $x \in \Gamma(B) \iff g(x) \in B$.

(g) Let $C \subseteq \mathbb{N}$ be a recursively enumerable set. By the projection theorem (1.8.4) there is a recursive set $D \subseteq \mathbb{N}$ such that $C = \{z \mid (\exists t)\ \langle z,t\rangle \in D\}$. Define a generalized unary oracle register machine M by the following flowchart:

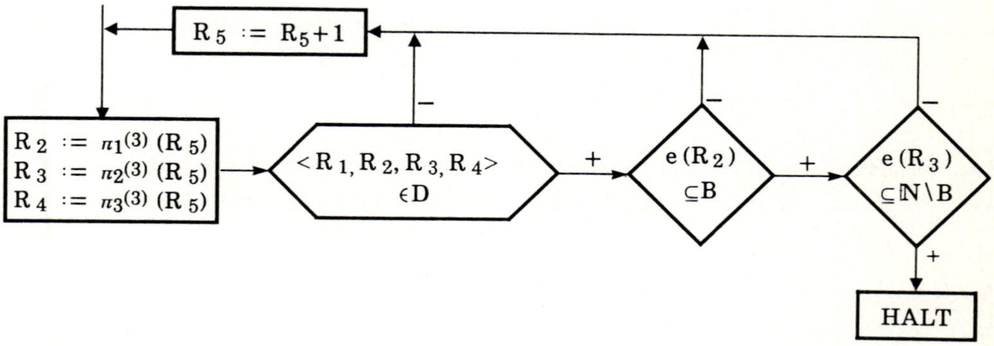

This flowchart can be refined into an oracle register machine flowchart. Define $\Gamma : 2^{\mathbb{N}} \longrightarrow 2^{\mathbb{N}}$ by $x \in \Gamma(B) :\Longleftrightarrow (B,x) \in \mathrm{dom}(f_M)$. Then
$x \in \Gamma(B) \Longleftrightarrow (\exists u,v)\ (\langle x,u,v\rangle \in C \wedge e_u \subseteq B \wedge e_v \subseteq \mathbb{N} \setminus B)$.

Similarly for the other cases of Example 1 oracle register machines can be used for specifying the intended computable operators.

Notice that in the cases (a), (b), and (f) only an enumeration procedure for B (and not the characteristic function) must be given by the oracle in order to informally be able to enumerate A. For describing this correctly another type of reduction procedures, the *enumeration operators*, are needed which are different from the operators deduced from oracle register machines in Example 3. Enumeration operators will be studied in Part 3 of this book.

Many parts of the theory of computability which we have developed so far can be relativized from the computable functions to the oracle computable functions. The necessary modifications in the definitions, theorems, and proofs are almost straightforward. Therefore we shall mention only the essentials and omit details. Since register machines have universal computational power the following definition is reasonable.

4 DEFINITION (*oracle-computability*)

A function

$$f : 2^{\mathbb{N}} \times \mathbb{N}^k \dashrightarrow \mathbb{N}$$

is called *oracle computable* (*o-computable*) iff $f = f_M$ for some oracle register machine M.

In Example 3 we have already used generalized oracle machines. Theorem 1.2.7 on generalized register machines can be easily transferred to oracle register machines. This simplifies the proofs that given functions are oracle computable considerably.

Stack machines over (Γ,Σ) can be generalized to *oracle stack machines* in a similar way as register machines. An oracle stack machine M over (Γ,Σ) computes a function

$$f_M : 2^{W(\Sigma)} \times (W(\Sigma))^k \dashrightarrow W(\Sigma)\ .$$

The data set is $2^{W(\Sigma)} \times (W(\Gamma))^{\mathbb{N}}$, and the essential new statement is the test "R_i" which tests whether the content of register R_i is in the oracle set. Theorem 1.6.6 on generalized stack machines can be easily generalized to oracle stack machines.

The connection between oracle stack computability and oracle register computability is given by a generalization of Theorem 1.7.5: Let Σ be an alphabet, let ν be a standard numbering of $W(\Sigma)$. Let $g : 2^{\mathbb{N}} \times \mathbb{N}^k \dashrightarrow \mathbb{N}$ and define $f : 2^{W(\Sigma)} \times (W(\Sigma))^k \dashrightarrow W(\Sigma)$ by

$$f(X,(w_1,\ldots,w_k)) := \nu g(\nu^{-1}X,(\nu^{-1}w_1,\ldots,\nu^{-1}w_k)) .$$

Then g is oracle register computable iff f is oracle stack computable. Notice that the sets X and $\nu^{-1}X$ have the same "degree of undecidability" (cf. Theorem 1.8.9).

Finally tape machines can be generalized to *oracle tape machines*. Since only one tape is available the questions "$w \in X$" for $w \in W(\Sigma)$ must be defined somewhat artificially. An oracle tape machine over (Γ,Σ,B) (i.e. with tape alphabet Γ, input/output alphabet Σ, and blank B) has oracle sets $X \subseteq W(\Sigma)$. In addition to the ordinary tape operations the test "Or" is admitted defined by

$$\text{"Or"}(X,[u,a,v]) := \begin{cases} + & \text{if } y \in X \\ - & \text{if } y \notin X \end{cases}$$

where y is the longest prefix of v with $y \in W(\Sigma)$ (c f. Definition 1.5.1). It can be shown that a function $f : 2^{W(\Sigma)} \times (W(\Sigma))^k \dashrightarrow W(\Sigma)$ is oracle tape computable iff it is oracle stack computable. The proof of this relativized property is slightly more complicated than the old proof (Theorem 1.6.7). The refinements of the statements simulating the oracle questions "R_i" and "Or", respectively, require some additional programming. Finally the lemma on auxiliary symbols (Lemma 1.5.3) can be generalized to oracle tape machines. Again some additional programming is necessary for refining the statement simulating the oracle question.

Our considerations show that the different types of oracle machines yield the same kind of computability on words or numbers. Many fundamental properties in recursion theory are derived from an admissible numbering φ of the set $P^{(1)}$ of the unary partial recursive functions. We shall introduce now a standard numbering η of the oracle computable functions $f : 2^{\mathbb{N}} \times \mathbb{N} \dashrightarrow \mathbb{N}$. Again this definition is only a slight generalization of the definition of φ (Def. 1.9.2, Def. 1.9.4). In Definition 1.9.2 the symbol Or is added to the alphabet Ω and the set $\{\text{"}(1^m\text{:Or},1^k,1^n)\text{"} \mid m,k,n \in \mathbb{N}\}$ is added to the set of test statements. Finally in Def. 1.9.2(4) the case

$\sigma(n) =$ 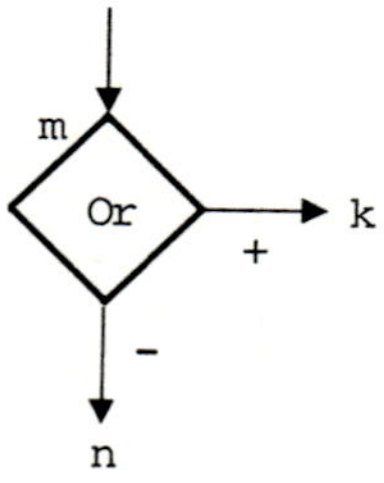

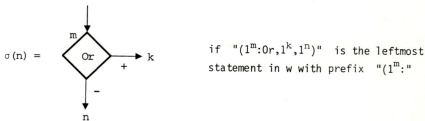

if "$(1^m\text{:Or},1^k,1^n)$" is the leftmost statement in w with prefix "$(1^m$:"

is added.

5 DEFINITION

(1) The standard numbering of the set

$$\{f : 2^{\mathbb{N}} \times \mathbb{N} \dashrightarrow \mathbb{N} \mid f \text{ oracle computable}\}$$

is denoted by η.

(2) Let $\hat{\eta}_i(A,x)$ be the number of steps which the i-th oracle tape machine needs for determining $\eta_i(A,x)$.

Similar to ordinary computability it is sufficient to consider the computable functions $f : 2^{\mathbb{N}} \times \mathbb{N} \dashrightarrow \mathbb{N}$, since a function $g : 2^{\mathbb{N}} \times \mathbb{N}^k \dashrightarrow \mathbb{N}$ is oracle computable iff the transformed function $h : 2^{\mathbb{N}} \times \mathbb{N} \dashrightarrow \mathbb{N}$ defined by $h(A,x) := g(A,(\pi^{(k)})^{-1}(x))$ is oracle computable. The definitions of φ and η are so similar that the proofs of the utm-theorem (Theorem 1.9.6) and the smn-theorem (1.9.7) can be easily generalized from φ to η.

6 THEOREM (*utm-, smn-theorem for* η)

(1) The universal function u of η defined by $u(A,(i,x)) := \eta_i(A,x)$ is oracle computable.

(2) For any oracle computable function $f : 2^{\mathbb{N}} \times \mathbb{N}^2 \dashrightarrow \mathbb{N}$ there is some total recursive function $r \in R^{(1)}$ with

$$f(A,(i,j)) = \eta_{r(i)}(A,j).$$

Notice that the function r which determines the new program is total recursive. It is not difficult to show that Blum's axioms hold in the relativized case.

7 THEOREM (*relativized complexity*)

(1) $\operatorname{dom} \eta_i = \operatorname{dom} \hat{\eta}_i$ for all $i \in \mathbb{N}$.

(2) There is an oracle computable total function $f : 2^{\mathbb{N}} \times \mathbb{N}^3 \longrightarrow \mathbb{N}$ such that for all $A \subseteq \mathbb{N}$, $i,x,t \in \mathbb{N}$:

$$f(A,(i,x,t)) = 0 \iff \hat{\eta}_i(A,x) = t .$$

Although the argument $A \subseteq \mathbb{N}$ for an oracle machine is generally infinite, for each finite computation of $\eta_i(A,x)$ only a finite subset $N_+(A,i,x) \subseteq A$ and a finite subset $N_-(A,i,x) \subseteq \mathbb{N} \setminus A$ are needed, since in finitely many steps of computation only finitely many questions "$z \in A$?" can be asked. Clearly, if $N_+(A,i,x) \subseteq B$ and $N_-(A,i,x) \subseteq \mathbb{N} \setminus B$, then $\eta_i(A,x) = \eta_i(B,x)$. Thus the behaviour of an oracle computable function on A is completely determined by its behaviour on the finite subsets of A. In Part 3 we shall express this as *continuity* w.r.t. an appropriate topology on $2^{\mathbb{N}}$. The following lemma gives some consequences of this finiteness, (2) generalizes Theorem 7(2) and Lemma 2.1(3). Remember that e is the standard numbering of the finite subsets of $\mathbb{N}$ (Def. 2.2.2).

8 LEMMA

For $A \subseteq \mathbb{N}$ and $i,x \in \mathbb{N}$ define

$N(A,i,x) := \{y \mid$ the i-th oracle tape machine with input (A,x) asks (after some steps) the question "$y \in A$?"$\}$,

$N_+(A,i,x) := A \cap N(A,i,x)$,

$N_-(A,i,x) := (\mathbb{N} \setminus A) \cap N(A,i,x)$.

Then the following properties hold.

(1) If $N_+(A,i,x) \subseteq B$ and $N_-(A,i,x) \subseteq \mathbb{N} \setminus B$, then

$$\eta_i(A,x) = \eta_i(B,x) \quad \text{and} \quad \hat{\eta}_i(A,x) = \hat{\eta}_i(B,x).$$

(2) The following set U is decidable:

$$\{\langle i,x,y,t,u,v\rangle \mid \eta_i(e_u,x) = y \wedge \hat{\eta}_i(e_u,x) = t \wedge N_+(e_u,i,x) = e_u \wedge N_-(e_u,i,x) = e_v\}.$$

(3) There are oracle computable functions $g, g_+, g_- : 2^{\mathbb{N}} \times \mathbb{N}^2 \dashrightarrow \mathbb{N}$ such that

$$N(A,i,x) = eg(A,i,x),$$

$$N_+(A,i,x) = eg_+(A,i,x),$$

$$N_-(A,i,x) = eg_-(A,i,x)$$

for all $A \subseteq \mathbb{N}$ and $i,x \in \mathbb{N}$ for which $\eta_i(A,x)$ exists.

(4) If $f : 2^{\mathbb{N}} \times \mathbb{N} \dashrightarrow \mathbb{N}$ is oracle computable then $g : \mathbb{N}^2 \dashrightarrow \mathbb{N}$ with $g(u,x) := f(e_u,x)$ is computable.

Proof

(1) (see discussion above)

(2) The proof is similar to that of the utm-theorem (6(1)) or of Theorem 7(2). For a given number i of an oracle tape machine M and given numbers x,y,t,u,v simulate the computation of M on input (e_u,x) step by step. Simultaneously the oracle requests are stored. Then after at most t steps the question $\langle i,x,y,t,u,v\rangle \in U$ can be easily

answered.

(3) Define g_+ as follows:

$$g_+(A,i,x) = \pi_1^{(2)}\mu\langle u,\langle y,t,v\rangle\rangle[e_u \subseteq A \wedge e_v \subseteq \mathbb{N}\setminus A \text{ and } \langle i,x,y,t,u,v\rangle \in U].$$

Therefore g_+ has the desired properties. The definition of g_- is similar, and g is oracle computable since union is (e^2,e)-computable.

(4) Let $i \in \mathbb{N}$ such that $f = \eta_i$. Then

$$f(e_u,x) = \pi_1^{(2)}\mu\langle y,\langle t,v\rangle\rangle[\langle i,x,y,t,u,v\rangle \in U],$$

hence g is computable.

Q.E.D.

Now let $A \subseteq \mathbb{N}$ be some arbitrary fixed subset of $\mathbb{N}$. We shall study those functions which would become computable if the set A were decidable. We reduce this definition to oracle computability (Def. 4).

9 DEFINITION (A-*computable*, A-*recursive*, A-*r.e.*)

(1) A function $f : \mathbb{N}^k \dashrightarrow \mathbb{N}$ is A-*computable* iff there is some oracle computable function $g : 2^{\mathbb{N}} \times \mathbb{N} \dashrightarrow \mathbb{N}$ such that $g(A,\overline{x}) = f(\overline{x})$ for all $\overline{x} \in \mathbb{N}^k$.

(2) A subset $B \subseteq \mathbb{N}^k$ is A-*recursive* (or A-*decidable*) iff there is some (total) A-computable function $f : \mathbb{N}^k \longrightarrow \mathbb{N}$ such that $B = f^{-1}\{0\}$.

(3) A subset $B \subseteq \mathbb{N}^k$ is A-*recursively enumerable* (A-*r.e.*) iff $B = \text{dom}(f)$ for some A-computable function $f : \mathbb{N}^k \dashrightarrow \mathbb{N}$.

Standard numberings of the A-computable functions $f : \mathbb{N} \dashrightarrow \mathbb{N}$ and of the A-r.e. subsets of $\mathbb{N}$ can be easily derived from Definition 5 (cf. Def. 2.3.8).

10 DEFINITION

(1) The standard numbering φ^A of the A-computable functions is defined by

$$\varphi_i^A(x) := \eta_i(A,x)$$

for all $i,x \in \mathbb{N}$.

(2) The standard complexity Φ^A of the numbering φ^A is defined by

$$\Phi_i^A(x) := \hat{\eta}_i(A,x)$$

for all $i,x \in \mathbb{N}$.

(3) The standard numbering of the A-r.e. subsets of $\mathbb{N}$ is defined by

$$W_i^A := \mathrm{dom}(\varphi_i^A)$$

for all $i \in \mathbb{N}$.

From Theorem 6 and Theorem 7 one concludes easily that the numbering φ^A satisfies a utm-theorem and an smn-theorem and that the pair (φ^A, Φ^A) satisfies a modification of Blum's axioms (see Definition 2.1.5).

11 THEOREM

(1) The universal function u of φ^A defined by $u(i,x) := \varphi_i^A(x)$ is A-computable.

(2) For each A-computable function $f : \mathbb{N}^2 \dashrightarrow \mathbb{N}$ there is some total recursive function $r : \mathbb{N} \longrightarrow \mathbb{N}$ such that

$$f(i,x) = \varphi_{r(i)}^A(x)$$

for all $i, x \in \mathbb{N}$.

(3) $\mathrm{dom}\, \varphi_i^A = \mathrm{dom}\, \Phi_i^A$ for all $i \in \mathbb{N}$.

(4) The set

$$\{(i,x,t) \mid \Phi_i^A(x) = t\}$$

is A-recursive.

Notice that the index function r which computes the number of a program is not only A-computable but absolutely computable.

The theory of (ordinary) computability which we have developed so far depends on the definition of the computable functions and on two numberings φ and Φ satisfying the conditions of Definition 2.1.5 (the utm-theorem, the smn-theorem, and Blum's axioms). The definition of A-computability is similar to that of computability and the numberings φ^A and Φ^A have the same formal properties as φ and Φ. This indicates that many theorems of ordinary recursion theory can be generalized to the relativized A-recursion theory (for any fixed set $A \subseteq \mathbb{N}$). We shall not develop a full relativized theory here but only outline some definitions and results of particular interest. The relativized proofs are usually very similar to the ordinary ones, therefore they are not given here.

The tupling function $\pi^{(k)}$ intermediates between k-ary and unary A-computable functions: $f : \mathbb{N} \dashrightarrow \mathbb{N}$ is A-computable iff $f\pi^{(k)}$ is A-computable. For convenience mainly unary functions are considered. The relativized projection theorem (Theorem 1.8.4) can be easily derived from Theorem 11(4). As a consequence we obtain the relativized version of Theorem 1.8.5.

12 THEOREM

Let $k \in \mathbb{N}$, $B \subseteq \mathbb{N}$. Then

$$B \text{ is A-recursive} \iff (B \text{ is A-r.e. and } \mathbb{N}\setminus B \text{ is A-r.e.})$$

The A-recursively enumerable subsets of $\mathbb{N}$ can be characterized in different ways according to Theorem 2.3.10. The following theorem lists some further interesting properties which generalize Theorems 2.5.2, 2.3.2, and 2.6.2.

13 DEFINITION (*relativized self applicability problem*)

$$K^A := \{i \in \mathbb{N} \mid i \in \mathrm{dom}(\varphi_i^A)\}$$

14 THEOREM

(1) The numberings φ^A, W^A, and cf_{K^A} are complete.

(2) K^A is A-r.e. but not A-recursive.

(3) K^A is 1-complete in the class RE^A of the A-r.e. sets (cf. Def. 2.6.1).

The next theorem brings computability and A-computability and the numberings φ and φ^A into relationship.

15 THEOREM

(1) $\varphi \le \varphi^A$ (especially any computable function is A-computable) for any $A \subseteq \mathbb{N}$.

(2) A is recursive $\iff$ each A-computable function is computable.

(3) $\varphi \equiv \varphi^A$ $\iff$ A is recursive.

Proof

(1) Consider Definitions 1.9.2 and 1.9.4. Then $\nu_{TP}(i)$ is the i-th tape program, tm(w) is the tape machine defined by the tape program w and $\iota^{-1} f_M \iota$ is the number function computed by the tape machine M, altogether

$$\varphi_i = \iota^{-1} f_{tm\nu_{TP}(i)} \iota .$$

The modification of these definitions to oracle tape programs TP' yields a numbering ν'_{TP} such that $\nu'_{TP}(i)$ is the i-th oracle tape program, a mapping tm' such that tm'(w) is the oracle tape machine defined by the program w, and η_i defined by

$$\eta_i(A,x) = \iota^{-1} f_{tm'\nu'_{TP}(i)}(\iota A, \iota(x)) ,$$

the function computed by i-th oracle machine. From Definition 1.9.2 and the definition of η (cf. Def. 5), obviously $TP \subseteq TP'$ and $\nu_{TP} \leq \nu'_{TP}$, i.e. $\nu_{TP}(i) = \nu'_{TP} r(i)$ for some $r \in R^{(1)}$. For any tape program $w \in TP$ we obtain

$$f_{tm(w)}(y) = f_{tm'(w)}(X,y)$$

for all $y \in W(\{1\})$ and all $X \subseteq W(\{1\})$, hence

$$\begin{aligned} \varphi^A_{r(i)}(x) &= \eta_{r(i)}(A,x) \\ &= \iota^{-1} f_{tm'\nu'_{TP} r(i)}(\iota(A), \iota(x)) \\ &= \iota^{-1} f_{tm\nu_{TP}(i)} \iota(x) \\ &= \varphi_i(x) \end{aligned}$$

for all $i, x \in \mathbb{N}$.

(2) Assume that A is not recursive. The function $f : \mathbb{N} \longrightarrow \mathbb{N}$ defined by $f(i) = (0$ if $i \in A$, 1 otherwise) is A-computable. It is not computable since A is not recursive. Therefore, there is some A-computable function which is not computable. Assume that A is recursive and let $f : \mathbb{N}^k \dashrightarrow \mathbb{N}$ be A-computable. Then there is some oracle register machine M with $f(\overline{x}) = f_M(A,\overline{x})$ for all $\overline{x} \in \mathbb{N}^k$. Let F be the flowchart of M. By Definition 2 the statements of F are from the set "$R_i := R_i+1$", "$R_i := R_i-1$", "$R_i = 0$", and "R_i" on the dataset $D = 2^{\mathbb{N}} \times \mathbb{N}^{\mathbb{N}}$. Define a simulation relation $Sim \subseteq D \times D'$, where $D' = \mathbb{N}^{\mathbb{N}}$, by $Sim := \{((A,d),d) \mid d \in \mathbb{N}^{\mathbb{N}}\}$. From F one easily constructs a flowchart of a generalized register machine such that F and F' are similar w.r.t. Sim (see Theorem 1.1.13). F' is obtained from F by replacing any statement "$R_i := R_i+1$", "$R_i := R_i-1$", or "$R_i = 0$" on $D = 2^{\mathbb{N}} \times \mathbb{N}^{\mathbb{N}}$ by the corresponding statement on $\mathbb{N}^{\mathbb{N}}$ and by replacing any test "R_i" on D by the test "$R_i \in A$" on D'. Then by Theorem 1.1.13, $f_F =_{Sim} f_{F'}$. Let M' be the k-ary generalized register machine with flowchart F'. Then by Definition 1.2.2 and 2:

$$\begin{aligned} f(\overline{x}) &= f_M(A,\overline{x}) \\ &= Of_F I^{(k)}(A,\overline{x}) \\ &= Of_F(A,(0,x_1,\dots,x_k,0,\dots)) \\ &= O(A, f_{F'}(0,x_1,\dots,x_k,0,\dots)) \qquad (\text{since } f_F =_{Sim} f_{F'}) \\ &= OCf_{F'} IC^{(k)}(\overline{x}) \\ &= f_{M'}(\overline{x}) \end{aligned}$$

for all $\overline{x} \in \mathbb{N}^k$. Since A is assumed to be recursive, $f_{M'}$ is computable by Theorem 1.2.7.

(3) "$\Longrightarrow$": (follows immediately from (2))
"$\Longleftarrow$": This is an effective version of (2). Assume that A is recursive. By the utm-theorem for φ^A there is some A-computable function f with $f(i,x) = \varphi_i^A(x)$. By (2), f is computable, hence $f(i,x) = \varphi_{r(i)}(x)$ by the smn-theorem for φ, where $r \in R^{(1)}$. We obtain $\varphi_i^A(x) = \varphi_{r(i)}(x)$ for all i,x, hence $\varphi^A \leq \varphi$. Together with (1) we obtain $\varphi \equiv \varphi^A$.
Q.E.D.

Finally we show that any oracle set A may be replaced by a more powerful one.

16 LEMMA (*change of oracle sets*)

Let $A,B,C \subseteq \mathbb{N}$, let B be A-recursive, let $f : \mathbb{N}^k \dashrightarrow \mathbb{N}$. Then:

(1) f is B-computable $\Longrightarrow$ f is A-computable,

(2) C is B-recursive $\Longrightarrow$ C is A-recursive,

(3) C is B-r.e. $\Longrightarrow$ C is A-r.e.

Proof

It suffices to prove (1). Let $M = (F, 2^{\mathbb{N}} \times \mathbb{N}^k, \mathbb{N}, I^{(k)}, O)$ be an oracle register machine such that $f_M(B,\overline{x}) = f(\overline{x})$ for all $\overline{x} \in \mathbb{N}^k$. Define a simulation relation

$$\text{Sim} := \{((B,d),(A,d)) \mid d \in \mathbb{N}^{\mathbb{N}}\}.$$

Since B is A-recursive, there is some oracle computable function $g : 2^{\mathbb{N}} \times \mathbb{N} \dashrightarrow \mathbb{N}$ such that g(A,x) exists for all x and $g(A,x) = 0 \Longleftrightarrow x \in B$. Transform the flowchart F into a flowchart F' by replacing any test "R_i" by the test "$g(Or,R_i) = 0$" where

$$\text{"}g(Or,R_i) = 0\text{"}(X,d) := \begin{cases} + & \text{if } g(X,d(i)) = 0 \\ - & \text{otherwise.} \end{cases}$$

Then F and F' are similar w.r.t. Sim, hence $f_F =_{\text{Sim}} f_{F'}$ by Theorem 1.1.13. Therefore, if $f_F(B,d) = (B,d')$ then $f_{F'}(A,d) = (A,d')$ by Definition 1.1.12 and $Of_F(B,d) = d'(0) = Of_{F'}(A,d)$. We obtain

$$\begin{aligned} f(x_1,\ldots,x_k) &= f_M(B,(x_1,\ldots,x_k)) \\ &= Of_F(B,(0,x_1,\ldots,x_k,0,\ldots)) \\ &= Of_{F'}(A,(0,x_1,\ldots,x_k,0,\ldots)) \\ &= f_{M'}(A,(x_1,\ldots,x_k)). \end{aligned}$$

M' is a generalized oracle register machine. Since g is oracle computable the oracle-version of Theorem 1.2.7 is applicable, hence $f_{M'}$ is oracle computable, and finally f is A-computable.
Q.E.D.

As an illustration of oracle computability, B-recursiveness, and B-recursive enumerability we extend Example 1.

17 EXAMPLE

(a) Let $f \in R^{(1)}$, define $g : 2^{\mathbb{N}} \times \mathbb{N} \longrightarrow \mathbb{N}$ by $g(C,x) = (0$ if $f(x) \in C$, 1 otherwise). Then g is oracle computable and A is B-recursive if Example 1(a) holds.

(b) Similarly, A is B-r.e., if Example 1(b) holds.

(c) A is B-recursive if Example 1(c) holds.

(d) (correspondingly)

(e) Define a function $f : 2^{\mathbb{N}} \times \mathbb{N} \dashrightarrow \mathbb{N}$ by

$$f(B,x) := \begin{cases} \text{div} & \text{if } n := \nu y[y > x \wedge y \in B] \text{ does not exist, otherwise} \\ 0 & \text{if } 1+n \in B \\ 1 & \text{if } 1+n \notin B . \end{cases}$$

The function f is not total, e.g. $f(\emptyset,0) = \text{div}$. If however B is an infinite set then f(B,x) exists for all $x \in \mathbb{N}$. In this case, A is B-recursive if Example 1(e) holds.

(f) A is B-r.e. if Example 1(f) holds.

(g) (correspondingly)

EXERCISES

1) Consider Example 1. For each of the cases (a),...,(g) decide which of the following properties hold.
   (a) B recursive ⇒ A recursive,
   (b) B recursive ⇒ A r.e.,
   (c) B r.e. ⇒ A recursive,
   (d) B r.e. ⇒ A r.e.
2) Verify the statements (c), (d), and (f) from Example 17.
3) Consider Example 1. Discuss the differences between the reductions given in the cases (a),...,(g).

4) Show that $f: 2^{\mathbb{N}} \times \mathbb{N} \longrightarrow \mathbb{N}$ defined by $f(A,n) = (0$ if $e_n \subseteq A$, 1 otherwise) is oracle computable.

5) Transfer the proof of Theorem 1.2.7 on generalized register machines to oracle machines.

6) Prove that a function is oracle tape computable iff it is oracle stack computable.

7) Generalize the proof of Lemma 1.5.3 on auxiliary symbols for tape machines to oracle tape machines.

8) Consider Lemma 8(2). Define η and $\hat{\eta}$ from the set U.

9) Let φ' be a numbering of the A-computable functions $f: \mathbb{N} \dashrightarrow \mathbb{N}$. Show that $\varphi' \equiv \varphi^A$ iff φ' satisfies the relativized utm-theorem and the relativized smn-theorem (Theorem 11).

10) Prove the relativized version of the projection theorem.

11) Prove Theorem 14.

12) Prove that the following sets are decidable:

$$\{\langle i,n,x,t\rangle \mid \hat{\eta}_i(e_n,x) = t\},$$
$$\{\langle i,n,x,y,t\rangle \mid \hat{\eta}_i(e_n,x) = t \wedge \eta_i(e_n,x) = y\}.$$

13) Derive Theorem 6(1) and Theorem 7(2) from Lemma 8(2).

14) Show that for any oracle computable $f: 2^{\mathbb{N}} \times \mathbb{N} \dashrightarrow \mathbb{N}$ there is some recursive set S such

$$f(A,x) = \pi_1^{(2)} \mu \langle y, \langle u,v,t\rangle\rangle\, [\langle x,y,t,u,v\rangle \in S \wedge e_u \subseteq A \wedge e_v \subseteq \mathbb{N}\setminus A].$$

2.11 Turing Reducibility and the Kleene Hierarchy

This chapter will be concerned with a very general kind of reducibility called *Turing reducibility*, and a classification of the arithmetical sets by the *Kleene hierarchy* or *arithmetical hierarchy*. Finally *truth-table reducibility* which is weaker than many-one reducibility but stronger than Turing reducibility is introduced. As a main tool we shall apply the relativized recursion theory introduced in Chapter 2.10. We prove some very basic facts and a deeper theorem by Friedberg and Muchnik which says that there are two recursively enumerable sets which are incomparable w.r.t. Turing reducibility. Among the possibly nonrecursive sets the arithmetical sets are of particular interest. They can be classified w.r.t. the degree of noncomputability by the Kleene hierarchy. Truth-table reducibility is defined as a special case of Turing reducibility. An extensive study and comparison of all the reducibilities is beyond the scope of this book.

In Chapter 2.3 we have defined many-one reducibility for sets: $A \leq B$ via $f \in R^{(1)}$, iff $x \in A \iff f(x) \in B$ for all $x \in \mathbb{N}$. Let $A \leq B$. Then any question "$x \in A$?" can be reduced to a question "$y \in B$?" where y can be determined by a computable function f. A more general kind of reducibility is obtained by admitting several questions "$y_o \in B$?", "$y_1 \in B$?" ... Oracle machines provide a tool for a formal definition of this reducibility.

1 DEFINITION (*Turing reducibility*)

Define two binary relations $(2^{\mathbb{N}}, \leq_T)$ and $(2^{\mathbb{N}}, \equiv_T)$ as follows.

(1) $A \leq_T B$ iff A is B-recursive (A is *Turing reducible* to B).

(2) $A \equiv_T B$ iff ($A \leq_T B$ and $B \leq_T A$) (A is *Turing equivalent* to B). The equivalence classes (cf. Theorem 3) are called *Turing degrees*.

2 EXAMPLE

Consider Example 2.10.1. In the cases (a), (c), (d), and (e) with infinite B, A is Turing reducible to B. The reducibilities are of different kinds of generality.

(a) Here $A \leq B$; only one question "$y \in B$?" has to be asked.

(c) At most 3 questions (a bounded number) "$y \in B$?" have to be asked for any $x \in \mathbb{N}$.

(d) The number of questions "$y \in B$?" depends computably on the input x (but not on the set B).

(e) The number of questions "$y \in B$?" depends on the input and on the set B. Note that the function f with

$$f(B,x) = \begin{cases} \text{div} & \text{if } a := 1 + \mu y[y > x \wedge x \in B] \text{ does not exist} \\ 0 & \text{if } a \notin B \\ 1 & \text{if } a \in B \end{cases}$$

is oracle computable but not total.

The following theorem summarizes the most basic properties of Turing reducibility.

3 THEOREM

(1) $(2^{\mathbb{N}}, \leq_T)$ is a pre-order.

(2) $A \leq B \implies A \leq_T B$ for any $A,B \subseteq \mathbb{N}$; but $\mathbb{N}\setminus K \leq_T K$ and not $\mathbb{N}\setminus K \leq K$.

(3) ($A \leq_T B$ and B recursive) $\implies$ A recursive for any $A,B \subseteq \mathbb{N}$ (but $\mathbb{N}\setminus K \leq_T K$ and K r.e. and $\mathbb{N}\setminus K$ not r.e.).

Proof

(1) For any $A \subseteq \mathbb{N}$, A is A-recursive, hence $A \leq_T A$. Let $A \leq_T B$ and $B \leq_T C$. By Lemma 2.10.16, A is C-recursive, hence $A \leq_T C$. Therefore $(2^{\mathbb{N}}, \leq_T)$ is a pre-order.

(2) Let $A \leq B$ via $f \in R^{(1)}$. The following function $g : 2^{\mathbb{N}} \times \mathbb{N} \longrightarrow \mathbb{N}$ is oracle computable:

$$g(C,x) := \begin{cases} 0 & \text{if } f(x) \in C \\ 1 & \text{otherwise .} \end{cases}$$

Then the function $h : \mathbb{N} \longrightarrow \mathbb{N}$ defined by $h(x) := g(B,x)$ is B-computable and $A = h^{-1}\{0\}$, hence $A \leq_T B$ (see Def. 2.10.9). The oracle computable function $g : 2^{\mathbb{N}} \times \mathbb{N} \longrightarrow \mathbb{N}$ with $g(C,x) = (1$ if $x \in C$, 0 otherwise) shows that $\mathbb{N}\setminus K \leq_T K$. Since $\mathbb{N}\setminus K$ is not r.e. and since K is m-complete in the class of r.e. sets, $\mathbb{N}\setminus K \leq K$ is false.

(3) Let $A \leq_T B$ and B recursive. Then $A = f^{-1}\{0\}$ for some B-computable function $f : \mathbb{N} \longrightarrow \mathbb{N}$. By Theorem 2.10.15, f is computable, therefore A is recursive.

Q.E.D.

By (1) Turing reducibility is a reasonable reducibility relation. Especially $(2^{\mathbb{N}}, \equiv_T)$ is an equivalence relation the equivalence classes of which are called *Turing degrees*. By (2) Turing reducibility is weaker than reducibility and the example $\mathbb{N}\setminus K \leq_T K$ shows that it is strictly weaker. The Turing degree of a nonrecursive recursively enumerable set A contains sets which are not even recursively enumerable (e.g. $\mathbb{N}\setminus K$). Property (3) generalizes Lemma 2.3.4(1) for reducibility, but the counterexample $\mathbb{N}\setminus K \le_T K$ shows that Lemma 2.3.4(2) cannot be generalized from reducibility to Turing reducibility. In Chapter 2.3 we proved the nonrecursiveness of several sets B by reduction, i.e. we proved $A \le B$ for some nonrecursive set A. By Theorem 3(3) it would suffice to prove $A \le_T B$ for some nonrecursive set A. In Chapter 2.3 we have constructed a recursively enumerable set S which is not recursive but for which $K \le S$ does not hold (Corollary 2.6.3). Thus the nonrecursiveness of S cannot be proved by (many-one) reduction to the unsolvability of the self applicability problem. The question arises whether $K \le_T A$ for any recursively enumerable nonrecursive set $A \subseteq \mathbb{N}$. This problem stated by Post in 1944 remained unsolved for twelve years. It was answered negatively by Friedberg and Muchnik who proved a slightly more general result.

4 <u>THEOREM</u> (*Friedberg-Muchnik*)

There are recursively enumerable sets $A, B \subseteq \mathbb{N}$ such that

$$A \not\le_T B \quad \text{and} \quad B \not\le_T A .$$

The proof is not trivial. It involves a new proof method called a *priority argument*.

<u>Proof</u>

(1) Two r.e. sets A and B will be constructed such that

$$(\forall j)\ (\exists y)\ \ (y \in A \iff y \in W_j^B)$$
$$(\forall j)\ (\exists y)\ \ (y \in B \iff y \in W_j^A) .$$

Assume $A \le_T B$. Then A is B-recursive, and $\mathbb{N}\setminus A$ is B-r.e. by Theorem 2.10.12. Hence $\mathbb{N}\setminus A = W_z^B$ for some $z \in \mathbb{N}$. But then $y \notin A \iff y \in W_z^B$ for all y, contradicting the above formula, hence $A \not\le_T B$. For the same reason, $B \not\le_T A$.

(2) By Lemma 2.10.8 (see Exercise 2.10(12)) the set $\{(u,j,x,t) \mid \hat{n}_j(e_u,x) \le t\}$ is decidable, and by Lemma 2.10.8 there is some computable function g such that $N\_(e_u,i,x) = e_{g(u,i,x)}$. We shall now informally describe a procedure for enumerating two sets A and B with the desired properties. The above observations will guarantee that the procedure is effective.

For bookkeeping purposes we introduce two (potentially) infinite lists, the A-*list* and the B-*list*, each of which has *positions* 0,1,2,... At any point in the computation, we shall have used only a finite portion of each list. During the computation *markers*, which are natural numbers, and *marks* (from the set {+,-}) may be put to positions (at most one marker and at most one mark for each position) or removed from positions. The following picture might show a snapshot of the list.

position	0	1	2	3	4	5	6	7	8	9	10	11	12
A-list			2				1	3	0				
		-	+	-		-		-					
B-list	0			2				1	3				
	+		-	-			-			-			

The procedure will guarantee the following properties:

- no + mark can be removed,
- in each list each marker $j \in \mathbb{N}$ will be used exactly once and moved only finitely often.

Let A be the set of positions in the A-list which receive a "+", and let B be the set of positions in the B-list which receive a "+"; then the following will hold:

- if y is the final position of marker j in the A-list, then $y \in A \iff y \in W_j^B$, and if y is the final position of marker j in the B-list, then $y \in B \iff y \in W_j^A$.

We shall say that a position k in a list is free if no position k' with $k' \geq k$ has a marker or a mark. The procedure operates in stages $1,2,3,\ldots$

Stage 1: Put marker 0 into position 0 in the A-list.

Stage 2: Put marker 0 into position 0 in the B-list.

For any $n \geq 1$ do the following.

Stage 2n+1:

Q_1: Put marker n into the smallest free position in the A-list.

Q_2: Let $u \in \mathbb{N}$ be such that e_u is the set of positions in the B-list which have the plus mark.

Q_3: For $j = 0,\ldots,n$ let $a_j^{(n)}$ be the position of marker j in the A-list. Let

$$S_n := \{j \leq n \mid \hat{n}_j(e_u, a_j^{(n)}) \leq n \text{ and position } a_j^{(n)} \text{ in the A-list has no } +\}.$$

Q_4: If $S_n = \emptyset$ then goto stage 2n+2.

Q_5: Let $i \in S_n$ be such that $a_i^{(n)} \leq a_j^{(n)}$ for all $j \in S_n$.

Q_6: Put the mark + into position $a_i^{(n)}$ in the A-list.

Q_7: Put the mark - into each position $b \in N_-(e_u, i, a_i^{(n)})$ of the B-list.

Q_8: On the B-list move all markers j with $i \leq j < n$ to free positions.

Stage 2n+2: (cf. Stage 2n+1)

R_1: Put marker n into the smallest free position in the B-list.

R_2: Let $v \in \mathbb{N}$ be such that e_v is the set of positions in the A-list which have the plus mark.

R_3: For $j = 0,\ldots,n$ let $b_j^{(n)}$ be the position of marker j in the B-list. Let

$$T_n := \{j \leq n \mid \hat{n}_j(e_v, b_j^{(n)}) \leq n \text{ and position } b_j^{(n)} \text{ in the B-list has no } +\}.$$

R_4: If $T_n = \emptyset$ then goto stage 2n+3.
R_5: Let $i \in T_n$ be such that $b_i^{(n)} \le b_j^{(n)}$ for all $j \in T_n$.
R_6: Put the mark + into position $b_i^{(n)}$ in the B-list.
R_7: Put the mark - into each position $a \in N\_(e_v, i, b_i^{(n)})$ of the A-list.
R_8: On the A-list move all markers j with $i < j \le n$ to free positions.
(End of stage 2n+2)

Now we shall analyze the algorithm. First we observe that each marker n will be put into the A-list exactly once and will not be removed from the list (correspondingly for the B-list). A plus mark may never be removed from a position (only minus marks may be replaced by plus marks). If a marker is moved (which is only possible in statement Q_8 or R_8) then it is moved to a greater position.

Proposition: In the A-list and in the B-list each marker m may be moved only finitely often.

Proof (by induction on m): If in some stage 2n+1, i is the number determined in statement Q_5 and $i \le j < n$, we say i moves j. If in some stage 2n+2, i is the number determined in statement R_5 and $i < j \le n$, we say i moves j. If i moves some j then its position obtains a plus mark (by Q_6 or R_6) and in this position it cannot move any marker again. The induction argument is as follows:
$m = 0$: Marker 0 in the A-list cannot be moved by any marker i from the B-list since $i < 0$ (see R_8) cannot be satisfied. Marker 0 in the B-list can be moved at most once for each position of marker 0 in the A-list, hence finitely often.
$m \Longrightarrow m+1$: Assume that each marker $j \le m$ can be moved only finitely often. Marker m+1 in the A-list can be moved at most once for any position of any marker $j \le m$ in the B-list, hence it can be moved only finitely often. Similarly marker m+1 in the B-list can be moved only finitely often.
q.e.d.

Therefore, each marker $x \in \mathbb{N}$ obtains its final position in the A-list which we call f(x). Let A be the set of positions in the A-list which finally receive a plus mark and let B be the set of positions on the B-list which finally receive a plus mark.

Proposition: For all $x \in \mathbb{N}$: $f(x) \in A \iff f(x) \in W_x^B$.

Proof: Assume $f(x) \in A$. Then position f(x) on the A-list receives a plus mark at some stage 2n+1. Let e_u be the set of positions in the B-list which have a plus mark at this time. By statement Q_7 each position $b \in N\_(e_u, x, f(x))$ in the B-list obtains a minus mark, and all markers j with $x \le j < n$ obtain positions greater than $m_o := \max N\_(e_u, x, f(x))$ by statement Q_8. Markers $j \ge n$ will be put only to positions greater than m_o in later stages. Suppose some position $b \in N\_(e_u, x, f(x))$ obtains a plus mark in some stage 2m+2 where $m \ge n$. Then some marker $j < x$ must have this position and j moves x in the A-list by statement R_8. Since by assumption x has obtained its final position in Stage 2n+1, this is a contradiction. We obtain

$N_-(e_u,x,f(x)) \subseteq \mathbb{N}\setminus B$. From statements Q_3 and Q_5 (where $i = x$) in Stage 2n+1 we know $\hat{n}_x(e_u,f(x)) \le n$. Since $N_+(e_u,x,f(x)) \subseteq e_u \subseteq B$, we may conclude $\hat{n}_x(B,f(x)) = \hat{n}_x(e_u,f(x)) \le n$ by Lemma 2.10.8, hence $f(x) \in W_x^B$.
On the other hand assume $f(x) \in W_x^B$. Let $t := \hat{n}_x(B,f(x))$ and $M := N_+(B,x,f(x))$. Then there is some stage 2m+1 with $m \ge t$ at the beginning of which every position $b \in M$ has already a plus mark in the B-list and marker x has its final position f(x) in the A-list. Consider the stages 2n+1 for $n \ge m$. Let u(n) be the number u from statement Q_2 in Stage 2n+1. Since $M \subseteq e_{u(n)} \subseteq B$ we have $\hat{n}_x(e_{u(n)},f(x)) = t \le m \le n$ by Lemma 2.10.8(1). (We have $N_+(B,x,f(x)) = M \subseteq e_{u(n)} \subseteq B$ and $N_-(B,x,f(x)) \subseteq \mathbb{N}\setminus B \subseteq \mathbb{N}\setminus e_{u(n)}$, hence $\hat{n}_x(B,f(x)) = \hat{n}_x(e_{u(n)},f(x)) = t$.) Therefore, $x \in S_n$ if position f(x) has no plus mark at the beginning of Stage 2n+1. There are only finitely many positions (at most f(x)) in the A-list which may have received a plus mark before position f(x). Therefore, if position f(x) does not have a plus mark at the beginning of stage 2m+1 it must receive a plus mark in one of the stages 2m+1, 2(m+1)+1, ..., 2(m+f(x))+1. Therefore $f(x) \in A$.
q.e.d.

Similarly $(\forall x)\ g(x) \in B \iff g(x) \in W_x^A$, where g(x) is the final position of x on the B-list, can be shown. Therefore neither $A \le_T B$ nor $B \le_T A$ holds as we have already proved. The procedure for constructing the marked lists is effective, hence the sets A and B are recursively enumerable.

Q.E.D.

By Theorem 3(2), A and B are incomparable w.r.t. m-reducibility. Clearly $\emptyset \le_T A \le_T K$ and $\emptyset \le_T B \le_T K$ by Theorem 3(2). As a corollary we can answer Post's problem.

5 <u>COROLLARY</u> (*Post's problem*)

There is a recursively enumerable set $A \subseteq \mathbb{N}$ with $\emptyset \not\equiv_T A$ and $K \not\equiv_T A$.

<u>Proof</u>

Consider A from Theorem 4. If $\emptyset \equiv_T A$ then A is recursive by Theorem 3(3). But then $A \le_T B$, a contradiction. If $K \equiv_T A$ then $B \le_T K \le_T A$ by Theorem 3(3) since $B \le K$, hence $B \le_T A$, a contradiction.
Q.E.D.

The above set A is recursively enumerable and not recursive. The nonrecursiveness, however, cannot be proved by Turing reduction to the unsolvability of the self applicability problem. A totally new proof idea is necessary, e.g. that one invented by

Friedberg and Muchnik. The study of the order $(2^{\mathbb{N}}, \leq_T)$ or the order of the corresponding Turing degrees especially on the recursively enumerable sets is an interesting but difficult area of research. Many deep results have been obtained so far mainly by use of priority proofs. These questions, however, are beyond the scope of this book. In Definition 2.10.13 we introduced the relativized self applicability problem K^A for $A \subseteq \mathbb{N}$. The mapping $h : A \longrightarrow K^A$ is called the *jump operator*.

6 DEFINITION (*jump*)

(1) For $A \subseteq \mathbb{N}$ define A', the *jump* of A, by

$$A' := K^A := \{x \mid \eta_x^A(x) \text{ exists}\} = \{x \mid x \in W_x^A\} .$$

(2) The n-*th jump* $A^{(n)}$ of $A \subseteq \mathbb{N}$ is defined inductively by

$$A^{(0)} := A , \quad A^{(n+1)} := (A^{(n)})' .$$

The following theorem summarizes some fundamental properties of the jump operation.

7 THEOREM

Let $A, B \subseteq \mathbb{N}$. Then the following properties hold.

(1) A' is A-recursively enumerable but not A-recursive.

(2) B is A-recursively enumerable $\iff B \leq_1 A'$.

(3) $A \leq_T B \iff A' \leq_1 B'$.

(4) $A \equiv_T B \iff A' \approx B'$.

Proof

(1) This is Theorem 2.10.14(2).

(2) This is a reformulation of Theorem 2.10.14(3).

(3) Assume $A \leq_T B$. By (1) A' is A-r.e., by Lemma 2.10.16(3), A' is B-r.e., and finally by (2), $A' \leq_1 B'$. On the other hand assume $A' \leq B'$. For any $C \subseteq \mathbb{N}$ we have

$$\begin{aligned} C \text{ is A-recursive} &\Longrightarrow C \text{ is A-r.e.} \\ &\Longrightarrow C \leq_1 A' \quad \text{(by (2))} \\ &\Longrightarrow C \leq_1 B' \\ &\Longrightarrow C \text{ is B-r.e.} \quad \text{(by (2))} . \end{aligned}$$

Since A and $\mathbb{N} \setminus A$ are A-recursive, A and $\mathbb{N} \setminus A$ are B-r.e., hence A is B-recursive by Theorem 2.10.12, i.e. $A \leq_T B$.

(4) Follows from (3) by Myhill's theorem (2.4.6).

Q.E.D.

By (3) and (4) the Turing order of the Turing degrees can be embedded into the $\le_1$-order of the isomorphism classes on $2^{\mathbb{N}}$. By (4) Turing equivalent sets have isomorphic jumps. For defining the jump operation we have used the special numbering η of the oracle computable functions $2^{\mathbb{N}} \times \mathbb{N} \dashrightarrow \mathbb{N}$. By Theorem 7(2) (or by Theorem 2.10.14(3)) a set $C \subseteq \mathbb{N}$ is isomorphic to the jump of A, iff it is 1-complete in the class of the A-r.e. sets. Thus the isomorphism class of A' can be defined without use of η. However, for proving the existence of A' a numbering like η (or some equivalent tool) seems to be necessary.

In Chapter 2.9 we have introduced the arithmetical sets $A \subseteq \mathbb{N}^k$ (Definition 2.9.7). Let $p \in L_A$ be a "basic" expression, i.e. $p = "t_1 = t_2"$ where t_1 and t_2 are terms. Let $x_1,\ldots,x_k$ be pairwise different variables such that $FV(p) \subseteq \{x_1,\ldots,x_k\}$ and let

$$M := \{(n_1,\ldots,n_k) \mid val[p : x_1/\underline{n}_1,\ldots,x_k/\underline{n}_k] = true\}.$$

Then obviously M is a recursive set. The considerations in Chapter 2.9 show that any arithmetical set can be obtained from recursive sets (such as the above set M) by finitely many applications of the operations negation, union, and projection. We shall show that the arithmetical sets are those sets which can be obtained from the recursive sets by finitely many applications of the operations of negation and projection. Note that K is the projection of a recursive set (projection theorem), that $K = \emptyset'$, and that the jump operator is related to Turing reducibility (Theorem 7). We shall now introduce the *Kleene-hierarchy* or *arithmetical hierarchy* which classifies the arithmetical sets w.r.t. to the number of projections and negations which are used for defining them from recursive sets.

8 <u>DEFINITION</u> (*standard numberings of the Kleene sets*)

For $n \ge 1$ define sets $\Pi_n \subseteq 2^{\mathbb{N}}$ and $\Sigma_n \subseteq 2^{\mathbb{N}}$ and standard numberings π_n of Π_n and σ_n of Σ_n inductively as follows:

$$\sigma_1(i) := \{x \mid (\exists y)\ \Phi_i(x) = y\},$$

$$\pi_n(i) := \mathbb{N} \setminus \sigma_n(i),$$

$$\sigma_{n+1}(i) := \{x \mid (\exists y)\ \langle x,y\rangle \in \pi_n(i)\},$$

$$\Sigma_n := \{\sigma_n(i) \mid i \in \mathbb{N}\},$$

$$\Pi_n := \{\pi_n(i) \mid i \in \mathbb{N}\}$$

for all $n \ge 1$. The sets Π_n and Σ_n are called *Kleene sets*.

(In this context π_1 and π_2 are not the projections of π^{-1}, where π is Cantor's pairing function, but the above numberings.) Note that $\sigma_1(i) = \{x \mid x \in \mathrm{dom}(\varphi_i)\} = W_i$ and $\pi_1(i) = \mathbb{N} \setminus W_i$. Then following lemma gives a direct notation with dots which is more instructive than the inductive definition.

9 LEMMA (*characterization of* σ_n *and* π_n)

If n is odd then

$$\sigma_n(i) = \{x \mid (\exists x_1)(\forall x_2)\dots(\exists x_n)\ \Phi_i\langle x,x_1,\dots,x_{n-1}\rangle = x_n\},$$

$$\pi_n(i) = \{x \mid (\forall x_1)(\exists x_2)\dots(\forall x_n)\ \Phi_i\langle x,x_1,\dots,x_{n-1}\rangle \neq x_n\}.$$

If n is even and $n > 0$ then

$$\sigma_n(i) = \{x \mid (\exists x_1)(\forall x_2)\dots(\forall x_n)\ \Phi_i\langle x,x_1,\dots,x_{n-1}\rangle \neq x_n\},$$

$$\pi_n(i) = \{x \mid (\forall x_1)(\exists x_2)\dots(\exists x_n)\ \Phi_i\langle x,x_1,\dots,x_{n-1}\rangle = x_n\}.$$

The lemma can be proved by induction on n. Remember that $\langle x_1,\dots,x_n\rangle = \langle\langle x_1,x_2\rangle,x_3,\dots,x_n\rangle$. In the above characterization, n is the number of alternating quantifiers $\exists$ and $\forall$. In the case of σ_n the first quantifier is $\exists$, in the case of π_n the first quantifier is $\forall$. In Lemma 9 we have used the special recursive sets $\{\langle i,x,x_1,\dots,x_n\rangle \mid \Phi_i\langle x,x_1,\dots,x_{n-1}\rangle = x_n\}$. We shall show that these sets can be replaced by arbitrary recursive sets. As a technical tool we prove the following lemma.

10 LEMMA

There are total recursive functions $p,q : \mathbb{N} \longrightarrow \mathbb{N}$ (i.e. $p,q \in R^{(1)}$) such that for all $n \in \mathbb{N}$ and for all $k \in \mathbb{N}$ with $\varphi_k \in R^{(1)}$ the following properties hold:

$$(\exists w)\ \varphi_k\langle u,w\rangle = 0 \iff (\exists w)\ \Phi_{p(k)}(u) = w,$$

$$(\forall w)\ \varphi_k\langle u,w\rangle = 0 \iff (\forall w)\ \Phi_{q(k)}(u) \neq w.$$

Proof

By Lemma 2.1.3(1) and by the translation lemma there is a function $p \in R^{(1)}$ such that

$$\varphi_{p(k)}(u) = \mu\langle w,t\rangle[\Phi_k\langle u,w\rangle = t \text{ and } \varphi_k\langle u,w\rangle = 0]$$

for all k and u. We obtain $(\exists w)\ \varphi_k\langle u,w\rangle = 0 \iff \varphi_{p(k)}(u)$ exists $\iff (\exists w)\ \Phi_{p(k)}(u) = w$ for all $k \in \mathbb{N}$. There is a function $r \in R^{(1)}$ with $\varphi_{r(k)}(u) = 1 \dot{-} \varphi_k(u)$ for all $k,u \in \mathbb{N}$. For all k with $\varphi_k \in R^{(1)}$ we obtain

$$(\forall w)\ \varphi_k\langle u,w\rangle = 0$$
$$\Longleftrightarrow \text{ not } (\exists w)\ \varphi_k\langle u,w\rangle \neq 0$$
$$\Longleftrightarrow \text{ not } (\exists w)\ \varphi_{r(k)}\langle u,w\rangle = 0$$
$$\Longleftrightarrow \text{ not } (\exists w)\ \Phi_{pr(k)}(u) = w \qquad (p \text{ from above})$$
$$\Longleftrightarrow (\forall w)\ \Phi_{pr(k)}(u) \neq w .$$

Define $q := pr$.

Q.E.D.

We are now able to prove the commonly used characterization of the classes Σ_n and Π_n $(n \geq 1)$.

11 <u>THEOREM</u> (*characterizations of* Σ_n *and* Π_n)

Let $n > 0$ and $M \subseteq \mathbb{N}$.

For even n the following equivalences hold:

$$M \in \Sigma_n \iff M = \{x \mid (\exists x_1)(\forall x_2) \ldots (\forall x_n)\ \langle x,x_1,\ldots,x_n\rangle \in Q\}$$
for some recursive set $Q \subseteq \mathbb{N}$.

$$M \in \Pi_n \iff M = \{x \mid (\forall x_1)(\exists x_2) \ldots (\exists x_n)\ \langle x,x_1,\ldots,x_n\rangle \in Q\}$$
for some recursive set $Q \subseteq \mathbb{N}$.

(correspondingly for odd n, where again the leftmost quantifier is $\exists$ in the case of Σ_n and $\forall$ in the case of Π_n)

<u>Proof</u>

"$\Longrightarrow$": The set $Q = \{\langle x,x_1,\ldots,x_n\rangle \mid \Phi_i\langle x,x_1,\ldots,x_{n-1}\rangle = x_n\}$ is recursive for each i and n. Hence, by Lemma 9, each $\sigma_n(i)$ can be written in the given form.

"$\Longleftarrow$": Consider Lemma 10. Let $u := \langle x,x_1,\ldots,x_{n-1}\rangle$, $w := x_n$, $\varphi_k :=$ characteristic function of Q . By Lemma 9 and Lemma 10 we obtain $M = \sigma_n q(k) \in \Sigma_n$.

The cases Π_n for even n and the cases Σ_n and Π_n for odd n are treated similarly.

Q.E.D.

The numberings σ_n and π_n and the classes Σ_n and Π_n are properly ordered.

12 THEOREM (*weak hierarchy theorem*)

(1) There are functions $h_1, h_2 \in R^{(1)}$ such that for all $n \geq 1$ and $i \in \mathbb{N}$

$$\sigma_n(i) = \sigma_{n+1} h_1(i) = \pi_{n+1} h_2\langle n,i\rangle$$
$$\pi_n(i) = \pi_{n+1} h_1(i) = \sigma_{n+1} h_2\langle n,i\rangle .$$

(2) For all $n \geq 1$:

$$\sigma_n \leq \sigma_{n+1} , \quad \sigma_n \leq \pi_{n+1} , \quad \pi_n \leq \sigma_{n+1} , \quad \pi_n \leq \pi_{n+1} .$$

(3) For all $n \geq 1$:

$$\Sigma_n \cup \Pi_n \subseteq \Sigma_{n+1} \cap \Pi_{n+1} .$$

Proof

It suffices to prove (1). First we prove $\sigma_n = \sigma_{n+1} h_1$ by induction on n. There is some $h_1 \in R^{(1)}$ such that

$$\varphi_{h_1(i)}\langle x,x_1\rangle = \begin{cases} 0 & \text{if } \Phi_i(x) \neq x_1 \\ \text{div} & \text{otherwise .} \end{cases}$$

Then for all $i,x,x_1 \in \mathbb{N}$:

$$\begin{aligned} x \in \sigma_1(i) &\iff (\exists x_1)\ \Phi_i(x) = x_1 \\ &\iff (\exists x_1)\ \varphi_{h_1(i)}\langle x,x_1\rangle = \text{div} \\ &\iff (\exists x_1)(\forall x_2)\ \Phi_{h_1(i)}\langle x,x_1\rangle \neq x_2 \\ &\iff x \in \sigma_2 h_1(i) . \end{aligned}$$

Thus we have proved $\sigma_1 = \sigma_2 h_1$. Assume that $\sigma_n = \sigma_{n+1} h_1$ has been proved for some $n \geq 1$. Then

$$\begin{aligned} \sigma_{n+1}(i) &= \{x \mid (\exists y)\ \langle x,y\rangle \notin \sigma_n(i)\} \\ &= \{x \mid (\exists y)\ \langle x,y\rangle \notin \sigma_{n+1} h_1(i)\} \\ &= \sigma_{n+2} h_1(i) . \end{aligned}$$

Therefore, $\sigma_n = \sigma_{n+1} h_1$ for all $n \in \mathbb{N}$. From $\pi_n(i) = \mathbb{N} \setminus \sigma_n(i)$ we obtain $\pi_n = \pi_{n+1} h_1$ for all n. Now we prove $\sigma_n \leq \pi_{n+1}$. By the translation lemma there is some $h \in R^{(1)}$ such that

$$\varphi_{h\langle i,n\rangle}\langle x,x_o,\ldots,x_{n-1},x_n\rangle = \begin{cases} 0 & \text{if } \Phi_i\langle x,x_1,\ldots,x_{n-1}\rangle \neq x_n \\ 1 & \text{otherwise .} \end{cases}$$

(Note that the value of the right hand side of the equation can be determined from $i,n,x,x_o,\ldots,x_n$ by a register machine). Let p and q be the functions from Lemma 10. For even n we obtain

$$\begin{aligned} x \in \sigma_n(i) &\iff (\forall x_o)\ (\exists x_1)\ \dots\ (\forall x_n)\quad \Phi_i\langle x,x_1,\dots,x_{n-1}\rangle \neq x_n \\ &\iff (\forall x_o)\ (\exists x_1)\ \dots\ (\forall x_n)\quad \varphi_{h\langle i,n\rangle}\langle x,x_o,\dots,x_n\rangle = 0 \\ &\iff (\forall x_o)\ (\exists x_1)\ \dots\ (\forall x_n)\quad \Phi_{qh\langle i,n\rangle}\langle x,x_o,\dots,x_{n-1}\rangle \neq x_n \\ &\iff x \in \pi_{n+1}\, q\, h\langle i,n\rangle\ . \end{aligned}$$

For odd n we obtain correspondingly

$$x \in \sigma_n(i) \iff x \in \pi_{n+1}\, p\, h\langle i,n\rangle\ .$$

Define $h_2 \in R^{(1)}$ by

$$h_2\langle n,i\rangle := \begin{cases} 0 & \text{if } n = 0 \\ qh\langle i,n\rangle & \text{if } n \neq 0 \text{ is even} \\ ph\langle i,n\rangle & \text{if } n \neq 0 \text{ is odd}\ . \end{cases}$$

Then $\sigma_n(i) = \pi_{n+1} h_2\langle n,i\rangle$ for all i. From $\pi_n(i) = \mathbb{N}\setminus\sigma_n(i)$ we obtain $\pi_n(i) = \sigma_{n+1} h_2\langle n,i\rangle$.
Q.E.D.

The order $(\{\Sigma_n, \Pi_n \mid n \geq 1\}, \subseteq)$ is called the *Kleene-hierarchy* or the *arithmetical hierarchy* (see below). Now for some sets M we determine an upper bound of the position of M in the Kleene-hierarchy.

13 EXAMPLE

(1) Let M be an r.e. set. By the projection theorem $M = \{x \mid (\exists t)\ \langle x,t\rangle \in Q\}$ for some recursive set Q, hence $M \in \Sigma_1$ by Theorem 11.

(2) Let $M := \{x \mid \varphi_x$ is a total function$\}$. Then $M = \{x \mid (\forall y)\ (\exists t)\ \Phi_x(y) = t\}$, hence $M \in \Pi_2$.

(3) Let $M := \{x \mid W_x$ is finite$\}$. Then

$$\begin{aligned} M &= \{x \mid (\exists y)\ (\forall z)\ (z > y \implies (\forall t)\ \Phi_x(z) \neq t)\} \\ &= \{x \mid (\exists y)\ (\forall z)\ (\forall t)\ (z > y \implies \Phi_x(z) \neq t)\} \\ &= \{x \mid (\exists y)\ (\forall u)\ (\pi_1^{(2)}(u) > y \implies \Phi_x \pi_1^{(2)}(u) \neq \pi_2^{(2)}(u))\} \\ &= \{x \mid (\exists y)\ (\forall u)\ \langle x,y,u\rangle \in Q\} \end{aligned}$$

for some recursive set Q, hence $M \in \Sigma_2$.

(4) Let $M = \{x \mid e_x \subseteq K\}$. Then

$$M = \{x \mid (\forall y)\ (\exists t)\ (y \in e_x \implies \Phi_y(y) = t)\},$$

hence $M \in \Pi_2$. We can, however, obtain a stronger result. Since $M = \{x \mid (\forall y \in e_x)\ (\exists t)\ \Phi_y(y) = t\}$, $x \in M$ iff there is a finite set $e_v = \{\langle y,t_y\rangle \mid y \in e_x\}$ which for each $y \in e_x$ encodes the corresponding value t_y. We obtain

$$M = \{x \mid (\forall y \in e_x)\ (\exists t)\ \Phi_y(y) = t\}$$
$$= \{x \mid (\exists v)\ (\forall y \in e_x)\ \Phi_y(y) = h(v,y)\}$$

where $h \in R^{(2)}$ is defined by

$$h(v,y) = \begin{cases} \mu t[\langle y,t\rangle \in e_v] & \text{if } y \in \pi_1^{(2)}(e_v) \\ 0 & \text{otherwise} . \end{cases}$$

Since the set $\{\langle x,v\rangle \mid (\forall y \in e_x)\ \Phi_y(y) = h(v,y)\}$ is recursive, $M \in \Sigma_1$ (by Theorem 11).

Note that we have not shown in any case that the class Π_n (or Σ_n) is minimal.

In general any set which is defined from recursive sets by the propositional operations and the quantifiers $(\forall x)$ and $(\exists x)$ is an element of some Σ_n or some Π_n. We shall now develop a method for transforming arbitrary definitions of the above type into a normal form corresponding to Lemma 9.

14 DEFINITION

(1) Define operations $\sim, \exists : 2^{2^{\mathbb{N}}} \longrightarrow 2^{2^{\mathbb{N}}}$ and $\vee : 2^{2^{\mathbb{N}}} \times 2^{2^{\mathbb{N}}} \longrightarrow 2^{2^{\mathbb{N}}}$ by

$$\sim\alpha := \{\mathbb{N} \setminus A \mid A \in \alpha\} ,$$

$$\exists\alpha := \{B \mid B = \{x \mid (\exists y)\ \langle x,y\rangle \in A\} \text{ for some } A \in \alpha\} ,$$

$$\alpha \vee \beta := \{A \cup B \mid A \in \alpha ,\ B \in \beta\} .$$

(2) Let $\hat{H}$ consist of those subsets of $2^{\mathbb{N}}$ which can be generated from the set

$$* := \{A \subseteq \mathbb{N} \mid A \text{ recursive}\}$$

in finitely many steps by the operators $\sim$, $\exists$, and $\vee$.

(3) Define the following abbreviations:

$\forall\alpha$ for $\sim\exists\sim\alpha$,

$\alpha \Longrightarrow \beta$ for $\sim\alpha\vee\beta$,

$\alpha \wedge \beta$ for $\sim(\sim\alpha\vee\sim\beta)$,

$\alpha \Longleftrightarrow \beta$ for $(\alpha \Longrightarrow \beta) \wedge (\beta \Longrightarrow \alpha)$.

The following lemma summarizes some basic properties of the set $\hat{H}$. Especially, by (1) the Kleene classes Σ_n and Π_n are elements of $\hat{H}$.

15 LEMMA

For all $\alpha,\beta,\alpha',\beta' \in \hat{H}$ the following holds:

(1) For $n \geq 1$, $\Sigma_n \in \hat{H}$ and $\Pi_n \in \hat{H}$, more precisely:

$$\Sigma_n = \underbrace{\exists\ \forall\ \exists\ \ldots}_{n\text{-times}} * \ , \quad \Pi_n = \underbrace{\forall\ \exists\ \forall\ \ldots}_{n\text{-times}} * .$$

(2) $A' \in \alpha$ if $A \in \alpha$ and $A' \leq A$.

(3) $\sim\alpha \subseteq \sim\alpha'$, $\exists\alpha \subseteq \exists\alpha'$ and $\alpha\vee\beta \subseteq \alpha'\vee\beta'$ if $\alpha \subseteq \alpha'$ and $\beta \subseteq \beta'$.

(4) $\alpha\vee\beta = \beta\vee\alpha$, $\sim\sim\alpha = \alpha$, $\alpha \subseteq \exists\alpha$, $\alpha \subseteq \forall\alpha$.

(5) $\exists\alpha\vee\beta \subseteq \exists(\alpha\vee\beta)$, $\exists\alpha\wedge\beta \subseteq \exists(\alpha\wedge\beta)$, $\forall\alpha\vee\beta \subseteq \forall(\alpha\vee\beta)$, $\forall\alpha\wedge\beta \subseteq \forall(\alpha\wedge\beta)$.

(6) $\exists\exists\alpha \subseteq \exists\alpha$, $\forall\forall\alpha \subseteq \forall\alpha$.

(7) $\alpha\vee\alpha \subseteq \alpha$, $\alpha\wedge\alpha \subseteq \alpha$.

(8) $\alpha\vee * \subseteq \alpha$, $\alpha\wedge * \subseteq \alpha$.

(9) Define operations $\forall_<$ and $\exists_<$ on the subsets of $2^{\mathbb{N}}$ by

$$\exists_<\gamma := \{B \mid B = \{x \mid (\exists y < x)\ \langle x,y\rangle \in A\} \text{ for some } A \in \gamma\}$$

and

$$\forall_<\gamma := \sim\exists_<\sim\gamma .$$

Then

$$\exists_<\alpha \subseteq \alpha \text{ and } \forall_<\alpha \subseteq \alpha.$$

Proof

(1) (immediate by Theorem 11)

(2) We prove the property by (structural) induction on the generation of $\hat{H}$.
$\alpha=*$: (see Lemma 2.3.4)
$\alpha=\sim\beta$: (Apply the property $A' \leq A \Leftrightarrow \mathbb{N}\setminus A' \leq \mathbb{N}\setminus A$)

$\alpha=\exists\beta$: By assumption $B' \in \beta$ if $B' \leq B \in \beta$. Let $A \in \alpha$ and $A' \leq A$ via $g \in R^{(1)}$. Then $A = \{x \mid (\exists y)\ \langle x,y\rangle \in B\}$ for some $B \in \beta$. Let $B' = \{\langle z,y\rangle \mid \langle g(z),y\rangle \in B\}$. Then $B' \leq B$, hence $B' \in \beta$, and $A' = \{z \mid (\exists y)\ \langle z,y\rangle \in B'\}$, hence $A' \in \exists\beta = \alpha$.
$\alpha=\beta\vee\gamma$: Let $A' = g^{-1}A$. $A = B \cup C$ with $B \in \beta$, $C \in \gamma$. By assumption $g^{-1}B \in \beta$, $g^{-1}C \in \gamma$, hence $g^{-1}A = g^{-1}(B) \cup g^{-1}(C) \in \beta\vee\gamma = \alpha$.

(3) (obvious from the definition)

(4) The first two properties are trivial. Let $A \in \alpha$. The case $A = \mathbb{N}$ is easy. Otherwise let $A' := \{\langle x,0\rangle \mid x \in A\}$. Then $A = \{x \mid (\exists y)\ \langle x,y\rangle \in A'\}$. Since $A' \leq A$ we have $A' \in \alpha$ by (2), hence $A \in \exists\alpha$. Furthermore $\alpha \subseteq \sim\sim\alpha \subseteq \sim\exists\sim\alpha = \forall\alpha$.

(5) Let $C \in \exists\alpha\vee\beta$. Then there are $A \in \alpha$ and $B \in \beta$ with $C = \{x \mid (\exists y)\ \langle x,y\rangle \in A \vee x \in B\}$. Let $B' = \{\langle x,y\rangle \mid y \in \mathbb{N},\ x \in B\}$. Then $B' \leq B$, hence $B \in \beta$ by (2), and $C = \{x \mid (\exists y)\ \langle x,y\rangle \in A \cup B'\}$, therefore $C \in \exists(\alpha\vee\beta)$. The second property is proved similarly. The last two ones are easy consequences.

(6) Let $B \in \exists\exists\alpha$. Then $B = \{x \mid (\exists y)(\exists z)\ \langle x,y,z\rangle \in A\}$ for some $A \in \alpha$. Let $A' = \{\langle x,\langle y,z\rangle\rangle \mid \langle x,y,z\rangle \in A\}$. Then $A' \leq A$, hence $A' \in \alpha$ by (2), and $B = \{x \mid (\exists w)\ \langle x,w\rangle \in A'\}$, hence $B \in \exists\alpha$. The proof of $\forall\forall\alpha \subseteq \forall\alpha$ follows from Def. 14(3).

(7) (easy by induction)

(8) (easy by induction)

(9) First we show $\forall_{<}\exists\alpha \subseteq \exists\forall_{<}\alpha$ for any α. Assume $B \in \forall_{<}\exists\alpha$. Then $B = \{x \mid (\forall y < x)(\exists z)\ \langle x,y,z\rangle \in A\}$ for some $A \in \alpha$. Let $h \in R^{(1)}$ be the function from Example 13(4). Let $A' = \{\langle x,v,y\rangle \mid \langle x,y,h(v,y)\rangle \in A\}$. Then $A' \leq A$, hence $A' \in \alpha$, and $B = \{x \mid (\exists v)(\forall y < x)\ \langle x,v,y\rangle \in A'\}$, hence $B \in \exists\forall_{<}\alpha$. Now the properties $\exists_{<}\alpha \subseteq \alpha$ and $\forall_{<}\alpha \subseteq \alpha$ can be proved by straightforward induction.
Q.E.D.

By use of the above rules and several simple derived ones we can easily determine upper bounds to the level in the Kleene-hierarchy for more complicated sets.

16 EXAMPLE

(1) Let $M = \{\langle i,j\rangle \mid \varphi_i = \varphi_j\}$. Then $z \in M$ iff

$$(\forall y)\ [[(\forall t)\ \Phi_{\pi_1^{(2)}(z)}(y) \neq t \wedge (\forall t)\ \Phi_{\pi_2^{(2)}(z)} \neq t] \vee$$
$$(\exists w)\ [(\exists t_1)\ (\Phi_{\pi_1^{(2)}(z)}(y) = t_1 \wedge \varphi_{\pi_1^{(2)}(z)}(y) = w)$$
$$\wedge\ (\exists t_2)\ (\Phi_{\pi_2^{(2)}(z)}(y) = t_2 \wedge \varphi_{\pi_2^{(2)}(z)}(y) = w)]] .$$

By Lemma 2.1.3 we obtain

$M \in \forall[[\forall{*}\wedge\forall{*}] \vee \exists[\exists{*}\wedge\exists{*}]]$

$\subseteq \forall[\forall{*}\vee\exists\exists{*}]$ (by Lemma 15(7))

$\subseteq \forall(\forall{*}\vee\exists{*})$ (by Lemma 15(6))

$\subseteq \forall\forall\exists({*}\vee{*})$ (by Lemma 15(5))

$\subseteq \forall\exists{*}$ (by Lemma 15(6),(7))

$= \Pi_2$

(2) Let $M = \{x \mid K \le W_x\}$. Then $x \in M$ iff K is reducible to W_x by some total function φ_y. We obtain

$$x \in M \iff (\exists y)\ [\varphi_y \in R^{(1)} \wedge (\forall z)\ (z \in K \iff \varphi_y(z) \in W_x)]\,.$$

Since $\{y \mid \varphi_y \in R^{(1)}\} \in \forall\exists*$ by Example 13(2) and since K is r.e. and $\{(y,z,x) \mid \varphi_y(z) \in W_x\}$ is r.e. we have by Lemma 15:

$$\begin{aligned}
M &\in \exists(\forall\exists* \wedge \forall(\exists* \iff \exists*)) \\
&\subseteq \exists\forall(\exists* \wedge (\exists* \iff \exists*)) && \text{(by (5) and (6))} \\
&\subseteq \exists\forall(\exists* \wedge (\exists* \Longrightarrow \exists*) \wedge (\exists* \Longrightarrow \exists*)) && \text{(by Def. of } \iff) \\
&\subseteq \exists\forall(\exists* \wedge (\forall* \vee \exists*)) && \text{(by (7) and Def. of } \Longrightarrow) \\
&\subseteq \exists\forall(\exists* \wedge (* \vee \exists*)) && \text{(by (5) and (6))} \\
&\subseteq \exists\forall\exists* \\
&\subseteq \Sigma_3
\end{aligned}$$

As in Example 13 we have not shown that the classifications are optimal.

The above method for transforming quantified expressions is called the *Tarski-Kuratowski algorithm*. It is not an algorithm in the sense of Church's thesis since it is nondeterministic and it does not yield a unique result. For example, the derivation in Example 16(2) could be changed as follows:

$$\begin{aligned}
M &\in \exists\forall(\exists* \wedge (\forall* \vee \exists*)) \\
&\subseteq \exists\forall\exists\forall\exists(* \wedge (* \vee *)) && \text{(by Lemma 15(5))} \\
&\subseteq \Sigma_5\,.
\end{aligned}$$

We are now able to prove that the arithmetical sets are exactly the sets from the classes Σ_n (and Π_n).

17 <u>THEOREM</u>

Let $k \ge 1$, $M \subseteq \mathbb{N}^k$. Then M is arithmetical iff $\pi^{(k)}M \in \Sigma_n$ for some n.

<u>Proof</u>

(1) We prove by induction on n: For all k and $M \subseteq \mathbb{N}^k$, M is arithmetical if $\pi^{(k)}M \subseteq \Sigma_n$.

<u>"n=1"</u>: Let $\pi^{(k)}M \in \Sigma_1$, then $\pi^{(k)}M$ is r.e., hence M is r.e. (see Lemma 1.8.6) and M

is arithmetical by Corollary 2.9.12.

"n ⟹ n+1": Assume M is arithmetical whenever $\pi^{(k)}M \in \Sigma_n$. Let $N \subseteq \mathbb{N}^k$ and $\pi^{(k)}N \in \Sigma_{n+1}$. Then by Definition 8, $\pi^{(k)}N = \{x \mid (\exists y)\ \langle x,y\rangle \notin A\}$ for some $A \in \Sigma_n$. By assumption, $M := (\pi^{(k+1)})^{-1}A$ is arithmetical, and we have

$$N = \{(a_1,\dots,a_k) \mid (\exists b)\ (a_1,\dots,a_k,b) \notin M\}.$$

Let p be an expression such that

$$M = \{(a_1,\dots,a_{k+1}) \mid val[p : x_1/\underline{a}_1,\dots,x_{k+1}/\underline{a}_{k+1}] = true\}.$$

Let $q := "(\exists x_{k+1}) \sim p"$. Then

$$N = \{(a_1,\dots,a_k) \mid val[q : x_1/\underline{a}_1,\dots,x_k/\underline{a}_k] = true\},$$

therefore N is arithmetical.

(2) We prove by structural induction on the expression p that $\pi^{(k)}M \in \Sigma_n$ for some n, if M can be represented by p.

$p = "t_1 = t_2"$: Let $M = \{(a_1,\dots,a_k) \mid val[p : x_1/\underline{a}_1,\dots,x_k/\underline{a}_k] = true\}$. Then M is recursive, hence $\pi^{(k)}M \in \Sigma_1$.

$p = "\sim q"$: Let $FV(p) \subseteq \{x_1,\dots,x_k\}$ and

$$M := \{(a_1,\dots,a_k) \mid val[p : x_1/\underline{a}_1,\dots,x_k/\underline{a}_k] = true\},$$

$$N := \{(a_1,\dots,a_k) \mid val[q : x_1/\underline{a}_1,\dots,x_k/\underline{a}_k] = true\}.$$

By assumption $\pi^{(k)}N \in \Sigma_n$ for some n. Since $M = \mathbb{N}^k \setminus N$, $\pi^{(k)}M = \mathbb{N} \setminus \pi^{(k)}N \in \Pi_n \subseteq \Sigma_{n+1}$.

$p = "q_1 \vee q_2"$: Let $FV(p) \subseteq \{x_1,\dots,x_k\}$, let M be as above and

$$N_i := \{(a_1,\dots,a_k) \mid val[q_i : x_1/\underline{a}_1,\dots,x_k/\underline{a}_k] = true\}$$

for $i = 1,2$. By assumption $\pi^{(k)}N_i \in \Sigma_n$ for some n. Since $M = N_1 \cup N_2$ we obtain $\pi^{(k)}M = \pi^{(k)}N_1 \cup \pi^{(k)}N_2 \in \Sigma_n$ by Lemma 15(7).

$p = "(\exists y)q"$: Let $FV(q) \subseteq \{x_1,\dots,x_k,y\}$, let M be as above and

$$N := \{(a_1,\dots,a_k,b) \mid val[q : x_1/\underline{a}_1,\dots,x_k/\underline{a}_k,y/\underline{b}] = true\}.$$

Then $M = \{(a_1,\dots,a_k) \mid (\exists b)\ (a_1,\dots,a_k,b) \in N\}$, hence $\pi^{(k)}M = \{x \mid (\exists b)\ \langle x,b\rangle \in \pi^{(k+1)}N\}$. By assumption $\pi^{(k+1)}N \in \Sigma_n$ for some n, hence $\pi^{(k+1)}N \in \Pi_{n+1}$ and $\pi^{(k)}M \in \Sigma_{n+2}$.

Q.E.D.

Thus the Kleene hierarchy classifies the arithmetical sets $M \subseteq \mathbb{N}$. It is customary to extend the Kleene sets to subsets $M \subseteq \mathbb{N}^k$ for any $k \geq 2$ by

$$M \in \Sigma_n :\Longleftrightarrow \pi^{(k)}M \in \Sigma_n, \quad M \in \Pi_n :\Longleftrightarrow \pi^{(k)}M \in \Pi_n.$$

In this case the arithmetical sets are exactly the sets from the classes Σ_n.

By the following fundamental lemma which connects the Kleene classes Σ_n with relativized computability the n-th jump of the empty set is 1-complete in Σ_n. This generalizes Theorem 2.6.2 for the recursively enumerable sets.

18 LEMMA

Let $B \subseteq \mathbb{N}$, let $n \in \mathbb{N}$. Then

$$B \in \Sigma_{n+1} \iff B \text{ is } \emptyset^{(n)}\text{-r.e.}$$

Proof

"$\Longrightarrow$": We prove the statement by induction on n.

"n=0": $B \in \Sigma_1 \Longrightarrow B$ is r.e. $\Longrightarrow B$ is $\emptyset$-r.e.

"$n \Longrightarrow n+1$": Assume $B \in \Sigma_{n+2}$. Then $B = \{x \mid (\exists y)\, \langle x,y\rangle \in C\}$ for some $C \in \Pi_{n+1}$. By the relativized projection theorem (Theorem 1.8.4, Chapter 2.10) B is C-r.e., since C is C-recursive. Then $B \leq_1 C'$ by Theorem 2.10.14. We obtain

$$\begin{aligned} C \in \Pi_{n+1} &\Longrightarrow \mathbb{N}\setminus C \in \Sigma_{n+1} \\ &\Longrightarrow \mathbb{N}\setminus C \text{ is } \emptyset^{(n)}\text{-r.e. (by induction)} \\ &\Longrightarrow \mathbb{N}\setminus C \leq \emptyset^{(n+1)} \qquad \text{(Theorem 7(2))} \\ &\Longrightarrow C \leq_T \mathbb{N}\setminus C \leq \emptyset^{(n+1)} \\ &\Longrightarrow B \leq_1 C' \leq_1 \emptyset^{(n+2)} \qquad \text{(Theorem 7(3))} \end{aligned}$$

"$\Longleftarrow$": We prove the statement by induction on n.

"n=0": $B = \emptyset$-r.e. $\Longrightarrow B$ is r.e. $\Longrightarrow B \in \Sigma_1$.

"$n \Longrightarrow n+1$": Assume that B is $\emptyset^{(n+1)}$-r.e. Then $B = \operatorname{dom} \varphi_i^{\emptyset^{(n+1)}}$ for some $i \in \mathbb{N}$ (Def. 2.10.9/10). From Lemma 2.10.8 we conclude: $x \in B$ iff

$$(\exists y)(\exists t)(\exists u)(\exists v)\, [e_u \subseteq \emptyset^{(n+1)} \wedge e_v \in \mathbb{N}\setminus\emptyset^{(n+1)} \wedge N_+(e_u,i,x) = e_u \wedge$$
$$\wedge\, N_-(e_u,i,x) = e_v \wedge \eta_i(e_u,x) = y \wedge \hat{\eta}_i(e_u,x) = t].$$

We have $e_z \subseteq X \iff (\forall i<z)\,(i \notin e_z \vee i \in X)$ for any $X \subseteq \mathbb{N}$. Since $\emptyset^{(n+1)}$ is $\emptyset^{(n)}$-r.e., $\emptyset^{(n+1)} \in \Sigma_{n+1}$ by induction, hence $\mathbb{N}\setminus\emptyset^{(n+1)} \in \Pi_{n+1}$. With Lemma 2.10.8(2) we obtain

$$\begin{aligned} B &\in \exists\exists\exists\exists\, [\forall_<(* \vee \Sigma_{n+1}) \wedge \forall_<(* \vee \Pi_{n+1}) \wedge *] \\ &\subseteq \exists\, (\forall_< \Sigma_{n+1} \wedge \forall_< \Pi_{n+1}) \\ &\subseteq \exists(\Sigma_{n+1} \wedge \Pi_{n+1}) \\ &\subseteq \exists(\Sigma_{n+2} \wedge \Sigma_{n+2}) \\ &\subseteq \Sigma_{n+2} \end{aligned}$$

by Lemma 15.

Q.E.D.

We can now prove some final results on the Kleene hierarchy.

19 THEOREM

Let $B \subseteq \mathbb{N}$ and $n > 0$. Then:

(1) $B \in \Sigma_n \iff B \leq_1 \emptyset^{(n)}$,

(2) $B \in \Pi_n \iff B \leq_1 \mathbb{N} \setminus \emptyset^{(n)}$,

(3) $B \in \Sigma_n \cap \Pi_n \iff B \leq_T \emptyset^{(n-1)}$,

(4) $\emptyset^{(n)} \in \Sigma_n \setminus \Pi_n$, $\mathbb{N} \setminus \emptyset^{(n)} \in \Pi_n \setminus \Sigma_n$,

(5) $\Sigma_n \cup \Pi_n \subsetneqq \Sigma_{n+1} \cap \Pi_{n+1}$.

This means that $\emptyset^{(n)}$ is 1-complete in Σ_n, $\mathbb{N} \setminus \emptyset^{(n)}$ is 1-complete in Π_n, $\emptyset^{(n-1)}$ is Turing-complete in $\Sigma_n \cap \Pi_n$, $\Sigma_n \setminus \Pi_n \neq \emptyset$, $\Pi_n \setminus \Sigma_n \neq \emptyset$, $\Sigma_n \cup \Pi_n \neq \Sigma_{n+1} \cap \Pi_{n+1}$.

Proof

(1) $B \in \Sigma_n \iff B$ is $\emptyset^{(n-1)}$-r.e. $\iff B \leq_1 \emptyset^{(n)}$.

(2) $B \in \Pi_n \iff \mathbb{N} \setminus B \in \Sigma_n \iff \mathbb{N} \setminus B \leq_1 \emptyset^{(n)} \iff B \leq_1 \mathbb{N} \setminus \emptyset^{(n)}$.

(3) $B \in \Sigma_n \cap \Pi_n \iff (B \in \Sigma_n \wedge \mathbb{N} \setminus B \in \Sigma_n)$

$\iff$ (B and $\mathbb{N} \setminus B$ are $\emptyset^{(n-1)}$-r.e.)

$\iff B$ is $\emptyset^{(n-1)}$-recursive

$\iff B \leq_T \emptyset^{(n-1)}$.

(4) $\emptyset^{(n)} \leq_1 \emptyset^{(n)}$, hence $\emptyset^{(n)} \in \Sigma_n$ (by (1)). Suppose $\emptyset^{(n)} \in \Pi_n$. Then $\emptyset^{(n)} \leq_T \emptyset^{(n-1)}$ and $\emptyset^{(n)}$ is $\emptyset^{(n-1)}$-recursive contradicting Theorem 2.10.14.

(5) For $A, B \subseteq \mathbb{N}$ define $A \oplus B = \{2x \mid x \in A\} \cup \{2x+1 \mid x \in B\}$. One easily shows:

$(A \leq_1 C \wedge B \leq_1 C) \iff (A \oplus B \leq_1 C)$

$(A \leq_T C \wedge B \leq_T C) \iff (A \oplus B \leq_T C)$.

Let $C := \emptyset^{(n)} \oplus (\mathbb{N} \setminus \emptyset^{(n)})$ (for $n > 0$). Since $\emptyset^{(n)} \leq_T \emptyset^{(n)}$ and $\mathbb{N} \setminus \emptyset^{(n)} \leq_T \emptyset^{(n)}$, $C \leq_T \emptyset^{(n)}$, hence $C \in \Sigma_{n+1} \cap \Pi_{n+1}$ (by (3)). Suppose $C \in \Sigma_n$. Then $C \leq_1 \emptyset^{(n)}$ (by (1)), $\mathbb{N} \setminus \emptyset^{(n)} \leq \emptyset^{(n)}$ (see above), $\mathbb{N} \setminus \emptyset^{(n)} \in \Sigma_n$ (by (1)) (contradiction to (4)). Therefore $C \notin \Sigma_n$. Similarly $C \notin \Pi_n$ is proved.

Q.E.D.

The Kleene hierarchy can be illustrated by the following diagram

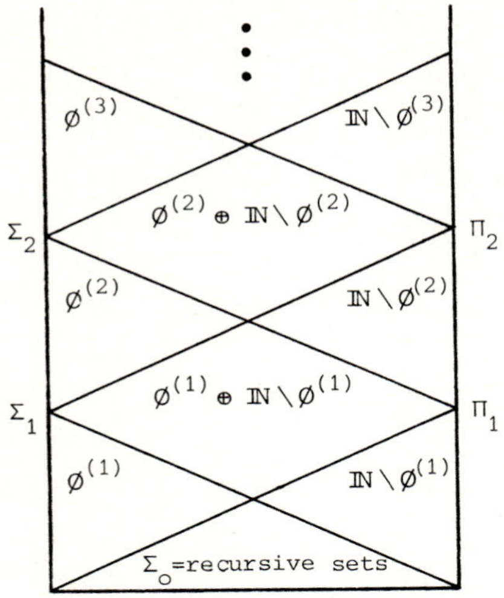

It is easy to define a set $M \subseteq \mathbb{N}$ which is not in the arithmetical hierarchy, i.e. which is not arithmetical.

20 LEMMA

The set $B := \{\langle n,i,a\rangle \mid a \in \sigma_{n+1}(i)\}$ is not arithmetical and $A \leq B$ for any arithmetical set $A \subseteq \mathbb{N}$.

Proof

Let A be an arithmetical set. Then $A = \sigma_{n+1}(i)$ for some $n, i \in \mathbb{N}$. Define $h \in R^{(1)}$ by $h(x) := \langle n,i,x\rangle$. Then $x \in A \iff h(x) \in B$, hence $A \leq B$. Suppose that B is arithmetical. Then $B \in \Sigma_n$ for some n, i.e. $B \leq_1 \emptyset^{(n)}$ for some n. But we know $\emptyset^{(n+1)} \leq B$ yielding the contradiction $\emptyset^{(n+1)} \leq \emptyset^{(n)}$.
Q.E.D.

By definition, the above set B is the "sum" of all arithmetical sets $B \subseteq \mathbb{N}$. The set $\{A \subseteq \mathbb{N} \mid A \leq B\}$ is called Σ_ω. We conclude the studies of the area beyond decidability by determining the exact position for some sets in the Kleene hierarchy.

21 <u>THEOREM</u>

The set $M := \{x \mid \varphi_x \in R^{(1)}\}$ is 1-complete in Π_2. Especially $M \approx \mathbb{N}\setminus\emptyset^{(2)}$ and $M \in \Pi_2 \setminus (\Pi_1 \cup \Sigma_1)$.

<u>Proof</u>

Let $A \in \Pi_2$. Then $A = \{x \mid (\forall y)(\exists z)\ \langle x,y,z\rangle \in B\}$ for some recursive set B. Define $h \in P^{(1)}$ by $h(x,y) := \mu z[\langle x,y,z\rangle \in B]$. By the injective translation lemma (Theorem 2.5.9) $h(x,y) = \varphi_{r(x)}(y)$ for some injective function $r \in R^{(1)}$. We obtain $x \in A \iff r(x) \in M$, hence $A \leq_1 M$. Since $M \in \Pi_2$ by Example 13(2), M is 1-complete in Π_2. Since $\mathbb{N}\setminus\emptyset^{(2)}$ is 1-complete in Π_2, $M \approx \mathbb{N}\setminus\emptyset^{(2)}$ by Myhill's theorem. Note that $M \notin \Sigma_1 \cup \Pi_1$ by Lemma 2.3.16.
Q.E.D.

22 <u>THEOREM</u>

The set $M = \{x \mid W_x \text{ is finite}\}$ is 1-complete in Σ_2.

<u>Proof</u>

From $M = \{x \mid (\exists y)(\forall z)(\forall t)\ (z > y \Longrightarrow \Phi_x(z) \neq t)\}$ we obtain $M \in \Sigma_2$. Assume $B \in \Sigma_2$. Then there is some recursive set A with

$$B = \{x \mid (\exists y)(\forall z)\ \langle x,y,z\rangle \in A\}\ .$$

By Theorem 2.5.9 there is an injective function $r \in R^{(1)}$ with

$$\varphi_{r(x)}(w) = \begin{cases} 0 & \text{if } (\forall y < w)\ (\exists z)\ \ \langle x,y,z\rangle \notin A \\ \text{div} & \text{otherwise}. \end{cases}$$

Then $x \in B \iff W_{r(x)}$ finite, hence $B \leq_1 M$.
Q.E.D.

23 <u>THEOREM</u>

The set $M = \{x \mid (\exists y)\ (y \in W_x \wedge W_y \text{ is infinite})\}$ is 1-complete in Σ_3.

<u>Proof</u>

Since $\{y \mid W_y \text{ is infinite}\} = \{y \mid (\forall n)(\exists m)(\exists t)\ (m > n \wedge \Phi_y(m) \leq t)\}$, we have $\{y \mid W_y \text{ is infinite}\} \in \Pi_2$ and

$$M \in \exists(\exists * \wedge \Pi_2) \subseteq \exists\exists(* \wedge \Pi_2) \subseteq \Sigma_3\ .$$

Let $C \in \Sigma_3$, i.e. $C = \{z \mid (\exists x_1)(\forall x_2)(\exists x_3)\ \langle z,x_1,x_2,x_3\rangle \in D\}$ for some recursive set D. By the translation lemma there is some $g \in R^{(1)}$ such that

$$\varphi_{g\langle x_1,z\rangle}(n) = \begin{cases} 0 & \text{if } (\forall m \le n)\ (\exists x_3)\ \langle z,x_1,m,x_3\rangle \in D \\ \text{div} & \text{otherwise.} \end{cases}$$

Then $W_{g\langle x_1,z\rangle}$ is infinite iff $(\forall x_2)\ (\exists x_3)\ \langle z,x_1,x_2,x_3\rangle \in D$. By the injective translation lemma there is some injective function $h \in R^{(1)}$ such that

$$\varphi_{h(z)}(y) = \mu x_1\ [g\langle x_1,z\rangle = y] .$$

We obtain

$$\begin{aligned} z \in C &\iff (\exists x_1)\ (\forall x_2)\ (\exists x_3)\ \ \langle z,x_1,x_2,x_3\rangle \in D \\ &\iff (\exists x_1)\ \ W_{g\langle x_1,z\rangle} \text{ is infinite} \\ &\iff (\exists y)\ \ (W_y \text{ is infinite and } (\exists x_1)\ g\langle x_1,z\rangle = y) \\ &\iff (\exists y)\ \ [W_y \text{ is infinite and } y \in W_{h(z)}] \\ &\iff h(z) \in M . \end{aligned}$$

Therefore, $C \le_1 M$ for any $C \in \Sigma_3$.
Q.E.D.

In Example 2.10.1 we have introduced different kinds of reducibilities. As we have seen in Example 2.11.2 in the cases (a), (c), (d), and (e) (with infinite B) we have $A \le_T B$. In the cases (c) and (d) the answer to "$x \in A$?" depends on finitely many questions $y \in B$ which depend on x but not on B. This special kind of Turing reducibility is called *truth-table reducibility* or *tt-reducibility*.

24 DEFINITION (*truth-table reducibility*)

(1) Define a predicate TC on $2^{\mathbb{N}} \times \mathbb{N}$ by

$$TC(B,u) \iff (\exists \langle y,z\rangle \in e_u)\ (e_y \subseteq B \wedge e_z \subseteq \mathbb{N}\setminus B)$$

(we say "B satisfies the truth-table condition u" iff TC(B,u) holds).

(2) Define truth-table reducibility $\le_{tt}$ on $2^{\mathbb{N}}$ by

$$A \le_{tt} B \ :\iff\ (\exists f \in R^{(1)})\ (\forall x)\ \ (x \in A \iff TC(B,f(x))) .$$

Suppose $A \le_{tt} B$. Then for deciding "$x \in A$?" determine f(x) and test whether B satisfies the truth-table condition f(x).

25 EXAMPLE

Consider Example 2.10.1(c) and (d).

(c) Define q such that $e_{q(x)} = \{<a,b>,<c,d>\}$ where $e_a = \{2x,4x\}$, $e_b = \emptyset$, $e_c = \{2x\}$, $e_d = \{5x\}$.

(d) Define q such that $e_{q(x)} = \{<x^2,0>,<0,2x>\}$.

Let $C \subseteq \mathbb{N}$ be a fixed set and let Q be any boolean expression constructed from atomic formulas "$y \in C$" (where $y \in \mathbb{N}$). Then Q can be transformed into equivalent expression Q' in disjunctive normal form which in general looks as follows:

$$Q' = "(Q_1 \wedge \overline{Q}_1) \vee (Q_2 \wedge \overline{Q}_2) \vee \dots \vee (Q_k \wedge \overline{Q}_k)"$$

where

$$Q_i = "x_{i1} \in C \wedge x_{i2} \in C \wedge \dots \wedge x_{im_i} \in C"$$

$$\overline{Q}_i = "y_{i1} \notin C \wedge y_{i2} \notin C \wedge \dots \wedge y_{in_i} \notin C" .$$

There are numbers x_i, y_i such that

$$e(x_i) = \{x_{i1}, \dots, x_{im_i}\} ,$$

$$e(y_i) = \{y_{i1}, \dots, y_{in_i}\}$$

and there is a number z such that

$$e(z) = \{<x_1,y_1>, \dots, <x_k,y_k>\} .$$

Then Q holds iff the set C satisfies the truth-table condition z. Thus we have shown that any boolean expression constructed from atomic formulas "$y \in C$" can be transformed into a truth-table condition which corresponds to the disjunctive normal form of this condition. The next theorem summarizes some basic properties of the relation $\leq_{tt}$.

26 THEOREM

(1) $\mathbb{N} \setminus A \leq_{tt} A$

(2) $A \leq B \implies A \leq_{tt} B \implies A \leq_T B$

(3) There are sets A,B with $A \leq_{tt} B$ and $A \not\leq B$.

(4) There are sets A,B with $A \leq_T B$ and $A \not\leq_{tt} B$.

(5) ($A \leq_{tt} B$ and B recursive) $\implies$ A recursive

(6) ($A \leq_{tt} B$ and $B \leq_{tt} C$) $\implies$ $A \leq_{tt} C$.

Proof

(1) Define $f \in R^{(1)}$ by $e_{f(x)} := \{\langle 0, 2^x \rangle\}$. Then $x \notin A \iff TC(A, f(x))$.

(2) Let $A \leq B$ via f. Define $q \in R^{(1)}$ by $e_{q(x)} = \{\langle 2^{f(x)}, 0 \rangle\}$, then $A \leq_{tt} B$ via q. Let $A \leq_{tt} B$ via $q \in R^{(1)}$. Then the function $f : 2^{\mathbb{N}} \times \mathbb{N} \longrightarrow \mathbb{N}$ defined by

$$f(B,x) = \begin{cases} 0 & \text{if } TC(B,q(x)) \\ 1 & \text{otherwise} \end{cases}$$

is oracle computable. Therefore A is B-recursive, hence $A \leq_T B$.

(3) Choose $A = K$ and $B = \mathbb{N} \setminus K$.

(4) Let $A := \{x \mid (\exists y)(\varphi_x(x) = y \wedge TC(K,y))\}$. Then $A \leq_T K$. Suppose, $A \leq_{tt} K$. Then $\mathbb{N} \setminus A \leq_{tt} K$ via some function $\varphi_a \in R^{(1)}$. We obtain

$$a \in \mathbb{N} \setminus A \iff TC(K, \varphi_a(a)) \iff a \in A,$$

i.e. a contradiction.

(5) $(A \leq_{tt} B \wedge B \text{ rec.}) \Longrightarrow (A \leq_T B \wedge B \text{ rec.})$ (by (2)) $\Longrightarrow A$ rec. (by Theorem 3(3)).

(6) Let $x \in A \iff TC(B, f(x))$ and $t \in B \iff TC(C, g(t))$ where $f, g \in R^{(1)}$. We obtain

$$x \in A \iff (\exists \langle y,z \rangle \in e_{f(x)}) ((\forall t \in e_y)\, t \in B \wedge (\forall t \in e_z)\, t \notin B)$$

$$t \in B \iff (\exists \langle u,v \rangle \in e_{g(t)}) (e_u \subseteq C \wedge e_v \subseteq \mathbb{N} \setminus C).$$

Therefore, from x a boolean expression Q with atomic formulas "$y \in C$" ($y \in \mathbb{N}$) can be constructed such that ($x \in A \iff Q$ is true). Q can be transformed into disjunctive normal form Q' and from the expression Q' a number z can be determined such that Q' is true $\iff TC(C,z)$. Note that z is independent of C. Therefore there is some computable function $h : \mathbb{N} \longrightarrow \mathbb{N}$ such that $x \in A \iff TC(C, h(x))$. We obtain $A \leq_{tt} C$.

Q.E.D.

For truth-table reducibility tt-cylinders can be defined which have properties similar to those of m-cylinders. It can be shown that m-reducibility and tt-reducibility already differ on the recursively enumerable sets and that tt-reducibility and T-reducibility also differ on the recursively enumerable sets. We conclude with a characterization of truth-table reducibility as a special case of Turing reducibility.

27 THEOREM

Let $A, B \subseteq \mathbb{N}$.

(1) $A \leq_T B$ iff $(\forall x)(x \in A \iff f(B,x) = 0)$ for some oracle computable function $f : 2^{\mathbb{N}} \times \mathbb{N} \dashrightarrow \mathbb{N}$ such that $(\forall x)\, f(B,x)$ exists.

(2) $A \leq_{tt} B$ iff $(\forall x)\ (x \in A \iff f(B,x) = 0)$ for some *total* oracle computable function $f : 2^{\mathbb{N}} \times \mathbb{N} \longrightarrow \mathbb{N}$.

Proof

(1) This follows immediately from the definitions 2.11.1 and 2.10.9.

(2) Assume $A \leq_{tt} B$. In the proof of Theorem 26(2) we have already defined a function f with the desired property. Assume $(\forall x)\ (x \in A \iff f(B,x) = 0)$ where $f : 2^{\mathbb{N}} \times \mathbb{N} \longrightarrow \mathbb{N}$ is a total oracle computable function. There is some i with $f = \eta_i$. On the set $2^{\mathbb{N}}$ define "open intervals" as follows:

$$[D,E] := \{A \subseteq 2^{\mathbb{N}} \mid D \subseteq A \wedge E \subseteq \mathbb{N} \setminus A\}$$

where D and E are finite subsets of $\mathbb{N}$ with $D \cap E = \emptyset$. A subset $X \subseteq 2^{\mathbb{N}}$ is called open (w.r.t. Cantor's topology) iff it is a union of open intervals, i.e. $X = \bigcup\{[D_j,E_j] \mid j \in I\}$. Cantor's topology will be used in Part 3 of this book. The relation to oracle computability is given by the following property which results from Lemma 2.10.8. Let $x \in \mathbb{N}$ and $B \subseteq \mathbb{N}$, define $B_+ := N_+(B,i,x)$ and $B_- := N_-(B,i,x)$. Then $B \in [B_+,B_-]$, $\eta_i(C,x) = \eta_i(B,x)$, and $\hat{\eta}_i(C,x) = \hat{\eta}_i(B,x)$ for all $C \in [B_+,B_-]$. The crucial property we shall use here is *compactness* of Cantor's space which we shall not prove here:

> Let $(O_j)_{j \in I}$ be a family of open subsets of $2^{\mathbb{N}}$ such that $2^{\mathbb{N}} = \bigcup\{O_j \mid j \in I\}$. Then there is a finite subset $J \subseteq I$ such that $2^{\mathbb{N}} = \bigcup\{O_j \mid j \in J\}$.

Let $x \in \mathbb{N}$. Since η_i is a total function $B_+ := N_+(B,i,x)$ and $B_- := N_-(B,i,x)$ exists for all $B \subseteq \mathbb{N}$. Since $B \in [B_+,B_-]$, we have $2^{\mathbb{N}} = \bigcup\{[B_+,B_-] \mid B \subseteq \mathbb{N}\}$. By compactness and the above observations there are open intervals $[D_1,E_1],\ldots,[D_k,E_k]$ for some k, such that $D_j = N_+(D_j,i,x)$ and $E_j = N_-(D_j,i,x)$ for $j = 1,\ldots,k$ and $2^{\mathbb{N}} = [D_1,E_1] \cup \ldots \cup [D_k,E_k]$. Therefore the following function $g : \mathbb{N} \dashrightarrow \mathbb{N}$ is total:

$$g(x) := \pi_2^{(2)} \mu\langle t,u\rangle[2^{\mathbb{N}} \subseteq \bigcup\{[e_a,e_b] \mid \langle a,b\rangle \in e_u\} \wedge$$
$$(\forall \langle a,b\rangle \in e_u)\ (\hat{\eta}_i(e_a,x) \leq t \wedge N_+(e_a,i,x) = e_a \wedge N_-(e_a,i,x) = e_b)]\ .$$

By Lemma 2.10.8, the property [...] is recursive in x, t, and u (see the exercises), hence g is computable. Since $\eta_i(e_a,x)$ exists for all $\langle a,b\rangle \in e_{g(x)}$ there is a total function $h \in R^{(1)}$ with

$$e_{h(x)} = \{\langle a,b\rangle \in e_{g(x)} \mid \eta_i(e_a,x) = 0\}\ .$$

We obtain for any $x \in \mathbb{N}$:

$$\begin{aligned} x \in A &\iff \eta_i(B,x) = 0 \\ &\iff (\exists \langle a,b\rangle \in e_{g(x)})\ (\eta_i(e_a,x) = 0 \wedge B \in [e_a,e_b]) \\ &\iff (\exists \langle a,b\rangle \in e_{h(x)})\ (e_a \subseteq B \wedge e_b \subseteq \mathbb{N} \setminus B) \\ &\iff TC(B,h(x))\ . \end{aligned}$$

Therefore, $A \leq_{tt} B$.
Q.E.D.

EXERCISES

(1) Modify the proof of Friedberg and Muchnik in order to show that there are three recursively enumerable sets A, B, and C which are pairwise incomparable w.r.t. Turing reducibility.

(2) Prove Lemma 9.

(3) Complete the proof of Theorem 11.

(4) Prove by direct diagonalization: $\Sigma_n \neq \Sigma_{n+1}, \Sigma_n \neq \Pi_{n+1}, \Pi_n \neq \Sigma_{n+1}, \Pi_n \neq \Pi_{n+1}$.

(5) Consider Definition 14. Show that each $\alpha \in H$ is one of the following sets: $*, \Sigma_n, \Pi_n, \Sigma_n \vee \Pi_n, \Sigma_n \wedge \Pi_n, (\Sigma_n \wedge \Pi_n) \vee \Sigma_n, (\Sigma_n \wedge \Pi_n) \vee \Pi_n$ for $n \geq 1$.

(6) Show that σ_n and π_n are complete numberings (cf. Def. 2.5.1).

(7) Consider the proof of Theorem 4. Let $f(x)$ be the final position of marker $x \in \mathbb{N}$ on the A-list. The function f has the property $(\forall x)(f(x) \in A \Leftrightarrow f(x) \in W_x^B)$. Show that f cannot be recursive.

(8) Consider the sets listed below Corollary 2.3.17. Classify these sets w.r.t. the Kleene hierarchy.

(9) Prove that $\{x \mid W_x = K\}$ is 1-complete in Π_2.

(10) Let $A = \{x \mid (\forall \langle y,z\rangle \in e_x)(y \in B \vee 2z \notin B)\}$. Prove $A \leq_{tt} B$.

(11) Show that there are recursively enumerable sets A and B such that $A \not\leq_{tt} B$ and $B \not\leq_{tt} A$.

(12) For $B \subseteq \mathbb{N}$ define the tt-cylindrification of B by $B^{tt} := \{y \mid TC(B,y) \text{ is true}\}$. Call $A \subseteq \mathbb{N}$ a tt-cylinder, if $A \equiv_1 B^{tt}$ for some $B \subseteq \mathbb{N}$. Prove the following properties (cf. Theorem 2.4.8).
   (a) $A \leq_1 A^{tt}$.
   (b) $A^{tt} \leq_{tt} A$.
   (c) A is a tt-cylinder $\Rightarrow$ A is a cylinder.
   (d) A is a tt-cylinder $\Leftrightarrow$ $(\forall B)(B \leq_{tt} A \Rightarrow B \leq_1 A)$.
   (e) $A \leq_{tt} B \Leftrightarrow A^{tt} \leq_1 B^{tt}$.

(13) Consider the definitions in the proof of Theorem 27.
   (a) Prove that $2^{\mathbb{N}}$ is compact w.r.t. Cantor's topology.
   (b) Prove that

$$\{u \mid 2^{\mathbb{N}} \subseteq \bigcup\{[e_a,e_b] \mid \langle a,b\rangle \in e_u \wedge e_a \cap e_b = \emptyset\}\}$$

is decidable.

(14) In the proof of Theorem 2.3.7 we have constructed a simple set S such that $\{0,1,\dots,2x\}\setminus S$ has at least $x+1$ elements. For $x\in\mathbb{N}$ let

$$S_x := \{2^x-1,2^x,\dots,2^{x+1}-2\}\ ,$$

define $S^* := S\cup\bigcup\{S_x \mid x\in K\}$.

(a) Show that $S_x\cap(\mathbb{N}\setminus S)\neq\emptyset$ for all x.

(b) S^* is simple.

(c) $B\leq_{tt} S^*$ for any r.e. set $B\subseteq\mathbb{N}$.

BIBLIOGRAPHICAL REMARKS

Post (1944) raised the question whether there are r.e. sets which are not Turing equivalent to $\emptyset$ or K. The question was solved independently by Muchnik (1956) and Friedberg (1957). The theory of Turing degrees is a difficult area of research. More details can be found in Rogers (1967), Shoenfield (1971), or Soare (1985).

2.12 Computational Complexity

The theory of computational complexity is concerned with measuring the difficulty of computations. Let P be a program of a programming language (e.g. PASCAL or "tape machines"). For any input x there is a computation $c(P,x) = (\alpha_o,\alpha_1,\dots)$ which is a sequence of configurations. If this sequence is infinite, the value $f_P(x)$, the result of applying program P to input x, does not exist, and the computational complexity $R_P(x)$ of the computation $c(P,x)$ is undefined. If $c(P,x) = (\alpha_o,\dots,\alpha_n)$ is finite, then the result $f_P(x)$ can be extracted from the last configuration α_n and the computational complexity is an appropriate function of the sequence $(\alpha_o,\dots,\alpha_n)$ There are many possibilities for defining $R_P(x)$. Examples:

- the length n of the computation,
- $\max\{\lg \nu_1(\alpha_i) \mid 0 \le i \le n\}$,
- $\Sigma\{\lg \nu_1(\alpha_i) \mid 0 \le i \le n\}$,
- $\nu_2^{-1}\ c(P,x)$

(where ν_1 is an "effective" notation of the configurations and ν_2 is an "effective" numbering of computations). A reasonable computational complexity measure should at least satisfy the following conditions:

- $(\forall x)\mathrm{dom}(f_P) = \mathrm{dom}(R_P)$ for all programs P
- $\{(P,x,t) \mid R_P(x) = t\}$ is decidable.

If we assume that programs are numbers and that the computed functions are from $P^{(1)}$, then the above conditions are Blum's axioms (B1) and (B2) from Definition 2.1.5. A pair (ψ,Ψ) satisfying Definition 2.1.5 is called a *Blum complexity measure*.

1 **DEFINITION** (*Blum complexity measure*)

A *Blum complexity measure* is a pair (ψ,Ψ), where $\psi: \mathbb{N} \longrightarrow P^{(1)}$ is a total numbering of $P^{(1)}$ and Ψ is a total numbering of a subset of $P^{(1)}$ such that the following axioms hold.

(utm) : $u_\psi \in P^{(2)}$, where $u_\psi(i,x) := \psi_i(x)$.
(smn) : $(\forall f \in P^{(2)})(\exists r \in R^{(1)})(\forall i,x)\ \psi_{r(i)}(x) = f(i,x)$.
(B1) : $(\forall i)\mathrm{dom}(\psi_i) = \mathrm{dom}(\Psi_i)$.
(B2) : $\{(i,x,t) \mid \Psi_i(x) = t\}$ is recursive.

Obviously, the pair (φ,Φ) fixed in Def. 2.1.5 is a Blum complexity measure. For any Ψ the properties $(\{(i,x,t) \mid \psi_i(x) \le t\}$ is recursive) and $(\{(i,x,t) \mid \psi_i(x) < t\}$ is recursive) are equivalent to Axiom (B2). Let $\psi: \mathbb{N} \longrightarrow P^{(1)}$ be any admissible numbering of $P^{(1)}$ (i.e. a numbering satisfying the smn-theorem and the utm-theorem). Then by Lemma 2.1.2 there is a numbering Ψ such that (ψ,Ψ) is a Blum complexity measure. The two axioms (B1) and (B2) are independent. If we define $\Psi_i(x) = 0$ for all i,x then (B2) holds but not (B1). If we define $\Psi_i(x) = \psi_i(x)$ for all i,x then (B1) holds but not (B2). There are many ways to construct a new Blum complexity measure from a given one.

2 EXAMPLE

The following definitions yield Blum complexity measures (φ,Ψ).

(1) $\Psi_i(x) := (\Phi_i(x))^2$.

(2) $\Psi_i(x) := \varphi_i(x) + \Phi_i(x)$.

(3) $\Psi_i(x) := \langle\varphi_i(x), \Phi_i(x)\rangle$.

(4) $\Psi_i(x) := (i^2 + x)\Phi_i(x)$.

(5) Let $A \subseteq \mathbb{N}$ be recursive such that $A \subseteq \{i \mid \varphi_i \in R^{(1)}\}$. Define

$$\Psi_i(x) := \begin{cases} 0 & \text{if } i \in A \\ \Phi_i(x) & \text{otherwise.} \end{cases}$$

The verification of Blum's axioms is left as an exercise.

By Lemma 2.1.3, the numbering Ψ satisfies the utm-theorem for any Blum complexity measure (ψ,Ψ). Many properties in complexity hold *infinitely often* or *almost everywhere*. As an example, let $f,g \in R^{(1)}$ be total recursive functions. ($f(x) \leq g(x)$ for almost all $x \in \mathbb{N}$) means that g grows faster than f. If g does not grow faster than f, then ($g(x) < f(x)$ for infinitely many $x \in \mathbb{N}$).

3 DEFINITION

(1) Let $P(x)$ be a predicate on $\mathbb{N}$. Then

$$(\forall_\infty x)\, P(x) :\iff (\exists y)(\forall x \geq y)\, P(x)\,,$$
$$(\exists_\infty x)\, P(x) :\iff (\forall y)(\exists x \geq y)\, P(x)\,.$$

(2) Let $f,g \in P^{(1)}$. We extend the $\leq$-relation on $\mathbb{N}$ as follows: $f(x) \leq g(x)$ iff:

$(x \in \mathrm{dom}(f) \cap \mathrm{dom}(g) \wedge f(x) \leq g(x))$ or $x \notin \mathrm{dom}(g)$.

By Theorem 1.9.14 there are partial recursive functions which cannot be extended to total recursive functions. As a consequence of the following lemma, $\varphi_i(x)$ can be computed from i, x, and $\Phi_i(x)$ by a total recursive function.

4 LEMMA

Let $f \in P^{(2)}$ be such that $(\forall i,x)(\Phi_i(x)$ exists $\Rightarrow f(i,x)$ exists).

(1) There is a function $h \in R^{(3)}$ such that

$$f(i,x) = h(i,x,\Phi_i(x))$$

whenever $\Phi_i(x)$ exists.

(2) There is an isotone function $g \in R^{(1)}$ such that for all i:

$$(\forall_\infty x) f(i,x) \leq g \max(x,\Phi_i(x)).$$

Proof

(1) Define $h \in P^{(3)}$ by

$$h(i,x,m) := \begin{cases} f(i,x) & \text{if } \Phi_i(x) = m \\ 0 & \text{otherwise.} \end{cases}$$

By assumption on f, h is a total function such that $f(i,x) = h(i,x,\Phi_i(x))$ if $\Phi_i(x)$ exists.

(2) Define

$$g(y) := \max \{h(i,x,m) \mid i \leq x \leq y,\ m \leq y\}.$$

Then $g \in R^{(1)}$ and g is isotone. Let $i,x \in \mathbb{N}$ and assume $x \geq i$. Assume that $\Phi_i(x)$ exists. For $y := \max \{x,\Phi_i(x)\}$ we obtain

$h(i,x,\Phi_i(x)) \in \{h(i,x,m) \mid i \leq x \leq y,\ m \leq y\}$, hence

$f(i,x) = h(i,x,\Phi_i(x)) \leq g(y)$. If $\Phi_i(x)$ does not exist, then

$f(i,x) \leq g \max(x,\Phi_i(x))$ by Def. 3(2).

Q.E.D.

Lemma 4 has interesting consequences. The values $\varphi_i(x)$ can be bounded by means of the complexity values $\Phi_i(x)$. Therefore a strongly increasing function must have high complexity.

5 COROLLARY

There is an isotone function $g \in R^{(1)}$ such that for all $i \in \mathbb{N}$:

$$(\forall_\infty x)\varphi_i(x) \leq g \max(x,\Phi_i(x)).$$

The proof follows immediately from Lemma 4. By the next theorem two complexity numberings Φ and Ψ for φ differ at most by a recursive function. Roughly speaking, for any i, Φ_i is strongly increasing iff Ψ_i is strongly increasing.

6 THEOREM

Let (φ,Ψ) be a Blum complexity measure. Then there is an isotone function $g \in R^{(1)}$ such that for all $i \in \mathbb{N}$:

- $(\forall_\infty x)\Psi_i(x) \leq g \max(x,\Phi_i(x))$
- $(\forall_\infty x)\Phi_i(x) \leq g \max(x,\Psi_i(x))$

Proof

By Lemma 4 there are isotone functions $g_1, g_2 \in R^{(1)}$ such that for all i and almost all x:

$\Psi_i(x) \leq g_1 \max(x,\Phi_i(x))$,

$\Phi_i(x) \leq g_2 \max(x,\Psi_i(x))$.

Define $g(x) := \max(g_1(x),g_2(x))$.

Q.E.D.

Theorem 6 can be used for transferring a property which has been proved for a standard complexity measure (e.g. time complexity for tape machines) to arbitrary complexity measures (see the proof of Theorem 7).

The converse of Corollary 5 is false: the computional complexity cannot be bounded uniformly by the computed values.

7 THEOREM

For all $g \in R^{(1)}$ there is some $i \in \varphi^{-1}(R^{(1)})$ with $(\exists_\infty x) g \max(x,\varphi_i(x)) < \Phi_i(x)$.

Proof

First we prove the statement for tape machine time complexity. Let ψ be the standard numbering of $P^{(1)}$ introduced explicitly in Chapter 1.9 (where it is denoted by φ). For any $i, x \in \mathbb{N}$ let $\Psi_i(x)$ be the number of steps which the tape machine (with number) i needs for input x (i.e. the word 1^x). Then (ψ,Ψ) is a Blum complexity measure. Let $f \in R^{(1)}$ be any total recursive function. Let j be the number of a tape machine which for input x first computes $f(x)$ and then prepares the output 0. Clearly $\psi_j(x) = 0$ and $\Psi_j(x) \geq f(x)$ for all x. Suppose there is some $g \in R^{(1)}$ such that for all i

$$(\forall_\infty x)\Psi_i(x) \le g\max(x,\psi_i(x)).$$

Choose $f(x) := g(x)+1$. Then for some x,

$$\Psi_j(x) \le g\max(x,\psi_j(x)) = g(x) < f(x) \le \Psi_j(x),$$

a contradiction. This proves the statement for the special case of (ψ,Ψ). From Theorem 1.9.10 we know $\varphi \equiv \psi$, hence $\psi_i = \varphi_{r(i)}$ for some $r \in R^{(1)}$. Suppose there is some $h \in R^{(1)}$ with

$$(\forall_\infty x)\Phi_i(x) \le h\max(x,\varphi_i(x))$$

for all $i \in \mathbb{N}$. Then $(\forall i)(\forall_\infty x)\Phi_{r(i)}(x) \le h\max(x,\psi_i(x))$. Since (ψ,Ψ') where $\Psi'_i := \Phi_{r(i)}$ is a Blum complexity measure, by Theorem 6 there is some $g' \in R^{(1)}$ with $(\forall i)(\forall_\infty x)\Psi_i(x) \le g'\max(x,\Psi'_i(x)) \le g'\max(x,h\max(x,\psi_i(x)))$. We may assume $(\forall x)h(x) \ge x$, hence $(\forall i)(\forall_\infty x)\Psi_i(x) \le g'h\max(x,\psi_i(x))$. As we have shown above, such a function $g := g'h$ does not exist, hence h does not exist.
Q.E.D.

From Corollary 5 we know that a strongly increasing computable function must have high computational complexity. We shall prove now that there are arbitrarily complex 0-1 valued computable functions.

8 THEOREM

There is some $p \in R^{(1)}$ such that for all i with $\varphi_i \in R^{(1)}$ the following properties hold.

(1) $\varphi_{p(i)} \in R^{(1)}$,

(2) $\text{range}(\varphi_{p(i)}) \subseteq \{0,1\}$,

(3) $(\varphi_k = \varphi_{p(i)} \Rightarrow (\forall_\infty x)\varphi_i(x) < \Phi_k(x))$ for all $k \in \mathbb{N}$.

If $\varphi_i \in R^{(1)}$, then $\varphi_{p(i)}$ is a 0-1 valued total recursive function such that for every program k which computes $\varphi_{p(i)}$ the complexity function Φ_k majorizes φ_i almost everywhere. In the proof $\varphi_{p(i)}$ is constructed by means of a diagonalization over all φ_k for which $(\exists_\infty x)\Phi_k(x) \le \varphi_i(x) < \infty$.

Proof

For any $i \in \mathbb{N}$ we define a sequence (M_n) of finite sets and a sequence (z_n) as follows.

$$M_o := \emptyset.$$

Assume that M_n has already been defined. Then determine $z_n \in \mathbb{N}$ and M_{n+1} as follows.

$y_n := \varphi_i(n)$

$Q_n := \{j \le n \mid \Phi_j(n) \le y_n\}$

if $Q_n \setminus M_n = \emptyset$

then: $z_n := 0$;

$M_{n+1} := M_n$

else: $m_n := \mathrm{Min}(Q_n \setminus M_n)$,

$z_n := 1 \dot{-} \varphi_{m_n}(n)$;

$M_{n+1} := M_n \cup \{m_n\}$.

Let M_{n+1} and z_n be not defined if M_n is not defined or $n \notin \mathrm{dom}(\varphi_i)$. By $g(i,n) := z_n$ a function $g \in P^{(2)}$ is defined. By the translation lemma there is some $p \in R^{(1)}$ with $\varphi_{p(i)}(n) = g(i,n)$. We shall prove now that p has the desired properties. Assume $\varphi_i \in R^{(1)}$. Then z_n is defined for all n, hence $\varphi_{p(i)}(n)$ exists for all n. Obviously $\varphi_{p(i)}(n) \in \{0,1\}$ for all n. It remains to prove (3). Let $k \in \mathbb{N}$ be a number with $\varphi_k \in R^{(1)}$ and $\Phi_k(n) \le \varphi_i(n) = y_n$ for infinitely many numbers n. We obtain $k \in Q_n$ for infinitely many n. Suppose $k \neq m_n$ for all n. Then $k \in Q_n \setminus M_n$ for infinitely many n. For each of these n, a value m_n is defined. These values m_n are pairwise different (by the construction). Therefore there is a step n for which $k \in Q_n \setminus M_n$ and $m_n > k$. This is a contradiction to $m_n = \mathrm{Min}(Q_n \setminus M_n)$. Therefore, for some n, $k = m_n$ and $\varphi_{p(i)}(n) = z_n = 1 \dot{-} \varphi_k(n)$, hence $\varphi_k \neq \varphi_{p(i)}$. This proves Property (3).
Q.E.D.

The total recursive functions which can be computed by a program whose complexity is bounded by $t : \mathbb{N} \longrightarrow \mathbb{N}$ form the *complexity class* C(t).

9 <u>DEFINITION</u> (*complexity class*)

For $t \in R^{(1)}$ define

$$C(t) := \{\varphi_i \in R^{(1)} \mid (\forall_\infty x)\Phi_i(x) \le t(x)\}$$

$$C^\circ(t) := \{f \in C(t) \mid \mathrm{range}(f) \subseteq \{0,1\}\}.$$

Every 0 - 1 valued function is the characteristic function of a set. Therefore $C^\circ(t)$ can be considered as a complexity class of sets. In the definition of C(t), finitely many exceptions $\Phi(x) \nleq f(x)$ are admitted. One reason for this is that for usual programming languages finitely many exceptions can be stored in an additional table and going through a table is not expensive. Another reason is that a stronger definition would not yield interesting results.

The main result of Theorem 8 can be formulated as follows: $\varphi_{p(i)} \in C^{\circ}(\Phi_{p(i)}) \setminus C(\varphi_i)$ whenever $\varphi_i \in R^{(1)}$. The compression theorem is a simple consequence.

10 THEOREM (*compression theorem*)

There is a function $h \in R^{(1)}$ such that

$$C(\varphi_i) \subsetneq C(\varphi_{h(i)})$$

whenever $\varphi_i \in R^{(1)}$.

Proof

There is some $h \in R^{(1)}$ with $\varphi_{h(i)}(n) = \max(\Phi_{p(i)}(n), \varphi_i(n))$ where p is from Theorem 8 (apply Lemma 2.1.3). By Theorem 8, h has the desired property.

Q.E.D.

Especially, there is no greatest complexity class. Is there a "computable operator" (see Part 3) $\Gamma : \mathbb{B} \dashrightarrow \mathbb{B}$ such that $\varphi_{h(i)} = \Gamma \varphi_i$? If we consider bounds Φ_i with $(\forall_\infty n) n \le \Phi_i(n)$, this is true.

11 LEMMA

There is a function $g \in R^{(1)}$ such that

$$C(\Phi_i) \subsetneq C(g\Phi_i)$$

for all i with $\Phi_i \in R^{(1)}$ and $(\forall_\infty n) n \le \Phi_i(n)$.

Proof

Since $\Phi \le \varphi$, $\Phi_i = \varphi_{r(i)}$ for some $r \in R^{(1)}$. By Theorem 10, $C(\varphi_{r(i)})$ is a proper subset of $C(\varphi_{hr(i)})$. By Lemma 4, there is some $g \in R^{(1)}$ such that $\varphi_{hr(i)}(x) \le g \max(x, \Phi_i(x))$ for almost all x. Therefore, $C(\Phi_i)$ is a proper subset of $C(g\,\Phi_i)$, if $\Phi_i \in R^{(1)}$ and $(\forall_\infty n) n \le \Phi_i(n)$.

Q.E.D.

By the following Gap Theorem Lemma 11 cannot be generalized to bounds φ_i instead of Φ_i.

12 THEOREM (*gap theorem*)

Let $g, t \in R^{(1)}$ be total recursive functions with $(\forall n) n \leq g(n)$. Then there is a function $f \in R^{(1)}$ such that

- $(\forall n) t(n) \leq f(n)$
- $C(f) = C(gf)$

Therefore, for any $g \in R^{(1)}$ there are arbitrarily large functions $f \in R^{(1)}$ such that between the complexity bound f and the complexity bound gf there is a gap (assume the case $(\forall n) n < g(n)$). The proof is easy.

Proof

Define $f : \mathbb{N} \dashrightarrow \mathbb{N}$ by:

$$f(n) := \mu k\, [t(n) \leq k \wedge (\forall i \leq n) \text{ not } k \leq \Phi_i(n) \leq g(k)].$$

The property [...] is decidable by Blum's axiom (B2), therefore f is computable. For given $n \in \mathbb{N}$ let

$$k_o := \max(\{\Phi_i(n) \mid i \leq n \wedge \Phi_i(n) \text{ exists}\} \cup \{t(n)\}) + 1.$$

Then $t(n) \leq k_o$ and $(\forall i \leq n)$ not $k_o \leq \Phi_i(n) \leq g(k_o)$. Therefore, f is total recursive. Obviously, $t(n) \leq f(n)$ for all n. Since $(\forall n) n \leq g(n)$, we obtain $C(f) \subseteq C(gf)$. Assume $h \in C(gf)$. Then there is some i such that $h = \varphi_i$ and $(\forall_\infty n) \Phi_i(n) \leq gf(n)$. For all $n \geq i$ the property $f(n) \leq \Phi_i(n) \leq gf(n)$ is false by the definition of f, hence $(\forall_\infty n) \Phi_i(n) \leq f(n)$. Therefore $h \in C(f)$.
Q.E.D.

If g is the function from Lemma 11, then the function f from Theorem 12 cannot be a complexity function Φ_k. Lemma 11 can be generalized from the numbering Φ to arbitrary measurable numberings of computable functions (as an exercise). A *measurable* numbering is a total numbering $\gamma : \mathbb{N} \longrightarrow T$ for some $T \subseteq P^{(1)}$ such that the set $\{(i,n,t) \mid \gamma_i(n) = t\}$ is decidable. Clearly, Φ is a measurable numbering. The set $R^{(1)}$ of the total recursive functions has no measurable numbering γ (as an exercise). This can also be concluded from Lemma 11 for measurable numberings and the gap theorem.

For every $t \in R^{(1)}$ we have defined the complexity class $C(t)$. The set $R^{(1)}$ has no measurable numbering γ. Is there a measurable numbering γ such that $\{C(t) \mid t \in R^{(1)}\} = \{C(\gamma(i)) \mid i \in \mathbb{N}\}$? The *naming theorem*, which we shall not prove here, gives a positive answer.

For our arbitrary complexity measure (φ, Φ) nothing can be said about the function g from Lemma 11. For Turing machine time or tape complexity very small functions may be chosen.

Any non empty complexity class $C(t)$ is not φ-recursively enumerable, i.e. $\{i \mid \varphi \in C(t)\}$ is not r.e. This follows immediately from Lemma 2.3.16. We shall prove, however, that sufficiently large complexity classes are *weakly* φ-r.e.

13 DEFINITION (*weakly* ν*-r.e. set*)

Let $\nu : \mathbb{N} \longrightarrow M$ be a total numbering, let $X \subseteq M$. X is weakly ν*-recursively enumerable* iff $X = \nu(A)$ for some r.e. set $A \subseteq \mathbb{N}$.

Every weakly φ-r.e. subset $X \subseteq R^{(1)}$ is contained in a complexity class $C(t)$.

14 LEMMA

Let $X \subseteq R^{(1)}$ be weakly φ-r.e. Then there is some $t \in R^{(1)}$ such that $X \subseteq C(t)$.

Proof

The case $X = \emptyset$ is trivial. If $X \neq \emptyset$, then there is some $f \in R^{(1)}$ such that $X = \{\varphi_{f(i)} \mid i \in \mathbb{N}\}$. Define $t \in R^{(1)}$ by

$$t(n) := \max\{\Phi_{f(i)}(n) \mid i \leq n\}.$$

Then t majorizes each function $\Phi_{f(i)} (i \in \mathbb{N})$ for all values $n \geq i$, hence $X \subseteq C(t)$.
Q.E.D.

15 THEOREM

Let $G = \{f \in R^{(1)} \mid (\forall_\infty n) f(n) = 0\}$. Let $t \in R^{(1)}$ be a complexity bound. Then $G \cup C(t)$ is weakly φ-r.e.

Proof

There is a function $q \in R^{(1)}$ such that

$$\varphi_{q\langle i,y,z\rangle}(x) = \begin{cases} \varphi_i(x) & \text{if } (\forall x' \leq x)[\Phi_i(x) \leq z \text{ if } x' \leq y, \text{ and } \Phi_i(x') \leq t(x') \text{ if } x' > y] \\ 0 & \text{otherwise .} \end{cases}$$

Let $A := \text{range}(q)$. We show $\varphi(A) = G \cup C(t)$.

Assume $f \in \varphi(A)$. Then $f = \varphi_{q<i,y,z>}$ for some $i,y,z \in \mathbb{N}$. If $(\forall x' \leq y)\Phi_i(x') \leq z$ and $(\forall x' > y)\Phi_i(x') \leq t(x')$, then $f = \varphi_i \in C(t)$, otherwise $f \in G$. Therefore $\varphi(A) \subseteq G \cup C(t)$. Assume $f \in G$. Then there are i,y,z with $f = \varphi_i$, $f(x) = 0$ for all $x > y$, $\Phi_i(x) \leq z$ for all $x \leq y$. We obtain $f = \varphi_{q<i,y,z>}$, therefore $f \in \varphi(A)$. Assume $f \in C(t)$. Then there are numbers i,y,z such that $f = \varphi_i$, $\Phi_i(x) \leq z$ for all $x \leq y$, and $\Phi_i(x) \leq t(x)$ for all $x > y$. We obtain $f = \varphi_{q<i,y,z>}$, therefore $f \in \varphi(A)$.
Q.E.D.

Since the above set G is weakly φ-r.e., $G \subseteq C(t_o)$ for some $t_o \in R^{(1)}$. Therefore, $C(t)$ is weakly φ-r.e. if $(\forall_\infty n)t_o(n) \leq t(n)$. Roughly speaking, $C(t)$ is weakly φ-r.e. if t is sufficiently large.

One of the most remarkable theorems of complexity theory is the *speedup theorem*. It states that for any recursive function r there is a function f such that any program i for f can be speeded up by an amount given by r. Especially the function f has no fastest program.

16 THEOREM (*speedup theorem*)

Let $r \in R^{(2)}$ be a total recursive function. Then there is some $f \in R^{(1)}$ with $\text{range}(f) \subseteq \{0,1\}$ such that

$$(\forall k \in \varphi^{-1}\{f\})(\exists j \in \varphi^{-1}\{f\})(\forall_\infty n)r(n,\Phi_j(n)) \leq \Phi_k(n).$$

Proof

The proof of the following proposition uses a diagonalization which is formally very similar to that of the proof of Theorem 8.

Proposition: There is a function $d \in R^{(3)}$ with the following properties.

(1) $\varphi_{d(u,v,s)}(n)$ exists for all $n \leq z+u$, if $(\forall w \leq z)\varphi_s(w)$ exists.

For all s with $\varphi_s \in R^{(1)}$:

(2) $\varphi_{d(0,0,s)} \neq \varphi_k$ if $(\exists_\infty n)[n \geq k$ and $\Phi_k(n) \leq \varphi_s(n-k)]$

(3) $\varphi_{d(u,v,s)} \in R^{(1)}$ for all u,v

(4) $(\forall u)(\exists v)\varphi_{d(u,v,s)} = \varphi_{d(0,0,s)}$

Proof

We modify the definition of the sequence z_n from the proof of Theorem 8 appropriately. For any input $u,v,s \in \mathbb{N}$ define a sequence (z_n) as follows (let e be the standard numbering of $E(\mathbb{N})$, Def. 2.2.1)

$\langle v_1, v_2, v_3\rangle := v$;

$z_n := \mu y\,[\langle n,y\rangle \in e(v_2)$ or $y = v_2]$ for all $n < v_1$.

$M_{v_1} := e(v_3)$;

for $n \geq v_1$ define z_n and M_{n+1} inductively as follows.

$Q_n := \{j \mid u \leq j \leq n \wedge \varphi_s(n-j)$ exists $\wedge\ \Phi_j(n) \leq \varphi_s(n-j)\}$

if $Q_n \setminus M_n = \emptyset$;

then: $z_n := 0$;

$M_{n+1} := M_n$

else: $m_n := \mathrm{Min}(Q_n \setminus M_n)$;

$z_n := 1 \dot{-} \varphi_{m_n}(n)$;

$M_{n+1} := M_n \cup \{m_n\}$

The values z_n and M_{n+1} are not defined if M_n is not defined or $\varphi_s(n-j)$ does not exist for some j with $u \leq j \leq n$. There is a function $d \in R^{(1)}$ such that $\varphi_{d(u,v,s)}(n) = z_n$ for all n. We show that d has the properties (1) to (4).

(1) Assume $(\forall w \leq z)\varphi_s(w)$ exists and $n \leq z+u$. It suffices to show that Q_n exists for $v_1 \leq n \leq z+u$, i.e. that $\varphi_s(n-j)$ exists for $v_1 \leq n \leq z+u$ and $u \leq j \leq n$. The inequalities yield $n-j \leq z+u-j \leq z$ in this case, hence $\varphi_{d(u,v,s)}(n)$ exists.

(2) We consider the case $u = v = 0$. Then $v_1 = v_3 = 0$, hence $M_o = e(0) = \emptyset$. As in the proof of Theorem 8 we conclude: If $\Phi_k(n) \leq \varphi_s(n-k)$ for infinitely many $n \geq k$, then there is some n with $m_n = k$. For this n we have $\varphi_{d(0,0,s)}(n) = z_n \neq \varphi_k(n)$, hence $\varphi_{d(0,0,s)} \neq \varphi_k$.

(3) This follows from (1).

(4) Consider the computation of the sequence $z_o, z_1, \ldots$ for input $u = 0$, $v = 0$, and s. Let $u' \in \mathbb{N}$. There is some v_1 such that $m_n > u'$ if m_n exists and $n \geq v_1$. Define v_2 by $e(v_2) = \{\langle n, z_n\rangle \mid n < v_1\}$ and v_3 by $e(v_3) = M_{v_1}$. Define $v' := \langle v_1, v_2, v_3\rangle$. Then the computation with input (u', v', s) yields the same sequence $z_o, z_1, \ldots$. This proves (4).

q.e.d.

Now we determine an appropriate number s. By the recursion theorem there is a number s such that

$$\varphi_s(0) = 0$$
$$\varphi_s(z+1) = \max\{r(z+u, \Phi_{d(u,v,s)}(z+u)) \mid u,v \le z\}.$$

We prove that $\varphi_s(z)$ exists for all z by induction. $\varphi_s(0)$ exists. Assume that $\varphi_s(w)$ exists for all $w \le z$. By Property (1) of the function d, $\varphi_s(z+1)$ exists. Therefore φ_s is a total recursive function. We define $f := \varphi_{d(0,0,s)}$. Then $f \in R^{(1)}$ (by (3)) and range(f) $\subseteq \{0,1\}$. Assume $\varphi_k = f$. Choose $u := k+1$ and some v (which exists by (4)) with $\varphi_{d(u,v,s)} = \varphi_{d(0,0,s)} = f$. Define $j := d(u,v,s)$. For almost all z we have

$$r(z+u, \Phi_{d(u,v,s)}(z+u)) \le \varphi_s(z+1)$$

by the properties of s. Replacing $z+u$ by n we obtain $r(n,\Phi_j(n)) \le \varphi_s(n-k)$ for almost all n. From (2) and $\varphi_k = \varphi_{d(0,0,s)}$ we obtain $\varphi_s(n-k) \le \Phi_k(n)$ for almost all n, therefore $r(n,\Phi_j(n)) \le \Phi_k(n)$ for almost all n.
Q.E.D.

The speedup theorem is interesting only if the function r is increasing. Notice that the complexity of any program of a function f which has an r-speedup must be considerably more increasing than r. The proof shows that a program for f can be computed from a program for r. The theorem has the form $(\forall k \ldots)(\exists j \ldots) \ldots$. Is there a computable function which for any $k \in \varphi^{-1}\{f\}$ determines an appropriate faster program j for f? The answer is "no" (without proof). In the theorem the property $r(n,\Phi_j(n)) \le \Phi_k(n)$ is only guaranteed for all $n \ge n_o$ where n_o depends on k and j. It can be shown that a bound n_o cannot be computed from k and j in general (without proof). These observations restrict the practical utility of the speedup theorem considerably.

The results from this recursion theoretic complexity theory hold for any concrete complexity measure, e.g. for Turing machine time complexity and tape complexity. Natural complexity measures have many interesting specific properties. For further information the reader should consult textbooks or other recent publications.

<u>EXERCISES</u>

(1) Prove Blum's axioms for the pairs (φ,Ψ) from Exercise 2.

(2) Let $h : \mathbb{N}^4 \longrightarrow \mathbb{N}$ be a total recursive function such that there is some $p \in R^3$ with $h(i,x,y,z) = t \Rightarrow z \le p(i,x,t)$. Define Ψ by

$$\Psi_i(x) := h(i,x,\varphi_i(x),\Phi_i(x)).$$

Show that (φ,Ψ) is a Blum complexity measure.

(3) Let ν be a numbering with $\nu(i)(x) = u(i,x)$ for some $u \in R^{(2)}$. Show that there is some total recursive function $h : \mathbb{N} \longrightarrow \mathbb{N}$ such that $(\forall_\infty n)\nu(i)(n) \le h(n)$ for all i.

(4) Let Ψ be a numbering of partial functions $f : \mathbb{N} \dashrightarrow \mathbb{N}$. Show that (φ, Ψ) is a Blum complexity measure iff $\Phi_i(x) = h(i,x,\Psi_i(x))$ for some $h \in R^{(3)}$.

(5) From Theorem 15 and Exercise 3 derive a simple proof of the following property: $(\forall t \in R^{(1)})(\exists f \in R^{(1)}) f \notin C(t)$ (see Theorem 8).

(6) Show that there are $f, g \in R^{(1)}$ with the following properties:

$$\varphi_i \circ \varphi_j = \varphi_{f<i,j>},$$

$$\Phi_{f<i,j>}(x) \le g \max(x, \Phi_i(x), \Phi_j(x)) \quad \text{for almost all } x.$$

(7) Show that there is a function $g \in R^1$ such that $C(\Phi_i) \subseteq C(q)$ where $q(n) = q \max(n, \Phi_i(n))$ for all i with $\Phi_i \in R^{(1)}$.

(8) Let $X \subseteq P^{(1)}$ be weakly φ-recursively enumerable. Show that $X = \varphi(B)$ for some recursive set $B \subseteq \mathbb{N}$. (Show that this can be proved for any total cylinder ν.)

(9) Let $(f_i)_{i \in \mathbb{N}}$ be a sequence of functions $f : \mathbb{N} \longrightarrow \mathbb{N}$ with the following properties:
- $(\forall i,x) f_i(x) \le f_{i+1}(x)$,
- the universal function v (defined by $v(i,x) = f_i(x)$) is computable.

Show that there is a function $f \in R^{(1)}$ such that

$$C(f) = \bigcup\{C(f_i) \mid i \in \mathbb{N}\}.$$

Hint: Define a total order on $\mathbb{N}$ by $(a,b) \le (a',b') :\Leftrightarrow (a < a' \text{ or } (a = a' \wedge b < b'))$. Define sets $L_n \subseteq \mathbb{N} \times \mathbb{N}$ and values $q(n)$ for $n = 0,1,2,\ldots$ inductively as follows:

$n = 0$: $L_o := \{(0,0)\}$, $q(0) := 0$

$n > 0$: if $\Phi_k(n) \le f_i(n)$ for all $(i,k) \in L_{n-1}$

then:

$L_n := L_{n-1} \cup \{(n,n)\}$

$q(n) := n$

else:

let (i_n,k_n) be the first pair (w.r.t. the above order) $(i,k) \in L_{n-1}$ with $\Phi_k(n) \not\le f_i(n)$. Define $L_n := (L_{n-1} \setminus \{(i_n,k_n)\}) \cup \{(n,k_n),(n,n)\}$

$q(n) := i_n$

Define f by $f(x) := f_{q(x)}(x)$.

BIBLIOGRAPHICAL NOTES

The recursion theoretic or axiomatic complexity theory has been introduced by M. Blum (1967). The main results of this paper are the speedup theorem and the compression theorem. An excellent overview of the theory of computational complexity is Hartmanis and Hopcroft (1971). Good representations of complexity theory can be found in Brainerd and Landweber (1974) and Schnorr (1974). There are only few comprehensive presentations of Turing machine complexity,e.g. Hopcroft and Ullmann (1979), Böhling and v.Braunmühl (1974), and Paul (1978). Most results are only published in Journals and conference proceedings.

Part 3: Type 2 Theory of Constructivity and Computability

In the first two parts of this book we have studied computability on the set $\mathbb{N}$ of natural numbers and on other denumerable sets using the concept of numbering. There are, however, sets for which our concepts do not apply, e.g. $P_\omega := 2^{\mathbb{N}}$ (subsets of $\mathbb{N}$), $\mathbb{B} := \mathbb{N}^{\mathbb{N}}$ (sequences of numbers), $\mathbb{C} := \{0,1\}^{\mathbb{N}}$ (0-1 sequences), $\mathbb{R}$ (set of real numbers), or $C[0;1]$ (for set of continuous functions $f : [0;1] \longrightarrow \mathbb{R}$). These sets are not denumerable but have the cardinality of the continuum. We shall call sets, the cardinality of which is not greater than that of the continuum, Type 2 sets and the elements of these sets will be called Type 2 objects. In Part 3 of this book we shall develop a theory of computability on Type 2 sets which will be called Type 2 recursion (or computability) theory. Type 2 recursion theory cannot be developed reasonably without considering topology. The topological aspects of this theory turn out to yield an interesting theory by themselves which can be interpreted as a general theory of constructivity on Type 2 sets. Thus we shall develop a general topological theory of constructivity and a more special theory of computability on Type 2 sets simultaneously. Notice that in the literature the term "constructive" has different meanings. We shall not introduce it formally but only use it for interpreting results.

The role of topology in Type 2 recursion theory can be explained roughly as follows. Any object x considered in Type 2 theory is defined as the limit of a sequence $(x_i)_{i \in \mathbb{N}}$ of finite objects, i.e. $x = \lim x_i$, thus any x_i can be considered as an approximation of the (infinite) object x. A property P of x can be considered as a kind of information $I(x)$ contained in x. In Type 2 theory those properties are considered for which $I(x)$ is the limit of the informations $I(x_i)$ of the finite approximate values, i.e. for which $I(x) = \lim I(x_i)$ if $x = \lim x_i$. Topology is a general theory in which limits and approximations can be investigated, therefore it is used as a tool for Type 2 theory. From time to time some basic definitions from topology will be inserted into the text. Readers who are not sufficiently familiar with these definitions should consult a textbook for more detailed information.

Type 2 theory of continuity and computability is still incomplete. This Part 3 of the book is only an attempt to present fundamentals of it.

In Part 1 we have defined computability explicitly on $\mathbb{N}$ and on $W(\Sigma)$ where Σ is an arbitrary alphabet. We have proved that computability on $W(\Sigma)$ can be reduced to computability on $\mathbb{N}$ and vice versa. In Chapter 3.1 we shall explicitly define computability and continuity on three different Type 2 sets and prove that the concepts can be reduced to each other. For the further studies computability on $\mathbb{B} := \mathbb{N}^{\mathbb{N}}$ is taken as a basis. A theory of computability and continuity on $\mathbb{B}$ which is formally similar to Type 1 recursion theory (see Part 2) is outlined in Chapter 3.2. A representation $\psi : \mathbb{B} \longrightarrow [\mathbb{B} \longrightarrow \mathbb{B}]$ of a certain class of continuous functions from $\mathbb{B}$ to $\mathbb{B}$ by elements of $\mathbb{B}$ is introduced as a counterpart of the standard numbering φ of $P^{(1)}$. In Chapter 3.3 representations are introduced. Again the formal similarity to the theory of numberings is stressed. Effectivity of representations is discussed in Chapter 3.4. Topological properties turn out to be essential. As a broad class of effective representations the admissible representations of T_o-spaces with countable bases are defined and investigated. The definitions are especially applicable to separable metric spaces. On the other hand, there are natural representations which are (probably) not admissible. The theory of cpo's which has been developed for purposes of programming language semantics constitutes an interesting model for studying Type 2 constructivity and computability. A topological framework for cpo's is developed in Chapter 3.5. Especially algebraic cpo's are introduced and the constructions of sum, product and function space are discussed. Aspects of Type 2 computability are investigated in Chapter 3.6. Two fundamental theorems relating computability w.r.t. numberings and computability w.r.t. representations are proved. Chapter 3.7 is devoted to the problem of constructing new domains (i.e. special constructive cpo's) which satisfy certain recursion equations. It is shown that the theory of cpo's itself can be applied for investigating the class of all domains. Finally in Chapter 3.8 the theory of representations is applied for studying constructivity and computability in Analysis. As an instructive example the determination of zeros of continuous functions on the real numbers is discussed in detail.

BIBLIOGRAPHICAL REMARKS

There is no comprehensive presentation of Type 2 computability in the literature. Parts of the theory can be found in Rogers (1967) and Davis (1958).

3.1 Type 2 Computability Models

In Type 1 recursion theory we have defined computability explicitly on numbers and on words and we have shown that both approaches are essentially equivalent (see Theorem 1.7.5). Computability on other denumerable sets can be reduced to computability on $\mathbb{N}$ via numberings or notations. In this chapter we shall introduce three explicit definitions of Type 2 computability and prove that they are essentially equivalent. Any "natural" kind of computability on some other Type 2 set should be reducible to any one of these three definitions by means of a representation.

The sets we shall consider are

- $\mathbb{C}_o$, the set of all finite and infinite 0-1-sequences,
- $\mathbb{B}_o$, the set of all finite and infinite sequences of natural numbers,
- $P_\omega := 2^{\mathbb{N}}$, the set of all subsets of $\mathbb{N}$.

Notice that these sets have the cardinality of the continuum.

As we have already mentioned topology plays a fundamental role in our theory. The first definition from topology is that of a topological space. A *topological space* is a pair (X,τ) where X is a set and $\tau \subseteq 2^X$ is a set of subsets of X such that the following properties hold:

(1) $\emptyset \in \tau$, $X \in \tau$.

(2) $A,B \in \tau \implies A \cap B \in \tau$.

(3) $\beta \subseteq \tau \implies \bigcup\beta \in \tau$.

The elements of X are called *points*, the elements of τ are called the *open sets* and τ is called *topology* of the space (X,τ). If $A \subseteq B \subseteq X$ such that $A \subseteq D \subseteq B$ for some open set $D \in \tau$, then B is called a *neighbourhood* of A (w.r.t. τ). If $x \in D \subseteq A \subseteq X$ for some $D \in \tau$, then A is called a neighbourhood of x. A subset $\beta \subseteq \tau$ of subsets of X is called a *base* of τ iff any $A \in \tau$ is the union of some subset of β. A set $\beta \subseteq 2^X$ is the base of a topology τ on X iff $X = \bigcup\beta$ and for each $B,B' \in \beta$ there is some $\alpha \subseteq \beta$ such that $B \cap B' = \bigcup\alpha$. In this case τ is uniquely determined: $\tau = \{\bigcup\alpha \mid \alpha \subseteq \beta\}$. Notice that τ is a base of τ. Let (X,τ) be a topological space, let $Y \subseteq X$. Then $\tau' := \{Y \cap A \mid A \in \tau\}$ is the topology on Y *induced* by τ. If $B = Y \cap A$ for some $A \in \tau$ we shall say "B is open in Y, w.r.t. τ".

First we consider the set P_ω. According to our philosophy we introduce a topology on P_ω.

1 DEFINITION (*standard topology* τ_E *on* P_ω)

Let $P_\omega := 2^{\mathbb{N}}$. For any finite subset $E \subseteq \mathbb{N}$ define $O_E := \{X \in P_\omega \mid E \subseteq X\}$. Let τ_E be the topology on P_ω defined by the base $\{O_E \mid E \subseteq \mathbb{N}$, E finite$\}$.

Clearly the set $\beta = \{O_E \mid E \subseteq \mathbb{N}$, E finite$\}$ is a base of a topology since $O_E \cap O_F = O_{E\cup F} \in \beta$ for finite sets E and F. Any $X \in P_\omega$ is the union of finite sets. It is uniquely determined by the set $B_X = \{E \subseteq X \mid E$ finite$\}$, i.e. $X = \bigcup B_X$. Moreover, each $X \in P_\omega$ is the union of a nondecreasing sequence $E_o, E_1, \ldots$ of finite sets, i.e. $X = \bigcup\{E_i \mid i \in \mathbb{N}\}$, therefore each Type 2 object X is the limit of a sequence of Type 1 objects.

Let (X,τ) and (X',τ') be topological spaces. A (possibly partial) function $f : X \dashrightarrow X'$ is called (τ,τ')-*continuous*, iff for any open set $A' \in \tau'$ there is some open set $A \in \tau$ with $f^{-1}(A') = A \cap \mathrm{dom}(f)$. In other words, f is (τ,τ')-continuous, iff $f^{-1}(A')$ is open w.r.t. the topology on dom(f) induced by τ for any open set $A' \in \tau'$. Let $\beta \subseteq \tau'$ be a base of τ'. Then each of the following conditions characterizes continuity of f.

- $(\forall A' \in \beta)\ (\exists A \in \tau)\quad f^{-1}A' = A \cap \mathrm{dom}(f)$,
- $(\forall A' \in \beta)\ (\forall x \in f^{-1}A')\ (\exists A \in \tau)\quad (x \in A \wedge f(A) \subseteq A')$.

We shall use these properties without further mention. The composition of continuous functions is continuous. If a set is open or a function is continuous w.r.t. standard topologies, we shall not mention these topologies explicitly.

We shall denote the set of the total continuous functions $\Gamma : P_\omega \longrightarrow P_\omega$ by $[P_\omega \longrightarrow P_\omega]$. Let $\Gamma \in [P_\omega \longrightarrow P_\omega]$. Then $\Gamma^{-1}O_F$ is open for every finite set $F \subseteq \mathbb{N}$. The topological properties of Γ are defined by the set $\{(E,F) \mid O_E \subseteq \Gamma^{-1}O_F\}$. Notice that $O_E \subseteq \Gamma^{-1}O_F \iff E \in \Gamma^{-1}O_F \iff \Gamma(E) \in O_F \iff F \subseteq \Gamma(E)$. We shall prove now that Γ is completely determined by the set $\{(E,F) \mid F \subseteq \Gamma(E)\}$.

2 THEOREM (*characterization of* $[P_\omega \longrightarrow P_\omega]$)

(1) Let $Z \subseteq \{(E,F) \mid E,F \in P_\omega$; E,F finite$\}$. Then the function $\Gamma_Z : P_\omega \longrightarrow P_\omega$ defined by

$$\Gamma_Z(A) := \bigcup\{F \mid (\exists E)\ ((E,F) \in Z \wedge E \subseteq A)\}$$

is continuous.

(2) For each continuous function $\Gamma : P_\omega \longrightarrow P_\omega$ the set $Z := \{(E,F) \mid E,F$ finite and $F \subseteq \Gamma(E)\}$ satisfies $\Gamma = \Gamma_Z$.

Notice that each Γ_Z is $\subseteq$-isotone, hence each continuous $\Gamma : P_\omega \longrightarrow P_\omega$ is isotone.

Proof

(1) Obviously $A \subseteq A' \Longrightarrow \Gamma_Z(A) \subseteq \Gamma_Z(A')$, hence Γ_Z is isotone. Let $C, D \in P_\omega$, D finite. Then

$$\begin{aligned} C \in \Gamma_Z^{-1} O_D &\Longrightarrow \Gamma_Z(C) \in O_D \\ &\Longrightarrow D \subseteq \Gamma_Z(C) = \bigcup \{F \mid (\exists E)\ ((E,F) \in Z \wedge E \subseteq C)\} \\ &\Longrightarrow (\exists G, \text{ finite})\ \ (D \subseteq \Gamma_Z(G) \wedge G \subseteq C) \quad (!) \\ &\Longrightarrow (\exists G, \text{ finite})\ \ (C \in O_G \subseteq \Gamma_Z^{-1}(O_D)) . \end{aligned}$$

Therefore Γ_Z is continuous.

(2) Let Γ be continuous. First we show that Γ is isotone. Assume $A \subseteq B$, D finite. Then

$$\begin{aligned} D \subseteq \Gamma(A) &\Longrightarrow A \in \Gamma^{-1} O_D \\ &\Longrightarrow (\exists E, \text{ finite})\ \ (A \in O_E \subseteq \Gamma^{-1} O_D) \quad \text{(by continuity of } \Gamma) \\ &\Longrightarrow (\exists E, \text{ finite})\ \ (B \in O_E \subseteq \Gamma^{-1} O_D) \\ &\Longrightarrow B \in \Gamma^{-1} O_D \\ &\Longrightarrow D \subseteq \Gamma(B) . \end{aligned}$$

This implies $\Gamma(A) \subseteq \Gamma(B)$. We show $D \subseteq \Gamma(A) \Longrightarrow D \subseteq \Gamma_Z(A)$ for finite D.

$$\begin{aligned} D \subseteq \Gamma(A) &\Longrightarrow (\exists E, \text{ finite})\ \ (A \in O_E \wedge O_E \subseteq \Gamma^{-1} O_D) \quad \text{(as above)} \\ &\Longrightarrow (\exists E, \text{ finite})\ \ (E \subseteq A \wedge D \subseteq \Gamma(E)) \\ &\Longrightarrow D \subseteq \bigcup \{F \mid (\exists E)\ (F \subseteq \Gamma(E) \wedge E \subseteq A)\} \\ &\Longrightarrow D \subseteq \Gamma_Z(A) . \end{aligned}$$

Therefore $\Gamma(A) \subseteq \Gamma_Z(A)$ for all $A \in P_\omega$. On the other hand, for any $k \in \mathbb{N}$ and $A \in P_\omega$ we have

$$\begin{aligned} k \in \Gamma_Z(A) &\Longrightarrow (\exists E,F, \text{ finite})\ \ (k \in F \wedge F \subseteq \Gamma(E) \wedge E \subseteq A) \\ &\Longrightarrow (\exists E, \text{ finite})\ \ (k \in \Gamma(E) \wedge \Gamma(E) \subseteq \Gamma(A)) \quad \text{(since } \Gamma \text{ is isotone)} \\ &\Longrightarrow k \in \Gamma(A) . \end{aligned}$$

Therefore $\Gamma_Z(A) \subseteq \Gamma(A)$ for all $A \in P_\omega$.

Q.E.D.

Any set $A \in P_\omega$ is uniquely determined by the (denumerable) set $M_1 = \{E \mid E \subseteq A,\ E \text{ finite}\}$ and any function $\Gamma \in [P_\omega \longrightarrow P_\omega]$ is uniquely determined by its "graph" $M_2 := \{(E,F) \mid E,F \text{ finite},\ F \subseteq \Gamma(E)\}$. Remember that we have already defined a standard numbering e of the set $E(\mathbb{N})$ of the finite subsets of $\mathbb{N}$ (Def. 2.2.2). We shall now apply Type 1 computability in order to define the computable elements of P_ω and of $[P_\omega \longrightarrow P_\omega]$. By the graph-theorem (2.3.14) a function $f : \mathbb{N} \dashrightarrow \mathbb{N}$ is computable iff its graph is recursively enumerable. This idea is generalized in the next definition.

3 <u>DEFINITION</u> (*computable elements of* P_ω *and* $[P_\omega \longrightarrow P_\omega]$)

(1) A set $A \in P_\omega$ is called *computable* iff

$$\{B \in E(\mathbb{N}) \mid B \subseteq A\}$$

is e-recursively enumerable.

(2) A function $\Gamma \in [P_\omega \longrightarrow P_\omega]$ is *computable* iff

$$\{(B,C) \in E(\mathbb{N}) \times E(\mathbb{N}) \mid C \subseteq \Gamma(B)\}$$

is [e,e]-recursively enumerable.

By Definitions 2.2.2, 2.2.11 and 2.2.14, $A \in P_\omega$ is computable iff $\{i \mid e_i \subseteq A\}$ is recursively enumerable, and $\Gamma \in [P_\omega \longrightarrow P_\omega]$ is computable iff the set $\{\langle i,j\rangle \mid e_j \subseteq \Gamma(e_i)\}$ is recursively enumerable. Obviously A is computable iff A is r.e. (see the exercises). If Z in Theorem 2(1) is [e,e]-r.e. then Γ_Z is computable (see Lemma 5). The computable functions $\Gamma : P_\omega \longrightarrow P_\omega$ are called enumeration operators. We define a standard numbering of the enumeration operators and a new kind of reducibility, *enumeration reducibility*.

4 <u>DEFINITION</u> (*enumeration operators, enumeration reducibility*)

(1) The computable functions $\Gamma \in [P_\omega \longrightarrow P_\omega]$ are called *enumeration operators*.

(2) Define a numbering Φ^e of the enumeration operators by

$$\Phi^e_n(A) := \bigcup \{e_j \mid (\exists i)\ \langle i,j\rangle \in W_n \wedge e_i \subseteq A\}$$

for all $n \in \mathbb{N}$ and $A \in P_\omega$.

(3) For $A,B \subseteq \mathbb{N}$ define $A \leq_e B$ (A is *enumeration reducible* to B), iff $A = \Gamma(B)$ for some enumeration operator $\Gamma : P_\omega \longrightarrow P_\omega$.

The enumeration operators are a reasonable subclass of $[P_\omega \longrightarrow P_\omega]$. The next lemma summarizes some properties.

5 LEMMA (*properties of enumeration operators*)

Let $\Gamma, \Gamma' \in [P_\omega \longrightarrow P_\omega]$.

(1) Γ is computable $\iff$ $\Gamma = \Phi^e_n$ for some $n \in \mathbb{N}$.

(2) $\Gamma\Gamma'$ is computable if Γ and Γ' are computable.

(3) $\Gamma(A)$ is r.e. if Γ is computable and A is r.e.

Proof

(1) Let Γ be computable. Then $W_n = \{\langle i,j\rangle \mid e_j \subseteq \Gamma(e_i)\}$ for some $n \in \mathbb{N}$, hence $\Gamma = \Phi^e_n$. Let $\Gamma = \Phi^e_n$. Then

$$e_k \subseteq \Gamma(e_m) \iff e_k \subseteq \bigcup\{e_j \mid (\exists i)\ \langle i,j\rangle \in W_n \wedge e_i \subseteq e_m\}.$$

Since e_k is finite, a finite union suffices hence $\{\langle m,k\rangle \mid e_k \subseteq \Gamma(e_m)\}$ is r.e. and Γ is computable.

(2) Let $m,n \in \mathbb{N}$. Then

$$\Phi^e_n\Phi^e_m(A) = \bigcup\{e_j \mid (\exists i)\ \langle i,j\rangle \in W_n \wedge e_i \subseteq \Phi^e_m(A)\},$$

and $e_i \subseteq \Phi^e_m(A)$ iff

$$(\exists b)(\exists a)\ [(\forall c \in e_a)\ c \in W_m \wedge e_i \subseteq \bigcup\{e_t \mid t \in \pi^{(2)}_2 e_a\} \wedge e_b = \bigcup\{e_s \mid s \in \pi^{(2)}_1 e_a\} \wedge e_b \subseteq A].$$

Therefore $\Phi^e_n\Phi^e_m = \Phi^e_k$ for some $k \in \mathbb{N}$.

(3) (as an exercise)

Q.E.D.

Assume $A \leq_e B$, i.e. $A = \Gamma(B)$ for some enumeration operator. If we had an oracle which enumerates B we could enumerate A. Remember that in the case of $A \leq_T B$ the characteristic function of A can be computed if we have an oracle which "computes" the characteristic function of B. The relation between Turing reducibility and enumeration reducibility is studied in an exercise. From Lemma 5 we easily conclude $(A \leq_e B \wedge B \leq_e C) \Longrightarrow A \leq_e C$ and $(A \leq_e B$ and B r.e.$) \Longrightarrow$ A r.e.

The next Type 2 set which we shall consider is the set $\mathbf{B}_o$ of all finite or infinite sequences of numbers. As for the case of P_ω we introduce a standard topology and characterize the continuous functions. The characterization then yields a definition of the computable functions $\Gamma : \mathbf{B}_o \longrightarrow \mathbf{B}_o$. The finite subsets of $\mathbb{N}$ will correspond to the finite sequences of numbers, and the inclusion order on P_ω will correspond to the prefix order on $\mathbf{B}_o$.

6 DEFINITION (*standard topology on* $\mathbf{B}_o$)

(1) Let $\mathbf{B}_o := \mathbb{N}^{\mathbb{N}} \cup W(\mathbb{N})$. For $w = a_o a_1 \ldots a_{k-1}$ where $a_i \in \mathbb{N}$ we define $w(i) = (a_i \text{ if } i < k,\ \text{div if } i \geq k)$.

(2) Define a partial order on $\mathbf{B}_o$ by $x \sqsubseteq y :\Longleftrightarrow$ (a), (b), or (c):

(a) $x,y \in W(\mathbb{N})$ and x is a prefix of y.

(b) $x \in W(\mathbb{N})$, $y \in \mathbb{N}^{\mathbb{N}}$ and $x = y(0)\,y(1) \ldots y(k-1)$ for some k .

(c) $x,y \in \mathbb{N}^{\mathbb{N}}$ and $x = y$.

If $x \sqsubseteq y$ we say "x approximates y" or "x is a prefix of y".

(3) Define a topology $\tau_{\mathbf{B}o}$ on $\mathbf{B}_o$ by the base

$$\beta = \{0_w \mid w \in W(\mathbb{N})\}$$

where

$$0_w = \{x \in \mathbf{B}_o \mid w \sqsubseteq x\} .$$

Therefore $x \sqsubseteq y$ iff x is a "segment" or "prefix" of y. 0_w is the set of all elements of $\mathbf{B}_o$ which have w as a prefix. Notice that $0_v \cap 0_w = \emptyset$ or $v \sqsubseteq w$ or $w \sqsubseteq v$ for any $v,w \in W(\mathbb{N})$. Therefore β is the base of a topology. A set $X \subseteq W(\mathbb{N})$ is *linearly ordered* iff $x \sqsubseteq y$ or $y \sqsubseteq x$ for any $x,y \in X$. A set $Z \subseteq W(\mathbb{N}) \times W(\mathbb{N})$ of pairs of words is *consistent*, iff for any finite subset $\{(x_1,y_1),\ldots,(x_n,y_n)\} \subseteq Z$, $\{y_1,\ldots,y_n\}$ is linearly ordered if $\{x_1,\ldots,x_n\}$ is linearly ordered. Every linearly ordered set $X \subseteq W(\mathbb{N})$ has a supremum in $\mathbf{B}_o$. The next theorem characterizes the set $[\mathbf{B}_o \longrightarrow \mathbf{B}_o]$ of the continuous functions from $\mathbf{B}_o$ to $\mathbf{B}_o$.

7 THEOREM (*characterization of* $[\mathbf{B}_o \longrightarrow \mathbf{B}_o]$)

(1) Let $Z \subseteq W(\mathbb{N}) \times W(\mathbb{N})$ be consistent. Then the function $\Gamma_Z : \mathbf{B}_o \longrightarrow \mathbf{B}_o$ defined by

$$\Gamma_Z(x) := \sup\{w \mid (\exists v)\ ((v,w) \in Z \wedge v \sqsubseteq x)\}$$

is continuous.

(2) For each continuous function $\Gamma : \mathbf{B}_o \longrightarrow \mathbf{B}_o$ the set $Z = \{(v,w) \mid w \sqsubseteq \Gamma(v)\}$ is consistent and satisfies $\Gamma = \Gamma_Z$.

Notice that each Γ_Z is $\sqsubseteq$-isotone, hence each continuous function $\Gamma : \mathbb{B}_o \longrightarrow \mathbb{B}_o$ is isotone. This theorem is very similar to Theorem 2, and its proof is very similar to that of Theorem 2 (see the exercises). For the set $W(\mathbb{N})$ we have defined a standard numbering ν^* (Def. 2.2.2). Computability on $\mathbb{B}_o$ is defined as follows (cf. Definition 3).

8 <u>DEFINITION</u> (*computability on* $\mathbb{B}_o$)

(1) An element $x \in \mathbb{B}_o$ is *computable* iff $\{w \in W(\mathbb{N}) \mid w \sqsubseteq x\}$ is ν^*-recursively enumerable.

(2) A function $\Gamma \in [\mathbb{B}_o \longrightarrow \mathbb{B}_o]$ is *computable* iff $\{(v,w) \mid w \sqsubseteq \Gamma(v)\}$ is $[\nu^*,\nu^*]$-recursively enumerable.

It is easy to show that each $x \in W(\mathbb{N})$ is computable and that $f \in \mathbb{N}^{\mathbb{N}}$ is computable in the above sense, iff f is computable in the common sense (i.e. $f \in R^{(1)}$). If $\Gamma, \Delta \in [\mathbb{B}_o \longrightarrow \mathbb{B}_o]$ are computable then $\Gamma\Delta$ is computable, and $\Gamma(x)$ is computable if Γ and x are computable. Corresponding to the definition of enumeration operators one could define a numbering of the computable functions from $\mathbb{B}_o$ to $\mathbb{B}_o$. One easily shows that Γ_Z is computable if Z is $[\nu^*,\nu^*]$-recursively enumerable (as an exercise).

Finally we define computability on $\mathbb{C}_o$, the set of all finite and infinite 0-1-sequences. $\mathbb{C}_o$ is a subset of $\mathbb{B}_o$, hence we could derive continuity and computability from the corresponding concepts on $\mathbb{B}_o$. Since computability on $\mathbb{C}_o$ is the most machine adequate one we prefer to write down the definitions and theorems explicitly. The prefix order on $\mathbb{C}_o$ is defined by 6(2).

9 <u>DEFINITION</u> (*standard topology on* $\mathbb{C}_o$)

Let $\mathbb{C}_o := \{0,1\}^{\mathbb{N}} \cup W(\{0,1\})$. Define a topology τ_{Co} on $\mathbb{C}_o$ by the base

$$\beta = \{Q_w \mid w \in W(\{0,1\})\}$$

where

$$Q_w := \{x \in \mathbb{C}_o \mid w \sqsubseteq x\} .$$

This definition corresponds to 6(3). τ_{Co} is the topology induced by τ_{Bo} on $\mathbb{C}_o$. The characterization of $[\mathbb{C}_o \longrightarrow \mathbb{C}_o]$, the continuous functions on $\mathbb{C}$, corresponds to Theorem 7.

10 THEOREM (*characterization of* $[\mathbb{C}_o \longrightarrow \mathbb{C}_o]$)

(1) Let $Z \subseteq (W(\{0,1\}))^2$ be consistent. Then the function $\Gamma_Z : \mathbb{C}_o \longrightarrow \mathbb{C}_o$ defined by

$$\Gamma_Z(x) := \sup\{w \mid (\exists v)\ ((v,w) \in Z \wedge v \sqsubseteq x)\}$$

is continuous.

(2) For each continuous function $\Gamma : \mathbb{C}_o \longrightarrow \mathbb{C}_o$ the set $Z = \{(v,w) \mid w \sqsubseteq \Gamma(v)\}$ is consistent and satisfies $\Gamma = \Gamma_Z$.

As in the former cases any continuous function is $\sqsubseteq$-isotone. Computability is defined accordingly.

11 DEFINITION (*computability on* $\mathbb{C}_o$)

(1) An element $x \in \mathbb{C}_o$ is *computable* iff $\{w \in W(\{0,1\}) \mid w \sqsubseteq x\}$ is recursively enumerable.

(2) A function $\Gamma \in [\mathbb{C}_o \longrightarrow \mathbb{C}_o]$ is *computable* iff $\{(v,w) \mid w \sqsubseteq \Gamma(v)\}$ is recursively enumerable.

An element $x \in \mathbb{C}_o$ is computable iff x is computable in $\mathbb{B}_o$. The computable functions on $\mathbb{C}_o$ are closed under composition and $\Gamma(x)$ is computable if Γ and x are computable. Again, Γ_Z is computable if Z is (consistent and) recursively enumerable.

We have now introduced three different topological spaces with three kinds of computability. We shall show that the three kinds of continuity and of computability are essentially equivalent. The tool is a generalization of the concept of numbering and of computability w.r.t. given numberings (see Chapter 2.2, especially Corollary 2.2.5, see also Theorem 1.7.5). Instead of standard numberings we shall use standard *representations*.

12 DEFINITION (*standard representation of* P_ω *by* $\mathbb{B}_o$)

Define $\gamma_1 : \mathbb{B}_o \dashrightarrow P_\omega$ by

$$\mathrm{dom}(\gamma_1) := \mathbb{B} := \mathbb{N}^{\mathbb{N}},$$

$$\gamma_1(p) := \{i \mid i+1 \in \mathrm{range}(p)\}$$

for all $p \in \mathbb{B}$. Then γ_1 is called the standard representation of P_ω by $\mathbb{B}_o$.

Obviously, γ_1 is surjective. We do not define $\gamma_1(p) := \text{range}(p)$ since $\emptyset$ is not the range of any $p \in \mathbf{B}$. If $\gamma_1(p) = A$ then p "enumerates" A. The representation $\gamma_1 : \mathbf{B}_o \dashrightarrow P_\omega$ has several remarkable properties which we shall need for the proof of Theorem 14.

13 LEMMA (*properties of* γ_1)

(1) Let $X \in P_\omega$. Then

$$X \text{ is open} \iff \gamma_1^{-1}X \text{ is open in } \mathbf{B}$$

(especially, γ_1 is continuous).

(2) The set

$$M := \{(w,E) \mid w \in W(\mathbb{N}),\ E \in E(\mathbb{N}),\ O_w \cap \mathbf{B} \subseteq \gamma_1^{-1} O_E\}$$

is $[\nu^*, e]$-r.e.

(3) There is an (ν^*, e)-computable function $f : W(\mathbb{N}) \longrightarrow E(\mathbb{N})$ with $\gamma_1(O_w) = O_{f(w)}$ for all $w \in W(\mathbb{N})$.

(4) Let $\delta : \mathbf{B}_o \dashrightarrow P_\omega$ be continuous, $\text{dom}(\delta) = \mathbf{B}$. Then there is some $\Sigma \in [\mathbf{B}_o \longrightarrow \mathbf{B}_o]$ such that

$$\delta(p) = \gamma_1 \Sigma(p) \quad \text{for all } p \in \mathbf{B}.$$

(5) If in addition $\{(w,E) \mid O_w \cap \mathbf{B} \subseteq \delta^{-1} O_E\}$ is $[\nu^*, e]$-r.e., then in (4) there is a computable function Σ.

By (1), τ_e is the final topology on P_ω w.r.t. γ_1 and τ_{Bo}. Final topologies will be considered in a later chapter. By (2) continuity of γ_1 is effective. By Property (3), γ_1 is an "effectively open" mapping. In (4) the property $\delta(p) = \gamma_1 \Sigma(p)$ means that δ can be "translated" into γ_1. Hence γ_1 is the most difficult continuous representation of P_ω w.r.t. continuous translation. Property (5) is the computable version of (4).

Proof

(1) Define $f : W(\mathbb{N}) \longrightarrow E(\mathbb{N})$ by $f(w) := \{i \mid (\exists j < lg(w))\ w(j) = i+1\}$. Obviously, $\gamma_1(O_w) = O_{f(w)} \subseteq P_\omega$. Let $X \subseteq P_\omega$ and assume that $\gamma_1^{-1}X$ is open in $\mathbf{B}$. Then there is some $I \subseteq W(\mathbb{N})$ with $\gamma_1^{-1}X = \bigcup \{O_w \mid w \in I\} \cap \mathbf{B}$, therefore $X = \bigcup \{O_{f(w)} \mid w \in I\}$, hence X is open. On the other hand, for any $E \in E(\mathbb{N})$ we have: $p \in \gamma_1^{-1} O_E \implies \gamma_1(p) \in O_E \implies E \subseteq \gamma_1(p) \implies (\exists w)\ (w \sqsubseteq p \wedge E \subseteq f(w)) \implies (\exists w)\ (p \in O_w \wedge \gamma_1(O_w) \subseteq O_E)$. Therefore $\gamma_1^{-1}X$ is open in $\mathbf{B}$ if X is open.

(3) The above function f is (ν^*, e)-computable.

(2) Since $0_w \cap \mathbf{B} \subseteq \gamma_1^{-1} 0_E \iff \gamma_1(0_w) \subseteq 0_E \iff 0_{f(w)} \subseteq 0_E \iff E \subseteq f(w)$, and since f is computable, the set M is r.e.

(4) For all $E \in E(\mathbb{N})$ and $x \in \mathbf{B}$ we have $E \subseteq \delta(x) \iff \delta(x) \in 0_E \iff x \in \delta^{-1} 0_E$ $\iff (\exists w \in W(\mathbb{N}))\ (x \in 0_w \wedge 0_w \cap \mathbf{B} \subseteq \delta^{-1} 0_E)$ by continuity of δ. Therefore

$$\delta(x) = \bigcup \{E \mid (\exists w)\ (w \sqsubseteq x \wedge 0_w \cap \mathbf{B} \subseteq \delta^{-1} 0_E)\}.$$

Let $((w_i, E_i))_{i \in \mathbb{N}}$ be a numbering of $\{(w,E) \mid 0_w \cap \mathbf{B} \subseteq \delta^{-1} 0_E\}$. There is an (e,ν^*)-computable function $g : E(\mathbb{N}) \longrightarrow W(\mathbb{N})$ with $fg(D) = D$ for any finite $D \subseteq \mathbb{N}$. Define a function $h : W(\mathbb{N}) \longrightarrow W(\mathbb{N})$ inductively as follows:

$$h(\varepsilon) := \varepsilon$$

$$h(ya) := h(y)\, g(\bigcup\{E_i \mid i \le lg(y) \wedge w_i \sqsubseteq ya\})\, 0$$

for all $y \in W(\mathbb{N})$ and $a \in \mathbb{N}$. Since $y \sqsubseteq y' \Longrightarrow h(y) \sqsubseteq h(y')$, the set $Z := \{(y, h(y)) \mid y \in W(\mathbb{N})\}$ is consistent (see Theorem 7). The function $\Sigma := \Gamma_Z$ is continuous by Theorem 7(1). For any $b \in \mathbb{N}$ and $x \in \mathbf{B}$ we obtain:

$$\begin{aligned} b \in \delta(x) &\iff (\exists E)\ (\exists w)\ (w \sqsubseteq x \wedge 0_w \cap \mathbf{B} \subseteq \delta^{-1} 0_E \wedge b \in E) \\ &\iff (\exists i)\ (w_i \sqsubseteq x \wedge b \in E_i) \\ &\iff (\exists v)\ (\exists i)\ (b \in E_i \wedge w_i \sqsubseteq v \wedge v \sqsubseteq x \wedge i < lg(v)) \\ &\iff (\exists v)\ (b \in fh(v) \wedge v \sqsubseteq x) \\ &\iff b \in \gamma_1 \sup\{h(y) \mid y \sqsubseteq x\} \\ &\iff b \in \gamma_1 \Gamma_Z(x). \end{aligned}$$

Therefore, $(\forall x \in \mathbf{B})\ \delta(x) = \gamma_1 \Sigma(x)$.

(5) If in addition $\{(w,E) \mid 0_w \cap \mathbf{B} \subseteq \delta^{-1} 0_E\}$ is $[\nu^*, e]$-r.e. then there is an $(1\!\!1_{\mathbb{N}}, [\nu^*, e])$-computable numbering $(w_i, E_i)_{i \in \mathbb{N}}$ of this set. Using this numbering in the above proof of Property (4), we obtain a (ν^*, ν^*)-computable function h, a $[\nu^*, \nu^*]$-r.e. set and therefore a computable function $\Sigma = \Gamma_Z$.
Q.E.D.

Continuity and computability on P_ω can be derived from continuity and computability on $\mathbf{B}_o$ via the standard representation γ_1.

14 THEOREM

(1) Let $A \in P_\omega$. Then A is computable iff $A = \gamma_1(p)$ for some computable element $p \in \mathbf{B}$.

(2) Let $\Gamma : P_\omega \longrightarrow P_\omega$ be a function. Then Γ is continuous iff $(\forall p \in \mathbf{B})\ \Gamma\gamma_1(p) = \gamma_1 \Sigma(p)$ for some continuous function $\Sigma : \mathbf{B}_o \longrightarrow \mathbf{B}_o$.

(3) Let $\Gamma : P_\omega \longrightarrow P_\omega$ be a function. Then Γ is computable iff $(\forall p \in \mathbf{B})$ $\Gamma\gamma_1(p) = \gamma_1\Sigma(p)$ for some computable function $\Sigma : \mathbf{B}_o \longrightarrow \mathbf{B}_o$.

By (1) the computable elements of P_ω are those which can be represented by computable elements of $\mathbf{B}$, by (2) and (3) the continuous (computable) functions $\Gamma : P_\omega \longrightarrow P_\omega$ are those which can be represented via γ_1 by continuous (computable) functions $\Sigma : \mathbf{B}_o \longrightarrow \mathbf{B}_o$. The following diagram illustrates this.

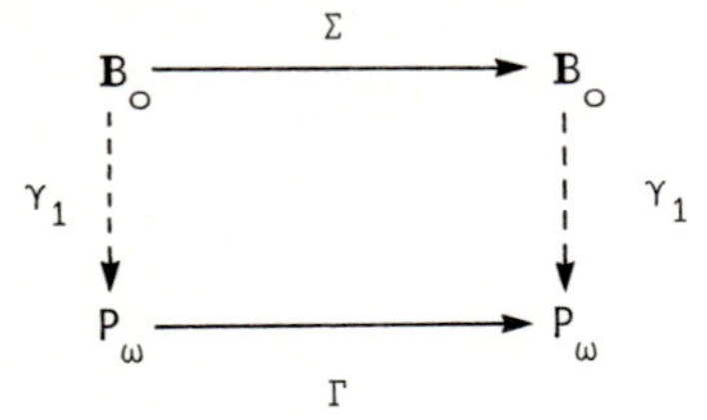

Proof

(1) For any $x \in P_\omega$ we have: x computable in $P_\omega \iff$ x is r.e. $\iff x = \gamma_1(p)$ for some $p \in R^{(1)}$ (by Theorem 2.3.10) $\iff x = \gamma_1(p)$ for some computable $p \in \mathrm{dom}(\gamma_1)$.

(2),(3) Let $\Gamma : P_\omega \longrightarrow P_\omega$ and $\Sigma : \mathbb{B}_o \longrightarrow \mathbb{B}_o$ be functions, let Σ be continuous and $(\forall x \in \mathbf{B})$ $\Gamma\gamma_1(x) = \gamma_1\Sigma(x)$. For finite $E \subseteq \mathbb{N}$ we have $\gamma_1^{-1}\Gamma^{-1}O_E = (\Gamma\gamma_1)^{-1}O_E =$ $= (\gamma_1\Sigma)^{-1}O_E \cap \mathbf{B} = \Sigma^{-1}\gamma_1^{-1}O_E \cap \mathbf{B} = \Sigma^{-1}(O_1 \cap \mathbf{B}) \cap \mathbf{B}$ (for some open $O_1 \subseteq \mathbf{B}_o$ since γ_1 is continuous) $= O_2 \cap \mathbf{B}$ (for some open $O_2 \subseteq \mathbf{B}_o$ since Σ is continuous and $\mathbf{B} \subseteq \Sigma^{-1}\mathbf{B}$). We obtain that $\gamma_1^{-1}(\Gamma^{-1}O_E)$ is open in $\mathbf{B}$, hence $\Gamma^{-1}O_E$ is open by Lemma 13(1). Therefore Γ is continuous. We determine O_1 and O_2.

$$O_1 = \bigcup\{O_w \mid O_w \cap \mathbf{B} \subseteq \gamma_1^{-1}O_E\},$$

$$O_2 = \bigcup\{\Sigma^{-1}O_w \mid O_w \cap \mathbf{B} \subseteq \gamma_1^{-1}O_E\}$$

$$= \bigcup\{O_y \mid (\exists w)\ (O_y \subseteq \Sigma^{-1}O_w \wedge O_w \cap \mathbf{B} \subseteq \gamma_1^{-1}O_E)\}.$$

With f and M from Lemma 13 we obtain $\Gamma^{-1}(O_E) = \gamma_1 O_2 = \bigcup\{O_{f(y)} \mid (\exists w)\ (w \sqsubseteq \Sigma(y) \wedge (w,E) \in M\}$. Therefore, $O_D \subseteq \Gamma^{-1}O_E$ iff there are words $y_1, w_1, \ldots, y_k, w_k$ such that $O_D \subseteq O_{f(y_1)} \cup \ldots \cup O_{f(y_k)}$, $w_i \sqsubseteq \Sigma(y_i)$, and $(w_i, E) \in M$ for $i = 1, \ldots, k$. If Σ is computable then by Lemma 13, the set $\{(D,E) \mid O_D \subseteq \Gamma^{-1}O_E\}$ is [e,e]-r.e., hence Γ is computable.

On the other hand, assume that Γ is continuous. Then $\Gamma\gamma_1$ is continuous. By Lemma 13(4), there is some $\Sigma \in [\mathbf{B}_o \longrightarrow \mathbf{B}_o]$ such that $\Gamma\gamma_1(p) = \gamma_1\Sigma(p)$ for all $p \in \mathbf{B}$. Assume additionally that Γ is computable. Then for $w \in W(\mathbb{N})$ and $E \in E(\mathbb{N})$ we have

$$O_w \cap \mathbf{B} \subseteq (\Gamma\gamma_1)^{-1}O_E$$

$$\iff \gamma_1(O_w) \subseteq \Gamma^{-1}O_E$$

$\iff O_{f(w)} \subseteq \Gamma^{-1} O_E$ (with f from Lemma 13)

$\iff E \subseteq \Gamma f(w)$.

Since f and Γ are computable, by Definition 3(2) the set $\{(E,w) \mid O_w \cap \mathbf{B} \subseteq (\Gamma\gamma_1)^{-1} O_E\}$ is $[e,\nu^*]$-r.e. Therefore, by Lemma 13(5) there is a computable function Σ with $\Gamma\gamma_1(p) = \gamma_1\Sigma(p)$ for all $p \in \mathbf{B}$.

Q.E.D.

Now we prove that continuity and computability on $\mathbf{B}_o$ can be derived from continuity and computability on $\mathbb{C}_o$ via a standard representation $\gamma_2 : \mathbb{C}_o \dashrightarrow \mathbf{B}_o$. A set of words V is called *prefixfree*, iff x is not a prefix of y and y is not a prefix of x for all $x,y \in V$.

15 DEFINITION (*standard representation of* $\mathbf{B}_o$ *by* $\mathbb{C}_o$)

(1) Define $\iota : \mathbb{N} \longrightarrow W(\{0,1\})$ by $\iota(i) := 1^i 0$. Extend ι to $W(\mathbb{N})$ by $\iota(i_1 \ldots i_n) := \iota(i_1)\iota(i_2)\ldots\iota(i_n)$.

(2) Define $\gamma_2 : \mathbb{C}_o \dashrightarrow \mathbf{B}_o$ by

$$\mathrm{dom}(\gamma_2) := \{\iota(i_1)\ldots\iota(i_k) \mid k,i_1,\ldots,i_k \in \mathbb{N}\}$$
$$\cup \{(\iota(i_o)\iota(i_1)\ldots) \mid i_n \in \mathbb{N} \text{ for all } n \in \mathbb{N}\}$$
$$\gamma_2(\iota(i_1)\ldots\iota(i_k)) := i_1\ldots i_k \in W(\mathbb{N})$$
$$\gamma_2(\iota(i_o)\iota(i_1)\ldots) := (i_o i_1 \ldots) \in \mathbf{B} = \mathbb{N}^{\mathbb{N}} .$$

Here we use the notation $(x_o x_1 \ldots) := \sup\{(x_o x_1 \ldots x_k) \mid k \in \mathbb{N}\}$ if $x_i \in W(\{0,1\})$ or $x_i \in W(\mathbb{N})$. Notice that γ_2 is welldefined since $\iota(\mathbb{N})$ is prefixfree. The function ι is effective, more precisely, ι is $(1\!\!1_{\mathbb{N}},\nu)$-computable where ν is a standard numbering of $W(\{0,1\})$. Subsequently we shall not consider the special definition of ι but only the properties: ι is injective, range(ι) is prefixfree, and ι is $(1\!\!1_{\mathbb{N}},\nu)$-computable. The following theorem corresponds to Theorem 14.

16 THEOREM

(1) Let $x \in \mathbf{B}_o$. Then x is computable iff $\gamma_2^{-1}(x)$ is computable.

(2) Let $\Gamma : \mathbf{B}_o \longrightarrow \mathbf{B}_o$ be a function. Then Γ is continuous iff $\Gamma = \gamma_2\Sigma\gamma_2^{-1}$ for some continuous function $\Sigma : \mathbb{C}_o \longrightarrow \mathbb{C}_o$.

(3) Let $\Gamma : \mathbf{B}_o \longrightarrow \mathbf{B}_o$ be a function. Then Γ is computable iff $\Gamma = \gamma_2\Sigma\gamma_2^{-1}$ for some computable function $\Sigma : \mathbb{C}_o \longrightarrow \mathbb{C}_o$.

Therefore continuity and computability on $\mathbb{B}_o$ can be defined by continuity and computability on $\mathbb{C}_o$ by means of the representation γ_2. The following diagram illustrates this.

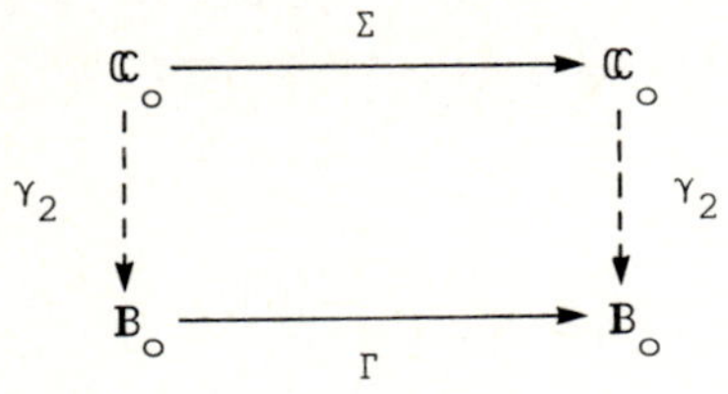

Notice that $\gamma_2(\mathbb{C}) = \mathbb{B}$ where $\mathbb{C} = \{0,1\}^{\mathbb{N}}$ and $\mathbb{B} = \mathbb{N}^{\mathbb{N}}$.

For proving Theorem 16 we need some effectivity properties of γ_2.

17 LEMMA *properties of* $\gamma_2 : \mathbb{C}_o \dashrightarrow \mathbb{B}_o$)

Let ν be a standard numbering of $W(\{0,1\})$.

(1) γ_2 and γ_2^{-1} are continuous.

(2) $\gamma_2^{-1} O_w = Q_{\iota(w)} \cap \mathrm{dom}(\gamma_2)$ for all $w \in W(\mathbb{N})$, where $\iota : W(\mathbb{N}) \longrightarrow W(\{0,1\})$ from Def. 15 is (ν^*,ν)-computable.

(3) The set $\{(v,w) \in W(\{0,1\}) \times W(\mathbb{N}) \mid O_w \subseteq \gamma_2 Q_v\}$ is $[\nu,\nu^*]$-r.e.

(4) Let $\delta : \mathbb{C}_o \dashrightarrow \mathbb{B}_o$ with $\mathrm{dom}(\delta) = \mathrm{dom}(\gamma_2)$ be continuous. Then there is some $\Sigma \in [\mathbb{C}_o \longrightarrow \mathbb{C}_o]$ with

$$\delta(p) = \gamma_2 \Sigma(p) \quad \text{for all} \quad p \in \mathrm{dom}(\delta).$$

(5) If in addition $\{(v,w) \in W(\mathbb{N}) \times W(\mathbb{N}) \mid \delta Q_{\iota(v)} \subseteq O_w\}$ is $[\nu^*,\nu^*]$-r.e., then in (4) there is a computable function Σ.

Proof

(2) For any $w \in W(\mathbb{N})$ we have

$$\gamma_2^{-1} O_w = Q_{\iota(w)} \cap \mathrm{dom}(\gamma_2).$$

Clearly ι is (ν^*,ν)-computable.

(1) By (2) γ_2 is continuous. For any $v \in W(\{0,1\})$ we have

$$\gamma_2(Q_v) = \bigcup \{O_w \mid v \sqsubseteq \iota(w)\},$$

hence $(\gamma_2^{-1})^{-1}(Q_v)$ is open. Therefore γ_2^{-1} is continuous.

(3) We have $O_w \subseteq \gamma_2 Q_v \iff v \sqsubseteq \iota(w)$, hence the set is $[\nu,\nu^*]$-r.e.

(4) For all $x \in \mathrm{dom}(\delta)$ and $w \in W(\mathbb{N})$ we have

$$w \sqsubseteq \delta(x) \iff \delta(x) \in O_w$$
$$\iff x \in \delta^{-1} O_w$$
$$\iff (\exists y \in W(\mathbb{N}))\ (x \in Q_{\iota(y)} \wedge Q_{\iota(y)} \cap \mathrm{dom}(\delta) \subseteq \delta^{-1} O_w)$$

since $x \in \mathrm{dom}(\gamma_2) = \mathrm{dom}(\delta)$ and δ is continuous. We obtain

$$\delta(x) = \sup\{w \mid (\exists y)\ (x \in Q_{\iota(y)} \wedge \delta Q_{\iota(y)} \subseteq O_w)\}$$
$$= \gamma_2 \sup\{\iota(w) \mid (\exists y)\ (x \in O_{\iota(y)} \wedge \delta Q_{\iota(y)} \subseteq O_w)\}.$$

With $Z := \{(\iota(y), \iota(w)) \mid \delta Q_{\iota(y)} \subseteq O_w\}$ we obtain

$$\delta(x) = \gamma_2 \sup\{\iota(w) \mid (\exists \iota(y))\ (\iota(y) \sqsubseteq x \wedge (\iota(y), \iota(w)) \in Z\}.$$

Since $\delta(x)$ exists, Z is consistent and $\delta(x) = \gamma_2 \Gamma_Z(x)$. Choose $\Sigma := \Gamma_Z$.

(5) If in addition $\{(v,w) \mid \delta Q_{\iota(v)} \subseteq O_w\}$ is $[\nu^*, \nu^*]$-r.e., then Z is $[\nu,\nu]$-r.e. and $\Sigma = \Gamma_Z$ is computable.

Q.E.D.

Notice that Lemma 13 and Lemma 17 are very similar. After these preparations it is not difficult to prove Theorem 16.

<u>Proof</u> (Theorem 16)

(1) For any $x \in \mathbf{B}_o$ we have: x computable $\iff$ $\{w \mid w \sqsubseteq x\}$ ν^*-r.e. $\iff$ $\{w \mid \iota(w) \sqsubseteq \gamma_2^{-1}(x)\}$ ν^*-r.e. $\iff$ $\{y \in W(\{0,1\}) \mid y \sqsubseteq \gamma_2^{-1}(x)\}$ ν-r.e. $\iff$ $\gamma_2^{-1}(x)$ computable.

(2) Let $\Gamma : \mathbf{B}_o \longrightarrow \mathbf{B}_o$ and $\Sigma : \mathbb{C}_o \longrightarrow \mathbb{C}_o$ be functions, let Σ be continuous and $\Gamma = \gamma_2 \Sigma \gamma_2^{-1}$. Then for any open $X \subseteq \mathbf{B}_o$ we have:

$\Gamma^{-1}(X)$

$= \gamma_2 \Sigma^{-1} \gamma_2^{-1}(X)$

$= \gamma_2 \Sigma^{-1}(O_1 \cap \mathrm{dom}(\gamma_2))$ for some open $O_1 \subseteq \mathbb{C}_o$ by continuity of γ_2

$= \gamma_2(O_2 \cap \Sigma^{-1}\mathrm{dom}(\gamma_2))$ for some open $O_2 \subseteq \mathbb{C}_o$ by continuity of Σ

$= \gamma_2(O_2)$ since $\mathrm{dom}(\gamma_2) \subseteq \Sigma^{-1}\mathrm{dom}(\gamma_2)$

$= (\gamma_2^{-1})^{-1} O_2$

$= O_3$ for some open $O_3 \subseteq \mathbf{B}_o$ since γ_2^{-1} is continuous.

Therefore Γ is continuous. For any $v, w \in W(\mathbb{N})$ we have

$$\begin{aligned}
& w \sqsubseteq \Gamma(v) \\
\iff & O_v \subseteq \Gamma^{-1} O_w \\
\iff & O_v \subseteq \gamma_2 \Sigma^{-1} \gamma_2^{-1} O_w \\
\iff & \gamma_2^{-1} O_v \subseteq \Sigma^{-1} \gamma_2^{-1} O_w \qquad \text{(since } \gamma_2 \text{ is injective)} \\
\iff & Q_{\iota(v)} \cap \mathrm{dom}(\gamma_2) \subseteq \Sigma^{-1}(Q_{\iota(w)} \cap \mathrm{dom}(\gamma_2)) \\
\iff & Q_{\iota(v)} \cap \mathrm{dom}(\gamma_2) \subseteq \Sigma^{-1} Q_{\iota(w)} \cap \mathrm{dom}(\gamma_2) \qquad \text{(since } \mathrm{dom}(\gamma_2) \subseteq \Sigma^{-1}\mathrm{dom}(\gamma_2)) \\
\iff & \iota(w) \sqsubseteq \Sigma\iota(v) .
\end{aligned}$$

If Σ is computable, then $\{(v,w) \mid w \sqsubseteq \Gamma(v)\}$ is r.e. by Lemma 17(2) and Definition 11(2), hence by Definition 8(2) Γ is computable. Thus we have proved the first implication of (2) and (3).
On the other hand, assume that $\Gamma : \mathbf{B}_o \longrightarrow \mathbf{B}_o$ is continuous. Then $\Gamma\gamma_2$ is continuous and $\mathrm{dom}(\Gamma\gamma_2) = \mathrm{dom}(\gamma_2)$. By Lemma 17(4) there is some continuous $\Sigma : \mathbb{C}_o \longrightarrow \mathbb{C}_o$ with $\Gamma\gamma_2(p) = \gamma_2\Sigma(p)$ for all $p \in \mathrm{dom}(\gamma_2)$, hence $\Gamma(x) = \gamma_2\Sigma\gamma_2^{-1}(x)$ for all $x \in \mathbf{B}_o$, i.e. $\Gamma = \gamma_2\Sigma\gamma_2^{-1}$. Assume additionally that Γ is computable. Then for any $v,w \in W(\mathbb{N})$ we have:

$$\begin{aligned}
\Gamma\gamma_2 Q_{\iota(v)} \subseteq O_w \iff & \gamma_2 Q_{\iota(v)} \subseteq \Gamma^{-1} O_w \\
\iff & O_v \subseteq \Gamma^{-1} O_w \qquad \text{(by Lemma 17(2))}.
\end{aligned}$$

By Definition 8(2), $\{(v,w) \mid \Gamma\gamma_2 Q_{\iota(v)} \subseteq O_w\}$ is $[\nu^*,\nu^*]$-r.e., hence $\Gamma\gamma_2(p) = \gamma_2\Sigma(p)$ for a computable function Σ by Lemma 17(5).

Q.E.D.

Notice the similarity between Theorem 14 and Theorem 16, Lemma 13 and Lemma 17 and between the corresponding proofs. Finally continuity and computability on $\mathbb{C}_o$ can be deduced from continuity and computability on P_ω by means of a standard representation $\gamma_3 : P_\omega \dashrightarrow \mathbb{C}_o$. In this case, an element $p \in \mathbb{C}_o$ will be represented by its graph $\{<i,p(i)> \mid i \in \mathrm{dom}(p)\}$.

18 <u>DEFINITION</u> (*standard representation of* $\mathbb{C}_o$ *by* P_ω)

Define $\bar{\gamma} : \mathbb{C}_o \longrightarrow P_\omega$ by

$$\bar{\gamma}(x) = \begin{cases} \{<i,x(i)> \mid i < \lg(x)\} & \text{if } x \in W(\{0,1\}) \\ \{<i,x(i)> \mid i \in \mathbb{N}\} & \text{if } x \in \{0,1\}^{\mathbb{N}} \end{cases}$$

Define $\gamma_3 : P_\omega \dashrightarrow \mathbb{C}_o$ by $\gamma_3 := \bar{\gamma}^{-1}$.

Notice that γ_3 is welldefined and injective since $\overline{\gamma}$ is injective. The next lemma which summarizes some basic properties of γ_3 corresponds to Lemma 13 and Lemma 17.

19 LEMMA (*properties of* $\gamma_3 : P_\omega \dashrightarrow \mathbb{C}_o$)

(1) γ_3 and γ_3^{-1} are continuous.

(2) $\gamma_3^{-1}Q_w = O_{\iota(w)} \cap \mathrm{dom}(\gamma_3)$ for all $w \in W(\{0,1\})$ where $\iota : W(\{0,1\}) \longrightarrow E(\mathbb{N})$ with $\iota(w) := \overline{\gamma}(w)$ is (ν,e)-computable (ν a standard numbering of $W(\{0,1\})$).

(3) The set $\{(D,w) \in E(\mathbb{N}) \times W(\{0,1\}) \mid Q_w \subseteq \gamma_3(O_D)\}$ is (e,ν)-r.e.

(4) Let $\delta : P_\omega \dashrightarrow \mathbb{C}_o$ with $\mathrm{dom}(\delta) = \mathrm{dom}(\gamma_3)$ be continuous. Then there is some $\Sigma \in [P_\omega \longrightarrow P_\omega]$ with $\delta(p) = \gamma_3\Sigma(p)$ for all $p \in \mathrm{dom}(\delta)$.

(5) If in addition $\{(v,w) \in (W(\{0,1\}))^2 \mid \delta O_{\iota(v)} \subseteq Q_w\}$ is r.e., then in (4) there is a computable function Σ.

The proof is very similar to the proof of Lemma 17. It is left as an exercise. Finally we formulate the counterpart of Theorem 16 and Theorem 14.

20 THEOREM

(1) Let $x \in \mathbb{C}_o$. Then x is computable iff $\gamma_3^{-1}(x)$ is computable.

(2) Let $\Gamma : \mathbb{C}_o \longrightarrow \mathbb{C}_o$ be a function. Then Γ is continuous iff $\Gamma = \gamma_3\Sigma\gamma_3^{-1}$ for some continuous function $\Sigma : P_\omega \longrightarrow P_\omega$.

(3) Let $\Gamma : \mathbb{C}_o \longrightarrow \mathbb{C}_o$ be a function. Then Γ is computable iff $\Gamma = \gamma_3\Sigma\gamma_3^{-1}$ for some computable function $\Sigma : P_\omega \longrightarrow P_\omega$.

Therefore, continuity and computability on $\mathbb{C}_o$ can be derived from continuity and computability on P_ω by means of the standard representation γ_3. The following diagram illustrates this.

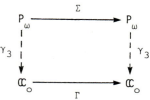

$$\begin{array}{ccc} P_\omega & \xrightarrow{\ \Sigma\ } & P_\omega \\ \gamma_3 \downarrow & & \downarrow \gamma_3 \\ \mathbb{C}_o & \xrightarrow[\ \Gamma\ ]{} & \mathbb{C}_o \end{array}$$

Since the proof of Theorem 20 is very similar to that of Theorem 16 it is left as an exercise.

Let (X,τ) and (X',τ') be two topological spaces. A mapping $f : X \longrightarrow X'$ is called a *homeomorphism*, iff f is bijective and both f and f^{-1} are continuous. The spaces (X,τ) and (X',τ') are called *homeomorphic*, iff there is a homeomorphism $f : X \longrightarrow X'$.

By Lemma 13, P_ω is homeomorphic to a factor of $\mathbb{B}$, by Lemma 17, $\mathbb{B}_o$ is homeomorphic to a subset of $\mathbb{C}_o$, and by Lemma 19, $\mathbb{C}_o$ is homeomorphic to a subset of P_ω. All the homeomorphisms are "effective". Each of the representations γ_1, γ_2, and γ_3 is the "most complicated" continuous function of the given type by Properties (4) and (5) of the above lemmas. We have defined three different kinds of Type 2 constructivity and computability and we have shown that they are essentially equivalent. The main theorems show how one kind of constructivity and computability can be reduced to any other one. In future we shall use that kind which is most convenient for the application in question. Constructivity and computability on P_ω are mainly used in abstract studies. The elements of $\mathbb{B}$ (which are the γ_1-names of the subsets of $\mathbb{N}$) can be considered as enumeration procedures of sets. The theory on $\mathbb{B}_o$ is mainly used if sequences (e.g. Cauchy sequences in analysis) are considered. The set $\mathbb{C}_o$ is used if concrete computability (especially computational complexity) is studied since in practice all objects in Type 2 theory are denoted (w.l.g.) by finite or infinite 0-1-sequences. There is a general theory which covers our three constructivity and computability approaches, the theory of *complete partial orders*, so called *cpo's*. We shall study cpo's in detail in later chapters.

Theorems 14, 16, and 20 show that for studying continuity and computability on $\mathbb{B}_o, \mathbb{C}_o$, and P_ω it suffices to consider the computable functions from $\mathbb{B}$ to $\mathbb{B}$ (or from $\mathbb{C}$ to $\mathbb{C}$). As a technical preparation we characterize the continuous functions $\Gamma : \mathbb{B} \longrightarrow \mathbb{B}_o$ and $\Gamma : \mathbb{C} \longrightarrow \mathbb{C}_o$, we define the computable functions $\Gamma : \mathbb{B} \longrightarrow \mathbb{B}_o$ and $\Gamma : \mathbb{C} \longrightarrow \mathbb{C}_o$ and characterize the computable functions $\Gamma : \mathbb{C} \longrightarrow \mathbb{C}_o$ by means of oracle computability. We start with some definitions.

21 DEFINITION

(1) Define $\mathbb{B} := \mathbb{N}^{\mathbb{N}}$ and $\mathbb{C} := \{0,1\}^{\mathbb{N}}$. For $p \in \mathbb{B}$ and $n \in \mathbb{N}$ define

$$p^{[n]} := p(0)\dots p(n-1) \in W(\mathbb{N}) .$$

(This definition applies to $\mathbb{C}$ since $\mathbb{C} \subseteq \mathbb{B}$.)

(2) For any $w \in W(\mathbb{N})$ let

$$[w] := \{p \in \mathbb{B} \mid w \sqsubseteq p\} .$$

The topology τ_B generated by the base $\beta = \{[w] \mid w \in W(\mathbb{N})\}$ on $\mathbb{B}$ is called *Baire's topology* and $(\mathbb{B}, \tau_B)$ is called *Baire's space.*

(3) For any $w \in W(\{0,1\})$ let

$$[\![w]\!] := \{p \in \mathbb{C} \mid w \sqsubseteq p\}.$$

The topology τ_C generated by the base $\beta = \{[\![w]\!] \mid w \in W(\{0,1\})\}$ on $\mathbb{C}$ is called *Cantor's topology* and $(\mathbb{C}, \tau_C)$ is called *Cantor's space.*

Obviously, τ_B is the topology on $\mathbb{B}$ induced by the topology τ_{Bo} (on $\mathbb{B}_o$), and τ_C is the topology on $\mathbb{C}$ induced by the topology τ_{Co} (on $\mathbb{C}_o$). Baire's and Cantor's topology will be our standard topologies on $\mathbb{B}$ and $\mathbb{C}$, respectively. The continuous functions $\mathbb{B} \longrightarrow \mathbb{B}_o$ $(\mathbb{C} \longrightarrow \mathbb{C}_o)$ are closely related to the continuous functions $\mathbb{B}_o \longrightarrow \mathbb{B}_o$ $(\mathbb{C}_o \longrightarrow \mathbb{C}_o)$.

22 LEMMA

A function $\Gamma : \mathbb{B} \longrightarrow \mathbb{B}_o$ $(\mathbb{C} \longrightarrow \mathbb{C}_o)$ is continuous iff Γ is the restriction of a continuous function $\Sigma : \mathbb{B}_o \longrightarrow \mathbb{B}_o$ $(\mathbb{C}_o \longrightarrow \mathbb{C}_o)$.

Proof

Assume that $\Sigma : \mathbb{B}_o \longrightarrow \mathbb{B}_o$ is continuous and $(\forall p \in \mathbb{B})\ \Sigma(p) = \Gamma(p)$. For any open set $X \subseteq \mathbb{B}_o$ we have $\Gamma^{-1}(X) = \Sigma^{-1}(X) \cap \mathbb{B}$, hence $\Gamma^{-1}X$ is open in $\mathbb{B}$. On the other hand assume that $\Gamma : \mathbb{B} \longrightarrow \mathbb{B}_o$ is continuous. Let Z be the set $Z := \{(v,w) \in W(\mathbb{N}) \times W(\mathbb{N}) \mid \Gamma([v]) \subseteq 0_w\}$. One easily shows that Z is consistent. Define $\Sigma := \Gamma_Z$ (Theorem 7). We obtain for any $p \in \mathbb{B}$ and $y \in W(\mathbb{N})$:

$$
\begin{aligned}
y \sqsubseteq \Gamma_Z(p) &\iff y \sqsubseteq \sup\{w \mid (\exists\, v)(v,w) \in Z \wedge v \sqsubseteq p\} \\
&\iff (\exists\, v,w)\ ((v,w) \in Z \wedge y \sqsubseteq w \wedge v \sqsubseteq p) \\
&\iff (\exists\, v,w)\ (\Gamma[v] \subseteq 0_w \wedge 0_w \subseteq 0_y \wedge p \in [v]) \\
&\iff (\exists\, v)\ (p \in [v] \wedge \Gamma[v] \subseteq 0_y) \\
&\iff \Gamma(p) \in 0_y \qquad \text{(by continuity of } \Gamma) \\
&\iff y \sqsubseteq \Gamma(p).
\end{aligned}
$$

Therefore, the continuous function Σ extends Γ. The case $\mathbb{C} \longrightarrow \mathbb{C}_o$ is proved correspondingly.

Q.E.D.

In general the function Σ is not uniquely determined by Γ (as an exercise). We shall call a function $\Gamma : \mathbb{B} \longrightarrow \mathbb{B}_o$ $(\mathbb{C} \longrightarrow \mathbb{C}_o)$ computable iff Γ is the restriction of a computable function $\Sigma : \mathbb{B}_o \longrightarrow \mathbb{B}_o$ $(\mathbb{C}_o \longrightarrow \mathbb{C}_o)$. This definition is justified by Lemma 22.

23 DEFINITION

(1) A function $\Gamma : \mathbb{B} \longrightarrow \mathbb{B}_o$ is *computable* iff $(\forall p \in \mathbb{B})\ \Gamma(p) = \Sigma(p)$ for some computable function $\Sigma : \mathbb{B}_o \longrightarrow \mathbb{B}_o$.

(2) A function $\Gamma : \mathbb{C} \longrightarrow \mathbb{C}_o$ is *computable* iff $(\forall p \in \mathbb{C})\ \Gamma(p) = \Sigma(p)$ for some computable function $\Sigma : \mathbb{C}_o \longrightarrow \mathbb{C}_o$.

The computable functions $\Gamma : \mathbb{C} \longrightarrow \mathbb{C}_o$ can be characterized by oracle machines (Chapter 2.10). This characterization explains how a computable function $\Gamma : \mathbb{C} \longrightarrow \mathbb{C}_o$ can really be computed.

24 THEOREM

Let $\Gamma : \mathbb{C} \longrightarrow \mathbb{C}_o$ be a function. Define $f_\Gamma : 2^{\mathbb{N}} \times \mathbb{N} \dashrightarrow \mathbb{N}$ by

$$f_\Gamma(A,n) := \Gamma(cf_A)(n) \qquad (A \subseteq \mathbb{N},\ n \in \mathbb{N}).$$

Then Γ is computable $\iff$ f_Γ is oracle computable.

Remember that $cf_A \in \mathbb{C}$ is the characteristic function of A. Thus with input (A,n) an oracle machine for f_Γ determines the n-th symbol of $\Gamma(cf_A) \in \mathbb{C}_o$. Especially $f_\Gamma(A,n) = \mathrm{div}$ if $\Gamma(cf_A) = w \in W(\{0,1\})$ and $n \geq lg(w)$ (see Def. 6(1)).

Proof

Assume that $\Gamma : \mathbb{C} \longrightarrow \mathbb{C}_o$ is computable. Let $\Sigma : \mathbb{C}_o \longrightarrow \mathbb{C}_o$ be a computable function which extends Γ (Def. 23). By Definition 11 the set $Z = \{(v,w) \mid w \sqsubseteq \Sigma(v)\}$ is recursively enumerable. By Theorem 10,

$$\Gamma(p) = \sup\{w \mid (\exists v)\ (v \sqsubseteq p \wedge (v,w) \in Z)\}$$

for all $p \in \mathbb{C}$. Let M be an oracle machine which for input $A := p^{-1}\{1\}$ and $n \in \mathbb{N}$ enumerates Z until a pair $(v,w) \in Z$ is found for which $v \sqsubseteq p$ and $lg(w) \geq n+1$. Then let $w(n)$ be the output of M. Clearly, $f_M = f_\Gamma$, hence f_Γ is oracle computable.
On the other hand assume that f_Γ is oracle computable. Then $f_\Gamma = \eta_i$ for some $i \in \mathbb{N}$ (see Def. 2.10.5). For any $v \in W(\{0,1\})$ define

$B_+^v := \{j < lg(v) \mid v(j) = 1\}$,

$B_-^v := \{j < lg(v) \mid v(j) = 0\}$.

Define $Z \subseteq (W(\{0,1\}))^2$ by

$$Z := \{(v,w) \mid (\forall n < lg(w))\ [\eta_i(B_+^v,n) = w(n) \wedge N_-(B_+^v,i,n) \subseteq B_-^v]\} .$$

By Lemma 2.10.8, Z is recursively enumerable. Since Z is consistent, $\Gamma_Z : \mathbb{C}_o \longrightarrow \mathbb{C}_o$ is computable. It suffices to show that $\Gamma_Z(p) = \Gamma(p)$ for all $p \in \mathbb{C}$. Let $y \in W(\{0,1\})$, $p \in \mathbb{C}$, and $A := p^{-1}\{1\}$. Then:

$$y \sqsubseteq \Gamma_Z(p)$$

$$\Longleftrightarrow (\exists (v,w) \in Z)\ (v \sqsubseteq p \wedge y \sqsubseteq w)$$

$$\Longleftrightarrow (\exists v,w)\ (v \sqsubseteq p \wedge y \sqsubseteq w \wedge (\forall n < lg(w))\ [\eta_i(B_+^v,n) = w(n) \wedge N_-(B_+^v,i,n) \subseteq B_-^v])$$

$$\Longleftrightarrow (\exists w)\ (y \sqsubseteq w \wedge (\forall n < lg(w))\ \eta_i(A,n) = w(n)) \qquad \text{(by Lemma 2.10.8)}$$

$$\Longleftrightarrow (\forall n < lg(y))\ \eta_i(A,n) = y(n)$$

$$\Longleftrightarrow y \sqsubseteq \Gamma(p) .$$

Therefore $\Gamma_Z(p) = \Gamma(p)$ for all $p \in \mathbb{C}$, hence Γ is computable.
Q.E.D.

For practical informal use it is convenient to consider a modified oracle machine model, the Type 2 machine. A Type 2 machine M reads its input $p \in \mathbb{C}$ from an input file and writes the output $x \in \mathbb{C}_o$ on to an output file. Its configuration can be illustrated by the following diagram.

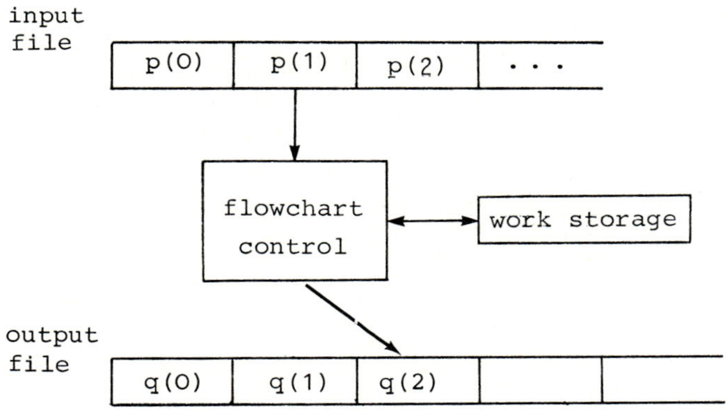

The machine is started with the input $p \in \mathbb{C}$ on the input file, the head on the first position, and with empty output file. From time to time the machine reads some symbol from the input file (and goes one position to the right) or prints some symbol on to the output file (and goes one position to the right). The actual computation is performed on the work storage which may contain tapes, stacks, counters, etc. The machine may halt or compute forever. The result $f_M(p)$ is the (finite or infinite) sequence $x \in \mathbb{C}_o$ generated on the output file. Notice that the head on the output file moves one-way.

Easy simulation arguments show that a function $\Gamma : \mathbb{C} \longrightarrow \mathbb{C}_o$ can be computed by a Type 2 machine, iff the function $f_\Gamma : 2^{\mathbb{N}} \times \mathbb{N} \dashrightarrow \mathbb{N}$ defined by $f_\Gamma(A,n) := \Gamma(cf_A)(n)$ is oracle computable. Therefore, by Theorem 24, $\Gamma : \mathbb{C} \longrightarrow \mathbb{C}_o$ is computable (according to Def. 23), iff it can be computed by a Type 2 machine. By means of $\gamma_2 : \mathbb{C}_o \dashrightarrow \mathbb{B}_o$ elements of $\mathbb{B}_o$ can be encoded by elements of $\mathbb{C}_o$. Let $\Delta : \mathbb{B} \longrightarrow \mathbb{B}_o$ and let M be a Type 2 machine. We shall say "M computes Δ" iff for any $p \in \mathbb{B}$ the function $f_M : \mathbb{C} \longrightarrow \mathbb{C}_o$ maps $\gamma_2^{-1}(p)$ to $\gamma_2^{-1}\Delta(p)$ (remember: $\gamma_2^{-1}(p) = 1^{p(0)}01^{p(1)}0\ldots$). By Theorem 16, $\Delta : \mathbb{B} \longrightarrow \mathbb{B}_o$ is computable iff some Type 2 machine computes Δ. In future we assume that Type 2 machines have inputs from $\mathbb{B}$ and outputs from $\mathbb{B}_o$.

Many basic properties in Type 1 recursion theory are proved by step counting arguments (projection theorem 1.8.4, Kleene's T-predicate 2.1.4, Blum's second axiom for tape machine computation time 2.1.5). Lemma 2.10.8(2) generalizes this concept to oracle tape machines. For Type 2 machines the following theorem can be proved.

25 <u>THEOREM</u>

Let M be a Type 2 machine. Then the following set $A \subseteq \mathbb{N}$ is recursive:

$\{\langle i,j,t\rangle \in \mathbb{N} \mid$ for any input $p \in \mathbb{B}$ with $\nu^*(i) \sqsubseteq p$ within at most t steps the machine reads at most the prefix $\nu^*(i)$ of p and writes at least $\nu^*(j)$ onto the output tape$\}$.

The almost obvious proof is left as an exercise. Let $Z := \{(\nu^*(i), \nu^*(j)) \mid (\exists t) \langle i,j,t\rangle \in A\}$. Then $\Gamma_Z : \mathbb{B}_o \longrightarrow \mathbb{B}_o$ (see Def. 8) is a computable extension of $f_M : \mathbb{B} \longrightarrow \mathbb{B}_o$. Any r.e. (consistent) set $Z \subseteq W(\mathbb{N}) \times W(\mathbb{N})$ is the projection of a recursive set D. In many proofs Theorem 7 and Definition 8 can replace Theorem 25.

By Theorem 7, $[\mathbb{B}_o \longrightarrow \mathbb{B}_o] = \{\Gamma_Z \mid Z \text{ consistent}\}$. For representing the continuous functions from $\mathbb{B}$ to $\mathbb{B}_o$ it suffices to consider consistent sets $Z \subseteq W(\mathbb{N}) \times W(\mathbb{N})$ which are graphs of functions.

26 THEOREM

Let $\Sigma : \mathbf{B} \longrightarrow \mathbf{B}_o$. Then Σ is continuous (computable) iff there is some $\sqsubseteq$-isotone ($\sqsubseteq$-isotone and computable) function $\gamma : W(\mathbb{N}) \longrightarrow W(\mathbb{N})$ such that for all $p \in \mathbf{B}$:

$$\Sigma(p) = \sup\{\gamma(u) \mid u \sqsubseteq p\} .$$

Proof

Assume that γ exists. Let $Z = \{(u,\gamma(u)) \mid u \in W(\mathbb{N})\}$. Then Z is consistent and $(\forall p \in \mathbf{B})\ \Sigma(p) = \Gamma_Z(p)$, hence Σ is continuous. If in addition γ is computable, Z is r.e. and Γ_Z and Σ are computable. On the other hand let Σ be continuous. There is some Z such that Γ_Z extends Σ. Let $(v_i,w_i)_{i\in\mathbb{N}}$ be an enumeration of Z. Define γ by

$$\gamma(u) := \sup\{w_i \mid v_i \sqsubseteq u \wedge i \le lg(u)\} .$$

Then γ is $\sqsubseteq$-isotone. It is not difficult to show that $x \sqsubseteq \Gamma_Z(p) = \Sigma(p) \iff x \sqsubseteq \sup\{\gamma(u) \mid u \sqsubseteq p\}$ for all $p \in \mathbf{B}$ and $x \in W(\mathbb{N})$ (as an exercise), therefore, an appropriate γ exists. If Σ is computable, then there is an $[\nu^*,\nu^*]$-r.e. set Z which has a computable enumeration $(v_i,w_i)_{i\in\mathbb{N}}$. In this case γ becomes computable.
Q.E.D.

EXERCISES

1) Let A be a subset of $\mathbb{N}$. Show that A is computable according to Definition 3(1) iff A is recursively enumerable.

2) Show that Γ_Z is computable if $Z \subseteq E(\mathbb{N}) \times E(\mathbb{N})$ is $[e,e]$-recursively enumerable (cf. Theorem 2).

3) Show that the numbering Φ^e is complete (cf. Def. 2.5.1).

4) Show that there is some $r \in R^{(2)}$ such that $\Phi^e_n \Phi^e_m = \Phi^e_{r(m,n)}$ for all $m,n \in \mathbb{N}$.

5) Show that $\Gamma : P_\omega \longrightarrow P_\omega$ is continuous, iff there is some $B \subseteq \mathbb{N}$ such that

$$\Gamma(A) = \{x \mid (\exists i)(\langle x,i\rangle \in B \wedge e_i \subseteq A)\} .$$

6) Show that there is some $r \in R^{(2)}$ such that $\Phi^e_m W_n = W_{r(m,n)}$ for all $m,n \in \mathbb{N}$.

7) For any $B \subseteq \mathbb{N}$ define $\delta(B) : P_\omega \longrightarrow P_\omega$ by

$$\delta(B)(A) = \cup\{e_i \mid (\exists j)(\langle i,j\rangle \in B \wedge e_j \subseteq A)\}.$$

(a) Show that $\Phi' : P_\omega \longrightarrow [P_\omega \longrightarrow P_\omega]$ with $\Phi'(B) := \Phi'_B := \delta(B)$ is a welldefined (total) and surjective function.

Define a pairing function $\oplus : P_\omega \times P_\omega \longrightarrow P_\omega$ by $A \oplus B := \{2i \mid i \in A\} \cup \{2i+1 \mid i \in B\}$.

(b) Show that there is a computable "universal" function $\Gamma_u : P_\omega \longrightarrow P_\omega$ such that $\Gamma_u(A \oplus B) = \Phi'_A(B)$ for all $A,B \in P_\omega$.

(c) Show that there is a computable function $\Sigma : P_\omega \longrightarrow P_\omega$ such that

$$\Phi'_{\Sigma(A \oplus B)}(C) = \Phi'_A(B \oplus C)$$

for all $A,B,C \in P_\omega$.

(d) Show that there is a computable function $\Delta : P_\omega \longrightarrow P_\omega$ with $\Phi'_{\Delta(A \oplus B)} = \Phi'_A \Phi'_B$ for all $A,B \in P_\omega$.

8) Show that A is B-recursively enumerable iff $A \leq_e B \oplus (\mathbb{N} \setminus B)$ ($\oplus$ is defined in Exercise 7).

9) Prove Theorem 7.

10) Consider Definition 8.

(a) Show that $f \in \mathbb{N}^{\mathbb{N}}$ is computable iff $f \in R^{(1)}$.

(b) Show that $\Gamma\Delta$ is computable if $\Gamma, \Delta : \mathbb{B}_o \longrightarrow \mathbb{B}_o$ are computable.

(c) Show that Γ_Z is computable if $Z \subseteq W(\mathbb{N}) \times W(\mathbb{N})$ is consistent and $[\nu^*, \nu^*]$-recursively enumerable.

11) Show that there is no continuous function $\gamma : P_\omega \longrightarrow \mathbb{B}_o$ such that $\gamma_1\gamma(A) = A$ for all $A \in P_\omega$ (see Def. 12).

12) Prove Lemma 19.

13) Prove Theorem 20.

14) Characterize those continuous functions $\Gamma : \mathbb{B} \longrightarrow \mathbb{B}_o$ which have a unique continuous extension $\Sigma : \mathbb{B}_o \longrightarrow \mathbb{B}_o$.

15) Let τ_E be the standard topology on P_ω. Let τ be the topology on P_ω induced by Cantor's topology:

$$X \in \tau :\Longleftrightarrow \{cf_A \mid A \in X\} \in \tau_C$$

for all $X \subseteq P_\omega$. Show that $X \in \tau_C \Longleftrightarrow (X \in \tau_E \wedge \{\mathbb{N} \setminus A \mid A \in X\} \in \tau_E)$ for all $X \subseteq P_\omega$. (This is the topological version of Theorem 1.8.5 which characterizes the recursive sets.)

16) Prove Theorem 25.

17) Complete the proof of Theorem 26.

BIBLIOGRAPHICAL NOTES

Rogers (1967) introduces the enumeration operators and reduces other kinds of type 2 computability to enumeration computability (§§ 9.7, 9,8, 15.3). Scott (1976) uses continuity and (enumeration) computability on P_ω as a basis of a theory of data types. A comparison of some kinds of type 2 operators is given by Barendregt and Longo (1983).

3.2 Recursion Theory on Baire's Space

In this chapter we lay the basis for a unified Type 2 recursion theory. Our investigations from Chapter 3.1 and especially Theorem 3.1.14 show that it suffices to study continuity and computability on Baire's space $\mathbb{B}$. We shall choose the set $\mathbb{B} = \mathbb{N}^{\mathbb{N}}$ as our standard set on which we develop a theory of continuity (w.r.t. Baire's topology) and of computability. The theory turns out to be formally similar to Type 1 recursion theory. Most definitions and theorems will appear in a topological and in a computational version in accordance with our previously explained program for Type 2 theory. First we introduce a representation $\hat{\Phi} : \mathbb{B} \longrightarrow [\mathbb{B} \longrightarrow \mathbb{B}_o]$ of the continuous functions from $\mathbb{B}$ to $\mathbb{B}_o$ which is effective: it satisfies the Type 2 utm-theorem and smn-theorem. From $\hat{\Phi}$ we derive a representation $\psi : \mathbb{B} \longrightarrow [\mathbb{B} \longrightarrow \mathbb{B}]$, where $[\mathbb{B} \longrightarrow \mathbb{B}]$ is the set of continuous functions $\Gamma : \mathbb{B} \dashrightarrow \mathbb{B}$ the domains of which are the G_δ-subsets of $\mathbb{B}$, and we derive a representation $\chi : \mathbb{B} \longrightarrow [\mathbb{B} \longrightarrow \mathbb{N}]$ of the set of the continuous functions $\Gamma : \mathbb{B} \dashrightarrow \mathbb{N}$ the domains of which are the open subsets of $\mathbb{B}$. The representations ψ and χ satisfy the utm-theorem and the smn-theorem. As a counterpart of the recursively enumerable subsets in Type 1 theory we study the open and the computably open subsets of $\mathbb{B}$. This Type 2 theory of open subsets of $\mathbb{B}$ is formally very similar to the Type 1 theory of the recursively enumerable sets.

The existence of an "effective" numbering φ of the set of unary partial recursive functions is one of the most fundamental properties in ordinary recursion theory. The representation $\hat{\Phi} : \mathbb{B} \longrightarrow [\mathbb{B} \longrightarrow \mathbb{B}_o]$ of the set $[\mathbb{B} \longrightarrow \mathbb{B}_o]$ of continuous functions from $\mathbb{B}$ to $\mathbb{B}_o$ has properties similar to those of φ. However, there seems to be a fundamental difference between $P^{(1)}$ which contains partial functions and the set $[\mathbb{B} \longrightarrow \mathbb{B}_o]$ which consists of total functions. This difference vanishes if we identify each function $f : \mathbb{N} \dashrightarrow \mathbb{N}$ with the total function $f_\perp : \mathbb{N} \longrightarrow \mathbb{N}_\perp$ where $\mathbb{N}_\perp := \mathbb{N} \cup \{\perp\}$ and

$$f_\perp(x) := \begin{cases} f(x) & \text{if } x \in \mathrm{dom}(f) \\ \perp & \text{otherwise} \end{cases}$$

or if for any $\Gamma : \mathbb{B} \longrightarrow \mathbb{B}_o$ we interpret $\Gamma(p) = \varepsilon$ as "$\Gamma(p)$ is divergent" and $\Gamma(p) \in \mathbb{B}$ by "$\Gamma(p)$ exists". Notice that in the second case $\Gamma(p)$ has a degree of *partial existence* between nonexistence and existence whenever $\Gamma(p) \in W(\mathbb{N})$.

1 DEFINITION

(1) Let $[\mathbb{B} \longrightarrow \mathbb{B}]$ be the set of all partial functions $\Gamma : \mathbb{B} \dashrightarrow \mathbb{B}$ such that Γ has a continuous extension $\Sigma : \mathbb{B}_o \longrightarrow \mathbb{B}_o$ with $\mathrm{dom}(\Gamma) = \mathbb{B} \cap \Sigma^{-1}(\mathbb{B})$.

(2) $\Gamma : \mathbb{B} \dashrightarrow \mathbb{B}$ is called *computable* iff Γ has a computable extension $\Sigma : \mathbb{B}_o \longrightarrow \mathbb{B}_o$ such that $\mathrm{dom}(\Gamma) = \mathbb{B} \cap \Sigma^{-1}(\mathbb{B})$.

(3) Let $[\mathbb{B} \longrightarrow \mathbb{N}]$ be the set of all partial functions $\Gamma : \mathbb{B} \dashrightarrow \mathbb{N}$ such that there is a continuous function $\Sigma : \mathbb{B}_o \longrightarrow \mathbb{B}_o$ with $\mathrm{dom}(\Gamma) = \mathbb{B} \cap \Sigma^{-1}(\mathbb{B}_o \setminus \{\varepsilon\})$ and $\Gamma(p) := \Sigma(p)(0)$ for all $p \in \mathrm{dom}(\Gamma)$.

(4) $\Gamma : \mathbb{B} \dashrightarrow \mathbb{N}$ is *computable* iff there is a computable function $\Sigma : \mathbb{B}_o \longrightarrow \mathbb{B}_o$ such that $\mathrm{dom}(\Gamma) = \mathbb{B} \cap \Sigma^{-1}(\mathbb{B}_o \setminus \{\varepsilon\})$ and $\Gamma(p) := \Sigma(p)(0)$ for all $p \in \mathrm{dom}(\Gamma)$.

The elements of $[\mathbb{B} \longrightarrow \mathbb{B}]$ are the "traces" of the elements of $[\mathbb{B}_o \longrightarrow \mathbb{B}_o]$ on $\mathbb{B}$. A function $\Gamma : \mathbb{B} \dashrightarrow \mathbb{B}$ is computable iff there is a Type 2 machine M with $f_M(p) \in \mathbb{B} \iff p \in \mathrm{dom}(\Gamma)$ for all $p \in \mathbb{B}$ and $f_M(p) = \Gamma(p)$ for all $p \in \mathrm{dom}(\Gamma)$. By Definition 1(3), $\Gamma \in [\mathbb{B} \longrightarrow \mathbb{N}]$ iff there is a function $\Sigma \in [\mathbb{B}_o \longrightarrow \mathbb{B}_o]$ such that $\Gamma(p) = \Sigma(p)(0)$ for all $p \in \mathbb{B}$. $\Gamma : \mathbb{B} \dashrightarrow \mathbb{N}$ is computable iff there is a Type 2 machine M such that $\Gamma(p) :=$ the first number of $f_M(p)$ for all $p \in \mathbb{B}$. Below the spaces $[\mathbb{B} \longrightarrow \mathbb{B}]$ and $[\mathbb{B} \longrightarrow \mathbb{N}]$ will be studied in more detail. We already mention that $\Sigma\Gamma \in [\mathbb{B} \longrightarrow \mathbb{B}]$ if Σ and Γ are in $[\mathbb{B} \longrightarrow \mathbb{B}]$ and that $\Sigma\Gamma$ is computable if Σ and Γ are additionally computable. As counterparts of Cantor's tupling functions $\mathbb{N}^k \longrightarrow \mathbb{N}$ we define standard tupling functions $\mathbb{B}^k \longrightarrow \mathbb{B}$, $\mathbb{B}^{\mathbb{N}} \longrightarrow \mathbb{B}$, and $\mathbb{N} \times \mathbb{B} \longrightarrow \mathbb{B}$.

2 DEFINITION (*standard tupling on* $\mathbb{B}$)

(1) Define $\Pi : \mathbb{B}^2 \longrightarrow \mathbb{B}$ by $\Pi(p,q)(2i) := p(i)$, $\Pi(p,q)(2i+1) := q(i)$.

(2) Define $\Pi^{(k)} : \mathbb{B}^k \longrightarrow \mathbb{B}$ for $k \geq 1$ inductively by $\Pi^{(1)}(q) = q$, $\Pi^{(k+1)}(q_1,\ldots,q_{k+1}) = \Pi(\Pi^{(k)}(q_1,\ldots,q_k),q_{k+1})$.
(Notation: $\langle q_1,\ldots,q_k\rangle := \Pi^{(k)}(q_1,\ldots,q_k)$)

(3) Define $\Pi^{(\infty)} : \mathbb{B}^{\mathbb{N}} \longrightarrow \mathbb{B}$ by $\Pi^{(\infty)}(p_o,p_1,\ldots)\langle i,j\rangle := p_i(j)$.
(Notation: $\langle p_i\rangle_i := \Pi^{(\infty)}(p_o,p_1,\ldots)$)

(4) Define $\Pi' : \mathbb{N} \times \mathbb{B} \longrightarrow \mathbb{B}$ by $\Pi'(n,p)(0) = n$, $\Pi'(n,p)(m+1) = p(m)$ for all $m,n \in \mathbb{N}$, $p \in \mathbb{B}$.
(Notation: $\langle n,p\rangle := \Pi'(n,p)$)

According to our philosophy topological properties have to be considered. The natural topologies on $\mathbb{B}^n$ and $\mathbb{B}^{\mathbb{N}}$ are the product topologies derived from the topology τ_B on $\mathbb{B}$. Let $(X_i,\tau_i)_{i\in I}$ be a family of topological spaces. Let $Y := \bigtimes_{i\in I} X_i$ be the product of the sets X_i and let β be the set of all products $\bigtimes_{i\in I} V_i$ where $V_i \in \tau_i$ and $V_i = X_i$ for all but finitely many $i \in I$. Then β is a base of a topology $\tau = \bigotimes_{i\in I}\tau_i$ on Y called the *product topology*. As an example let $(X_i,\tau_i) = (\mathbb{N},2^{\mathbb{N}})$ for all $i \in \mathbb{N}$. ($\tau = 2^{\mathbb{N}}$ is the *discrete topology* on $\mathbb{N}$.) Then $\bigotimes_{i\in\mathbb{N}}\tau_i$ is Baire's topology τ_B on $\mathbb{N}^{\mathbb{N}} = \mathbb{B}$ (as an exercise). The projections $pr_i : Y \longrightarrow X_i$ are (τ,τ_i)-continuous. The product topology $\tau = \bigotimes_{i\in I}\tau_i$ is the coarsest topology on Y (i.e. the smallest subset of 2^Y which is a topology) such that the projections become continuous.

As the standard topology on $\mathbb{N}$ we consider the discrete topology $\tau_N := 2^{\mathbb{N}}$. The tupling functions have very nice topological and computational properties.

3 THEOREM

(1) The tupling functions $\pi^{(k)}$ (for $k \geq 1$), $\pi^{(\infty)}$, and π' are homeomorphisms (w.r.t. the standard topologies).

(2) The projections of the inverses of $\pi^{(k)}$ $(k \geq 1)$, $\pi^{(\infty)}$, and π' are computable functions $\mathbb{B} \longrightarrow \mathbb{B}$ or $\mathbb{B} \longrightarrow \mathbb{N}$, respectively.

For becoming conversant with topological techniques we prove the theorem in detail.

Proof

(1) Obviously the tupling functions are bijective. We show that $\pi : \mathbb{B}^2 \longrightarrow \mathbb{B}$ is continuous. It suffices to prove that $\pi^{-1}[w]$ is open for any $w \in W(\mathbb{N})$. Let $w \in W(\mathbb{N})$. There are numbers $x_1,\ldots,x_i,y_1,\ldots,y_j$ such that $i = j$ and $w = x_1y_1\ldots x_jy_j$ or $i = j+1$ and $w = x_1y_1\ldots x_jy_jx_{j+1}$. Let $x := x_1\ldots x_i$ and $y := y_1\ldots y_j$. Then $\pi^{-1}[w] = [x] \times [y]$ which is an open set w.r.t. the product topology on $\mathbb{B} \times \mathbb{B}$. Therefore π is continuous. For proving continuity of π^{-1} it suffices to show that $\pi([x] \times [y])$ is open for any $x,y \in W(\mathbb{N})$. For words $u = u_1\ldots u_k$ and $v = v_1\ldots v_k$ $(u_i,v_i \in \mathbb{N})$ define $h(u,v) := u_1v_1\ldots u_kv_k$. Let $x,y \in W(\mathbb{N})$. Assume w.l.g. $lg(x) \leq lg(y)$. Then

$$\begin{aligned}\pi([x]\times[y]) &= \bigcup\{\pi([xv]\times[y]) \mid v \in W(\mathbb{N}),\ lg(xv) = lg(y)\}\\ &= \bigcup\{[h(xv,y)] \mid v \in W(\mathbb{N}),\ lg(xv) = lg(y)\}\end{aligned}$$

which is an open subset of $\mathbf{B}$. Therefore Π^{-1} is continuous. By induction on k we prove that $\Pi^{(k)}$ is a homeomorphism. Obviously $\Pi^{(1)}$ is a homeomorphism. Assume that $\Pi^{(k)}$ is a homeomorphism. Then the mapping $H : \mathbf{B}^{k+1} \longrightarrow \mathbf{B} \times \mathbf{B}$ defined by $H(p_1,\dots,p_{k+1}) := (<p_1,\dots,p_k>,p_{k+1})$ is a homeomorphism, and $\Pi^{(k+1)}$ is a homeomorphism since $\Pi^{(k+1)} = \Pi H$ and Π is a homeomorphism. We show that $\Pi^{(\infty)}$ is a homeomorphism. Define a mapping $S : W(\mathbb{N}) \longrightarrow \bigcup\{(W(\mathbb{N})\setminus\{\varepsilon\})^k \mid k\in\mathbb{N}\}$ by

$$S(y) := (x_o,\dots,x_k) \quad \text{where} \quad (\forall i,j)x_i(j) = y<i,j> \quad \text{(see Def. 3.1.6(1))}.$$

Let $w \in W(\mathbb{N})$. Then

$$(\Pi^{(\infty)})^{-1}[w] = [x_o] \times [x_1] \times \dots \times [x_k] \times \mathbf{B} \times \dots$$

where $S(w) = (x_o,\dots,x_k)$. This set is open, hence $\Pi^{(\infty)}$ is continuous. On the other hand, for proving continuity of $(\Pi^{(\infty)})^{-1}$ it suffices to show that

$$M := \Pi^{(\infty)}([x_o] \times [x_1] \times \dots \times [x_k] \times \mathbf{B} \times \dots)$$

is open for any tuple $(x_o,\dots,x_k) \in (W(\mathbb{N}))^{k+1}$, $k \in \mathbb{N}$. Since

$$M = \bigcup\{[y] \mid (\exists n)(\exists v_o,\dots,v_n)\ S(y) = (x_o v_o,\dots,x_k v_k,v_{k+1},\dots,v_n)\},$$

M is open. Thus we have shown that $\Pi^{(\infty)}$ is a homeomorphism. The proof that Π' is a homeomorphism is left as an exercise.

(2) A function $\Sigma : \mathbf{B} \longrightarrow \mathbf{B}$ is computable iff there is a Type 2 machine which with input p (encoded by γ_2) yields the output $\Sigma(p)$ (encoded by γ_2) for any $p \in B$ (Def. 1(2), Theorem 3.1.16, Theorem 3.1.24, and comment on Type 2 machines). Define $\Sigma_1 : \mathbb{B} \longrightarrow \mathbb{B}$ by $\Sigma_1(p)(i) := p(2i)$ for all $p\in\mathbb{B}$, $i\in\mathbb{N}$. Then obviously Σ_1 can be computed by a Type 2 machine and $pr_1\Pi^{-1} = \Sigma_1$ is computable. The second projection Σ_2 is computable since $\Sigma_2(p)(i) = p(2i+1)$. An easy induction shows that the projections of $(\Pi^{(k)})^{-1}$ are computable. The i-th projection Σ_i of $(\Pi^{(\infty)})^{-1}$ has the property $\Sigma_i(p)(k) = p<i,k>$. Therefore Σ_i is computable. For similar reasons the projections of $(\Pi')^{-1}$ are computable.

Q.E.D.

In Type 1 recursion theory we have defined the k-ary computable functions explicitly and then we have shown that the tupling functions $\pi^{(k)}$ are computable and that $f : \mathbb{N}^k \dashrightarrow \mathbb{N}$ is computable iff its transform $g = f(\pi^{(k)})^{-1} : \mathbb{N} \dashrightarrow \mathbb{N}$ is computable. In Type 2 theory we define computability of functions on tuples from computability of unary functions by means of the standard tupling functions which by Theorem 3 possess all the necessary topological and computational properties. Thus a function $\Sigma : A \dashrightarrow B$ where $A \in \{\mathbf{B}^k, \mathbf{B}^{(\infty)}, \mathbb{N}\times\mathbf{B}\}$ and $B \in \{\mathbf{B}, \mathbf{B}_o, \mathbb{N}\}$ is called computable iff its transform $\Sigma\Delta^{-1}$, where Δ is the appropriate tupling function, is computable. For example each of the tupling functions is computable by this definition.

We shall now define a representation $\hat{\psi} : \mathbf{B} \longrightarrow [\mathbf{B} \longrightarrow \mathbf{B}_o]$ of the continuous functions from $\mathbf{B}$ to $\mathbf{B}_o$. By Lemma 3.1.22 and Theorem 3.1.7 it suffices to define a representation of the consistent sets $Z \subseteq W(\mathbb{N}) \times W(\mathbb{N})$.

4 DEFINITION *(standard representation $\hat{\psi}$ of $[\mathbb{B} \longrightarrow \mathbb{B}_o]$)*

(1) Define a surjective function $\delta : \mathbb{B} \longrightarrow 2^{W(\mathbb{N}) \times W(\mathbb{N})}$ by

$$\delta(p) := \{(\nu^*(i), \nu^*(j)) \mid (\exists k)\; p(k) = 1 + \langle i,j \rangle\}$$

for all $p \in \mathbf{B}$ where ν^* is the standard numbering of $W(\mathbb{N})$.

(2) Define $X \subseteq W(\mathbb{N}) \times W(\mathbb{N})$ by

$$X := \{(w, x0^n) \mid x \text{ is the longest consistent prefix of } w \text{ and } lg(w) = n + lg(x)\},$$

where x is called consistent iff $\{(\nu^*(i), \nu^*(j)) \mid (\exists k)\; x(k) = 1 + \langle i,j \rangle\}$ is consistent (see the explanation before Def. 3.1.7).

(3) Define $\hat{\psi} : \mathbf{B} \longrightarrow [\mathbf{B} \longrightarrow \mathbf{B}_o]$ by

$$\hat{\psi}_p(q) := \hat{\psi}(p)(q) := \Gamma_{\delta\Gamma_X(p)}(q)$$

for all $p,q \in \mathbf{B}$ (see Theorem 3.1.7 for Γ_X).

The function $\hat{\psi}$ is welldefined: The set X is itself consistent, hence Γ_X is welldefined. For any $p \in \mathbf{B}$, $\delta\Gamma_X(p)$ is consistent, and if $\delta(p)$ is consistent then $\delta(p) = \delta\Gamma_X(p)$. Therefore $\delta\Gamma_X$ is a representation of the set of consistent subsets of $W(\mathbb{N}) \times W(\mathbb{N})$ and $\hat{\psi}$ is a welldefined surjective mapping. The representation $\hat{\psi}$ satisfies the Type 2 versions of the utm-theorem and the smn-theorem.

5 THEOREM *(utm-, smn-theorem for $\hat{\psi}$)*

(1) The universal function $\Delta_u : \mathbf{B} \longrightarrow \mathbf{B}_o$ of $\hat{\psi}$ defined by $\Delta_u\langle p,q \rangle := \hat{\psi}_p(q)$ is computable.

(2) For any computable function $\Gamma : \mathbf{B} \longrightarrow \mathbf{B}_o$ there is a computable function $\Sigma : \mathbf{B} \longrightarrow \mathbf{B}$ with

$$\hat{\psi}_{\Sigma(p)}(q) = \Gamma\langle p,q \rangle \quad \text{for all } p,q \in \mathbf{B}.$$

Notice that Σ in (2) is a total function. The universal function Δ_u is computable by a Type 2 machine M which with input $\langle p,q \rangle$ yields the output $\hat{\psi}_p(q)$.

Before studying the proof of Theorem 5 the reader should repeat the proofs of the Type 1 utm-theorem and the Type 1 smn-theorem (see Chapter 1.9).

Proof

(1) We define a Type 2 machine M which for input <p,q> yields the value $\hat{\psi}_p(q)$. The machine M operates in stages $n = 0,1,2,\ldots$

Stage n:

x_n := the longest prefix of $p^{[n]} = p(0)\ldots p(n-1)$ which is consistent;

$z_n := \sup\{v \mid (\exists u)\ ((u,v) \in \delta(x_n) \wedge u \sqsubseteq q^{[n]})\}$

(where $\delta(x_n) := \{(\nu^*(i),\nu^*(j)) \mid (\exists k)\ x_n(k) = 1 + \langle i,j\rangle\}$);

lengthen the output from Stage (n-1) in order to obtain z_n on the output tape. Notice that the output z_{n-1} from Stage (n-1) is a prefix of the output z_n from Stage n. Therefore M is welldefined. We show that $f_M\langle p,q\rangle = \hat{\psi}_p(q)$ for all $p,q \in \mathbf{B}$. For any $y \in W(\mathbb{N})$ and $p,q \in \mathbf{B}$ we have

$$\begin{aligned} y \sqsubseteq \hat{\psi}_p(q) &\iff y \sqsubseteq \sup\{v \mid (\exists u)\ ((u,v) \in \delta\Gamma_X(p) \wedge u \sqsubseteq q)\} \\ &\iff (\exists u,v)\ \ (y \sqsubseteq v \wedge u \sqsubseteq q \wedge (u,v) \in \delta\Gamma_X(p)) \\ &\iff (\exists u,v)\ (\exists n)\ \ (y \sqsubseteq v \wedge u \sqsubseteq q^{[n]} \wedge (u,v) \in \delta(x_n)) \\ &\iff (\exists n)\ \ y \sqsubseteq z_n \\ &\iff y \sqsubseteq f_M\langle p,q\rangle , \end{aligned}$$

hence $\hat{\psi}_p(q) = f_M\langle p,q\rangle$ for all $p,q \in \mathbf{B}$. Therefore, Δ_u is computable.

(2) Let Γ be computable. By Definition 3.1.23 there is a computable function $\Delta : \mathbf{B}_o \longrightarrow \mathbf{B}_o$ which extends Γ. Define

$$Z := \{(y,v) \mid v \sqsubseteq \Delta(y)\} .$$

Then Z is $[\nu^*,\nu^*]$-r.e. and $\Delta = \Gamma_Z$.

For any $p \in \mathbf{B}$ define

$$Y(p) := \{(u,v) \mid ([p^{[\lg(u)]},u],v) \in Z\}$$

where $[x_1x_2\ldots x_n, y_1y_2\ldots y_n] := x_1y_1\ldots x_ny_n$ for $x_i, y_i \in \mathbb{N}$. Since Z is consistent, Y(p) is consistent for any $p \in \mathbf{B}$. We prove $\Gamma_{Y(p)}(q) = \Gamma_Z\langle p,q\rangle$ for any $p,q \in \mathbf{B}$. For any $x \in W(\mathbb{N})$ we have

$$x \sqsubseteq \Gamma_Z\langle p,q\rangle \iff x \sqsubseteq \sup\{v \mid (\exists y)\ ((y,v) \in Z \wedge y \sqsubseteq \langle p,q\rangle)\} .$$

Since Δ is isotone on $\mathbf{B}_o$, and since <p,q> is infinite we may choose y with lg(y) even. Therefore

$$\begin{aligned} x \sqsubseteq \Gamma_Z\langle p,q\rangle &\iff x \sqsubseteq \sup\{v \mid (\exists y)\ (\lg(y) \text{ even} \wedge (y,v) \in Z \wedge y \sqsubseteq \langle p,q\rangle)\} \\ &\iff (\exists v,y)\ \ (x \sqsubseteq v \wedge \lg(y) \text{ even} \wedge (y,v) \in Z \wedge y \sqsubseteq \langle p,q\rangle) \end{aligned}$$

$\iff (\exists u,v,w)\ \ (x \sqsubseteq v \wedge w \sqsubseteq p \wedge u \sqsubseteq q \wedge ([w,u],v) \in Z)$

$\iff (\exists u,v)\ \ (x \sqsubseteq v \wedge u \sqsubseteq q \wedge ([p^{[lg\ u]},u],v) \in Z)$

$\iff (\exists u,v)\ \ (x \sqsubseteq v \wedge u \sqsubseteq q \wedge (u,v) \in Y(p))$

$\iff x \sqsubseteq \Gamma_{Y(p)}(q)$.

Since Z is recursively enumerable there is a computable function $\Sigma : \mathbb{B} \longrightarrow \mathbb{B}$ such that $Y(p) = \delta\Sigma(p)$ for any $p \in \mathbb{B}$ (construct a Type 2 machine). For any $p,q \in \mathbb{B}$ we obtain $\Gamma<p,q> = \Gamma_Z<p,q> = \Gamma_{Y(p)}(q) = \Gamma_{\delta\Sigma(p)}(q) = \Gamma_{\delta\Gamma_X\Sigma(p)}(q)$ (since $\delta\Sigma(p)$ is consistent) $= \hat{\Psi}_{\Sigma(p)}(q)$.

Q.E.D.

As in Type 1 recursion theory the smn-theorem and the utm-theorem open a rich and elegant theory of computability and in this case also of continuity. Two other versions of the smn-theorem, the "topological" and the "uniform" version, can be easily derived.

6 COROLLARY

(1) There is a computable function $\Sigma : \mathbb{B} \longrightarrow \mathbb{B}$ with

$$\hat{\Psi}_{\Sigma<p,q>}(r) = \hat{\Psi}_p<q,r>$$

for all $p,q,r \in \mathbb{B}$.

(2) For any continuous function $\Gamma : \mathbb{B} \longrightarrow \mathbb{B}_o$ there is a continuous function $\Sigma : \mathbb{B} \longrightarrow \mathbb{B}$ with

$$\hat{\Psi}_{\Sigma(p)}(q) = \Gamma<p,q>$$

for all $p,q \in \mathbb{B}$.

Proof

(1) Define $\Omega : \mathbb{B} \longrightarrow \mathbb{B}$ by $\Omega<<p,q>,r> = <p,<q,r>>$, and $\Gamma : \mathbb{B} \longrightarrow \mathbb{B}_o$ by $\Gamma := \Delta_u\Omega$. Then Γ is computable by Theorem 5(1) (use a Type 2 machine). By Theorem 5(2) there is a function $\Sigma : \mathbb{B} \longrightarrow \mathbb{B}$ with $\Gamma<p,q> = \hat{\Psi}_{\Sigma(p)}(q)$. We obtain $\hat{\Psi}_p<q,r> = \Delta_u<p,<q,r>> = \Gamma<<p,q>,r> = \hat{\Psi}_{\Sigma<p,q>}(r)$.

(2) There is some $r \in \mathbb{B}$ with $\Gamma = \hat{\Psi}_r$. By (1), $\Gamma<p,q> = \hat{\Psi}_{\Delta<r,p>}(q)$ for some computable function $\Delta : \mathbb{B} \longrightarrow \mathbb{B}$. Define Σ by $\Sigma(p) := \Delta<r,p>$. Then Σ is continuous.

Q.E.D.

As in Type 1 recursion theory the smn-theorem and the utm-theorem determine $\hat{\Psi}$ uniquely up to equivalence. We introduce representations and reducibility and equivalence for representations. Again the definition splits into a topological and a more restricted computational version.

7 DEFINITION (*representations, t-reducibility, c-reducibility*)

(1) A *representation* of a set M is a (partial) surjective function $\delta : \mathbf{B} \dashrightarrow M$.

(2) Define the following relations on the class of representations.

$$\delta \leq_t \delta' \;:\Longleftrightarrow\; (\exists \Gamma : \mathbf{B} \dashrightarrow \mathbf{B}, \text{ continuous})(\forall p \in \mathrm{dom}(\delta))\;\; \delta(p) = \delta'\Gamma(p)$$

$$\delta \leq_c \delta' \;:\Longleftrightarrow\; (\exists \Gamma : \mathbf{B} \dashrightarrow \mathbf{B}, \text{ computable})(\forall p \in \mathrm{dom}(\delta))\;\; \delta(p) = \delta'\Gamma(p)$$

$$\delta \equiv_t \delta' \;:\Longleftrightarrow\; (\delta \leq_t \delta' \wedge \delta' \leq_t \delta)$$

$$\delta \equiv_c \delta' \;:\Longleftrightarrow\; (\delta \leq_c \delta' \wedge \delta' \leq_c \delta)$$

This definition is the counterpart of Definition 1.9.9 for numberings. The index t denotes topological reducibility or equivalence, the index c computational reducibility or equivalence. The relations $\leq_t$ and $\leq_c$ are pre-orders and $\equiv_t$ and $\equiv_c$ are equivalence relations. (Notice that $\Sigma\Gamma \in [B \longrightarrow B]$ (and $\Sigma\Gamma$ is computable) if $\Sigma, \Gamma \in [B \longrightarrow B]$ (and Σ and Γ are computable.)

Since the universal function Δ_u of $\hat{\Psi}$ is not only continuous but even computable we prove the computational version of the equivalence theorem. There is, of course, a weaker topological version (as an exercise).

8 THEOREM (*characterization of* $\hat{\Psi}$)

Let δ be a total representation of $[\mathbf{B} \longrightarrow \mathbf{B}_o]$, then (1) and (2) are equivalent.

(1) $\delta \equiv_c \hat{\Psi}$.

(2) δ satisfies the (computational) utm-theorem and the (computational) smn-theorem.

Since the proof is formally similar to the proof of the corresponding Type 1 theorem (1.9.10) we omit it.

9 DEFINITION (*standard representations of* $[\mathbb{B} \longrightarrow \mathbb{B}]$ *and* $[\mathbb{B} \longrightarrow \mathbb{N}]$)

(1) Define $\psi : \mathbb{B} \longrightarrow [\mathbb{B} \longrightarrow \mathbb{B}]$ by

$$\psi_p(q) := \psi(p)(q) := \begin{cases} \hat{\Psi}_p(q) & \text{if } \hat{\Psi}_p(q) \in \mathbb{B} \\ \text{div} & \text{otherwise} \end{cases}$$

for all $p,q \in \mathbb{B}$.

(2) Define $\chi : \mathbb{B} \longrightarrow [\mathbb{B} \longrightarrow \mathbb{N}]$ by

$$\chi_p(q) := \chi(p)(q) := \begin{cases} \hat{\Psi}_p(q)(0) & \text{if } \hat{\Psi}_p(q) \neq \varepsilon \\ \text{div} & \text{otherwise} \end{cases}$$

for all $p,q \in \mathbb{B}$.

It follows from the definitions (1 and 4) that ψ and χ are welldefined representations of $[\mathbb{B} \longrightarrow \mathbb{B}]$ and $[\mathbb{B} \longrightarrow \mathbb{N}]$, respectively. Obviously, for computable functions from $[\mathbb{B} \longrightarrow \mathbb{B}]$ and $[\mathbb{B} \longrightarrow \mathbb{N}]$ exist computable names $p \in \mathbb{B}$ w.r.t. ψ or χ, respectively. In Type 1 theory the domains of the partial recursive functions are the recursively enumerable sets. We shall show now that the domains of the functions from $[\mathbb{B} \longrightarrow \mathbb{N}]$ are the open subsets of $\mathbb{B}$ and that the domains of the functions from $[\mathbb{B} \longrightarrow \mathbb{B}]$ are the G_δ-subsets of $\mathbb{B}$. (A G_δ-subset of a topological space is a countable intersection of open subsets.) We shall immediately prove computably uniform versions of these characterizations.

10 DEFINITION (*representations of open and* G_δ*-sets*)

(1) Define a representation ω of $O(\mathbb{B})$, the open subsets of $\mathbb{B}$ (cf. Def. 3.1.21) by

$$\omega(p) := \bigcup \{[\nu^*(j)] \mid j+1 \in \text{range}(p)\}$$

for all $p \in \mathbb{B}$.

(2) Define a representation ξ of the G_δ-subsets of $\mathbb{B}$ by

$$\xi(p) := \bigcap_{i \in \mathbb{N}} S_i \quad \text{where} \quad S_i = \bigcup \{[\nu^*(j)] \mid \langle i,j \rangle + 1 \in \text{range}(p)\}$$

for all $p \in \mathbb{B}$.

The representation ω corresponds to the characterization of the recursively enumerable sets by (modified) ranges of computable functions, the "enumeration"-characterization. Property (1) of the next theorem corresponds to the property $W \equiv V_2$ from Theorem 2.3.10 for recursively enumerable sets.

11 THEOREM

(1) Define a representation ω' of subsets of $\mathbf{B}$ by $\omega'(p) := \mathrm{dom}(\chi_p)$. Then

$$\omega \equiv_c \omega' .$$

(2) Define a representation ξ' of subsets of $\mathbf{B}$ by $\xi'(p) := \mathrm{dom}(\psi_p)$. Then

$$\xi \equiv_c \xi' .$$

Notice that the representations are not only topologically but even computationally equivalent.

Proof

"$\omega \le_c \omega'$": Let M be a Type 2 machine which on input $\langle p,q \rangle$, where $p,q \in \mathbf{B}$, works in stages $n = 0,1,2,...$ as follows.

Stage$\langle i,k \rangle$: if $p(i) \neq 0$ and $\nu^*(p(i)-1) = q^{[k]}$ then write the number $0 \in \mathbb{N}$ onto the output tape.

Since $f_M : \mathbf{B} \longrightarrow \mathbf{B}_o$ is computable, by the computational smn-theorem for $\hat{\Psi}$ (Theorem 5(2)) there is a computable function $\Sigma : \mathbf{B} \longrightarrow \mathbf{B}$ with $f_M\langle p,q \rangle = \hat{\Psi}_{\Sigma(p)}(q)$.

We obtain for any $p,q \in \mathbf{B}$:

$$q \in \omega(p) \iff (\exists\, i,k)\ (p(i) \neq 0 \wedge \nu^*(p(i)-1) = q^{[k]})$$

$$\iff \hat{\Psi}_{\Sigma(p)}(q) \neq \varepsilon$$

$$\iff q \in \mathrm{dom}(\chi_{\Sigma(p)}) = \omega'\Sigma(p) .$$

Therefore $\omega \le_c \omega'$.

"$\omega' \le_c \omega$": By Theorem 5, Def. 3.1.8, and Def. 3.1.23 there is an r.e. set Z such that $\Gamma_Z\langle p,q \rangle = \hat{\Psi}_p(q)$ for all $p,q \in \mathbf{B}$. By the projection theorem there is a recursive set $B \subseteq \mathbb{N}^3$ such that

$$Z = \{(\nu^*(m), \nu^*(n)) \mid (\exists\, t)\ (m,n,t) \in B\} .$$

Define $\Sigma : \mathbf{B} \longrightarrow \mathbf{B}$ by

$$\Sigma(p)\langle m,n,i,j,t \rangle := \begin{cases} j+1 & \text{if } (m,n,t) \in B \wedge \lg(\nu^*(i)) = \lg(\nu^*(j)) \\ & \quad \wedge\ \nu^*(m) \sqsubseteq [\nu^*(i), \nu^*(j)] \wedge \nu^*(i) \sqsubseteq p \wedge n \neq 0 \\ 0 & \text{otherwise} \end{cases}$$

for all $p \in \mathbf{B}$ and $m,n,i,j,t \in \mathbb{N}$. Remember that $\nu^*(n) = \varepsilon \iff n = 0$. (We have used the notation $[x_1 \ldots x_n, y_1 \ldots y_n] := x_1 y_1 \ldots x_n y_n$ for $x_i, y_i \in \mathbb{N}$.) The function Σ can be computed by a Type 2 machine, hence Σ is computable. For any $p,q \in \mathbf{B}$ we obtain

$$q \in \omega'(p) \iff \Gamma_Z\langle p,q \rangle \neq \varepsilon$$

$$\iff (\exists\, (v,w) \in Z)\ (v \sqsubseteq \langle p,q \rangle \wedge w \neq \varepsilon)$$

$$\begin{aligned}\iff\ & (\exists m,n,i,j,t)\ \ (lg(\nu^*(i)) = lg(\nu^*(j))\ \wedge\ \nu^*(m) \sqsubseteq [\nu^*(i),\nu^*(j)] \\ & \qquad \wedge\ \nu^*(i) \sqsubseteq p\ \wedge\ \nu^*(j) \sqsubseteq q\ \wedge\ (m,n,t) \in B\ \wedge\ n \neq 0) \\ \iff\ & (\exists j)\ \ (j+1 \in \text{range}\,\Sigma(p)\ \wedge\ \nu^*(j) \sqsubseteq q) \\ \iff\ & q \in \omega\Sigma(p)\,.\end{aligned}$$

This shows $\omega' \leq_c \omega$.

"$\xi \leq_c \xi'$": Define a function $\Delta : \mathbf{B} \longrightarrow \mathbf{B}_o$ as follows:

$$\Delta\langle p,q\rangle(n) = \begin{cases} 0 & \text{if } \{\langle j,k\rangle \mid p(k) = \langle i,j\rangle + 1\ \wedge\ \nu^*(j) \sqsubseteq q\} \neq \emptyset \quad \text{for all } i \leq n \\ \text{div} & \text{otherwise}\,.\end{cases}$$

The function Δ is computable by means of a Type 2 machine. By Theorem 5(2) there is a computable function $\Sigma : \mathbf{B} \longrightarrow \mathbf{B}$ with $\Delta\langle p,q\rangle = \hat{\psi}_{\Sigma(p)}(q)$ for all $p,q \in \mathbf{B}$. We obtain

$$\begin{aligned} q \in \xi(p) \iff\ & (\forall i)(\exists j)(\exists k)\ \ (p(k) = \langle i,j\rangle + 1\ \wedge\ \nu^*(j) \sqsubseteq q) \\ \iff\ & (\forall n)\ \ \Delta\langle p,q\rangle(n) \text{ exists} \\ \iff\ & q \in \text{dom}(\psi_{\Sigma(p)}) \\ \iff\ & q \in \xi'\Sigma(p)\end{aligned}$$

for all $p,q \in \mathbf{B}$, hence $\xi \leq_c \xi'$.

"$\xi' \leq_c \xi$": Let B be the set from the proof of $\omega' \leq_c \omega$. Define a function $\Sigma : \mathbf{B} \longrightarrow \mathbf{B}$ as follows:

$$\Sigma(p)\langle i,j,k,m,n,t\rangle := \begin{cases} \langle i,n\rangle + 1 & \text{if } lg(\nu^*(m)) = lg(\nu^*(n))\ \wedge\ \nu^*(j) \sqsubseteq [\nu^*(m),\nu^*(n)] \\ & \qquad \wedge\ \nu^*(m) \sqsubseteq p\ \wedge\ \langle j,k,t\rangle \in B\ \wedge\ lg(\nu^*(k)) \geq i \\ 0 & \text{otherwise}\,.\end{cases}$$

Then Σ is computable. For any $p,q \in \mathbf{B}$ we obtain

$$\begin{aligned} q \in \xi'(p) \iff\ & (\forall i)\ \ \hat{\psi}_p(q)(i) \text{ exists} \\ \iff\ & (\forall i)(\exists (u,v) \in Z)(\exists x,y)\ \ (lg(x) = lg(y)\ \wedge\ u \sqsubseteq [x,y] \\ & \qquad \wedge\ x \sqsubseteq p\ \wedge\ y \sqsubseteq q\ \wedge\ lg(v) \geq i) \\ \iff\ & (\forall i)(\exists j,k,m,n,t)\ \ (lg(\nu^*(m)\ ) = lg(\nu^*(n))\ \wedge\ \nu^*(j) \sqsubseteq [\nu^*(m),\nu^*(n)] \\ & \qquad \wedge\ \nu^*(m) \sqsubseteq p\ \wedge\ \langle j,k,t\rangle \in B\ \wedge\ lg(\nu^*(k)) \geq i \\ & \qquad \wedge\ \nu^*(n) \sqsubseteq q) \\ \iff\ & (\forall i)(\exists n)\ \ (\langle i,n\rangle + 1 \in \text{range}\Sigma(p)\ \wedge\ \nu^*(n) \sqsubseteq q) \\ \iff\ & q \in \xi\Sigma(p)\,,\end{aligned}$$

hence $\xi' \leq_c \xi$.

Q.E.D.

By Theorem 11, every function $\Gamma \in [\mathbf{B} \longrightarrow \mathbb{N}]$ has an open domain. We shall show that $[\mathbf{B} \longrightarrow \mathbb{N}]$ is the set of all continuous functions $\Sigma : \mathbf{B} \dashrightarrow \mathbb{N}$ with open domain. Furthermore, we show that any (partial) continuous function $\Delta : \mathbf{B} \dashrightarrow \mathbb{N}$ can be extended to a function $\Gamma \in [\mathbf{B} \longrightarrow \mathbb{N}]$. Hence the set $[\mathbf{B} \longrightarrow \mathbb{N}]$ represents "essentially" every continuous function $\Delta : \mathbf{B} \dashrightarrow \mathbb{N}$. Notice that there is no representation $\delta : \mathbf{B} \dashrightarrow X$ of the set X of all the partial continuous functions $\Delta : \mathbf{B} \dashrightarrow \mathbb{N}$ since the cardinality of X is greater than that of $\mathbf{B}$.

12 THEOREM (*characterization of* $[\mathbf{B} \longrightarrow \mathbb{N}]$, *extension theorem*)

(1) $[\mathbf{B} \longrightarrow \mathbb{N}]$ is the set of all continuous functions $\Sigma : \mathbf{B} \dashrightarrow \mathbb{N}$ such that $\mathrm{dom}(\Sigma)$ is open.

(2) For any continuous function $\Sigma : \mathbf{B} \dashrightarrow \mathbb{N}$ there is a function $\Sigma' \in [\mathbf{B} \longrightarrow \mathbb{N}]$ which extends Σ.

Proof

(1) Let $\Sigma : \mathbf{B} \dashrightarrow \mathbb{N}$ be continuous and let $\mathrm{dom}(\Sigma)$ be open. Define $Z := \{(w,n) \in (W(\mathbb{N}))^2 \mid [w] \subseteq \mathrm{dom}(\Sigma) \wedge \Sigma([w]) = \{n\}\}$. If $w \sqsubseteq w'$, $(w,n) \in Z$ and $(w',n') \in Z$, then $n = n'$. Therefore Z is consistent. Define $\Sigma' \in [\mathbf{B} \longrightarrow \mathbb{N}]$ by $\Sigma'(p) := \Gamma_Z(p)(0)$ (Theorem 3.1.7). For any $p \in \mathbf{B}$ and $n \in \mathbb{N}$ we obtain:

$$\begin{aligned}
\Sigma(p) = n &\iff (\exists w)\ (p \in [w] \wedge \Sigma([w]) = \{n\} \text{ (since } \Sigma \text{ is continuous))}\\
&\iff (\exists w)\ (p \in [w] \wedge [w] \subseteq \mathrm{dom}(\Sigma) \wedge \Sigma([w]) = \{n\} \text{ (since } \mathrm{dom}(\Sigma) \text{ is open))}\\
&\iff (\exists w)\ (w \sqsubseteq p \wedge (w,n) \in Z)\\
&\iff n \sqsubseteq \Gamma_Z(p)\\
&\iff \Sigma'(p) = n\,.
\end{aligned}$$

Therefore $\Sigma = \Sigma' \in [\mathbf{B} \longrightarrow \mathbb{N}]$. On the other hand assume $\Sigma \in [\mathbf{B} \longrightarrow \mathbb{N}]$. By Theorem 11, $\mathrm{dom}(\Sigma)$ is an open subset of $\mathbf{B}$. The function $H : \mathbf{B}_o \dashrightarrow \mathbb{N}$ defined by $H(x) :=$ (the first number (symbol) of x) is continuous since $H^{-1}\{n\} = 0_n$ (see Def. 3.1.6). Remember that we consider the discrete topology on $\mathbb{N}$. By Def. 9, there is a continuous function $\Gamma : \mathbf{B} \longrightarrow \mathbf{B}_o$ with $\Sigma = H\Gamma$. Therefore Σ is continuous.

(2) Let $\Sigma : \mathbf{B} \dashrightarrow \mathbb{N}$ be continuous. Define Z by $Z := \{(w,n) \mid \Sigma([w]) = \{n\}\}$. Then Z is consistent. Define $\Sigma' \in [\mathbf{B} \longrightarrow \mathbb{N}]$ by $\Sigma'(p) = H\Gamma_Z(p)$. Then Σ' extends Σ:

$$\begin{aligned}
\Sigma(p) = n &\implies (\exists w)\ (\Sigma([w]) = \{n\} \wedge p \in [w])\\
&\implies (\exists w)\ (w \sqsubseteq p \wedge (w,n) \in Z)\\
&\implies n \sqsubseteq \Gamma_Z(p)\\
&\implies \Sigma'(p) = n
\end{aligned}$$

Q.E.D.

A corresponding theorem can be proved for the space $[\mathbb{B} \longrightarrow \mathbb{B}]$.

13 THEOREM (*characterization of* $[\mathbb{B} \longrightarrow \mathbb{B}]$, *extension theorem*)

(1) $[\mathbb{B} \longrightarrow \mathbb{B}]$ is the set of all continuous functions $\Sigma : \mathbb{B} \dashrightarrow \mathbb{B}$ such that $\mathrm{dom}(\Sigma)$ is a G_δ-set.

(2) Any continuous function $\Sigma : \mathbb{B} \dashrightarrow \mathbb{B}$ can be extended into a function $\Sigma' \in [\mathbb{B} \longrightarrow \mathbb{B}]$.

Proof

Let $\Sigma \in [\mathbb{B} \longrightarrow \mathbb{B}]$. Then $\mathrm{dom}(\Sigma)$ is a G_δ-set by Theorem 11, and Σ is continuous as the restriction of a continuous function $\Delta : \mathbb{B} \longrightarrow \mathbb{B}_o$. On the other hand let $\Sigma : \mathbb{B} \dashrightarrow \mathbb{B}$ be continuous. Define

$$Z := \{(x,y) \mid \Sigma[x] \subseteq [y] \text{ and } \Sigma[x] \neq \emptyset\} .$$

Then Z is consistent. For any $p \in \mathrm{dom}(\Sigma)$ and $u \in W(\mathbb{N})$ we obtain

$$\begin{aligned} u \sqsubseteq \Sigma(p) &\Longrightarrow \Sigma(p) \in [u] \\ &\Longrightarrow (\exists w)\ (p \in [w] \wedge \Sigma[w] \subseteq [u]) \quad \text{(since } \Sigma \text{ is continuous)} \\ &\Longrightarrow (\exists v,w)\ (p \in [w] \wedge \Sigma[w] \subseteq [v] \wedge u \sqsubseteq v) \\ &\Longrightarrow (\exists v,w)\ (u \sqsubseteq v \wedge w \sqsubseteq p \wedge (w,v) \in Z) \\ &\Longrightarrow u \sqsubseteq \Gamma_Z(p) . \end{aligned}$$

This shows that Γ_Z extends Σ, hence Σ has an extension $\Sigma' \in [\mathbb{B} \longrightarrow \mathbb{B}]$. Assume additionally that $\mathrm{dom}(\Sigma)$ is a G_δ-set. By Theorem 11 there is some $\Delta \in [\mathbb{B} \longrightarrow \mathbb{B}]$ such that $\mathrm{dom}(\Sigma) = \mathrm{dom}(\Delta)$. Δ is the restriction of some $\Gamma_Y \in [\mathbb{B}_o \longrightarrow \mathbb{B}_o]$. Define

$$X := \{(x,y) \in Z \mid (\exists (u,v) \in Y)\ (u \sqsubseteq x \wedge \lg(y) \leq \lg(v))\},$$

let $\Gamma \in [\mathbb{B} \longrightarrow \mathbb{B}]$ be the restriction of Γ_X to $\mathbb{B} \cap \Gamma_X^{-1}(\mathbb{B})$. Then Γ extends Σ and $\mathrm{dom}(\Gamma) = \mathrm{dom}(\Sigma)$ (as an exercise), hence $\Sigma \in [\mathbb{B} \longrightarrow \mathbb{B}]$.
Q.E.D.

From Theorem 5 we can derive easily that the representations χ and ψ satisfy the utm-theorem and the smn-theorem.

14 THEOREM (*utm-, smn-theorem for* χ)

(1) The universal function of χ is computable.

(2a) $(\forall \Gamma \in [\mathbb{B} \longrightarrow \mathbb{N}]$, computable$)(\exists \Sigma : \mathbb{B} \longrightarrow \mathbb{B}$, computable$)$
$(\forall p,q)\ \ \Gamma\langle p,q\rangle = \chi_{\Sigma(p)}(q)$.

(2b) $(\forall \Gamma \in [\mathbb{B} \longrightarrow \mathbb{N}])(\exists \Sigma \in [\mathbb{B} \longrightarrow \mathbb{B}]$, total)
$(\forall p,q) \quad \Gamma\langle p,q\rangle = \chi_{\Sigma(p)}(q)$.

(2c) $(\exists \Sigma : \mathbb{B} \longrightarrow \mathbb{B}$, computable)
$(\forall p,q,r) \quad \chi_p\langle q,r\rangle = \chi_{\Sigma\langle p,q\rangle}(r)$.

Property (1) is the *utm-theorem*, Property (2a) the *computational translation lemma*, Property (2b) the *continuous translation lemma*, and Property (2c) the *uniform (computational) smn-theorem*.

Proof

Define $H : \mathbb{B}_o \dashrightarrow \mathbb{N}$ by $H(x) :=$ "the first symbol of x" . Then $\chi_p = H\hat{\psi}_p$ for all p, and by Def. 1, $\chi(p)$ is computable if $\hat{\psi}(p)$ is computable.

(1) Let Δ_u be the universal function of $\hat{\psi}$ (Theorem 5). Then $\chi_p(q) = H\hat{\psi}_p(q) = H\Delta_u\langle p,q\rangle$, hence $H\Delta_u$ is the universal function of χ and it is computable by Def. 1.

(2a) Let $\Gamma \in [\mathbb{B} \longrightarrow \mathbb{N}]$ be computable. Then $\Gamma = H\Gamma'$ for some computable $\Gamma' \in [\mathbb{B} \longrightarrow \mathbb{B}_o]$. By Theorem 5 there is a computable function $\Sigma : \mathbb{B} \longrightarrow \mathbb{B}$ with

$$\Gamma\langle p,q\rangle = H\Gamma'\langle p,q\rangle = H\hat{\psi}_{\Sigma(p)}(q) = \chi_{\Sigma(p)}(q) .$$

(2b) and (2c) can be derived from (2a) or from Corollary 6.

Q.E.D.

Like φ and $\hat{\psi}$, χ is characterized up to equivalence by the utm-theorem and the smn-theorem (14(2a)).

15 THEOREM (*characterization of* χ)

Let δ be a total representation of $[\mathbb{B} \longrightarrow \mathbb{N}]$. Then (1) and (2) are equivalent.

(1) $\delta \equiv_c \chi$.

(2) δ satisfies the (computational) translation lemma and the utm-theorem.

The proof is formally similar to the proof of the corresponding Type 1 theorem (1.9.10). It is left as an exercise. The smn-theorem and the utm-theorem and the characterization theorem hold correspondingly for the representation ψ of $[\mathbb{B} \longrightarrow \mathbb{B}]$. The proofs are very similar to the former ones. We leave them as exercises.

16 THEOREM (*utm-, smn-theorem for* ψ)

(1) The universal function of ψ is computable.

(2a) $(\forall \Gamma \in [\mathbb{B} \longrightarrow \mathbb{B}]$, computable$)$ $(\exists \Sigma : \mathbb{B} \longrightarrow \mathbb{B}$, computable$)$
$(\forall p,q)\ \ \Gamma\langle p,q\rangle = \psi_{\Sigma(p)}(q)$.

(2b) $(\forall \Gamma \in [\mathbb{B} \longrightarrow \mathbb{B}])$ $(\exists \Sigma \in [\mathbb{B} \longrightarrow \mathbb{B}]$, total$)$
$(\forall p,q)\ \ \Gamma\langle p,q\rangle = \psi_{\Sigma(p)}(q)$.

(2c) $(\exists \Sigma : \mathbb{B} \longrightarrow \mathbb{B}$, computable$)$
$(\forall p,q,r)\ \ \psi_p\langle q,r\rangle = \psi_{\Sigma\langle p,q\rangle}(r)$.

17 THEOREM (*characterization of* ψ)

Let δ be a total representation of $[\mathbb{B} \longrightarrow \mathbb{B}]$. Then (1) and (2) are equivalent.

(1) $\delta \equiv_c \psi$.

(2) δ satisfies the (computational) translation lemma and the utm-theorem.

The advantage of our approach to Type 2 recursion theory is the formal analogy between the properties of φ on the one hand and of Φ, ψ, and χ on the other hand. Several parts of Type 1 theory can be easily transferred to Type 2 theory. For most of the definitions and theorems there are two versions, a general topological one and a more special computational one. We shall not develop both branches completely but only transfer some basic diagonalizations, the concept of precompleteness and some aspects of the theory of recursively enumerable sets to Type 2 theory. In definitions we shall mostly formulate the computational version. The corresponding topological version can be easily derived if necessary. Usually positive results will be proved in a computational version ("there is a computable ...") and negative results in a topological version ("there is no continuous ...").

The smn- and the utm-theorem can be used for showing the effectivity of operations on $[\mathbb{B} \longrightarrow \mathbb{N}]$, $[\mathbb{B} \longrightarrow \mathbb{B}]$, etc. There are, e.g., computable (computational version!) total functions $\Sigma,\Delta : \mathbb{B} \longrightarrow \mathbb{B}$ such that

$$\varphi_i\chi_p = \chi_{\Sigma\langle i,p\rangle} \qquad (\text{for all } i \in \mathbb{N},\ p \in \mathbb{B}),$$

$$\psi_p\psi_q = \psi_{\Delta\langle p,q\rangle} \qquad (\text{for all } p,q \in \mathbb{B}).$$

These properties correspond to Lemma 1.9.12. For the proof apply the utm-theorem for φ, ψ, and χ and show that functions Σ_1 and Δ_1 with

$$H\Sigma_1\langle\langle i,p\rangle,q\rangle = \varphi_i\chi_p(q)$$

$$\Delta_1\langle\langle p,q\rangle,r\rangle = \psi_p\psi_q(r)$$

(where $H(x) :=$ "the first symbol of x" for $x \in \mathbf{B}_o$) can be computed by Type 2 machines. The smn-theorems yield the desired computable functions. Notice that $\Sigma\Gamma$ is not necessarily an element of $[\mathbf{B} \longrightarrow \mathbb{N}]$ if $\Gamma \in [\mathbf{B} \longrightarrow \mathbf{B}]$ and $\Sigma \in [\mathbf{B} \longrightarrow \mathbb{N}]$. Choose, e.g., Γ such that dom(Γ) is not open (see the exercises) and define Σ by $\Sigma(p) = 0$ for all $p \in \mathbf{B}$. Then dom($\Sigma\Gamma$) is not open, hence $\Sigma\Gamma \notin [\mathbf{B} \longrightarrow \mathbb{N}]$ by Theorem 12. Since $\Sigma\Gamma$ is continuous it has an extension in $[\mathbf{B} \longrightarrow \mathbb{N}]$.

In Type 1 recursion theory we have shown by diagonalization that there is a partial recursive function which cannot be extended to a total recursive function (Theorem 1.9.14). Type 2 versions of this theorem can be formulated as follows.

18 THEOREM (*non-extensible functions*)

(1) There is a computable function $\Gamma \in [\mathbf{B} \longrightarrow \mathbb{N}]$ which has no total continuous extension.

(2) There is a computable function $\Gamma \in [\mathbf{B} \longrightarrow \mathbf{B}]$ which has no total continuous extension.

Proof

(1) (This is a translation of the proof of Theorem 1.9.14)
Define $\Gamma : \mathbf{B} \dashrightarrow \mathbb{N}$ by $\Gamma(p) := \chi_p(p) + 1$. By the utm-theorem for χ, Γ is computable. Assume that Γ has a continuous total extension $\Sigma : \mathbf{B} \longrightarrow \mathbb{N}$. Then Σ diagonalizes over all continuous total functions $\Delta : \mathbf{B} \longrightarrow \mathbb{N}$: Let $\Delta : \mathbf{B} \longrightarrow \mathbb{N}$ be continuous. Then $\Delta = \chi_q$ for some $q \in \mathbf{B}$. Since $\chi_q(q)$ exists, $\Sigma(q) = \Gamma(q) = \chi_q(q) + 1 \neq \chi_q(q) = \Delta(q)$, hence $\Sigma \neq \Delta$. Therefore, Γ has no total continuous extension.

(2) (as an exercise)

Q.E.D.

The open subsets of $\mathbf{B}$ in our topological Type 2 theory and the computably open (see Def. 19) in our computational Type 2 theory correspond to the recursively enumerable sets in ordinary recursion theory.

19 DEFINITION (*open, clopen subsets of* $\mathbf{B}$)

Let A be a subset of $\mathbf{B}$. Then define:

A is *t-open* $:\Longleftrightarrow$ A is open.

A is *c-open* $:\Longleftrightarrow$ $A = \omega'(p)$ for some computable function $p \in \mathbf{B}$.

A is *t-clopen* $:\Longleftrightarrow$ A open and $\mathbf{B}\setminus A$ open.

A is *c-clopen* $:\Longleftrightarrow$ A c-open and $\mathbf{B}\setminus A$ c-open.

(Usually we shall say *clopen* instead of *t-clopen*, *provable* instead of *c-open*, and *decidable* instead of *c-clopen*.)

Remember that $\omega \equiv_c \omega'$ by Theorem 11. Since $\Gamma(p)$ is computable if Γ and p are computable, A is c-open iff $A = \omega(p)$ for some computable function $p \in \mathbf{B}$. The definition of the clopen subsets is derived from Theorem 1.8.5 (A recursive $\Longleftrightarrow$ (A r.e. $\wedge$ $\mathbb{N}\setminus A$ r.e.)). The following theorem which corresponds to Theorem 1.8.5 shows that the t-clopen (c-clopen) sets can be defined as those ones which have continuous (computable) characteristic functions.

20 <u>THEOREM</u>

A set $A \subseteq \mathbf{B}$ is t-clopen (c-clopen) iff $A = \Gamma^{-1}\{0\}$ for some total continuous (computable) function $\Gamma : \mathbf{B} \longrightarrow \mathbb{N}$.

Notice that Γ must be a total function. The easy proof is left as an exercise. Also a uniform version which corresponds to Lemma 2.3.9(1)(2) can be proved:

- There is a computable function $\Gamma : \mathbf{B} \dashrightarrow \mathbf{B}$ such that $\chi_{\Gamma<p,q>}$ is total and $(\chi_{\Gamma<p,q>})^{-1}\{0\} = \omega'(p)$ if $\omega'(q) = \mathbf{B}\setminus\omega'(p)$.
- There are computable functions $\Gamma_1, \Gamma_2 : \mathbf{B} \dashrightarrow \mathbf{B}$ with $\omega'\Gamma_1(p) = \chi_p^{-1}\{0\}$, $\omega'\Gamma_2(p) = \mathbf{B}\setminus\chi_p^{-1}\{0\}$ for all p such that χ_p is total.

(as an exercise). But it is not possible to go continuously from an enumeration index to a characteristic function index for a t-clopen set $A \subseteq \mathbb{B}$. This property, which corresponds to Lemma 2.3.9(3) for r.e. sets, can be derived from the following lemma (as an exercise).

21 <u>LEMMA</u>

There is no continuous function $\Gamma \in [\mathbf{B} \longrightarrow \mathbf{B}]$ such that $p \in \mathrm{dom}(\Gamma)$ and

$$\omega\Gamma(p) = \mathbb{B}\setminus\omega(p)$$

for all p such that $\omega(p)$ is t-clopen.

Therefore complementation on the t-clopen sets is not continuous w.r.t. the representation ω. Since $\omega \equiv_c \omega'$ we can formulate Lemma 21 for ω' instead of ω.

Proof

Suppose there is a continuous function $\Gamma \in [\mathbb{B} \longrightarrow \mathbb{B}]$ with $\omega\Gamma(p) = \mathbb{B} \setminus \omega(p)$ if $\omega(p)$ is clopen. Define $p(x) = 0$ for all $x \in \mathbb{N}$. Then $\omega(p) = \emptyset$ and $p \in \mathrm{dom}(\Gamma)$. Since $\omega\Gamma(p) = \mathbb{B} \neq \emptyset$ there is some n with $\Gamma(p)(n) \neq 0$, hence $\Gamma(p) \in [w]$ for some $w \notin W(\{0\})$. Since Γ is continuous there is some $v \in W(\mathbb{N})$ with $p \in [v]$ and $\Gamma[v] \subseteq [w]$. Clearly $v = 0^m$ for some m. Define $r \in \mathbb{B}$ by $r(k) = 0$ if $k < m$, $k - m$ if $k \geq m$). Then $r \in [v]$, $\omega(r) = \mathbb{B}$, $r \in \mathrm{dom}(\Gamma)$ and $\Gamma(r) \in \Gamma[v] \subseteq [w]$, hence $\omega\Gamma(r) \neq \emptyset$. This contradicts $\omega\Gamma(r) = \mathbb{B} \setminus \omega(r) = \emptyset$.

Q.E.D.

Also the characterizations of the recursively enumerable sets by projections can be transferred to Type 2 theory. We immediately prove a uniform version (cf. Theorem 2.3.10).

22 THEOREM (*uniform projection theorem*)

(1) There is a total computable function $\Sigma \in [\mathbb{B} \longrightarrow \mathbb{B}]$ such that $\chi_{\Sigma(p)}$ is total and

$$\omega(p) = \{q \mid (\exists i \in \mathbb{N})\ \chi_{\Sigma(p)}\langle i,q\rangle = 0\}$$

for all $p \in \mathbb{B}$.

(2) There is a computable total function $\Gamma \in [\mathbb{B} \longrightarrow \mathbb{B}]$ with

$$\omega\Gamma(p) = \{q \mid (\exists i \in \mathbb{N})\ \langle i,q\rangle \in \omega(p)\}\ .$$

By (1) any t-open (c-open) set is the projection of a t-clopen (c-clopen) set, and by (2) the projection of any t-open (c-open) set is t-open (c-open).

Proof

(1) By Theorem 14(2a) there is a computable total function $\Sigma : \mathbb{B} \longrightarrow \mathbb{B}$ with

$$\chi_{\Sigma(p)}\langle i,q\rangle = \begin{cases} 0 & \text{if } p(i) \neq 0 \wedge \nu^*(p(i)-1) \sqsubseteq q \\ 1 & \text{otherwise}, \end{cases}$$

for all $p,q \in \mathbb{B}$ and $i \in \mathbb{N}$. We obtain

$$q \in \omega(p) \iff (\exists i)\ (p(i) \neq 0 \wedge q \in [\nu^*(p(i)-1)])$$

$$\iff (\exists i)\ \chi_{\Sigma(p)}\langle i,q\rangle = 0$$

for all $p,q \in \mathbb{B}$.

(2) By constructing a Type 2 machine one shows easily that there is a computable

function $\Delta : \mathbb{B} \dashrightarrow \mathbb{N}$ with

$$\Delta\langle p,q\rangle = \begin{cases} 0 & \text{if } (\exists i,j)\ (p(j) \neq 0 \wedge \nu^*(p(j)-1) \sqsubseteq \langle i,q\rangle) \\ \text{div} & \text{otherwise} \end{cases}$$

for all $p,q \in \mathbb{B}$. By the smn-theorem there is a computable total function $\Sigma : \mathbb{B} \longrightarrow \mathbb{B}$ with $\chi_{\Sigma(p)}(q) = \Delta\langle p,q\rangle$. We obtain

$$q \in \mathrm{dom}(\chi_{\Sigma(p)}) \iff (\exists i,j)\ (p(j) \neq 0 \wedge \nu^*(p(j)-1) \sqsubseteq \langle i,q\rangle)$$

$$\iff (\exists i)\ \langle i,q\rangle \in \omega(p)\ .$$

By Theorem 11, $\mathrm{dom}(\chi_{\Sigma(p)}) = \omega\Gamma(p)$ for some computable total $\Gamma : \mathbb{B} \longrightarrow \mathbb{B}$. This function Γ has the desired property.

Q.E.D.

The theory of m-reducibility on $2^{\mathbb{N}}$ has a counterpart in Type 2 theory.

23 DEFINITION (*reducibility for subsets of* $\mathbb{B}$)

Let A,B be subsets of $\mathbb{B}$. Define

$$A \le_t B \;:\iff\; A = \Gamma^{-1}B \quad \text{for some total} \quad \Gamma \in [\mathbb{B} \longrightarrow \mathbb{B}]\ ,$$

$$A \equiv_t B \;:\iff\; (A \le_t B \wedge B \le_t A)\ ,$$

$$A \le_c B \;:\iff\; A = \Gamma^{-1}B \quad \text{for some total computable} \quad \Gamma \in [\mathbb{B} \longrightarrow \mathbb{B}]\ ,$$

$$A \equiv_c B \;:\iff\; (A \le_c B \wedge B \le_c A)\ .$$

If $A = \Gamma^{-1}B$ for some total $\Gamma \in [\mathbb{B} \longrightarrow \mathbb{B}]$ and B is open (clopen) then clearly A is open (clopen), and A is c-open (c-clopen) if B is c-open (c-clopen) and $A \le_c B$. These properties correspond to Lemma 2.3.4 of Type 1 theory.

We have defined topological and computational reducibility and equivalence for subsets of $\mathbb{B}$. The corresponding 1-reducibilities can be defined accordingly. However, seemingly 1-reducibility in Type 1 theory and Type 2 theory differ in some aspects which are worth being investigated in more detail. If the cylindrification of $A \subseteq \mathbb{B}$ is defined by $\langle A, \mathbb{B}\rangle$ then a (topological and a computational) counterpart of the cylinder theorem (2.4.8) can be proved. However, Myhill's theorem on isomorphism doesn't seem to be true in Type 2 theory. Concepts like creativity and completeness can be transferred to Type 2 theory. The Type 2 self applicability problem is complete and creative.

24 DEFINITION

(1) $K_\chi := \{p \in \mathbf{B} \mid p \in \operatorname{dom} \chi_p\}$ (*self applicability problem*).

(2) $K^o_\chi := \{\langle p,q\rangle \mid p \in \operatorname{dom} \chi_q\}$ (*halting problem*).

(3) $A \subseteq \mathbf{B}$ is *t-complete* (*c-complete*) in $X \subseteq 2^{\mathbf{B}}$ iff $A \in X$ and $B \leq_t A$ $(B \leq_c A)$ for all $B \in X$.

(4) $A \subseteq \mathbf{B}$ is *t-productive* (*c-productive*) iff there is some continuous (computable) function $\Gamma : \mathbf{B} \dashrightarrow \mathbf{B}$ such that

$$\omega(q) \subseteq A \implies (q \in \operatorname{dom}(\Gamma) \wedge \Gamma(q) \in A \setminus \omega(q))$$

for all $q \in \mathbf{B}$.

(5) A is *t-creative* (*c-creative*) iff A is t-open (c-open) and $\mathbf{B} \setminus A$ is t-productive (c-productive).

Some interesting properties of K_χ are summarized in the following theorem.

25 THEOREM (*properties of* K_χ)

(1) $K_\chi \equiv_c K^o_\chi$.

(2) K_χ is c-open.

(3) $\mathbf{B} \setminus K_\chi$ is not t-open.

(4) K_χ is c-complete in the class of c-open subsets of $\mathbf{B}$.

(5) $\mathbf{B} \setminus K_\chi$ is c-productive.

(6) K_χ is c-creative.

All the proofs are very easy and formally equivalent to the proofs of the corresponding Type 1 properties of K (see Part 2 of this book). Many questions are still open: Is m-completeness equivalent to 1-completeness? Is creativity equivalent to completeness? Is productivity of A equivalent to $\mathbf{B} \setminus K_\chi \leq A$? Is there always a total productive function? Simple Type 2 sets S can be defined. The complement of S should not only be infinite but should have non-zero measure. Notice that all these questions can be discussed in a purely topological manner and in a more special computational one.

As a last example we introduce effective inseparability on Baire's space $\mathbf{B}$.

26 DEFINITION (*effective inseparability*)

$A, B \subseteq \mathbf{B}$ are t-(c-)*effectively inseparable* iff $A \cap B = \emptyset$ and there is some (computable) $\Gamma \in [\mathbf{B} \longrightarrow \mathbf{B}]$ such that $\langle p,q\rangle \in \mathrm{dom}(\Gamma)$ and $\Gamma\langle p,q\rangle \in \mathbf{B} \setminus (\omega'(p) \cup \omega'(q))$ for all $p,q \in \mathbf{B}$ with $A \subseteq \omega'(p)$, $B \subseteq \omega'(q)$, $\omega'(p) \cap \omega'(q) = \emptyset$.

The next lemma corresponds to Lemma 2.6.13/14.

27 LEMMA

(1) $\{p \mid \chi_p(p) = 0\}$ and $\{p \mid \chi_p(p) = 1\}$ are c-effectively inseparable.

Let $A, B \subseteq \mathbf{B}$ t-(c-)effectively inseparable. Then

(2) A and B are not t-clopen.

(3) If $A \subseteq A'$, $B \subseteq B'$ and $A' \cap B' = \emptyset$, then A' and B' are t-(c-)effectively inseparable.

(4) If $\Gamma : \mathbf{B} \longrightarrow \mathbf{B}$ is continuous (computable) and $\Gamma(A) \cap \Gamma(B) = \emptyset$ then $\Gamma(A)$ and $\Gamma(B)$ are t-(c-)effectively inseparable.

Proof

(1) By the smn-theorem there is a computable function $\Gamma : \mathbf{B} \longrightarrow \mathbf{B}$ with

$$\chi_{\Gamma\langle p,q\rangle}(r) = \begin{cases} 0 & \text{if} \quad r \in \mathrm{dom}(\chi_p) \wedge r \notin \mathrm{dom}(\chi_q) \\ 1 & \text{if} \quad r \notin \mathrm{dom}(\chi_p) \wedge r \in \mathrm{dom}(\chi_q) \\ \in\{0,1\} & \text{if} \quad r \in \mathrm{dom}(\chi_p) \cap \mathrm{dom}(\chi_q) \\ \mathrm{div} & \text{otherwise}. \end{cases}$$

Then Γ has the desired properties (cf. the proof of Lemma 2.6.14).

(2) - (4) (see the proof of Lemma 2.6.13)

Q.E.D.

EXERCISES

1) (a) For $i \in \mathbb{N}$ let τ_i be the discrete topology on $\mathbb{N}$. Show: $\tau_{\mathbf{B}} = \bigotimes_{i \in \mathbb{N}} \tau_i$.
   (b) For $i \in \mathbb{N}$ let τ_i be the discrete topology on $\{0,1\}$. Show: $\tau_{\mathbf{C}} = \bigotimes_{i \in \mathbb{N}} \tau_i$

2) Show that $\pi' : \mathbb{N} \times \mathbb{B} \longrightarrow \mathbb{B}$ is a homeomorphism.

3) Let $\Gamma : \mathbb{B} \longrightarrow \mathbb{B}_o$ and $\Gamma' : \mathbb{B} \dashrightarrow \mathbb{N}$ be functions such that $\Gamma'\langle n,p\rangle = \Gamma(p)(n)$ for all $n \in \mathbb{N}$, $p \in \mathbb{B}$. Prove:
   (a) Γ continuous $\iff$ Γ' continuous.
   (b) Γ computable $\iff$ Γ' computable.

4) Let $\Gamma_i \in [\mathbb{B} \longrightarrow \mathbb{B}]$ be computable, $p_i, q_i \in \mathbb{B}$, and $\Gamma_i(p_i) = q_i$ for $i = 1,\dots,s$. Show that there is a computable function $\Gamma \in [\mathbb{B} \longrightarrow \mathbb{B}]$ such that $\Gamma(p_i) = q_i$ for $i = 1,\dots,s$.

5) Consider the proof of the smn-theorem (5(2)). Show in detail that Σ exists.

6) (a) Prove Theorem 8.
   (b) Formulate and prove the topological version of Theorem 8.

7) Show that ξ from Definition 10 is a representation of the G_δ-subsets of $\mathbb{B}$.

8) Complete the proof of Theorem 13: Show that Γ extends Σ and that $\mathrm{dom}(\Gamma) = \mathrm{dom}(\Sigma)$.

9) Prove Theorems 15, 16, and 17.

10) Show that there is a G_δ-subset of $\mathbb{B}$ which is not open.

11) Let $\Gamma \in [\mathbb{B} \longrightarrow \mathbb{B}]$ and $\Sigma \in [\mathbb{B} \longrightarrow \mathbb{N}]$. Show that $\Sigma\Gamma$ has a computable extension if Σ and Γ are computable.

12) Prove that there are computable functions $\Sigma, \Gamma : \mathbb{B} \longrightarrow \mathbb{B}$ with

$$\chi_{\Sigma<i,p>} = \varphi_i \chi_p ,$$
$$\psi_{\Gamma<p,q>} = \psi_p \psi_q$$

for all $p, q \in \mathbb{B}$, $i \in \mathbb{N}$.

13) (a) Prove Theorem 18.
   (b) Is there a computable function $\Gamma \in [\mathbb{B} \longrightarrow \mathbb{B}]$ which has no continuous extension Σ such that $\mathrm{dom}(\Sigma)$ contains a non-empty open subset?

14) (a) Prove Theorem 20.
   (b) Formulate and prove the computably uniform version of Theorem 20.

15) Prove Theorem 25.

16) For $A \subseteq \mathbb{B}$ define the cylindrification $c(A)$ by $c(A) := <A, \mathbb{B}> = \{<p,q> \mid p \in A, q \in \mathbb{B}\}$. Formulate and prove a computational cylinder theorem for subsets of $\mathbb{B}$ which corresponds to Theorem 2.4.8.

17) Complete the proof of Lemma 27.

18) Let $\Gamma : \mathbb{B} \dashrightarrow \mathbb{N}$ be a function. Show:
   (a) $\Gamma \in [\mathbb{B} \longrightarrow \mathbb{N}] \iff \{<i,q> \mid \Gamma(q) = i\}$ is open in $\mathbb{B}$.
   (b) Γ is computable $\iff \{<i,q> \mid \Gamma(q) = i\} = \omega(p)$ for some computable $p \in \mathbb{B}$ (cf. the graph Theorem 2.3.14).

BIBLIOGRAPHICAL NOTES

The computable operators $\Gamma \in [\mathbb{B} \longrightarrow \mathbb{B}]$ are the general recursive operators from Rogers (1967). The kind of type 2 theory on Baire's space presented here is from Weihrauch (1985).

3.3 Representations

In Chapter 3.1 we have introduced Type 2 constructivity and computability on the spaces P_ω, $\mathbb{B}_o$, and $\mathbb{C}_o$ explicitly and we have shown that each of these concepts can be derived from any other one. In Chapter 3.2 we have chosen Baire's space $\mathbb{B}$ as our basic Type 2 space. We have developed a theory of constructivity and a more special theory of computability both of which are formally very similar to ordinary Type 1 recursion theory. In this chapter the basic Type 2 theory on Baire's space will be extended to a theory of representations.

Constructivity and computability on sets with cardinality not greater than that of the continuum can be reduced to Type 2 theory on $\mathbb{B}$ by means of representations. The elements of $\mathbb{B}$ serve as names of the elements of the set M under consideration. The theory of representations has a structure similar to that of the theory of numberings. As basic Type 2 theory the theory of representations splits into a constructive (topological) one and a more special computational one. We introduce relative constructivity and computability of functions and the relativized concepts of "open" and "clopen" for sets. The representation $\mathbb{M}$ of P_ω to be defined below has many properties which formally correspond to the properties of the numbering W of the recursively enumerable subsets of $\mathbb{N}$. The theory of precompleteness can be transferred to Type 2 theory. However the theory of cylinders doesn't seem to be as simple as in Type 1 theory. For example, the precomplete representation $\mathbb{M}$ has only certain weak cylinder properties. The recursion theorem and two versions of Rice's theorem are easy consequences of precompleteness.

1 DEFINITION (*representation*)

Let M be a set. A *representation* of M is a partial surjective function

$$\delta : \mathbb{B} \dashrightarrow M .$$

An element $m \in M$ is δ-computable iff $m = \delta(p)$ for some computable function $p : \mathbb{N} \longrightarrow \mathbb{N}$.

In the previous chapters we have already introduced several representations:

$\Phi : \mathbb{B} \longrightarrow [\mathbb{B} \longrightarrow \mathbb{B}_o]$ (Def. 3.2.4)

$\psi : \mathbb{B} \longrightarrow [\mathbb{B} \longrightarrow \mathbb{B}]$ (Def. 3.2.9)

$\chi : \mathbb{B} \longrightarrow [\mathbb{B} \longrightarrow \mathbb{N}]$ (Def. 3.2.9)

$\omega : \mathbf{B} \longrightarrow O(\mathbf{B})$ (Def. 3.2.10)

$\omega' : \mathbf{B} \longrightarrow O(\mathbf{B})$ (Theorem 3.2.11)

$\xi : \mathbf{B} \longrightarrow G_\delta(\mathbf{B})$ (Def. 3.2.10)

$\xi' : \mathbf{B} \longrightarrow G_\delta(\mathbf{B})$ (Theorem 3.2.11)

The restriction of γ_1 to $\mathbf{B}$ (see Def. 3.1.12) yields a representation $\mathbf{M}$ of P_ω which corresponds to the characterization of the recursively enumerable sets by enumeration. Below we define another representation of P_ω by interpreting names $p \in \mathbf{B}$ as characteristic functions which corresponds to the definition of the recursive sets. Finally the inverses of the tupling functions from Def. 3.2.2 are representations.

2 <u>DEFINITION</u> (*some standard representations*)

(1) $1\!\!1_{\mathbb{B}} : \mathbf{B} \longrightarrow \mathbf{B}$,

$1\!\!1_{\mathbb{B}}(q) := q$

(2) $\delta_{\mathbb{N}} : \mathbf{B} \longrightarrow \mathbb{N}$,

$\delta_{\mathbb{N}}(q) := q(0)$

(3) $\mathbf{M} : \mathbf{B} \longrightarrow P_\omega$,

$\mathbf{M}(p) := \{i \mid i+1 \in \mathrm{range}(p)\}$

(4) $\mathbf{M}^c : \mathbf{B} \longrightarrow P_\omega$,

$\mathbf{M}^c(p) := \mathbb{N} \setminus \mathbf{M}(p)$

(5) $\mathbf{M}_{cf} : \mathbf{B} \longrightarrow P_\omega$,

$\mathbf{M}_{cf}(p) := p^{-1}\{0\}$

(6) The inverses of $\pi^{(k)}$, $\pi^{(\infty)}$, and π' are standard representations.

(7) $\mathbb{P} : \mathbf{B} \dashrightarrow PF := \{f : \mathbb{N} \dashrightarrow \mathbb{N}\}$,

$\mathbb{P}(p) = f \;:\Longleftrightarrow\; \mathrm{graph}(f) = \mathbf{M}_p$

(where $\mathrm{graph}(f) := \{\langle i, f(i)\rangle \mid i \in \mathrm{dom}(f)\}$)

Any representation δ of a set M induces a theory of constructivity (topology) and a theory of computability on M. The following definitions correspond to those for numberings (Chapter 2.2).

3 DEFINITION (*relative continuity and computability*)

Let $\delta : \mathbb{B} \dashrightarrow M$ and $\delta' : \mathbb{B} \dashrightarrow M'$ be representations and let $f = (M, M', \rho)$ be a correspondence.

(1) f is (δ,δ')-*continuous* iff there is some (continuous) function $\Gamma \in [\mathbb{B} \longrightarrow \mathbb{B}]$ such that

$$(\delta(p)\ ,\ \delta'\Gamma(p)) \in \rho$$

for all $p \in \delta^{-1}\mathrm{dom}(f)$.

(2) f is *strongly* (δ,δ')-*continuous* iff there is some (continuous) function $\Gamma \in [\mathbb{B} \longrightarrow \mathbb{B}]$ such that

$$(\forall p \in \delta^{-1}\mathrm{dom}(f)) \quad (\delta(p)\ ,\ \delta'\Gamma(p)) \in \rho$$

and

$$(\forall p \in \delta^{-1}(M \setminus \mathrm{dom}(f))) \quad p \notin \mathrm{dom}(\Gamma)$$

(correspondingly for *computable* instead of *continuous*)

The correspondence f is (δ,δ')-computable iff for any δ-name p of some $x \in \mathrm{dom}(f)$ a δ'-name q such that $(p,q) \in \rho$ can be computed. The correspondence f is strongly computable, iff the function Γ in addition respects the domain of f. If the correspondence f is a partial function Definition 3 can be expressed as follows.

4 COROLLARY

Let $f : M \dashrightarrow M'$ be a function, let $\delta : \mathbb{B} \dashrightarrow M$ and $\delta' : \mathbb{B} \dashrightarrow M'$ be representations.

(1) f is (δ,δ')-continuous iff there is some (continuous) $\Gamma \in [\mathbb{B} \longrightarrow \mathbb{B}]$ such that

$$(\forall p \in \mathrm{dom}(f\delta)) \quad f\delta(p) = \delta'\Gamma(p)\ .$$

(2) f is strongly (δ,δ')-continuous iff in addition to (1) $p \notin \mathrm{dom}(\Gamma)$ whenever $p \in \mathrm{dom}(\delta) \setminus \mathrm{dom}(f\delta)$.

(Correspondingly for computable instead of continuous.)

The following diagram illustrates Corollary 5.

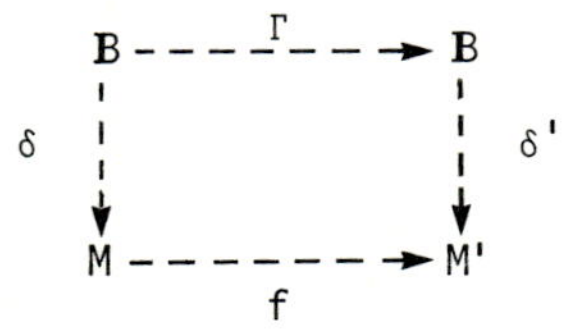

If $f=(M,M',\rho)$ is a correspondence, $\delta : \mathbf{B} \dashrightarrow M$ is a representation, and $\nu : \mathbb{N} \dashrightarrow M'$ is a numbering, (δ,ν)-continuity and (δ,ν)-computability are defined accordingly via continuous (computable) functions $\Gamma \in [\mathbf{B} \longrightarrow \mathbb{N}]$. We do not formulate these definitions explicitly.

5 EXAMPLES

(1) Let $\omega : \mathbf{B} \longrightarrow O(\mathbf{B})$ be the representation of the open subsets of $\mathbf{B}$ from Definition 3.2.10. Define a correspondence $f = (O(\mathbf{B}),\mathbf{B},\rho)$ by $(X,q) \in \rho :\Longleftrightarrow q \in X$. Then f is strongly $(\omega, 1\!\!1_{\mathbf{B}})$-computable. This means that there is a computable function $\Sigma : \mathbf{B} \dashrightarrow \mathbf{B}$ such that $\Sigma(q) \in \omega(q)$ if $\omega(q) \neq \emptyset$ and $\Sigma(q) = \mathrm{div}$ if $\omega(q) = \emptyset$. The computable function Σ determines a "witness" for the property "$\omega(q) \neq \emptyset$" iff $\omega(q)$ is not empty. For given $q \in \mathbf{B}$ determine $\Sigma(q)$ as follows. If $(\forall i)\ q(i) = 0$ then $q \notin \mathrm{dom}(\Sigma)$. Otherwise let $i := \mu j[q(j) \neq 0]$, $k := q(i) - 1$, and let $\Sigma(q)$ be the function $p \in \mathbf{B}$ defined by $\nu^*(k) \sqsubseteq p$ and $p(i) = 0$ for $i \geq lg(\nu^*(k))$. Obviously Σ is computable and $\Sigma(q) \in \omega(q)$ if $\omega(q) \neq \emptyset$. Therefore the correspondence f is strongly $(\omega, 1\!\!1_{\mathbf{B}})$-computable.

(2) The identity function on $G_\delta(\mathbf{B})$, the set of G_δ-subsets of $\mathbf{B}$, is (strongly) (ξ,ξ')-computable by Theorem 3.2.11.

The following lemma on effectivity on P_ω illustrates important features of our Type 2 theory. Its proof is easy and straightforward.

6 LEMMA

(1) Consider the following correspondences f and f'.

$$f = (P_\omega, \mathbb{N}, \rho) \quad \text{with} \quad (A,i) \in \rho \iff i \in A,$$

$$f' = (P_\omega, \mathbb{N}, \rho) \quad \text{with} \quad (A,i) \in \rho \iff i \notin A.$$

Then

f and f' are strongly $(\mathbf{M}_{cf}, 1\!\!1_{\mathbb{N}})$-computable,

f is strongly $(\mathbf{M}, 1\!\!1_{\mathbb{N}})$-computable,

f' is not $(\mathbf{M}, 1\!\!1_{\mathbb{N}})$-continuous.

(2) The function $g : P_\omega \longrightarrow P_\omega$ with $g(A) := \mathbb{N} \setminus A$ (i.e. complementation) is $(\mathbf{M}_{cf},\mathbf{M}_{cf})$-computable but not $(\mathbf{M},\mathbf{M})$-continuous.

(3) $\mathbf{M}_{cf} \leq_c \mathbf{M}$, $\mathbf{M}_{cf} \leq_c \mathbf{M}^c$, $\mathbf{M} \not\leq_t \mathbf{M}^c$, $\mathbf{M}^c \not\leq_t \mathbf{M}$, $\mathbf{M} \not\leq_t \mathbf{M}_{cf}$, $\mathbf{M}^c \not\leq_t \mathbf{M}_{cf}$ (see Lemma 9).

The above correspondence f is associated with the property $Q : (\forall A \in P_\omega)(\exists i)$ $(A \neq \emptyset \Longrightarrow i \in A)$. Q is "computably constructive" w.r.t. the characteristic function representation $\mathbf{M}_{cf}$ and w.r.t. the enumeration representation $\mathbf{M}$. On the other hand, the property $(\forall A \in P_\omega)(\exists i)\ (A \neq \mathbb{N} \Longrightarrow i \notin A)$ is computably constructive w.r.t. $\mathbf{M}_{cf}$ but not even (topologically) constructive w.r.t. the enumeration representation $\mathbf{M}$. If $\mathbf{M}(p) = A \neq \emptyset$ a prefix of p suffices to determine some $i \in A$. But no prefix of p suffices to determine an element $j \notin A$ (if $A \neq \mathbb{N}$). The representation $\mathbf{M}$ lists all positive informations "$i \in A$", the representation $\mathbf{M}^c$ lists all negative informations "$j \notin A$", and the representation $\mathbf{M}_{cf}$ lists the positive as well as the negative informations. By (1) it is not possible to obtain continuously (i.e. from a prefix) any negative information from a positive listing by $\mathbf{M}$ (cf. Lemma 3.2.21 and Lemma 2.3.9).

Proof

(1) Define $\Gamma : \mathbf{B} \dashrightarrow \mathbb{N}$ by $\Gamma(p) := \mu i[p(i) = 0]$. Then Γ is computable and f is strongly $(\mathbf{M}_{cf}, 1\!\!1_{\mathbb{N}})$-computable via Γ. For f' define Γ' by $\Gamma'(p) := \mu i[p(i) \neq 0]$. Define $\Sigma : \mathbf{B} \dashrightarrow \mathbb{N}$ as follows. $\Sigma(p) = \text{div}$ if $(\forall i)\ p(i) = 0$, otherwise let $i := \mu j[p(j) \neq 0]$, $\Sigma(p) := p(i) - 1$. Then Σ is computable and f is strongly $(\mathbf{M}, 1\!\!1_{\mathbb{N}})$-computable via Σ. Now assume that f' is $(\mathbf{M}, 1\!\!1_{\mathbb{N}})$-continuous. Then there is a continuous function $\Sigma : \mathbf{B} \dashrightarrow \mathbb{N}$ such that $\Sigma(p) \notin \mathbf{M}(p)$ if $\mathbf{M}(p) \neq \mathbb{N}$. Define $q \in \mathbf{B}$ by $(\forall i)\ q(i) = 0$. Then $\mathbf{M}(q) = \emptyset$, hence $k := \Sigma(q)$ exists. Since Σ is continuous, there is some $w \in W(\mathbb{N})$ such that $q \in [w]$ and $\Sigma([w]) = \{\Sigma(q)\}$. Then $w = 0^n$ for some n. Define $r \in \mathbf{B}$ by $r(n) = k + 1$, $r(i) = 0$ for $i \neq n$. Then $r \in [w]$, $r \in \text{dom}(\Sigma)$, $\Sigma(r) = k$, and $\mathbf{M}(r) = \{k\}$ in contradiction to the property $\Sigma(r) \notin \mathbf{M}(r)$ required for Σ. Therefore, f' is not $(\mathbf{M}, 1\!\!1_{\mathbb{N}})$-continuous.

(2) Define $\Sigma : \mathbf{B} \longrightarrow \mathbf{B}$ by $\Sigma(p)(n) := 1 \dot{-} p(n)$. Then $g\mathbf{M}_{cf}(p) = \mathbf{M}_{cf}\Sigma(p)$ for all $p \in \mathbf{B}$ and Σ is computable. Therefore g is $(\mathbf{M}_{cf}, \mathbf{M}_{cf})$-computable. On the other hand, assume that g is $(\mathbf{M}, \mathbf{M})$-continuous. Then there is a continuous function $\Sigma : \mathbf{B} \longrightarrow \mathbf{B}$ with $\mathbf{M}\Sigma(p) = \mathbb{N} \setminus \mathbf{M}(p)$ for all $p \in \mathbf{B}$. By (1) there is a continuous function $\Gamma : \mathbf{B} \dashrightarrow \mathbb{N}$ such that $\Gamma(p) \in \mathbf{M}(p)$ if $\mathbf{M}(p) \neq \emptyset$ since f is $(\mathbf{M}, 1\!\!1_{\mathbb{N}})$-continuous. For any $p \in \mathbf{B}$ we obtain

$$\begin{aligned} \mathbf{M}(p) \neq \mathbb{N} &\Longrightarrow \mathbf{M}\Sigma(p) \neq \emptyset \\ &\Longrightarrow \Gamma\Sigma(p) \in \mathbf{M}\Sigma(p) \\ &\Longrightarrow \Gamma\Sigma(p) \notin \mathbf{M}(p)\ . \end{aligned}$$

The function $\Gamma\Sigma : \mathbf{B} \dashrightarrow \mathbb{N}$ is continuous. By Theorem 3.2.12, $\Gamma\Sigma$ can be extended to a function $\Delta \in [\mathbf{B} \longrightarrow \mathbb{N}]$, for which $\Delta(p) \notin \mathbf{M}(p)$ if $\mathbf{M}(p) \neq \mathbb{N}$ holds. Since f' in (1) is not $(\mathbf{M}, 1\!\!1_{\mathbb{N}})$-continuous, we have a contradiction.

(3) Define $\Sigma : \mathbf{B} \longrightarrow \mathbf{B}$ by

$$\Sigma(p)(n) = \begin{cases} n+1 & \text{if } p(n)=0 \\ 0 & \text{otherwise} \end{cases}$$

for all $p \in \mathbf{B}$ and $n \in \mathbb{N}$. Then Σ is computable and $\mathbf{M}_{cf}(p) = \mathbf{M}\Sigma(p)$ for all $p \in \mathbf{B}$. The case $\mathbf{M}_{cf} \leq_c \mathbf{M}^c$ is proved correspondingly. Assume $\mathbf{M} \leq_t \mathbf{M}^c$. Then $\mathbf{M}(p) = \mathbf{M}^c\Sigma(p) = \mathbb{N} \setminus \mathbf{M}\Sigma(p)$ for some $\Sigma \in [\mathbf{B} \longrightarrow \mathbf{B}]$, hence complementation is $(\mathbf{M},\mathbf{M})$-continuous (contradiction to (2)). Therefore, $\mathbf{M} \not\leq_t \mathbf{M}^c$. Similarly $\mathbf{M}^c \not\leq_t \mathbf{M}$ is proved. $\mathbf{M} \leq_t \mathbf{M}_{cf}$ would imply $\mathbf{M} \leq_t \mathbf{M}^c$, and $\mathbf{M}^c \leq_t \mathbf{M}_{cf}$ would imply $\mathbf{M}^c \leq_t \mathbf{M}$, hence $\mathbf{M} \not\leq_t \mathbf{M}_{cf}$ and $\mathbf{M}^c \not\leq_t \mathbf{M}_{cf}$.

Q.E.D.

Notice that in Lemma 6 the positive results can be formulated in the form "there is a computable ..." and that the negative results have the form "there is no continuous ...".

As in Type 1 theory we derive relative decidability from relative computability (see Def. 2.2.11). Again we have a weak topological and a strong computational version.

7 <u>DEFINITION</u> (*relative constructivity of sets*)

Let M be a set and let $\delta : \mathbf{B} \dashrightarrow M$ be a representation of M. Let $X \subseteq M$ be a subset of M.

(1) X is *δ-open* iff there is a strongly $(\delta, 1\!\!1_{\mathbb{N}})$-continuous function $f : M \dashrightarrow \mathbb{N}$ with $X = \text{dom}(f)$.

(2) X is *δ-provable* iff there is a strongly $(\delta, 1\!\!1_{\mathbb{N}})$-computable function $f : M \dashrightarrow \mathbb{N}$ with $X = \text{dom}(f)$.

(3) X is *δ-clopen* iff there is a $(\delta, 1\!\!1_{\mathbb{N}})$-continuous function $f : M \longrightarrow \mathbb{N}$ with $X = f^{-1}\{0\}$.

(4) X is *δ-decidable* iff there is a $(\delta, 1\!\!1_{\mathbb{N}})$-computable functions $f : M \longrightarrow \mathbb{N}$ with $X = f^{-1}\{0\}$.

A more direct characterization is easily obtained from Corollary 4.

8 <u>COROLLARY</u>

Let $\delta : \mathbf{B} \dashrightarrow M$ be a representation and let $X \subseteq M$ be a subset of M.

(1) X is δ-open (δ-provable) iff there is some continuous (computable) $\Sigma \in [\mathbb{B} \longrightarrow \mathbb{N}]$ such that $p \in \mathrm{dom}(\Sigma) \iff \delta(p) \in X$ for all $p \in \mathrm{dom}(\delta)$.

(2) X is δ-clopen (δ-decidable) iff there is some continuous (computable) function $\Sigma \in [\mathbb{B} \longrightarrow \mathbb{N}]$ with ($\Sigma(q) = 0$ if $\delta(q) \in X$, and $\Sigma(q) = 1$ if $\delta(q) \notin X$) for all $q \in \mathrm{dom}(\delta)$.

Clearly $X \subseteq \mathbb{B}$ is open (c-open, t-clopen, c-clopen) iff it is $1\!\!1_{\mathbb{B}}$-open (-provable, clopen, decidable) (see Def. 3.2.19). On P_ω we have introduced a topology τ_E explicitly. By Lemma 3.1.13, $X \in \tau_E \iff X$ is $\mathbf{M}$-open. Theorem 2.2.13 can be transferred to representations: $A \subseteq M$ is δ-clopen (δ-decidable) iff A and $M \setminus A$ are δ-open (δ-provable) (as an exercise).

Reducibility for representations can be defined via relative computability (cf. Lemma 2.2.7, Def. 3.2.7).

9 LEMMA

Let δ be a representation of M, let δ' be a representation of M'. Then $\delta \le_t \delta'$ ($\delta \le_c \delta'$) iff $M \subseteq M'$ and $1\!\!1_{M,M'}$, the injective embedding of M into M', is (δ,δ')-continuous ((δ,δ')-computable).

The proof is easy (see the proof of Lemma 2.2.7).

Lemma 2.2.6, Lemma 2.2.8, and Lemma 2.2.10 can be transferred to Type 2 theory in a topological and a computational version. We only formulate Conclusion 2.2.9 in a Type 2 version.

10 THEOREM

Two representations of a set M induce the same kind of constructivity (computability) on M iff they are topologically (computationally) equivalent.

There are some natural operations by which new representations can be constructed from given ones (cf. Definition 2.2.14).

11 DEFINITION

Let $\delta_i : \mathbb{B} \dashrightarrow M_i$ be a representation of M_i $(i \in \mathbb{N})$ and let $\nu : \mathbb{N} \dashrightarrow S$ be a numbering of S.

(1) The representation $[\delta_1,\dots,\delta_k]$ of $M_1 \times \dots \times M_k$ (where $k \geq 1$) is defined by

$$\mathrm{dom}[\delta_1,\dots,\delta_k] := \langle \mathrm{dom}(\delta_1),\mathrm{dom}(\delta_2),\dots,\mathrm{dom}(\delta_k)\rangle$$

$$[\delta_1,\dots,\delta_k]\langle q_1,\dots,q_k\rangle := (\delta_1(q_1),\dots,\delta_k(q_k))$$

for all $\langle q_1,\dots,q_k\rangle \in \mathrm{dom}[\delta_1,\dots,\delta_k]$.
If $\delta_1 = \delta_2 = \dots = \delta_k = \delta$ we define $\delta^k := [\delta_1,\dots,\delta_k]$.

(2) The representation $[\delta_i]_i$ of the set of sequences $\bigtimes_{i\in\mathbb{N}} M_i$ is defined by

$$\langle p_i\rangle_i \in \mathrm{dom}[\delta_i]_i \;:\Longleftrightarrow\; (\forall i)\; p_i \in \mathrm{dom}(\delta_i),$$

$$[\delta_i]_i\langle p_i\rangle_i \;:=\; (\delta_o(p_o),\delta_1(p_1),\dots).$$

If $\delta_i = \delta$ for all $i \in \mathbb{N}$, we write $\delta^\infty := [\delta_i]_i$.

(3) The representation $[\nu,\delta_o]$ of $S \times M_o$ is defined by

$$\mathrm{dom}[\nu,\delta_o] \;:=\; \{\langle i,p\rangle \mid i \in \mathrm{dom}(\nu),\; p \in \mathrm{dom}(\delta_o)\},$$

$$[\nu,\delta_o]\langle i,p\rangle \;:=\; (\nu(i),\delta_o(p))$$

for all $\langle i,p\rangle \in \mathrm{dom}[\nu,\delta_o]$.

(4) The representation $\delta_1 \sqcup \delta_2$ of $M_1 \cup M_2$ is defined by

$$(\delta_1 \sqcup \delta_2)(p) := \begin{cases} \delta_1(q) & \text{if } p = 2q \text{ and } q \in \mathrm{dom}(\delta_1) \\ \delta_2(q) & \text{if } p = 2q{+}1 \text{ and } q \in \mathrm{dom}(\delta_2) \\ \mathrm{div} & \text{otherwise} \end{cases}$$

(where $(2q)(i) := 2q(i)$, $(2q{+}1)(i) := 2q(i)+1$ for all q and i).

(5) The representation $\delta_1 \sqcap \delta_2$ of $M_1 \cap M_2$ is defined by

$$\mathrm{dom}(\delta_1 \sqcap \delta_2) \;:=\; \{\langle p_1,p_2\rangle \mid p_1 \in \mathrm{dom}(\delta_1) \wedge p_2 \in \mathrm{dom}(\delta_2) \wedge \delta_1(p_1) = \delta_2(p_2)\}$$

$$(\delta_1 \sqcap \delta_2)\langle p_1,p_2\rangle \;:=\; \delta_1(p_1)$$

for all $\langle p_1,p_2\rangle \in \mathrm{dom}(\delta_1 \sqcap \delta_2)$.

(6) The representation $[\delta_o \longrightarrow \delta_1]$ of the strongly (δ_o,δ_1)-continuous functions $M_o \dashrightarrow M_1$ is defined as follows:

$$p \in \mathrm{dom}[\delta_o \longrightarrow \delta_1] \;:\Longleftrightarrow\; \begin{cases} \psi_p(\mathrm{dom}(\delta_o)) \subseteq \mathrm{dom}(\delta_1) \text{ and} \\ (\forall q,q' \in \mathrm{dom}(\delta_o))\; (\delta_o q = \delta_o q' \implies \\ \qquad \delta_1\psi_p(q) = \delta_1\psi_p(q')) \end{cases}$$

$$[\delta_o \longrightarrow \delta_1](p)(x) \;:=\; \delta_1\psi_p(q) \text{ for some } q \in \delta_o^{-1}\{x\}$$

for all $p \in \mathrm{dom}[\delta_o \longrightarrow \delta_1]$ and $x \in M_o$.

By applying Definition 11 we are able to formulate relative constructivity (computability) of k-ary and of ω-ary functions.

12 EXAMPLES

(1) The function $f: P_\omega \times P_\omega \longrightarrow P_\omega$ with $f(A,B) := A \cup B$ is $(\mathbf{M}^2, \mathbf{M})$-computable: Let Γ be the identity on $\mathbb{B}$. Then $\mathbf{M}\Gamma\langle p,q\rangle = \mathbf{M}(p) \cup \mathbf{M}(q) = f(\mathbf{M}(p), \mathbf{M}(q)) = f\mathbf{M}^2\langle p,q\rangle$.

(2) Intersection on P_ω is $(\mathbf{M}^2, \mathbf{M})$-computable (as an exercise).

(3) Intersection and union on P_ω are $(\mathbf{M}^2_{cf}, \mathbf{M}_{cf})$-computable (as an exercise).

(4) The function $f: P_\omega^{\mathbb{N}} \longrightarrow P_\omega$ with $f(A_o, A_1, \ldots) = \bigcup\{A_i \mid i \in \mathbb{N}\}$ (i.e. infinite union) is $(\mathbf{M}^\infty, \mathbf{M})$-computable (as an exercise) but not $(\mathbf{M}^\infty_{cf}, \mathbf{M}_{cf})$-continuous. Assume to the contrary that f is $(\mathbf{M}^\infty_{cf}, \mathbf{M}_{cf})$-continuous. Then there is a continuous function $\Gamma : \mathbb{B} \longrightarrow \mathbb{B}$ with

$$\mathbf{M}_{cf}\Gamma\langle p_o, p_1, \ldots\rangle = \mathbf{M}_{cf}(p_o) \cup \mathbf{M}_{cf}(p_1) \cup \ldots$$

The value $a := \Gamma\langle p_o, p_1, \ldots\rangle(0)$ depends on the infinitely many values $p_o(0)$, $p_1(0)$, $p_2(0), \ldots$:

$$a = 0 \iff (\exists i)\ p_i(0) = 0$$

This is impossible if Γ is continuous. We give a more formal argument. Let $q(i) = 1$ for all i. Then $\Gamma(q) = \langle i, r\rangle$ for some $i \neq 0$, $r \in \mathbb{B}$. Since Γ is continuous, $\Gamma[q^{[n]}] \subseteq [i]$ for some $n \in \mathbb{N}$. There are $\langle s_o, s_1, \ldots\rangle \in [q^{[n]}]$ and $\kappa \in \mathbb{N}$ such that $s_k(0) = 0$. We obtain $0 \in \mathbf{M}_{cf}(s_o) \cup \mathbf{M}_{cf}(s_1) \cup \ldots$ and $0 \notin \mathbf{M}_{cf}\Gamma\langle s_o, s_1, \ldots\rangle$, a contradiction.

By Lemma 6 and Example 12 the numbering W of the recursively enumerable sets has properties which are formally similar to those of $\mathbf{M}$, and the numbering Z of the recursive sets has properties which are formally similar to those of $\mathbf{M}_{cf}$, and what is more, the proofs are similar (cf. Theorem 2.3.13). Notice however, that $\mathrm{range}(\mathbf{M}_{cf}) = \mathrm{range}(\mathbf{M})$ but $\mathrm{range}(Z) \neq \mathrm{range}(W)$.

By the next lemma which is a counterpart of Lemma 2.2.15, equivalent representations yield equivalent constructs.

13 LEMMA

(1) Suppose $\delta_i \leq_t \delta'_i$ $(i \in \mathbb{N})$ and let ν, ν' be numberings with $\mathrm{range}(\nu) \subseteq \mathrm{range}(\nu')$. Then:

$$[\delta_1, \ldots, \delta_k] \leq_t [\delta'_1, \ldots, \delta'_k],$$

$[\delta_i]_i \le_t [\delta'_i]_i$,

$[\nu,\delta_1] \le_t [\nu',\delta_1]$,

$\delta_1 \sqcup \delta_2 \le_t \delta'_1 \sqcup \delta'_2$,

$\delta_1 \sqcap \delta_2 \le_t \delta'_1 \sqcap \delta'_2$,

$[\delta'_1 \longrightarrow \delta_2] \le_t [\delta_1 \longrightarrow \delta'_2]$.

(2) Suppose $\delta_i \le_c \delta'_i$ and $\nu \le \nu'$. Then

$[\delta_1,\ldots,\delta_k] \le_c [\delta'_1,\ldots,\delta'_k]$,

$[\nu,\delta_1] \le_c [\nu',\delta'_1]$,

$\delta_1 \sqcup \delta_2 \le_c \delta'_1 \sqcup \delta'_2$,

$\delta_1 \sqcap \delta_2 \le_c \delta'_1 \sqcap \delta'_2$,

$[\delta'_1 \longrightarrow \delta_2] \le_c [\delta_1 \longrightarrow \delta'_2]$.

The proof is left as an exercise. Notice that in the constructive case (1) we do not require $\nu \le \nu'$ but only $\mathrm{range}(\nu) \subseteq \mathrm{range}(\nu')$ which means that ν is "constructively" reducible to ν'. For proving $[\delta_i]_i \le_c [\delta'_i]_i$ the universal function of the family Γ_i of the reducing functions must be computable.

In Chapter 2.4 we have defined Sup and Inf for pre-orders. For representations we have the two pre-orders $\le_t$ and $\le_c$ which yield Sup_t and Inf_t, and Sup_c and Inf_c, respectively. The next lemma corresponds to Lemma 2.4.14.

14 LEMMA

Let δ_1,δ_2 be representations. Then

(1) $\delta_1 \sqcup \delta_2 \in \mathrm{Sup}_c\{\delta_1,\delta_2\} \subseteq \mathrm{Sup}_t\{\delta_1,\delta_2\}$

(2) $\delta_1 \sqcap \delta_2 \in \mathrm{Inf}_c\{\delta_1,\delta_2\} \subseteq \mathrm{Inf}_t\{\delta_1,\delta_2\}$

Proof

(1) The essential part of the proof is to show $\delta_1 \sqcup \delta_2 \in \mathrm{Sup}_c\{\delta_1,\delta_2\}$ and $\delta_1 \sqcup \delta_2 \in \mathrm{Sup}_t\{\delta_1,\delta_2\}$ (as an exercise).

(2) (cf. the proof of Lemma 2.4.14) $\delta_1 \sqcap \delta_2\langle p,q\rangle = \delta_1(p) = \delta_2(q)$, hence $\delta_1 \sqcap \delta_2 \le_c \delta_1$ and $\delta_1 \sqcap \delta_2 \le_c \delta_2$ by Theorem 3.2.3. Assume $\delta \le_c \delta_1$ via Γ_1 and $\delta \le_c \delta_2$ via Γ_2. Define $\Gamma : \mathbb{B} \dashrightarrow \mathbb{B}$ by $\Gamma(p) := \langle\Gamma_1(p),\Gamma_2(p)\rangle$. Then $\delta \le_c \delta_1 \sqcap \delta_2$ via Γ, hence

$\delta_1 \sqcap \delta_2 \in Inf_c\{\delta_1,\delta_2\}$. The property $\delta_1 \sqcap \delta_2 \in Inf_t\{\delta_1,\delta_2\}$ is proved correspondingly. The inclusions in (1) and (2) follow from $(\delta \leq_c \delta' \Rightarrow \delta \leq_t \delta')$. Details are left as an exercise.
Q.E.D.

The next lemma is a further example of the formal correspondence between Type 1 and Type 2 theory (cf. Lemma 2.3.9).

15 LEMMA

$\mathbf{M}_{cf} \equiv_c \mathbf{M} \sqcap \mathbf{M}^c$

Proof

By Lemma 6, $\mathbf{M}_{cf} \leq_c \mathbf{M}$ and $\mathbf{M}_{cf} \leq_c \mathbf{M}^c$, hence $\mathbf{M}_{cf} \leq_c \mathbf{M} \sqcap \mathbf{M}^c$ (Lemma 14). The proof of $\mathbf{M} \sqcap \mathbf{M}^c \leq_c \mathbf{M}_{cf}$ corresponds to that of Lemma 2.3.9 (b). Define $\Sigma : \mathbf{B} \dashrightarrow \mathbb{N}$ and $\Gamma : \mathbf{B} \longrightarrow \mathbf{B}_o$ as follows.

$$\Sigma\langle n,\langle p,q\rangle\rangle := \mu t[p(t) = n+1 \vee q(t) = n+1]$$

$$\Gamma\langle p,q\rangle(n) := \begin{cases} 0 & \text{if } (\forall m < n)\ \Gamma\langle p,q\rangle(m) \text{ exists and } s := \Sigma\langle n,\langle p,q\rangle\rangle \text{ exists} \\ & \text{and } p(s) = n+1 \\ 1 & \text{if } (\forall m < n)\ \Gamma\langle p,q\rangle(m) \text{ exists and } s := \Sigma\langle n,\langle p,q\rangle\rangle \text{ exists} \\ & \text{and } p(s) \neq n+1 \\ \text{div} & \text{otherwise.} \end{cases}$$

Then Σ and Γ are computable and $\mathbf{M}_{cf}\Gamma\langle p,q\rangle = (\mathbf{M} \sqcap \mathbf{M}^c)\langle p,q\rangle$ for all $\langle p,q\rangle \in dom(\mathbf{M} \sqcap \mathbf{M}^c)$.
Q.E.D.

1-reducibility is a special kind of reducibility for representations. $\delta \leq_{1t} \delta'$ $(\delta \leq_{1c} \delta')$ iff there is an injective continuous (computable) function $\Gamma : \mathbf{B} \dashrightarrow \mathbf{B}$ with $\delta(q) = \delta'\Gamma(q)$ for all $q \in dom(\delta)$. Although a counterpart of Myhill's theorem (2.4.6) doesn't seem to hold, the theory of cylinders can be transferred to Type 2 theory (essentially Def. 2.4.7 and Theorem 2.4.8). The representation δ is a *t-cylinder* iff $\delta \equiv_{1t} c(\delta')$ for some δ' where $c(\delta')\langle p,q\rangle := \delta'\langle p\rangle$ for all $p,q \in \mathbf{B}$; *c-cylinders* are defined correspondingly.

16 THEOREM

The representation $\Phi : \mathbf{B} \longrightarrow [\mathbf{B} \longrightarrow \mathbf{B}_o]$ is a c-cylinder.

Proof

Consider Definition 3.2.4. Let $Z \subseteq W(\mathbb{N}) \times W(\mathbb{N})$ be consistent, let $Y \subseteq W(\mathbb{N}) \times \{\varepsilon\}$. Then $Z \cup Y$ is consistent and $\Gamma_Z = \Gamma_{Z \cup Y}$. Define $\Sigma : \mathbb{B} \longrightarrow \mathbb{B}$ by

$$\Sigma\langle p,q\rangle(2n) = p(n)$$

$$\Sigma\langle p,q\rangle(2n+1) = \langle q(n),0\rangle + 1 .$$

Then Σ is injective, computable, and $\delta\Gamma_X\Sigma\langle p,q\rangle = \delta\Gamma_X(p) \cup Y$ for some $Y \subseteq W(\mathbb{N}) \times \{\varepsilon\}$ (remember $\nu^*(0) = \varepsilon$). Therefore, $\Phi_{\Sigma\langle p,q\rangle} = \Phi_p$ for all q. Since $\Phi \leq_{1c} c(\Phi)$, it suffices to show $c(\Phi) \leq_{1c} \Phi$. We have $c(\Phi)\langle p,q\rangle = \Phi(p) = \Phi\Sigma\langle p,q\rangle$ for all $\langle p,q\rangle \in \mathbb{B}$, hence $c(\Phi) \leq_{1c} \Phi$.

Q.E.D.

A sophisticated proof in Type 1 theory (Theorem 2.5.9) shows that φ' is a cylinder if $\varphi \equiv \varphi'$. Is δ a cylinder whenever $\delta \equiv_c \Phi$? This problem is not yet solved. As a corollary of Lemma 16 we obtain that the representations ψ and χ are c-cylinders and that the set K_X is a c-cylinder (as an exercise). The representation $\mathbf{M}$ is not a cylinder since the empty set has only one name, the constant 0 function. Nevertheless, $\mathbf{M}$ has certain weak cylinder properties which are invariant w.r.t. equivalence.

17 THEOREM (*many-one properties of* $\mathbf{M}$)

(1) There is a (total) representation δ_o of P_ω such that $\delta_o \equiv_c \mathbf{M}$ and:

- $\delta_o^{-1}\{\emptyset\}$ has one element,
- $\delta_o^{-1}\{A\}$ is denumerable for every finite set $A \in P_\omega$,
- $\delta_o^{-1}\{A\}$ has the cardinality of the continuum for every infinite set $A \in P_\omega$.

(2) Let δ be a representation of P_ω such that $\delta \equiv_c \mathbf{M}$.

- There is a computable function $\Delta : \mathbb{B} \dashrightarrow \mathbb{B}$ such that for all $p \in \mathrm{dom}(\delta)$ with $\delta(p) \neq \emptyset$ the following holds:

  $\delta(p) = \delta\Delta\langle n,p\rangle$ for all $n \in \mathbb{N}$,

  $\Delta\langle n,p\rangle \neq \Delta\langle m,p\rangle$ for all m,n with $m \neq n$.

- There is a computable function $\Gamma : \mathbb{B} \dashrightarrow \mathbb{B}$ such that for all $p \in \mathrm{dom}(\delta)$ such that $\delta(p)$ is infinite the following holds:

  $\delta(p) = \delta\Gamma\langle p,q\rangle$ for all $q \in \mathbb{B}$,

  $\Gamma\langle p,q\rangle \neq \Gamma\langle p,r\rangle$ for all $q,r \in \mathbb{B}$ with $q \neq r$.

Proof

(1) Let $Q := \{p \in \mathbb{B} \mid (\forall m,n,\ m \neq n)\ (p(m) = p(n) \Longrightarrow p(m) = 0)\}$. Define two computable functions $\Sigma, \Sigma' : \mathbb{B} \longrightarrow \mathbb{B}$ as follows.

$$\Sigma(p)(n) := \begin{cases} p(n) & \text{if } p(n) = 0 \text{ or } p(n) \notin \{\Sigma(p)(i) \mid i < n\} \\ 1 + \max\{\Sigma(p)(i) \mid i < n\} & \text{otherwise,} \end{cases}$$

$$\Sigma'(p)(n) := \begin{cases} p(n) & \text{if } p(n) = 0 \text{ or } p(n) \notin \{\Sigma'(p)(i) \mid i < n\} \\ 0 & \text{otherwise.} \end{cases}$$

Σ and Σ' have the following properties: $\Sigma(\mathbb{B}) = Q$, $\Sigma'(\mathbb{B}) = Q$, $\Sigma(q) = \Sigma'(q) = q$ for $q \in Q$, and $\mathbf{M}(p) = \mathbf{M}\Sigma'(p)$ for all $p \in \mathbb{B}$. Define δ_o by $\delta_o := \mathbf{M}\Sigma$. Then $\delta_o \leq_c \mathbf{M}$ and $\mathrm{range}(\delta_o) = P_\omega$ since $\mathbf{M}(Q) = P_\omega$. For any $p \in \mathbb{B}$ we have $\mathbf{M}(p) = \mathbf{M}\Sigma'(p) = \mathbf{M}\Sigma\Sigma'(p) = \delta_o\Sigma'(p)$, hence $\mathbf{M} \leq_c \delta_o$. Obviously $\delta_o(p) = \emptyset \Longleftrightarrow (\forall n)\ p(n) = 0$. Let $A \in P_\omega$, $A \neq \emptyset$, be finite. If $p(n) \neq 0$ for infinitely many n, then $\delta_o(p) = \mathbf{M}\Sigma(p)$ is infinite, hence $\delta_o(p) = A \Longrightarrow p(n) = 0$ almost everywhere. Therefore $\{p \mid \delta_o(p) = A\}$ is denumerable. Let A be infinite. Then $\{p \in Q \mid \mathbf{M}(p) = A\}$ has the cardinality of $\mathbb{B}$, hence $\delta_o^{-1}\{A\}$ has the cardinality of $\mathbb{B}$.

(2) There are computable functions $\Sigma, \Sigma' : \mathbb{B} \dashrightarrow \mathbb{B}$ with $\mathbf{M} = \delta\Sigma$ and $\delta(p) = \mathbf{M}\Sigma'(p)$ for all $p \in \mathrm{dom}(\delta)$. Let $p \in \mathrm{dom}(\delta)$, $\delta(p) \neq \emptyset$. Then $\delta\Sigma\langle 0^n, \Sigma'(p)\rangle = \delta(p)$ for all $n \in \mathbb{N}$ (where $\langle w,q\rangle(k) := (w(k)$ if $k < \lg(w)$, $q(k - \lg(w))$ otherwise$)$). Assume that $\{\Sigma\langle 0^n, \Sigma'(p)\rangle \mid n \in \mathbb{N}\}$ is finite. Then there is some $s \in \mathbb{B}$ with $s = \Sigma\langle 0^n, \Sigma'(p)\rangle$ for infinitely many n. Define $\tilde{0} \in \mathbb{B}$ by $(\forall n)\ \tilde{0}(n) = 0$. We show that continuity of Σ implies $s = \Sigma(\tilde{0})$. Let $t := \Sigma(\tilde{0})$, $m \in \mathbb{N}$. Then there is some k with $\Sigma[0^k] = \Sigma[\tilde{0}^{[k]}] \subseteq [t^{[m]}]$. There is some $n > k$ with $\Sigma\langle 0^n, \Sigma'(p)\rangle = s$, hence $s \in \Sigma[0^k] \subseteq [t^{[m]}]$. We conclude $s = t = \Sigma(\tilde{0})$. There is some n such that $\delta(p) = \delta\Sigma\langle 0^n, \Sigma'(p)\rangle = \delta(s) = \delta\Sigma(\tilde{0}) = \mathbf{M}(\tilde{0}) = \emptyset$ in contradiction to $\delta(p) \neq \emptyset$. Therefore if $\delta(p) \neq \emptyset$, the set $\{\Sigma\langle 0^n, \Sigma'(p)\rangle \mid n \in \mathbb{N}\}$ is infinite. It is now easy to define a computable operator Δ with the desired properties. The proof is similar to that of Theorem 2.4.18 on negative numberings.

Now we study the case that $\delta(p)$ is infinite. Let $\mathbf{M} \leq_c \delta$ via Σ and $\delta \leq_c \mathbf{M}$ via Σ'. There is a computable function $\Delta' : \mathbb{B} \dashrightarrow \mathbb{N}$ such that

$$\Delta'\langle 0,p\rangle = p(j) \quad \text{where} \quad j = \mu i[p(i) \neq 0],$$

$$\Delta'\langle n,p\rangle = p(j) \quad \text{where} \quad j = \mu i[p(i) \neq 0 \wedge (\forall k < n)p(i) \neq \Delta'\langle k,p\rangle].$$

Thus $\Delta'\langle n,p\rangle$ is "1 + n-th element of $\mathbf{M}(p)$" if it exists. There is a computable function $\Delta : \mathbb{B} \dashrightarrow \mathbb{N}$ such that $\Delta\langle n,p\rangle = \Delta'\langle n,\Sigma'(p)\rangle$ for all $p \in \mathrm{dom}(\Sigma')$. Then $\Delta\langle n,p\rangle$ is "1 + the n-th element of $\delta(p)$" if $p \in \mathrm{dom}(\delta)$. By Theorem 3.1.26 there is an $\sqsubseteq$-isotone computable function $\gamma : W(\mathbb{N}) \longrightarrow W(\mathbb{N})$ such that $\Sigma(p) = \sup\{\gamma(u) \mid u \sqsubseteq p\}$ for all $p \in \mathbb{B}$. We define a function $\Gamma_1 : \mathbb{B} \dashrightarrow \mathbb{B}$ by a Type 2 machine. With input $\langle p,q\rangle \in \mathbb{B}$ the machine operates in stages $n = 0,1,2,\ldots$ as follows. Let $v_n \in W(\mathbb{N})$ be the word on the output tape at the beginning of Stage n. Set $v_o := \varepsilon$.

Stage n:

$a_n := \Delta\langle n,p\rangle$

$k := \min\{j>0 \mid \gamma(v_n a_n 0^j)$ and $\gamma(v_n 0^j)$ are incomparable w.r.t. $\sqsubseteq\}$

$$v_{n+1} := \begin{cases} v_n a_n 0^k & \text{if } q(n)=0 \\ v_n 0^k a_n & \text{otherwise}. \end{cases}$$

Now assume that $\delta(p)$ is infinite, and $q \in \mathbf{B}$ is arbitrary. $\Delta\langle n,p\rangle$ exists for all n. Assume that v_n exists. We show that v_{n+1} exists also. Assume that $\gamma(v_n a_n 0^j)$ and $\gamma(v_n 0^j)$ are comparable for all j. Since $\Sigma : \mathbf{B} \longrightarrow \mathbf{B}$ is total, γ is unbounded on each $\sqsubseteq$-ascending sequence, therefore $\Sigma\langle v_n a_n,\tilde{0}\rangle = \Sigma\langle v_n,\tilde{0}\rangle$ and $\mathbb{M}\langle v_n a_n,\tilde{0}\rangle = \mathbb{M}\langle v_n,\tilde{0}\rangle$, but by our construction $a_n - 1$ is in the first set and not in the second one. Therefore v_{n+1} exists. This consideration shows that $\Gamma_1\langle p,q\rangle$ exists. Obviously $\mathbb{M}\,\Gamma_1\langle p,q\rangle = \delta(p)$, hence $\delta\Sigma\Gamma_1\langle p,q\rangle = \delta(p)$ if $\delta(p)$ is infinite and $q \in \mathbb{B}$. Let $q' \in \mathbf{B}$ such that $\{i \mid q(i)=0\} \neq \{i \mid q'(i)=0\}$. Let $n \in \mathbb{N}$ be minimal with $q(n)=0 \iff q'(n) \neq 0$. Let v'_n be the output of the machine with input $\langle p,q'\rangle$ before Stage n. Then $v_n = v'_n$ but $v_{n+1} \neq v'_{n+1}$, and $\gamma(v_{n+1})$ and $\gamma(v'_{n+1})$ are incomparable, therefore $\Sigma\Gamma_1\langle p,q\rangle \neq \Sigma\Gamma_1\langle p,q'\rangle$. Define $\Gamma_2 : \mathbf{B} \longrightarrow \mathbb{B}$ by $\Gamma_2(a_0 a_1 a_2 \ldots) := (0^{a_0}10^{a_1}1\ldots)$ and $\Gamma : \mathbf{B} \dashrightarrow \mathbb{B}$ by $\Gamma\langle p,q\rangle := \Sigma\Gamma_1\langle p,\Gamma_2(q)\rangle$. Then Γ has the desired properties.

Q.E.D.

Precomplete numberings play an important role in Type 1 recursion theory (see Chapter 2.5, 2.6). In Type 2 theory a constructive and a computational version of precompleteness can be defined. We consider the general case of partial representations.

18 DEFINITION (*precomplete representations*)

(1) A total representation $\delta : \mathbf{B} \longrightarrow M$ is t-*precomplete* (c-*precomplete*) iff for every continuous (computable) function $\Gamma \in [\mathbf{B} \longrightarrow \mathbf{B}]$ there is some continuous (computable) total function $\Delta : \mathbf{B} \longrightarrow \mathbf{B}$ such that

$$(\forall p \in \mathrm{dom}(\Gamma))\quad \delta\Gamma(p) = \delta\Delta(p).$$

(2) A representation $\delta : \mathbf{B} \dashrightarrow M$ is t-*precomplete* (c-*precomplete*) iff the extended total representation $\overline{\delta} : \mathbf{B} \longrightarrow M_\perp$, defined by $M_\perp := M \cup \{\perp\}$ (where $\perp \notin M$) and

$$\overline{\delta}(p) := \begin{cases} \delta(p) & \text{if } p \in \mathrm{dom}(\delta) \\ \perp & \text{otherwise} \end{cases}$$

is t-precomplete (c-precomplete).

We have already several precomplete representations.

19 LEMMA

The representations $\mathbf{M}, \hat{\psi}, \psi, \chi$ and the characteristic function $c : \mathbf{B} \longrightarrow \{0,1\}$ of K_χ are c-precomplete and t-precomplete.

Proof

$\mathbf{M}$: Let $\Gamma \in [\mathbf{B} \longrightarrow \mathbf{B}]$ be a continuous function. By Theorem 3.1.26 there is an isotone $\gamma : W(\mathbb{N}) \longrightarrow W(\mathbb{N})$ with $\Gamma(p) = \sup\{\gamma(u) \mid u \sqsubseteq p\}$ for all $p \in dom(\Gamma)$. Define γ' inductively by $\gamma'(\varepsilon) := \varepsilon$, $\gamma'(un) = \gamma'(u)\,0\,\gamma(un)$ for all $u \in W(\mathbb{N})$, $n \in \mathbb{N}$. Define $\Gamma' \in [\mathbf{B} \longrightarrow \mathbf{B}]$ by $\Gamma'(p) := \sup\{\gamma'(u) \mid u \sqsubseteq p\}$. Then Γ' is total and $\mathbf{M}\Gamma'(p) = \mathbf{M}\Gamma(p)$ for all $p \in dom(\Gamma)$. If Γ is computable, there is some computable γ, hence a computable function Γ'.

$\hat{\psi}$: (This case is proved by using the utm-theorem and the smn-theorem, see the proof of Theorem 2.5.2.)

ψ, χ : There are functions H_1, H_2 with $\psi = H_1\hat{\psi}$ and $\chi = H_2\hat{\psi}$.

K_χ : (see the proof of Theorem 2.5.2)

Q.E.D.

Application of the utm-theorem and the smn-theorem shows that c-precompleteness implies t-precompleteness. If δ and δ' are total representations, δ is c-precomplete and $\delta \equiv_c \delta'$, then δ' is c-precomplete. If $\delta : \mathbf{B} \longrightarrow M$ is precomplete and $H : M \longrightarrow M'$ is surjective, then $H\delta$ is precomplete (cf. Theorem 2.5.4). If δ and δ' are precomplete then $[\delta, \delta']$ is precomplete. As in Type 1 theory the precomplete representations are exactly those ones which satisfy the recursion theorem.

20 THEOREM (*recursion theorem*)

Let $\delta : \mathbf{B} \dashrightarrow M$ be a representation. Then δ is t-precomplete (c-precomplete) iff it satisfies the t-recursion theorem (c-recursion theorem) (*).

(*) There is some total continuous (computable) function $\Omega : \mathbf{B} \longrightarrow \mathbf{B}$ such that

$$\delta\Omega(p) = \delta\psi_p\Omega(p)$$

for all $p \in \mathbf{B}$ such that ψ_p is total.

The proof corresponds to that of Theorem 2.5.5. As an immediate consequence we obtain that any (δ,δ)-continuous function $f: M \longrightarrow M$ has a fixed point if δ is t-precomplete (cf. Corollary 2.5.6). This fixed point has a computable name, if δ is c-precomplete and f is (δ,δ)-computable. There are two versions of Rice's theorem for precomplete representations (see Theorem 2.5.8, Theorem 2.6.15).

21 THEOREM (*Rice*)

Let $\delta: \mathbf{B} \longrightarrow M$ be a t-precomplete representation of M. Let $M_o \subseteq M$. Then (1) and (2) hold.

(1) $\delta^{-1}(M_o) \not\leq_t \delta^{-1}(M \setminus M_o)$

(2) If $\delta^{-1}(M_o)$ is clopen then $M_o = M$ or $M_o = \emptyset$.

For a proof see the proof of Theorem 2.5.8. Notice that any c-version of Theorem 21 is weaker.

22 THEOREM (*Rice*)

Let $\delta: \mathbf{B} \longrightarrow M$ be a total t-precomplete (c-precomplete) representation, let $M_1, M_2 \subseteq M$ with $M_1, M_2 \neq \emptyset$ and $M_1 \cap M_2 = \emptyset$. Then:

(1) There are t-effectively inseparable t-open (c-open) sets B_1, B_2 and a total (computable) function $\Gamma \in [\mathbb{B} \longrightarrow \mathbb{B}]$ with $B_1 \subseteq \delta^{-1}M_1$ and $B_2 \subseteq \delta^{-1}M_2$.

(2) $\delta^{-1}M_1$ and $\delta^{-1}M_2$ are t-effectively (c-effectively) inseparable.

(3) $\delta^{-1}M_1$ is t-creative (c-creative) if it is t-open (c-open).

(4) $\delta^{-1}M_1$ is not t-clopen.

The proof is analogous to that of Theorem 2.6.15.

EXERCISES

1) Define an "effective" representation of $\bigcup_n \mathbb{B}^n$.

2) Let $\Gamma: \mathbb{B} \dashrightarrow \mathbb{N}$ be a function. Show:

(a) $\Gamma \in [\mathbb{B} \longrightarrow \mathbb{N}]$ iff dom(Γ) is open and Γ is strongly $(\mathbb{I}_{\mathbb{B}}, \delta_{\mathbb{N}})$-continuous.

(b) Γ is computable iff dom(Γ) is ω-computable and Γ is strongly $(\mathbb{I}_{\mathbb{B}}, \delta_{\mathbb{N}})$-computable.

(c) There is a strongly $(\Pi_{\mathbb{B}}, \delta_{\mathbb{N}})$-computable function which is not in $[\mathbb{B} \longrightarrow \mathbb{N}]$.

3) Let $f: \mathbb{N} \dashrightarrow \mathbb{N}$ be a function. How are computability and strong $(\delta_{\mathbb{N}}, \delta_{\mathbb{N}})$-computability related?

4) Prove Corollary 8.

5) Characterize the $\mathbb{M}_{cf}$-open subsets of P_ω.

6) Show that intersection on P_ω is $(\mathbb{M}^2, \mathbb{M})$-computable.

7) Show that intersection and union on P_ω are $(\mathbb{M}^2_{cf}, \mathbb{M})$-computable.

8) Prove Lemma 13.

9) Complete the proof of Lemma 14.

10) Let $\delta: \mathbb{B} \dashrightarrow M$ be a representation and let A be a subset of M. Show:
A δ-decidable iff A and $M \setminus A$ are δ-provable.

11) Prove the c-cylinder theorem for representations.

12) Prove that the representations ψ and χ and the set K_χ are cylinders.

13) Restrict $\mathbb{M}$ to δ by defining $\mathrm{dom}(\delta) := \{p \mid p \text{ nondecreasing}\}$. Show:
$\mathbb{M}_{cf} \leq_c \delta$, $\delta \not\leq_t \mathbb{M}_{cf}$.

14) Prove the constructive version of Theorem 17(2).

15) Define the operator Δ in the proof of Theorem 17(2).

16) Show that $\mathbb{M}_{cf}$ is not t-precomplete.

17) Prove that any c-precomplete representation is t-precomplete.

18) Prove Theorem 21(2) directly for the case $\delta = \mathbb{M}$. Does the theorem hold for $\delta = \mathbb{M}_{cf}$?

19) Let $\delta: \mathbb{B} \dashrightarrow M$ be a partial representation. Let δ be precomplete and $M_o \subseteq M$.
Show:
$\delta^{-1}(M_o) \not\leq_t \mathbb{B} \setminus \delta^{-1}(M_o)$.

20) Let $A, B \in P_\omega$. Show:
(a) $A \leq_e B$ (i.e. A is enumeration reducible to B) iff $\Gamma(B) = A$ for some $(\mathbb{M}, \mathbb{M})$-computable function $\Gamma: P_\omega \longrightarrow P_\omega$.
(b) $A \leq_T B$ (i.e. A is Turing reducible to B) iff $\Gamma(B) = A$ for some $(\mathbb{M}_{cf}, \mathbb{M}_{cf})$-computable function $\Gamma: P_\omega \dashrightarrow P_\omega$.
(c) $A \leq_{tt} B$ (i.e. A is truth-table reducible to B) iff $\Gamma(B) = A$ for some total $(\mathbb{M}_{cf}, \mathbb{M}_{cf})$-computable function $\Gamma: P_\omega \longrightarrow P_\omega$.

BIBLIOGRAHICAL NOTES

Some further results on representations can be found in Kreitz and Weihrauch (1985).

3.4 Effective Representations

It cannot be expected that arbitrary representations have interesting constructive or computational properties. In this chapter we introduce some types of "effective" representations. For any topological space with T_o-topology and countable base a distinguished equivalence class of effective representations (the *admissible representations*) can be introduced by natural topological requirements. These requirements correspond to the axiomatic characterization of the numbering φ of the partial recursive functions by the smn-theorem and the utm-theorem (see Chapter 2.1). Final topologies which play an important role in this theory are studied in advance. Admissible representations have several natural properties; especially for admissible representations of T_o-spaces topological continuity coincides with continuity w.r.t. the representations. For any given numbering of a base of a T_o-space, we define the computationally admissible representations. For separable metric spaces the *Cauchy-representations* are introduced which turn out to be admissible. The concept of admissible representations is sufficiently powerful in order to define constructivity and computability in a natural way in functional analysis and measure theory.

In Chapter 2.8 we have introduced trees with ω-branching. We shall construct standard representations for such sets of trees (cf. Def. 2.8.13) which for example induce a representation of the whole set $\mathbb{O}$ of countable ordinals.

Any representation $\delta : \mathbf{B} \dashrightarrow M$ induces a topology on M, the final topology τ_δ.

1 <u>DEFINITION</u> (*final topology*)

Let $\delta : \mathbf{B} \dashrightarrow M$ be a representation. Then $\tau_\delta \subseteq 2^M$ defined by
$X \in \tau_\delta :\Longleftrightarrow \delta^{-1}X$ is open (in $\mathrm{dom}(\delta)$) is called the *final topology* of δ.

Notice that on $\mathrm{dom}(\delta)$ we consider the topology induced by Baire's topology. Clearly, τ_δ is a topology on M: $\emptyset \in \tau_\delta$; $M \in \tau_\delta$; let $X, Y \in \tau_\delta$, then $\delta^{-1}(X \cap Y) = \delta^{-1}X \cap \delta^{-1}Y$ is an open subset of $\mathrm{dom}(\delta)$; let $X_i \in \tau_\delta$ for $i \in I$, then $\delta^{-1} \bigcup \{X_i \mid i \in I\}$ $= \bigcup \{\delta^{-1}X_i \mid i \in I\}$ is an open subset of $\mathrm{dom}(\delta)$, hence $\bigcup \{X_i \mid i \in I\} \in \tau_\delta$. Any representation δ is (τ_B, τ_δ)-continuous (see Def. 3.1.21).

2 EXAMPLES

(1) $\mathbb{M}$:

The final topology of $\mathbb{M}$ on P_ω is τ_E, the standard topology on P_ω (see Def. 3.1.1). This follows immediately from Lemma 3.1.13.

(2) $\mathbb{M}_{cf}$:

For any finite subsets $c,d \subseteq \mathbb{N}$ define the interval $[c;d] \subseteq P_\omega$ by

$$[c;d] = \{A \mid c \subseteq A \subseteq \mathbb{N} \setminus d\} .$$

For $v \in W(\mathbb{N})$ define

$$c_v := \{i < lg(v) \mid v(i) = 0\} ,$$
$$d_v := \{i < lg(v) \mid v(i) \neq 0\} .$$

Then $\mathbb{M}_{cf}[v] = [c_v;d_v]$. On the other hand, for any interval $[c;d]$ we have $\mathbb{M}_{cf}^{-1}[c;d] = \bigcup \{[v] \mid c \subseteq c_v \wedge d \subseteq d_v\}$, i.e. $[c;d] \in \tau_{\mathbb{M}_{cf}}$. Let $X \subseteq P_\omega$ be open w.r.t. $\tau_{\mathbb{M}_{cf}}$. Then $\mathbb{M}_{cf}^{-1}X = \bigcup\{[v] \mid v \in V\}$ for some $V \subseteq W(\mathbb{N})$. We obtain $X = \bigcup \{\mathbb{M}_{cf}[v] \mid v \in V\}$ $= \bigcup \{[c_v;d_v] \mid v \in V\}$. This shows that the set of intervals $[c;d]$ is a base of the final topology of $\mathbb{M}_{cf}$.

(3) $\mathbf{M}^c$:

The set of all $\langle e \rangle := \{A \in P_\omega \mid A \subseteq \mathbb{N} \setminus e\}$ for finite $e \in P_\omega$ is a base of the final topology of $\mathbf{M}^c$ (as an exercise).

(4) δ_N :

The final topology of δ_N is the discrete topology on $\mathbb{N}$.

(5) The final topology of the inverse of $\Pi^{(k)}$ $(\Pi^{(\infty)}, \Pi')$ is the product topology on $\mathbf{B}^k$ $(\mathbf{B}^{\mathbb{N}}, \mathbb{N}\times\mathbf{B})$ since $\Pi^{(k)}$ $(\Pi^{(\infty)}, \Pi')$ is a homeomorphism.

In Definition 3.3.7 we have introduced the δ-open subsets of M, where δ is a representation of M. The final topology of δ is the set of δ-open subsets of M.

3 THEOREM

Let $\delta : \mathbf{B} \dashrightarrow M$ be a representation, let $A \subseteq M$ be a subset of M. Then

$$A \text{ is } \delta\text{-open} \iff A \in \tau_\delta .$$

Proof

A is δ-open $\Longleftrightarrow$ (by Corollary 3.3.8) $\delta^{-1}A = \mathrm{dom}(\Sigma) \cap \mathrm{dom}(\delta)$ for some $\Sigma \in [\mathbb{B} \longrightarrow \mathbb{N}]$ $\Longleftrightarrow$ (by Theorem 3.2.11(1) $\delta^{-1}A$ is open in $\mathrm{dom}(\delta) \Longleftrightarrow A \in \tau_\delta$.

Q.E.D.

We shall study the behaviour of the final topologies w.r.t. reduction, sup, inf, and product of representations. We introduce the following notations.

4 DEFINITION

(1) Let (M,τ) be a topological space and let $A \subseteq M$. Then let $\tau|_A := \{X \cap A \mid X \in \tau\}$ be the topology on A induced by τ.

Let (M_1,τ_1) and (M_2,τ_2) be topological spaces.

(2) A topology $\sup(\tau_1,\tau_2)$ on $M_1 \cup M_2$ is defined by

$$\sup(\tau_1,\tau_2) = \{X \subseteq M_1 \cup M_2 \mid X \cap M_1 \in \tau_1 \wedge X \cap M_2 \in \tau_2\}.$$

(3) A topology $\inf(\tau_1,\tau_2)$ on $M_1 \cap M_2$ is defined by the base

$$\{X_1 \cap X_2 \mid X_1 \in \tau_1,\ X_2 \in \tau_2\}.$$

It is easy to verify that $\sup(\tau_1,\tau_2)$ is a topology on $M_1 \cup M_2$ and $\inf(\tau_1,\tau_2)$ is a topology on $M_1 \cap M_2$.

5 LEMMA

Let δ_i be a representation of M_i with final topology τ_i $(i = 1,2,\ldots)$. Then:

(1) $\delta_1 \leq_t \delta_2 \implies \tau_2|_{M_1} \subseteq \tau_1$

(especially $\delta_1 \equiv_t \delta_2 \implies \tau_1 = \tau_2$)

(2) $\sup(\tau_1,\tau_2) = \tau_{\delta_1 \sqcup \delta_2}$

(3) $\inf(\tau_1,\tau_2) \subseteq \tau_{\delta_1 \sqcap \delta_2}$

(4) $\tau_1 \otimes \ldots \otimes \tau_n \subseteq \tau_{[\delta_1,\ldots,\delta_n]}$

(5) $\bigotimes_{i\in\mathbb{N}} \tau_i \subseteq \tau_{[\delta_i]_{i\in\mathbb{N}}}$

Proof

Let $A_i := \mathrm{dom}(\delta_i)$ and $\delta_i' := \delta_i|_{A_i}$.

(1) Suppose $\delta_1 \leq_t \delta_2$. Then there is a continuous function $\Sigma : A_1 \longrightarrow A_2$ such that $\delta_1' = \delta_2'\Sigma$. It suffices to show $X \cap M_1 \in \tau_1$ for every $X \in \tau_2$:

$$\begin{aligned} X \in \tau_2 &\Longrightarrow \delta_2'^{-1}X \text{ is open in } A_2 \\ &\Longrightarrow \Sigma^{-1}\delta_2'^{-1}X \text{ is open in } A_1 \\ &\Longrightarrow \delta_1'^{-1}X \text{ is open in } A_1 \\ &\Longrightarrow \delta_1'^{-1}(X \cap M_1) \text{ is open in } A_1 \\ &\Longrightarrow X \cap M_1 \in \tau_1 . \end{aligned}$$

(2) Suppose $X \in \sup(\tau_1, \tau_2)$. Then there are $V_i \subseteq W(\mathbb{N})$ with $\delta_i^{-1}(X \cap M_i) = A_i \cap \bigcup\{[w] \mid w \in V_i\}$ for $i = 1,2$. Define $V := \{2\cdot w \mid w \in V_1\} \cup \{2w+1 \mid w \in V_2\}$ (where $(2w)(i) := 2\cdot w(i)$, $(2w+1)(i) := 2\cdot w(i)+1$ for all w and all i). We obtain

$$\begin{aligned} (\delta_1 \sqcup \delta_2)^{-1}X &= \{2q \mid \delta_1(q) \in X\} \cup \{2q+1 \mid \delta_2(q) \in X\} \qquad \text{(by Def. 3.3.11)} \\ &= \{2q \mid \delta_1(q) \in X \cap M_1\} \cup \{2q+1 \mid \delta_2(q) \in X \cap M_2\} \\ &= \{2q \mid q \in A_1 \cap \bigcup\{[w] \mid w \in V_1\}\} \cup \{2q+1 \mid q \in A_2 \cap \bigcup\{[w] \mid w \in V_2\}\} \\ &= (2A_1 \cap \bigcup\{[2w] \mid w \in V_1\}) \cup ((2A_2+1) \cap \bigcup\{[2w+1] \mid w \in V_2\}) \\ &= (2A_1 \cup (2A_2+1)) \cap \bigcup\{[x] \mid x \in V\} \\ &= \mathrm{dom}(\delta_1 \sqcup \delta_2) \cap \bigcup\{[x] \mid x \in V\} , \end{aligned}$$

hence $X \in \tau_{\delta_1 \sqcup \delta_2}$.

On the other hand suppose $X \in \tau_{\delta_1 \sqcup \delta_2}$. Since $\delta_1 \leq_t \delta_1 \sqcup \delta_2$ and $\delta_2 \leq_t \delta_1 \sqcup \delta_2$ we obtain $X \cap M_1 \in \tau_1$ and $X \cap M_2 \in \tau_2$ (Lemma 3.3.14, (1) of this lemma), hence $X \in \sup(\tau_1, \tau_2)$ by Definition 4.

(3) It suffices to prove $X_1 \cap X_2 \in \tau_{\delta_1 \sqcap \delta_2}$ if $X_1 \in \tau_1$ and $X_2 \in \tau_2$. Suppose $X_1 \in \tau_1$, $X_2 \in \tau_2$. Since $\delta_1 \sqcap \delta_2 \leq_t \delta_1$ and $\delta_1 \sqcap \delta_2 \leq_t \delta_2$, by (1) we obtain $X_1 \cap M_2 \in \tau_{\delta_1 \sqcap \delta_2}$ and $X_2 \cap M_1 \in \tau_{\delta_1 \sqcap \delta_2}$, hence $X_1 \cap X_2 = X_1 \cap M_2 \cap X_2 \cap M_1 \in \tau_{\delta_1 \sqcap \delta_2}$.

(4) (similar to (5))

(5) It suffices to prove $0 \in \tau_{[\delta_i]_i}$ for any base element 0 of $\otimes \tau_i$. Let $0 = 0_o \times 0_1 \times \ldots$ where $0_i \in \tau_i$ and $0_i = M_i$ for almost all i. Then $[\delta_i]_i^{-1}0 = \pi^{(\infty)}(\delta_o^{-1}0_o \times \delta_1^{-1}0_1 \times \ldots)$ is open in $\mathrm{dom}[\delta_i]_i$, hence $0 \in \tau_{[\delta_i]_i}$.

Q.E.D.

Later we shall define representations δ and δ' of the real numbers with $\delta \not\equiv_t \delta'$ but $\tau_\delta = \tau_{\delta'}$. This shows that the equivalence in Lemma 5(1) does not hold in general. Define a standard representation ω_δ of the final topology τ_δ of the representation $\delta : \mathbb{B} \dashrightarrow M$ as follows.

$$\omega_\delta(p) := X \; :\Longleftrightarrow \; \delta^{-1}X = \mathrm{dom}(\chi_p) \cap \mathrm{dom}(\delta)$$

for all $p \in \mathbb{B}$ and $X \subseteq M$. Then constructive and computational versions w.r.t. standard representations of the properties from Lemma 5 can be proved.

We have defined a topology τ_δ on M for any representation $\delta : \mathbf{B} \dashrightarrow M$, and we have defined (δ_1,δ_2)-continuity (Corollary 3.3.4). This raises the question whether (δ_1,δ_2)-continuity is equivalent to $(\tau_{\delta_1},\tau_{\delta_2})$-continuity. The answer is negative in general but there is a distinguished class of representations which have this property. The spaces we shall consider are the T_o-*spaces with countable bases*. A topological space (M,τ) is a T_o-*space* (and τ is a T_o-*topology*) iff

$$(\forall x,y \in M) \quad (V(x) = V(y) \Longrightarrow x = y) ,$$

where $V(x)$ is the set of neighbourhoods of x (see Chapter 3.1). Therefore, (M,τ) is a T_o-space, iff every $x \in M$ is uniquely determined by its set $V(x)$ of neighbourhoods. A set β of subsets of M is a *base* of $V(x)$, iff $\beta \subseteq V(x)$ and $(\forall A \in V(x))(\exists B \in \beta)\; B \subseteq A$. If β is a base of $V(x)$, then $V(x) = \{A \mid (\exists B \in \beta)\; B \subseteq A\}$. Therefore, in a T_o-space every point x is uniquely determined by any base β of $V(x)$. Below we shall use names of such bases as names of x. Many interesting topological spaces are T_o-spaces with countable bases.

6 EXAMPLES (T_o-*spaces with countable bases*)

(1) (P_ω,τ_E) (see Definition 3.1.1). The set $\{O_E \mid E \subseteq \mathbb{N}, \text{ finite}\}$ is a denumerable base. If $V(X) = V(Y)$ then $X \in O_E \Longleftrightarrow Y \in O_E$ for all finite E, therefore $E \subseteq X \Longleftrightarrow E \subseteq Y$ for all finite E, hence $X = Y$.

(2) $(\mathbf{B}_o,\tau_{Bo})$ (see Definition 3.1.6). The set $\beta = \{O_w \mid w \in W(\mathbb{N})\}$ is a denumerable base. Let $x \in O_w \Longleftrightarrow y \in O_w$ for all $w \in W(\mathbb{N})$. Then $w \sqsubseteq x \Longleftrightarrow w \sqsubseteq y$ for all $w \in W(\mathbb{N})$, hence $x = y$.

(3) $(\mathbb{C}_o,\tau_{Co})$ (see Definition 3.1.9) is a T_o-space with countable base (as an exercise).

(4) $(\mathbf{B},\tau_B)$ (see Definition 3.2.21) is a T_o-space with a countable base (as an exercise).

(5) The set $\mathbb{N}$ with the discrete topology is a T_o-space with countable base.

(6) The real line $(\mathbb{R},\tau_R)$ where τ_R is the set of unions of open intervals is a T_o-space with countable base. The set $\beta := \{(p;q) \mid p,q \in \mathbb{Q},\; p < q\}$ where

$(p;q) = \{x \in \mathbb{R} \mid p < x < q\}$ is a countable base of τ_R. If $x \neq y$ then there is some $(p;q) \in \beta$ with $x \in (p;q)$ and $y \notin (p;q)$, hence $(\mathbb{R}, \tau_R)$ is a T_o-space.

(7) Let (M,d) be a *metric space*. This means that M is a set of points and $d : M \times M \longrightarrow \mathbb{R}$ is a mapping (the *distance*) satisfying the axioms $d(x,y) \geq 0$, $d(x,x) = 0$, $d(x,y) = 0 \Longrightarrow x = y$, $d(x,y) = d(y,x)$, $d(x,y) \leq d(x,z) + d(z,y)$ for all $x,y,z \in M$. The distance d induces a topology τ on M as follows: The set $\{B(x;\varepsilon) \mid x \in M,\ \varepsilon \in \mathbb{R},\ \varepsilon > 0\}$ is a base of τ, where $B(x;\varepsilon) := \{y \in M \mid d(x,y) < \varepsilon\}$ is the *open ball* with *center* x and *radius* ε. The space (M,τ) is a T_o-space since different points can be separated by open balls. A subset $A \subseteq M$ is called *dense*, iff $(\forall x \in M)(\forall \varepsilon > 0)(\exists a \in A)\ d(a,x) < \varepsilon$. If a metric space (M,d) has a denumerable dense subset A, (in this case (M,d) is called *separable*) then the set $\{B(a;q) \mid a \in A;\ q \in \mathbb{Q},\ q > 0\}$ is a base of the topology τ on M. Therefore, (M,τ) is a T_o-space with countable base, if (M,d) is separable.

(8) Let C[0;1] be the set of all continuous functions $f : [0;1] \longrightarrow \mathbb{R}$ from the unit interval of $\mathbb{R}$ to $\mathbb{R}$. Define a distance on C[0;1] by $d(f,g) := \sup\{|f(x) - g(x)| \mid x \in [0;1]\}$. Then $(C[0;1],d)$ is a separable metric space. Dense subsets are $A_1 :=$ the set of all polynomials with rational coefficients, $A_2 :=$ the set of all trigonometric polynomials with rational coefficients, $A_3 :=$ the set of all polygons (= piecewise linear functions) with rational break points.

(9) Let (M,τ) be a T_o-space with countable base and let $A \subseteq M$. Then $(A, \tau|_A)$ is a T_o-space with countable base.

(10) Let $(M_i,\tau_i)_{i \in I}$ be a family of T_o-spaces with countable bases where I is finite or denumerable. Then the product space is a T_o-space with countable base.

Let (M,τ) be a T_o-space with countable base. We shall assume that a total numbering $U : \mathbb{N} \longrightarrow \beta$ of a base β of τ is given. In order to avoid technical complications we shall not consider partial numberings although this might yield a more general and elegant theory. We shall define a standard representation δ_U of M in such a way that $p \in \mathrm{dom}(\delta_U)$ iff $\{U_i \mid i \in \mathbb{M}_p\}$ is a base of some set V(x) of neighbourhoods. Since we have a T_o-space, x is uniquely determined by p. At first we study only topological properties.

7 DEFINITION (*standard representation*)

Let (M,τ) be a T_o-space, let β be a base of τ and let $U : \mathbb{N} \longrightarrow \beta$ be a total numbering of β. The *standard representation* $\delta_U : \mathbb{B} \dashrightarrow M$ *of* M *w.r.t.* U is defined as follows.

$$\delta_U(p) = x :\iff \{U_i \mid i \in \mathbb{M}_p\} \text{ is a base of the neighbourhoods } V(x)$$

for all $p \in \mathbb{B}$ and $x \in M$.

Notice that δ_U is welldefined since (M,τ) is a T_o-space. The representation δ_U has some remarkable properties.

8 LEMMA (*properties of* δ_U)

(1) δ_U is continuous.

(2) δ_U is an open mapping (i.e. A open $\Longrightarrow$ $\delta_U(A)$ open).

(3) τ is the final topology of δ_U.

(4) Let $\xi : \mathbb{B} \dashrightarrow M$ be a function. Then ξ is continuous iff $(\forall p \in \mathrm{dom}(\xi))$ $\xi(p) = \delta_U \Sigma(p)$ for some $\Sigma \in [\mathbb{B} \longrightarrow \mathbb{B}]$.

(5) Let (M',τ') be a topological space, let $H : M \dashrightarrow M'$ be a function such that $H\delta_U : \mathbb{B} \dashrightarrow M'$ is continuous. Then H is continuous.

(6) δ_U is c-precomplete.

The properties (3) and (4) correspond to Properties (1) and (4) from Lemma 3.1.13, Lemma 3.1.17, and Lemma 3.1.19. Especially by (4), δ_U can be called the most difficult continuous function from $\mathbb{B}$ to M.

Proof

(1) It suffices to show that $\delta_U^{-1}U_i$ is open in $\mathrm{dom}(\delta_U)$ for any i. For any $p \in \mathrm{dom}(\delta_U)$ we have $p \in \delta_U^{-1}U_i$ iff $(\exists j)(j \in \mathbb{M}_p$ and $U_j \subseteq U_i)$, therefore

$$\delta_U^{-1}U_i = \bigcup\{[w] \mid (\exists j,k)(w(k) = j+1 \text{ and } U_j \subseteq U_i)\} \cap \mathrm{dom}(\delta_U).$$

(2) It suffices to show that $\delta_U[w]$ is open for any $w \in W(\mathbb{N})$. We have $\delta_U[w] = \bigcap\{U_i \mid (\exists j < \lg(w))\ w(j) = i+1\}$. Therefore δ_U is an open mapping.

(3) This follows immediately from (1) and (2).

(4) Let $\xi : \mathbb{B} \dashrightarrow M$ be continuous. Define a mapping $\Sigma : \mathbb{B} \longrightarrow \mathbb{B}$ by

$$\Sigma(p)\langle n,i\rangle := \begin{cases} i+1 & \text{if } \nu^*(n) \sqsubseteq p \wedge \xi[\nu^*(n)] \subseteq U_i \\ 0 & \text{otherwise.} \end{cases}$$

Then Σ is continuous and for any $p \in \mathrm{dom}(\xi)$ and any $i \in \mathbb{N}$ we have $\xi(p) \in U_i \iff$ (by continuity of ξ) $(\exists n)\ (\nu^*(n) \sqsubseteq p \wedge \xi[\nu^*(n)] \subseteq U_i) \iff i \in \mathbf{M}\Sigma(p)$.

We obtain for $p \in \mathrm{dom}(\xi)$: $\{U_i \mid i \in \mathbb{M}\,\Sigma(p)\}$ is a base of the neighbourhoods of $\xi(p)$, hence $\xi(p) = \delta_U \Sigma(p)$ by the definition of δ_U.

On the other hand let $\Sigma \in [\mathbb{B} \longrightarrow \mathbb{B}]$ such that $\xi(p) = \delta_U \Sigma(p)$ for all $p \in \mathrm{dom}(\xi)$. Then ξ is continuous since δ_U and Σ are continuous.

(5) Let $H\delta_U$ be continuous. Let $O' \in \tau'$ be open. Then there is some open set $O \subseteq \mathbb{B}$ such that $H^{-1}(O') = \delta_U (H\delta_U)^{-1} O' = \delta_U(O \cap \mathrm{dom}(H\delta_U)) = \delta_U(O \cap \delta_U^{-1}\mathrm{dom}(H)) \overset{!}{=} \delta_U(O) \cap \mathrm{dom}(H)$. By Property (2) H is continuous.

(6) Since $\mathbb{M}$ is c-precomplete (Lemma 3.3.19) and $\delta_U = H\,\mathbb{M}$ for some surjective function H, δ_U is c-precomplete.

Q.E.D.

As a corollary we obtain a characterization of the t-equivalence class of δ_U.

9 COROLLARY (*characterizations of* δ_U)

Let δ be a representation of M. Then the following properties are equivalent:

(1) $\delta \equiv_t \delta_U$.

(2) δ is continuous and $\delta' \leq_t \delta$ for all continuous representations δ' of M.

(3) δ is continuous and for all continuous functions $\xi : \mathbb{B} \dashrightarrow M$ there is some $\Sigma \in [\mathbb{B} \longrightarrow \mathbb{B}]$ with $\xi(p) = \delta\Sigma(p)$ for all $p \in \mathrm{dom}(\xi)$.

Proof

"(1) $\Longrightarrow$ (3)": Suppose $\delta \equiv_t \delta_U$. From $\delta \leq_t \delta_U$ and Lemma 8(4) we conclude that δ is continuous. Let $\xi : \mathbb{B} \dashrightarrow M$ be continuous. Then $\xi(p) = \delta_U \Sigma(p)$ for all $p \in \mathrm{dom}(\xi)$ by Lemma 8(4). Let $\delta_U \leq_t \delta$ via $\Gamma \in [\mathbb{B} \longrightarrow \mathbb{B}]$. Then $\xi(p) = \delta\Gamma\Sigma(p)$ for all $p \in \mathrm{dom}(\xi)$ where $\Gamma\Sigma \in [\mathbb{B} \longrightarrow \mathbb{B}]$.

"(3) $\Longrightarrow$ (2)": (obvious)

"(2) $\Longrightarrow$ (1)": Since δ is continuous, we have $\delta \leq_t \delta_U$ by Lemma 8(4). Since δ_U is continuous, $\delta_U \leq_t \delta$.

Q.E.D.

Since $\delta \equiv_t \delta_U$ iff 9(2) holds, the equivalence class $\{\delta \mid \delta \equiv_t \delta_U\}$ is independent of the numbering U of a base of τ. The property $\delta \leq_t \delta_U$ informally means that the elements of M can be constructively analyzed with respect to U: given a name p one can enumerate constructively a base $\{U_i \mid i \in I\}$ of $V\delta(p)$, the set of neighbourhoods of $\delta(p)$. This property corresponds to the utm-theorem from Type 1 recursion theory. The property $\delta_U \leq_t \delta$ can be interpreted as follows: from any enumeration of a base of $V(x)$ for some x a δ-name p of x can be found constructively. This property which expresses the "effective synthesis" corresponds roughly to the smn-theorem of Type 1 recursion theory. We shall call the representations which are t-equivalent to δ_U, t-admissible.

10 DEFINITION (*t-admissible representations*)

(1) Let (M,τ) be a T_0-space with countable base, let $\delta : \mathbb{B} \dashrightarrow M$ be a representation. Then δ is *t-admissible w.r.t.* τ, iff δ is (τ_B,τ)-continuous and $\delta' \leq_t \delta$ for any (τ_B,τ)-continuous representation δ' of M.

(2) Let M be a set and let $\delta : \mathbb{B} \dashrightarrow M$ be a representation. Then δ is *t-admissible* iff τ_δ is a T_0-topology with countable base and $\delta' \leq_t \delta$ for any (τ_B,τ_δ)-continuous representation δ' of M.

Definition 10(2) is reasonable since $\tau_\delta = \tau$ if δ is t-admissible w.r.t. τ (Lemma 8(3), Corollary 9, Lemma 5(1)). Examples of t-admissible representations will be given below. At first we prove that for admissible representations continuity and continuity w.r.t. to the representations coincide. The proof follows easily from Lemma 8.

11 THEOREM (*basic theorem*)

Let δ (δ') be a t-admissible representation of the T_0-space (M,τ) ((M',τ')) with countable base. Let $F : M \dashrightarrow M'$ be a function. Then:

$$F \text{ is } (\tau,\tau')\text{-continuous} \iff F \text{ is } (\delta,\delta')\text{-continuous}.$$

Proof

Since t-equivalent representations yield the same kind of constructivity we may assume that δ and δ' are standard representations. Suppose that F is (τ,τ')-continuous. By Lemma 8(1), $F\delta : \mathbb{B} \dashrightarrow M'$ is continuous, by Lemma 8(4) for δ' there is some $\Sigma \in [\mathbb{B} \longrightarrow \mathbb{B}]$ with $F\delta(p) = \delta'\Sigma(p)$ for all $p \in \mathrm{dom}(F\delta)$. Therefore F is (δ,δ')-continuous. On the other hand let F be (δ,δ')-continuous. Then there is some $\Gamma \in [\mathbb{B} \longrightarrow \mathbb{B}]$ with $F\delta(p) = \delta'\Gamma(p)$ for all $p \in \mathrm{dom}(F\delta)$. By Lemma 8(1) for δ', $\delta'\Gamma$ is continuous, hence $F\delta$ is continuous. By Lemma 8(5) for δ, F is (τ,τ')-continuous.
Q.E.D.

As we have seen our constructive theory of admissibility is independent of any particular numbering of a base of the topology. This cannot be expected for the computability theory. A computationally admissible representation δ should be t-admissible in any case. We choose δ_U as the standard c-admissible (w.r.t. U) representation.

12 DEFINITION (*c-admissible representations*)

Let (M,τ) be a T_o-space and let U be a total numbering of a base of τ. Then a representation δ of M is *c-admissible w.r.t.* U, iff $\delta \equiv_c \delta_U$.

It is not quite clear whether there are other t-admissible representations for which the attribute "c-admissible w.r.t. U" is appropriate. Obviously every c-admissible representation is t-admissible. Under certain conditions on numberings U and V of spaces, $\delta_U \equiv_c \delta_V$. It seems to be difficult to formulate necessary and sufficient conditions.

13 LEMMA

Let U and V be total numberings of bases of a T_o-space; then:

$$U \le V \implies \delta_U \le_c \delta_V ,$$

$$\{(i,j) \mid U_i \subseteq V_j\} \text{ r.e. } \implies \delta_U \le_c \delta_V .$$

Proof (as an exercise)

The following example shows that commonly used representations are c-admissible w.r.t. commonly used numberings of bases.

14 LEMMA (*examples for c-admissible representations*)

(1) Let U with $U(i) := O_{e(i)} = \{A \in P_\omega \mid e(i) \subseteq A\}$ be a numbering of a base of (P_ω, τ_E) (see Def. 3.1.1, Def. 2.2.2). Then the representation $\mathbf{M}$ is c-admissible w.r.t. U.

(2) Let U with $U(i) := [\nu^*(i)]$ be a numbering of a base of $(\mathbb{B}, \tau_B)$ (see Def. 3.2.21). Then $1\!\!1_{\mathbb{B}}$ is c-admissible w.r.t. U.

(3) Let ν be a standard numbering of $W(\{0,1\})$ and let U with $U(i) := [\![\nu(i)]\!]$ be a numbering of a base of $(\mathbb{C}, \tau_c)$ (see Def. 3.1.21). Then the representation δ of $\mathbb{C}$ defined by $\delta(p)(i) := 1 \dot{-} p(i)$ is c-admissible w.r.t. U.

In each of the cases it can be shown that the given representation is c-equivalent to the standard representation δ_U (see the exercises). By the following theorem the admissible representations are closed w.r.t. basic operations.

15 THEOREM

Let (M_i, τ_i) be a T_o-space, let U_i be a total numbering of a base of τ_i, let $\delta_i := \delta_{U_i}$ $(i = 0,1,2,\ldots)$.

(1) Define a numbering U of a base of $\tau_1 \otimes \ldots \otimes \tau_k$ by

$$U\langle i_1,\ldots,i_k\rangle := U_1(i_1) \times \ldots \times U_k(i_k) .$$

Then $[\delta_1,\ldots,\delta_n]$ is c-admissible w.r.t. U.

(2) Define a numbering U of a base of $\inf(\tau_1,\tau_2)$ by

$$U\langle i_1,i_2\rangle := U_1(i_1) \cap U_2(i_2) .$$

Then $\delta_1 \sqcap \delta_2$ is c-admissible w.r.t. U.

(3) Let $M \subseteq M_o$, let $\tau = \{A \cap M \mid A \in \tau_o\}$ be the topology induced on M by τ_o. Assume that there exists a total numbering U which is (recursively) equivalent to U' defined by

$$U'(i) := \begin{cases} U_o(i) \cap M & \text{if } U_o(i) \cap M \neq \emptyset \\ \text{div} & \text{otherwise} . \end{cases}$$

Define a representation δ of M by

$$\delta(p) = \begin{cases} \delta_o(p) & \text{if } p \in \delta_o^{-1}(M) \\ \text{div} & \text{otherwise} . \end{cases}$$

Then δ is c-admissible w.r.t. U.

The proof is left as an exercise. As a corollary we obtain t-admissibility in the above cases.

16 COROLLARY

Let (M_i,τ_i) be a topological space and let δ_i be a t-admissible representation w.r.t. τ_i $(i = 0,1,2,\dots)$. Then:

(1) $[\delta_1,\dots,\delta_k]$ is t-admissible and

$$\tau_1 \otimes \dots \otimes \tau_k = \tau_{[\delta_1,\dots,\delta_k]} .$$

(2) $\delta_1 \sqcap \delta_2$ is t-admissible and

$$\inf(\tau_1,\tau_2) = \tau_{\delta_1 \sqcap \delta_2} .$$

(Compare Corollary 16 with Lemma 5(3) and (4).)
In general $\sup(\tau_1,\tau_2)$ is not a T_o-topology if τ_1 and τ_2 are T_o-topologies. Hence in general $\delta_1 \sqcup \delta_2$ is not t-admissible. It does not seem to be likely that the representations $\hat{\psi}$, ψ, χ, ω, ω', ξ, and ξ' (see Chapter 3.2) are t-admissible according to Definition 10(2). Therefore, totally new or more general concepts for justifying constructivity are needed.

Metric spaces are T_o-spaces of particular interest. For completeness we recapitulate some basic definitions. A *pseudometric space* is a pair (M,d), where M is a set and $d : M \times M \longrightarrow \mathbb{R}$ is a function such that the following properties hold for all $x,y, \in M$.

(M 1) $d(x,y) \geq 0$,

(M 2) $d(x,y) = d(y,x)$,

(M 3) $d(x,x) = 0$,

(M 4) $d(x,y) \leq d(x,z) + d(z,y)$.

(M,d) is called a *metric space*, if in addition

(M 5) $d(x,y) = 0 \implies x = y$.

Let (M,d) be a pseudometric space. A natural factorization yields a metric space. Define an equivalence relation on M by $x \sim y \iff d(x,y) = 0$, define $M_\sim := \{x_\sim \mid x \in M\}$ where $x_\sim := \{y \mid x \sim y\}$ and $d_\sim : M_\sim \times M_\sim \longrightarrow \mathbb{R}$ by $d_\sim(x_\sim,y_\sim) := d(x,y)$. Then $(M_\sim,d_\sim)$ is a metric space the points of which are the "distance-0-sets" of (M,d).

Let (M,d) be a pseudometric space. The topology τ on M induced by d is defined by the base $\{B(x;\varepsilon) \mid x \in M,\ \varepsilon \in \mathbb{R},\ \varepsilon > 0\}$ where $B(x;\varepsilon) = \{y \in M \mid d(x,y) < \varepsilon\}$ is the *open ball* with *center* x and *radius* ε. Notice that a pseudometric space has a T_o-topology iff it is a metric space. We shall be interested in metric spaces the topology of which has a countable base. A topological space (M,τ) is called *separable* iff there is a countable *dense* subset, i.e. a subset $X \subseteq M$ such that $cls(X) = M$. ($cls(X)$ is the *closure* of X, i.e. the smallest closed set $Y \subseteq M$ with $X \subseteq Y$.)

A metric space is separable iff its topology has a countable base. (Notice that there is a separable topological space which has no countable base.) Let (M,τ) be a topological space with countable base β. From each $Y \in \beta$ select an element $y \in Y$. Let $A \subseteq M$ be the set of these elements y. Then A is denumerable. By definition $M \setminus \mathrm{cls}(A)$ is an open set B with $B \cap A = \emptyset$. But $C \cap A \neq \emptyset$ for any nonempty open set $C \subseteq M$. Therefore, $\mathrm{cls}(A) = M$ and the space (M,τ) is separable. On the other hand let (M,d) be a separable metric space. Then there is some countable set $A \subseteq M$ such that $M = \mathrm{cls}(A)$. The set of open balls $\{B(a;2^{-n}) \mid a \in A,\ n \in \mathbb{N}\}$ is a countable base of the topology of (M,d).

Separable metric spaces can be defined constructively from a (numbering of a) dense subset. For example, the real line $(\mathbb{R},d)$ is the greatest metric space in which the space $(\mathbb{Q},d')$ of the rational numbers with the absolute value of the difference as distance is dense. The metric space $(\mathbb{R},d)$ can be defined by Cauchy completion of $(\mathbb{Q},d')$. Below we shall generalize this idea and construct an admissible representation of the completion of a countable metric space.

First we show that for separable metric spaces admissible representations can be introduced by means of Cauchy sequences.

17 DEFINITION (*Cauchy-representation*)

Let (M,d) be a separable metric space, let α be a total numbering of a dense subset M_o of M. Define a representation δ_α of M as follows.

$$p \in \mathrm{dom}(\delta_\alpha) \;:\Longleftrightarrow\; (\forall m,n,\ m>n)\ d(\alpha p(m),\alpha p(n)) < 2^{-n} \text{ and } \lim_n \alpha p(n) \in M,$$

$$\delta_\alpha(p) := \lim_n \alpha p(n)$$

for all $p \in \mathrm{dom}(\delta_\alpha)$. δ_α is called the *Cauchy-representation of* (M,d) *w.r.t.* α.

Roughly speaking the names of an $x \in M$ are the Cauchy sequences on M_o which converge to x with speed 2^{-n}. Notice that $d(\delta_\alpha(p), \alpha p(n)) \le 2^{-n}$ for all n. Clearly $\mathrm{range}(\delta_\alpha) = M$ since for any $x \in M$ there is such a sequence. From the numbering α a numbering U of a base of the topology of (M,d) can be derived canonically.

18 THEOREM

Let (M,d), M_o,α, and δ_α be as in Def. 17. Define a numbering U of open balls by

$$U\langle i,n\rangle := B(\alpha(i)\,;2^{-n}).$$

Then U is a numbering of a base of the topology of (M,d) and:

(1) $\delta_\alpha \equiv_t \delta_U$ (i.e. δ_α is t-admissible)

(2) If (M,d) has no isolated points then $\delta_\alpha \equiv_c \delta_U$.

Proof

"$\delta_\alpha \leq_c \delta_U$": Let $\delta_\alpha(p) = x$. Then $Z_p := \{B(\alpha p(n+1) ; 2^{-n}) \mid n \in \mathbb{N}\}$ is a base of the set V(x) of neighbourhoods of x. Define $\Gamma : \mathbb{B} \longrightarrow \mathbb{B}$ by $\Gamma(q)(n) := 1 + \langle q(n+1), n\rangle$ for all $q \in \mathbb{B}$ and $n \in \mathbb{N}$. Then $\delta_\alpha(p) = x = \delta_U \Gamma(p)$. Since Γ is computable, we have shown $\delta_\alpha \leq_c \delta_U$. Let $q \in \mathbb{B}$ such that $\mathbb{M}_q = \{\langle i,j\rangle \mid \{\alpha(i)\} = U\langle i,j\rangle\}$. Define a function $\Sigma : \mathbb{B} \longrightarrow \mathbb{B}_o$ as follows.

$$\Sigma\langle p,q\rangle(N) = \begin{cases} \pi_1^{(4)} \mu\langle i,n,j,k\rangle[p(j) = \langle i,n\rangle + 1 \text{ and } (n > N \text{ or } q(k) = \langle i,n\rangle + 1)] \\ \qquad \text{if } (\forall N' < N)\, \Sigma\langle p,q\rangle(N') \text{ exists} \\ \text{div} \quad \text{otherwise .} \end{cases}$$

Then $\delta_U(p) = \delta_\alpha \Sigma\langle p,q\rangle$ for all $p \in \text{dom}(\delta_U)$. The smn-theorem yields $\delta_U \leq_t \delta_\alpha$. If (M,d) has no isolated points, $(\forall i) q(i) = 0$, hence $\delta_U \leq_c \delta_\alpha$.
Q.E.D.

In Definition 17 the normed convergence (e.g. with 2^{-n}) of the names is essential since the "naive" Cauchy-representation is not t-admissible if the metric space has at least two points.

19 EXAMPLE (*naive Cauchy-representation*)
Let (M,d) be a metric space, let α be a total numbering of a dense subset M_o of M. Define the naive Cauchy-representation δ of M w.r.t. α as follows.

$$\text{dom}(\delta) := \{p \mid (\alpha p(i)) \text{ is a Cauchy sequence with } \lim_i \alpha p(i) \in M\},$$

$$\delta(p) := \lim_i \alpha p(i)$$

for all $p \in \text{dom}(\delta)$. We show that the final topology of δ is $\tau_\delta = \{\emptyset, M\}$. Let $A \in \tau_\delta$, $A \neq \emptyset$. Then $\delta^{-1}A$ is open in dom(δ). Let $\delta(p) \in A$. Then there is some $w \sqsubseteq p$ with $\delta[w] \subseteq A$. By the definition of δ we have $\delta[w] = M$, hence $A = M$. This shows that M is the only non-empty set in τ_δ.

Every metric space can be embedded into a complete metric space. There is a standard construction for completing a metric space. Most of the metric spaces of practical interest are defined as such completions. The process of completion of a countable metric space automatically leads to a Cauchy-representation.

20 DEFINITION (*constructive completion*)

Let (M_o, d_o) be a countable pseudometric space, let α be a total numbering of M_o. Define a pseudometric space (M', d') as follows

$$M' := \{p \in \mathbf{B} \mid (\forall m > n)\ d_o(\alpha p(m), \alpha p(n)) < 2^{-n}\},$$

$$d'(p,q) := \lim_n d_o(\alpha p(n), \alpha q(n))$$

for all $p,q \in M'$. Define a representation $\overline{\delta}_\alpha$ by

$$\mathrm{dom}(\overline{\delta}_\alpha) := M',$$

$$\overline{\delta}_\alpha(p) := \{q \mid d'(p,q) = 0\}.$$

On $M := \mathrm{range}(\overline{\delta}_\alpha)$ define a metric d by

$$d(\overline{\delta}_\alpha(p), \overline{\delta}_\alpha(q)) := d'(p,q)$$

for all $p,q \in \mathrm{dom}(\overline{\delta}_\alpha)$. (M,d) is called the *standard completion* of (M_o, d_o) and $\overline{\delta}_\alpha$ the *standard representation* of (M,d) w.r.t. α.

If we define $p \sim q :\Longleftrightarrow d'(p,q) = 0$, then $\overline{\delta}_\alpha(p) = \{q \mid p \sim q\}$, $M = M'_\sim$ and $d = d'_\sim$. By standard arguments it can be shown that Definition 20 is correct: d' is a pseudometric and d is a welldefined metric on M. The following lemma summarizes essential properties of (M,d) and $\overline{\delta}_\alpha$.

21 LEMMA

Consider Definition 20.

(1) The metric space (M,d) is separable and (Cauchy-) complete.

(2) $\overline{\delta}_\alpha$ is a t-admissible representation of (M,d).

(3) Define $\iota : M_o \longrightarrow M$ by $\iota(x) = \overline{\delta}_\alpha(i,i,i,\dots)$ where $i \in \alpha^{-1}\{x\}$ is arbitrarily chosen. Then $d_o(x,y) = d(\iota(x), \iota(y))$ for all $x,y \in M_o$, and ι is injective if (M_o, d_o) is a metric space.

(4) Define a numbering $\overline{\alpha}$ by $\overline{\alpha}(i) := \iota\alpha(i)$. Then $\overline{\delta}_\alpha \equiv \delta_{\overline{\alpha}}$ (where $\delta_{\overline{\alpha}}$ is the Cauchy-representation w.r.t. $\overline{\alpha}$, see Def. 17).

The proof of this lemma is left to the reader. By Theorem 18 and Lemma 21, the representation $\overline{\delta}_\alpha$ of the completion can be called c-effective w.r.t. α.

Many metric spaces of practical interest are complete and have a dense denumerable subset for which a canonical numbering exists. These numberings imply c-admissible representations. Although for complete metric spaces Definition 17 and Definition 20 yield c-equivalent representations, Definition 20 is more satisfactory from the constructive point of view. The following examples show that for many concrete interesting metric spaces Definition 17 or Definition 20 yield natural representations.

22 EXAMPLES

(1) The discrete metric on $\mathbb{N}$.

For $i,j \in \mathbb{N}$ define $d(i,j) = (0$ if $i = j$, 1 otherwise$)$. Obviously $\mathbb{N}$ is dense in $\mathbb{N}$. Define $\alpha : \mathbb{N} \longrightarrow \mathbb{N}$ by $\alpha(i) := i$. Consider the representation δ_α from Definition 17. Then $\mathrm{dom}(\delta_\alpha)$ is the set of constant functions and $\delta_\alpha(p) = p(0)$ for all $p \in \mathrm{dom}(\delta_\alpha)$. Obviously, $\delta_\alpha \equiv_c \delta_{\mathbb{N}}$ (see Def. 3.3.2(2)).

(2) Baire's space

Baire's space $(\mathbb{B}, \tau_{\mathbb{B}})$ is metrizable. For any $p,q \in \mathbb{B}$ define

$$d(p,q) = \begin{cases} 0 & \text{if } p = q \\ 2^{-n} & \text{where } n = \mu t[p(t) \neq q(t)] \text{ otherwise}. \end{cases}$$

Then the open balls $B(p;2^{-n}) = [p^{[n+1]}]$ are a base of $\tau_{\mathbb{B}}$ (see Definition 3.1.21). Define a numbering α of a subset B_o of $\mathbb{B}$ by

$$\alpha(i) := \langle \nu^*(i), f_o \rangle$$

where $(\forall n)\ f_o(n) = 0$. Then B_o is a dense subset of $\mathbb{B}$. Let δ_α be the Cauchy-representation of $\mathbb{B}$ derived from the numbering α according to Definition 17. Then $\delta_\alpha \equiv_c 1\!\!1_{\mathbb{B}}$ can be easily shown. Notice that the metric space $(\mathbb{B}, d)$ is complete.

(3) The real numbers

Let $(\mathbb{Q}, d_o)$ be the metric space of rational numbers where $d_o(p,q) := |p - q|$, let ν_Q be a standard numbering of $\mathbb{Q}$, e.g. $\nu_Q\langle i,j,k\rangle := (i-j) / (1+k)$. Consider Definition 20. The set M' consists of those $p \in \mathbb{B}$ such that the sequence $\nu_Q p$ is a Cauchy sequence which converges with speed 2^{-n}. The equivalence classes $X_p := \{q \mid d'(p,q) = 0\}$ are called the real numbers. The space (M,d) is the real line, and the representation $\overline{\delta}_{\nu_Q}$ is c-admissible. Let U be the numbering of balls defined in Theorem 18, i.e. $U\langle i,n\rangle = B(\nu_Q(i);2^{-n})$ which is the open interval $(\nu_Q(i) - 2^{-n}; \nu_Q(i) + 2^{-n})$. Then $\delta_U \equiv_c \overline{\delta}_{\nu_Q}$. Define a numbering V of open intervals as follows:

$$V\langle i,j\rangle := \begin{cases} (\nu_Q(i) ; \nu_Q(j)) & \text{if } \nu_Q(i) < \nu_Q(j) \\ (0;1) & \text{otherwise}. \end{cases}$$

Then $\{(i,j) \mid U_i \subseteq V_j\}$ and $\{(i,j) \mid V_i \subseteq U_j\}$ are r.e., hence $\delta_U \equiv_c \delta_V$ by Lemma 13.

(4) The L^p-spaces

Consider the closed interval [0;1] on the real line. A simple rational step function is a function $s : [0;1] \longrightarrow \mathbb{R}$ such that there are rational numbers p,q,r with $0 \le p < q \le 1$ and $s(x) = (r \text{ if } p < x < q,\ 0 \text{ otherwise})$. The integral $\int s\,dx$ is defined by $\int s\,dx = (q-p)\cdot r$. A rational step function is a finite sum $s = s_1 + \ldots + s_n$ of simple rational step functions. The integral of s is defined by $\int s\,dx = \int s_1\,dx + \ldots + \int s_n\,dx$. Let SF be the set of all rational step functions. Notice that SF is countable. Let ν be a standard numbering of SF. For any p, where $1 \le p < \infty$, a pseudometric space (SF, d_p) can be defined by $d_p(s,s') := (\int |s(x) - s'(x)|^p\,dx)^{1/p}$. For any p, Definition 20 yields a metric space (L^p, d_p) together with an admissible representation δ. The L^p-spaces are studied in functional analysis. Our standard definition of δ induces a natural theory of constructivity and computability on these spaces.

(5) The Borel-sets

Consider the closed interval [0;1] on the real line. For any interval $I = [p;q]$, $I = (p;q]$, $I = [p;q)$, or $I = (p;q)$ where $0 \le p \le q \le 1$ define $\mu_o(I) := q - p$. For any finite set $\{I_1, \ldots, I_k\}$ of pairwise disjoint intervals define $\mu_o(I_1 \cup \ldots \cup I_k) := \mu_o(I_1) + \ldots + \mu_o(I_k)$. Let M_o be the set of finite disjoint unions of intervals with rational endpoints on [0;1]. For $x,y \in M_o$ define $d_o(x,y) := \mu_o(x\backslash y \cup y\backslash x)$. Then (M_o, d_o) is a pseudometric space. A standard numbering ν of M_o can be defined easily. By Definition 20 a metric space (M,d) and an admissible representation δ is given. M is the set of Borel-sets B on [0;1] factorized by the null-sets N on [0;1], i.e. $M = B / N$, and $\mu : M \longrightarrow \mathbb{R}$ with $\mu(y) := d(y,N)$ is the Lebesgue-Borel measure on M.

The above examples show that our theory supplies very natural basic definitions for constructive and computational functional analysis and measure theory. In each of the examples the pseudometric space (M_o, d_o) is easy to understand. Notice that other definitions of the real numbers IR, of the spaces L^p and of B/N are not simpler. In contrast to the classical definitions in our definition the p-integrable functions and the Borel sets do not appear explicitly. The set of p-integrable functions, e.g., has a cardinality which is greater than that of the continuum and therefore it is not accessible in our constructive theory.

In Chapter 2.7 we have constructed effective numberings of sets which can be generated from some initial set via some functions. These numberings are based on standard numberings of generation trees. In Chapter 2.8 we have defined trees with possibly ω-ary branching (Def. 2.8.7) and we showed how these trees can be interpreted as generation rules if an algebra is given (Def. 2.8.10). It is not difficult to define a standard representation of the set of trees $T(\sigma)$ over the signature σ. Consider the definitions from Chapter 2.8.

23 DEFINITION (*standard representation of trees*)

Let $\sigma : \mathbb{N} \dashrightarrow \mathbb{N}$ be a signature, let $T(\sigma)$ be the set of trees over σ (cf. Def. 2.8.7). Define a mapping $N : T(\sigma) \longrightarrow 2^{\mathbb{B}}$ inductively by the following condition:

$$N(t) = \begin{cases} \{(0,j,0,\ldots)\} & \text{if } t = j \in \mathbb{N} \\ \{<i+1,<p_1,\ldots,p_k>> \mid p_1 \in N(t_1),\ldots,p_k \in N(t_k)\} & \text{if } t = (i,t_1,\ldots,t_k) \\ \{<i+1,<p_o,p_1,\ldots>> \mid (\forall i)\ p_j \in N(t_j)\} & \text{if } t = (i,t_o,t_1,\ldots)\ . \end{cases}$$

Define $\delta_\sigma : \mathbb{B} \dashrightarrow T(\sigma)$ by $\mathrm{dom}(\delta_\sigma) := \bigcup \{N(t) \mid t \in T(\sigma)\}$ and $\delta_\sigma(p) = t$ if $p \in N(t)$.

Obviously, δ_σ is a representation of $T(\sigma)$. From any $p \in \mathrm{dom}(\delta_\sigma)$ one can effectively determine the root and names of the direct subtrees of $\delta_\sigma(p)$. Unfortunately, the final topology of δ_σ is not a T_o-topology in general. Therefore the concept of admissibility is not applicable to δ_σ.

Consider the algebra $\hat{A}$ from Definition 2.8.17. Let $H : T(\sigma) \dashrightarrow \mathbb{O}$ be the evaluation mapping associated with $\hat{A}$. Then $H\delta_\sigma$ is a standard representation of the set $\mathbb{O}$ of countable ordinals. The final topology of $H\delta_\sigma$, however, is not a T_o-topology.

Consider the algebra $\hat{A}$ from Example 2.8.12(2) and let H be the corresponding evaluation mapping. Then $H\delta_\sigma$ is a representation of the real numbers. One can show $H\delta_\sigma \equiv_c \delta_U$, where δ_U is from Example 22(3).

EXERCISES

1) Characterize the final topology of the representation $\mathbb{M}^c$ of P_ω.

2) Prove that $\mathbb{M} \sqcup \mathbb{M}^c$ has the final topology $\{\emptyset, P_\omega\}$.

3) Define a representation $\delta : \mathbb{B} \longrightarrow P_\omega$ by $\delta<p,q> := \mathbb{M}_p \setminus \mathbb{M}_q$. Show:
   (a) $\mathbb{M} \leq_c \delta$,
   (b) $\mathbb{M}^c \leq_c \delta$,
   (c) $\delta \not\leq_t \mathbb{M}$,
   (d) $\delta \not\leq_t \mathbb{M}^c$.

4) Let (M_i, τ_i) $(i = 1,2)$ be topological spaces. Show that $\sup(\tau_1,\tau_2)$ and $\inf(\tau_1,\tau_2)$ are topologies.

5) Define $\alpha: P_\omega \longrightarrow \mathbb{C}$ by $\alpha(A) :=$ the characteristic function of A. Show that α is a homeomorphism (i.e. α is bijective, and α and α^{-1} are continuous) w.r.t. to the spaces (P_ω, τ) and $(\mathbb{C}, \tau_C)$, where τ is the final topology of $\mathbb{M}_{cf}$.

6) Let δ_i be representations of M_i with final topologies $\tau_i (i = 1,2)$. Prove: $\tau_1 \otimes \tau_2 \subseteq \tau_{[\delta_1, \delta_2]}$.

7) Show that $(\mathbb{C}_o, \tau_{Co})$ and $(\mathbb{B}_o, \tau_{Bo})$ are T_o-spaces with countable bases.

8) Let (M, τ) be a T_o-space with countable base, let $A \subseteq M$. Show that $(A, \tau|_A)$ is a T_o-space with countable base.

9) Let $(M_i, \tau_i)_{i \in I}$ be a family of T_o-spaces with countable bases where I is finite or countable. Show that the space $(\mathsf{X} M_i, \otimes \tau_i)$ is a T_o-space with countable base.

10) Prove Lemma 13.

11) Prove Lemma 14.

12) Prove Theorem 15.

13) Find an example of two admissible representations δ_1 and δ_2 of a set M such that $\delta_1 \sqcup \delta_2$ is not admissible.

14) Let (M, τ) be a T_o-space with countable base and let U be a total numbering of a base. Define a representation δ of M as follows:

$$p \in \mathrm{dom}(\delta) \;:\Longleftrightarrow\; \mathbb{M}_p = \{i \mid x \in U_i\} \text{ for some } x \in M$$
$$\delta(p) \;:\Longleftrightarrow\; \text{the unique } x \text{ with } x \in U_i \text{ for all } i \in \mathbb{M}_p$$

for $p \in \mathrm{dom}(\delta)$.

(a) Prove $\delta \equiv_t \delta_U$.

(b) Suppose that $\{(i,j) \mid U_i \subseteq U_j\}$ is recursively enumerable. Prove $\delta \equiv_c \delta_U$.

15) Show that $(\pi^{(\infty)})^{-1}, (\pi^{(k)})^{-1}$, and $(\pi')^{-1}$ are t-admissible representations.

16) By Corollary 9, any t-admissible representation $\delta : \mathbb{B} \dashrightarrow M$ is maximal in the class of continuous functions $\zeta : \mathbb{B} \dashrightarrow M$. Show that generally δ is not maximal in the class of all continuous functions $X \longrightarrow M$, where (X, τ_X) is an arbitrary topological space.
(Hint: Choose $\delta = \mathbb{M}$ and let $\zeta : P_\omega \longrightarrow P_\omega$ be the identity on P_ω.)

17) Prove Lemma 20.

18) Let δ_o be the representation of $\mathbb{R}$ from Example 22(3). Define a metric space $(\mathbb{Q}_d, d_d)$ by $\mathbb{Q}_d = \{(i-k)/2^n \mid i,k,n\ \mathbb{N}\}$ and $d_d(x,y) := |x-y|$. Let ν be a standard numbering of $\mathbb{Q}_d$. Let (M_1, d_1) be the metric space and let δ_1 be the representation of M_1 from Definition 20. Show that there is a bijection $\iota : M_1 \longrightarrow \mathbb{R}$ such that $d_1(x,y) = |\iota(x) - \iota(y)|$ and that $\delta_o \equiv_c \iota\delta_1$.

19) Let δ_o be the representation of $\mathbb{R}$ from Example 22(3). Let δ' be the restriction of δ_o to $[-1;1]$, i.e. $\mathrm{dom}(\delta') := \delta_o^{-1}[-1;1]$. Define a representation

$\delta : \mathbb{B} \dashrightarrow [-1;1]$ by $\mathrm{dom}(\delta) := \{p \in \mathbb{B} \mid \mathrm{range}(p) \subseteq \{0,1,2\}\}$, $\delta(p) := \Sigma\{(p(i)-1) \cdot 2^{-i} \mid i \geq 1\}$. (Hence in the sequence $p(1), p(2), \ldots$ the number 0 is interpreted as digit "-1", 1 as digit "0" and 2 as digit "1".) Prove $\delta \equiv_c \delta_o$.

20) Consider Definition 20. Replace "2^{-n}" in the definition of M' by "1/(1+ n)". Show that $\delta_\alpha \equiv_c \delta'$ for the resulting representation δ'.

21) A subset X of a metric space (M,d) is called compact iff for every set D of open subsets of M with $X \subseteq \cup D$ there is a finite subset D_1 of D with $X \subseteq \cup D_1$.
(a) Show that Cantor's space $(\mathbb{C}, d)$ is compact.
(b) Let $X \subseteq \mathbb{B}$ be a subset of Baire's space. Show that X is compact iff X is closed and there is some $g \in \mathbb{B}$ with $(\forall f \in X)(\forall n) f(n) \leq g(n)$.

22) Let $\hat{A}$ be the algebra from Definition 2.8.17, let $H : T(\sigma) \dashrightarrow \mathbb{D}$ be the evaluation mapping associated with $\hat{A}$. Let δ_σ be the representation of the trees over σ (Def. 23). Show that the final topology of $H\delta_\sigma$ does not satisfy the T_o-property.

23) Consider the algebra from Example 2.8.12(2) and let H be the corresponding evaluation mapping. Prove $H\delta_\sigma \equiv_c \delta_U$ (δ_U from Example 22(3)).

24) Consider the naive Cauchy representation δ from Example 19. Show that every continuous function $f : M \longrightarrow M$ is (δ,δ)-continuous. Is every total (δ,δ)-continuous function continuous?

25) Let M be a separable metric space. Show that there is a total admissible representation of M.

26) Consider the definitions from Theorems 17 and 18. Let ν be a total numbering of positive real numbers such that there are total recursive functions $r,s : \mathbb{N} \longrightarrow \mathbb{N}$ with

$$\nu(i) \geq 2^{-r(i)}$$
$$2^{-i} \geq \nu s(i)$$

for all $i \in \mathbb{N}$. Define a numbering V of open balls by $V\langle i,n \rangle := B(\alpha(i);\nu(n))$. Prove: $\delta_U \equiv_c \delta_V$.

BIBLIOGRAPHICAL NOTES

Admissible representations have been introduced and investigated by Kreitz and Weihrauch (1985).

3.5 Complete Partial Orders

In Chapter 3.1 we have defined constructivity and computability on the sets P_ω, $\mathbb{B}_o$, and $\mathbb{C}_o$ explicitly (Def. 3.1.3, 3.1.8, 3.1.10). The three definitions are very similar. They are special cases of a general theory, the theory of *complete partial orders* (*cpo*'s). Complete partial orders are used as domains for the semantics (the *denotational semantics*) of programming languages. But independently of this application they are an interesting general model for studying Type 2 constructivity and computability. We shall not develop a general theory of cpo's but essentially study a special class of cpo's, the class of boundedly-complete algebraic cpo's with countable basis. This chapter contains the topological framework. CPO's and the continuous functions are defined. Algebraic cpo's are introduced. For any algebraic cpo a topology can be defined such that order-continuity and topological continuity coincide. It is shown that the class of cpo's is closed w.r.t. sum and product. The most remarkable property is that the space of the continuous functions between two cpo's is a cpo again. The algebraic basises of the standard sum, product, and function space of b-complete algebraic cpo's are defined explicitly. Finally the recursion theorem for cpo's is proved. Constructivity and computability are investigated in the next two chapters.

As we have already mentioned, the (infinite) Type 2 objects usually are defined as limits of sets or sequences of finite Type 1 objects. In the previous chapters we have used topology for specifiying the limiting process. Now we shall consider limits defined on partial orders. (We shall show, however, that these concepts can be expressed topologically as well.)

A *partial order* is a pair $(D,\sqsubseteq)$ where D is a set, $\sqsubseteq\, \subseteq D\times D$, such that $x\sqsubseteq x$, $(x\sqsubseteq y\wedge y\sqsubseteq z)\Rightarrow x\sqsubseteq z$, and $(x\sqsubseteq y\wedge y\sqsubseteq x)\Rightarrow x=y$ for all $x,y,z\in D$. We write $x\sqsubset y$ if $x\sqsubseteq y$ and $x\neq y$. A subset $M\subseteq D$ is called *directed* iff $M\neq\emptyset$ and $(\forall x,y\in M)(\exists z\in M)(x\sqsubseteq z\wedge y\sqsubseteq z)$. A *chain* (more precisely an ω-chain) is a sequence $(x_i)_{i\in\mathbb{N}}$ such that $x_i\sqsubseteq x_{i+1}$ for all i. Obviously $\{x_i \mid i\in\mathbb{N}\}$ is directed if $(x_i)_{i\in\mathbb{N}}$ is a chain. An element $x\in D$ is the *least upper bound* of a set $M\subseteq D$ iff $(\forall y\in M)y\sqsubseteq x$ and $(\forall y\in M)y\sqsubseteq z\Rightarrow x\sqsubseteq z$ for all $z\in D$. If x is the least upper bound of M we write $x=\sqcup M$ or $x=\sup M$. If $\sup\{x,y\}$ exists, the value is usually denoted by $x\sqcup y$.

1 **DEFINITION** *(complete partial order, cpo)*

A *complete partial order* is a triple $\overline{D}=(D,\sqsubseteq,\perp)$ with:

(1) $(D,\sqsubseteq)$ is a partial order.

(2) $\perp$ is the least element of $(D,\sqsubseteq)$, i.e. $\perp \in D$ and $\perp \sqsubseteq x$ for all $x \in D$ ($\perp$ is called *bottom*).

(3) $\sqcup M$ exists for every directed subset M of D.

We shall interpret a partial order $(D,\sqsubseteq)$ as an order of *information*: if $x \sqsubseteq y$ then the information given by y is greater or equal to that one given by x. A related interpretation of $\sqsubseteq$ is that by *approximation*: if $x \sqsubseteq y$, then x *approximates* y, or y is at least as precise as x. The element $\perp$ (bottom) represents the least amount of information (no information). In Example 3 below bottom can be considered as a name of "div". Every partial function $f : \mathbb{N} \dashrightarrow \mathbb{N}$ can be extended to a total function $f' : \mathbb{N} \longrightarrow \mathbb{N}_\perp$ by setting $f'(x) := \perp$ if $x \notin dom(f)$. The examples from Chapter 3.1 show how objects can be approximated from below.

2 <u>EXAMPLES</u>

(1) Let $D = \{\perp, \top\}$ ($\top$ is called *top*), $\sqsubseteq := \{(\perp,\top),(\perp,\perp),(\top,\top)\}$. Then $(D,\sqsubseteq,\perp)$ is a cpo.

(2) Let $D = \{\perp, t, f\}$ (t = true, f = false), $\sqsubseteq := \{(\perp,t),(\perp,f)\} \cup \{(d,d) \mid d \in D\}$. Then $(D,\sqsubseteq,\perp)$ is a cpo.

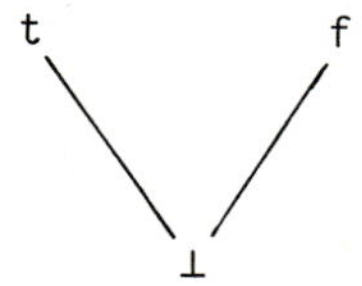

(3) Let $D = \mathbb{N}_\perp := \mathbb{N} \cup \{\perp\}$, where $\perp \notin \mathbb{N}$, $\sqsubseteq := \{(\perp,i) \mid i \in \mathbb{N}\} \cup \{(d,d) \mid d \in D\}$. Then $(D,\sqsubseteq,\perp)$ is the *flat* cpo derived from $\mathbb{N}$.

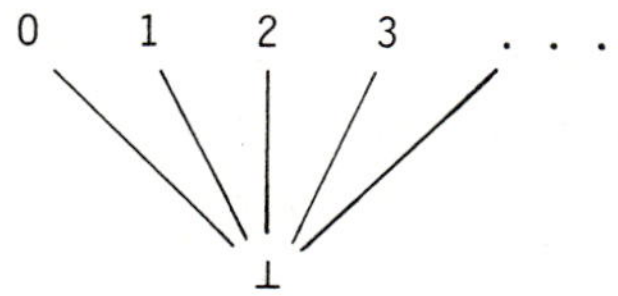

(4) $(P_\omega, \subseteq, \emptyset)$ is a cpo. Notice that $\sqcup M = \cup M$ exists for all $M \subseteq P_\omega$.

(5) $(\mathbb{B}_o, \sqsubseteq, \varepsilon)$ is a cpo (see Definition 3.1.6). Let $M \subseteq \mathbb{B}_o$ be directed. If $x,y \in M$, then $x \sqsubseteq z$ and $y \sqsubseteq z$ for some $z \in M$, therefore both x and y are prefixes of z, hence $x \sqsubseteq y$ or $y \sqsubseteq x$. Therefore any directed set is linearly ordered. Every linearly ordered subset $M \subseteq \mathbb{B}_o$ has a least upper bound. Either M has

a longest word x, then $\sqcup M = x$; or M has no longest word, then $\sqcup M := p \in \mathbb{B}$ where $p(i) = n$ if $w(i) = n$ for some $w \in M$. We have already used the cpo properties implicitly.

(6) $(\mathbb{C}_o, \sqsubseteq, \varepsilon)$ is a cpo.

(7) $(\mathbb{P}, \sqsubseteq, \bot)$ where $\mathbb{P} := \{f : \mathbb{N} \dashrightarrow \mathbb{N}\}$, $f \sqsubseteq g$ iff $\text{graph}(f) \subseteq \text{graph}(g)$, $\bot(n) = \text{div}$ for all n, is a cpo. Let $M \subseteq \mathbb{P}$ be directed. If $f, g \in M$ then f and g have a common extension in M, hence $f(n) = g(n)$ if $n \in \text{dom}(f) \cap \text{dom}(g)$. Therefore $f \in \mathbb{P}$ with $f(n) = (i$ if $g(n) = i$ for some $g \in M$, div otherwise) is welldefined, and $f = \sqcup M$.

(8) Define $(D, \sqsubseteq, \bot)$ as follows. $D := \{[a;b] \subseteq \mathbb{R} \mid a, b \in \mathbb{R}, a \le b\} \cup \{\mathbb{R}\}$ where $[a;b] = \{c \in \mathbb{R} \mid a \le c \le b\}$, $x \sqsubseteq y :\iff y \subseteq x$ for all $x, y \in D$, $\bot := \mathbb{R}$. Then $(D, \sqsubseteq, \bot)$ is a cpo, the cpo of closed intervals on $\mathbb{R}$ (as an exercise).

(9) Define $(D, \sqsubseteq, \bot)$ by $D := \mathbb{R} \cup \{+\infty, -\infty\}$, $\sqsubseteq := \le$, $\bot := -\infty$. Then $(D, \sqsubseteq, \bot)$ is a cpo.

(10) Let (X, d) be a complete metric space. (A metric space is complete iff $\lim x_i$ exists for every Cauchy sequence $(x_i)_{i \in \mathbb{N}}$.) Let $A \subseteq X$ be a dense subset of X. Define $\overline{D} := (D, \sqsubseteq, \bot)$ as follows.

$$\begin{aligned} D &:= \{\bot\} \cup (A \times \mathbb{N}) \cup X \\ \sqsubseteq &:= \{(x,x) \mid x \in D\} \cup \{(\bot, x) \mid x \in D\} \\ &\quad \cup \{((a,m),(b,n)) \mid d(a,b) + 2^{-n} < 2^{-m};\ a, b \in A;\ m, n \in \mathbb{N}\} \\ &\quad \cup \{((a,n),x) \mid d(a,x) < 2^{-n};\ x \in X;\ a \in A;\ n \in \mathbb{N}\}\ . \end{aligned}$$

Then $(D, \sqsubseteq, \bot)$ is a cpo (as an exercise). The element (a,n) can be considered as a "formal" ball with center a and radius 2^{-n}. Examples (5) and (6) can be considered as special cases.

(11) Let (A, τ) be a topology. Then $M := (\tau, \subseteq, \emptyset)$ is a cpo since τ is closed w.r.t. arbitrary union.

The natural mappings between cpo's are those ones which preserve order and sup's of directed sets. In future we shall use the some symbols "$\sqsubseteq$" (for the order) and "$\bot$" (for the minimum) for different cpo's if no confusion is possible.

3 <u>DEFINITION</u> ($(\overline{D}_1, \overline{D}_2)$-*continuous mappings*)

Let $\overline{D} := (D_1, \sqsubseteq_1, \bot_1)$ and $\overline{D}_2 = (D_2, \sqsubseteq_2, \bot_2)$ be cpo's. Let $f : D_1 \longrightarrow D_2$ be a total function. Then f is called $(\overline{D}_1, \overline{D}_2)$-*continuous* iff the following properties hold.

(1) f is $(\sqsubseteq_1, \sqsubseteq_2)$-isotone.

(2) $f(\sqcup_1 M) = \sqcup_2 \{f(x) \mid x \in M\}$ for any $\sqsubseteq_1$-directed set $M \subseteq D_1$.

Notice that $\{f(x) \mid x \in M\}$ is directed if f is isotone and M is directed.

4 EXAMPLES

Let $\overline{D}_i := (D_i, \sqsubseteq, \perp)$ be the cpo from Example 2(i) for $i = 1, \ldots, 11$.

(1) Any isotone function $f: D_i \longrightarrow D_j$ $(i,j \leq 3)$ is $(\overline{D}_i, \overline{D}_j)$-continuous (trivial).

(2) Define $f: P_\omega \longrightarrow P_\omega$ by $f(X) := X \cup \{2x \mid x \in X\}$. Obviously, f is $\subseteq$-isotone. Furthermore, f is $(\overline{D}_4, \overline{D}_4)$-continuous (as an exercise).

(3) Define $f: P_\omega \longrightarrow \mathbb{R}$ by $f(A) := \Sigma\{2^{-i} \mid i \in A\}$. Then f is $(\overline{D}_4, \overline{D}_9)$-continuous.

(4) Consider Example 2(8). Define $f: D_8 \longrightarrow D_8$ by

$$f(\mathbb{R}) := \mathbb{R},$$
$$f[a;b] := [\min\{z^2 \mid z \in [a;b]\};\ \max\{z^2 \mid z \in [a;b]\}].$$

Then f is $(\overline{D}_8, \overline{D}_8)$-continuous.

(5) Define $f: \mathbb{C}_o \longrightarrow \mathbb{B}_o$ by $f(w) := w$ for all $w \in W(\{0,1\})$. Then f is $(\overline{D}_6, \overline{D}_5)$-continuous.

Let $\overline{A}_1 = (A_1, \leq_1)$ and $\overline{A}_2 = (A_2, \leq_2)$ be partial orders. A function $f: A_1 \longrightarrow A_2$ is a homomorphism (w.r.t. $(\overline{A}_1, \overline{A}_2)$) iff $x \leq y \Rightarrow f(x) \leq f(y)$ for all $x,y \in A_1$. $\overline{A}_1$ and $\overline{A}_2$ are isomorphic iff there is a bijection $f: A_1 \longrightarrow A_2$ with $x \leq y \Leftrightarrow f(x) \leq f(y)$ for all $x,y \in A_1$. This means $\overline{A}_1$ and $\overline{A}_2$ are identical up to a renaming of the elements. If two cpo's are isomorphic (as partial orders) the isomorphism mapping preserves sup's.

5 LEMMA *(isomorphism of cpo's)*

Let $\overline{D}_1 = (D_1, \sqsubseteq_1, \perp_1)$ and $\overline{D}_2 = (D_2, \sqsubseteq_2, \perp_2)$ be cpo's, let $f: D_1 \longrightarrow D_2$ be a bijection. Then (1) and (2) are equivalent.

(1) $(\forall x,y \in D_1)(x \sqsubseteq_1 y \Leftrightarrow f(x) \sqsubseteq_2 f(y))$ (i.e. $(D_1, \sqsubseteq_1)$ and $(D_2, \sqsubseteq_2)$ are *order isomorphic*).

(2) f and f^{-1} are continuous (i.e. $\overline{D}_1$ and $\overline{D}_2$ are *continuously isomorphic* cpo's).

The proof is left as an exercise. Obviously the above isomorphism maps the bottom onto the bottom, i.e. $f(\perp_1) = \perp_2$.

In many cases a cpo $\overline{D}=(D,\sqsubseteq,\bot)$ is spanned by a (proper) subset $B\subseteq D$ in the following sense: For each $x\in D$ there is some directed subset $M\subseteq B$ with $x=\sqcup M$. Such a set B is called a *generating system*. In any case, D itself is a generating system.

6 EXAMPLE

Consider the cpo's from Example 2. Then the following sets are generating systems.

(1) $\{\bot,\top\}$ is the only generating system.

(2) $\{\bot,t,f\}$ is the only generating system.

(3) $\mathbb{N}_\bot$ is the only generating system.

(4) $E(\mathbb{N})=\{A\subseteq\mathbb{N}\mid A \text{ finite}\}$ is a generating system.

(5) $W(\mathbb{N})$ is a generating system.

(6) $W(\{0,1\})$ is a generating system.

(7) The set $\{f:\mathbb{N}\dashrightarrow\mathbb{N}\mid \mathrm{dom}(f) \text{ is finite}\}$ is a generating system.

(8) The set $\{\mathbb{R}\}\cup\{[p;q]\mid p<q, p,q\in\mathbb{Q}\}$ is a generating system.

(9) $\mathbb{Q}\cup\{-\infty\}$ is a generating system.

(10) $\{\bot\}\cup(A\times\mathbb{N})$ is a generating system.

(11) Let β be a base of τ such that $A,B\in\beta \Rightarrow A\cup B\in\beta$. Then $\beta\cup\{\emptyset\}$ is a generating system. Notice that $\emptyset\cup\{[\![w]\!]\mid w\in W(\{0,1\})\}$ is not a generating system for the cpo $(\tau_c,\subseteq,\emptyset)$ (cf. Def. 3.1.21).

We shall call an element $x\in D$ *compact*, if for any directed set $M\subseteq D, x\sqsubseteq\sqcup M \Rightarrow x\sqsubseteq m$ for some $m\in M$. This means that x is an indispensable component of any y with $x\sqsubseteq y$.

7 DEFINITION *(compact elements, algebraic cpo, basis)*

Let $\overline{D}=(D,\sqsubseteq,\bot)$ be a cpo.

(1) x is called *compact* (or *finite*) if for any directed set $M\subseteq D$ the following holds $x\sqsubseteq\sqcup M \Rightarrow (\exists m\in M)\, x\sqsubseteq m$.

(2) $\overline{D}$ is called *algebraic* iff $B:=\{x\in D\mid x \text{ compact}\}$ is a *generating system* of $\overline{D}$ (this means that for any $x\in D$ there is a directed subset $A\subseteq B$ with $x=\sqcup A$). In this case, B is called the *basis* (more precisely the *algebraic basis*) of $\overline{D}$.

8 EXAMPLE

Consider the cpo's from Examples 2 and 6. The following sets consist of the compact elements.

(1) $\{\perp,\top\}$
(2) $\{\perp,t,f\}$
(3) $\mathbb{N}_\perp$
(4) $E(\mathbb{N})$
(5) $W(\mathbb{N})$
(6) $W(\{0,1\})$
(7) $\{f : \mathbb{N} \dashrightarrow \mathbb{N} \mid dom(f) \text{ finite}\}$
(8) $\{\mathbb{R}\}$
(9) $\{-\infty\}$
(10) $\{\perp\} \cup (A \times \mathbb{N})$
(11) Consider Cantor's space $(\mathbb{C},\tau_C)$ and the cpo $(\tau_C,\subseteq,\emptyset)$. Then $\emptyset$ is the only compact element (as an exercise).

For any cpo any generating system includes the compact elements. If B is the basis of an algebraic cpo D, then for any $x \in D$ the set $B_x := \{b \in B \mid b \sqsubseteq x\}$ is directed and $x = \sqcup B_x$. Notice that $\perp$ is always compact.

9 LEMMA

(1) Let $\overline{D} = (D,\sqsubseteq,\perp)$ be a cpo, let $M \subseteq D$ be a generating system, and let $b \in D$ be compact. Then $b \in M$.
(2) Let $\overline{D}$ be an algebraic cpo with basis B. Then for any $x \in D$ the set $B_x := \{b \in B \mid b \sqsubseteq x\}$ is directed and $x = \sqcup B_x$. Especially, $x = y \Leftrightarrow B_x = B_y$.

Proof

(1) There is some directed set $M_o \subseteq M$ with $b = \sqcup M_o$. Since b is compact, $b \sqsubseteq m$ for some $m \in M_o$. Since $m \sqsubseteq b$, we obtain $b = m \in M_o \subseteq M$.
(2) There is some $C \subseteq B$, C directed, with $x = \sqcup C$. For any $a_1,a_2 \in B$ we have

$$\begin{aligned} a_1,a_2 \sqsubseteq x = \sqcup C &\Rightarrow (\exists c_1,c_2 \in C)(a_1 \sqsubseteq c_1 \wedge a_2 \sqsubseteq c_2) \quad \text{(by compactness)} \\ &\Rightarrow (\exists c \in C)\ a_1,a_2 \sqsubseteq c \quad \text{(since } C \text{ is directed)} \\ &\Rightarrow (\exists c \in B_x)\ a_1,a_2 \sqsubseteq c. \end{aligned}$$

Therefore, B_x is directed and $x = \sqcup C \sqsubseteq \sqcup B_x \sqsubseteq x$.

Q.E.D.

Therefore, if $\overline{D}$ is an algebraic cpo, then the basis B consisting of the compact elements is the minimal generating system of $\overline{D}$. The pair $(B,\sqsubseteq)$ is a partial order. For any partial order $(A,\leq)$ with minimum there is an algebraic cpo $\overline{D} = (D,\sqsubseteq,\perp)$ with basis B such that $(A,\leq)$ is order isomorphic to $(B,\sqsubseteq)$. $\overline{D}$ can be constructed by d-*completion*.

10 DEFINITION *(d-completion of a partial order with minimum)*

Let $(A,\leq)$ be a partial order, let $\perp_o$ be the minimum of A. Define a structure $\overline{D}=(D,\sqsubseteq,\perp)$ as follows.

$$D := \{X\subseteq A \mid X \text{ is } \leq\text{-directed and } \leq\text{-saturated}\},$$
$$X\sqsubseteq Y :\iff X\subseteq Y,$$
$$\perp := \{\perp_o\},$$

where X is $\leq$-*saturated* if $(x\in X \wedge y\leq x) \Rightarrow y\in X$ for all $y\in A$. Then $\overline{D}$ is called the *d-completion of* $(A,\leq)$.

Thus the elements of the d-completion of $(A,\leq)$ are the $\leq$-directed and $\leq$-saturated subsets of A. By the following theorem there is a correspondence between the partial orders with minimum and the algebraic cpo's, which is one-one up to isomorphism. Especially up to isomorphism, any algebraic cpo is the d-completion of its basis.

11 THEOREM

(1) Let $(A,\leq)$ be a partial order with minimum. Then its d-completion is an algebraic cpo with the basis $B=\{\iota(a)\mid a\in A\}$ where $\iota(a)=\{b\in A\mid b\leq a\}$. Furthermore, ι is an isomorphism from $(A,\leq)$ to $(B,\sqsubseteq)$.

(2) Let $\overline{D}=(D,\sqsubseteq,\perp)$ be an algebraic cpo. Let $\overline{E}$ be the d-completion of $(B,\sqsubseteq)$. Then $f: D\longrightarrow E$ with $f(x):=B_x=\{b\in B\mid b\sqsubseteq x\}$ is an isomorphism from $\overline{D}$ to $\overline{E}$.

Proof

(1) Since $a\leq b \iff \iota(a)\subseteq\iota(b)$, ι is an isomorphism. Let $(D,\sqsubseteq,\perp)$ be the d-completion of $(A,\leq)$. Obviously, $\perp=\{\perp_o\}$ is the minimum of $\overline{D}$. Let $\alpha\subseteq D$ be $\sqsubseteq$-directed. Let $Z:=\cup\alpha$. Since each $X\in\alpha$ is $\leq$-saturated, Z is $\leq$-saturated. Since α is $\sqsubseteq$-directed and each $X\in\alpha$ is $\leq$-directed, Z is directed. This shows $Z\in D$. Since $X\sqsubseteq Y\iff X\subseteq Y$ on D, Z is the least upper bound of α in $\overline{D}$. Therefore, $\overline{D}$ is a cpo. Assume $a\in A, \alpha\subseteq D$ $\sqsubseteq$-directed and $\iota(a)\sqsubseteq\bigsqcup\alpha$. Then $a\in\iota(a)\subseteq\cup\alpha=\bigsqcup\alpha$. Therefore, there is some $X\in\alpha$ with $a\in X$. Since X is $\leq$-saturated, $\iota(a)\subseteq X$, hence $\iota(a)\sqsubseteq X$. Therefore, $\iota(a)$ is compact for any $a\in A$. It remains to show that B is a generating system. Assume $X\in D$. Since X is $\leq$-directed the set $C:=\{\iota(a)\mid a\in X\}$ is $\sqsubseteq$-directed. Since X is $\leq$-saturated, we obtain $\bigsqcup C=\cup C=X$. Therefore B is the algebraic basis of $\overline{D}$.

(2) If $f(x) = f(y)$ then $x = \sqcup B_x = \sqcup f(x) = \sqcup f(y) = \sqcup B_y = y$, hence f is injective. Let $X \in E$. Then $X \subseteq B$ and X is $\sqsubseteq$-directed. Let $x := \sqcup X$. For any $b \in B$ we have $b \in B_x \Leftrightarrow b \sqsubseteq \sqcup X \Leftrightarrow (\exists a \in X) b \sqsubseteq a$ (since b is compact and X is $\sqsubseteq$-directed) $\Leftrightarrow b \in X$ (since X is $\sqsubseteq$-saturated). Therefore $X = B_x = f(x)$, and f is surjective. Obviously, $x \sqsubseteq y \Leftrightarrow f(x) \sqsubseteq f(y)$. Therefore f is an isomorphism.
Q.E.D.

Let $\overline{D}_1, \overline{D}_2$ be cpo's. Let M be a generating system of $\overline{D}_1$, let $f : D_1 \longrightarrow D_2$ be $(\overline{D}_1, \overline{D}_2)$-continuous. For any $x \in D_1$ there is a directed set $A \subseteq M$ such that $x = \sqcup_1 A$. By continuity of f we obtain

$$f(x) = f \sqcup_1 A = \sqcup_2 fA .$$

Therefore, f is determined uniquely by its values on the generating set M. Obviously, f is isotone on M. In general not every isotone function on a generating system can be extended to a continuous function. However, for algebraic cpo's the following theorem holds.

12 <u>THEOREM</u> *(extension theorem)*

Let $\overline{D}_1 = (D_1, \sqsubseteq, \perp)$ be an algebraic cpo with basis B, let $\overline{D}_2 = (D_2, \sqsubseteq, \perp)$ be a cpo. Let $f : B \longrightarrow D_2$ be isotone. Then there is a unique continuous extension $\overline{f} : D_1 \longrightarrow D_2$ of f where $\overline{f}$ can be defined by

$$\overline{f}(x) := \sqcup\{f(b) \mid b \in B_x\} .$$

<u>Proof</u>

We show that $\overline{f}$ is welldefined. Since $B_x = \{b \in B \mid b \sqsubseteq x\}$ is directed and f is isotone, $\overline{f}(x) = \sqcup fB_x$ exists. For any $b \in B$ we have $\overline{f}(b) = \sqcup fB_b = f(b)$, hence $\overline{f}$ extends f. Assume $x \sqsubseteq y$. Then $B_x \subseteq B_y$ and $\overline{f}(x) = \sqcup fB_x \sqsubseteq \sqcup fB_y = \overline{f}(y)$, hence $\overline{f}$ is isotone. Let $X \subseteq D$ be directed. Since $\overline{f}$ is isotone the set $\{\overline{f}(x) \mid x \in X\}$ is directed and $\overline{f}(x) \sqsubseteq \overline{f} \sqcup X$ for any $x \in X$, hence $\sqcup\{\overline{f}(x) \mid x \in X\} \sqsubseteq \overline{f} \sqcup X$. On the other hand,

$$\begin{aligned}\overline{f} \sqcup X &= \sqcup\{f(b) \mid b \in B \text{ and } b \sqsubseteq \sqcup X\} \quad \text{(by definition of } \overline{f}\text{)}\\ &= \sqcup\{f(b) \mid b \in B \text{ and } (\exists x \in X) b \sqsubseteq x\} \quad \text{(since } b \text{ is compact)}\\ &\sqsubseteq \sqcup\{\overline{f}(x) \mid x \in X\} \quad \text{(since } b \sqsubseteq x \Rightarrow f(b) \sqsubseteq \overline{f}(x)\text{)} .\end{aligned}$$

Therefore, $\overline{f}$ is continuous. Let $f' : D_1 \longrightarrow D_2$ be another continuous function which extends f. Then $f'(x) = f' \sqcup B_x = \sqcup f' B_x = \sqcup f B_x = \overline{f}(x)$ for any $x \in D_1$, hence $f' = \overline{f}$.
Q.E.D.

Theorem 12 corresponds to similar theorems from analysis. Let $f: [0;1] \longrightarrow \mathbb{R}$ be a continuous function from the interval $[0;1] \subseteq \mathbb{R}$ to the set of real numbers $\mathbb{R}$. Let $X \subseteq [0;1]$ be a dense subset (e.g. the rational numbers from $[0;1]$). Then f is determined uniquely by its values on X. Notice that $g :=$ (the restriction of f to X) is uniformly continuous. On the other hand, every uniformly continuous function $g: X \longrightarrow \mathbb{R}$ has a unique continuous (even uniformly continuous) extension $f: [0;1] \longrightarrow \mathbb{R}$. Notice that in the case of Theorem 12, the function $f: B \longrightarrow D_2$ is isotone iff it is continuous.

For each of the cpo's $(P_\omega, \subseteq, \emptyset)$, $(\mathbb{B}_o, \sqsubseteq, \varepsilon)$, and $(\mathbb{C}_o, \sqsubseteq, \varepsilon)$ we introduced in Chapter 3.1 there is a standard T_o-topology associated with it $(\tau_E, \tau_{Bo}, \tau_{Co})$. We shall show now that for every algebraic cpo $\overline{D}$ there is a T_o-topology τ, the so-called Scott topology, such that $\overline{D}$-continuity and τ-continuity coincide.

13 DEFINITION *(Scott topology)*

Let $\overline{D} = (D, \sqsubseteq, \bot)$ be an algebraic cpo with basis B. The Scott-topology $\tau \subseteq 2^D$ of $\overline{D}$ is defined by the topological base

$$\beta := \{O_b \mid b \in B\}$$

where

$$O_b := \{x \in D \mid b \sqsubseteq x\} .$$

It remains to show that β is a base of a topology.

14 LEMMA

Let τ be the Scott topology of an algebraic cpo $\overline{D}$.

(1) τ is welldefined.

(2) τ is a T_o-topology.

Proof

(1) It suffices to show that for any $a, b \in B$ there is some subset $\alpha \subseteq \beta$ such that $O_a \cap O_b = \cup\, \alpha$. Let $x \in O_a \cap O_b$. Since $x = \sqcup B_x$ and B_x is directed (Lemma 9) there is some $c \in B_x$ with $a \sqsubseteq c$ and $b \sqsubseteq c$. For any $y \in O_c$ we have $a \sqsubseteq c \sqsubseteq y$ and $b \sqsubseteq c \sqsubseteq y$, hence $y \in O_a \cap O_b$. Therefore $x \in O_c$ and $O_c \subseteq O_a \cap O_b$. For each

$x \in O_a \cap O_b$ there is some c_x with the above property. Then

$$O_a \cap O_b = \cup\{O_{c_x} \mid x \in O_a \cap O_b\}.$$

(2) Let $x,y \in D$ and $\{O_b \mid x \in O_b\} = \{O_b \mid y \in O_b\}$. Then $b \sqsubseteq x \Longleftrightarrow b \sqsubseteq y$ for all $b \in B$, hence $B_x = B_y$ and $x = y$ by Lemma 9. Therefore τ is a T_o-topology.
Q.E.D.

Let $\overline{D}_i$ be an algebraic cpo with basis $B_i (i = 1,2)$. Let $f: D_1 \longrightarrow D_2$ be $(\overline{D}_1,\overline{D}_2)$-continuous. Then f is uniquely determined by its values on B_1. By Lemma 9, f is uniquely determined by the set $\{(a_1,a_2) \in B_1 \times B_2 \mid a_2 \sqsubseteq f(a_1)\}$. Special cases have been considered in Theorems 3.1.2(2), 3.1.8(2), and 3.1.11(2). Since any $(\overline{D}_1,\overline{D}_2)$-continuous function is isotone, the property $a_2 \sqsubseteq f(a_1)$ is equivalent to $f\,O_{a_1} \subseteq O_{a_2}$. We have used this relation repeatedly in Chapter 3.1. It remains to show that sup-continuity for cpo's coincides with topological continuity w.r.t. the Scott topologies.

15 THEOREM *(sup-continuous = top-continuous)*

Let $\overline{D}_i = (D_i,\sqsubseteq,\bot)$ be an algebraic cpo with Scott topology τ_i $(i = 1,2)$. Let $f: D_1 \longrightarrow D_2$ be a function. Then (1) and (2) are equivalent.
(1) f is $(\overline{D}_1,\overline{D}_2)$-continuous.
(2) f is (τ_1,τ_2)-continuous.

Proof

For $i = 1,2$ let B_i be the basis of $\overline{D}_i$. Assume that f is $(\overline{D}_1,\overline{D}_2)$-continuous. It suffices to show that for each $x \in D_1$ and $b \in B_2$ with $f(x) \in O_b$ there is some $a \in B_1$ with $x \in O_a$ and $f(O_a) \subseteq O_b$. For any $x \in D_1$ and $b \in B_2$ we have

$$\begin{aligned} f(x) \in O_b &\Rightarrow b \sqsubseteq f(x) = f(\sqcup B_x) = \bigsqcup\{f(a) \mid a \in B_x\} \\ &\Rightarrow (\exists a \in B_1)(b \sqsubseteq f(a) \wedge a \in B_x) \quad \text{(since } b \text{ is compact)} \\ &\Rightarrow (\exists a \in B_1)(f(a) \in O_b \wedge x \in O_a) \\ &\Rightarrow (\exists a \in B_1)(f(O_a) \subseteq O_b \wedge x \in O_a) \quad \text{(since } f \text{ is isotone).} \end{aligned}$$

On the other hand, assume that f is (τ_1,τ_2)-continuous. First we show that f is $(\overline{D}_1,\overline{D}_2)$-isotone. Assume $x \sqsubseteq y$. Then for any $b \in B_2$ we have:

$$\begin{aligned} b \sqsubseteq f(x) &\Rightarrow f(x) \in O_b \\ &\Rightarrow (\exists a \in B_1)(x \in O_a \wedge f(O_a) \subseteq O_b) \quad \text{(by continuity of } f) \\ &\Rightarrow (\exists a \in B_1)(y \in O_a \wedge f(O_a) \subseteq O_b) \quad \text{(since } x \sqsubseteq y) \\ &\Rightarrow f(y) \in O_b \\ &\Rightarrow b \sqsubseteq f(y). \end{aligned}$$

This shows $B_{f(x)} \subseteq B_{f(y)}$, hence $f(x) \sqsubseteq f(y)$. Now let $X \subseteq D$ be directed. Since f is isotone, we have $\sqcup f X \sqsubseteq f \sqcup X$. For any $b \in B_2$ we have

$$\begin{aligned} b \sqsubseteq f \sqcup X &\Rightarrow f \sqcup X \in O_b \\ &\Rightarrow (\exists a \in B_1)(\sqcup X \in O_a \wedge f(O_a) \subseteq O_b) \quad \text{(by } (\tau_1,\tau_2)\text{-continuity)} \\ &\Rightarrow (\exists a \in B_1)(a \sqsubseteq \sqcup X \wedge f(a) \in O_b) \\ &\Rightarrow (\exists a \in B_1)(\exists x \in X)(a \sqsubseteq x \wedge b \sqsubseteq f(a)) \quad \text{(since } a \text{ is compact)} \\ &\Rightarrow (\exists x \in X)(b \sqsubseteq f(x)) \quad \text{(since } f \text{ is isotone)} \\ &\Rightarrow b \sqsubseteq \sqcup f X. \end{aligned}$$

Therefore $f \sqcup X \sqsubseteq \sqcup f X$ by Lemma 9.
Q.E.D.

The above theorem essentially generalizes Theorems 3.1.2, 3.1.7, and 3.1.10 which connect approximation-continuity with topological continuity.

At the beginning of this chapter we have interpreted $x \sqsubseteq y$ by "the information given by y is greater or equal to that one given by x". If $x_1 \sqsubseteq y$ and $x_2 \sqsubseteq y$, for some y, the information given by x_1 and the information given by x_2 may be called consistent. Therefore it is reasonable to call a set X *consistent*, iff it is *bounded* (i.e. $(\forall x \in X) x \sqsubseteq y$ for some y). It is desirable to have a name for the information given by X in this case. Formally this means that every bounded set X should have a least upper bound y. CPO's with this property are called *boundedly-complete*.

16 <u>DEFINITION</u> *(b-completeness, fb-completeness)*

Let $\overline{A} = (A,\leq)$ be a partial order.
(1) $\overline{A}$ is called b-*complete* iff $\sqcup X$ exists for every non-empty bounded set $X \subseteq A$.
(2) $\overline{A}$ is called fb-*complete* iff $\sqcup X$ exists for every non-empty finite bounded set $X \subseteq A$.

For example, the partial order $(P_\omega, \subseteq)$ is b-complete. By the following theorem, b-completeness of an algebraic cpo can be characterized by fb-completeness on the basis.

17 <u>THEOREM</u>

Let $\overline{D} = (D,\sqsubseteq,\perp)$ be an algebraic cpo with basis B. Let $\overline{B} := (B,\sqsubseteq_o)$ be the partial order induced by $\overline{D}$ on B. Then (1,), (2), and (3) are equivalent.

(1) $\overline{D}$ is b-complete.

(2) $\overline{D}$ is fb-complete.

(3) $\overline{B}$ is fb-complete.

Furthermore, if $\overline{D}$ is b-complete, then $\sqcup_o E = \sqcup E \in B$ for any not empty, finite, and bounded subset $E \sqsubseteq B$ (where $\sqcup_o$ is the sup-operation w.r.t. the order $\sqsubseteq_o$).

Proof

"(1) $\Rightarrow$ (2)": (obvious)

"(2) $\Rightarrow$ (3)": Assume that $\overline{D}$ is fb-complete. Let $E \subseteq B$ be finite and bounded (in B). Then E is bounded in D. Therefore $\sqcup E = x$ for some $x \in D$. Then $e \sqsubseteq x$ for all $e \in E$. Since $B_x = \{b \in B \mid b \in x\}$ is directed, there is some $b \in B_x$ with $e \sqsubseteq b$ for all $e \in E$, hence $\sqcup E \sqsubseteq b \sqsubseteq x$. This shows $\sqcup E = b \in B$. Obviously, b is an upper bound of E in B (w.r.t. $\sqsubseteq_o$). Since $\sqcup E \sqsubseteq \sqcup_o E$ in any case, $b = \sqcup_o E$. Therefore $\overline{B}$ is fb-complete and $\sqcup_o E = \sqcup E \in B$ for any finite set $E \subseteq B$.

"(3) $\Rightarrow$ (1)": Let $\overline{B}$ be fb-complete. Let $X \subseteq D$ be bounded by $w \in D$. Define

$$Z := \bigcup \{B_x \mid x \in X\}.$$

Let $E \subseteq Z$ be finite. Then $(\forall e \in E) e \sqsubseteq w$, hence $E \subseteq B_w$. Since B_w is directed, E is bounded by some $b \in B_w$, hence $\sqcup_o E$ exists. Define

$$Y := \{\sqcup_o E \mid E \subseteq Z,\ E \text{ finite}\}.$$

Since $\sqcup_o E_1 \sqsubseteq \sqcup_o (E_1 \cup E_2)$ and $\sqcup_o E_2 \sqsubseteq \sqcup_o (E_1 \cup E_2)$, Y is directed. Since $b \sqsubseteq x \in X \Rightarrow b \in Z \Rightarrow b \in Y$, we obtain $B_x \subseteq Y$ for any $x \in X$, hence $x = \sqcup B_x \sqsubseteq \sqcup Y$ for any $x \in X$. Therefore $\sqcup Y \in D$ is an upper bound of X. Let w be any upper bound of X. Then w is an upper bound of Z, $\sqcup_o E \sqsubseteq w$ for any finite $E \subseteq Z$ (see above), and hence $\sqcup Y \sqsubseteq w$. Therefore, $\sqcup Y$ is the least upper bound of X.
Q.E.D.

The following example gives a cpo which is not b-complete.

18 EXAMPLE

We consider a special case of Example 2(10). Let $X = \mathbb{R}^2$ and $A \subseteq \mathbb{R}^2$ be a dense subset in the plane $\mathbb{R}^2$ with Euclidean distance. By Examples 6(10) and 8(10), $\overline{D}$ is an algebraic cpo with basis $\{\bot\} \cup (A \times \mathbb{N})$. We have $(a,n) \sqsubseteq (b,m)$ iff $\overline{B}(b;2^{-m}) \subseteq B(a;2^{-n})$ where $\overline{B}$ denotes the closed ball. The set $\{(a,n),(b,m)\}$ is consistent if the intersection $B(a;2^{-n}) \cap B(b;2^{-n})$ is not empty. The least upper bound of two consistent balls must be represented by the intersection which in general is not a ball. This shows that $\overline{D}$ is not b-complete.

Any partial order can be embedded into an fb-complete partial order. Let $(A,\leq)$ be a partial order.
Define $(C,\sqsubseteq')$ as follows.

$$C := \{E \subseteq A \mid E \text{ finite and bounded}\}$$
$$E \sqsubseteq' F :\Longleftrightarrow (\forall e \in E)(\exists f \in F)e \leq f.$$

Then $(C,\sqsubseteq')$ is a pre-order. For any bounded finite set $X \subseteq C$ we have $\cup X \in C$ and $\cup X \in \mathrm{Sup}\ X$ (Def. 2.4.2). The mapping $\iota : b \longrightarrow \{b\}$ embeds A isotone into C. Factorization of $(C,\sqsubseteq')$ by the equivalence relation derived from $\sqsubseteq'$ yields an fb-complete partial order which extends $(A,\leq)$.

There are constructions which generate new cpo's from given ones: The *sum* of two cpo's is a cpo, the *product* of two cpo's is a cpo, and the *function space* between two cpo's is a cpo. Several subclasses of cpo's have the same closure properties, especially the b-complete algebraic cpo's. These closure properties, where the closure under function space construction is the most remarkable one, among others justify the detailed investigation of cpo's.

19 <u>DEFINITION</u> *(standard sum of cpo's)*

Let $\overline{D}_i = (D_i, \sqsubseteq_i, \perp_i)$ be cpo's $(i = 1,2)$. The *standard sum* $\overline{D} = (D, \sqsubseteq, \perp)$ of $\overline{D}_1$ and $\overline{D}_2$ is defined as follows:

$$\perp := \emptyset\ ,$$
$$D := (\{1\} \times D_1) \cup (\{2\} \times D_2) \cup \{\perp\}$$
$$\sqsubseteq := \{(\perp, d) \mid d \in D\}$$
$$\cup \{((1,x),(1,y)) \mid x,y \in D_1, x \sqsubseteq_1 y\}$$
$$\cup \{((2,x),(2,y)) \mid x,y \in D_2, x \sqsubseteq_2 y\}\ .$$

Notation: $(D_1 + D_2) := D$, $[\overline{D}_1 + \overline{D}_1] := \overline{D}$

The carrier of the standard sum is the disjoint union of the carriers D_1 and D_2 plus a new bottom element. The order $\sqsubseteq$ is essentially the disjoint union of $\sqsubseteq_1$ and $\sqsubseteq_2$. The properties "cpo", "algebraic cpo", and "b-complete algebraic cpo" are preserved under sum.

The next lemma summarizes the most important properties of $[\overline{D}_1 + \overline{D}_2]$.

20 LEMMA *(properties of the standard sum)*

Let $\overline{D}$ be sum of $\overline{D}_1$ and $\overline{D}_2$ (see Def. 19). Then the following properties hold

(1) $\overline{D} = [\overline{D}_1 + \overline{D}_2]$ is a cpo.

(2) Define $\iota_1 : D_1 \longrightarrow D$ and $\iota_2 : D_2 \longrightarrow D$ by $\iota_1(x) := (1,x)$ and $\iota_2(y) = (2,y)$. Then ι_1 and ι_2 are continuous and the triple $(\overline{D}, \iota_1, \iota_2)$ satisfies Property (*).

(*) Let $\overline{C}$ be a cpo, let $f_1 : D_1 \longrightarrow C$ and $f_2 : D_2 \longrightarrow C$ be continuous mappings. Then there is a unique continuous mapping $f : D \longrightarrow C$ such that

$$f_1 = f\iota_1 \quad \text{and} \quad f_2 = f\iota_2 \quad \text{and} \quad f(\bot) = \bot .$$

(3) If B_i is an algebraic basis of $\overline{D}_i$ $(i = 1,2)$, then $\overline{D}$ is algebraic and

$$B = \{\bot\} \cup (\{1\} \times B_1) \cup (\{2\} \times B_2)$$

is the algebraic basis of $\overline{D}$.

(4) If $\overline{D}_1$ and $\overline{D}_2$ are b-complete algebraic cpo's, then $\overline{D}$ is a b-complete algebraic cpo.

The proof is easy. In Case (2) notice that ι_1 and ι_2 are continuous and injective, $\text{range}(\iota_1) \cap \text{range}(\iota_2) = \emptyset$, and $\text{range}(\iota_1) \cup \text{range}(\iota_2) = D \setminus \{\bot\}$. For algebraic cpo's, the universal property (*) characterizes $[\overline{D}_1 + \overline{D}_2]$ up to isomorphism.

21 LEMMA *(characterization of the sum)*

Let $\overline{D}_1$ and $\overline{D}_2$ be algebraic cpo's. Then an algebraic cpo $\overline{E}$ is isomorphic to $[\overline{D}_1 + \overline{D}_2]$ iff there are continuous functions $h_1 : D_1 \longrightarrow E$ and $h_2 : D_2 \longrightarrow E$ such that the triple $(\overline{E}, h_1, h_2)$ satisfies Condition (*) from Lemma 20.

Proof

First assume that functions h_1 and h_2 exist such that $(\overline{E}, h_1, h_2)$ satisfies Property (*): for any pair of continuous functions $f_1 : D_1 \longrightarrow C$ and $f_2 : D_2 \longrightarrow C$ there is a unique continuous mapping $f : E \longrightarrow C$ such that $f_1 = fh_1$, $f_2 = fh_2$, and $f(\bot) = \bot$.

Consider the special case $C = D_1$, $f_1(x) = x$, $f_2(x) = \bot$. Since $f_1 = fh_1$ and f_1 is injective, h_1 is injective. Since h_1 and f are isotone we obtain $x \sqsubseteq y \Rightarrow h_1(x) \sqsubseteq h_1(y) \Rightarrow fh_1(x) \sqsubseteq fh_1(y) \Rightarrow x \sqsubseteq y$. Therefore, $\overline{D}_1$ and ($\overline{E}$ restricted to $h_1(D_1)$) are order isomorphic. (Notice that $fh_1(D_1) = D_1$.)

Correspondingly, h_2 is injective and $\overline{D}_2$ is order isomorphic to $\overline{E}$ restricted to $h_2(D_2)$.

Consider the special case $C = \{\bot,\top\}, \bot \sqsubseteq \top, f_1(x) = \top, f_2(x) = \bot$. Since $f_1 = fh_1$ and $f(\bot) = \bot$ we have $h_1(x) \neq \bot$ for $x \in D_1$. Suppose $x_1 \in D_1, x_2 \in D_2$ and $h_1(x_1) \sqsubseteq h_2(x_2)$. Then $\top = f_1(x_1) = fh_1(x_1) \sqsubseteq fh_2(x_2) = f_2(x_2) = \bot$ (contradiction). Similarly $h_2(x) \neq \bot$ and not $h_2(x_2) \sqsubseteq h_1(x_1)$ is proved. Therefore, the sets $\{\bot\}$, $h_1(D_1)$, and $h_2(D_2)$ are pairwise disjoint and $y_1 \in h_1(D_1)$ and $y_2 \in h_2(D_2)$ are incomparable. Suppose $X = E \setminus (\{\bot\} \cup h_1(D_1) \cup h_2(D_2))$ is not empty. Since $\overline{E}$ restricted to $(\{\bot\} \cup h_1(D_1) \cup h_2(D_2))$ is an algebraic cpo by the above observations (indeed it is isomorphic to $[\overline{D}_1 + \overline{D}_2]$), there must be some basis element $a \in X$.
Consider the special case $C = \{\bot,\top\}, \bot \sqsubseteq \top$,

$$f_1(x) := (\top \text{ if } a \sqsubseteq h_1(x), \bot \text{ otherwise}) \ (x \in D_1),$$
$$f_2(x) := (\top \text{ if } a \sqsubseteq h_2(x), \bot \text{ otherwise}) \ (x \in D_2).$$

Define $f, f' : E \longrightarrow C$ by

$$f(y) = (\top \text{ if } a \sqsubseteq y, \bot \text{ otherwise}) \ (y \in E),$$
$$f'(y) = (\top \text{ if } a \sqsubseteq y \text{ and } a \neq y, \bot \text{ otherwise} \ (y \in E)).$$

Then f and f' are two different continuous functions with the desired properties. We obtain $X = \emptyset$ by the uniqueness requirement. Therefore, E is the disjoint union of $\{\bot\}, h_1(D_1)$, and $h_2(D_2)$. Consider the following diagram (where $D = [D_1 + D_2]$):

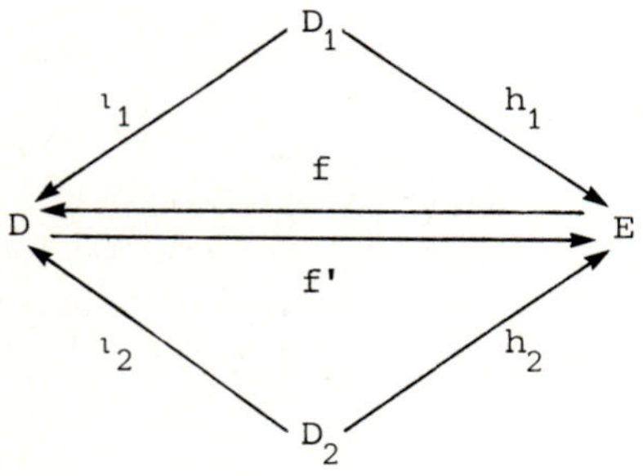

Since $(\overline{E}, h_1, h_2)$ satisfies (*), there is a continuous function $f : E \longrightarrow D$ such that $f(\bot) = \bot, fh_1 = \iota_1, fh_2 = \iota_2$. By Lemma 20(2) there is a continuous function $f' : D \longrightarrow E$ such that $f'(\bot) = \bot, f'\iota_1 = h_1, f'\iota_2 = h_2$. We obtain $ff'\iota_1 = \iota_1, ff'\iota_2 = \iota_2, ff'(\bot) = \bot$, therefore ff' is the identity on D. Similarly we obtain $f'fh_1 = h_1, f'fh_2 = h_2$, $f'f(\bot) = \bot$, hence $f'f$ is the identity on $E = \{\bot\} \cup h_1(D_1) \cup h_2(D_2)$. Therefore, $\overline{D}$ and $\overline{E}$ are isomorphic.

To show the inverse is left as an exercise.
Q.E.D.

Each cpo which is isomorphic to $[\overline{D}_1 + \overline{D}_2]$ can therefore be called a *sum* of $\overline{D}_1$ and $\overline{D}_2$. A computational special case will be considered in Chapter 3.7.

22 EXAMPLE
Let $\overline{D}$ be the one-element cpo $\overline{D} = (\{\bot\},\{(\bot,\bot)\},\bot)$. Then $[\overline{D}+\overline{D}]$ is isomorphic to the cpo from Example 2(2).

The standard product of two cpo's is defined as follows.

23 DEFINITION *(standard product of cpo's)*

Let $\overline{D}_i = (D_i, \sqsubseteq_i, \bot_i)$ be cpo's $(i = 1,2)$. The *standard product* $\overline{D} = (D, \sqsubseteq, \bot)$ of $\overline{D}_1$ and $\overline{D}_2$ is defined as follows:

$$D := D_1 \times D_2,$$
$$\bot := (\bot_1, \bot_2),$$
$$(d_1,d_2) \sqsubseteq (e_1,e_2) \;:\Leftrightarrow\; (d_1 \sqsubseteq e_1 \wedge d_2 \sqsubseteq e_2)$$

for all $(d_1,d_2),(e_1,e_2) \in D$.
Notation: $[\overline{D}_1 \times \overline{D}_2] := \overline{D}$

The standard product has the following properties.

24 LEMMA *(properties of the standard product)*

Consider Definition 23. The standard product $[\overline{D}_1 \times \overline{D}_2]$ has the following properties.

(1) $[D_1 \times D_2]$ is a cpo.

(2) Define $pr_1 : D \longrightarrow D_1$ and $pr_2 : D \longrightarrow D_2$ by $pr_1(x,y) = x$ and $pr_2(x,y) = y$. Then pr_1 and pr_2 are continuous and the triple $(\overline{D}, pr_1, pr_2)$ satisfies Property (*).

(*) Let $\overline{C}$ be a cpo, let $g_1 : C \longrightarrow D_1$ and $g_2 : C \longrightarrow D_2$ be continuous mappings. Then there is a unique continuous mapping $g : C \longrightarrow D$ such that

$$g_1 = pr_1 g \quad\text{and}\quad g_2 = pr_2 g.$$

(3) If B_i is an algebraic basis of $D_i (i = 1,2)$, then $[\overline{D}_1 \times \overline{D}_2]$ is algebraic and $B = B_1 \times B_2$ is the basis.

(4) If $\overline{D}_1$ and $\overline{D}_1$ are b-complete algebraic cpo's then $[\overline{D}_1 \times \overline{D}_2]$ is b-complete algebraic.

The proof is easy. Notice that pr_1 and pr_2 are continuous. In (2) define $g(x) := (g_1(x), g_2(x))$. The isomorphism class of $[\overline{D}_1 \times \overline{D}_2]$ can be characterized by a universal property.

25 LEMMA *(characterization of the product)*

Let $\overline{E} = (E, \sqsubseteq, \bot)$ be a cpo. Then $\overline{E}$ is isomorphic to $[\overline{D}_1 \times \overline{D}_2]$ iff there are continuous functions $h_1 : E \longrightarrow D_1$ and $h_2 : E \longrightarrow D_2$ such that the triple $(\overline{E}, h_1, h_2)$ satisfies Condition (∗) from Lemma 24.

Proof

Let $(\overline{E}, h_1, h_2)$ satisfy Condition (∗). Let z and z' be elements of E such that $(x_1, x_2) := (h_1(z), h_2(z)) = (h_1(z'), h_2(z'))$. Consider $C = \{\bot, \top\}, \bot \sqsubseteq \top, f_1(\bot) = f_2(\bot) = \bot$, $f_1(\top) = x_1, f_2(\top) = x_2$. Define $f, f' := C \longrightarrow E$ by $f(\bot) = f'(\bot) = \bot, f(\top) = z, f'(\top) = z'$. Since $h_1(\bot) = h_2(\bot) = \bot$, the two functions f and f' satisfy the desired properties and we obtain $f = f'$, i.e. $z = z'$, by the uniqueness requirement. Therefore $(h_1, h_2) : E \longrightarrow D_1 \times D_2$ is injective. Consider $\overline{C} = [\overline{D}_1 \times \overline{D}_2] = D, f_1 = pr_1, f_2 = pr_2$. By assumption on E there is a continuous function $f : D \longrightarrow E$ such that $x_i = pr_i(x_1, x_2) = h_i f(x_1, x_2)(i = 1,2)$, i.e. $(h_1, h_2) f = \mathbb{1}_D$. Especially, (h_1, h_2) is surjective. Therefore, (h_1, h_2) and f are bijective. Since $(\overline{D}, pr_1, pr_2)$ satisfies Property (∗) there is a continuous function $f' : E \longrightarrow D$ such that $h_1 = pr_1 f'$, $h_2 = pr_2 f'$, hence $(h_1, h_2) = (pr_1 f', pr_2 f') = f'$. This shows that $f' = f^{-1}$ is continuous. Therefore $\overline{D}$ and $\overline{E}$ are isomorphic.

The second part of the proof is left as an exercise.
Q.E.D.

Each cpo which is isomorphic to the standard product $[\overline{D}_1 \times \overline{D}_2]$ is called a *product* of $\overline{D}_1$ and $\overline{D}_2$. Computable products will be considered in Chapter 3.7.

On the product space sup's may be performed on the projections separately, and a function defined on the product space is continuous if all its sections are continuous. Note that this is not true for arbitrary topological spaces; counterexample: $f : \mathbb{R}^2 \longrightarrow \mathbb{R}$, $f(x,y) := xy/(x^2 + y^2)$ if $(x,y) \neq (0,0), f(0,0) = 0$.

26 LEMMA

Let $\overline{D} = (D_i, \sqsubseteq_i, \bot_i)$ be cpo's $(i = 0,1,2)$, let $\overline{D} = (D, \sqsubseteq, \bot)$ be the standard product of $\overline{D}_1$ and $\overline{D}_2$.

(1) Let $X \subseteq D$ be directed, $X_1 := pr_1(X), X_2 := pr_2(X)$.
Then:
- X_1 and X_2 are directed
- $(\forall y \in X_1 \times X_2)(\exists x \in X) y \sqsubseteq x$
- $\sqcup X = (\sqcup_1 X_1, \sqcup_2 X_2) = \sqcup(X_1 \times X_2)$

(2) Let $f: D_1 \times D_2 \longrightarrow D_o$ be a function. For $x \in D_1$ and $y \in D_2$ define

$$f_{1x} : D_2 \longrightarrow D_o,$$
$$f_{2y} : D_1 \longrightarrow D_o$$

by $f_{1x}(y) := f_{2y}(x) := f(x,y)$. Then f is continuous iff $(\forall x \in D_1) f_{1x}$ is continuous and $(\forall y \in D_2) f_{2y}$ is continuous.

(3) Let $\overline{D}_1$ and $\overline{D}_2$ be algebraic cpo's. Then the product of the Scott topologies of $\overline{D}_1$ and $\overline{D}_2$ is the Scott topology of $[\overline{D}_1 \times \overline{D}_2]$.

Proof

(1) Let X be directed. For any $x_1, y_1 \in D_1$ we have

$$\begin{aligned} x_1, y_1 \in X_1 &\Rightarrow (\exists x_2, y_2)(x_1,x_2),(y_1,y_2) \in X \\ &\Rightarrow (\exists x_2,y_2)(\exists (z_1,z_2) \in X)((x_1,x_2),(y_1,y_2) \sqsubseteq (z_1,z_2)) \\ &\Rightarrow (\exists z_1 \in X_1) x_1, y_1 \sqsubseteq_1 z_1 . \end{aligned}$$

Therefore X_1 is $\sqsubseteq_1$-directed. The case of X_2 is proved correspondingly. For any $(y_1,y_2) \in D_1 \times D_2$ we have

$$\begin{aligned} (y_1,y_2) \in X_1 \times X_2 &\Rightarrow (\exists z_1,z_2)(z_1,y_2),(y_1,z_2) \in X \\ &\Rightarrow (\exists z_1,z_2)(\exists (x_1,x_2) \in X)(z_1,y_2),(y_1,z_2) \sqsubseteq (x_1,x_2) \\ &\Rightarrow (\exists (x_1,x_2) \in X)(y_1,y_2) \sqsubseteq (x_1,x_2). \end{aligned}$$

This proves the second statement. For any $(x_1,x_2) \in X$, $(x_1,x_2) \sqsubseteq (\sqcup_1 X_1, \sqcup_2 X_2)$, hence $\sqcup X \sqsubseteq (\sqcup_1 X_1, \sqcup_2 X_2)$. Let (y_1,y_2) be an upper bound of X. Then (y_1,y_2) is an upper bound of $X_1 \times X_2$ by the second statement, hence y_i is an upper bound of X_i, i.e. $\sqcup_i X_i \sqsubseteq y_i$ for $i = 1,2$. Therefore, $(\sqcup_1 X_1, \sqcup_2 X_2)$ is the least upper bound of X. Replacing X by $X_1 \times X_2$ we obtain that $(\sqcup_1 X_1, \sqcup_2 X_2)$ is the least upper bound of $X_1 \times X_2$.

(2) Assume that f is continuous, let $x \in D_1$. Let $Y \subseteq D_2$ be directed. Then $\{x\} \times Y$ is directed and $f_{1x} \sqcup_2 Y = f(x, \sqcup_2 Y) = f \sqcup (\{x\} \times Y) = \sqcup_o f(\{x\} \times Y) = \sqcup_o f_{1x} Y$. Continuity of f_{2y} is proved correspondingly. Now, assume that f_{1x} and f_{2y} are continuous for all $x \in D_1$ and $y \in D_2$. Let $(x_1,x_2),(y_1,y_2) \in D_1 \times D_2$ such

that $(x_1,x_2) \sqsubseteq (y_1,y_2)$. Then $f(x_1,x_2) = f_{1x_1}(x_2) \sqsubseteq_o f_{1x_1}(y_2) = f_{2y_2}(x_1) \sqsubseteq_o f_{2y_2}(x_2)$ $= f(x_2,y_2)$. Therefore f is isotone. Let $X \subseteq D_1 \times D_2$ be directed. By (1) $X_1 \times X_2$ is directed and $\forall z \in f(X_1 \times X_2)$ there is some $y \in fX$ with $x \sqsubseteq y$ since f is isotone. Therefore, $\sqcup_o f(X) = \sqcup_o f(X_1 \times X_2)$. With $z := \sqcup_2 X_2$ we obtain

$$
\begin{aligned}
f \sqcup X &= f(\sqcup_1 X_1, z) && \text{(by (1))}\\
&= f_{2z} \sqcup_1 X_1 \\
&= \sqcup_o f_{2z} X_1 && \text{(by continuity of } f_{2z})\\
&= \sqcup_o \{f(x,z) \mid x \in X_1\}\\
&= \sqcup_o \{f_{1x} \sqcup_2 X_2 \mid x \in X_1\}\\
&= \sqcup_o \{\sqcup_o f_{1x} X_2 \mid x \in X_1\} && \text{(by continuity of } f_{1x})\\
&= \sqcup_o \{\sqcup_o f(\{x\} \times X_2) \mid x \in X_1\}\\
&= \sqcup_o f(X_1 \times X_2)\\
&= \sqcup_o f(X) \quad .
\end{aligned}
$$

Therefore, f is continuous.

(3) Let B_i be the algebraic basis and let τ_i be the Scott topology of $\overline{D}_i$. Let $O^1_b := \{x \in D_1 \mid b \sqsubseteq x\}$, $O^2_c := \{x \in D_2 \mid c \sqsubseteq x\}$. The sets $O^1_b \times O^2_c$, where $b \in B_1$ and $e \in B_2$ are a basis of $\tau_1 \otimes \tau_2$. The sets $O_{(b,c)} = \{(x,y) \in D_1 \times D_2 \mid (b,c) \sqsubseteq (x,y)\}$ where $b \in B_1$ and $c \in B_2$ are a basis of the Scott topology of $\overline{D}$. The two topologies τ and $\tau_1 \otimes \tau_2$ are equal since $O^1_b \times O^2_c = O_{(b,c)}$.

Q.E.D.

By Property (3) of the above lemma, for algebraic cpo's a binary function $f: D_1 \times D_2 \longrightarrow D_3$ is continuous iff it is continuous w.r.t. to the product cpo $[\overline{D}_1 \times \overline{D}_2]$. The most interesting construction is that of the function space between two cpo's.

27 <u>DEFINITION</u> *(standard space of continuous functions)*

Let $\overline{D}_i = (D_i, \sqsubseteq_i, \bot_i)$ be cpo's $(i = 1,2)$. The *standard function space* $\overline{D} = (D, \sqsubseteq, \bot)$ from $\overline{D}_1$ to $\overline{D}_2$ is defined as follows.

$D := \{f : D_1 \longrightarrow D_2 \mid f \text{ is } (\overline{D}_1, \overline{D}_2)\text{-continuous}\}$

$\bot(x) := \bot_2$ for all $x \in D_1$

$f \sqsubseteq g :\iff f(x) \sqsubseteq_2 g(x)$ for all $x \in D_1$.

<u>Notation:</u> $[\overline{D}_1 \longrightarrow \overline{D}_2] := \overline{D}$, $(D_1 \longrightarrow D_2) := D$

The following lemma summarizes some important properties of the space of continuous functions.

28 LEMMA

Let $\overline{D}_i = (D_i, \sqsubseteq_i, \perp_i)$ be cpo's $(i=0,1,2)$. Then the standard space $\overline{D} = [\overline{D}_1 \longrightarrow \overline{D}_2]$ has the following properties.

(1) $\overline{D}$ is a cpo with $(\sqcup F)\, x = \sqcup_2\{f(x) \mid f \in F\}$ for any $x \in D_1$ and any directed $F \subseteq D$.

(2a) The evaluation function $\Gamma : D \times D_1 \longrightarrow D_2$ with $\Gamma(f,x) := f(x)$ is $([\overline{D} \times \overline{D}_1], \overline{D}_2)$-continuous.

(2b) Let $\Gamma : D_o \times D_1 \longrightarrow D_2$ be $([\overline{D}_o \times \overline{D}_1], \overline{D}_2)$-continuous. Then the function $\Delta : D_o \longrightarrow D$ defined by

$$\Delta(x)(y) = \Gamma(x,y)$$

for all $x \in D_o, y \in D_1$ is $(\overline{D}_o, \overline{D})$-continuous.

(3) Let $\overline{D}_i$ be a b-complete algebraic cpo with basis $B_i (i = 1,2)$. Then $\overline{D} = [\overline{D}_1 \longrightarrow \overline{D}_2]$ is a b-complete algebraic cpo. Define

$$SB := \{(a \longrightarrow b) \mid a \in B_1, b \in B_2\},$$

where $(a \rightarrow b) \in \overline{D}$ is the *step function* defined by

$$(a \longrightarrow b)(x) := \begin{cases} b & \text{if } a \sqsubseteq x \\ \perp_2 & \text{otherwise.} \end{cases}$$

Then

$$B = \{\sqcup F \mid F \subseteq SB,\ F \text{ not empty, finite, and bounded}\}$$

is the algebraic basis of $\overline{D}$. Furthermore the following properties hold.

(a) $(a \longrightarrow b) \sqsubseteq f \iff b \sqsubseteq fa \quad (a \in B_1, b \in B_2, f \in D)$.

(b) Let $F = \{(a_o \longrightarrow b_o), \ldots, (a_n \longrightarrow b_n)\}$. Then the following properties are equivalent:

- $\sqcup F$ exists,
- F is bounded (in D),
- $(\forall J \subseteq \{0,\ldots,n\})(\{a_i \mid i \in J\}$ bounded $\Rightarrow \{b_i \mid i \in J\}$ bounded$)$.

(c) $(\sqcup F)(x) = \sqcup\{b_i \mid a_i \sqsubseteq x\}$ if $(F = \{(a_o \longrightarrow b_o), \ldots, (a_n \longrightarrow b_n)\}$ and $\sqcup F$ exists$)$.

Proof

(1) Obviously $(D, \sqsubseteq)$ is a partial order with minimum $\perp$ since $\perp$ is a continuous function. Assume $F \subseteq (D_1 \longrightarrow D_2)$, F directed. Define $h : D_1 \longrightarrow D_2$ by $h(x) := \sqcup_2\{f(x) \mid f \in F\}$. The function h is welldefined since $\{fx \mid f \in F\}$ is directed for all $x \in D_1$. Obviously, h is isotone. Let $X \subseteq D_1$ be directed. Then $\sqcup\, hX$ exists since h is isotone and

$$\begin{aligned} h \sqcup_1 X &= \sqcup_2\{f \sqcup_1 X \mid f \in F\} \\ &= \sqcup_2\{\sqcup_2 f(X) \mid f \in F\} \qquad (\text{since } F \subseteq (D_1 \longrightarrow D_2)) \\ &= \sqcup_2\{f(x) \mid f \in F, x \in X\} \\ &= \sqcup_2\{\sqcup_2\{f(x) \mid f \in F\} \mid x \in X\} \\ &= \sqcup_2\{h(x) \mid x \in X\} \\ &= \sqcup_2\ hX. \end{aligned}$$

Therefore h is continuous. Let $g \in (D_1 \longrightarrow D_2)$ such that $(\forall f \in F) f \sqsubseteq g$. Then $(\forall f \in F) f(x) \sqsubseteq_2 g(x), \sqcup_2\{f(x) \mid f \in F\} \sqsubseteq_2 g(x), h(x) \sqsubseteq_2 g(x)$ for all $x \in D_1$, hence $h = \sqcup F$. Therefore, $\overline{D}$ is a cpo and $(\sqcup F)x = \sqcup_2\{f(x) \mid f \in F\}$.

(2a) By Lemma 26(2) it suffices to show that the sections of Γ are continuous. Let $f \in (D_1 \longrightarrow D_2)$. Then $\Gamma_{1f}(x) = \Gamma(f,x) = f(x)$ for all x. Therefore Γ_{1f} is continuous. Let $x \in D_2$. Let $f_1, f_2 \in (D_1 \longrightarrow D_2)$, $f_1 \sqsubseteq f_2$. Then $\Gamma_{2x}(f_1) = f_1(x) \sqsubseteq_2 f_2(x) = \Gamma_{2x}(f_2)$, hence Γ_{2x} is isotone. Let $F \subseteq (D_1 \longrightarrow D_2)$ be directed. Then $\sqcup \Gamma_{2x} F = \sqcup_2\{fx \mid f \in F\} = (\sqcup F)(x) = \Gamma_{2x} \sqcup F$. Therefore Γ_{2x} is continuous. By Lemma 26(2), Γ is continuous.

(2b) Since $\Delta(x) = \Gamma_{1x}$ for any $x \in D_o$, range$(\Delta) \subseteq D$ by Lemma 26(2). Δ is isotone since Γ is isotone. Let $X \subseteq D_o$ be directed. Then

$$\begin{aligned}
\Delta(\sqcup_o X)(y) &= \Gamma(\sqcup_o X, y) \\
&= \Gamma \sqcup (X \times \{y\}) \\
&= \sqcup_2 \Gamma(X \times \{y\}) \\
&= \sqcup_2\{\Delta(x)(y) \mid x \in X\} \\
&= \sqcup\ \{\Delta(x) \mid x \in X\}(y) \qquad \text{(by (1))}
\end{aligned}$$

for all $y \in D_1$. Therefore Δ is continuous.

(3) From now we shall omit the indices of $\sqsubseteq$ and $\perp$. It is easy to show that $(a \longrightarrow b)$ is continuous for $a \in B_1$ and $b \in B_2$. We show Property (a). Assume $(a \longrightarrow b) \sqsubseteq f$. Then $b = (a \longrightarrow b)(a) \sqsubseteq f(a)$. Assume $b \sqsubseteq f(a)$. If $a \sqsubseteq x$ then $(a \longrightarrow b)(x) = b \sqsubseteq f(a) \sqsubseteq f(x)$, otherwise $(a \longrightarrow b)(x) = \perp \sqsubseteq f(x)$. Therefore $(a \longrightarrow b)(x) \sqsubseteq f(x)$ for all $x \in D_1$. We prove (b). If $\sqcup F$ exists then F is bounded. Assume $f \in D$ is an upper bound of F. Let $a_i \sqsubseteq x$ for all $i \in J$. Then $b_i = (a_i \longrightarrow b_i)(x) \sqsubseteq f(x)$ for all $i \in J$, hence $f(x)$ is an upper bound of $\{b_i \mid i \in J\}$. Assume that the third property holds. Define $h : D_1 \longrightarrow D_2$ by

$$h(x) := \sqcup \{f(x) \mid f \in F\}.$$

Then $h(x) = \sqcup\{b_i \mid a_i \sqsubseteq x, i \leq n\}$. By our assumption $h(x)$ exists since $\overline{D}_2$ is b-complete. Let $X \subseteq D$ be directed. Then $h \sqcup X = \sqcup\{f \sqcup X \mid f \in F\} = \sqcup\{\sqcup\{fx \mid x \in X\} \mid f \in F\} = \sqcup\{\sqcup\{fx \mid f \in F\} \mid x \in X\} = \sqcup\{h(x) \mid x \in X\}$, hence h is continuous. Obviously h is an upper bound of F. If g is another upper bound of F then for any x: $h(x) = \sqcup\{f(x) \mid f \in F\} \sqsubseteq g(x)$. Therefore $\sqcup F$ exists and $h = \sqcup F$. Property (c) follows immediately from the above considerations.

So far we have proved (a), (b), and (c) and we have shown that the set $B \subseteq D$ is welldefined. We show that each $(a \longrightarrow b)$ is compact. Let $F \subseteq D$ be directed, assume $(a \longrightarrow b) \sqsubseteq \sqcup F$. Then $b \sqsubseteq (\sqcup F)(a)$ (by (a)), i.e. $b \sqsubseteq \sqcup\{fa \mid f \in F\}$. Since b is compact, $b \sqsubseteq f(a)$, i.e. $(a \longrightarrow b) \sqsubseteq f$, for some $f \in F$. Therefore $(a \longrightarrow b)$ is compact. Since in general $\sqcup F$ is compact if F is a finite set of compact elements and $\sqcup F$ exists, each $b' \in B$ is compact. We show that B is a basis. Let $f \in D$,

$$M_f := \{(a \longrightarrow b) \mid (a \longrightarrow b) \sqsubseteq f\}.$$

Then f is an upper bound of M_f. Let $g \in D$ be another upper bound of M_f. We have $b \sqsubseteq fa \Rightarrow (a \longrightarrow b) \sqsubseteq f \Rightarrow (a \longrightarrow b) \sqsubseteq g \Rightarrow b \sqsubseteq g(a)$, hence $f(a) = \sqcup\{b \mid b \sqsubseteq f(a)\} \sqsubseteq \sqcup\{b \mid b \sqsubseteq g(a)\} = g(a)$ for any $a \in B_1$. Therefore $f \sqsubseteq g$, and $f = \sqcup M_f$. The set M_f is not directed in general. Since M_f is bounded by f, each finite subset $F \subseteq M_f$ is bounded, hence $\sqcup F$ exists for each finite subset $F \subseteq M_f$. We obtain

$$f = \sqcup\{\sqcup F \mid F \subseteq M_f,\ F \text{ finite},\ F \neq \emptyset\}.$$

Each $\sqcup F$ is an element of B and the set $\{\sqcup F \mid F \subseteq M_f,\ F \text{ finite},\ F \neq \emptyset\}$ is directed. Therefore, B is a basis of D. It remains to show that B is fb-complete (see Theorem 17). For $i = 1,\ldots,n$ let $F_i \subseteq SB$ be finite and bounded. Let $\{\sqcup F_i \mid i = 1,\ldots,n\}$ be bounded. Then $\cup F_i$ is bounded and $\sqcup \cup F_i = \sqcup\{\sqcup F_i\}$.

Q.E.D.

Properties (2a) and (2b) characterize the standard product uniquely up to isomorphism.

29 LEMMA *(characterization of the function space)*

Let $\overline{E}$ be a cpo. Then $\overline{E}$ is isomorphic to $\overline{D} = [\overline{D}_1 \longrightarrow \overline{D}_2]$ iff there is an $([\overline{E} \times \overline{D}_1], \overline{D}_2)$-continuous function $\Gamma : E \times D_1 \longrightarrow D_2$ such that (1) and (2) hold.

(1) $(\forall x \in D)\Gamma(e,x) = \Gamma(e',x) \Rightarrow e = e'$.

(2) For any $([\overline{D}_o \times \overline{D}_1], \overline{D}_2)$-continuous function $\Sigma : D_o \times D_1 \longrightarrow D_2$ there is a $(\overline{D}_o, \overline{E})$-continuous function $\Delta : D_o \longrightarrow E$ such that

$$\Gamma(\Delta(x), y) = \Sigma(x,y)$$

for all $x \in D_o, y \in D_1$.

Γ is called the *universal* function, the *apply* function, or the *evaluation* function. Condition (1) guarantees that the elements of E can be considered as functions rather than as names of functions. Condition (2) is a constructive cpo-version of the translation lemma (Theorem 1.9.7). Lemma 29 corresponds to the Type 1 characterization of the standard numbering φ by the smn-theorem and the utm-theorem (Theorem 1.9.10).

Proof

Assume there is some continuous $\Gamma' : E \times D_1 \longrightarrow D_2$ such that (1) and (2) are satisfied. Since $\Gamma : D \times D_1 \longrightarrow D_2$ with $\Gamma(f,x) = f(x)$ is continuous, there is some continuous $\Delta' : D \longrightarrow E$ such that $f(x) = \Gamma'(\Delta'(f),x)$ for all $f \in D, x \in D_1$. Since Γ' is continuous, by Lemma 28 (2b) there is a continuous function $\Delta : E \longrightarrow D$ such that $\Gamma'(z,x) = \Delta(z)(x)$ for all $z \in E, x \in D_1$. We obtain $f(x) = \Delta\Delta'(f)(x)$ hence

and

$$\delta_\beta(p) = \delta_\beta\Sigma(p).$$

If $\{<i,j>|\beta(i) \sqsubseteq \beta(j)\}$ is r.e., then there are computable functions Γ and Σ in (2) and (3), respectively.

Proof

(1) For any $p \in \mathbb{B}$ and $x \in D$ we have:

$x = \delta_\beta(p)$

$\Longrightarrow \{U_\beta(i)|i \in \mathbb{M}_p\}$ is a base of $V(x)$ (cf. Def. 3.4.7)

$\Longrightarrow (\forall i \in \mathbb{M}_p) x \in U_\beta(i) \wedge (\forall X \in V(x))(\exists i \in \mathbb{M}_p) U_\beta(i) \subseteq X$

$\Longrightarrow (\forall i \in \mathbb{M}_p)\beta(i) \sqsubseteq x \wedge (\forall i,j \in \mathbb{M}_p)(\exists k \in \mathbb{M}_p) U_\beta(k) \subseteq U_\beta(i) \cap U_\beta(j)$

$\wedge (\forall m)(\exists i \in \mathbb{M}_p)(x \in U_\beta(m) \Longrightarrow U_\beta(i) \subseteq U_\beta(m))$

$\Longrightarrow (\forall i \in \mathbb{M}_p)\beta(i) \sqsubseteq x \wedge \{\beta(i)|i \in \mathbb{M}_p\}$ is directed

$\wedge (\forall m)(\exists i \in \mathbb{M}_p)(\beta(m) \sqsubseteq x \Longrightarrow \beta(m) \sqsubseteq \beta(i))$

$\Longrightarrow \{\beta(i)|i \in \mathbb{M}_p\}$ is directed and $x = \bigsqcup\{\beta(i)|i \in \mathbb{M}_p\}$.

On the other hand

$\{\beta(i)|i \in \mathbb{M}_p\}$ is directed and $x = \bigsqcup\{\beta(i)|i \in \mathbb{M}_p\}$

$\Longrightarrow (\forall m)(\beta(m) \sqsubseteq x \Longrightarrow (\exists i \in \mathbb{M}_p)\beta(m) \sqsubseteq \beta(i)) \wedge (\forall i \in \mathbb{M}_p)\beta(i) \sqsubseteq x$

$\Longrightarrow \{U_\beta(i)|i \in \mathbb{M}_p\}$ is a base of $V(x)$

$\Longrightarrow x = \delta_\beta(p)$.

(2) For $w \in W(\mathbb{N})$ define $\mathbb{M}(w) := \{i|(\exists k < lg(w))w(k) = i+1\}$. For $r,p \in \mathbb{B}$ define a function $h : \mathbb{N} \longrightarrow W(\mathbb{N})$ as follows:

$h(0) := \varepsilon$

$h(n+1) :=$ some $v \in W(\mathbb{N})$ such that $i \in \mathbb{M}(v) \Longleftrightarrow (\exists j \in \mathbb{M}(p^{[n]}))<i,j> \in \mathbb{M}(r^{[n]})$.

Then define $\Gamma' : \mathbb{B} \longrightarrow \mathbb{B}_o$ by

$\Gamma'<r,p> := h(0)h(1)h(2)\ldots$

Γ' is computable by a Type 2 machine. Let $\Gamma'' \in [\mathbb{B} \longrightarrow \mathbb{B}]$ be the canonical restriction of Γ'. By the translation lemma (Theorem 3.2.16(2a)) there is a total computable function $\Delta : \mathbb{B} \longrightarrow \mathbb{B}$ such that $\psi_{\Delta(r)}(p) = \Gamma''<r,p> = \Gamma'<r,p>$ for all $<r,p> \in \mathrm{dom}(\Gamma'')$. Since each $\beta(i)$ is compact, for any $p \in \mathrm{dom}(\delta_\beta)$ we have $\beta(i) \sqsubseteq \delta_\beta(p) \Longleftrightarrow (\exists j \in \mathbb{M}_p)\beta(i) \sqsubseteq \beta(j)$. There is some $r \in \mathbb{B}$ such that $\mathbb{M}(r) = \{<i,j>|\beta(i) \sqsubseteq \beta(j)\}$. Then $\mathbb{M}\Gamma'<r,p> = \{i|\beta(i) \sqsubseteq \delta_\beta(p)\}$ for any $p \in \mathrm{dom}(\delta_\beta)$. Therefore $\Gamma := \psi_{\Delta(r)}$ has the desired property. If $\{<i,j>|\beta(i) \sqsubseteq \beta(j)\}$ is r.e. then there is some computable r, and Γ becomes computable.

(3) Define a function $\Sigma' : \mathbb{B} \longrightarrow \mathbb{B}_o$ as follows:

$\Sigma'<r,p>(0) := 1 + i_o$ (where $\beta(i_o) = \bot$).

For any $n \geq 0$ define

$$\Sigma'<r,p>(n+1) := \begin{cases} \text{div if } \Sigma'<r,p>(n) = \text{div} \\ \Sigma'<r,p>(n) \text{ if } p(n+1) = 0 \text{ and } \Sigma'<r,p>(n) \text{ exists.} \end{cases}$$

Otherwise let k,j be the numbers with $p(n+1) = 1+k$ and $\Sigma'\langle r,p\rangle(n) = 1+j$. Define

$$\Sigma'\langle r,p\rangle(n+1) := 1 + \pi_1^{(4)}\mu\langle m,m_1,m_2,m_3\rangle[p(m_1) = 1 + m \wedge r(m_2) = 1 + \langle k,m\rangle \wedge r(m_3) = 1 + \langle j,m\rangle].$$

The function Σ' is computable. Let $\Sigma'' \in [\mathbb{B} \longrightarrow \mathbb{B}]$ be the canonical restriction of Σ'. By the translation lemma there is a computable function $\Delta : \mathbb{B} \longrightarrow \mathbb{B}$ with $\Sigma''\langle r,p\rangle = \psi_{\Delta(r)}(p)$. There is some $r \in \mathbb{B}$ with $\mathbb{M}(r) = \{\langle i,j\rangle \mid \beta(i) \sqsubseteq \beta(j)\}$. The function $\Sigma := \psi_{\Delta(r)}$ has the desired properties. If $\{\langle i,j\rangle \mid \beta(i) \sqsubseteq \beta(j)\}$ is r.e., then r and Σ can be chosen to be computable.

Q.E.D.

The representation δ_β from Definition 31 is admissible. Therefore by Theorems 3.4.11 and 3.5.15 the $(\overline{D},\overline{D}')$-continuous cpo-functions are exactly the $(\delta_\beta,\delta_{\beta'})$-continuous cpo-functions.

Let $\overline{D}_i = (D_i,\sqsubseteq,\bot,\beta_i)$ be constructive cpo's with standard representations δ_i (see Def. 31) for $i = 1,2$. Constructivity and computability on the set $D_1 \times D_2$ is defined canonically by the representation $[\delta_1,\delta_2]$ (see Def. 3.3.11). By Corollary 3.4.16, the final topology of $[\delta_1,\delta_2]$ is the product of the final topologies of δ_1 and δ_2, i.e. the Scott topologies of $\overline{D}_1$ and $\overline{D}_2$. From Lemma 3.5.26(3) we know that the Scott topology on $[\overline{D}_1 \times \overline{D}_2]$ is equal to the final topology of $[\delta_1,\delta_2]$. We shall now define a constructive product of constructive cpo's by additionally defining a numbering of the basis of the product cpo.

33 <u>DEFINITION</u> *(constructive product)*

Let $\overline{D}_i = (D_i,\sqsubseteq,\bot_i,\beta_i)$ be a constructive cpo $(i = 1,2)$. Let $(D,\sqsubseteq,\bot)$ be the standard product of $(D_1,\sqsubseteq,\bot_1)$ and $(D_2,\sqsubseteq,\bot_2)$ according to Definition 3.5.23. Define a numbering β of the basis B (cf. Lemma 3.5.26(3)) by

$$\beta\langle i,j\rangle := (\beta_1(i),\beta_2(j)).$$

Then $[\overline{D}_1 \times \overline{D}_2] := (D,\sqsubseteq,\bot,\beta)$ is called the *constructive product* (or simply the *product*) of $\overline{D}_1$ and $\overline{D}_2$.

Notice that $\beta = [\beta_1,\beta_2]$ by Definition 2.2.14. For the set $D_1 \times D_2$ we have now different canonical representations: The representation $[\delta_1,\delta_2]$ and the standard representation δ of $[\overline{D}_1 \times \overline{D}_2]$. Fortunately these two representations are computationally equivalent and therefore induce the same kind of constructivity and computability.

34 LEMMA

Let $\overline{D}_i = (D_i, \sqsubseteq, \bot, \beta_i)$ be constructive cpo's with standard representations $\delta_i (i = 1,2)$. Let δ be the standard representation of $[\overline{D}_1 \times \overline{D}_2]$. Then

$$\delta \equiv_c [\delta_1, \delta_2].$$

Proof

By Definition 33 and Theorem 32(1),

$$\delta(p) = \sqcup\{(\beta_1(i), \beta_2(j)) \mid \langle i,j\rangle \in \mathbb{M}_p\}$$

and by Def. 3.3.11,

$$[\delta_1, \delta_2]\langle p,q\rangle = (\delta_1(p), \delta_2(q)) = (\sqcup\{\beta_1(i) \mid i \in \mathbb{M}_p\}, \sqcup\{\beta_2(j) \mid j \in \mathbb{M}_q\}).$$

Now it can be easily proved that δ and $[\delta_1, \delta_2]$ are computationally equivalent (as an exercise, use Lemma 3.5.26).

Q.E.D.

EXERCISES

1) Consider Example 2. In each case i $(i = 1,\dots,11)$ verify that $\overline{D}_i = (D_i, \sqsubseteq_i, \bot_i)$ is a cpo.
2) Show that the cpo from Example 2(5) is a special case of Example 2(10).
3) Let $\overline{D}_i$ $(i = 4,7)$ be the cpo from Example 2(i). Define $\Gamma : \mathbb{P} \longrightarrow P_\omega$ by $\Gamma(p) := \mathrm{dom}(p)$. Show that Γ is $(\overline{D}_7, \overline{D}_4)$-continuous.
4) Let $\overline{D}_i = (D_i, \sqsubseteq, \bot)$ be cpo's $(i = 1,2)$. Show that $\overline{D}_1$ and $\overline{D}_2$ are isomorphic iff there is some function $f : D_1 \longrightarrow D_2$ with $x \sqsubseteq y \Leftrightarrow f(x) \sqsubseteq f(y)$.
5) Prove the statements from Example 4.
6) Prove the statements from Example 5.
7) Prove the statements from Example 8.
8) Let $\overline{D} = (D, \sqsubseteq, \bot)$ be a cpo. Define a relation $< \subseteq D \times D$ as follows:

   $$x < y :\Longleftrightarrow (\forall M \subseteq D, \text{ directed})(y \sqsubseteq \sqcup M \Rightarrow (\exists m \in M)\, x \sqsubseteq m).$$

   (Therefore x is compact iff $x < x$.) Characterize the relation $<$ for all the cases of Example 2.
9) Define $\overline{D} := (D, \sqsubseteq, \bot)$ as follows:

   $$D := P_\omega \times P_\omega$$
   $$(A_1, A_2) \sqsubseteq (B_1, B_2) :\Longleftrightarrow (A_1 \subseteq B_1 \wedge B_2 \subseteq A_2)$$
   $$\bot := (\emptyset, \mathbb{N}).$$

   Prove that $\overline{D}$ is a b-complete algebraic cpo. Characterize the (algebraic) basis of $\overline{D}$.

10) Let $\overline{\mathbb{Q}} := \mathbb{Q} \cup \{-\infty, \infty\}$. Show that the d-completion of $(\overline{\mathbb{Q}}, \leq, -\infty)$ is isomorphic to the cpo $\overline{D}_9$ from Example 2.
11) Characterize those cpo's $\overline{D}$ for which the d-completion of $\overline{D}$ is isomorphic to $\overline{D}$.
12) Consider the cpo $\overline{D} = (D, \sqsubseteq, \bot)$ from Example 2(8). Define an injective mapping $\iota : \mathbb{R} \longrightarrow D$ by $\iota(x) := [x;x]$. Let $f : \mathbb{R} \longrightarrow \mathbb{R}$ be a function. Show that f is continuous iff there is a $(\overline{D},\overline{D})$-continuous function $\overline{f} : D \longrightarrow D$ with $f(x) = \iota^{-1}\overline{f}\iota(x)$ for all $x \in \mathbb{R}$.
13) Show that the extension theorem (Theorem 12) cannot be generalized in such a way that the algebraic basis B is replaced by an arbitrary generating system.
14) Define the fb-completion of a partial order $\overline{A}$ formally, prove that the resulting cpo $\overline{B}$ is fb-complete, and show that $\overline{B}$ is (up to equivalence) the smallest fb-complete partial order into which $\overline{A}$ can be embedded.
15) Let $\mathbb{O}$ be the set of countable ordinals. For $\alpha \in \mathbb{O}$ let $X_\alpha := \{\beta \mid \beta \leq \alpha\}$. Show that $(X_\alpha, \leq, 0)$ is a b-complete algebraic cpo. Characterize the algebraic basis. Is $(\mathbb{O}, \leq, 0)$ a cpo?
16) Consider Example 2(10). Show that the topology induced on X by the Scott topology is the topology derived from the metric.
17) Prove Lemma 20.
18) Complete the proof of Lemma 21.
19) Define a cpo $\overline{D}$ such that $\overline{D}$ is isomorphic to $[\overline{D} + \overline{D}]$.
20) Let $\overline{D}_1$ and $\overline{D}_2$ be algebraic cpo's. Characterize the Scott topologies of $[\overline{D}_1 + \overline{D}_2]$ and $[\overline{D}_1 \times \overline{D}_2]$ by the Scott topologies of $\overline{D}_1$ and $\overline{D}_2$.
21) Prove Lemma 24.
22) Complete the proof of Lemma 25.
23) Complete the proof of Lemma 29.
24) Let $\overline{D}_o, \overline{D}_1$, and $\overline{D}_2$ be b-complete algebraic cpo's. Prove that each of the following pairs of cpo's is isomorphic.
    (a) $[\overline{D}_o + \overline{D}_1]$ and $[\overline{D}_1 + \overline{D}_o]$.
    (b) $[\overline{D}_o \times \overline{D}_1]$ and $[\overline{D}_1 \times \overline{D}_o]$.
    (c) $[\overline{D}_o \times [\overline{D}_1 \times \overline{D}_2]]$ and $[[\overline{D}_o \times \overline{D}_1] \times \overline{D}_2]$
    (d) $[[\overline{D}_o \times \overline{D}_1] \longrightarrow \overline{D}_2]$ and $[\overline{D}_o \longrightarrow [\overline{D}_1 \longrightarrow \overline{D}_2]]$.
    (e) $[[\overline{D}_o \longrightarrow \overline{D}_1] \times [\overline{D}_o \longrightarrow \overline{D}_2]]$ and $[\overline{D}_o \longrightarrow [\overline{D}_1 \times \overline{D}_2]]$.
25) Let $\overline{D}$ be a cpo, let $f : D \longrightarrow D$ be isotone (not necessarily continuous). Show that f has a least fixed point. (Hint: Define an ordinal sequence x_α inductively by $x_o = \bot$, $x_{\alpha+1} = f(x_\alpha)$, $x_\beta = \sqcup\{x_\alpha \mid \alpha < \beta\}$ if β is a limit ordinal.)
26) Consider the proof of Theorem 32(3). Verify that Σ has the desired properties.
27) Prove Lemma 34.

BIBLIOGRAPHICAL NOTES

One of the pioneering papers in which the use of cpo's is suggested for defining the semantics of programming languages is Scott (1970). There are a large number of publications on cpo's but most of them are not selfcontained or are difficult to read. Good books treating the theory of cpo's are Stoy (1977), Milne and Strachey (1976), and Loeckx and Sieber (1984). In particular two unpublished papers by D. Scott (1981) (1982) are worth reading.

3.6 Type 1 Computability and Type 2 Computability

For any representation δ there is a derived numbering ν_δ, defined by $\nu_\delta(i) := \delta\varphi_i$, of the δ-computable elements. In this chapter the relation between δ-computability and ν_δ-computability is investigated. It is easy to show that the restriction of a (δ,δ')-computable function to the computable elements is $(\nu_\delta,\nu_{\delta'})$-computable. The converse does not seem to be true in general. Only for two special cases a positive answer is known: for "effective" metric spaces (special cases have been proved independently by Ceitin, by Kreisel, Lacombe, and Shoenfield, and by Moschovakis) and for "computable" cpo's (a special case has been proved by Myhill and Sheperdson). As a corollary we obtain a theorem which characterizes the ν_δ-r.e. subsets of the δ-computable elements for "computable" cpo's (Rice / Shapiro theorem). The proofs of the main theorems are rather sophisticated.

In Chapters 3.1 and 3.2 we have investigated computability and constructivity for functions on Baire's space $\mathbb{B}$. We have already defined the computable elements of $\mathbb{B}$ (namely the total recursive functions) in Part 1. If a set M is represented by a representation δ, then the δ-computable elements of M are those with computable names. The δ-computable elements can be numbered canonically.

1 <u>DEFINITION</u> (*standard numbering of δ-computable elements*)

Let $\delta : \mathbb{B} \dashrightarrow M$ be a representation.

(1) $x \in M$ is called δ-computable iff $x = \delta(p)$ for some computable $p \in \mathbb{B}$.

(2) The standard numbering $\nu_\delta : \mathbb{N} \dashrightarrow M_c$ of the set of δ-computable elements is defined by

$$\mathrm{dom}(\nu_\delta) := \{i \mid \varphi_i \in \mathrm{dom}(\delta)\},$$

$$\nu_\delta(i) := \delta\varphi_i$$

for all $i \in \mathrm{dom}(\nu_\delta)$.

Since φ is a precomplete numbering, ν_δ is precomplete for any representation δ.

2 EXAMPLES

(1) The $\mathbb{M}$-computable elements are the recursively enumerable subsets of $\mathbb{N}$, and $\nu_{\mathbb{M}}$ is the numbering V_2 which is equivalent to the standard numbering W (where $W_i = \mathrm{dom}(\varphi_i)$) of the set of r.e. subsets of $\mathbb{N}$ (see Theorem 2.3.10).

(2) The $\mathbb{M}_{cf}$-computable elements are the recursive subsets of $\mathbb{N}$. The standard numbering ν of the set of $\mathbb{M}_{cf}$-computable elements is the numbering Z from Definition 2.3.8.

(3) The $1\!\!1_{\mathbb{B}}$-computable elements of $\mathbb{B}$ are the total recursive functions. $\nu_{1\!\!1_{\mathbb{B}}}$ is the restriction of φ to $\{i \mid \varphi_i \in R^{(1)}\}$.

(4) The computable elements of $[\mathbb{B} \longrightarrow \mathbb{B}_o]$ ($[\mathbb{B} \longrightarrow \mathbb{B}]$, $[\mathbb{B} \longrightarrow \mathbb{N}]$) (Def. 3.1.23, 3.2.1) are the $\hat{\psi}$-(ψ-, χ-) computable elements (Def. 3.2.4, 3.2.9).

Computable functions on $\mathbb{B}$ map computable elements uniformly into computable elements.

3 THEOREM

(1) There is a computable function $f : \mathbb{N}^3 \dashrightarrow \mathbb{N}$ such that

$$f(i,j,x) = \hat{\psi}(\varphi_i)(\varphi_j)(x)$$

for all i,j,x with $\varphi_i, \varphi_j \in \mathbb{B}$.

(2) There is a computable function $g : \mathbb{N}^2 \longrightarrow \mathbb{N}$ such that

$$\varphi_{g(i,j)} = \psi(\varphi_i)(\varphi_j)$$

for all i,j with $\varphi_i, \varphi_j \in \mathbb{B}$ and $\varphi_j \in \mathrm{dom}(\psi(\varphi_i))$.

(3) There is a computable function $h \in P^{(2)}$ such that

$$\chi(\varphi_i)(\varphi_j) = h(i,j)$$

for all i,j with $\varphi_i, \varphi_j \in \mathbb{B}$.

Notice that in (2) the equation may fail if $\varphi_j \notin \mathrm{dom}\psi(\varphi_i)$. The representations ψ and χ are introduced in Chapter 3.2. By Property (2), the restriction of any computable function $\Gamma : \mathbb{B} \dashrightarrow \mathbb{B}$ to the computable elements is (φ,φ)-computable, by (3) the restriction of any computable function $\Sigma \in [\mathbb{B} \longrightarrow \mathbb{N}]$ to $R^{(1)}$ is strongly $(\varphi, 1\!\!1_{\mathbb{N}})$-computable (see Chapter 2.2).

Proof

(1) Let $\Delta_u : \mathbf{B} \longrightarrow \mathbf{B}_o$ be the universal function of the representation $\hat{\Psi} : \mathbf{B} \longrightarrow [\mathbf{B} \longrightarrow \mathbf{B}_o]$. By Theorem 3.2.5, Definition 3.1.23, and Definition 3.1.8, Δ_u has a computable extension $\Gamma : \mathbf{B}_o \longrightarrow \mathbf{B}_o$ for which the set $Z = \{(v,w) \subseteq W(\mathbb{N}) \times W(\mathbb{N}) \mid w \sqsubseteq \Gamma(v)\}$ is $[\nu^*,\nu^*]$-r.e. There is some total recursive function $r : \mathbb{N} \longrightarrow \mathbb{N}$ such that $Z = \{(\nu^*(i),\nu^*(j)) \mid \langle i,j\rangle \in \text{range}(r)\}$. Define $p \in P^{(3)}$ by

$$p(i,j,x) = \pi_1^{(3)}\mu\langle n,m,t\rangle\ [(\forall k \le m)(\Phi_i(k) \le t \wedge \Phi_j(k) \le t) \wedge \lg \nu^*\pi_1 r(n) \le m \wedge \nu^*\pi_1 r(n) \sqsubseteq \langle\varphi_i,\varphi_j\rangle \wedge \lg \nu^*\pi_2 r(n) > x]$$

for all $i,j,x \in \mathbb{N}$ (where $\langle\varphi_i,\varphi_j\rangle(2m) := \varphi_i(m)$, $\langle\varphi_i,\varphi_j\rangle(2m+1) := \varphi_j(m)$, cf. Def. 3.2.2, and $v \sqsubseteq \varphi_k$ iff $v(x) = \varphi_k(x)$ for all $x < \lg(v)$).

Define $f : \mathbb{N}^3 \dashrightarrow \mathbb{N}$ by

$$f(i,j,x) := \nu^*\pi_2 r p(i,j,x)(x)\ .$$

Then f is computable and $f(i,j,x) = \hat{\Psi}(\varphi_i)(\varphi_j)(x)$ if $\varphi_i,\varphi_j \in R^{(1)}$.

(2) By the translation lemma for φ (Theorem 1.9.7) there is a function $g \in R^{(2)}$ with $\varphi_{g(i,j)}(x) = f(i,j,x)$. This function has the desired property.

(3) Define h by $h(i,j) := f(i,j,0)$.

Q.E.D.

The numberings derived from the representations $\hat{\Psi}$, ψ, and χ satisfy smn- and utm-theorems (cf. Chapter 2.1).

4 THEOREM

(1) The numbering $\nu_{\hat{\Psi}}$ of the computable functions from $[\mathbf{B} \longrightarrow \mathbf{B}_o]$ satisfies the utm-theorem and the translation lemma:

(a) There is a computable function $\Gamma : \mathbf{B} \longrightarrow \mathbf{B}_o$ with

$$\Gamma\langle i,p\rangle = \nu_{\hat{\Psi}}(i)(p)$$

whenever $\varphi_i, p \in \mathbf{B}$.

(b) For all computable functions $\Delta : \mathbf{B} \longrightarrow \mathbf{B}_o$ there is a function $g \in R^{(1)}$ such that

$$\nu_{\hat{\Psi}} g(i)(p) = \Delta\langle i,p\rangle$$

for all $\langle i,p\rangle \in \mathbf{B}$.

(2) (correspondingly for ψ instead of $\hat{\Psi}$)

(3) (correspondingly for χ instead of $\hat{\Psi}$)

Proof

(1) Let $r : \mathbb{N} \longrightarrow \mathbb{N}$ be the computable function defined in the proof of Theorem 3(1). Define a computable function $\Gamma_1 : \mathbb{B} \dashrightarrow \mathbb{N}$ by

$$\Gamma_1\langle i,x,p\rangle := \pi_1^{(3)}\mu\langle n,m,t\rangle[(\forall k \le m)\Phi_i(k) \le t \wedge \lg \nu^*\pi_1 r(n) \le m \wedge \lg \nu^*\pi_2 r(n) > x \wedge \nu^*\pi_1 r(n) \sqsubseteq \langle\varphi_i,p\rangle]$$

and define Γ by

$$\Gamma\langle i,p\rangle(x) := \nu^*\pi_2 r\Gamma_1\langle i,x,p\rangle(x) .$$

Then Γ is computable (by a Type 2 machine) and has the desired properties. On the other hand, let $\Delta : \mathbb{B} \longrightarrow \mathbb{B}_o$ be computable. There are computable functions $\Delta_1 : \mathbb{B} \longrightarrow \mathbb{B}$ and $s : \mathbb{N} \longrightarrow \mathbb{N}$ such that $\Delta_1\langle\varphi_{s(i)},p\rangle = \langle i,p\rangle$ for all $\langle i,p\rangle \in \mathbb{B}$. By the translation lemma (Theorem 3.2.5) for $\hat{\Psi}$ there is a computable function $\Sigma : \mathbb{B} \longrightarrow \mathbb{B}$ with $\Delta\Delta_1\langle q,p\rangle = \hat{\Psi}_{\Sigma(q)}(p)$ for all $p,q \in \mathbb{B}$. By Theorem 3 there is a function $t \in R^{(1)}$ with $\Sigma(\varphi_i) = \varphi_{t(i)}$ if $\varphi_i \in R^{(1)}$. We obtain $\Delta\langle i,p\rangle = \Delta\Delta_1\langle\varphi_{s(i)},p\rangle = = \hat{\Psi}_{\varphi_{ts(i)}}(p) = \nu_{\Psi}(ts(i))(p)$. Define $g := ts$.

(2) and (3) are left to the exercises.

Q.E.D.

In Chapter 3.1 (Theorem 24) we have characterized the computable functions $\Gamma : \mathbb{C} \longrightarrow \mathbb{C}_o$ by means of oracle machines (Chapter 2.10). On the other hand, oracle computability can be defined via computability on $\mathbb{B}$. Define a numbering ζ of functions $2^{\mathbb{N}} \times \mathbb{N} \dashrightarrow \mathbb{N}$ as follows:

$$\zeta(i)(A,n) := \nu_\chi(i)\langle n,cf_A\rangle$$

Then ζ is a (partial) numbering of the oracle computable functions $2^{\mathbb{N}} \times \mathbb{N} \dashrightarrow \mathbb{N}$ which is equivalent to the standard numbering η from Def. 2.10.5 (as an exercise).

The restriction of a (δ,δ')-computable function to the computable elements is $(\nu_\delta,\nu_{\delta'})$-computable. We prove a uniform version.

5 THEOREM (*(δ,δ')-computability* $\Longrightarrow$ *$(\nu_\delta,\nu_{\delta'})$-computability*)

There is a total recursive function $r \in R^{(1)}$ with the following property. If $\delta : \mathbb{N} \dashrightarrow M$ and $\delta' : \mathbb{N} \dashrightarrow M'$ are representations and $f : M \dashrightarrow M'$ is (δ,δ')-computable via $\psi(\varphi_i)$, then the restriction $\overline{f}$ of f to the δ-computable elements of M is $(\nu_\delta,\nu_{\delta'})$-computable via $\varphi_{r(i)}$.

Proof

Let $g \in R^{(2)}$ be the function from Theorem 3(2) with $\varphi_{g(i,j)} = \psi(\varphi_i)(\varphi_j)$ for all i,j with $\varphi_i \in \mathbf{B}$ and $\varphi_j \in \mathrm{dom}(\psi(\varphi_i))$. By the translation lemma there is a function $r \in R^{(1)}$ with $g(i,j) = \varphi_{r(i)}(j)$. Let f be (δ,δ')-computable via $\psi(\varphi_i)$. Then for any $j \in \mathrm{dom}(\nu_\delta)$ we have $\overline{f}\nu_\delta(j) = f\delta\varphi_j = \delta'\psi(\varphi_i)(\varphi_j) = \delta'\varphi_{g(i,j)} = \nu_{\delta'}\varphi_{r(i)}(j)$.

Q.E.D.

6 COROLLARY

(1) If $f : M \dashrightarrow M'$ is (δ,δ')-computable then f maps δ-computable elements to δ'-computable elements.

(2) If $f : M \dashrightarrow M'$ is (δ,δ')-computable, then its restriction to the δ-computable elements is $(\nu_\delta,\nu_{\delta'})$-computable.

(3) If $\delta \leq_c \delta'$ then $\nu_\delta \leq \nu_{\delta'}$.

Is every $(\nu_\delta,\nu_{\delta'})$-computable function (δ,δ')-computable? Only very few partial answers are known. Below we shall prove two positive cases, one for cpo's and one for metric spaces.

In Definition 3.3.2 we have introduced the standard representation $\delta_{\mathbb{N}} : \mathbf{B} \longrightarrow \mathbb{N}$ by $\delta_{\mathbb{N}}(p) := p(0)$. Computability w.r.t. $\delta_{\mathbb{N}}$ has already been investigated in Exercises 3.3.2 and 3.3.3. The next theorem shows that effectivity w.r.t. a numbering ν and w.r.t. its derived representation $\nu\delta_{\mathbb{N}}$ are almost the same. The proof is left as an exercise.

7 THEOREM

(1) Let $\delta : \mathbf{B} \dashrightarrow M$ be a representation, let $\nu : \mathbb{N} \dashrightarrow S$ be a numbering and let $f : M \dashrightarrow S$ be a function. Then

f is (δ,ν)-continuous $\iff$ f is $(\delta,\nu\delta_{\mathbb{N}})$-continuous,

f is strongly (δ,ν)-continuous $\Longrightarrow$ f is strongly $(\delta,\nu\delta_{\mathbb{N}})$-continuous.

(correspondingly for *computable* instead of *continuous*)

(2) Let $\nu : \mathbb{N} \dashrightarrow S$ and $\nu' : \mathbb{N} \dashrightarrow S'$ be numberings, let $f : S \dashrightarrow S'$ be a function. Then

f is (ν,ν')-computable $\iff$ f is $(\nu\delta_{\mathbb{N}},\nu')$-computable.

(correspondingly for *strongly computable* instead of *computable*)

For metric spaces there is a weak inverse of Corollary 6(2). It states that under certain conditions a $(\nu_\delta,\nu_{\delta'})$-computable function is continuous and even (δ,δ')-computable. As a natural starting point we choose admissible representations δ (Definition 3.4.17, Theorem 3.4.18) and the derived numberings ν_δ. For proving the theorem, additional effectivity properties are needed. Slightly more special cases of Theorem 8 have been proved independently by Ceitin, by Kreisel, Lacombe, and Shoenfield, and by Moschovakis.

8 THEOREM (*CKLSM*)

Let (M,d) ((M',d')) be a metric space, let α (α') be a total numbering of a dense subset, and let δ_α (δ'_α) be the Cauchy-representation of (M,d) w.r.t. α (of (M',d') w.r.t. α'). Define $\nu_\alpha := \nu_{\delta_\alpha}$ and $\nu'_\alpha := \nu_{\delta'_\alpha}$. Additionally assume the following properties:

(a) $\{\langle i,j,k\rangle \mid d(\alpha(i),\alpha(j)) < \nu_Q(k)\}$ is r.e.,

(b) $\{\langle i,j,k\rangle \mid d'(\alpha'(i),\alpha'(j)) < \nu_Q(k)\}$ is r.e.,

(c) $\{\langle i,j,k\rangle \mid d'(\alpha'(i),\alpha'(j)) > \nu_Q(k)\}$ is r.e.

(where ν_Q is the standard numbering of the rational numbers). Let $f : M_c \dashrightarrow M'_c$ be a (ν_α,ν'_α)-computable function from the δ_α-computable elements of M to the δ'_α-computable elements of M'. Assume that there is some r.e. set $E \subseteq \mathrm{dom}(f\nu_\alpha)$ such that $\nu_\alpha(E)$ is dense in dom(f). Define $F : M \dashrightarrow M'$ by

$$\mathrm{dom}(F) := \mathrm{dom}(f) , \quad F(x) := f(x) \quad \text{for all } x \in \mathrm{dom}(f) .$$

Then F is $(\delta_\alpha,\delta'_\alpha)$-computable. Especially, F and f are continuous.

There are special cases in which the assumption that E exists can be omitted, but it is unknown whether it is necessary for the general case. Therefore, there might exist (ν_α,ν'_α)-computable functions which are not continuous.

Proof

Let $U_{\langle i,n\rangle} := B(\alpha(i);2^{-n})$ and define $\delta : \mathbb{B} \dashrightarrow M$ by $\delta(p) = x$, iff $\{U_k \mid k \in \mathbb{M}_p\}$ is a base of neighbourhoods of x and $(\forall m)(\exists\langle i,n\rangle \in \mathbb{M}_p) m \le n$. Then $\delta \equiv_c \delta_\alpha$ and $\nu := \nu_\delta \equiv \nu_\alpha$. Define U', δ', and ν' correspondingly for (M',d') and α'. It suffices to show the Theorem for $(\delta,\delta',\nu,\nu')$ instead of $(\delta_\alpha,\delta'_\alpha,\nu_\alpha,\nu'_\alpha)$. Since f is (ν,ν')-computable and φ is precomplete, there is some $g \in R^{(1)}$ such that $f\nu(i) = \nu' g(i)$ for all $i \in \mathrm{dom}(f\nu)$. For $y,n \in \mathbb{N}$ define $Y(y,n) \subseteq M$ as follows:

$$Y(y,n) \text{ exists} \;:\Longleftrightarrow\; \{0,\dots,n\} \subseteq \mathrm{dom}(\varphi_y)$$

$$Y(y,n) := \bigcap \{U_i \mid (\exists j \le n)\ \varphi_y(j) = 1+i\}$$

Accordingly $Y'(y,n)$ is defined by means of U'. Define a predicate Cons on $\mathbb{N}^2$ as follows:

$$\mathrm{Cons}(y,n) \;:\Longleftrightarrow\; (\exists i)\ \alpha'(i) \in Y'(g(y),n)$$

Especially $\mathrm{Cons}(y,n)$ is false if $Y'(g(y),n)$ does not exist. Therefore, $\mathrm{Cons}(y,n)$ holds iff the word $\varphi_{g(y)}(0)\dots\varphi_{g(y)}(n)$ is the prefix of some $p \in \mathrm{dom}(\delta')$. Define a set $A \subseteq \mathbb{N}$ as follows. $\langle y,z,m\rangle \in A$ iff

$$(\exists i,j,\bar{n},c,d)\ [\mathrm{Cons}(y,\bar{n}) \wedge \varphi_{g(y)}(\bar{n}) = 1 + \langle i,c\rangle$$
$$\wedge\ 1 + \langle j,d\rangle \in \mathrm{range}\ \varphi_{g(z)} \wedge d'(\alpha'(i),\alpha'(j)) + 2^{-c} + 2^{-d} < 2^{-m}]\ .$$

By Property (b), the set A is recursively enumerable. If $y,z \in \mathrm{dom}(f\nu)$ and $m \in \mathbb{N}$, then $\langle y,z,m\rangle \in A \Longleftrightarrow d'(\nu'g(y),\nu'g(z)) < 2^{-m}$. Let $a \in \mathbb{N}$ such that $A = \mathrm{dom}\ \Phi_a$. Define a set $B \subseteq \mathbb{N}$ as follows. $\langle y,m,w,k\rangle \in B$ iff

$$k \in E \wedge \nu(k) \in Y(y,w) \wedge (\exists \bar{m},i,c)\ [\mathrm{Cons}(y,\bar{m}) \wedge c > m \wedge \varphi_{g(y)}(\bar{m}) = 1 + \langle i,c\rangle$$
$$\wedge\ d'(\alpha'(i),\nu'g(k)) > 2^{-m} + 2^{-c}]\ .$$

By Properties (a) and (c), B is recursively enumerable. The property $(\exists \bar{m},i,c)\ [\dots]$ guarantees that $\nu'g(k) \notin Y'(g(y),\bar{m})$ for some $\bar{m}$ with $\mathrm{Cons}(y,\bar{m})$. Let $b \in \mathbb{N}$ such that $B = \mathrm{dom}\ \Phi_b$. Define $h \in P^{(3)}$ by

$$h(y,m,w) := \pi_1 \mu\langle k,t\rangle[\Phi_b\langle y,m,w,k\rangle = t]\ .$$

Thus, $h(y,m,w)$ is "the first" $k \in \mathbb{N}$ such that $\langle y,m,w,k\rangle \in B$. By the recursion theorem for φ (Corollary 2.5.7(3)) there is some function $r \in R^{(2)}$ with

$$\varphi_{r(y,m)}(x) = \begin{cases} \varphi_y(x) & \text{if } \Phi_a\langle y,r(y,m),m\rangle \not< x \\ \varphi_k(x) & \text{if } w := \Phi_a\langle y,r(y,m),m\rangle < x \text{ exists and } k := h(y,m,w) \text{ exists} \\ \text{div} & \text{otherwise} \end{cases}$$

for all $y,m,x \in \mathbb{N}$.

<u>Proposition 1</u>: $\Phi_a\langle y,r(y,m),m\rangle$ exists if $y \in \mathrm{dom}(f\nu)$ and $m \in \mathbb{N}$.

<u>Proof (1)</u>: Suppose that $\Phi_a\langle y,r(y,m),m\rangle$ does not exist. Then $\varphi_{r(y,m)} = \varphi_y$, hence $f\nu r(y,m) = f\nu(y)$, and $f\nu r(y,m)$ and $f\nu(y)$ have neighbourhood balls the centers of which have distance less than 2^{-m}. Therefore $\langle y,r(y,m),m\rangle \in A$, which is a contradiction.
q.e.d. (1)

<u>Proposition 2</u>: If $w := \Phi_a\langle y,r(y,m),m\rangle$ exists then $h(y,m,w)$ does not exist.

<u>Proof (2)</u>: Suppose that $k := h(y,m,w)$ exists. Then $\langle y,m,w,k\rangle \in B$. Since $\nu(k) \in Y(y,w)$, $\varphi_{r(y,m)}$ enumerates a base of the neighbourhoods of $\nu(k)$, hence

$\nu r(y,m) = \nu(k)$. Since $k \in \mathrm{dom}(f\nu)$, we obtain $\nu' gr(y,m) = \nu' g(k)$. Since $\Phi_a \langle y,r(y,m),m \rangle$ exists there are numbers $i',j',\bar{n},c',d'$ such that $\mathrm{Cons}(y,\bar{n})$, $\varphi_{g(y)}(\bar{n}) = 1 + \langle i',c' \rangle$, $1 + \langle j',d' \rangle \in \mathrm{range}\ \varphi_{gr(y,m)}$ and

$$d'(\alpha'(i'),\alpha'(j')) + 2^{-c'} + 2^{-d'} < 2^{-m} .$$

We obtain

$$\begin{aligned} d'(\alpha'(i'),\nu' g(k)) &= d'(\alpha'(i'),\nu' gr(y,m)) \\ &\le d'(\alpha'(i'),\alpha'(j')) + d'(\alpha'(j'),\nu' gr(y,m)) \\ &< 2^{-m} - 2^{-c'} - 2^{-d'} + 2^{-d'} \\ &= 2^{-m} - 2^{-c'} . \end{aligned}$$

Since $\langle y,m,w,k \rangle \in B$, there are numbers $\bar{m},i,c$ such that $\mathrm{Cons}(y,\bar{m})$, $\varphi_{g(y)}(\bar{m}) = 1 + \langle i,c \rangle$, and

$$d'(\alpha'(i),\nu' g(k)) > 2^{-m} + 2^{-c} .$$

Since $\mathrm{Cons}(y,\bar{m})$ and $\mathrm{Cons}(y,\bar{n})$, the intersection $B(\alpha'(i');2^{-c'}) \cap B(\alpha'(i);2^{-c})$ contains some $v \in M'$.

The above inequalities yield:

$$\begin{aligned} d'(v,\nu' g(k)) &\le d'(v,\alpha'(i')) + d'(\alpha'(i'),\nu' g(k)) \\ &< 2^{-c'} + 2^{-m} - 2^{-c'} \\ &= 2^{-m} \end{aligned}$$

and

$$\begin{aligned} d'(v,\nu' g(k)) &\ge d'(\alpha'(i),\nu' g(k)) - d'(v,\alpha'(i)) \\ &> 2^{-m} + 2^{-c} - 2^{-c} \\ &= 2^{-m} . \end{aligned}$$

This is a contradiction.

q.e.d. (2)

As an immediate consequence we obtain Proposition 3.

Proposition 3: Let $m,y,w,k,\bar{m},i,c$ be numbers which satisfy the following properties:

- $w = \Phi_a \langle y,r(y,m),m \rangle$
- $k \in E$
- $\nu(k) \in Y(y,w)$
- $\mathrm{Cons}(y,\bar{m})$
- $\varphi_{g(y)}(\bar{m}) = 1 + \langle i,c \rangle$
- $c > m$

Then $d'(\alpha'(i),\nu'g(k)) < 2\cdot 2^{-m}$.

Proof (3): (immediate from Proposition 2 and the definition of B)
We define a computable function $\Gamma : \mathbb{B} \longrightarrow \mathbb{B}_o$ as follows.

$$\Gamma(p)(m) := 0 \quad \text{if} \quad m<3$$

Let $m \geq 3$. If $\Gamma(p)(m-1)$ does not exist then $\Gamma(p)(m) := \text{div}$. Assume that $\Gamma(p)(m-1)$ exists. Find "the first" tuple $\langle y,w,k,\overline{m},i,c\rangle$ such that

$$(\forall w' \leq w)\ \varphi_y(w') = p(w')$$

and that the assumptions of Proposition 3 are satisfied. Since all the conditions are recursively enumerable there is a computable procedure which possibly does not halt for finding an appropriate tuple (use a computation time argument). Define

$$\Gamma(p)(m) := \begin{cases} 1+\langle i,m-3\rangle & \text{if the search is successful} \\ \text{div} & \text{otherwise .} \end{cases}$$

The function Γ is computable. Consider $z \in \text{dom}(f\nu)$. It remains to show that $\delta'\Gamma\varphi_z = f\delta\varphi_z (= f\nu(z))$. First, we show that for all $m \geq 3$ there exist numbers $y,w,k,\overline{m},i,c$ such that the tuple $(m,y,w,k,\overline{m},i,c)$ satisfies the conditions from Prop. 3. Choose $y := z$, $w := \Phi_a\langle z,r(z,m),m\rangle$. Since $\nu(z) \in Y(z,w)$ and $\nu(E)$ is dense in $\text{dom}(f)$, $\nu(k) \in Y(z,w)$ for some $k \in E$. Since $\nu'g(z) = f\nu(z)$ exists, there are numbers $\overline{m},i,c$ with $\text{Cons}(z,\overline{m})$, $\varphi_{g(z)}(\overline{m}) = 1+\langle i,c\rangle$, and $c>m$. Therefore, $\Gamma(\varphi_z)(m)$ exists for all m. Now consider $m \geq 3$. Let $y,w,k,\overline{m},i,c$ be numbers with $\Gamma(\varphi_z)(m) = 1+\langle i,m-3\rangle$ such that the numbers $m,y,w,k,\overline{m},i,c$ satisfy the assumptions of Prop. 3. By Prop. 1, $w_z := \Phi_a\langle z,r(z,m),m\rangle$ exists. Since $\nu(E)$ is dense in $\text{dom}(f)$ there is some $k_z \in E$ with $\nu(k_z) \in Y(z,w) \cap Y(z,w_z)$. Since $(\forall w' \leq w)\varphi_y(w') = \varphi_z(w')$, $\nu(k_z) \in Y(z,w) = Y(y,w)$. From Prop. 3 for $(m,y,w,k_z,\overline{m},i,c)$ we obtain

$$d'(\alpha'(i),\nu'g(k_z)) < 2\cdot 2^{-m} .$$

For z,w_z, and k_z there are numbers $\overline{m}_z,i_z,c_z$ such that $(m,z,w_z,k_z,\overline{m}_z,i_z,c_z)$ satisfy the assumptions of Prop. 3. We obtain

$$d'(\alpha'(i_z),\nu'g(k_z)) < 2\cdot 2^{-m}$$

by Prop. 3 and from the properties of i_z and c_z

$$d'(\alpha'(i_z),\nu'g(z)) \leq 2^{-c_z} < 2^{-m} .$$

The triangle inequality yields

$$d'(\alpha'(i),\nu'g(z)) < 5\cdot 2^{-m}$$

hence $f\nu(z) = \nu'g(z) \in U'_{\langle i,m-3\rangle}$. Therefore, the function $\Gamma(\varphi_z) \in \mathbb{B}$ enumerates a basis of the neighbourhoods of $f\nu(z)$, hence $\delta'\Gamma\varphi_z = f\nu(z) = F\delta\varphi_z$. This shows that the function F is (δ,δ')-computable.
Q.E.D.

The following corollary of Theorem 8 has originally been proved by Kreisel, Lacombe, and Shoenfield.

9 COROLLARY

Let $f : R^{(1)} \dashrightarrow \mathbb{N}$ be a function such that:

(1) f is $(\varphi', 1_{\mathbb{N}})$-computable, where $\varphi' : \mathbb{N} \dashrightarrow R^{(1)}$ is defined by restriction of φ.

(2) There is some recursively enumerable set $E \subseteq \mathrm{dom}(f\varphi')$ such that $\varphi'(E)$ is dense in dom(f).

Then there is a computable function $\Gamma \in [\mathbf{B} \longrightarrow \mathbb{N}]$ which extends f.

Proof

Define a numbering $\alpha : \mathbb{N} \longrightarrow A \subseteq \mathbb{B}$ by $\alpha(i) := (\nu^*(i),0,0,\ldots)$ (see Example 3.4.22(2)). Then $\delta_\alpha \equiv_c 1_{\mathbb{B}}$ and $\nu_\alpha \equiv \varphi'$. Consider the discrete metric space $(\mathbb{N}, d')$ from Example 3.4.22(1). Define α' by $\alpha'(i) := i$. Then $\nu'_\alpha \equiv 1_{\mathbb{N}}$. We conclude that f is $(\nu_\alpha, \nu'_\alpha)$-computable. The conditions (a), (b), and (c) are satisfied by α and α'. Since $\varphi' \equiv \nu_\alpha$, there is some r.e. set $\overline{E} \subseteq \mathrm{dom}(f\nu_\alpha)$ such that $\nu_\alpha(\overline{E})$ is dense in dom(f). By Theorem 8, f has a $(\delta_\alpha, \delta'_\alpha)$-computable extension $F : \mathbb{B} \dashrightarrow \mathbb{N}$. Since $\delta_\alpha \equiv_c 1_B$, there is some computable function $\Sigma : \mathbb{B}_o \longrightarrow \mathbb{B}_o$ with $F(p) = \mathrm{IF}\, 1_B(p) = \delta'_\alpha \Sigma(p) = \Sigma(p)(0)$ for all $p \in \mathrm{dom}(f)$. Let $\Gamma \in [\mathbb{B} \longrightarrow \mathbb{N}]$ be the restriction of Σ according to Definition 3.2.1.
Q.E.D.

Corollary 9 does not state, however, that f is the restriction of some computable $\Gamma \in [\mathbf{B} \longrightarrow \mathbb{N}]$ to $R^{(1)}$.

10 THEOREM (*Friedberg*)

There is a strongly $(\varphi', 1_{\mathbb{N}})$-computable function $f : R^{(1)} \dashrightarrow \mathbb{N}$ which satisfies Condition 2 of Corollary 9 and which is not the restriction of some continuous function $\Gamma \in [\mathbf{B} \longrightarrow \mathbb{N}]$ to $R^{(1)}$.

Proof

Define $\psi \in P^{(1)}$ by

$$\psi(x) := \begin{cases} 0 & \text{if } (\forall y \le x)\ \varphi_x(y) = 0 \text{ or } (\exists z)\ [\varphi_x(z) \text{ exists and } \varphi_x(z) \neq 0 \\ & \wedge (\forall y < z)\ \varphi_x(y) = 0 \wedge (\exists x' < z)\ (\forall u \le z)\ \varphi_{x'}(u) = \varphi_x(u)] \\ \text{div} & \text{otherwise}. \end{cases}$$

It can be shown that $\psi(x) = \psi(w)$ if $\varphi_x = \varphi_w$ for all $x, w \in \mathrm{dom}(\varphi')$. Define $f : R^{(1)} \dashrightarrow \mathbb{N}$ by $f(\varphi'_x) := \psi(x)$. Then f is welldefined and strongly $(\varphi', 1\!\!1_{\mathbb{N}})$-computable. It can be shown that there is an r.e. set $E \subseteq \mathrm{dom}(f\varphi')$ such that $\varphi'(E)$ is dense in dom(f) (as an exercise). Suppose that f is the restriction of $\Gamma \in [\mathbb{B} \longrightarrow \mathbb{N}]$ to $R^{(1)}$. Obviously f_o with $(\forall n)\ f_o(n) = 0$ is in dom(f), hence in dom(Γ). Since Γ is continuous there is some $n \in \mathbb{N}$ such that $[0^n] \subseteq \mathrm{dom}(\Gamma)$, hence $[0^n] \cap R^{(1)} \subseteq \mathrm{dom}(f)$. For any k the function g_k defined by

$$g_k(i) = \begin{cases} 0 & \text{if } i \neq n \\ k & \text{if } i = n \end{cases}$$

is computable hence $g_k \in \mathrm{dom}(f)$. There is some fixed $k > 0$ such that $(\varphi_y(0), \ldots, \varphi_y(n)) \neq (g_k(0), \ldots, g_k(n))$ for all $y < n$. There is some $x > n$ with $\varphi_x = g_k$. Then $f(g_k) = f(\varphi_x) = \psi(x) = \text{div}$ by definition of ψ. This shows $g_k \notin \mathrm{dom}(f)$, a contradiction.

Q.E.D.

As we know, every continuous function $\Sigma : \mathbb{B} \dashrightarrow \mathbb{B}$ has an extension in $[\mathbb{B} \longrightarrow \mathbb{B}]$ (Theorem 3.2.13). Can F in Theorem 8 be extended to a strongly (δ, δ')-computable function? We give positive answer for a special case. More general results can be obtained.

11 THEOREM

Consider Example 3.4.22(3), let $\delta := \delta_U$ and $\nu := \nu_\delta$. Let $f : \mathbb{R}_c \longrightarrow \mathbb{R}_c$ be (ν, ν)-computable. Then f can be extended to a strongly (δ, δ)-computable function $F : \mathbb{R} \dashrightarrow \mathbb{R}$.

It can be shown that the domain of a strongly (δ, δ)-computable function is a computable G_δ-subset of $\mathbb{R}$. The δ-computable numbers $\mathbb{R}_c$ are not a G_δ-subset of $\mathbb{R}$ (as an exercise). The proof of Theorem 11 is left as an exercise.

In Chapter 5 we have studied complete partial orders from the order theoretical and topological point of view. Definition 3.5.31 and Theorem 3.5.32 lead to a natural theory of constructivity and computability on cpo's. In order to obtain interesting and simple results we shall consider algebraic cpo's with denumerable basis and a numbering β of the basis such that $\{\langle i,j\rangle \mid \beta(i) \sqsubseteq \beta(i)\}$ is recursively enumerable (cf. Theorem 3.5.32).

12 DEFINITION (*computable cpo*)

(1) A *computable cpo* is a quadruple $\overline{D} = (D, \sqsubseteq, \bot, \beta)$ such that $(D, \sqsubseteq, \bot)$ is an algebraic cpo and β is a total numbering of its basis such that $\{\langle i,j\rangle \mid \beta(i) \sqsubseteq \beta(j)\}$ is r.e.

(2) Define the representation δ_β of D by

$$p \in \mathrm{dom}(\delta_\beta) \;:\Longleftrightarrow\; \{\beta(i) \mid i \in \mathbf{M}_p\} \text{ is directed}$$

$$\delta_\beta(p) := \sqcup \{\beta(i) \mid i \in \mathbf{M}_p\} \quad \text{for } p \in \mathrm{dom}(\delta_\beta)\,.$$

By Theorem 3.5.32, the definition of δ_β is equivalent to that from Definition 3.5.31 which is canonical because of topological reasons. Many important cpo's are computable according to Definition 12.

13 EXAMPLES

Consider Examples 3.5.2(i). The following numberings yield computable cpo's.

(i=1): Define $\beta(0) := \bot$, $\beta(n+1) := \top$ for all $n \in \mathbb{N}$.

(i=2): Define $\beta(0) := \bot$, $\beta(1) := t$, $\beta(n+2) := f$ for all $n \in \mathbb{N}$.

(i=3): Define $\beta(0) := \bot$, $\beta(n+1) := n$.

(i=4): Define $\beta(i) := e_i$ (Def. 2.2.2).

(i=5): Define $\beta(i) := \nu^*(i)$ (Def. 2.2.2).

(i=6): Let β be a standard numbering of $W(\{0,1\})$.

(i=7): Define $\beta(i)(n) := \mu y[\langle n,y\rangle \in e_i]$.

(i=10): $\{\bot\} \cup A \times \mathbb{N}$ is the basis. Suppose that α is a total numbering of A such that $\{\langle i,j,k\rangle \mid d(\alpha(i),\alpha(j)) < \nu_Q(k)\}$ is recursively enumerable. Define β by $\beta(0) := \bot$, $\beta(1+\langle i,n\rangle) := (\alpha(i),n)$.

For computable cpo's the δ_β-computable elements and the δ_β-computable functions can be characterized directly by means of β.

14 THEOREM

Let $(D,\sqsubseteq,\bot,\beta)$ and $(D',\sqsubseteq,\bot,\beta')$ be computable cpo's.

(1) For any $x \in D$ the following properties are equivalent:

(a) x is δ_β-computable (Def. 1)

(b) there is some r.e. set $A \subseteq \mathbb{N}$ such that $\{\beta(i) \mid i \in A\}$ is directed and $x = \sqcup\{\beta(i) \mid i \in A\}$.

(c) $\{i \mid \beta(i) \sqsubseteq x\}$ is r.e.

(2) Let $f : D \longrightarrow D'$ be continuous. Then the following properties are equivalent:

(a) f is $(\delta_\beta, \delta_{\beta'})$-computable,

(b) there is some r.e. set $C \subseteq \mathbb{N}$ such that for any $i \in \mathbb{N}$ the set $Y_i := \{\beta'(j) \mid \langle i,j\rangle \in C\}$ is directed and $f\beta(i) = \sqcup Y_i$,

(c) the set $Y := \{\langle i,j\rangle \mid \beta'(j) \sqsubseteq f\beta(i)\}$ is r.e.

Proof

(1) This follows from the definitions and from Theorem 3.5.32.

(2) Let f be $(\delta_\beta, \delta_{\beta'})$-computable. There is a computable function $\Gamma \in [\mathbf{B} \longrightarrow \mathbf{B}]$ such that $f\delta_\beta p = \delta_{\beta'}\Gamma(p)$ for all $p \in \mathrm{dom}(\delta_\beta)$. For any $i \in \mathbb{N}$ define $g_i \in \mathbf{B}$ by $g_i(n) := i+1$. Then $\delta_\beta(g_i) = \beta(i)$ and $f\beta(i) = f\delta_\beta(g_i) = \delta_{\beta'}\Gamma(g_i)$. Define $C := \{\langle i,j\rangle \mid (\exists k)\ \Gamma(g_i)(k) = 1+j\}$. Then C has the desired property.
Consider (b). Let $X := \{\langle i,j\rangle \mid (\exists k)\ (\beta'(j) \sqsubseteq \beta'(k) \wedge \beta'(k) \sqsubseteq f\beta(i))\}$. Then X is r.e. and $X = \{\langle i,j\rangle \mid \beta'(j) \sqsubseteq f\beta(i)\} = Y$.
Consider (c). Since f is continuous we obtain

$$\begin{aligned} f\sqcup\{\beta(i) \mid i \in T\} &= \sqcup\{f\beta(i) \mid i \in T\} \\ &= \sqcup\{\sqcup\{\beta'(j) \mid \beta'(j) \sqsubseteq f\beta(i)\} \mid i \in T\} \\ &= \sqcup\{\beta'(j) \mid (\exists i)\ (\beta'(j) \sqsubseteq f\beta(i) \wedge i \in T)\} \end{aligned}$$

for any $T \subseteq \mathbb{N}$ such that $\{\beta(i) \mid i \in T\}$ is directed. The case $T = \mathbf{M}_p$ suggests the following definition. Let $h \in R^{(1)}$ such that $Y = \mathrm{range}(h)$. Define $\Gamma : \mathbf{B} \longrightarrow \mathbf{B}$ by

$$\Gamma(p)\langle i,j,k,n\rangle = \begin{cases} 1+j & \text{if } \langle i,j\rangle = h(n) \text{ and } p(k) = i+1 \\ 0 & \text{otherwise.} \end{cases}$$

Then for any $p \in \mathrm{dom}(\delta_\beta)$ we obtain $f\delta_\beta(p) = \delta_{\beta'}\Gamma(p)$. Since Γ is computable, f is $(\delta_\beta, \delta_{\beta'})$-computable.

Q.E.D.

By Theorem 14, the definition of computability on P_ω (Def. 3.1.3) coincides with computability w.r.t. δ_4, the standard representation of the computable cpo $(P_\omega, \subseteq, \emptyset, e)$

from Example 13(4). The corresponding remark holds for the cpo's with carrier $\mathbb{B}_o$ (Example 13(5)) and $\mathbb{C}_o$ (Example 13(6)). Therefore the theory of cpo's generalizes the explicit definitions of computability from Chapter 3.1. As another example consider the cpo $(\mathbb{P}, \sqsubseteq, \bot, \beta)$ from Example 13(7). Then the δ_β-computable elements are exactly the partial recursive functions. Let $\nu_\beta := \nu_{\delta_\beta}$ be the numbering of the computable elements of $\mathbb{P}$ derived from δ_β according to Definition 1. Then ν_β is equivalent to φ, the standard numbering of $P^{(1)}$.

A function $f : D \longrightarrow D'$ on algebraic cpo's is continuous iff $f^{-1}O$ is open for any open set $O \subseteq D'$ (w.r.t. Scott's topology). We prove now that this property is "computably effective" for computable functions.

15 THEOREM

Let $\overline{D} = (D, \sqsubseteq, \bot, \beta)$ and $\overline{D}' = (D', \sqsubseteq, \bot, \beta')$ be computable cpo's, let U_β ($U_{\beta'}$) be the standard numbering of a base of Scott's topology on $\overline{D}$ (on $\overline{D}'$) (see Definition 3.5.31). Let $f : D \longrightarrow D'$ be a function. Then f is computable iff there is a function $h \in R^{(1)}$ such that

$$f^{-1}(U_{\beta'}(j)) = \cup \{U_\beta(i) \mid i \in W_{h(j)}\}$$

for all $i \in \mathbb{N}$.

Proof

Let f be computable. Then f is continuous and $\{\langle i,j\rangle \mid \beta'(j) \sqsubseteq f\beta(i)\}$ is r.e. There is some $h \in R^{(1)}$ with $W_{h(j)} = \{i \mid \beta'(j) \sqsubseteq f\beta(i)\}$. For any $x \in D$ and $j \in \mathbb{N}$ we obtain

$$\begin{aligned} x \in f^{-1}U_{\beta'}(j) &\iff f(x) \in U_{\beta'}(j) \\ &\iff \beta'(j) \sqsubseteq f(x) = \sqcup \{f\beta(i) \mid \beta(i) \sqsubseteq x\} \\ &\iff (\exists i) \quad (\beta(i) \sqsubseteq x \wedge \beta'(j) \sqsubseteq f\beta(i)) \\ &\iff (\exists i \in W_{h(j)}) \quad x \in U_\beta(i) \\ &\iff x \in \cup \{U_\beta(i) \mid i \in W_{h(j)}\}. \end{aligned}$$

On the other hand, let $h \in R^{(1)}$ be a function with the above property. Then f is continuous since $f^{-1}O$ is open for any open set. We show Property 2(c) of Theorem 14. For any $i,j \in \mathbb{N}$ we have

$$\begin{aligned} \beta'(j) \sqsubseteq f\beta(i) &\iff f\beta(i) \in U_{\beta'}(j) \\ &\iff \beta(i) \in f^{-1}U_{\beta'}(j) \end{aligned}$$

$$\iff (\exists k)\ (k \in W_{h(i)} \wedge \beta(i) \in U_\beta(k))$$

$$\iff (\exists k)\ (k \in W_{h(i)} \wedge \beta(k) \sqsubseteq \beta(i))\ .$$

Therefore, $\{\langle i,j\rangle \mid \beta'(j) \sqsubseteq f\beta(i)\}$ is r.e. and f is computable by Theorem 14.
Q.E.D.

We return to our previous question on the relation between δ-computability and ν_δ-computability. For computable cpo's and their canonical representations there is a strong positive answer.

16 THEOREM (*Myhill / Shepherdson*)

Let $(D,\sqsubseteq,\perp,\beta)$ be a computable cpo, let $\delta := \delta_\beta$, $\nu := \nu_\delta$, D_c := the set of δ-computable elements of D. Let $(D',\sqsubseteq,\perp,\beta')$ be another computable cpo with corresponding parameters δ', ν', and D'_c. For any computable $f : D \longrightarrow D'$ define $Tr(f) : D_c \longrightarrow D'_c$ by $Tr(f)(x) = f(x)$ for all $x \in D_c$ (see Corollary 6(2)).

(1) Let $f : D \longrightarrow D'$ be (δ,δ')-computable. Then $Tr(f)$ is (ν,ν')-computable.

(2) Let $g : D_c \longrightarrow D'_c$ be (ν,ν')-computable. Then there is a unique (δ,δ')-computable function $f : D \longrightarrow D'$ such that $Tr(f) = g$.

Property (1) is Corollary 6(2). There is a similarity between Theorem 8 and Property (2). Notice that in the case of cpo's only total functions are considered.

Proof

(1) (by Corollary 6(2))

(2) First we show that g is isotone and even continuous. Since the basis B of D is a subset of D_c, g is isotone on the basis. By the extension theorem (3.5.12) there is a unique continuous extension $f : D \longrightarrow D'$. Since g is continuous, f extends g. Finally Property 2(c) of Theorem 14 is proved.

Proposition 1: g is isotone.

Proof (1): Let $i,j \in \mathrm{dom}(\nu)$ such that $\nu(i) \sqsubseteq \nu(j)$. Suppose that $g\nu(i) \sqsubseteq g\nu(j)$ is false. By Lemma 3.5.9 there is some $k \in \mathbb{N}$ such that $\beta'(k) \sqsubseteq g\nu(i)$ and $\beta'(k) \not\sqsubseteq g\nu(j)$. There is a function $s \in R^{(1)}$ such that

$$\varphi_{s(z)}(n) = \begin{cases} \varphi_i(n) & \text{if } \Phi_z(z) \not\leq n \\ \varphi_j(n-m) & \text{if } m := \Phi_z(z) \leq n \end{cases} .$$

We obtain $\nu s(z) = \delta\varphi_{s(z)} = \delta\varphi_i = \nu(i)$ if $z \notin K$ and $\nu s(z) = \nu(j)$ if $z \in K$. (Notice that $\varphi_{s(z)} \in \mathrm{dom}(\delta)$ for all z since $\delta\varphi_i \sqsubseteq \delta\varphi_j$.) Therefore $\beta'(k) \sqsubseteq g\nu s(z)$ iff $z \notin K$ by assumption on k. Since g is (ν,ν')-computable there is some $t \in P^{(1)}$ such that $g\nu(n) = \nu' t(n)$ for all $n \in \mathrm{dom}(\nu)$. For any $z \in \mathbb{N}$ we obtain

$$z \notin K \iff \beta'(k) \sqsubseteq g\nu s(z) = \nu' ts(z) = \delta'\varphi_{ts(z)}$$

$$\iff (\exists m,n)\ (\beta'(k) \sqsubseteq \beta'(n) \wedge \varphi_{ts(z)}(m) = 1+n)\ .$$

Therefore, $\mathbb{N}\setminus K$ is recursively enumerable, a contradiction.
q.e.d. (1)

Proposition 2: g is continuous.

Proof (2): The essential part is to prove $g\nu(j) \sqsubseteq \sqcup\{g\beta(i) \mid \beta(i) \sqsubseteq \nu(j)\}$ for all $j \in \mathrm{dom}(\nu)$. Suppose that $j \in \mathrm{dom}(\nu)$ and there is some $k \in \mathbb{N}$ with $\beta'(k) \sqsubseteq g\nu(j)$ and $\beta'(k) \not\sqsubseteq \sqcup\{g\beta(i) \mid \beta(i) \sqsubseteq \nu(j)\}$. By Theorem 3.5.32(3) we may assume $\beta(\varphi_j(n) - 1) \sqsubseteq \beta(\varphi_j(n+1) - 1)$ for all n. There is a computable function $r \in R^{(1)}$ such that

$$\varphi_{r(z)}(n) = \begin{cases} \varphi_j(n) & \text{if } \Phi_z(z) \not\leq n \\ \varphi_j(m) & \text{if } m := \Phi_z(z) \leq n\ . \end{cases}$$

If $z \notin K$, then $\nu r(z) = \delta\varphi_{r(z)} = \delta\varphi_j = \nu(j)$, and if $z \in K$, then $\nu r(z) = \beta(i) \sqsubseteq \nu(j)$ for some $i \in \mathbb{N}$. We obtain $z \notin K$ iff $\beta'(k) \sqsubseteq g\nu r(z)$. Let $t \in P^{(1)}$ with $g\nu(n) = \nu' t(n)$ for all $n \in \mathrm{dom}(\nu)$. Then $z \notin K \Leftrightarrow \beta'(k) \sqsubseteq \nu' tr(z)$, hence $\mathbb{N}\setminus K$ is r.e., a contradiction. Now we prove continuity of g. Let $x \in D_c$ and $Y \subseteq D_c$ such that Y is directed and $x = \sqcup Y$. Since g is isotone, g(Y) is directed and $g(y) \sqsubseteq g(x)$ for all $y \in Y$, hence $\sqcup g(Y) \sqsubseteq g(x)$. Let $\beta(i) \sqsubseteq x$. Then $\beta(i) \sqsubseteq y$ for some $y \in Y$, hence $g\beta(i) \sqsubseteq g(y)$ for some $y \in Y$. We obtain

$$gx \sqsubseteq \sqcup\{g\beta(i) \mid \beta(i) \sqsubseteq x\} \sqsubseteq \sqcup g(Y) \sqsubseteq gx\ .$$

Therefore g is continuous.
q.e.d. (2)

It remains to prove that $Z := \{\langle i,j\rangle \mid \beta'(j) \sqsubseteq f\beta(i)\}$ is recursively enumerable. There is $q \in R^{(1)}$ such that $(\forall n)\ \varphi_{q(i)}(n) = i+1$. Then $\beta(i) = \nu q(i)$ and

$$\begin{aligned} \beta'(j) \sqsubseteq f\beta(i) &\iff \beta'(j) \sqsubseteq f\nu q(i) \\ &\iff \beta'(j) \sqsubseteq g\nu q(i) \\ &\iff \beta'(j) \sqsubseteq \nu' tq(i) \\ &\iff (\exists m,n)\ (\beta'(j) \sqsubseteq \beta'(m) \wedge \varphi_{tq(i)}(n) = 1+m)\ . \end{aligned}$$

Therefore, Z is recursively enumerable. By Theorem 14, f is (δ,δ')-computable.

Q.E.D.

In Chapter 2.3 we have studied, among others, the φ-r.e. subsets of $P^{(1)}$. Lemma 2.3.16 gives necessary conditions for φ-r.e. subsets. We shall now, as a corollary of the Myhill/Shepherdson theorem, prove a characterization of the ν_β-r.e. subsets of D_c, the δ_β-computable elements of a computable cpo. Lemma 2.3.16 is a simple consequence of this theorem.

17 <u>THEOREM</u> (*Rice / Shapiro*)

Let $(D,\sqsubseteq,\bot,\beta)$ be a computable cpo with standard representation δ_β of D and standard numbering ν_β of the set D_c of the δ_β-computable elements. Then

$$X \text{ is } \nu_\beta\text{-r.e.} \iff (\exists Y \subseteq D)\ (Y \text{ is } \delta_\beta\text{-provable} \wedge X = Y \cap D_c)$$

for any $X \subseteq D_c$.

<u>Proof</u>

Let $(D',\sqsubseteq,\bot,\beta')$ be the cpo D_1 from our examples, i.e. $D' = \{\bot,\top\}$, $\sqsubseteq = \{(\bot,\bot),(\top,\top),(\bot,\top)\}$, $\beta'(0) = \bot$, $\beta'(n+1) = \top$. Let $\delta' := \delta_{\beta'}$ and $\nu' := \nu_{\delta'}$. The following propositions characterize the δ-provable sets and the ν-r.e. sets.

<u>Proposition 1</u>: Let ν be a numbering of a set S. Then $X \subseteq S$ is ν-r.e. iff the function $f : S \longrightarrow D'$ with $(f(x) = \top \iff x \in X)$ is (ν,ν')-computable.

<u>Proof (1)</u>: (as an exercise)

<u>Proposition 2</u>: Let δ be a representation of a set M. Then $Y \subseteq M$ is δ-provable iff the function $f : M \longrightarrow D'$ with $(f(x) = \top \iff x \in Y)$ is (δ,δ')-computable.

<u>Proof (2)</u>: (as an exercise)

Now assume that $X \subseteq D_c$ is ν_β-r.e. By Proposition 1 there is a (ν_β,ν')-computable function $f : D_c \longrightarrow D' = D'_c$ such that $X = f^{-1}\{\top\}$. Let $h : D \longrightarrow D'$ be the (δ_β,δ')-computable extension of f (from Theorem 16(2)). Then $Y := h^{-1}\{\top\}$ is δ-provable and $X = Y \cap D_c$. On the other hand let Y be δ-provable and $X = Y \cap D_c$. By Proposition 2 there is a (δ_β,δ')-computable function $h : D \longrightarrow D'$ such that $Y = h^{-1}\{\top\}$. By Theorem 16(1), $f := \mathrm{Tr}(h) : D_c \longrightarrow D'$ is (ν_β,ν')-computable and $f^{-1}\{\top\} = Y \cap D_c = X$, hence X is ν_β-r.e.

Q.E.D.

In Definition 2.8.7 we have introduced the set $T(\sigma)$ of trees over the signature σ which may have ω-ary branching. In Definition 3.4.23 we have defined a standard representation $\delta_\sigma : \mathbb{B} \dashrightarrow T(\sigma)$ of the set $T(\sigma)$, and in Definition 2.8.13 we have introduced a standard numbering ν_σ of the computable trees from $T(\sigma)$. These two definitions are not independent.

18 THEOREM

Let σ be a signature, let $T(\sigma)$ be the set of trees over σ, let δ_σ be the standard representation of $T(\sigma)$, and let ν_σ be the standard numbering of the set $T_c(\sigma)$ of the computable elements of $T(\sigma)$. Then

$$\nu_\sigma \equiv \nu_{\delta_\sigma},$$

especially, $T_c(\sigma)$ is the set of δ_σ-computable elements.

The proof is left as an exercise. A relation between ν_σ-computability and δ_σ-computability which goes beyond Corollary 6 is not known in this case. Consider the algebra $\hat{A} = (\mathbb{O}, \hat{f}, \nu_o)$ with signature σ from Definition 2.8.17 and let $\hat{\nu}$ be the standard numbering of the computable ordinals. Define a standard representation δ of the set $\mathbb{O}$ by $\delta = H\delta_\sigma$. Then $\hat{\nu} \equiv \nu_\delta$ by Theorem 18, i.e. the numbering ν_δ of the δ-computable ordinals derived from the standard representation δ of $\mathbb{O}$ is equivalent to the standard numbering of the computable ordinals.

EXERCISES

1) Complete the proof of Theorem 4.

2) Let (M,τ) be T_o-space (see Chapter 3.4) and let U be a numbering of a base of τ. Let δ_U be the standard representation of M w.r.t. U. Let M_c be the set of δ_U-computable elements of M. Show that a numbering ν of M_c is equivalent to ν_{δ_U}, iff the following properties (1) and (2) hold.

   (1) There is an r.e. set $A \subseteq \mathbb{N}$ such that for any $i \in \mathrm{dom}(\nu)$ the set $\{U_j \mid \langle i,j\rangle \in A\}$ is a base of the neighbourhoods of $\nu(i)$.

   (2) There is a function $f \in P^{(1)}$ such that $\nu f(i) = x$ whenever $\{U_j \mid j \in W_i\}$ is a base of neighbourhoods of $x \in M_c$.

3) Let η be the standard numbering of the oracle computable functions $2^{\mathbb{N}} \times \mathbb{N} \dashrightarrow \mathbb{N}$ (see Definition 2.10.5). Let χ be the standard representation of $[\mathbb{B} \longrightarrow \mathbb{N}]$ (Definition 3.2.9). Define a numbering ζ of functions $2^{\mathbb{N}} \times \mathbb{N} \dashrightarrow \mathbb{N}$ by

   $$\zeta(i)(A,n) := \nu_\chi(i)\langle n, cf_A\rangle .$$

   Prove $\eta \equiv \zeta$.

4) Prove Theorem 7.

5) Let δ, δ' be representations. Prove the following properties:

- $\nu_{[\delta,\delta']} \equiv [\nu_\delta, \nu_{\delta'}]$
- $\nu_{\delta \sqcup \delta'} \equiv \nu_\delta \sqcup \nu_{\delta'}$
- $\nu_{\delta \sqcap \delta'} \equiv \nu_\delta \sqcap \nu_{\delta'}$

6) Consider the proof of Theorem 10. Show that there is a recursively enumerable set $E \subseteq \mathrm{dom}(f\varphi')$ such that $\varphi'(E)$ is dense in dom(f).

7) Let $X \subseteq \mathbb{R}$ be a denumerable set which is dense in $\mathbb{R}$. Show that X is not a G_δ-subset of $\mathbb{R}$.

8) Prove Theorem 11.

9) Show that the cpo's defined in Example 13 are computable.

10) Consider Theorem 14(2). Each of the cases (a), (b), and (c) gives rise to a representation of the continuous functions $f : D \longrightarrow D'$ (cf. Def. 3.3.11(6)). Define these representations and show that they are c-equivalent.

11) Consider Theorem 15. Define a representation $\overline{\delta}$ of continuous functions $f : D \longrightarrow D'$ as follows.

$$p \in \mathrm{dom}(\overline{\delta}) \;:\Longleftrightarrow\; (\forall j)\;\; f^{-1}U_{\beta'}(j) = \cup\,\{U_\beta(i) \mid \langle i,j\rangle \in \mathbf{M}_p\} \text{ for some continuous } f : D \longrightarrow D'.$$

$\overline{\delta}(p)$:= the continuous $f : D \longrightarrow D'$ such that the above property holds.

Prove: $\overline{\delta} \equiv_c [\delta_\beta \longrightarrow \delta_{\beta'}]$ (Def. 3.3.11(6)).

12) Prove a uniform version of the Myhill/Shepherdson theorem:

(a) There is some $h \in P^{(1)}$ such that Tr(f) is (ν,ν')-computable via $\varphi_{h(i)}$ if $f : D \longrightarrow D'$ is (δ,δ')-computable via $\psi(\varphi_i)$ (for all $i \in \mathbb{N}$).

(b) There is some $h \in P^{(1)}$ such that $\mathrm{Tr}([\delta \longrightarrow \delta'](\varphi_{h(i)}))$ extends $g : D_c \longrightarrow D'_c$ if g is (ν,ν')-computable via φ_i.

13) Let $(D, \sqsubseteq, \bot, \beta)$ be a computable cpo.

(a) Show that there is a total representation δ of D such that $\delta \equiv_c \delta_\beta$. Show that such a representation δ is precomplete.

(b) Show that there is a total numbering ν of D_c such that $\nu \equiv \nu_\beta$. Show that such a numbering ν is precomplete.

14) Let $(D',\sqsubseteq,0,\beta')$ be the computable cpo defined by $D' = \{0,1\}$, $\sqsubseteq := \{(0,0),(0,1),(1,1)\}$, $\beta'(0) = 0$, $\beta'(n+1) = 1$. Let $\delta' := \delta_{\beta'}$, $\nu' := \nu_{\delta'}$.

(a) Show that ν' is equivalent to the numbering cf_K, the characteristic function of K (see Theorem 2.5.2).

(b) Let ν be a numbering of a set S, let $X \subseteq S$. Show that X is ν-r.e. iff the function $f: \delta \longrightarrow D'$ with $X = f^{-1}\{1\}$ is (ν,ν')-computable.

(c) Let δ be a representation of a set M, let $X \subseteq M$. Show that X is δ-provable iff the function $f: M \longrightarrow D'$ with $X = f^{-1}\{1\}$ is (δ,δ')-computable.

15) Prove Theorem 18.

16) Show that Lemma 2.3.16 follows from Theorem 17.

BIBLIOGRAPHICAL NOTES

Special versions of Theorem 8 have been proved independently by Ceitin (1959), Kreisel, Lacombe, and Shoenfield (1959) and Moschovakis (1964). A proof of the Kreisel, Lacombe, and Shoenfield version can be found in Rogers (1967). Theorem 10 is from Friedberg (1957). The first version of Theorem 16 for the cpo $\mathbb{P}$ of partial functions has been proved by Myhill and Shepherdson (1955). A more general version for recursive domains is from Egli and Constable (1976). A generalization to certain computable cpo's is from Weihrauch and Deil (1980). Spreen and Young (1984) proved a unified general version of Theorem 8 and Theorem 16. The original version of Theorem 17 is from Rice (1956). Its deduction from Theorem 16 is from Weihrauch and Deil (1980).

3.7 Solving Domain Equations

As we have already noted, cpo's are used for defining the semantics of programming languages. In the theory of semantics, cpo's which satisfy certain recursion equations are needed. Different formalisms for solving such recursion equations have been developed. In this chapter we shall use the cpo theory itself for studying an appropriate class of cpo's. We shall construct a "super cpo", the elements of which are cpo's and solve fixed point equations by applying the fixed point operator to appropriate computable functions on the super cpo.

In Chapter 3.5, Def. 31, we have introduced constructive cpo's. A constructive cpo is a quadruple $(D,\sqsubseteq,\perp,\beta)$ where $(D,\sqsubseteq,\perp)$ is an algebraic cpo and β is a total numbering of its basis B. Now we shall admit that β is a partial numbering. Since we wish that our class of cpo's is closed w.r.t. function space construction we shall consider b-complete cpo's (cf. Def. 3.5.16).

1 DEFINITION (*domain, recursive domain*)

(1) A *domain* is a quadruple $\overline{D} = (D,\sqsubseteq,\perp,\beta)$ such that $(D,\sqsubseteq,\perp)$ is a b-complete algebraic cpo and β is a partial numbering of its algebraic basis. Let DOM_o be the class of all domains.

(2) Define a mapping rel on DOM_o by

$$rel(D,\sqsubseteq,\perp,\beta) := (A,\rho)$$

$$A := dom(\beta)$$

$$\rho := \{(i,j) \in A \times A \mid \beta(i) \sqsubseteq \beta(j)\}$$

(3) A domain $\overline{D} = (D,\sqsubseteq,\perp,\beta)$ is called *recursive* iff the following conditions hold (where $(A,\rho) := rel(\overline{D})$):

(a) A is recursively enumerable.

(b) There is a computable function $f : \mathbb{N}^2 \dashrightarrow \mathbb{N}$ such that $A \times A \subseteq dom(f)$ and

$$f(i,j) = 0 \iff (i,j) \in \rho \quad (\iff \beta(i) \sqsubseteq \beta(j))$$

for all $(i,j) \in A \times A$.

(c) There is a computable function $g : \mathbb{N} \dashrightarrow \mathbb{N}$ such that $\{n \mid e_n \subseteq dom(\beta)\} \subseteq dom(g)$ and

$$g(n) = 0 \iff \beta e_n \text{ is bounded w.r.t. } \rho$$

for all n with $e_n \subseteq \mathrm{dom}(\beta)$.

(d) There is a computable function $h : \mathbb{N} \dashrightarrow \mathbb{N}$ such that

$\beta h(n) = \sqcup_\rho \beta e_n$

if $e_n \subseteq \mathrm{dom}(\beta)$ and βe_n is bounded, w.r.t. ρ .

Remember that by Lemma 2.4.15, $(\exists \beta, \text{total})\ \beta' \equiv \beta$ if dom(β') is recursively enumerable. Obviously every domain with total β is a constructive cpo (Def. 3.5.31), and every recursive domain with total β is a computable cpo (Def. 3.6.12). The constructive cpo's defined in Example 3.6.13 (1) to (7) are recursive domains. Therefore, recursive domains are of particular interest. As we know from Chapter 3.5, every algebraic cpo is determined uniquely up to isomorphism by its basis, and the partial order on the basis of a domain is determined by the pre-order $\{(i,j) \mid \beta(i) \sqsubseteq \beta(j)\}$.

Our main goal is to perform constructions on the class of all domains. Of course, this class has no representation because it is too large; however, it can be partitioned into a sufficiently small set of classes each of which consists of constructively indistinguishable domains.

2 DEFINITION (*constructive equivalence*)

Two domains $\overline{D}_1$ and $\overline{D}_2$ are *constructively equivalent* iff $\mathrm{rel}(\overline{D}_1) = \mathrm{rel}(\overline{D}_2)$.

If $\overline{D}_1$ and $\overline{D}_2$ are constructively equivalent, they are indistinguishable from the constructive point of view. The constructive equivalence class of a domain $\overline{D} = (D, \sqsubseteq, \bot, \beta)$ is uniquely determined by the set $\rho = \{(i,j) \mid \beta(i) \sqsubseteq \beta(j)\}$. From ρ a standard representative of the equivalence class can be constructed. In Chapter 3.5 we have defined the d-completion of a partial order with minimum. The relation ρ is a pre-order which by canonical factorization yields a partial order of equivalence classes [i] together with a numbering β' of these classes defined by $\beta'(i) := [i]$. Notice that $\rho = \{(i,j) \mid \beta'(i) \sqsubseteq \beta'(j)\}$. Therefore d-completion of the partial order on the classes [i] would yield a domain which is constructively equivalent to $\overline{D}$. Below we shall define explicitly the constructive d-completion of appropriate pre-orders.

It is convenient to generalize some concepts from *partial orders* to *pre-orders*. Let $\overline{M} = (M, \rho)$ be a pre-order. Define

$\mathrm{Min}(\overline{M}) = \{m \in M \mid (\forall m' \in M)\ m \rho m'\}$.

Each $m \in \mathrm{Min}(\overline{M})$ is called a *minimum* of $\overline{M}$. For $Y \subseteq M$ the set Sup Y of *least upper bounds* of Y has already been introduced in Def. 2.4.2. A subset $Y \subseteq M$ is *bounded* iff $(\forall y \in Y)\ y \rho a$ for some $a \in M$. A subset $Y \subseteq M$ is called *directed* iff $(\forall a,b \in Y)\ (\exists c \in Y)\ (a \rho c \wedge b \rho c)$, and Y is called *saturated* iff $(\forall y \in Y)\ (\forall m \in M)\ (m \rho y \Longrightarrow m \in Y)$. The pre-order is called *fb-complete* iff $\mathrm{Sup}\, Y \neq \emptyset$ for every finite, non-empty, and bounded subset $Y \subseteq M$.

3 DEFINITION (*constructive d-completion*)

(1) Let

$$D'_s := \{(A,\rho) \mid A \subseteq \mathbb{N},\ \rho \subseteq A \times A,\ (A,\rho) \text{ is an fb-complete pre-order with } \mathrm{Min}(A,\rho) \neq \emptyset\}.$$

(2) For each $(A,\rho) \in D'_s$ define the *d-completion* $(D,\sqsubseteq,\bot,\beta)$ as follows.

$D := \{y \subseteq A \mid y \text{ is } \rho\text{-directed and } \rho\text{-saturated}\}$,

$B := \{\{k \in A \mid k \rho i\} \mid i \in A\}$,

$\bot := \mathrm{Min}(A,\rho)$,

$\sqsubseteq\ := \{(x,y) \subseteq D \times D \mid x \subseteq y\}$,

$\mathrm{dom}(\beta) := A$,

$\beta(i) := \{k \in A \mid k \rho i\}$.

(3) Define a set DOM and a total surjective mapping $\mathrm{cpl} : D' \longrightarrow \mathrm{DOM}$ by

$\mathrm{cpl}(x) :=$ the d-completion of x .

(4) Define a mapping $\zeta : \mathrm{DOM}_o \longrightarrow \mathrm{DOM}$ by

$\zeta(\overline{D}) := \mathrm{cpl}(\mathrm{rel}(\overline{D}))$.

The d-completion of an fb-complete pre-order with minimum on some $A \subseteq \mathbb{N}$ is a domain, and the set DOM of these d-completions represents the constructive equivalence classes of domains. The representative $\zeta(D,\sqsubseteq,\bot,\beta)$ of the constructive equivalence class of $(D,\sqsubseteq,\bot,\beta)$ can be defined directly as follows: $(D',\sqsubseteq',\bot',\beta') := \zeta(D,\sqsubseteq,\bot,\beta)$ where

$D' := \{\{i \mid \beta(i) \sqsubseteq x\} \mid x \in D\}$,

$\bot' := \{i \mid \beta(i) \sqsubseteq \bot\}$,

$\mathrm{dom}(\beta') := \mathrm{dom}(\beta)$,

$\beta'(k) := \{i \mid \beta(i) \sqsubseteq \beta(k)\}$ for all $k \in \mathrm{dom}(\beta)$,

$d' \sqsubseteq e' \;:\Longleftrightarrow\; d' \subseteq e'$ for all $d', e' \in D'$.

The following lemma summarizes the basic properties of the d-completion cpl.

4 LEMMA (*properties of d-completion*)

(1) $\mathrm{cpl}(x)$ is a domain for any $x \in D'_s$ (i.e. $\mathrm{DOM} \subseteq \mathrm{DOM}_o$).

(2) $\zeta(\overline{D}) = \overline{D}$ for any $\overline{D} \in \mathrm{DOM}$.

(3) $\zeta(\overline{D}_1) = \zeta(\overline{D}_2) \iff \overline{D}_1$ and $\overline{D}_2$ are constructively equivalent.

The proof is not difficult (as an exercise).
The reader should compare Definition 3 with Definition 3.5.10 of the d-completion of a partial order with minima. By Lemma 4, ζ maps each domain $\overline{D}$ to its constructively equivalent uniquely determined representative from DOM. Furthermore, the completion mapping $\mathrm{cpl} : D'_s \longrightarrow \mathrm{DOM}$ is bijective. Instead of the whole class DOM_o of domains we shall now investigate the set DOM of representatives. We shall show that by defining $\sqsubseteq$, $\bot$, and β appropriately, we obtain a computable cpo $(\mathrm{DOM} \cup \{\bot\}, \sqsubseteq, \bot, \beta)$ which allows approximation on the set DOM of domains to be described adequately. Since we shall define $\sqsubseteq$, $\bot$, and β by means of properties of the relations $(A,\rho) = \mathrm{rel}(\overline{D})$, it is more convenient to use a cpo the elements of which are fb-complete pre-orders (A,ρ) with minimum.

5 DEFINITION (*super cpo $\overline{D}_s$*)

Define $\overline{D}_s := (D_s, \sqsubseteq, \bot_s, \beta_s)$, where β_s is a total numbering of a set $B_s \subseteq D_s$, as follows.

(1) $D_s := \{(\emptyset,\emptyset)\} \cup D'_s$.

(2) $B_s := \{(A,\rho) \in D_s \mid A \text{ finite}\}$.

(3) $\bot_s := (\emptyset,\emptyset)$.

(4) β_s is a standard numbering of B_s.

(5) For $(A,\rho), (B,\sigma) \in D_s$ define $(A,\rho) \sqsubseteq (B,\sigma)$ by the following conditions.

(a) $A \subseteq B$.

(b) $(\forall i,j \in A)\ (i \rho j \iff i \sigma j)$.

(c) $\mathrm{Min}(\rho) \subseteq \mathrm{Min}(\sigma)$.

(d) (E σ-bounded $\Rightarrow$ E ρ-bounded) for every non-empty finite $E \subseteq A$.

(e) $\mathrm{Sup}_\rho(E) \subseteq \mathrm{Sup}_\sigma(E)$ for every non-empty finite $E \subseteq A$.

The set D'_s has no object with no information. Therefore, a minimum $(\emptyset,\emptyset)$ has to be added explicitly. Notice that $(\emptyset,\emptyset)$ has no d-completion since a cpo must have at least one element. Part(5) of the definition is the most interesting one. If $(A,\rho) \sqsubseteq (B,\sigma)$ then the pre-order (B,σ) can be obtained from the pre-order (A,ρ) by adding vertices and edges provided that the following restrictions are observed.

- No new edge (i,j) may be added for $i,j \in A$ (by (b)).
- If $A \neq \emptyset$ then no "strictly smaller minimum" may be added (by (c)).
- If $E \subseteq A$, $E \neq \emptyset$, is not bounded, no upper bound for E may be added (by (d)).
- If $E \subseteq A$, $E \neq \emptyset$, is bounded (in A), then no "strictly smaller upper bound" may be added (by (e)).

The conditions guarantee that we shall be able to determine a minimum, to decide $i\rho j$, to decide boundedness, and to determine a least upper bound of a finite subset of (A,ρ) from an approximation of (A,ρ) by a directed set of basis elements. For illustrating the definition we give examples of directed subsets of D_s.

6 <u>EXAMPLES</u> (*directed subsets of* D_s)
Consider Examples 3.5.2 and 3.6.13.

(a) The following sequence of elements of $\mathbf{B}_s$ is increasing:

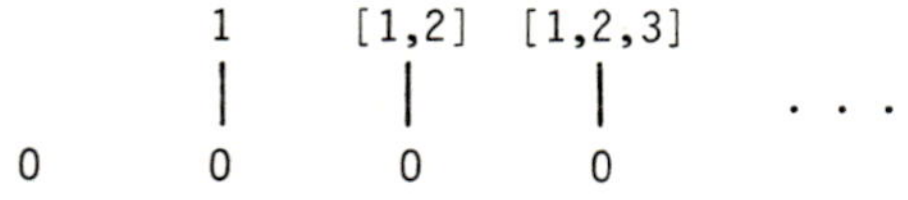

(Numbers which are equivalent are written within brackets.)
The least upper bound of this sequence is the relation $(\mathbb{N},\rho)$ where $\rho = \{(i,j) \mid \beta_1(i) \sqsubseteq \beta_1(j)\}$, β_1 from 3.6.13(1).

(b) The following sequence of elements of B_s is increasing:

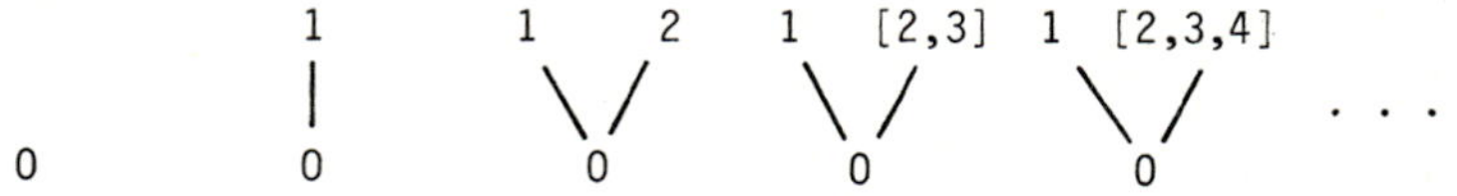

It has the least upper bound $(\mathbb{N},\rho)$, where $\rho = \{(i,j) \mid \beta_2(i) \sqsubseteq \beta_2(j)\}$, β_2 from 3.6.13(2).

(c) The following sequence on B_s is increasing.

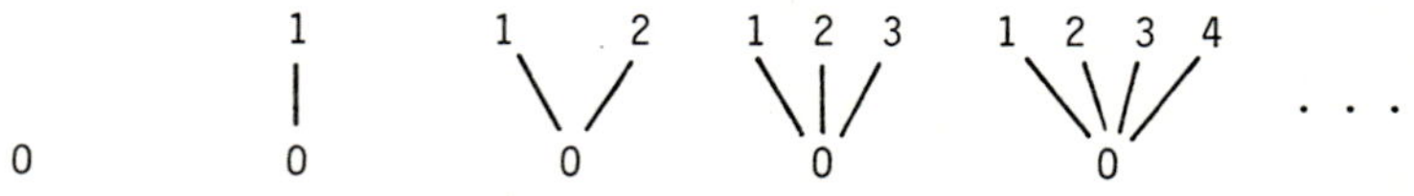

It has the limit $(\mathbb{N},\rho)$ where $\rho = \{(i,j) \mid \beta_3(i) \sqsubseteq \beta_3(j)\}$, β_3 from 3.6.13(3).

(d) The following sequence on B_s is increasing. (Here $\{n_1,\ldots,n_k\}$ denotes the number $m \in \mathbb{N}$ with $e_m = \{n_1,\ldots,n_k\}$.)

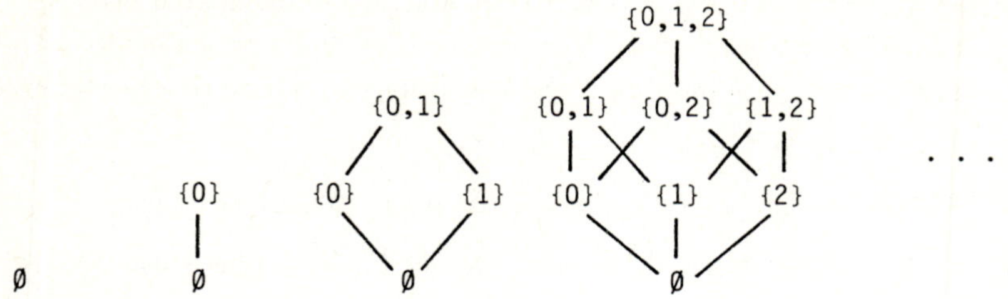

Its limit is the relation $(\mathbb{N},\rho)$ with $\rho = \{(i,j) \mid e_i \subseteq e_j\}$, see 3.6.13(4).

(e) Let β be a bijective standard numbering of $W(\{0,1\})$. We shall denote $i \in \mathbb{N}$ by $\beta(i)$. The following sequence on B_s is increasing.

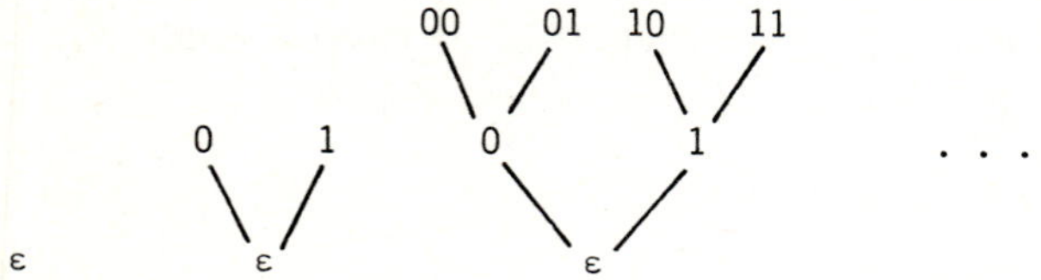

Its limit is the relation $(\mathbb{N},\rho)$ where $\rho = \{(i,j) \mid \beta(i) \sqsubseteq \beta(j)\}$ (see 3.6.13(6)).

The examples show how different domains, more precisely the pre-orders $\{(i,j) \mid \beta(i) \sqsubseteq \beta(j)\}$ characterizing the constructive equivalence classes of these domains, can be generated in $\overline{D}_s$ by chains of basis elements. The laborious but straightforward proof of the next theorem gives some more insight into the definition of $\overline{D}_s$.

7 <u>THEOREM</u>

$\overline{D}_s = (D_s, \sqsubseteq, \bot_s, \beta_s)$ is a constructive cpo such that $\{(i,j) \mid \beta(i) \sqsubseteq \beta(j)\}$ is decidable. Especially, $\overline{D}_s$ is a computable cpo (see Def. 3.6.12).

By the following counterexample $\overline{D}_s$ is not a domain. The two elements

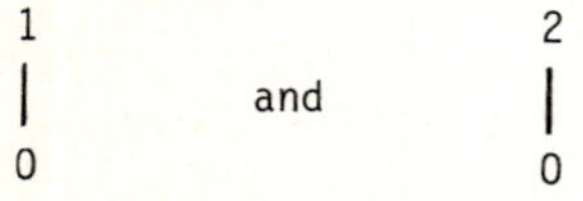

have different incomparable minimal upper bounds:

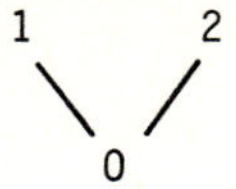

and

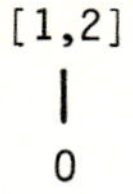

and

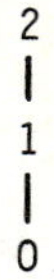

Proof (of Theorem 7)

Proposition 1: $(D_s, \sqsubseteq)$ is a partial order with minimum $(\emptyset,\emptyset)$.

Proof (1): (easy exercise)

Our next aim is to show that $(D_s, \sqsubseteq, \perp_s)$ is a cpo. Let $X \subseteq D_s$ be a non-empty directed set. If $X = \{(\emptyset,\emptyset)\}$, then $\perp_s = \sqcup X$. Assume X is not trivial. For any $x \in D_s$ define $(A_x, \rho_x) := x$. Define a pair (A,ρ) by

$A := \cup \{A_x \mid x \in X\}$,

$\rho := \cup \{\rho_x \mid x \in X\}$.

We want to show $(A,\rho) \in D_s$ and $(A,\rho) = \sqcup X$.

Proposition 2: (A,ρ) is a pre-order.

Proof (2): (as an exercise, use directedness of X)

Proposition 3: $\mathrm{Min}(A,\rho) \neq \emptyset$

Proof (3): Since X is not trivial $(B,\sigma) \in X$ for some $B \neq \emptyset$. Using directedness of X one can show that $\mathrm{Min}(B,\sigma) \subseteq \mathrm{Min}(A,\rho)$.
(as an exercise)

Proposition 4: (A,ρ) is fb-complete.

Proof (4): Let $\{a_1,\ldots,a_n\} \subseteq A$ be ρ-bounded by $b \in A$. Then there are elements $x_i = (A_i,\rho_i) \in X$ with $(a_i,b) \in \rho_i$ for $i = 1,\ldots,n$. Since X is directed, the set $\{x_1,\ldots,x_n\}$ has an upper bound $x \in X$. Then $(a_i,b) \in \rho_x$ for $i = 1,\ldots,n$. Since $\{a_1,\ldots,a_n\}$ is bounded in x, there is some least upper bound $a \in \mathrm{Sup}_x\{a_1,\ldots,a_n\}$. Let $c \in A$ be any upper bound of $\{a_1,\ldots,a_n\}$ in ρ. By the same reasons as above, there is some $y \in X$ such that $(a_i,c) \in \rho_y$ for $i = 1,\ldots,n$. Since X is directed there is an upper bound $z \in X$ of x and y. Since $\{a_1,\ldots,a_n\}$ is bounded in x, y, and z, by (e) we obtain $a \in \mathrm{Sup}_x\{a_1,\ldots,a_n\} \subseteq \mathrm{Sup}_z\{a_1,\ldots,a_n\}$, and c is an upper bound of $\{a_1,\ldots,a_n\}$ in z, hence $(a,c) \in \rho_z$, hence $(a,c) \in \rho$. Therefore $a \in \mathrm{Sup}_\rho\{a_1,\ldots,a_n\}$.
q.e.d. (4)

Proposition 5: $(\forall x \in X)\ \ x \sqsubseteq (A,\rho)$

Proof (5): (as an exercise)

Proposition 6: (A,ρ) is the least upper bound of X.

Proof (6): (as an exercise)

So far it is shown that $(D_s,\sqsubseteq,\bot_s)$ is a cpo.

Proposition 7: B_s consists of compact elements.

Proof (7): (as an exercise)

Let $z \in D_s$, $X_z := \{x \in B_s \mid x \sqsubseteq z\}$. We have to show that X_z is directed and that $z = \sqcup X_z$. For $z = \bot_s$ this is obvious. Assume $z \neq \bot_s$. For any finite $E \subseteq A_z$, $E \neq \emptyset$, with $E \cap \mathrm{Min}(z) \neq \emptyset$ define (where for $G \subseteq \mathbb{N}$, min G is the smallest $i \in G$)

$$A_E := E \cup \{\min \mathrm{Sup}_z C \mid C \subseteq E,\ C \neq \emptyset,\ C \text{ bounded in } z\},$$

$$\rho_E := \rho_z \cap A_E \times A_E .$$

We want to show that (A_E,ρ_E) is a basis element smaller than z.

Proposition 8: $(A_E,\rho_E) \in B_s$, $(A_E,\rho_E) \sqsubseteq z$

Proof (8): A_E is not empty and finite. (A_E,ρ_E) is a pre-order with minimum. We show that (A_E,ρ_E) is fb-complete. Let $B \subseteq A_E$, $B \neq \emptyset$, be bounded in (A_E,ρ_E). B can be decomposed as follows:

$$B = \{b_1,\dots,b_j, \min \mathrm{Sup}_z C_1, \dots, \min \mathrm{Sup}_z C_k\}$$

where $b_1,\dots,b_j \in E$ and $C_1,\dots,C_k \subseteq E$. Since B is bounded, the set $F := \{b_1,\dots,b_j\} \cup C_1 \cup \dots \cup C_k$ is a non empty subset of E which is bounded in z. Therefore, $a := \min \mathrm{Sup}_z F \in A_E$, and $a \in \mathrm{Sup}_{\rho_E}(B)$. For proving $(A_E,\rho_E) \sqsubseteq z$ we have to show Conditions (a),...,(e) of Def. 5(5). Obviously, (a), (b), and (c) hold. Let $D \subseteq A_E$, $D \neq \emptyset$, D bounded in z. Then $a := \min \mathrm{Sup}_z D \in A_E$. Especially, D is bounded in (A_E,ρ_E), $a \in \mathrm{Sup}_{\rho_E} D$, and finally $\mathrm{sup}_{\rho_E} D \subseteq \mathrm{Sup}_z D$. Therefore $(A_E,\rho_E) \sqsubseteq z$.
q.e.d. (8)

Proposition 9: X_z is directed

Proof (9): Let $x,y \in B_s$, $x \sqsubseteq z$, $y \sqsubseteq z$. If $x = \bot_s$ or $y = \bot_s$ nothing else is to prove. Assume $x \neq \bot_s$, $y \neq \bot_s$. Let $E := A_x \cup A_y$. Then $E \subseteq A_z$, $E \neq \emptyset$ and E contains a minimum of z. We know $(A_E,\rho_E) \in X_z$ by Proposition 8. We have to show $x,y \sqsubseteq (A_E,\rho_E)$. It suffices to show $x \sqsubseteq (A_E,\rho_E)$. It is not difficult to verify (a), (b), and (c) from Def. 5(5). Let $F \subseteq A_x$ be not empty and bounded in (A_E,ρ_E). Then F is bounded in z (since $(A_E,\rho_E) \sqsubseteq z$) and F is bounded in x (since $x \sqsubseteq z$). Therefore, Property (d) holds. Let $a \in \mathrm{Sup}_x F$. Then $a \in \mathrm{Sup}_z F$ (since $x \sqsubseteq z$) and $a \in \mathrm{Sup}_v F$ since $v := (A_E,\rho_E) \sqsubseteq z$ and $a \in A_E$. This proves Property (e).
q.e.d. (9)

Proposition 10: $z = \sqcup X_z$

Proof (10): (as an exercise)

So far we have shown that $(D_s, \sqsubseteq, \bot_s)$ is an algebraic cpo with basis B_s. Since β_s is an "effective" numbering of the set B_s which consists only of finite objects, the set $\{(i,j) \mid \beta_s(i) \sqsubseteq \beta_s(j)\}$ is recursive.

Q.E.D.

Let δ_s be the standard representation of the computable cpo $\overline{D}_s$ according to Definition 3.6.12. Then from any δ_s-name p of some $(A,\rho) \in D_s$, a minimum, an enumeration procedure for A, a decision procedure for ρ, a decision procedure for boundedness, and a procedure for computing least upper bounds can be computed and vice versa. This is formulated more precisely in the following lemma. (The representation $\mathbb{P}$ of $PF = \{f : \mathbb{N} \dashrightarrow \mathbb{N}\}$ is from Def. 3.3.2)

8 LEMMA

Let δ_s be the standard representation of the super cpo $\overline{D}_s$.

(1) There are computable operators $\Gamma_o : \mathbb{B} \dashrightarrow \mathbb{N}$ and $\Gamma_1, \ldots, \Gamma_4 : \mathbb{B} \dashrightarrow \mathbb{B}$ such that for all $p \in dom(\delta_s)$ with $(A,\rho) := \delta_s(p) \neq (\emptyset,\emptyset)$, $p \in dom(\Gamma_i)$ $(i = 0,\ldots,4)$ and:

- $\Gamma_o(p) \in Min(A,\rho)$.
- $\mathbb{M}\Gamma_1(p) = A$.
- $\mathbb{P}\Gamma_2(p)\langle i,j\rangle = \begin{cases} 0 & \text{if } (i,j) \in \rho \\ 1 & \text{otherwise} \end{cases}$ for all $i,j \in A$.
- $\mathbb{P}\Gamma_3(p)(i) = \begin{cases} 0 & \text{if } e_i \text{ is } \rho\text{-bounded} \\ 1 & \text{otherwise} \end{cases}$ for all i with $e_i \subseteq A$.
- $\mathbb{P}\Gamma_4(p)(i) \in Sup_\rho e_i$ if $e_i \subseteq A$ and e_i is ρ-bounded.

(2) On the other hand, there is a computable operator $\Gamma : \mathbb{B} \dashrightarrow \mathbb{B}$ with the following property. If $(A,\rho) \in D_s$ with $A \neq 0$, and $n_o \in \mathbb{N}$ and $q_1,\ldots,q_4 \in \mathbb{B}$ satisfy the following properties:

- $n_o \in Min(A,\rho)$.
- $\mathbb{M}(q_1) = A$.
- $\mathbb{P}(q_2)\langle i,j\rangle = \begin{cases} 0 & \text{if } (i,j) \in \rho \\ 1 & \text{otherwise} \end{cases}$ for all $i,j \in A$.
- $\mathbb{P}(q_3)(i) = \begin{cases} 0 & \text{if } e_i \text{ is } \rho\text{-bounded} \\ 1 & \text{otherwise} \end{cases}$ for all i with $e_i \subseteq A$.
- $\mathbb{P}(q_4)(i) \in Sup_\rho e_i$ if $e_i \subseteq A$ and e_i is ρ-bounded.

Then $(A,\rho) = \delta_s \Gamma\langle n_o, q_1, \ldots, q_4\rangle$.

Proof

(1) By Definition 3.6.12, $p \in dom(\delta_s) \iff \{\beta_s(i) \mid i \in \mathbf{M}_p\}$ is directed, and $\delta_s(p) = \sqcup\{\beta_s(i) \mid i \in \mathbf{M}_p\}$. Compute $\Gamma_o : \mathbb{B} \dashrightarrow \mathbb{N}$ as follows:

Input: $p \in \mathbb{B}$.
Find the first $n \in \mathbf{M}_p$ such that $\beta_s(n) \neq (\emptyset,\emptyset)$.
Determine a minimum $m \in Min(\beta_s(n))$.
Output: m.

By Property 5(5)(c), Γ_o has the desired property. Define $\Gamma_1 : \mathbb{B} \dashrightarrow \mathbb{B}$ as follows.

$$\Gamma_1(p)\langle i,j,n\rangle = \begin{cases} 1+i & \text{if } (\exists (A,\rho))\ [p(j) = 1+n \wedge \beta_s(n) = (A,\rho) \wedge i \in A] \\ 0 & \text{otherwise}. \end{cases}$$

Then Γ_1 is computable and has the desired property. Define $\Gamma_2 : \mathbb{B} \dashrightarrow \mathbb{B}$ as follows.

$$\Gamma_2(p)\langle i,j,k,n\rangle = \begin{cases} 1+\langle\langle i,j\rangle,0\rangle & \text{if } (\exists (A,\rho))\ [p(k) = 1+n \wedge \beta_s(n) = (A,\rho) \\ & \qquad \wedge \langle i,j\rangle \in \rho] \\ 1+\langle\langle i,j\rangle,1\rangle & \text{if } (\exists (A,\rho))\ [p(k) = 1+n \wedge \beta_s(n) = (A,\rho) \\ & \qquad \wedge i \in A \wedge j \in A \wedge (i,j) \notin \rho] \\ 0 & \text{otherwise}. \end{cases}$$

Then Γ_2 has the desired property. Appropriate functions Γ_3 and Γ_4 can be defined accordingly.

(2) Compute $\Gamma : \mathbb{B} \dashrightarrow \mathbb{B}$ as follows

$$\Gamma\langle n_o,q_1,q_2,q_3,q_4\rangle\langle k,n\rangle := \begin{cases} 1+n & \text{if } \beta_s(n) = (\emptyset,\emptyset) \text{ or the conditions} \\ & \text{listed below hold.} \\ 0 & \text{otherwise.} \end{cases}$$

The conditions are as follows: (define $(A,\rho) := \beta_s(n)$)

- $n_o \in Min(A,\rho)$.
- $A \subseteq \{q_1(j) - 1 \mid j \leq k,\ q_1(j) \neq 0\}$.
- For all $i,j \in A$:
  $(i,j) \in \rho \implies (\exists j \leq k)\ q_2(j) = 1 + \langle\langle i,j\rangle,0\rangle$,
  $(i,j) \notin \rho \implies (\exists j \leq k)\ q_2(j) = 1 + \langle\langle i,j\rangle,1\rangle$.
- For all i with $e_i \subseteq A$:
  e_i is ρ-bounded $\implies (\exists j \leq k)\ q_3(j) = 1 + \langle i,0\rangle$,
  e_i is not ρ-bounded $\implies (\exists j \leq k)\ q_3(j) = 1 + \langle i,1\rangle$.
- For all i with $e_i \subseteq A$, e_i ρ-bounded:
  $(\exists k_1,k_2)\ [k_1 \leq k \wedge q_4(k_1) = 1 + \langle i,k_2\rangle \wedge k_2 \in Sup_\rho(e_i)]$.

Then Γ has the desired properties (as an exercise).

Q.E.D.

9 COROLLARY

Assume $(A,\rho) \in D_s$, $A \neq \emptyset$. Then (A,ρ) is δ_s-computable iff $(A,\rho) = \mathrm{rel}(\overline{D})$ for some recursive domain $\overline{D}$.

Proof

This follows from the fact that computable operators map computable functions into computable functions.

Q.E.D.

Lemma 8 and its corollary show that the concepts "domain" and "recursive domain" are presented adequately by the cpo $\overline{D}_s$. For each $x \in D_s$, $x \neq (\emptyset,\emptyset)$, there is the d-completion $\mathrm{cpl}(x) \in \mathrm{DOM}$. We know from Chapter 3.5 that the b-complete algebraic cpo's are closed w.r.t. to sum, product, and function space operation. By adding appropriate numberings of basises, the definitions of sum, product, and function space can be extended to domains.

10 DEFINITION (*standard sum, product, and function space of domains*)

Let $\overline{D}_i = (D_i, \sqsubseteq, \bot_i, \beta_i)$ be domains.

(1) Let $(D,\sqsubseteq,\bot)$ be the standard sum of $(D_1,\sqsubseteq,\bot_1)$ and $(D_2,\sqsubseteq,\bot_2)$ according to Def. 3.5.19. Define a numbering β of the basis B (cf. Lemma 3.5.20(3)) as follows:

$$\beta(n) := \begin{cases} (1,\beta_1(i)) & \text{if } n = \langle 1,i\rangle \\ (2,\beta_2(i)) & \text{if } n = \langle 2,i\rangle \\ \bot & \text{if } n = 0 \\ \mathrm{div} & \text{otherwise}. \end{cases}$$

Then $[\overline{D}_1 + \overline{D}_2] := (D,\sqsubseteq,\bot,\beta)$ is the *standard sum* of $\overline{D}_1$ and $\overline{D}_2$.

(2) Let $(D,\sqsubseteq,\bot)$ be the standard product of $(D_1,\sqsubseteq,\bot_1)$ and $(D_2,\sqsubseteq,\bot_2)$ according to Def. 3.5.23. Define a numbering β of the basis B (cf. Lemma 3.5.24(3)) by

$$\beta\langle i,j\rangle := (\beta_1(i),\beta_2(j)).$$

Then $[\overline{D}_1 \times \overline{D}_2] := (D,\sqsubseteq,\bot,\beta)$ is called the *standard product* of $\overline{D}_1$ and $\overline{D}_2$.

(3) Let $(D,\sqsubseteq,\bot)$ be the standard function space from $(D_1,\sqsubseteq,\bot_1)$ to $(D_2,\sqsubseteq,\bot_2)$ with standard basis B (see Def. 3.5.27, Lemma 3.5.28). Define a numbering β of B as follows:

$$\beta(n) := \begin{cases} f & \text{if } e_n \neq \emptyset \text{ and } f := \sqcup\{(\beta_1(i) \longrightarrow \beta_2(j)) \mid \langle i,j\rangle \in e_n\} \text{ exists} \\ \mathrm{div} & \text{otherwise}. \end{cases}$$

Then $[\overline{D}_1 \longrightarrow \overline{D}_2] := (D, \sqsubseteq, \bot, \beta)$ is called the *standard function domain* of $\overline{D}_1$ and $\overline{D}_2$.

Obviously, in each of the three cases, β is a numbering of the algebraic basis of the constructed cpo. The operations of the standard sum, standard product, and standard function space respect constructive equivalence.

11 LEMMA

Let $\overline{D}_i$ and $\overline{E}_i$ be constructively equivalent $(i = 1,2)$. Then the following pairs are constructively equivalent:

(a) $[\overline{D}_1 + \overline{D}_2]$ and $[\overline{E}_1 + \overline{E}_2]$,

(b) $[\overline{D}_1 \times \overline{D}_2]$ and $[\overline{E}_1 \times \overline{E}_2]$,

(c) $[\overline{D}_1 \longrightarrow \overline{D}_2]$ and $[\overline{E}_1 \longrightarrow \overline{E}_2]$.

The proof follows from the definitions.

We want to show that sum, product, and function space are computable operations on the set DOM (or on the domain $\overline{D}_s$). The standard sum $\overline{D}$ of $\overline{D}_1, \overline{D}_2 \in \mathrm{DOM}$ is not in DOM. Since $\overline{D}$ and $\zeta(\overline{D})$ are isomorphic, $\zeta(\overline{D})$ may be called "sum" of $\overline{D}_1$ and $\overline{D}_2$ (see Lemma 3.5.21). We shall define a function sum: $D_s \times D_s \longrightarrow D_s$ explicitly which is computable and satisfies

$$\mathrm{sum}(x_1, x_2) = \mathrm{rel}[\mathrm{cpl}(x_1) + \mathrm{cpl}(x_2)] .$$

Corresponding functions prd for the product and fct for the function space are introduced.

12 DEFINITION (*constructive sum, product, and function space*)

(1) Define a mapping $\mathrm{sum} : D_s \times D_s \longrightarrow D_s$ as follows:

$$(A, \rho) =: \mathrm{sum}((A_1, \rho_1), (A_2, \rho_2))$$

where

$$A := \langle 1, A_1 \rangle \cup \langle 2, A_2 \rangle \cup \{0\}$$

$$\rho := \{(\langle 1,i \rangle, \langle 1,j \rangle) \mid (i,j) \in \rho_1\} \cup \{(\langle 2,i \rangle, \langle 2,j \rangle) \mid (i,j) \in \rho_2\} \cup \{(0,x) \mid x \in A\} .$$

(2) Define a mapping $prd : D_s \times D_s \longrightarrow D_s$ as follows:

$$(A,\rho) =: prd((A_1,\rho_1),(A_2,\rho_2))$$

where

$$A := \langle A_1,A_2\rangle$$

$$\rho := \{(\langle i_1,i_2\rangle,\langle j_1,j_2\rangle) \mid (i_1,j_1)\in\rho_1 \wedge (i_2,j_2)\in\rho_2\} .$$

(3) Define a mapping $fct : D_s \times D_s \longrightarrow D_s$ as follows:

$$(A,\rho) =: fct((A_1,\rho_1),(A_2,\rho_2))$$

where

$$A := \{n \mid e_n \neq \emptyset \wedge e_n \subseteq \langle A_1,A_2\rangle \wedge (\forall E \subseteq e_n , E \neq \emptyset)$$
$$(\pi_1 E\ \rho_1\text{-bounded} \implies \pi_2 E\ \rho_2\text{-bounded})\} ,$$

$$(m,n)\in\rho :\iff (\forall \langle a,b\rangle \in e_m)\ b\rho_2 Sup_{\rho_2}\{d \mid \langle c,d\rangle \in e_n \wedge c\rho_1 a\}$$

for all $m,n\in A$. (We define $Sup_{\rho_2}(\emptyset) := Min(\rho_2)$.)

13 LEMMA

Let $x_1,x_2 \in D_s$, $x_1,x_2 \neq (\emptyset,\emptyset)$. Then the following properties hold.

(1) $cpl\ sum(x_1,x_2) = \varsigma[cpl(x_1) + cpl(x_2)]$

(2) $cpl\ prd(x_1,x_2) = \varsigma[cpl(x_1) \times cpl(x_2)]$

(3) $cpl\ fct(x_1,x_2) = \varsigma[cpl(x_1) \longrightarrow cpl(x_2)]$

Proof

(1) Let $\bar{D} = (D,\sqsubseteq,\bot,\beta) = [cpl(x_1) + cpl(x_2)]$ and $(A,\rho) = sum(x_1,x_2)$. It suffices to show $\rho = \{(i,j) \mid \beta(i) \sqsubseteq \beta(j)\}$. This follows immediately from Def. 10, Def. 12, and Def. 3.5.19.

(2) (correspondingly)

(3) Let $x_1 = (A_1,\rho_1)$, $x_2 = (A_2,\rho_2)$, $\bar{D} = (D,\sqsubseteq,\bot,\beta) = [cpl(x_1) \longrightarrow cpl(x_2)]$, and $(A,\rho) = fct(x_1,x_2)$. It suffices to show $A = dom(\beta)$ and $\rho = \{(i,j) \mid \beta(i) \sqsubseteq \beta(j)\}$. We have:

$$n \in dom(\beta)$$

$$\iff e_n \neq \emptyset \wedge e_n \subseteq \langle A_1,A_2\rangle \wedge \sqcup\{(\beta_1(i) \longrightarrow \beta_2(j)) \mid \langle i,j\rangle \in e_n\} \text{ exists}$$

$$\iff e_n \neq \emptyset \wedge e_n \subseteq \langle A_1,A_2\rangle \wedge (\forall E \subseteq e_n , E \neq \emptyset)\ (\beta_1\pi_1 E \text{ bounded} \implies \beta_2\pi_2 E \text{ bounded})$$

$$\iff n \in A ,$$

and for all $m,n \in dom(\beta)$ we obtain

$$\beta(m) \sqsubseteq \beta(n)$$

$$\iff \sqcup \{(\beta_1(a) \longrightarrow \beta_2(b)) \mid \langle a,b\rangle \in e_m\} \sqsubseteq \beta(n)$$

$$\iff (\forall \langle a,b\rangle \in e_m) \quad \beta_2(b) \sqsubseteq \beta(n)\beta_1(a)$$

$$\iff (\forall \langle a,b\rangle \in e_m) \quad \beta_2(b) \sqsubseteq \sqcup\{\beta_2(d) \mid \langle c,d\rangle \in e_n \wedge \beta_1(c) \sqsubseteq \beta_1(a)\}$$

$$\iff (m,n) \in \rho .$$

Q.E.D.

As a corollary we obtain that sum, prd, and fct are welldefined. If $x,y \neq (\emptyset,\emptyset)$ then sum(x,y), prd(x,y), and fct(x,y) are elements of D_s by lemma 12. If $x = (\emptyset,\emptyset)$ or $y = (\emptyset,\emptyset)$ then $sum(x,y) \in D_s'$ and $prd(x,y) = fct(x,y) = (\emptyset,\emptyset)$. We want to show that the three functions are computable on $\overline{D}_s$.

14 THEOREM

8 The functions sum, prd, and fct are computable on $\overline{D}_s$.

Proof

We consider the function sum. Let $\overline{D} := (D,\sqsubseteq,\perp,\beta) := [\overline{D}_s \times \overline{D}_s]$ be the constructive product if $\overline{D}_s$ with itself (Def. 3.5.33). Then $B := B_s \times B_s$ is the basis of $\overline{D}$. Let δ be the standard representation of $\overline{D}$.

Proposition 1: $sum(x,y) \sqsubseteq sum(x',y')$ if $x \sqsubseteq x'$ and $y \sqsubseteq y'$.

Proof (1): (easy)

Proposition 2: sum restricted to B and B_s is (β,β_s)-computable .

Proof (2): (obvious)

Proposition 3: $sum(z) = \sqcup\{sum(b) \mid b \in B , b \sqsubseteq z\}$ for all $z \in D$.

Proof (3): Since sum is isotone, $\sqcup\{\ldots\} \sqsubseteq sum(z)$. Assume $z = ((A_1,\rho_1),(A_2,\rho_2))$, $sum(z) = (A,\rho)$. Let $(m,n) \in \rho$. By using the fact that $\overline{D}_s$ is an algebraic cpo with basis B_s it can be shown that $(m,n) \in \rho'$ for some $A' \subseteq \mathbb{N}$ such that $(A',\rho') \in B$ and $(A',\rho') \sqsubseteq z$.

q.e.d. (3)

By Propositions 1 and 3, $sum : D \longrightarrow D_s$ is continuous. Since δ and δ_s are admissible representations, sum is (δ,δ_s)-continuous.

By Proposition 2 and Theorem 3.6.14, sum is (δ,δ_s)-computable, and by Lemma 3.5.34, the function sum is $([\delta_s,\delta_s],\delta_s)$-computable. For the functions prd and fct the proofs are similar. In each case it suffices to show the three corresponding propositions. The straightforward proofs are left to the exercises.
(Warning: The proofs for fct are laborious.)

Q.E.D.

Lemma 13 and Theorem 14 can be expressed as follows: the operations sum, product, and function space are computable on the set DOM of domains. For every sum there is a pair of injections by Lemma 3.5.21. For the sum on DOM the injections are computable and can be determined by computable operations. Correspondingly the projections for the product (Lemma 3.5.25) and the evaluation function and the "smn-function" for the function space (see Lemma 3.5.29) are computable and can be determined effectively. We shall not formulate and prove all of these effectivity properties in detail. We shall only define the standard representations which are used for the formulations.

15 DEFINITION

(1) Define $\tilde{\delta} : \mathbb{B} \dashrightarrow \mathrm{DOM}$ by $\tilde{\delta}(p) := \mathrm{cpl}\ \delta_s(p)$.

(2) For any $p \in \mathrm{dom}(\tilde{\delta})$ where $\tilde{\delta}(p) = (D,\sqsubseteq,\bot,\beta)$ let δ^p be the standard representation of $\tilde{\delta}(p)$, i.e.

$$\delta^p(q) = x \ :\Longleftrightarrow\ \mathbf{M}_q = \{i \in \mathrm{dom}(\beta) \mid \beta(i) \sqsubseteq x\}\ .$$

If we define $\mathrm{SUM}(\overline{D}_1,\overline{D}_2) := \zeta[\overline{D}_1 + \overline{D}_2]$, then by Lemma 13 and Theorem 14, SUM (on DOM) is $([\tilde{\delta},\tilde{\delta}],\tilde{\delta})$-computable.

Now an extensive theory of constructivity and computability on domains can be developed. As an example we shall only show how domains with prescribed properties can be determined by solving *fixed point equations* on the set DOM of domains. For showing that our solutions are recursive domains we shall apply the following lemma.

16 LEMMA (*computable fixed points*)

Let $\overline{D}$ be a computable cpo (Def. 3.6.12) with standard representation δ. Let $f : D \longrightarrow D$ be a (δ,δ)-computable function. Then the fixed point Fix(f) is δ-computable (cf. Theorem 3.6.14, Theorem 3.5.30).

Proof

From the proof of the fixed point theorem we know $Fix(f) = \sqcup\{f^i\bot \mid i \in \mathbb{N}\}$. Let $\overline{D} = (D,\sqsubseteq,\bot,\beta)$ with basis B. Since $\overline{D}$ is an algebraic cpo we have

$$b \sqsubseteq fy \iff (\exists c \in B)\ (b \sqsubseteq fc \wedge c \sqsubseteq y)$$

for any $b \in B$ and $y \in D$. We obtain: $\beta(k) \sqsubseteq Fix(f)$, iff

$$(\exists i,n_o,\dots,n_i \in \mathbb{N})\ [k = n_o \wedge (\forall j < i)\ \beta(n_j) \sqsubseteq f\beta(n_{j+1}) \wedge \beta(n_i) = \bot].$$

Since f is a computable function, by Theorem 3.6.14(2) and Theorem 3.6.14(1), Fix(f) is a computable element of $\overline{D}$.

Q.E.D.

The first class of equations we shall solve is of type

$$\overline{D} = \zeta[f_1(\overline{D}) + f_2(\overline{D})],$$

where f_1 and f_2 are $(\tilde{\delta},\tilde{\delta})$-computable (or continuous) functions on DOM.

17 THEOREM

Let $g_i : D_s \longrightarrow D_s$ be (δ_s,δ_s)-continuous functions; define f_i: DOM $\longrightarrow$ DOM by $f_i(\overline{D}) :=$ cpl g_i rel$(\overline{D})$ $(i = 1,2)$. Then there is a domain $D \in$ DOM such that

$$\overline{D} = \zeta[f_1(\overline{D}) + f_2(\overline{D})].$$

If g_1 and g_2 are (δ_s,δ_s)-computable, then there is a recursive domain $\overline{D}$ satisfying the above equation.

Proof

Define $g : D_s \longrightarrow D_s$ by $g(x) := sum(g_1(x),g_2(x))$, let $x_o := Fix(g)$ be the least fixed point of g. Then $x_o = sum(g_1(x_o),g_2(x_o))$. We have $x_o \neq (\emptyset,\emptyset)$ by Definition 12, hence $\overline{D} := cpl(x_o)$ exists. From Lemma 13 we obtain $\overline{D} = \zeta[f_1(\overline{D}) + f_2(\overline{D})]$. If g_1 and g_2 are computable, then g is computable, x_o is computable by Lemma 16, and $\overline{D}$ is recursive by Corollary 9.

Q.E.D.

18 EXAMPLES

The following functions may be chosen for f_1 or f_2.

$\overline{D} \mapsto \overline{D}_o$,

$\overline{D} \mapsto \overline{D}$,

$\overline{D} \mapsto \zeta[\overline{D} + \overline{D}]$,

$\overline{D} \mapsto \zeta[\overline{D} \times \overline{D}]$,

$\overline{D} \mapsto \zeta[\overline{D} \longrightarrow \overline{D}]$,

$\overline{D} \mapsto \zeta[\overline{D} \longrightarrow \overline{D}_o]$,

$\overline{D} \mapsto \zeta[[\overline{D}_1 \times \overline{D}] \longrightarrow [\overline{D} \times \overline{D}]]$

where $\overline{D}_o$ and $\overline{D}_1$ are any constant domains from DOM. Each of the following equations has a solution in DOM.

$\overline{D} = \zeta[\overline{D}_o + \overline{D}]$,

$\overline{D} = \zeta[[\overline{D} \longrightarrow \overline{D}_o] + [\overline{D} \times \overline{D}]]$,

$\overline{D} = \zeta[\overline{D}_o + [[\overline{D}_1 \times \overline{D}] \longrightarrow [\overline{D} \times \overline{D}]]]$,

$\overline{D} = \zeta[\overline{D} + [\overline{D} \longrightarrow [\overline{D} \times \overline{D}]]]$.

The following examples show how fixed points are generated step by step.

19 EXAMPLES

(1) Let $\overline{D}_o := \mathrm{cpl}(x_o)$, where $x_o = (\{3\},\{(3,3)\}) \in D_s$. Let $f(x) := \mathrm{sum}(x_o,x)$ on D_s. The least fixed point Fix(f) is the least upper bound of the sequence $\bot_s, f\bot_s, f^2\bot_s, \ldots$. The sequence can be represented graphically as follows.

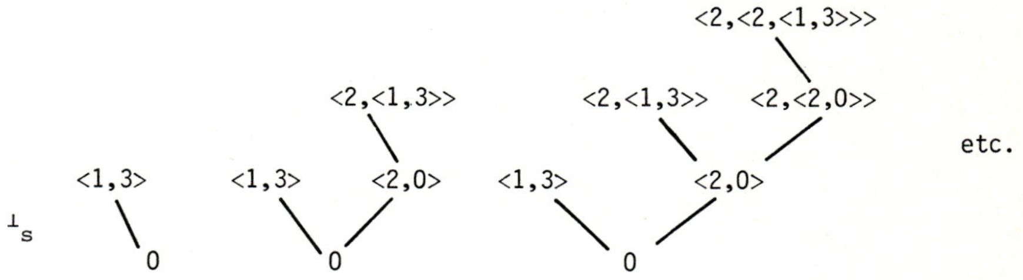

Therefore, $(A,\rho) := \mathrm{Fix}(f)$ can be represented by the following graph.

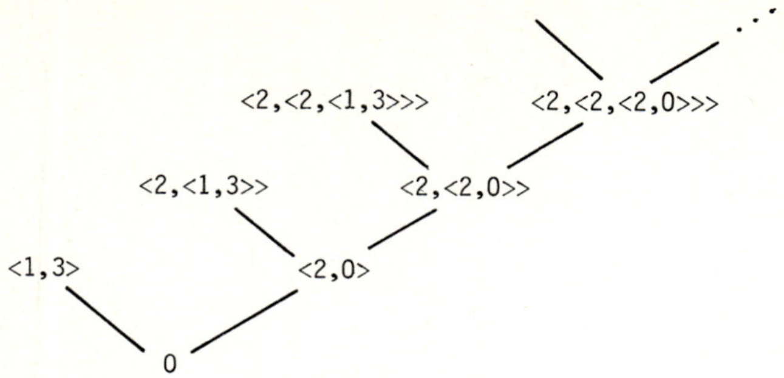

Let $\overline{D} := \mathrm{cpl}(\mathrm{Fix}(f))$. Then $\overline{D} = \zeta[\overline{D}_o + \overline{D}]$.
The basis B of $\overline{D}$ consists of the sets $\{k \in A \mid k \rho i\}$ with $i \in A$ and $D = B \cup \{d\}$ where

$$d = \{0,\langle 2,0\rangle,\langle 2,\langle 2,0\rangle\rangle,\langle 2,\langle 2,\langle 2,0\rangle\rangle\rangle,\dots\} .$$

(2) If $\overline{D}_i = \mathrm{cpl}(x_i)$ $(i = 1,2)$, then $\mathrm{sum}(x_1,x_2)$ can be represented informally as follows.

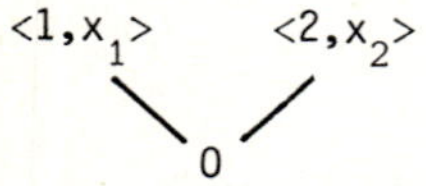

If in (1) $\overline{D}_o = \mathrm{cpl}(x_o)$ is an arbitrary domain, then correspondingly a domain $\overline{D}$ with $\overline{D} = \zeta[\overline{D}_o + \overline{D}]$ is obtained which can be represented by $x \in D_s$ with $\overline{D} = \mathrm{cpl}(x)$ as follows.

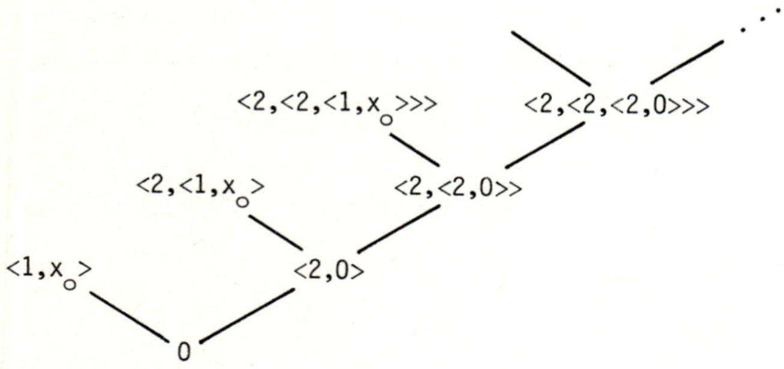

The property $x = \mathrm{sum}(x_o,x)$ is obvious from the figure.

(3) Let $x_o := (\{3\},\{(3,3)\})$, $x_1 := (\{4,5\},\{(4,4),(4,5),(5,5)\})$. Define $f : D_s \longrightarrow D_s$ by $f(x) := \mathrm{sum}(x_o,\mathrm{prd}(x_1,x))$. The sequence $\bot_s, f\bot_s, f^2\bot_s, \dots$ can be represented as follows.

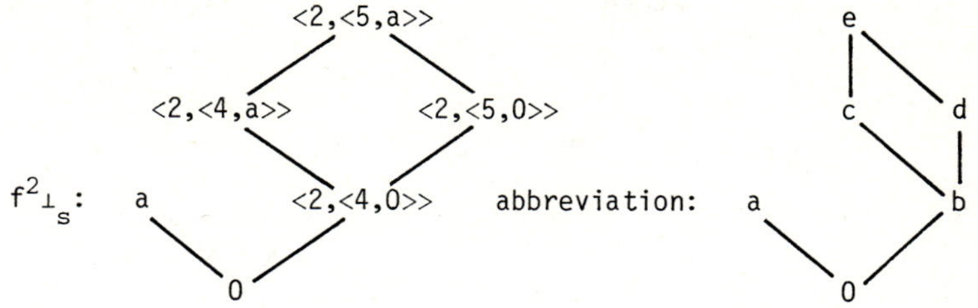

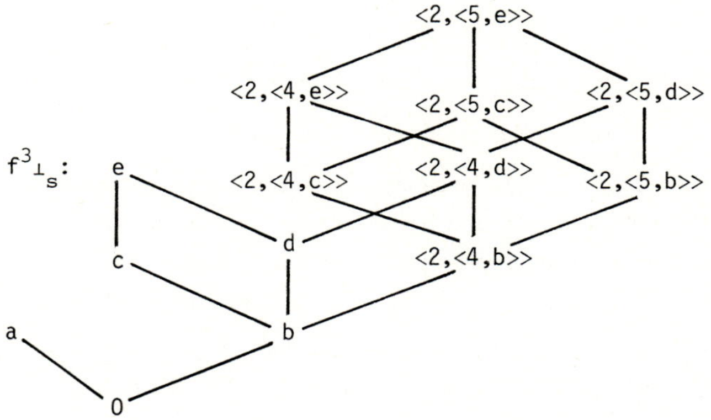

The next element $f^4\bot_s$ is even more complicated. The figures show the property $\bot_s \sqsubseteq f\bot_s \sqsubseteq f^2\bot_s \sqsubseteq f^3\bot_s$ very clearly.

(4) Let x_o and x_1 be the elements of D_s from (3). Define $f : D_s \longrightarrow D_s$ by $f(x) := \mathrm{sum}(x_o, \mathrm{fct}(x_1, x))$. Since the elements $f^i\bot_s$ become very complicated, we shall only present the (finite) domains $\mathrm{cpl}(f^i\bot_s)$ for $i = 1,2,3$ graphically. Notice that a finite domain is the partial order on its basis, and that a function is continuous iff it is isotone in this case.

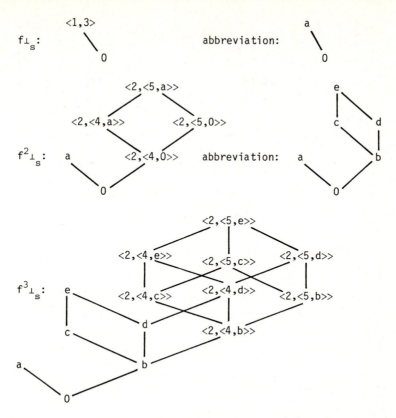

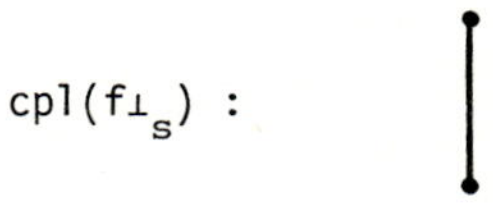

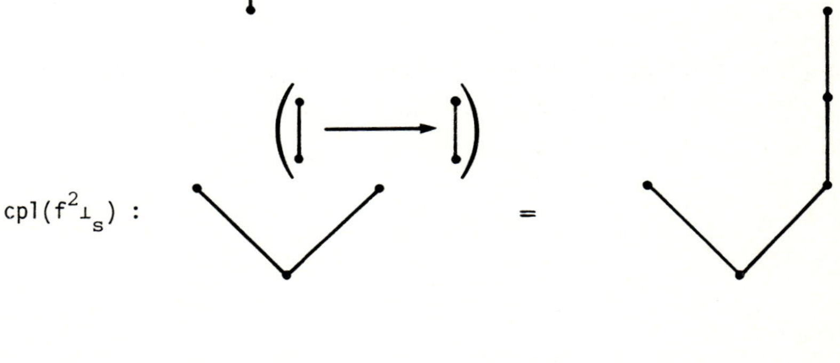

$cpl(f^3 \bot_s)$: 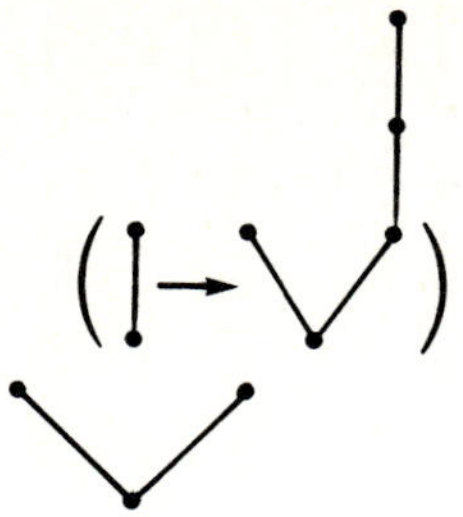 = 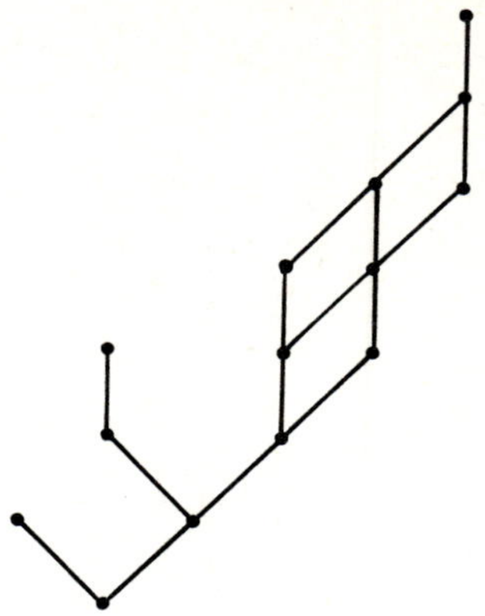

By Theorem 3.5.30, the fixed point Fix(f) depends continuously (even computably) on f. In our examples, f depends computably on the parameters x_o and x_1. Hence the fixed point is a computable function of the parameters x_o and x_1. Notice that we have proved not only isomorphism of $\overline{D}$ and $\zeta[f_1(\overline{D}) + f_2(\overline{D})]$ but equality in Theorem 17.

In Theorem 17, the sum operation guarantees that $x_o = Fix(g) = \sqcup g^n(\bot_s)$ is not equal to $\bot_s = (\emptyset,\emptyset)$. Therefore, $cpl(x_o)$ exists. The additional conditions $g_i(x) \neq \bot_s$ if $x \neq \bot_s$ imply that $f_1(\overline{D})$ and $f_2(\overline{D})$ exist. Similar theorems can be proved for the product and function space operations. Since $prd(x,y) = \bot_s \iff fct(x,y) = \bot_s \iff (x = \bot_s \text{ or } y = \bot_s)$, we shall require $g_1(\bot_s) \neq \bot_s$ and $g_2(\bot_s) \neq \bot_s$ in addition.

20 THEOREM

Let $g_i : D_s \longrightarrow D_s$ be (δ_s,δ_s)-continuous functions such that $g_i(x) \neq \bot_s$ for all $x \in D_s$, define $f_i : DOM \longrightarrow DOM$ by $f_i(\overline{D}) := cpl\ g_i\ rel(\overline{D})$ $(i = 1,2)$. Then the following equations have solutions in DOM.

(1) $\overline{D} = \zeta[f_1(\overline{D}) \times f_2(\overline{D})]$,

(2) $\overline{D} = \zeta[f_1(\overline{D}) \longrightarrow f_2(\overline{D})]$.

If g_1 and g_2 are computable, then in both cases there are recursive solutions.

Proof

The proof corresponds to that of Theorem 17.

(1) Define $g(x) := \mathrm{prd}(g_1(x), g_2(x))$. The assumptions guarantee that $x_o := \mathrm{Fix}(g) \neq \bot_s$ and that $\mathrm{cpl}\ g_1(x_o)$ and $\mathrm{cpl}\ g_2(x_o)$ exist.

(2) (correspondingly)

Q.E.D.

21 EXAMPLES

The standard examples for g_1 and g_2 are constant functions $x \longrightarrow x_o$ (where $x_o \neq \bot_s$) or sums $x \longrightarrow \mathrm{sum}(\ldots,\ldots)$. Among others the following equations have solutions in DOM.

$$\overline{D} = \zeta[\overline{D}_o \longrightarrow \overline{D}_o] ,$$

$$\overline{D} = \zeta[[\overline{D} + \overline{D}] \times \overline{D}_o] ,$$

$$\overline{D} = \zeta[[[\overline{D} \longrightarrow \overline{D}] + \overline{D}_o] \longrightarrow [\overline{D} + \overline{D}_o]] .$$

Our method does not work for equations like $\overline{D} = \zeta[\overline{D} \times \overline{D}]$ and $\overline{D} = \zeta[\overline{D} \longrightarrow \overline{D}]$. The special form of our standard product (depending on Cantor's pairing function) admits a simple trick for finding a nontrivial solution for the equation $\overline{D} = \zeta[\overline{D} \times \overline{D}]$.

22 THEOREM

8 The equation $\overline{D} = \zeta[\overline{D} \times \overline{D}]$ has a nontrivial solution in DOM.

Proof

Define $g : D_s \longrightarrow D_s$ by $g(x) := \mathrm{prd}(x,x)$. (Notice that $g(\bot_s) = \bot_s$). Let $y := (A,\rho) = (\{0,1\},\{(0,0),(0,1),(1,1)\})$. Let $(B,\sigma) := g(y)$. Then $B = \langle A,A\rangle = \{\langle 0,0\rangle,\langle 0,1\rangle,\langle 1,0\rangle,\langle 1,1\rangle\}$. Since $0 = \langle 0,0\rangle$ and $1 = \langle 1,0\rangle$ we have $0\sigma 1$ and not $1\sigma 0$, hence $y \sqsubseteq g(y)$ (see Def. 5). As in the proof of the fixed point theorem, one easily shows that $x_o = \sqcup\{g^n(y) \mid n \in \mathbb{N}\}$ is the least fixed point of g with $y \sqsubseteq x_o$. $\overline{D} := \mathrm{cpl}(x_o)$ is a nontrivial solution of the equation $\overline{D} = \zeta[\overline{D} \times \overline{D}]$.

Q.E.D.

The above method can be applied to similar situations e.g. to equations $\overline{D} = \zeta[\overline{D} \times \overline{D}_o]$ if $(A,\rho) := rel(\overline{D}_o)$ has the properties: $0 \in Min(A,\rho)$ and $0\rho 1$ and not $1\rho 0$ (as an exercise). For more general cases the reqirement that $\overline{D}$ has to be equal to $\zeta h(\overline{D})$ seems to be too strong. Instead of equality we shall consider *recursive isomorphism*. Two cpo's are isomorphic iff there is a bijection α such that $x \sqsubseteq y \iff \alpha(x) \sqsubseteq \alpha(y)$. Two algebraic cpo's are isomorphic iff the induced orderings on the basises are isomorphic.

23 <u>DEFINITION</u> (*recursive isomorphism of domains*)

Let $\overline{D} = (D_i, \sqsubseteq, \bot, \beta_i)$ be a domain with basis B_i $(i = 1,2)$.

(1) $\overline{D}_1$ and $\overline{D}_2$ are called *isomorphic*, iff $(B_1, \sqsubseteq)$ and $(B_2, \sqsubseteq)$ are isomorphic partial orders.

(2) $\overline{D}_1$ and $\overline{D}_2$ are called *recursively isomorphic*, iff there is a bijection $\iota : B_1 \longrightarrow B_2$ with

$$b \sqsubseteq b' \iff \iota(b) \sqsubseteq \iota(b') \qquad (\forall b,b' \in B_1)$$

and

$$\iota\beta_1 \equiv \beta_2 .$$

By the following lemma there are sums, products and function spaces with special properties.

24 <u>LEMMA</u>

For $n \in \mathbb{N}$ let $X_n := \{(A,\rho) \in D_s \mid \langle a,b\rangle \in A \Rightarrow a \leq n\}$.

(1) For any $n \geq 1$ there is a computable function $sum_n : D_s \times D_s \longrightarrow D_s$ such that $range(sum_n) \subseteq X_n$, $cpl\ sum_n(rel(\overline{D}_1), rel(\overline{D}_2))$ is recursively isomorphic to $[\overline{D}_1 + \overline{D}_2]$, and $x \sqsubseteq sum_n(x,y)$ if $x \in X_{n-1}$. (Correspondigly with sum'_n and $y \sqsubseteq sum'_n(x,y)$.)

(2) For any $n \geq 1$ there is a computable function $prd_n : D_s \times D_s \longrightarrow D_s$ such that $range(prd_n) \subseteq X_n$, $cpl\ prd_n(rel(\overline{D}_1), rel(\overline{D}_2))$ is recursively isomorphic to $[\overline{D}_1 \times \overline{D}_2]$, and $x \sqsubseteq prd_n(x,y)$ if $x \in X_{n-1}$ and $y \neq \bot$. (Correspondingly with prd'_n and $y \sqsubseteq prd'_n(x,y)$.)

(3) For any $n \geq 1$ there is a computable function $fct_n : D_s \times D_s \longrightarrow D_s$ such that $range(fct_n) \subseteq X_n$, $cpl\ fct_n(rel(\overline{D}_1), rel(\overline{D}_2))$ is recursively isomorphic to $[\overline{D}_1 \longrightarrow \overline{D}_2]$, and $y \sqsubseteq fct_n(x,y)$ if $y \in X_{n-1}$ and $x \neq \bot$.

For the proof the facts that $\overline{D}_1$ and $\overline{D}_2$ can be embedded into $[D_1 + D_2]$ and $[\overline{D}_1 \times \overline{D}_2]$ and that $\overline{D}_2$ can be embedded into $[\overline{D}_1 \longrightarrow \overline{D}_2]$ are used. Instead of a complete proof we only define as an example a function prd_n. For (A_1,ρ_1), $(A_2,\rho_2) \in D_s$ define $(A,\rho) = prd_n((A_1,\rho_1),(A_2,\rho_2))$ as follows. Let $(A',\rho') := prd((A_1,\rho_1),(A_2,\rho_2))$. Define a function $q : A' \longrightarrow \mathbb{N}$ by

$$q\langle a_1,a_2\rangle = \begin{cases} a_1 & \text{if } a_2 \in Min(\rho_2) \text{ and } a_1 \in \langle\{1,\dots,n-1\},\mathbb{N}\rangle \\ \langle n,\langle a_1,a_2\rangle\rangle & \text{otherwise.} \end{cases}$$

Let $A := range(q)$ and $a'\rho'b' \Longleftrightarrow : q(a')\rho q(b')$.

Then the function prd_n has the desired properties. In each of the three cases the computable translation functions for the numberings of the basises which determine the isomorphism can be computed from x and y. We show by two examples how "homogeneous" domain isomorphisms can be solved.

25 EXAMPLE

Problem: Let $\overline{D}_o$ and $\overline{D}_1$ be recursive domains such that $x_o := rel(\overline{D}_o)$ and $x_1 := rel(\overline{D}_1)$ have the following graphs:

x_o :

x_1 :

Find a recursive domain $\overline{D}$ which is recursively isomorphic to $[\overline{D} \times \overline{D}_1]$ such that $\overline{D}_o$ can be embedded into $\overline{D}$.

Solution: Notice that $0 = \langle 0,0\rangle, 1 = \langle 1,0\rangle, 2 = \langle 0,1\rangle$. Define $g : D_s \longrightarrow D_s$ by $g(x) = prd_3(x,x_1)$. Then g is computable and $x_o \sqsubseteq g(x_o)$. Let $x := \bigsqcup g^i(x_o)$, then x is smallest $y \in D_s$ with $x_o \sqsubseteq y$ and $g(y) = y$. Since g is computable, x is a computable element of D_s. The following diagram shows the first three elements of the sequence $x_o, g(x_o), g^2(x_o), \dots$.

x_o:

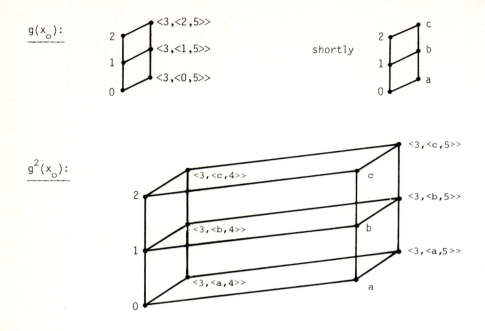

$\underline{g(x_o):}$

$\underline{g^2(x_o):}$

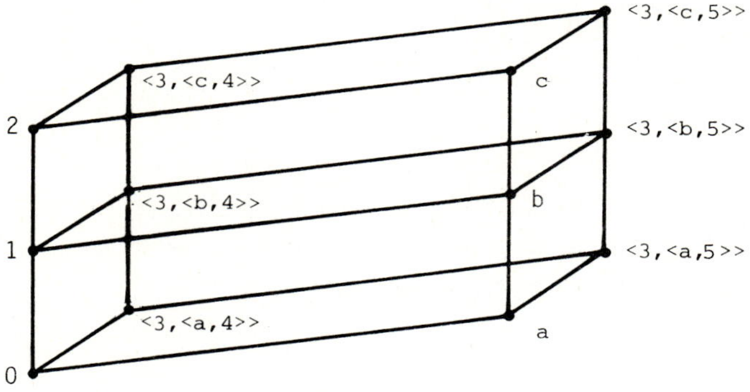

Let $\overline{D} := \text{cpl}(x)$. Since $x_o \sqsubseteq x$, $\overline{D}_o$ can be embedded into $\overline{D}$, and since $\overline{D} = \text{cpl}(x) = \text{cpl } g(x) = \text{cpl } \text{prd}_3(x,x_1) = \text{cpl } \text{prd}_3(\text{rel}(\overline{D}), \text{rel}(\overline{D}_1))$, $\overline{D}$ is recursively isomorphic to $[\overline{D} \times \overline{D}_1]$. Notice that the embedding and the isomorphism can be determinded effectively.

26 <u>EXAMPLE</u>

<u>Problem:</u> Let $\overline{D}_o$, $\overline{D}_2$ be recursive domains. Find a recursive domain $\overline{D}$ such that $\overline{D}_o$ can be embedded into $\overline{D}$ and $\overline{D}$ is recursively isomorphic to $[[\overline{D} + \overline{D}_2] \times [\overline{D} \longrightarrow \overline{D}]]$.

<u>Solution:</u> Let $(A_o, \rho_o) := \text{rel}(D_o)$. Define $\overline{D}_1 := \text{cpl}(x_1)$, where $x_1 := (A_1, \rho_1)$, $A_1 := \{\langle 0,a\rangle \mid a \in A_o\}$, $\rho_1 = \{(\langle 0,a\rangle, \langle 0,b\rangle) \mid a \rho_o b\}$. Then D_o and D_1 are recursively isomorphic, and $x_1 \in X_o$. Define $g : D_s \longrightarrow D_s$ by $g(x) := \text{prd}_2'(\text{sum}(x,x_2), \text{fct}_1(x,x))$. Then g is computable and $x_1 \sqsubseteq \text{fct}_1(x_1,x_1) \sqsubseteq g(x_1)$. Let $y := \bigsqcup g^i(x_1)$. Then y is computable, $x_1 \sqsubseteq y$, and $y = g(y)$. Therefore, D_o can be embedded into $D := \text{cpl}(y)$, D is a recursive domain and recursively isomorphic to $[[D + D_2] \times [D \longrightarrow D]]$.

The formalism allows one to show that the solutions of the equations can be determined concretely as well as the isomorphism and embeddings in the last two cases. For technical reasons we have used numbers $i \in \mathbb{N}$ and functions $p \in \mathbb{B} = \mathbb{N}^{\mathbb{N}}$ as names. In practice it is more convenient to use words and ω-sequences of words as names. This change, however, does not affect the essentials of the approach.

EXERCISES

1) Show that the computable cpo's from Example 3.6.13(1) to (7) are recursive domains.

2) Let $\overline{D} = (D, \sqsubseteq, \bot, \beta)$ be a domain. Define

$$D' := \{\{i \mid \beta(i) \sqsubseteq x\} \mid x \in D\} ,$$

$$\bot' := \{i \mid \beta(i) \sqsubseteq \bot\} ,$$

$$\mathrm{dom}(\beta') := \mathrm{dom}(\beta) ,$$

$$\beta'(k) := \{i \mid \beta(i) \sqsubseteq \beta(k)\} \quad (\text{for all } k \in \mathrm{dom}(\beta)) ,$$

$$d' \sqsubseteq' e' :\Longleftrightarrow d' \subseteq e' \quad (\text{for all } d', e' \in D') .$$

Show: $(D', \sqsubseteq', \bot', \beta') = \mathrm{cpl}(\mathrm{rel}(\overline{D}))$ (see Def. 3).

3) Prove Lemma 4.

4) Complete the proof of Theorem 7.

5) Complete the proof of Lemma 8.

6) Prove Lemma 11.

7) Prove Lemma 13(2).

8) Complete the proof of Theorem 14.

9) Solve the domain equation $\overline{D} = \zeta[\overline{D} + \overline{D}]$ according to the proof of Theorem 17. Present $\mathrm{rel}(\overline{D})$ graphically.

10) Prove Theorem 20 in detail.

11) Complete the proof of Theorem 22.

12) Let $\overline{D}_o$ be a domain such that $(A, \rho) := \mathrm{rel}(\overline{D}_o)$ has the properties $0 \in \mathrm{Min}(A, \rho)$, $(0,1) \in \rho$, $(1,0) \notin \rho$. Solve the domain equation $\overline{D} = \zeta[\overline{D} \times \overline{D}_o]$.

13) Prove Lemma 24.

14) Let $\overline{D}_o, \overline{D}_1$ be domains. Solve the following domain isomorphisms with the additional condition that $\overline{D}_o$ can be computably embedded into $\overline{D}$.

(a) $\overline{D} \cong [\overline{D} \times \overline{D}_1]$

(b) $\overline{D} \cong [\overline{D} \longrightarrow \overline{D}]$

(c) $\overline{D} \cong [\overline{D}_1 \longrightarrow \overline{D}]$

(d) $\overline{D} \cong [\overline{D} + \overline{D}]$

15) Define nontrivial domains $\overline{D}_1$ and $\overline{D}_2$ such that $\overline{D}_1$ cannot be embedded into $[\overline{D}_1 \longrightarrow \overline{D}_2]$. Discuss the problem of solving isomorphisms $\overline{D} \cong [\overline{D} \longrightarrow \overline{D}_2]$.

BIBLIOGRAPHICAL NOTES

In the past several strategies for solving domain equations have been proposed (see e.g. Scott 1976, 1982). It has been guessed for a long time that domain equations can be solved by determining fixed points of continuous operators in an appropriate domain. Scott (1982) suggests this method explicitly, chapter 7 shows that it works. A similiar approach has been presented by Larsen and Winskel (1984).

3.8 Applications to Analysis

Type 2 theory of continuity and computability has interesting applications in Analysis. In this chapter some basic questions on constructivity in Analysis are studied by means of the tools which have been developed in the preceding chapters.

First, representations of the real numbers are investigated. It is shown that several known ones are unnatural already because of topological reasons. The standard numbering ρ is admissible according to the definitions from Chapter 3.4. As examples, computability w.r.t. ρ of the product and of the exponential function are proved in detail. The main part of each of these proofs is a careful estimation of convergence. The set of computable numbers is introduced, and an example shows that diagonalizations on the set of computable real numbers resemble the diagonalizations on the set $R^{(1)}$ of total recursive functions. As an instructive example for demonstrating the character of the Type 2 theory on $\mathbb{R}$ derived from the general theory of representations the determination of zeros of continuous real functions is studied in detail.

There are only very few representations of $\mathbb{R}$ which are of interest. They are given in the following definition.

1 <u>DEFINITION</u> *(representations of* $\mathbb{R}$*)*

Let ν_Q be the standard numbering of the rational numbers ($\nu_Q\langle i,j,k\rangle := (i-j)/(1+k)$). Define representations $\rho, \rho_<$, and $\rho_>$ of the set $\mathbb{R}$ of the real numbers as follows.

(1) $x = \rho(p)$ iff

$(\forall m,n)(m > n \Rightarrow |\nu_Q p(m) - \nu_Q p(n)| < 2^{-n}) \wedge x = \lim_n \nu_Q p(n)$,

(2) $x = \rho_<(p)$ iff

$(\forall n)\nu_Q p(n) < \nu_Q p(n+1) \wedge x = \lim_n \nu_Q p(n)$,

(3) $x = \rho_>(p)$ iff

$(\forall n)\nu_Q p(n) > \nu_Q p(n+1) \wedge x = \lim_n \nu_Q p(n)$,

for all $p \in \mathbb{B}$ and $x \in \mathbb{R}$.

For any $x \in \mathbb{R}$ let $M_< := \{q \in \mathbb{Q} \mid q < x\}$ be the rational left cut of x and let $M_> := \{q \in \mathbb{Q} \mid q > x\}$ be the rational right cut of x. From any $\rho_<$-name p of x the set $M_<$ can be constructed, from any $\rho_>$-name p of x the set $M_>$ can be constructed. The converses are also true. From $M_<$ a $\rho_<$-name p of x can be constructed etc.

Since the set $\mathbb{Q}$ of rational numbers is dense in $\mathbb{R}$, ρ is the Cauchy-representation of the real line w.r.t. the numbering $\nu_{\mathbb{Q}}$ according to Def. 3.4.17. Consider Definition 3.4.12 of c-admissibility.

2 THEOREM

(1) The representation ρ is c-admissible w.r.t. the numbering U defined by

$$U\langle i,n\rangle := B(\nu_{\mathbb{Q}}(i);\ 2^{-n}) \subseteq \mathbb{R}.$$

The final topology τ_ρ of ρ is the topology generated by the open intervals on $\mathbb{R}$.

(2) The representation $\rho_<$ is c-admissible w.r.t. the numbering $U_<$ defined by

$$U_<(i) := \{x \in \mathbb{R} \mid \nu_{\mathbb{Q}}(i) < x\} \subseteq \mathbb{R}.$$

The final topology of $\rho_<$ is $\tau_< := \{\{y \mid x < y\} \mid x \in \mathbb{R}\} \cup \{\emptyset, \mathbb{R}\}$.

(3) The representation $\rho_>$ is c-admissible w.r.t. the numbering $U_>$ defined by

$$U_>(i) := \{x \in \mathbb{R} \mid \nu_{\mathbb{Q}}(i) > x\} \subseteq \mathbb{R}.$$

The final topology of $\rho_>$ is

$$\tau_> := \{\{y \mid y < x\} \mid x \in \mathbb{R}\} \cup \{\emptyset, \mathbb{R}\}.$$

Proof

(1) (by Theorem 3.4.18)

(2) Obviously, range$(U_<)$ is a base of the topology $\tau_<$ on $\mathbb{R}$ and $(\mathbb{R}, \tau_<)$ is a T_o-space. Let $\delta_< := \delta_{U_<}$ be the standard representation of $\mathbb{R}$ w.r.t. $U_<$ according to definition 3.4.7. By Definition 3.4.12 it remains to show that $\rho_<$ and $\delta_<$ are c-equivalent. By Definition 3.4.7, if $\delta_<(p) = x$, then $\nu_{\mathbb{Q}}\mathbb{M}_p$ is a set of rational numbers less than x with least upper bound x. Therefore a $\rho_<$-name q of x can be computed from p, hence $\delta_< \leq_c \rho_<$. The relation $\rho_< \leq_c \delta_<$ can be shown easily.

(3) (similar to the proof of (2))

Q.E.D.

The three representations $\rho, \rho_<$, and $\rho_>$ are related as follows.

3 THEOREM

(1) $\rho \equiv_c \rho_< \sqcap \rho_>$ (i.e. $\rho \in \mathrm{Inf}_c\{\rho_<, \rho_>\}$),

(2) not $\rho_< \leq_t \rho_>$, not $\rho_> \leq_t \rho_<$.

Proof

(1) We show $\rho \le_c \rho_<$. If $\rho(p) = x$, then

$$\nu_Q p(n) - 2 \cdot 2^{-n} < x < \nu_Q p(n) + 2 \cdot 2^{-n}.$$

Define $\Gamma : IB \dashrightarrow IB$ such that

$$\Gamma(p)(0) = \mu y[\nu_Q(y) = \nu_Q p(0) - 2]$$
$$\Gamma(p)(n+1) = \pi_1 \mu\langle y,m\rangle[\nu_Q\Gamma(p)(n) < \nu_Q(y) = \nu_Q p(m) - 2 \cdot 2^{-m}]$$

for all $n \in IN$ and $p \in IB$. Then Γ is computable and $\rho(p) = \rho_<\Gamma(p)$ for all $p \in \mathrm{dom}(\rho)$. Similarly, $\rho \le_c \rho_>$ is proved. Therefore, $\rho \le_c \rho_< \sqcap \rho_>$. On the other hand, define $\Gamma : IB \dashrightarrow IB$ by

$$\Gamma\langle p_1, p_2\rangle(n) := p_1(\mu m[\nu_Q p_2(m) - \nu_Q p_1(m) < 2^{-n}])$$

for all $p_1, p_2 \in IB$ and $n \in IN$. Then $(\rho_< \sqcap \rho_>)q = \rho\Gamma(q)$ for all $q \in \mathrm{dom}(\rho_< \sqcap \rho_>)$.

(2) Assume $\rho_< \le_t \rho_>$. Then $\tau_> \subseteq \tau_<$ by Lemma 3.4.5. This is incompatible with Theorem 2. Similarly, $\rho_> \le_t \rho_<$ is false.

Q.E.D.

The representation ρ (or a c-equivalent one) is commonly used in computational or recursive analysis. Since τ_ρ is the usual topology on the real numbers it is (up to t-equivalence) the most natural representation of IR (see Chapter 3.4). The definitions of $\rho, \rho_<$, and $\rho_>$ do not depend on the choice of $\mathbb{Q}$ as a dense subset of IR. Let $\nu : IN \longrightarrow \chi$ be a total numbering of a subset $\chi \in IR$ such that there are functions $p, q \in R^{(1)}$ with $|\nu p\langle i,n\rangle - \nu_Q(i)| < 2^{-n}$ and $|\nu_Q q\langle i,n\rangle - \nu(i)| < 2^{-n}$, then replacing ν_Q by ν in Definition 1 yields a c-equivalent representation. As an example consider the numbering ν defined by $\nu\langle i,j,k\rangle := (i - j) \cdot 10^{-k}$. There are other commonly used representations of the real numbers which are unreasonable for purely topological reasons. Among these are the m-adic representations.

4 DEFINITION *(m-adic representation)*

Let $m \in IN$, $m \ge 2$. Define $\delta_m : IB \dashrightarrow IR$ by

$$\mathrm{dom}(\delta_m) := \{p \in IB \mid (\forall i \ge 1) p(i) < m\}$$
$$\delta_m(p) := \pi_1 p(0) - \pi_2 p(0) + \Sigma\{p(i) m^{-i} \mid i \ge 1\}.$$

δ_m is called m-*adic representation* of IR.

5 THEOREM

For any $m \ge 2$, the final topology of δ_m is the standard topology on IR (i.e. τ_ρ), but δ_m is not t-admissible. Especially the function $x \longmapsto (m^2 - 1) \cdot x$ is not (δ_m, δ_m)-continuous (see the basis theorem 3.4.11).

Proof

It is an easy exercise to prove $\delta_m \leq_c \rho$. Therefore $\tau_\rho \subseteq \tau_{\delta_m}$. Suppose, $X \subseteq \mathbb{R}$ is δ_m-open, i.e. $\delta_m^{-1} X = A \cap \mathrm{dom}(\delta_m)$ for some open subset $A \subseteq \mathbb{B}$. Let x be an element of X, let $p \in \delta_m^{-1}\{x\}$. Case 1: $p = (w,0,0,\dots)$ for some $w \in W(\mathbb{N})$. Since $\delta_m^{-1}X$ is open, $[w0^k] \cap \mathrm{dom}(\delta_m) \subseteq \delta_m^{-1}X$, hence $[x;\ x + m^{-i}) \subseteq X$ for some k and i. Furthermore $x = \delta_m(q)$ for some $q = (v, m-1, m-1, \dots)$. For a similar reason as above $(x - m^{-j}; x] \subseteq X$. Therefore, $x \in O \subseteq X$ for some $O \in \tau_\rho$.

Case 2: $p = (w, m-1, m-1, \dots)$ for some $w \in W(\mathbb{N})$. This is treated correspondingly.

Case 3: not Case 1 or Case 2. Since $\delta_m^{-1}\{X\}$ is open, $[p^{[k]}] \cap \mathrm{dom}(\delta_m) \subseteq \delta_m^{-1} X$ for some k. Let

$$p_1 := (p^{[k]}, 0, 0, \dots) \quad \text{and} \quad p_2 := (p^{[k]}, m-1, m-1, \dots).$$

Then $p_1 \neq p$ and $p_2 \neq p$ by assumption and $x \in (\delta_m(p_1); \delta_m(p_2)) \subseteq X$. In each of the three cases, x has an open τ_ρ-neighbourhood, hence X is τ_ρ-open. This shows $\tau_\rho = \tau_{\delta_m}$. If δ_m is admissible, then by Theorem 3.4.11 any (τ_ρ, τ_ρ)-continuous function is (δ_m, δ_m)-continuous. Clearly, the function $f: \mathbb{R} \longrightarrow \mathbb{R}$ with $f(x) = (m^2 - 1) \cdot x$ is (τ_ρ, τ_ρ)-continuous. Assume that f is (δ_m, δ_m)-continuous. Then there is a continuous function $\Gamma: \mathbb{B} \dashrightarrow \mathbb{B}$ such that $f\delta_m(p) = \delta_m \Gamma(p)$ for all $p \in \mathrm{dom}(\delta_m)$. Let

$$p := (0,0,0,1,0,1,\dots)$$

$$p_k := (0,0,\underbrace{0,1,0,1,\dots,0,1}_{k\text{-times}},0,0,\dots)$$

$$q_k := (0,0,\underbrace{0,1,0,1,\dots,0,1}_{k\text{-times}},0,1,1,0,0,\dots)$$

for $k \in \mathbb{N}$. Then $\lim p_k = \lim q_k = p$ in Baire's space. The condition on Γ implies

$$\Gamma(p_k) = (0,0,\underbrace{m-1,m-1,\dots,m-1}_{(2k-1)\text{-times}},c_0,c_1,\dots) \quad \text{for certain } c_i \in \{0,\dots,m-1\}$$

$$\Gamma(q_k) = (0,1,\underbrace{0,0,\dots,0}_{2k\text{-times}},d_0,d_1,\dots) \quad \text{for certain } d_i \in \{0,\dots,m-1\}$$

Therefore $\lim \Gamma(p_k) \neq \lim \Gamma(q_k)$, and Γ cannot be continuous. Therefore, f is not (δ_m, δ_m)-continuous and δ_m is not admissible.

Q.E.D.

The commonly used functions in analysis like $x + y$, x^n, $\sin(x)$, $\exp(x)$, $\log_x(y)$, etc. are not even continuous but computable w.r.t. ρ. Notice that the ρ-computable functions are closed under substitution. As examples we prove that the product and the exponential function on $\mathbb{R}$ are computable w.r.t. ρ.

6 EXAMPLES

(1) We show that $f:\mathbb{R}^2 \longrightarrow \mathbb{R}$ defined by $f(x,y) := x \cdot y$ is (ρ^2,ρ)-computable. We define a computable operator $\Gamma:\mathbb{B} \dashrightarrow \mathbb{B}$ which transforms any ρ^2-name of $(x,y) \in \mathbb{R}^2$ into a ρ-name of $x \cdot y \in \mathbb{R}$. Let $\rho^2\langle p,q\rangle = (x,y)$ (cf. Def. 3.3.11). Then the sequence $(a_i)_{i\in\mathbb{N}}$ with $a_i := \nu_Q p(i) \cdot \nu_Q q(i)$ converges to $x \cdot y$. It remains to choose a "computable" subsequence (b_i) in order to satisfy the Cauchy condition (Def. 1(1)). Define a function $r:\mathbb{N} \longrightarrow \mathbb{N}$ with the following property. Let $k \in \mathbb{N}$ be the least number with $k \geq |\nu_Q p(0)|+1$ and $k \geq |\nu_Q q(0)| + 1$. Then $|\nu_Q p(n)| \leq k$ and $|\nu_Q q(n)| \leq k$ for all $n \in \mathbb{N}$. Let $n_o \in \mathbb{N}$ be the least number with $2(2k+1) \cdot 2^{-n_o} < 1$. Let $r:\mathbb{N} \longrightarrow \mathbb{N}$ be a function with

$$\nu_Q r(n) = \nu_Q p(n_o + n) \cdot \nu_Q q(n_o + n)$$

for all $n \in \mathbb{N}$. Since $\nu_Q p(n_o + n) + \varepsilon_n = x$ and $\nu_Q q(n_o + n) + \varepsilon'_n = y$ where $|\varepsilon_n|, |\varepsilon'_n| \leq 2^{-n_o - n}$, we have

$$\begin{aligned} |xy - \nu_Q r(n)| &= |\nu_Q p(n_o + n)\varepsilon'_n + \nu_Q q(n_o + n)\varepsilon_n + \varepsilon_n\varepsilon'_n| \\ &\leq (2k+1) \cdot 2^{-n_o - n} \\ &< \tfrac{1}{2} \cdot 2^{-n} \end{aligned}$$

for any n. Therefore, the sequence $(\nu_Q r(n))$ converges to xy, and for any m,n with $m \geq n$ we have $|\nu_Q r(n) - \nu_Q r(m)| \leq |\nu_Q r(n) - xy| + |\nu_Q r(m) - xy| < 2^{-n}$. This shows $\rho(r) = xy$. There is a computable function $\Gamma:\mathbb{B} \dashrightarrow \mathbb{B}$ which determines some r from $\langle p,q\rangle \in B$. Therefore, $x \cdot y$ is (ρ^2,ρ)-computable.

(2) We show that the exponential function $\exp:\mathbb{R} \longrightarrow \mathbb{R}$ is computable. By definition, $e^x = \exp(x) = \sum_i x^i/i!$ for all $x \in \mathbb{R}$. An easy estimation yields for all n:

$$\exp(x) = \Sigma\{x^i/i! \mid i < n\} + r_n(x)$$

where

$$|r_n(x)| \leq 2|x|^n/n! \qquad \text{if } |x| \leq (n+1)/2.$$

Especially, for all x with $|x| \leq 1$:

$$\exp(x) = 1 + r_1(x)$$

where

$$|r_1(x)| \leq 2|x|.$$

Let $\rho(p) = x$. For any $n \in \mathbb{N}$ determine $q(n) \in \mathbb{N}$ as follows:

- Let $k \in \mathbb{N}$ be the least number such that $|\nu_Q p(0)| + 2 \leq k$.
- Let $m \in \mathbb{N}$ be the least number with $4 \cdot 3^k \cdot 2^{-m} < \frac{1}{4}\, 2^{-n}$.
- Let $x_m := \nu_Q p(m)$.
- Let $N \in \mathbb{N}$ be the least number with $x_m \leq (N+1)/2$ and $2 \cdot x_m^N/N! < \frac{1}{4}\, 2^{-n}$.
- Determine $q(n)$ such that $\nu_Q q(n) = \Sigma\{x_m^i/i! \mid i < N\}$.

We obtain

$$x = x_m + \varepsilon_m \qquad \text{for some } \varepsilon_m \in \mathbb{R} \text{ with } |\varepsilon_m| < 2 \cdot 2^{-m}$$

and

$$|e^x - e^{x_m}| = e^{x_m}|e^{\varepsilon_m} - 1|$$
$$\le e^{x_m} \cdot 2|\varepsilon_m| \qquad \text{(since } m \ge 1 \text{ and } |\varepsilon_m| \le 1)$$
$$\le 3^k \cdot 4 \cdot 2^{-m} \qquad \text{(since } x_m \le k \text{ and } e < 3)$$
$$< \frac{1}{4} 2^{-n} \qquad \text{(by the definition of } m).$$

Furthermore we have

$$|e^{x_m} - \nu_{\mathbb{Q}}q(n)| \le |r_N(x_m)| \le 2|x_m|^N / N! < \frac{1}{4} 2^{-n}.$$

The triangle inequality yields $|e^x - \nu_{\mathbb{Q}}q(n)| < \frac{1}{2} 2^{-n}$ for all n, hence $|\nu_{\mathbb{Q}}q(n) - \nu_{\mathbb{Q}}q(n')| < 2^{-n}$ for all $n' > n$. Therefore, $\exp(x) = \rho(q)$. There is a computable operator $\Gamma : \mathbb{B} \dashrightarrow \mathbb{B}$ which determines q from p, hence $\exp$ is (ρ,ρ)-computable.

The essential part of each of the above proofs is the careful estimation of convergence.

Because of their natural properties (see Theorem 2) mainly the representations $\rho, \rho_<$, and $\rho_>$ are considered in recursive analysis. Each of the above representations defines a numbering of computable real numbers according to Definition 3.6.1.

7 DEFINITION *(computable real numbers)*

Define $\nu_< := \nu_{\rho_<}$, $\nu_> := \nu_{\rho_>}$. Define:

x is *computable*: $\iff x \in \text{range}(\nu_\rho)$,
x is *left-computable*: $\iff x \in \text{range}(\nu_<)$,
x is *right-computable*: $\iff x \in \text{range}(\nu_>)$.

Most of the real numbers used in analysis are computable, e.g. the rational numbers, the algebraic numbers, the number $e = \Sigma\{1/k! \mid k \in \mathbb{N}\}$, the number π, logarithms of rational numbers, etc. Notice that (ρ,ρ)-computable functions map computable numbers into computable numbers. The following lemma gives some simple properties of the numberings $\nu_\rho, \nu_<$, and $\nu_>$.

8 LEMMA

(1) $\nu_\rho \equiv \nu_< \sqcap \nu_>$

(2) Let $A \subseteq \mathbb{N}$ be recursively enumerable and not recursive. Then

$x_A := \Sigma\{4^{-i} \mid i \in A\}$
is left-computable and not computable.

(3) The function $x \longmapsto -x$ is $(\nu_<, \nu_>)$-computable.

Proof

(1) The proof is similar to that of Theorem 3(1), or it can be derived from Theorem 3(1) by means of Exercise 3.6(5).

(2) There is a total-recursive injective function $f: \mathbb{N} \longrightarrow \mathbb{N}$ with $A = \mathrm{range}(f)$. There is a total-recursive function p such that $\nu_Q p(n) = \Sigma\{4^{-f(j)} \mid j \le n\}$. Then $x_A = \delta_<(p)$, hence x_A is $\delta_<$-computable, i.e. left-computable. Assume that x_A is computable. Then $x_A = \rho(p)$ for some computable $p \in \mathbb{B}$. Consider $n \in \mathbb{N}$. Let $x_n := \Sigma\{4^{-i} \mid i \in A, i \le n\}$ and $r_n := \Sigma\{4^{-i} \mid i \in A, i > n\}$. Then $x_A = x_n + r_n$ and $r_n \le \frac{1}{3} 4^{-n}$. Notice that $(n \in A \iff 4^n x_n$ is odd). We determine $4^n x_n$. Let $y_n := \nu_Q p(2n+3)$. Then $|x_A - y_n| \le 2^{-2n-3} = \frac{1}{8} 4^{-n}$, hence $|x_n - y_n| \le r_n + \frac{1}{8} 4^{-n} \le \frac{11}{24} 4^{-n} < \frac{1}{2} 4^{-n}$, i.e. $|4^n x_n - 4^n y_n| < \frac{1}{2}$. Therefore, $4^n x_n$ is the integer part of $4^n y_n + \frac{1}{2}$. We obtain $n \in A \iff \lfloor 4^n y_n + \frac{1}{2} \rfloor$ is odd, for all n, hence A is decidable (contradiction).

(3) (obvious)

Q.E.D.

Notice that in the proof $(\nu_Q p(n))_{n \in \mathbb{N}}$ is a computable increasing bounded sequence of rational numbers the limit x_A of which is not ν_ρ-computable. The sequence does not converge computably i.e. for no computable isotone and unbounded function $h: \mathbb{N} \longrightarrow \mathbb{N}$ $|x_A - \nu_Q p(n)| < 2^{-h(n)}$. Otherwise x_A would be a computable real number.

Since ν_δ is precomplete for any representation δ, the numberings $\nu_\rho, \nu_<$, and $\nu_>$ are precomplete. The numbering ν_ρ of the computable real numbers resembles the numbering φ' of the set $R^{(1)}$ of the total recursive functions, where $\varphi'(i) := (\varphi_i$ if $\varphi_i \in R^{(1)}$, div otherwise). Notice that in both cases the computable elements of a metric space are numbered. As a consequence the theory of computational complexity (Chapter 2.12) can be transferred from $R^{(1)}$ to $\mathbb{R}_c$, the computable elements of $\mathbb{R}$. Complexity classes of real numbers can be defined and a compression theorem and a speedup theorem can be proved for real numbers. Real numbers like e, π, etc. are very easily computable. The proof of the next lemma is an example for diagonalization on $\mathbb{R}_c$.

9 LEMMA

(1) Let $A \subseteq \mathrm{dom}(\nu_\rho)$ be recursively enumerable. Then there is a computable number x with $x \notin \nu_\rho(A)$.

(2) There is no total numbering ν of $\mathbb{R}_c$ with $\nu \leq \nu_\rho$.

Proof

(1) If $A = \emptyset$ we are finished. Consider $A \neq \emptyset$. Then there is a computable function $f : \mathbb{N} \longrightarrow \mathbb{N}$ with $A = \mathrm{range}(f)$. Define a function $\Gamma : \mathbb{C} \longrightarrow \mathbb{R}$ as follows.

$$\Gamma(p) := \Sigma\{3 \cdot p(n) \cdot 4^{-n} \mid n \in \mathbb{N}\}.$$

Thus the elements of $\Gamma(p)$ can be presented by 4-adic numbers in which only the digits 0 or 3 appear.

Proposition: If $p(n) \neq q(n)$ then $|\Gamma(p) - \Gamma(q)| \geq 2 \cdot 4^{-n}$.

Proof: Let $p(n) \neq q(n)$, let $m \leq n$ be the least number with $p(m) \neq q(m)$. Since $\Sigma\{3 \cdot p(i) \cdot 4^{-i} \mid i > m\} \leq 4^{-m}$ and $\Sigma\{3 \cdot q(i) \cdot 4^{-i} \mid i > m\} \leq 4^{-m}$ we obtain $\Gamma(q) - \Gamma(p) \geq 3 \cdot 4^{-m} - 4^{-m} = 2 \cdot 4^{-m}$ if $p(m) = 0$ and similarly $\Gamma(p) - \Gamma(q) \geq 2 \cdot 4^{-m}$ if $q(m) = 0$. Therefore, $|\Gamma(p) - \Gamma(q)| \geq 2 \cdot 4^{-m} \geq 2 \cdot 4^{-n}$.
q.e.d.

As a simple consequence we obtain that Γ is injective. Now an easy diagonalization yields a computable number $x \notin \nu_\rho(A)$. Define $p \in \mathbb{C}$ inductively as follows.

$$p(n) := \begin{cases} 0 & \text{if } \Sigma\{3 \cdot p(i) \cdot 4^{-i} \mid i < n\} + 2 \cdot 4^{-n} < \nu_{\mathbb{Q}}\varphi_{f(n)}(2n+1) \\ 1 & \text{otherwise.} \end{cases}$$

Consider $n \in \mathbb{N}$, let $x_n := \nu_\rho f(n) = \rho\varphi_{f(n)}$. If $p(n) = 0$ then

$$\begin{aligned} \Gamma(p) &\leq \Sigma\{3 \cdot p(i) \cdot 4^{-i} \mid i < n\} + 4^{-n} \\ &< \nu_{\mathbb{Q}}\varphi_{f(n)}(2n+1) - 4^{-n} \\ &< x_n + 2 \cdot 2^{-2n-1} - 4^{-n} \\ &= x_n , \end{aligned}$$

if $p(n) = 1$ then

$$\begin{aligned} x_n &< \nu_{\mathbb{Q}}\varphi_{f(n)}(2n+1) + 2 \cdot 2^{-2n-1} \\ &\leq \Sigma\{3p(i) \cdot 4^{-i} \mid i < n\} + 3 \cdot 4^{-n} \\ &= \Sigma\{3p(i) \cdot 4^{-i} \mid i \leq n\} \\ &\leq \Gamma(p). \end{aligned}$$

Therefore $\Gamma(p) \notin \nu_\rho(A)$, and $x := \Gamma(p)$ has the desired properties.

(2) If $\nu \leq \nu_\rho$, then $(\forall i)\nu(i) = \nu_\rho f(i)$ for some $f \in R^{(1)}$. Let $A := \mathrm{range}(f)$. Then A is r.e., $A \subseteq \mathrm{dom}(\nu_\rho)$, and $\nu_\rho(A) = \mathbb{R}_c$, which is impossible by (1).

Q.E.D.

Notice that $\Gamma : \mathbb{C} \longrightarrow \mathbb{R}$ in the above proof induces a homeomorphism between Cantor's space $\mathbb{C}$ and *Cantor's discontinuum* range$(\Gamma) \subseteq \mathbb{R}$. Diagonalizations on $\mathbb{R}$ or $\mathbb{R}_c$ are usually performed on Cantor's discontinuum defined in this or a similar way.

Computability on $\mathbb{R}$ w.r.t. ρ and on $\mathbb{R}_c$, the set of computable elements of $\mathbb{R}$, w.r.t. ν_ρ are related by Ceitin's theorem (Theorems 3.6.8 and Theorem 3.6.5). If $f : \mathbb{R} \dashrightarrow \mathbb{R}$ is (ρ,ρ)-computable then the restriction of f to $\mathbb{R}_c$ is (ν_ρ,ν_ρ)-computable. On the other hand, if $f : \mathbb{R}_c \dashrightarrow \mathbb{R}_c$ is (ν_ρ,ν_ρ)-computable, then f considered as a function on $\mathbb{R}$ is (ρ,ρ)-computable if there is some r.e. set $A \subseteq \text{dom}(f\nu_\rho)$ such that $\nu_\rho(A)$ is dense in dom(f). There are two important schools of *recursive analysis*. The *Polish school* investigates (ρ,ρ)-computability of functions on the whole set of real numbers, the *Russian school* investigates (ν_ρ,ν_ρ)-computability on the set $\mathbb{R}_c$ of the ρ-computable real numbers. Many results can be transferred from one approach to the other by means of Ceitin's theorem. The Russian recursive analysis gives rise to some formal paradoxes. There is, e.g., a function $f : \mathbb{R}_c \dashrightarrow \mathbb{R}_c$ which is (ν_ρ,ν_ρ)-computable and continuous on the closed interval $\{x \in \mathbb{R}_c \mid 0 \leq x \leq 1\}$ but not uniformly continuous. This formal paradox is solved by the fact that such a function is defined only on $[0;1] \cap \mathbb{R}_c$ and cannot be extended to a continuous function $\overline{f} : [0;1] \longrightarrow [0;1]$ (see the exercises).

Below we shall investigate the determination of zeros of continuous real functions. This is an instructive example for demonstrating the difference between classical analysis and the kind of constructive and recursive theory considered in this book. Among others we shall investigate the following questions:

- Is there a procedure (continuous or computable) for determining a zero from f?
- Is there a computable zero if f is computable?

For simplicity we shall consider only the set of continuous functions $f : [0;1] \longrightarrow \mathbb{R}$ which is usually denoted by $C[0,1]$. With the distance d, where

$$d(f,g) := \max\{|f(x) - g(x)| \mid x \in [0;1]\},$$

$(C[0,1],d)$ is a complete separable metric space. Examples of countable dense subsets are

- the polynomials with rational coefficients,
- the trigonometric polynomials with rational coefficients,
- the polygons with rational vertices.

Each of these sets can be numbered canonically, and the derived Cauchy-representations (see Def. 3.4.17) can be shown to be c-equivalent to each other. For being more concrete, let α be a total numbering of the set Pg of polygons on $[0;1]$ defined as follows: $\alpha(m) = f \in \text{Pg}$ iff there are numbers $i_o, j_o, \ldots, i_n, j_n \in \mathbb{N}$ with

$0=\nu_Q(i_o)<\ldots<\nu_Q(i_n)=1$ such that $f\nu_Q(i_k)=\nu_Q(j_k)$ for $k=0,\ldots,n$, f is obtained by linear interpolation between the vertices $(\nu_Q(i_k),\nu_Q(j_k))$ and $\nu^*(m)=\langle i_o,j_o\rangle\ldots\langle i_n,j_n\rangle\in W(\mathbb{N})$ (see Def. 2.2.2). Let δ_α be the derived representation of $C[0;1]$ according to Definition 3.4.17.

From our framework in Chapters 3.3 and 3.4 another representation of $C[0;1]$ can be derived from ρ. Since our representation ρ of $\mathbb{R}$ is admissible, a function f on $\mathbb{R}$ is continuous iff it is (ρ,ρ)-continuous (Theorem 3.4(11)). Every (ρ,ρ)-continuous function f is "computed" by some continuous function $\Gamma:\mathbb{B}\dashrightarrow\mathbb{B}$. We shall now use the ψ-names (see Def. 3.2.9) of Γ as names of f. Define a representation $\overline{\delta}$ of $C[0;1]$ as follows.

$$\overline{\delta}(p)=f \iff (\forall q\in\rho^{-1}[0;1])f\rho(q)=\rho\psi_p(q).$$

We shall prove that $\overline{\delta}$ and δ_α are c-equivalent representations. First we show that a modulus of uniform continuity for $\overline{\delta}(p)$ can be determined from p by means of a computable operator.

10 THEOREM

There is a computable operator $\Delta:\mathbb{B}\dashrightarrow\mathbb{B}$ such that $\mathrm{dom}(\overline{\delta})\subseteq\mathrm{dom}(\Delta)$ and for all $p\in\mathrm{dom}(\overline{\delta})$:

$$(\forall x,y\in[0;1])(|x-y|<2^{-\Delta(p)(n)}\Rightarrow|f(x)-f(y)|<2^{-n})$$

where $f:=\overline{\delta}(p)$.

Proof

Let $f=\overline{\delta}(p)$, $x=\rho(q)\in[0;1]$. Then for any $n\in\mathbb{N}$,

$$|f(x)-\nu_Q\psi_p(q)(n)|<2^{-n}.$$

By Theorem 3.2.16, the universal function Γ of ψ, defined by $\Gamma\langle p,q\rangle:=\psi_p(q)$ is computable. Let M be a type 2 machine for Γ. Then, for determining $\psi_p(q)(n)=\Gamma\langle p,q\rangle(n)$, M reads at most a prefix $q^{[m]}$ of q for some m if $\langle p,q\rangle\in\mathrm{dom}\,\Gamma$. Therefore, $\Gamma\langle p,q'\rangle(n)=\Gamma\langle p,q\rangle(n)$ if $q'^{[m]}=q^{[m]}$ and

$$|f(y)-\nu_Q\Gamma\langle p,q\rangle(n)|\le 2^{-n}$$

for all $y\in\rho([q^{[m]}]\cap[0;1])$. For input $p\in\mathbb{B}$ and $n\in\mathbb{N}$ determine $\Delta(p)(n)$ as follows:

By applying Theorem 3.1.25 to the universal function Γ generate a complete list of those words $wi\in W(\mathbb{N})$, where $w\in W(\mathbb{N})$ and $i\in\mathbb{N}$, such that there is some $q\in\rho^{-1}[0;1]$ with $wi\sqsubseteq q$ and for determining $\Gamma\langle p,q\rangle(n+3)$ the machine for Γ reads at most the prefix wi of q. Let w_ki_k be the k'th word in this list.

Define:

$$
\begin{aligned}
a_k &:= \nu_Q(i_k),\\
m_k &:= \lg(w_k),\\
I_k &:= (a_k - 2^{-m_k};\ a_k + 2^{-m_k}),\\
N &:= \min\{j \mid [0;1] \subseteq \cup\{I_k \mid k \le j\}\},\\
\Delta(p)(n) &:= \max\{m_k \mid k \le N\}.
\end{aligned}
$$

By this specification a computable function $\Delta : \mathbb{B} \dashrightarrow \mathbb{B}$ is defined. Suppose $p \in \mathrm{dom}(\bar{\delta})$. Let $\rho(q') = x \in [0;1]$ and define $q \in \mathbb{B}$ by $q(i) := q'(i+1)$. Then $\rho(q) = x$ and $|x - \nu_Q q(i)| = |x - \nu_Q q'(i+1)| \le 2^{-i-1} < 2^{-i}$. This shows that for any $x \in [0;1]$ there is some number k such that $x \in I_k$. Therefore, $\{I_k \mid k \in \mathbb{N}\}$ is a covering of the compact set $[0;1] \subseteq \mathbb{R}$. By the Heine-Borel theorem there is a finite subcovering, hence N and $\Delta(p)(n)$ exist. We conclude that $\Delta(p)$ exists for all $p \in \mathrm{dom}(\bar{\delta})$. Let $x,y \in [0;1]$, $x < y$, $|x - y| < 2^{-\Delta(p)(n)}$. We shall show that there are two intervals $I_i, I_j, i,j \le N$, with $x \in I_i, y \in I_j$ and $I_i \cap I_j \neq \emptyset$. Let I_i be an interval $I_k, k \le N$, with $x \in I_k$ and greatest $r_k = a_k + 2^{-m_k}$. If $y \in I_i$ set $j := i$. If $y \notin I_i$, let I_j be an interval I_k with $\sup I_i \in I_j$. The above maximality condition excludes $x \in I_j$. Since the length of I_j is greater than $|x - y|$, we have $y \in I_j$. Let $z \in I_i \cap I_j$. Since $y,z \in I_j$ there are functions $q_y, q_z \in [w_j i_j]$ such that $y = \rho(q_y)$ and $z = \rho(q_z)$. We obtain $\Gamma\langle p,q_y\rangle(n+3) = \Gamma\langle p,q_z\rangle(n+3)$, hence

$$
\begin{aligned}
|f(y) - f(z)| &\le |f(y) - \nu_Q\Gamma\langle p,q_y\rangle(n+3)| + |f(z) - \nu_Q\Gamma\langle p,q_z\rangle(n+3)|\\
&\le 2 \cdot 2^{-n-3}\\
&\le 2^{-n-2}.
\end{aligned}
$$

For a similar reason $|f(x) - f(z)| \le 2^{-n-2}$, hence $|f(x) - f(y)| < 2^{-n}$.
Q.E.D.

11 THEOREM

Let δ_α and $\bar{\delta}$ be the representations of $C[0;1]$ defined above. Then $\bar{\delta} \equiv_c \delta_\alpha$.

Proof

(1) Let $f = \bar{\delta}(p)$. Let $\Delta : \mathbb{B} \dashrightarrow \mathbb{B}$ be the operator determining the modulus of continuity from Theorem 10. We show how from p and any n a polygon g_n can be determined such that $(g_n)_{n\in\mathbb{N}}$ is a Cauchy sequence with $d(g_n, g_m) < 2^{-n}$ for $m \ge n$ which converges to f. Let $N' := \Delta(p)(n+4) + 1$. For $k = 0,\dots N$, $N = 2^{N'}$, define $i_k \in \mathbb{N}, x_k, y_k \in Q$ and $q_k \in \mathbb{B}$ such that $x_k = \nu_Q(i_k) = k \cdot 2^{-N'}$, $q_k = (i_k, i_k, \dots)$, and $y_k = \nu_Q\psi_p(q_k)(n+4)$. Let g_n be the polygon defined by the vertices $(x_o,y_o),(x_1,y_1),\dots,(x_N,y_N)$. For any $k < N$ and any $x \in \mathbb{R}$ with $x_k \le x \le x_{k+1}$

we obtain by the definitions and Theorem 10:

$$\begin{aligned}|f(x)-g_n(x)| &\le |f(x)-f(x_k)|+|f(x_k)-y_k|+|y_k-g_n(x)|\\ &< 2^{-n-4}+2^{-n-4}+|y_k-y_{k+1}|\\ &\le 2^{-n-3}+|y_k-f(x_k)|+|f(x_k)-f(x_{k+1})|+|y_{k+1}-f(x_{k+1})|\\ &< 2^{-n-3}+2^{-n-4}+2^{-n-4}+2^{-n-4}\\ &< 2^{n-1}\ .\end{aligned}$$

For any $m>n$ and for all $x\in[0;1]$ we have

$$|g_n(x)-g_m(x)|\le|g_n(x)-f(x)|+|g_m(x)-f(x)|<2^{-n}.$$

Therefore the sequence (g_n) has the desired properties. Let $j_n\in\mathbb{N}$ be the least α-number of g_n. Then $\Gamma:\mathbb{B}\dashrightarrow\mathbb{B}$ defined by $\Gamma(p)(n)=j_n$ has the property $\overline{\delta}(p)=\delta_\alpha\Gamma(p)$ for all $p\in\mathrm{dom}(\overline{\delta})$.

(2) Let $\alpha:\mathbb{N}\longrightarrow Pg$ be the numbering of polygons introduced above.

Proposition: There is a computable operator $\Omega:\mathbb{B}\dashrightarrow\mathbb{B}$ such that $\alpha(i)\rho(q)=\rho\Omega\langle i,q\rangle$ for all $i\in\mathbb{N}$ and $q\in\rho^{-1}[0;1]$.

Proof: (as an exercise)

Define $\Sigma':\mathbb{B}\dashrightarrow\mathbb{B}$ by

$$\Sigma'\langle p,q\rangle(n) := \Omega\,\langle p(n+2),q\rangle(n+2)$$

for all $n\in\mathbb{N}$, $p,q\in\mathbb{B}$. Then Σ' is computable. Let $f\in C[0;1]$, $n\in\mathbb{N}$, $p,q\in\mathbb{B}$, $x\in[0;1]$ with $p\in\mathrm{dom}(\delta_\alpha)$, $x=\rho(q)$, and $f=\delta_\alpha(p)$. Then

$$\begin{aligned}&|f(x)-\nu_Q\Sigma'\langle p,q\rangle(n)|\\ &\le |f(x)-\rho\Omega\,\langle p(n+2),q\rangle|+|\rho\Omega\,\langle p(n+2),q\rangle-\nu_Q\Omega\,\langle p(n+2),q\rangle(n+2)|\\ &\le |f(x)-\alpha p(n+2)(x)|+2^{-n-2}\\ &\le 2^{-n-1}\end{aligned}$$

and

$$\begin{aligned}&|\nu_Q\Sigma'\langle p,q\rangle(n)-\nu_Q\Sigma'\langle p,q\rangle(m)|\\ &\le |\nu_Q\Sigma'\langle p,q\rangle(n)-f(x)|+|\nu_Q\Sigma'\langle p,q\rangle(m)-f(x)|\\ &\le 2^{-n-1}+2^{-m-1}\\ &< 2^{-n}\end{aligned}$$

for all $m>n$. Therefore, $f(x)=\rho\Sigma'\langle p,q\rangle$. By the smn-theorem for ψ there is some computable function $\Sigma:\mathbb{B}\longrightarrow\mathbb{B}$ with $\Sigma'\langle p,q\rangle=\psi_{\Sigma(p)}(q)$. We conclude $\delta_\alpha(p)=\overline{\delta}\Sigma(p)$ for all $p\in\mathrm{dom}(\delta_\alpha)$, hence $\delta_\alpha\le_c\overline{\delta}$.

Q.E.D.

The Theorem shows that $\overline{\delta}$ as well as δ_α are natural representations of the set $C[0;1]$. Now we shall study the determination of zeros for functions from $C[0;1]$ from the constructive point of view. We shall prove negative results of the form "there is no continuous ..." and positive results of the form "there is a computable ...".

By the next theorem and its corollary the determination of zeros is not (δ_α,ρ)-continuous.

12 THEOREM

Let $k\in\mathbb{N}$, $k\geq 2$ and let $X_k\subseteq C[0;1]$ be the set of continuous functions $f\in C[0;1]$ which have exactly k zeros. Then there is no continuous function $\Gamma:\mathbb{B}\dashrightarrow\mathbb{B}$ with

$$\delta_\alpha(p)(\rho\Gamma(p))=0$$

for all p with $\delta_\alpha(p)\in X_k$.

Proof

We consider the case $k=2$. The cases $k>2$ are treated similarly. Define a function $F:\mathbb{R}\longrightarrow C[0;1]$ as follows: $F(x)$ is the polygon with the vertices

$$(0,1),(\tfrac{1}{4},x),(\tfrac{1}{2},1),(\tfrac{3}{4},-x),(1,1)\ .$$

Notice that $F(x)$ has exactly two zeros for any $x\in\mathbb{R}$. The function F is continuous, hence (ρ,δ_α)-continuous since ρ and δ_α are t-admissible (see Theorem 3.4.11). Therefore $(\forall p\in \mathrm{dom}(\rho))F\rho(p)=\delta_\alpha\Sigma(p)$ for some continuous function $\Sigma:\mathbb{B}\dashrightarrow\mathbb{B}$. Assume that Γ exists. Then $\rho\Gamma\Sigma(p)$ is a zero of the polygon $F\rho(p)$ for any $p\in\mathrm{dom}(\rho)$. Since ρ,Γ, and Σ are continuous, $\rho\Gamma\Sigma$ must be continuous. Consider $p_o\in\mathbb{B}$ with $(\forall i\in\mathbb{N})p_o(i)=0$. Then $\rho(p_o)=0\in\mathbb{R}$, hence $\rho\Gamma\Sigma(p_o)=\frac{1}{4}$ or $\rho\Gamma\Sigma(p_o)=\frac{3}{4}$. Assume w.l.g. $\rho\Gamma\Sigma(p_o)=\frac{1}{4}$. For any n let $i_n\in\mathbb{N}$ be a number with $\nu_Q(i_n)=2^{-n-1}$ and define $q_n\in\mathbb{B}$ by

$$q_n(i)=\begin{cases}0 & \text{if } i<n\\ i_n & \text{if } i\geq n\ .\end{cases}$$

Then $\rho(q_n)=2^{-n-1}$ and the sequence (q_n) converges to p_o. But the sequence $\rho\Gamma\Sigma(q_n)$ converges to $\frac{3}{4}$ and not to $\rho\Gamma\Sigma(p_o)=\frac{1}{4}$. Therefore $\rho\Gamma\Sigma$ is not continuous in p_o (contradiction). This shows that Γ cannot exist.
Q.E.D.

Obviously, Theorem 12 holds correspondingly for any set $Y\subseteq C[0;1]$ with $X_k\subseteq Y$ such that each $f\in Y$ has a zero, instead of X.

13 COROLLARY

There is no continuous function $\Gamma:\mathbb{B}\dashrightarrow\mathbb{B}$ such that $\rho\Gamma(p)$ is a zero of $\delta_\alpha(p)$ if $\delta_\alpha(p)$ has a zero. Especially there is no (δ_α,ρ)-computable function $F: C[0;1]\dashrightarrow\mathbb{R}$ such that $fF(f)=0$ if f has a zero.

Although there is no continuous procedure for determining a ρ-name of a zero, a $\rho_<$-name of the minimal zero and a $\rho_>$-name of the maximal zero can be determined.

14 THEOREM

Define functions Z_{min} and $Z_{max} : C[0;1] \dashrightarrow \mathbb{R}$ as follows:

$$Z_{min}(f) := \min f^{-1}\{0\},$$
$$Z_{max}(f) := \max f^{-1}\{0\}$$

(where $\min(\emptyset)$ and $\max(\emptyset)$ are undefined). Then Z_{min} is strongly $(\delta_\alpha,\rho_<)$-computable and Z_{max} is strongly $(\delta_\alpha,\rho_>)$-computable.

Proof

There is a computable function $\Gamma : \mathbb{B} \dashrightarrow \mathbb{B}$ such that

$$\nu_Q\Gamma(p)(m) = \begin{cases} \min\{x\in[0;1] \mid |\alpha p(m)(x)| \le 2^{-m}\} \\ \quad \text{if } \Gamma(p)(m') \text{ exists for all } m' < m \\ \text{div otherwise.} \end{cases}$$

(Notice that the polygons α_i have rational vertices.) Assume $p \in \mathrm{dom}(\delta_\alpha)$. Then $d(\alpha p(n),\delta_\alpha(p)) \le 2^{-n}$ for any $n\in\mathbb{N}$ since δ_α is a Cauchy representation. We distinguish two cases.

Case 1: $\delta_\alpha(p)$ has no zero.

Then $\Gamma(p)(m)$ does not exist for some m, hence $\Gamma(p)$ does not exist.

Case 2: $\delta_\alpha(p)$ has a zero.

Let $x_o := Z_{min}(f)$ be the least zero of $f = \delta_\alpha(p)$. Then $\Gamma(p)(m)$ exists and $\nu_Q\Gamma(p)(m) \le x_o$ for all m. Let $\varepsilon \in \mathbb{R}, \varepsilon > 0$. Then there is some $\delta > 0$ with $|f(x)| > \delta$ for all $x < x_o - \varepsilon$ by continuity of f. Hence, $|x_o - \nu_Q\Gamma(p)(m)| \le \varepsilon$ if $2^{-m} \le \delta$. These considerations show $x_o = \sup\{\nu_Q\Gamma(p)(m) \mid m\in\mathbb{N}\}$.

We determine a sequence of rational numbers according to Def. 1(2) in two steps. There are computable functions $\Sigma,\Delta : \mathbb{B} \dashrightarrow \mathbb{B}$ with

$$\nu_Q\Sigma(p)(m) = \max\{\nu_Q\Gamma(p)(m') \mid m' \le m\}$$

and

$$\nu_Q\Delta(p)(m) = \nu_Q\Sigma(p)(m) - 2^{-m}$$

for all $p\in\mathbb{B}$ and $m\in\mathbb{N}$. Then $\Delta(p)$ exists iff $\Gamma(p)$ exists iff $\delta_\alpha(p)$ has a zero, and $\rho_<\Delta(p) = \sup\{\nu_Q\Gamma(p)(m) \mid m\in\mathbb{N}\} = x_o$ if $\delta_\alpha(p)$ has a zero. Therefore Z_{min} is $(\delta_\alpha,\rho_<)$-computable. The case of Z_{max} is proved correspondingly.

Q.E.D.

If f has exactly one zero then $Z_{max} = Z_{min}$. By Theorem 3, a ρ-name of the zero can be determined in this case.

15 COROLLARY

Define $F_1 : C[0;1] \dashrightarrow \mathbb{R}$ by $dom(F_1) := \{f \in C[0;1] \mid f$ has one and only one zero$\}$
$F_1(f)$:= the unique $x \in \mathbb{R}$ with $f(x) = 0$
for all $f \in dom(f\ )$. Then F_1 is strongly (δ_α, ρ)-computable.

Proof

Let Γ_{min} and Γ_{max} be the functions from Theorem 13 for computing Z_{min} and Z_{max}, respectively. Define computable functions $\Sigma, \Delta : \mathbb{B} \dashrightarrow \mathbb{B}$ as follows:

$$\Sigma(p)(n) := \mu m[\nu_Q \Gamma_{max}(p)(m) - \nu_Q \Gamma_{min}(p)(m) < 2^{-n}],$$
$$\Delta(p)(n) := \Gamma_{max}(p)\Sigma(p)(n)$$

for all $p \in \mathbb{B}$ and $n \in \mathbb{N}$. Then for any $p \in dom(\delta_\alpha)$, $\Delta(p)$ exists iff $\delta_\alpha(p)$ has exactly one zero, and $\rho\Delta(p)$ is the zero of $\delta_\alpha(p)$ in this case. Therefore, F_1 is strongly (δ_α, ρ)-computable.
Q.E.D.

Corollary 15 cannot be generalized to functions with two or more zeros by Theorem 12.

By the intermediate value theorem from classical analysis, a function $f \in C[0;1]$ has a zero if $f(0) \cdot f(1) < 0$. Notice that the negative result from Theorem 12 is obtained by using a function which has no values below zero. We shall now study the set of functions $f \in C[0;1]$ with $f(0) \cdot f(1) < 0$. This additional condition shifts the border line between non effectivity and effectivity. The following theorem improves Corollary 13.

16 THEOREM

Let V be the set of all functions $f \in C[0;1]$ with $f(0) \cdot f(1) < 0$. Then there is no continuous function $\Gamma : \mathbb{B} \dashrightarrow \mathbb{B}$ such that $\rho\Gamma(p)$ is a zero of $\delta_\alpha(p)$ for all $p \in \delta_\alpha^{-1}(V)$.

Proof

Define $G : \mathbb{R} \longrightarrow C[0;1]$ as follows: $G(x)$ is the polygon with the vertices $(0,-1)$, $(\frac{1}{3}, x), (\frac{2}{3}, x), (1,1)$. Then G is continuous, hence (ρ, δ_α)-continuous. Therefore, there is some continuous function $\Sigma : \mathbb{B} \dashrightarrow \mathbb{B}$ with $G\rho(p) = \delta_\alpha\Sigma(p)$ for all $p \in dom(\rho)$. Define $p_o \in \mathbb{B}$ by $(\forall i) p_o(i) = 0$. Then $\rho(p_o) = 0$. Assume that Γ exists. Then $x_o := \rho\Gamma\Sigma(p_o)$ is a zero of $G(0)$, hence $\frac{1}{3} \le x_o \le \frac{2}{3}$. Consider the case $x_o \neq \frac{2}{3}$. Define $p_i \in \mathbb{B}$ by $p_i(n) = (0$ if $n < i$, $\langle 0,1,2^i-1 \rangle$ otherwise$)$. Then $\lim p_i = p_o$ and

$\lim \rho\Gamma\Sigma(p_i) = \frac{2}{3} \neq \rho\Gamma\Sigma(p_o)$. Therefore $\rho\Gamma\Sigma$ is not continuous, hence Γ cannot be continuous. The case $x_o \neq \frac{1}{3}$ is treated correspondingly.
Q.E.D.

In the proof the polygon $f_o \in C[0;1]$ with the vertices $(0,-1),(\frac{1}{3},0),(\frac{2}{3},0),(1,1)$ gives rise to a non-continuous jump of the zero. The function f_o is zero on an interval of $[0;1]$. By excluding this, a positive result is obtained.

17 THEOREM

Let Y be the set of all functions $f \in C[0;1]$ with (1) and (2):
(1) $f(0) \cdot f(1) < 0$,
(2) for no open interval $I \subseteq [0;1]$, $(\forall x \in I) f(x) = 0$.
Then there is a computable function $\Gamma : \mathbb{B} \dashrightarrow \mathbb{B}$ such that $\rho\Gamma(p)$ is a zero of $\delta_\alpha(p)$ for all $p \in \delta_\alpha^{-1}(Y)$.

Proof

Let $f \in Y$ and $a,b \in \mathbb{R}$ with $0 \le a < b \le 1$ and $f(a) \cdot f(b) < 0$. Then for any $\varepsilon > 0$ there are $a',b' \in \mathbb{Q}$ with $a \le a' < b' \le b$, $f(a') \cdot f(b') < 0$, and $b' - a' \le \varepsilon$. We explain how to compute $\Gamma(p)$. Define two sequences $(i_n),(j_n)$ inductively as follows:

$$i_o := 0 ,$$
$$j_o := 1 .$$

(Then $\nu_Q(i_o) = 0$, $\nu_Q(j_o) = 1$.) For $n \ge 1$ define

$$\langle i_n, j_n\rangle := \pi_1 \mu \langle\langle i,j\rangle,m\rangle\, [\nu_Q(i_{n-1}) \le \nu_Q(i) < \nu_Q(j) \le \nu_Q(j_{n-1}),\ \nu_Q(j) - \nu_Q(i) \le 2^{-n},\ |x| > 2^{-m},\ |y| > 2^{-m}, \text{ and } x \cdot y < 0 \text{ where } x := \alpha(p(m))\nu_Q(i),\ y := \alpha(p(m))\nu_Q(j)].$$

By definition of δ_α, i_n and j_n exist for any $n \in \mathbb{N}$ if $p \in \delta_\alpha^{-1}(Y)$, and obviously, $x_o := \lim \nu_Q(i_n) = \lim \nu_Q(j_n)$ is a zero of $\delta_\alpha(p)$. Define $\Gamma : \mathbb{B} \dashrightarrow \mathbb{B}$ such that $\Gamma(p) = (i_1, i_2, i_3, \ldots)$. Then $\rho\Gamma(p)$ is a zero of $f = \delta_\alpha(p)$.
Q.E.D.

Theorem 17 does not guarantee $\rho\Gamma(p) = \rho\Gamma(p')$ if $\delta_\alpha(p) = \delta_\alpha(p')$, i.e. Theorem 17 does not express that there is a (δ_α,ρ)-computable function which determines zeros on Y. By the next theorem and its corollary such a function does not exist.

18 THEOREM

Let Z be the set of all functions $f \in C[0;1]$ with $f(0) \cdot f(1) < 0$ which have at most 3 zeros. Then there is no continuous (i.e. (δ_α,ρ)-continuous) function $F: C[0;1] \dashrightarrow \mathbb{R}$ with $fF(f) = 0$ for all $f \in Z$.

Proof

Define $G: \mathbb{R} \longrightarrow C[0;1]$ as follows: $G(x)$ is the polygon with vertices $(0,-1), (\frac{1}{3},x), (\frac{2}{3},x-1), (1,1)$. Then G is continuous. Let $F: C[0;1] \dashrightarrow \mathbb{R}$ be a function such that $F(f)$ is a zero of f for any $f \in Z$. Then $FG(x)$ is a zero of $G(x)$ for any $x \in \mathbb{R}$. An easy consideration shows that FG cannot be continuous, hence F cannot be continuous.

Q.E.D.

19 COROLLARY

There is no continuous function $F: C[0;1] \dashrightarrow \mathbb{R}$ such that $fF(f) = 0$ for any $f \in Y$ (Y from Theorem 17).

Our last question concerns computability of zeros of computable functions. As a negative result we prove that there is a computable function $f \in C[0;1]$ which has many zeros but no computable one.

20 THEOREM

There is a δ_α-computable function $f: [0;1] \longrightarrow \mathbb{R}$ such that $f(x) > 0$ for every ρ-computable number $x \in [0;1]$ and the set $f^{-1}\{0\}$ has measure not less than $\frac{1}{2}$.

Proof

For any $n = \langle j,k \rangle$ determine $p_n : [0;1] \longrightarrow \mathbb{R}$ as follows. If $\Phi_j(j+4) \neq k$ then $(\forall x) p_n(x) = 0$. If $\Phi_j(j+4) = k$, let $a := \nu_Q \varphi_j(j+4)$, let $q_n : \mathbb{R} \longrightarrow \mathbb{R}$ be the "polygon" with the vertices $(-\infty,0), (a-2^{-j-3},0), (a,2^{-j-3}), (a+2^{-j-3},0), (\infty,0)$, and let p_n be the restriction of q_n to $[0;1]$. There is a computable function $r \in R^{(1)}$ with $\alpha r(n) = \Sigma\{p_i \mid i \leq n\}$ for all $n \in \mathbb{N}$, where α is the standard numbering of the rational polygons. An easy estimation shows $r \in \mathrm{dom}(\delta_\alpha)$. Define $f := \delta_\alpha(r)$. Then f is δ_α-computable and $f(x) = \Sigma\{p_n(x) \mid n \in \mathbb{N}\}$ for all x. For any $n \in \mathbb{N}$ we have $\mu\{x \mid p_n(x) \neq 0\} \leq 2^{-n-2}$. Therefore, the measure of $\{x \in [0;1] \mid f(x) \neq 0\}$ is not greater than $\frac{1}{2}$, hence $f^{-1}\{0\}$ has measure not less than $\frac{1}{2}$. It remains to show

that f has no computable zero. Let $x_o \in [0;1]$ be a computable number. Then $x_o = \rho\varphi_j$ for some $j \in \mathbb{N}$. Let $k := \Phi_j(j+4)$. Then for $n := \langle j,k\rangle$, $q_n(x) \neq 0$ for $a - 2^{-j-3} < x < a + 2^{-j-3}$, where $a = \nu_{\mathbb{Q}}\varphi_j(j+4)$, hence $p_n(x_o) \neq 0$ and $f(x_o) \neq 0$.
Q.E.D.

Notice: Since $\delta_\alpha \equiv_c \overline{\delta}$ and ψ_p is computable if p is computable, $f \in C[0;1]$ is δ_α-computable iff it can be extended to a (ρ,ρ)-computable function $f' : \mathbb{R} \dashrightarrow \mathbb{R}$.

Our last result is a positive one.

21 <u>THEOREM</u>

Let $f \in C[0;1]$ be a δ_α-computable function with zeros. Then:
(1) $\min f^{-1}\{0\}$ is $\rho_<$-computable (i.e. left-computable).
(2) $\max f^{-1}\{0\}$ is $\rho_>$-computable (i.e. right-computable).
(3) If x is an isolated zero of f, then x is computable.
(4) If $f(0) \cdot f(1) < 0$ then f has a computable zero.

<u>Proof</u>
(1) and (2) follow from Theorem 14. If x_o is isolated, then x_o has a closed neighbourhood $[a;b]$ where $a,b \in \mathbb{Q}$, in which it is the only zero. Corollary 15 holds correspondingly for functions on $[a;b]$ instead of $[0;1]$. This proves (3). Assume $f(0) \cdot f(1) < 0$. If f is not constantly zero on any open interval, then the computable function Γ from Theorem 17 yields a computable zero from any computable $p \in \delta_\alpha^{-1}\{f\}$. Otherwise there is an open interval $I \subseteq [0;1]$ with $(\forall x \in I) f(x) = 0$. Notice that I contains computable numbers.
Q.E.D.

The example of determination of zeros shows how a simple concept from classical analysis gives rise to several different questions and results on constructivity and computability in that kind of Type 2 theory which is being developed in Part 3 of this book. Even more interesting results can be obtained by investigating the computational complexity of computable real functions. The following theories form a hierarchy in analysis.
(1) classical analysis,
(2) Type 2 theory of constructivity,
(3) Type 2 theory of computability,
(4) Type 2 theory of computational complexity,
(5) numerical analysis.
The five theories can be very roughly distinguished as follows. In classical analysis the pure existence of single objects is investigated. Type 2 constructivity theory

studies whether objects (the existence of which is guaranteed) can be constructed by a continuous procedure , while Type 2 computability theory is concerned with computable procedures. Type 2 computational complexity asks whether objects can be easily computed, and finally numerical analysis is essentially interested in computations on real computers. A negative result on level i give a negative result on level $i+1$: An object which does not exist cannot be computed, if there is no continuous procedure there is no computable one, if there is no computable procedure there is no easily computable one, and if a function is not easily computable it cannot be executed on real computers.

EXERCISES

1) Define a representation δ of $\mathbb{R}$ as follows

$$p \in \mathrm{dom}(\delta) :\iff p(i_o) = 3 \text{ for exactly one number } i_o \in \mathbb{N} \text{ and } p(i) \le 2 \text{ for all } i \neq i_o.$$

$$p(a_n, a_{n-1}, \dots, a_o, 3, b_1, b_2, \dots) := \Sigma\{(a_i - 1)2^i \mid i \le n\} + \Sigma\{(b_i - 1)2^{-i} \mid i \in \mathbb{N}\}$$

Prove: $\delta \equiv_c \rho$.

(Remark: δ is a 2-adic representation with positive and negative digits.)

2) Prove Theorem 2(3).

3) Prove that $x \longmapsto \sin x$ is (ρ,ρ)-computable.

4) Show that $x \longmapsto -x$ is $(\delta_<, \delta_>)$-computable.

5) Define the left cut representation δ_L based on the numbering ν_Q of the rational numbers $\mathbb{Q}$ as follows.

$$\delta_L(p) = x :\iff \nu_Q \mathbb{M}_{cf}(p) = \{r \in \mathbb{Q} \mid r < x\}$$

(i.e. $p(i) = 0 \iff \nu_Q(i) < x$). Characterize the final topology of δ_L and show that δ_L is admissible. (Notice that τ_{δ_L} depends on $\mathbb{Q}$.)

6) Let ν' be the restriction of $\nu_<$ to the ρ-computable numbers. Show that ν' is not reducible to $\nu_>$.

(Hint: cf. Lemma 2.3.9, use $h \in R^{(1)}$ with

$$\nu_Q \varphi_{h(i)}(n) = \begin{cases} -2^{-i} & \text{if } \Phi_i(i) \not\le n \\ 1 - 2^{-i} & \text{if } \Phi_i(i) \le n.) \end{cases}$$

7) Define representations δ and δ' of $\mathbb{R}$ as follows

$$\delta(p) = x :\iff x = \sup \nu_Q \mathbb{M}_p,$$
$$\delta'(p) = x :\iff x = \sup \nu_Q \mathbb{M}_p \wedge (\forall i \in \mathbb{M}_p) \nu_Q(i) < x.$$

Show: $\delta \equiv_c \rho_<$ and $\delta' \equiv_c \rho_<$.

8) Prove: $\nu_Q \le \nu_<$, $\nu_Q \le \nu_>$, $\nu_Q \le \nu_\rho$.

9) Let $A \subseteq \mathbb{N}$ be an r.e. set which is not recursive. Show that $\Sigma\{2^{-i} \mid i \in A\}$ is $\rho_<$-computable and not computable.

10) Let ν be a numbering of the computable real numbers which satisfies the following properties:
(1) The set $\{(i,m,n) \mid \nu_{\mathbb{Q}}(m) < \nu(i) < \nu_{\mathbb{Q}}(n)\}$ is r.e.
(2) There is a computable function $h: \mathbb{N} \dashrightarrow \mathbb{N}$ such that

$$\nu h\langle i,j\rangle = \sup \nu_{\mathbb{Q}} W_i = \inf \nu_{\mathbb{Q}} W_j$$

for all $i,j \in \mathbb{N}$ with $\sup \nu_{\mathbb{Q}} W_i = \inf \nu_{\mathbb{Q}} W_j$.
Show: $\nu \equiv \nu_\rho$
(Property (1) can be called a utm-theorem and Property (2) an smn-theorem for ν, see Def. 2.1.5.)

11) Define a representation $\rho^b_<$ of $\mathbb{R}$ as follows:

$$\rho^b_< \langle n,p\rangle = x \;:\Longleftrightarrow\; (\rho_<(p) = x \text{ and } x \le n).$$

Let $\nu^b_<$ be the canonical numbering derived from $\rho^b_<$.
Show: $\rho \le \rho^b_<$, $\rho^b_< \le \rho_<$, $\rho_< \not\le \rho^b_<$, $\rho^b_< \not\le \rho$,

$$\nu_\rho \le \nu^b_<, \; \nu^b_< \le \nu_<, \; \nu_< \not\le \nu^b_<, \; \nu^b_< \not\le \nu_\rho .$$

12) Let $\Gamma: \mathbb{C} \longrightarrow X \subseteq \mathbb{R}$ be the surjective mapping with
$\Gamma(p) = \Sigma\{3p(n) \cdot 4^{-n} \mid n \in \mathbb{N}\}$.
Show that Γ is a homeomorphism between Cantor's space and the subspace X of $\mathbb{R}$ (cf. the proof of Lemma 9).

13) Construct a continuous function $f: \mathbb{R} \dashrightarrow \mathbb{R}$ such that $\mathbb{R}_c \subseteq \mathbb{R}$ and f is not uniformly continuous on $\mathrm{dom}(f) \cap [0;1]$. (Hint: Consider the proof of Theorem 20, define partial polygons with vertices $(a - 2^{-j-3},0)(a,1),(a + 2^{-j-3},0)$.)

14) Define a representation δ_s of sequences S on $\mathbb{R}$ as follows:
$\delta_s\langle p_o,p_1,\dots\rangle = (x_o,x_1,\dots)$
iff

$$(\forall i)(\rho(p_i) = x_i \text{ and } (\forall j > i) \mid x_i - x_j \mid < 2^{-i}) .$$

Prove that the limit function $\lim: S \longrightarrow \mathbb{R}$ is (δ_s,ρ)-computable.

15) Let $h \in R^{(1)}$ be a computable function with $\mathrm{range}(h) \subseteq \mathrm{dom}(\nu_\rho)$. Let $r > 0$ be the radius of convergence of the power series $\Sigma \nu_\rho h(i) x^i$.
Show that the function $f_r: \mathbb{R} \dashrightarrow \mathbb{R}$ with $\mathrm{dom}(f_r) = (-r;r)$ and
$f_r(x) := \Sigma \nu_\rho h(i) x^i$ for $x \in (-r;r)$
is (ρ,ρ)-computable.

16) Define a representation $\overline{\rho}$ of the complex numbers CN by
$\overline{\rho}\langle p,q\rangle := \rho(p) + i \cdot \rho(q)$. Show that the functions $(z,z') \longmapsto z + z'$, $z \longrightarrow \exp(z)$ are computable w.r.t. $\overline{\rho}$.

17) Let $\alpha: \mathbb{N} \longrightarrow Pg$ be the standard numbering of the rational polygons on $[0;1]$.

Show that there is a computable function $\Omega : \mathbb{B} \dashrightarrow \mathbb{B}$ with $\rho\Omega\langle i,p\rangle = \alpha_i \rho(p)$ for all $i \in \mathbb{N}$ and $p \in \rho^{-1}[0;1]$.

18) Let δ_α be the standard representation of $C[0;1]$. Show that there is a computable function $\Delta : \mathbb{B} \dashrightarrow \mathbb{B}$ such that
$\rho\Delta\langle p,q\rangle = \delta_\alpha(p)\rho(q)$
for all $p \in \mathrm{dom}(\delta_\alpha)$ and $q \in \rho^{-1}[0;1]$.

19) Discuss provability and decidability w.r.t. ρ of the following sets (see Definition 3.3.7):
$\{0\}, \{x \mid x < 0\}, \{x \mid x \neq 0\}, \{(x,y) \mid x = y\}$,
$\{(x,y) \mid x < y\}, \{(x,y) \mid x \leq y\}, \{(x,y) \mid x > y\}, \{(x,y) \mid x \neq y\}$.

20) Let $X := \mathbb{B} \setminus \mathrm{dom}(\rho)$. Is X (a) provable, (b) clopen, (c) c-complete in $\{A \subseteq \mathbb{B} \mid A \text{ open}\}$, (d) c-creative? Is the characteristic function of X a precomplete representation?

21) Show that $\{f \in C[0;1] \mid f(0) \cdot f(1) < 0\}$ is δ_α-provable but not δ_α-clopen.

22) Let $\max : C[0;1] \longrightarrow \mathbb{R}$ be the maximum function.
(1) Show that max is (δ_α,ρ)-computable.
(2) Let $X \subseteq C[0;1]$ be the set of functions with exactly one maximum. Show that the function $f \longmapsto x_{max}$ on X is (δ_α,ρ)-computable.
(3) Show that there is no continuous function $\Gamma : \mathbb{B} \dashrightarrow \mathbb{B}$ such that $\delta_\alpha(p)$ has a maximum at $\rho\Gamma(p)$ for any $p \in \mathrm{dom}(\delta_\alpha)$.

BIBLIOGRAPHICAL NOTES

There are many approaches for studying effectivity in analysis. The attempts can roughly be divided into three classes. The constructivists only study "constructive" objects and only use "constructive" proofs e.g. by using intuitionistic logic (Brouwer (1924-26), Lorenzen (1965), Bishop (1967), Bridges (1979), et al.). A good overview over aspects of constructive mathematics is gives by Troelstra (1977). The other two attempts are based on recursion theory. The "Russian school" starts with an "effective" partial numbering (equivalent to ν_ρ in our framework) of the set $\mathbb{R}_c$ of computable real numbers and investigates ν_ρ-computability on $\mathbb{R}_c$ (Ceitin (1962), Kushner (1973), Aberth (1980), et al.). The "Polish school" investigates computability on $\mathbb{R}$ w.r.t. a representation of $\mathbb{R}$ which is equivalent to our representation ρ (Turing (1936), Grzegorczyk (1957), Klaua (1961), et al.). Most of the mathematicians familiar with the constructivistic objections to classical mathematics concede their validity but remain unconvinced that there is any satisfactory alternative. The approach presented in this book is a further development of the Polish approach. Some more details can be found in the papers by Kreitz and by Weihrauch from 1984 to 1986. Computational complexity of real functions has been investigated by Ko and Friedman (1982).

Bibliography

Aberth, O.:
Computable analysis, McGraw-Hill, New York, 1980

Ackermann, W.:
Zum Hilbertschen Aufbau der reellen Zahlen, Math. Ann. 99, 118-133 (1928)

Barendregt, Henk; Longo, Giuseppe:
Recursion theoretic operators and morphisms on numbered sets, Fundamenta Mathematicae CXIX, 49-62 (1983)

Bird, Richard:
Programs and machines, John Wiley, New York, 1976

Bishop, Erret:
Foundations of constructive analysis, McGraw-Hill, New York, 1967

Blum, Manuel:
A machine-independent theory of the complexity of the recursive functions, Journal of the ACM 14, 322-336 (1967)

Böhling, K. H.;v. Braunmühl, B.:
Komplexität bei Turingmaschinen, Bibliographisches Institut, Mannheim, 1974

Börger, Egon:
Berechenbarkeit, Komplexität, Logik, Vieweg, Wiesbaden, 1985

Boolos, George; Jeffrey, Richard:
Computability and logic, Cambridge University Press, Cambridge, 1974

Brainerd, Walter S.; Landweber, Lawrence H.:
Theory of computation, John Wiley, New York, 1974

Bridges, D. S.:
Constructive functional analysis, Pitman, London, 1979

Brouwer, L.E. J.:
Zur Begründung der intuitionistischen Mathematik I, II, III, Mathematische Annalen 93, 244-258 (1924); 95, 453-473 (1925); and 96, 451-489 (1926)

Ceitin, G. S.:
Algorithmic operators in constructive complete separable metric spaces (in Russian), Doklady Akad, Nauk 128, 49-52 (1959)

Ceitin, G. S.:
Algorithmic operators in constructive metric spaces, Trudy Mat- Inst. Steklov 67, 295-361 (1962)

Church, Alonzo:
An unsolvable problem of elementary number theory, American Journal of Mathematics 58, 345-363 (1936)

Church, Alonzo:
The constructive second number class, Bulletin of the American Mathematical Society 44, 224-232 (1938)

Cutland, Nigel:
Computability, Cambridge University Press, Cambridge, 1980

Davis, Martin:
Computability and unsolvability, McGraw-Hill, New York, 1958

Egli, H.; Constable, R.L.:
Computability concepts for programming language semantics, Theoretical Computer Science 2, 133-145 (1976)

Ershov, Ju. L.:
Theorie der Numerierungen I, Zeitschrift für mathematische Logik und Grundlagen der Mathematik 19, 289-388 (1973)

Ershov, Ju. L.:
Theorie der Numerierungen II, Zeitschrift für mathematische Logik und Grundlagen der Mathematik 21, 473-584 (1975)

Friedberg, Richard M.:
Two recursively enumerable sets of incomparable degrees of unsolvability (solution of Post's problem 1944), Proceedings of the National Academy of Sciences 43, 236-238 (1957)

Gödel, Kurt:
Über formal unentscheidbare Sätze der Prinzipia Mathematica und verwandter Systeme, I, Monatshefte für Mathematik und Physik 38, 173-198 (1931)

Grzegorczyk, A.:
On the definition of computable real continuous functions, Fund. Math. 44, 61-71 (1957)

Hartmanis, Juris; Hopcropft, John E.:
An overview of the theory of computational complexity, Journal of the ACM 18, 444-475 (1971)

Heidler, Klaus; Hermes, Hans; Mahn, Friedrich-K.:
Rekursive Funktionen, Bibliographisches Institut, Mannheim, 1977

Hennie, Fred:
Introduction to computability, Addison-Wesley, Reading, MA, 1977

Hermes, Hans:
Aufzählbarkeit, Entscheidbarkeit, Berechenbarkeit, 3rd ed., Springer-Verlag, Berlin, Heidelberg, 1978

Hopcropft, John E.; Ullmann, Jeffrey D.:
Introduction to automata theory, languages, and computation, Addison-Wesley, Reading, MA, 1979

Jones, Neil D.:
Computability theory, Academic Press, New York, 1977

Klaua, D.:
Konstruktive Analysis, Deutscher Verlag der Wissenschaften, Berlin, 1961

Kleene, Stephan C.:
General recursive functions of natural numbers, Mathematische Annalen 112, 727-742 (1936)

Kleene, Stephan C.:
On the notation for ordinal numbers, Journal of Symbolic Logic 3, 150-155 (1938)

Kleene, Stephan C.:
Introduction to metamathematics, Van Nostrand, Princeton, 1952

Ko, Ker-I; Friedman, Harvey:
Computational complexity of real functions, Theoretical Computer Science 20, 323-352 (1982)

Kreisel, G.; Lacombe, D.; Shoenfield, J.:
Partial recursive functionals and effective operations. Constructivity in Mathematics (A. Heyting, ed.), 195-207, North-Holland, Amsterdam, 1959

Kreitz, Christoph; Weihrauch, Klaus:
Compactness in constructive analysis revisited, Informatik-Berichte, Fernuniversität, Hagen (1984) and Annals of Pure and Applied Logic (1986)

Kreitz, Christoph; Weihrauch, Klaus:
A unified approach to constructive and recursive analysis.In: Computation and proof theory,(M.M. Richter et al., eds.),Springer-Verlag, Berlin, Heidelberg, 1984

Kreitz, Christoph; Weihrauch, Klaus:
Theory of representations, Theoretical Computer Science 38, 35-53 (1985)

Kushner, B.A.:
Lectures on constructive mathematical analysis (in Russian), Monographs in mathematical logic and foundations of mathematics, Izdat. "Nauka", Moscow, 1973

Larsen, K.G.; Winskel, G.:
Using information systems to solve recursive domain equations effectively. In Semantics of data types (G.Kahn et al., eds.), 109-120, Springer-Verlag, Berlin, Heidelberg, 1984

Loeckx, Jacques:
Algorithmentheorie, Springer-Verlag, Berlin, Heidelberg, 1976

Loeckx, Jacques; Sieber, Kurt:
The foundation of program verification, Teubner, Stuttgart, and John Wiley, New York, 1984

Lorenzen, P.:
Differential und Integral - eine konstruktive Einführung in die klassische Analysis, Akademische Verlagsgesellschaft, Frankfurt, 1965

Luckham, D.C.; Park, D.M.R.; Paterson, M.S.:
On formalized computer programs, Journal of Computer and System Sciences 4, 220-249 (1970)

Machtey, Michael; Young, Paul:
An introduction to the general theory of algorithms, North-Holland, Amsterdam, 1978

Malcev, A.I.:
Algorithmen und rekursive Funktionen, Vieweg, Wiesbaden, 1974

Manna, Zohor:
Mathematical theory of computation, McGraw-Hill, New York, 1974

Markov, A.A.:
The theory of algorithms (in Russian), Trudy Mathematicheskogo Instituta imeni V.A. Steklova 38, 176-189 (1951)

Matijasevic, Ju. V.:
Enumerable sets are diophantine, Soviet Math. Dokl. 11.2, 354-358 (1970)

Milne, R.; Strachey, C.:
A theory of programming language semantics, John Wiley, New York, 1976

Moschavakis, Y.N.:
Recursive metric spaces, Fundamenta mathematicae LV, 215-238 (1964)

Muchnik, A.A.:
On the unsolvability of the problem of reducibility in the theory of algorithms (in Russian), Doklady Akad. Nauk SSSR 108, 114-119 (1956)

Myhill, John:
Creative sets, Zeitschrift für mathematische Logik und Grundlagen der Mathematik 1, 97-1o8 (1955)

Myhill, J.: Shepherdson, J.C.:
Effective operations on partial recursive functions, Zeitschrift für mathematische Logik und Grundlagen der Mathematik 1, 310-317 (1955)

Paul, Wolfgang J.:
Komplexitätstheorie, Teubner, Stuttgart, 1978

Peter, Rosza:
Rekursive Funktionen, Academiai Kiado, Budapest, 1951

Post, Emil L.:
Finite combinatory processes - formulation, I, Journal of Symbolic Logic 1, 103-105 (1936)

Post, Emil L.:
Recursively enumerable sets of positive integers and their decision problems, Bulletin of the American Mathematical Society 50, 284-316 (1944)

Post, Emil L.:
A variant of a recursively unsolvable problem, Bulletin of the American Mathematical Society 52, 264-268 (1946)

Post, Emil L.:
Recursive unsolvability of a problem of Thue, Journal of Symbolic Logic 12, 1-11 (1947)

Reiser, Angelika; Weihrauch, Klaus:
Natural numberings and generalized computability, Elektronische Informationsverarbeitung und Kybernetik 16, 11-20 (1980)

Rice, H. Gordon:
On completely recursively enumerable classes and their key arrays, Journal of Symbolic Logic 21, 304-308 (1956)

Robinson, J.:
General recursive functions, Proceedings of the American Mathematical Society 1, 703-718 (1950)

Rogers, Hartley Jr.:
Gödel numberings of partial recursive functions, Journal of Symboloc Logic 23, 331-341 (1958)

Rogers, Hartley Jr.:
Theory of recursive functions and effective computability, McGraw-Hill, New York, 1967

Rosser, J. Barkley:
Extensions of some theorems of Gödel and Church, Jounal of Symbolic Logic 1, 87-91 (1936)

Schnorr, Claus P.:
Rekursive Funktionen und ihre Komplexität, Teubner, Stuttgart, 1974

Schütte, Kurt:
Proof Theory, Springer-Verlag, Berlin, Heidelberg, 1977

Scott, Dana:
Some definitional suggestions for automata theory, Journal of Computer and System Sciences 1, 187-212 (1967)

Scott, Dana:
Outline of a mathematical theory of computation, 4th Annual Princeton Conference on Information and System Sciences, 169-176 (1970)

Scott,Dana:
Data types as lattices, SIAM J. Comp. 5, 522-587 (1976)

Scott,Dana:
Lectures on a mathematical theory of computation, Technical Monograph PRG-19, May 1981, Oxford University Computing Laboratory

Scott, Dana:
Domains for denotational semantics, A corrected and expanded version of a paper for ICALP'82, Denmark, July 1982 (1982)

Shepherdson,J.C.; Sturgis, H.E.:
Computability of recursive functions, Journal of the ACM 10, 217-255 (1963)

Shoenfield, Joseph R.:
Mathematical logik, Addison-Wesley, Reading, MA, 1967

Shoenfield, Joseph R.:
Degrees of unsolvability, North-Holland, Amsterdam, 1971

Soare, R.:
Recursively enumerable sets and degrees, Springer-Verlag, Berlin, Heidelberg (to be published)

Spreen, Dieter; Young, Paul:
Effective operators in a topological setting. In: Computation and proof theory (M.M.Richter et al., eds.), Springer-Verlag, Berlin, Heidelberg, 1984

Stoy, Joseph E.:
Denotational semantics: the Scott-Strachey approach to programming language theory, MIT Press, Cambridge, MA, 1977

Thue, A.:
Probleme über Veränderungen von Zeichenreihen nach gegebenen Regeln, Skr. Vidensk. Selks. Kristiania I, 10 (1914)

Troelstra, A.S.:
Aspects of constructive mathematics. In: Handbook of mathematical logics (J. Barwise,ed.), North-Holland, Amsterdam, 1977

Turing, Alan M.:
On computable numbers, with an application to the Entscheidungsproblem, Proceedings of the London Mathematical Society (2)42, 230-265 (1936)

Weihrauch, Klaus; Deil, Thomas:
Berechenbarkeit auf cpo's, Schriften zur Angew. Math. u. Informatik Nr.63, RWTH Aachen (1980)

Weihrauch, Klaus; Kreitz, Christoph:
Representations of the real numbers and of the open subsets of the set of real numbers, Annals of Pure and Applied Logic (1986)

Weihrauch, Klaus:
Type 2 recursion theory, Theoretical Computer Science 38, 17-33 (1985)

Index of Notations

(Entries are listed in order of occurrence in text)

Subject Index